AF180043

Advances in Spatial Science

Editorial Board
David F. Batten
Manfred M. Fischer
Geoffrey J.D. Hewings
Peter Nijkamp
Folke Snickars (Coordinating Editor)

Springer
Berlin
Heidelberg
New York
Barcelona
Budapest
Hong Kong
London
Milan
Paris
Santa Clara
Singapore
Tokyo

Titles in the Series

Cristoforo S. Bertuglia,
Manfred M. Fischer
and *Giorgio Preto* (Eds.)
Technological Change,
Economic Development and Space
XVI, 354 pages. 1995. ISBN 3-540-59288-1

Harry Coccossis and
Peter Nijkamp (Eds.)
Overcoming Isolation
Information and Transportation
Networks in Development
Strategies for Peripheral Areas
VIII, 272 pages. 1995. ISBN 3-540-59423-X

Luc Anselin and
Raymond J.G.M Florax (Eds.)
New Directions in Spatial
Econometrics
XIX, 420 pages. 1995. ISBN 3-540-60020-5

Heikki Eskelinen and
Folke Snickars (Eds.)
Competitive European Peripheries
VIII, 271 pages. 1995. ISBN 3-540-60211-9

Jeroen C.J.M. van den Bergh,
Peter Nijkamp
and *Piet Rietveld* (Eds.)
Recent Advances in Spatial
Equilibrium Modelling
VIII, 392 pages. 1996. ISBN 3-540-60708-0

Peter Nijkamp, Gerard Pepping
and *David Banister*
Telematics and Transport
Behaviour
XII, 227 pages. 1996. ISBN 3-540-60919-9

David F. Batten and *Charlie*
Karlsson (Eds.)
Infrastructure and the
Complexity of Economic Development
VIII, 298 pages. 1996. ISBN 3-540-61333-1

Tönu Puu
Mathematical Location and
Land Use Theory
IX, 294 pages. 1997. ISBN 3-540-61819-8

Yee Leung
Intelligent Spatial Decision
Support Systems
XV, 470 pages. 1997. ISBN 3-540-62518-6

Cristoforo S. Bertuglia,
Silvana Lombardo and *Peter Nijkamp*
Innovative Behaviour in Space
and Time
X, 437 pages. 1997. ISBN 3-540-62542-9

Anna Nagurney · Stavros Siokos

Financial Networks

Statics and Dynamics

With 58 Figures
and 10 Tables

Springer

Anna Nagurney
University of Massachusetts
School of Management
Amherst, MA 01003, USA

Stavros Siokos
University of Massachusetts
Department of Mechanical and Industrial Engineering
Amherst, MA 01003, USA

ISBN 3-540-63116-X Springer-Verlag Berlin Heidelberg New York

Cataloging-in-Publication Data applied for
Die Deutsche Bibliothek - CIP-Einheitsaufnahme
Nagurney, Anna: Financial network : statistics and dynamics; with 10 tables / Anna Nagurney; Stavros Siokos. - Berlin; Heidelberg; New York; Barcelona; Budapest; Hong Kong; London; Milan; Paris; Santa Clara; Singapore; Tokyo :
Springer 1997
(Advances in spatial science)
ISBN 3-540-63116-X

This work is subject to copyright. All rights are reserved, whether the whole or part of the material is concerned, specifically the rights of translation, reprinting, reuse of illustrations, recitation, broadcasting, reproduction on microfilm or in any other way, and storage in data banks. Duplication of this publication or parts thereof is permitted only under the provisions of the German Copyright Law of September 9, 1965, in its current version, and permission for use must always be obtained from Springer-Verlag. Violations are liable for prosecution under the German Copyright Law.

© Springer-Verlag Berlin · Heidelberg 1997
Printed in Germany

The use of registered names, trademarks, etc. in this publication does not imply, even in the absence of a specific statement, that such names are exempt from the relevant protective laws and regulations and therefore free for general use.

Hardcover design: Erich Kirchner, Heidelberg
SPIN 10549331 42/2202-5 4 3 2 1 0 - Printed on acid-free paper

To our families

Preface

Finance is concerned with the study of capital flows over time and space in the presence of risk. The existence of distinct sectors in economies, the proliferation of new financial instruments, coupled with the increasing diversification of portfolios internationally, along with governmental policy interventions, as well as the presence of transaction costs, have all brought added complexities to this general problem domain. In this economic and financial environment there is a clear need for the development and harnessing of appropriate and rigorous methodological tools, along with computer resources, for financial and quantitative analyses.

Congruent with the need for analytical and computational tools that are based on theory and can efficiently handle financial problems of sufficient generality and detail is that the tools also provide added insight into the behavior and structure of these large-scale, interacting and competitive systems, consisting of multiple sectors and multiple financial instruments. Indeed, what is sought is generality supported by increased clarity.

In this volume we present a theory of multi-sector, multi-instrument financial systems based on the visualization of such systems as networks consisting of nodes and links and the associated flows. Importantly, the depiction of such problems as networks adds a graphic dimension to the understanding of the fundamental underlying economic structure and its evolution over time. Our framework also depends crucially on the methodologies of finite-dimensional variational inequality theory for the exploration of statics and equilibrium states and on projected dynamical systems theory for the study of dynamics and disequilibrium behavior. At the same time, visualization and formulation of financial problems as network flow problems provide one with the opportunity of applying network-based algorithms, coupled with the aforementioned methodologies, for computational purposes.

The recognition of the pivotal role of computational methodologies in finance and their application dates to the early 1950's, beginning with the seminal work of Markowitz and his contributions to quadratic programming in the framework of portfolio optimization problems. In fact, the classical mean-variance portfolio optimization problem is a network optimization problem.

In addition to quadratic programming and, of course, linear programming, the field of finance has made use in recent years of such optimization techniques as nonlinear programming and stochastic programming as well as network programming and integer programming. Finance has also benefited from advances in partial differential equations for both modeling and computation purposes. The primary focus in much of the literature, however, has been on the individual sector or agent and, as such, optimization techniques are a natural tool since the emphasis is on a single objective function subject to the appropriate constraints.

Here, in contrast, the topic of concern is the entire financial economy as an embodiment of the individual sectors in conjunction with their particular behavior and their interactions over space and time through, for example, price signals. Consequently, extensions/generalizations of basic optimization techniques are required, which can elucidate both questions of statics revolving around the equilibrium state and of the dynamics of the system in disequilibrium.

Such tools and their application for financial modeling, qualitative analysis, and computation, are the focus of this book.

This book is divided into six major parts, beginning with the introduction and overview and the economic and finance foundations chapters of Part I, and ending with the empirical analysis chapter of Part VI. The book contains fifteen chapters, with a Sources and Notes section concluding each chapter, along with references.

Part I provides the background and context for the book in terms of economics and basic finance. Part II lays the methodological foundations of finite-dimensional variational inequality and optimization theory, projected dynamical systems theory, and network theory at a level that is utilized in Parts III, IV, and V. Parts III and IV develop the financial models, along with their qualitative properties, and provide algorithms for their solution, with numerical examples for illustrative purposes. Part V discusses flow of funds accounts and their network structure whereas Part VI concludes this volume with a discussion of empirical analysis.

In particular, in Part II we demonstrate how the mathematical tools can be utilized for both qualitative analysis and computational purposes. The presentation therein is such that the reader can familiarize oneself with these topics at first reading and can delve more deeply through additional citations, depending on one's needs and interests.

In Part III, single country, multi-sector, multi-instrument financial models are developed, beginning with perfect market models (in the absence of transaction costs and policy interventions). We present first static models, focusing on the variational inequality formulations of the governing equilibrium conditions, and then derive their dynamic counterparts. In these models, not only are the optimal composition of assets and liabilities for each sector determined, but also the equilibrium instrument prices. We also discuss extensions to the basic financial equilibrium models that incorporate such features as futures and options in order to model the possibility of hedging. We identify the network structure(s) out of equilibrium as well as in equilibrium and demonstrate how the network structure can be exploited for computational purposes.

Subsequently, we consider the case of imperfect markets in which the sectors are subjected to transaction costs and policy interventions in the form of taxes and price bounds, i. e., price floors and ceilings. We derive the new equilibrium conditions along with the variational inequality formulations and discuss the effects on the financial networks of such market imperfections. Finally, we study dynamic counterparts of these models both from a qualitative perspective as well as computationally.

In Part IV, we turn to international finance and present multi-country, multi-sector, multi-currency, multi-instrument financial models in which not only is the optimal composition of assets and liabilities for each sector determined, but also the instrument prices in terms of a basic currency, as well as the exchange rates. This part, hence, adds an international dimension to the single country (and single currency) models of Part III. Again, we begin with the perfect market assumption and consider both static and dynamic models. Subsequently, we relax this assumption in order to treat taxes, transaction costs, and price bounds. In this part, unlike in Part III, the static and dynamic models are developed within the same chapters, in order to see the synthesis immediately.

Part V focuses on flow of funds accounts and their estimation as the solution of optimization problems and identifies and exploits the network structure of this general equilibrium system. Therein the accounts are related to the financial models in Part III.

Finally, Part VI provides an accompaniment to the theoretical foundations of financial networks through discussions of empirical analysis.

The financial network framework developed here captures the essential components of the economic structure of financial macro systems in both a visual medium and mathematically and can be utilized for modeling, analysis, and computation purposes.

The intended audience for this book includes students, researchers, and practitioners in finance, in computational economics, and in operations research and management science, who are interested in the formulation, qualitative analysis, and computation of financial equilibrium problems in both static and dynamic settings.

The writing of this book was made possible, in part, by the sponsorship of the Royal Institute of Technology (KTH) in Stockholm, Sweden, while the first author was a Distinguished Guest Professor there in 1996. The support of Dr. Janne Carlsson, President of KTH and Dr. Ingmar Grenthe, Vice

President of KTH, is acknowledged. The hospitality of the host institution and, in particular, the Divisions of Regional Planning and Optimization and Systems Theory at KTH are warmly appreciated. The support of Swedish academic colleagues, notably, Professor Folke Snickars of the Department of Infrastructure and Planning, Division of Regional Planning, Professor Anders Lindqvist of the Department of Mathematics, Division of Optimization and Systems Theory, and Professor Börje Johansson of Regional Planning at KTH and Ënkoping University in this endeavor is also recognized as is the support of Dr. Åke Andersson, Director of the Institute of Future Studies in Stockholm. The friendship and hospitality of Dr. Anders Forsgren and Dr. Xioaming Hu of the Division of Optimization and Systems Theory at KTH as well as Lars Lindqvist of Regional Planning at KTH are appreciated. The first author acknowledges helpful conversations with Professor David E. Boyce of the University of Illinois at Chicago who spent part of his sabbatical leave at KTH as a Guest Professor of Regional Planning. The presence and wisdom of Professor Martin Beckmann of Brown University, an intellectual godfather, are also acknowledged.

The research described herein was supported, in addition, in part, by a National Science Foundation Faculty Award for Women, NSF Grant No. DMS-9024071 and by an earlier grant from the Economic Research Service of the United States Department of Agriculture.

The resources of the Illinois National Center for Supercomputer Applications at the University of Illinois at Urbana, Illinois and at the Cornell Theory Center at Cornell University in Ithaca, New York were utilized for the computational work.

We are grateful to our families and collaborators and, in particular, to Dr. Sten Thore, formerly of the IC^2 Institute at the University of Texas at Austin and to Professors Ding Zhang and June Dong of the State University of New York at Oswego, without whom this book would not have been possible. We also acknowledge the support of Professor Richard Giglio of the Department of Mechanical and Industrial Engineering at the University of Massachusetts at Amherst.

Finally, we would like to thank Dean Tom O'Brien of the School of Management, Professor Nelson Lacey, Chair of the Department of Finance and Operations Management at the University of Massachusetts at Amherst, and Professor Ben Branch, as well as Professor Thomas Schneeweis, Director, and Professor Hossein Kazemi, Associate Director, of the Center for International Security and Derivative Markets at the School of Management at the University of Massachusetts at Amherst for their collegiality and support in our research endeavors.

Contents

Part I Background

1 Introduction and Overview

Networks of economic activity are pervasive in today's societies in the form of transportation networks, telecommunication networks, energy networks, and a variety of trade networks. Flows on such networks correspond, respectively, to vehicles, messages, fuel, and products. The challenges in studying economic networks arise from their, typically, large-scale nature, and from the distinct behaviors of the economic network agents and their interactivity.

For example, in congested urban transportation networks, travelers (unilaterally) seek to determine their user cost-minimizing routes of travel between their origin and destination nodes and, hence, compete on the network, whereas in telecommunication networks, the network manager may have the authority to control the routes that the messages take so as to minimize the total system cost or traffic delays. In such physical networks the nodes correspond to intersections and the links to roads or communication media. One is interested in such settings in predicting the flows on the links and/or paths and in determining the resulting costs. In addition, one may be interested in evaluating the effects of alterations to the existing network topology as well as the effects of policy interventions on the resulting flows.

Networks consist of nodes, links and associated costs, plus supplies / demands (sometimes determined endogenously) of the flow commodity, along with the underlying behavioral principle (i.e., optimization, competitive equilibrium, etc.). Nodes are natural decision points, whereas links represent choices with the flow on a particular link representing the volume of the entity. For example, in finance, a node may represent a portfolio-optimizing agent, the links the choices of instruments to invest in, and the flow on a link the size of the investment. Associated with each link may be a risk and/or a return in the form of a "cost." The topology of the network, in turn, can represent the linkages among different agents and their portfolios. In addition, market clearing conditions, a fundamental equilibrium concept, can be represented through the appropriate subnetwork topology depicting that the total supply of an instrument is equal to the total demand. Another important feature of network modeling for financial problems is that of arc multipliers, which may be added to a network to reflect gains/losses in the flow as the links are traversed.

Networks and network theory can provide a formalism for modeling many complex systems in which the movement or flow of an entity over space and time is critical. In addition, they provide a graphical snapshot of a system with accompanying structural insights which may not be apparent in a purely mathematical formulation. Network-based algorithms typically dramatically outperform general-purpose algorithms and, hence, provide computational advantages. Moreover, further computational efficiencies may be gained through the exploitation of any special network structure underlying a problem.

To-date, such fields and application areas as transportation and logistics as well as telecommunications have made wide use of network models and algorithms. Networks have also been utilized to model economic systems such as spatial oligopolistic markets, human migration problems, and spatial price equilibrium problems.

Financial networks date to Quesnay (1758), who in his **Tableau Economique**, conceptualized the circular flow of funds in an economy as a network. His basic idea has been utilized in the construction of flow of funds accounts, which are primarily a statistical description of the flows of money and credit in an economy (cf. Cohen (1987)). What the flow of funds accounts in matrix form, however, fail to illuminate is the behavior on a micro level of the various financial sectors in an economy, such as banks, households, insurance companies, etc.

Copeland, in his 1952 book, recognized the idea of conceptualizing the inter-relationships of financial funds as a network, raised the question, "Does money flow like water or electricity?" and devoted a section to this topic. Furthermore, he provided a "wiring diagram for the main money circuit." Interestingly, Enke in 1951, had proposed electronic circuits as a means of solving spatial price equilibrium problems, in which goods are produced, consumed, and traded, in the presence of transportation costs. Such analogue computational devices, however, were soon to be superseded by digital computers, accompanied by parallel developments in computational methodologies, based on mathematical programming techniques.

In 1960, Fei proposed the "method of a linear graph" (or linear network) for the study of the credit system and expressed hope that with the aid of linear graph theory more meaningful theorems could be developed in the field of money and banking.

Thore, in 1969, was the first to introduce networks, along with the mathematics, for the study of systems of linked portfolios. His work benefited from the 1967 paper of Charnes and Cooper which pointed out that systems of linked accounts could be represented as a network, where the nodes depict the balance sheets and the links – the credit and debit entries. Thore's contribution was in the context of credit networks, with the explicit goal of providing a tool for the use in the study of the propagation of money and credit streams in an economy, based on a theory of the behavior of banks and other financial institutions. The credit network recognized that these sectors interact and its solution made use of linear programming. Thore, subsequently (cf. Thore (1970)), extended the basic network model to handle holdings of financial reserves in the case of uncertainty. The approach made use of two-stage linear programs under uncertainty (cf. Ferguson and Dantzig (1956) and Dantzig and Madansky (1961)).

In 1975, Storoy, Thore, and Boyer presented a network representation of the interconnection of capital markets and showed how decomposition theory of mathematical programming could be exploited for the computation of equilibrium. The utility functions facing a sector were no longer restricted to being linear functions. In 1980, Thore, in a book, further investigated network models of linked portfolios, financial intermediation, and decentralization/decomposition theory. Computational techniques to handle such problems were not, however, at that time sufficiently developed for implementation in practice.

In 1984, Thore proposed an international financial network for the Eurodollar market and viewed it as a logistical system, exploiting ideas of Samuelson (1952) and Takayama and Judge (1971) from spatial economics, who had proposed mathematically rigorous reformulations of spatial price equilibrium conditions. As in Thore's preceding papers on financial networks, the micro-behavioral unit consisted of the individual bank, savings and loan, or other financial intermediary and the portfolio choices were described in some optimizing framework, with the portfolios being linked together into a network with a separate portfolio visualized as a node and assets and liabilities as directed links.

Interestingly, the aforementioned contributions identified networks as a tool for the study of entire financial systems consisting of multiple, interacting economic agents. In such systems, equilibrium was a central concept, along with the role of prices in the equilibrating mechanism. Rigorous approaches that characterized the formulation of equilibrium and the corresponding price determination were greatly influenced by the Arrow-Debreu economic model (cf. Arrow (1951), Debreu (1951)), a general description of which is presented in Chapter 2. Moreover, the importance of the inclusion of dynamics in the study of such systems was explicitly emphasized (see, also, Thore and Kydland (1972)).

Network models have also been proposed for financial problems characterized by a single objective function to be optimized such as in portfolio optimization and asset allocation problems, currency translation, and risk management problems, among others. We now briefly highlight this literature recognizing that it was, of course, the innovative work of Markowitz (1952, 1959) that started a new era in financial economics and became the basis for many financial optimization models that exist in our day.

Interestingly, although many financial optimization problems (including the work by Markowitz) had an underlying network structure, and the advantages of network programming were becoming increasingly evident (cf. Charnes and Cooper (1958)), not many financial network optimization models were developed until some time later, with the exception of several early models due to Charnes and Miller (1957) and Charnes and Cooper (1961). Indeed, it was not until the last years of the sixties and the first years of the seventies that the network setting started to be extensively used for financial applications.

Among the first financial network optimization models that appeared in the literature were a series of currency translating models. Rutenberg (1970) suggested that the translation among different currencies could be performed through the use of arc multipliers. The network model that he developed was a multiperiod one with linear costs on the arcs (a characteristic common to the earlier financial networks models). The nodes of such generalized networks represented a particular currency in a specific period and the flow on the arcs the amount of cash moving from one period and/or currency to another. Related financial network models were subsequently developed by Christofides, Hewins, and Salkin (1979) and Shapiro and Rutenberg (1976), among others. In most of these models, the currency prices were determined according to the amount of capital (network flow) that was moving from one currency (node) to the other.

A series of cash management problems were also modeled as networks (cf. Barr (1972), Srinivasan (1974)), with a significant contribution being the introduction (cf. Crum (1976)) of a generalized linear network model for the cash management of a multi-national firm. The arcs in the network represented possible cash flow patterns and the multipliers incorporated costs, fees, liquidity changes, and exchange rates. A series of related cash management problems were modeled as network problems in the years that followed (see, e.g., Crum and Nye (1981), Crum, Klingman, and Tavis (1983)), thereby, further extending the applicability of network programming in financial applications. The focus therein was on linear network flow problems in which the cost on an arc was a linear function of the flow.

Crum, Klingman, and Tavis (1979), in turn, showed how contemporary financial capital allocation problems could be modeled as an integer generalized network problem, in which the flows on particular arcs were forced to be integers.

Note that in many financial network optimization problems the objective function must be nonlinear due to the modeling of the risk function and, hence, typically, such financial problems lie in the domain of nonlinear, rather than linear, network flow problems. Mulvey (1987) presented a collection of nonlinear financial network models that were based on previous cash flow and portfolio models in which the original authors (e.g., Rudd and Rosenberg (1979), Soenen (1979)) did not realize (nor exploit) the underlying network structure. He also recognized that the Markowitz (1952, 1959) mean-variance minimization problem was, in fact, a network optimization problem with a nonlinear objective function.

Lastly, a part of the optimization literature on financial networks focused on variables that were stochastic and had to be treated as random variables in the optimization procedure. Obviously, due to the fact that most financial optimization problems are of large size, the incorporation of stochastic variables made the problems more complicated and difficult to model and compute. A part of the literature (see, e.g., Mulvey (1987), Mulvey and Vladimirou (1989, 1991)), although emphasizing stochastic financial networks, consisted of a series of different theories and techniques (e.g., purchase power priority, arbitrage theory, scenario aggregation) that were then utilized for the estimation of the stochastic elements in the network in order to be able to represent them as a series of deterministic equivalents. The large size and the computational complexity of stochastic networks limited their usage to specially structured problems where general computational techniques and algorithms could be applied. We refer the reader to Rudd and Rosenberg (1979), Wallace (1986), and Rockafellar and Wets (1991) for a more detailed discussion on aspects of realistic portfolio optimization and implementation issues related to stochastic financial networks.

The focus in the financial network optimization literature, however, has been on individual optimization problems and not on the financial systems in disequilibrium or in equilibrium nor on the interactions among the individual sectors, with each facing his own utility function. Nevertheless, such single "agent" models serve as building blocks of financial systems models and clearly emphasize the advantages of network modeling and computation.

In this book, we develop a theory of financial networks as a foundation for the study of financial flows in economies. Such a theory has both historical support as well as timeliness in view of both the increasing globalization of financial decision-making and the dramatic technological developments in methodologies and computer advances of the past two decades. In addition, the rapidity of response required in the present competitive environment demands powerful, rigorous tools for both the qualitative and quantitative evaluation of the behavior and responsiveness of financial systems.

The theory makes use of finite-dimensional variational inequality theory for the formulation, analysis, and computation of the equilibrium asset and liability patterns, as well as the equilibrium prices in the multiple sector, multiple instrument economies. It also makes use of projected dynamical systems theory in order to study the disequilibrium behavior of the financial systems both from a qualitative perspective, in terms of, for example, stability analysis, as well as from a computational viewpoint, in terms of continuous time adjustment processes and discrete time algorithms for their approximation. Hence, both statics and dynamics are crucial features of the new theoretical framework.

Finite-dimensional variational inequality theory is a well-known methodology for the study of equilibrium problems arising in settings as diverse as the afore-mentioned congested urban transportation systems, in spatial economics in the case of spatial price equilibrium problems and a variety of oligopolistic market problems, and in general economic equilibrium problems. Although an equilibrium problem need not have a network structure in order to be formulated and studied as a variational inequality problem, interestingly, many that have been studied thus, in fact, do (cf. the book by Nagurney (1993) and the references therein).

The first use of finite-dimensional variational inequality theory for the computation of multi-sector, multi-instrument financial equilibria is due to Nagurney, Dong, and Hughes (1992), who recognized the network structure underlying the subproblems encountered in their proposed decomposition scheme. Hughes and Nagurney (1992) and Nagurney and Hughes (1992) had earlier proposed the formulation and solution of estimation of financial flow of funds accounts as network optimization problems. Their proposed optimization scheme fully exploited the special network structure of these problems. Nagurney and Siokos (1997) then developed an international financial equilibrium model utilizing finite-dimensional variational inequality theory for the first time in that framework.

Although finite-dimensional variational inequality theory is a powerful unifying methodology in that it contains, as special cases, such mathematical programming problems as: nonlinear equations, optimization problems, and complementarity problems, it is, nevertheless, static in scope in that it focuses on the equilibrium state. Projected dynamical systems theory, on the other hand, which was introduced by Dupuis and Nagurney (1993) and Zhang and Nagurney (1995) (see also the book by Nagurney and Zhang (1996)), is concerned not only with the equilibrium or stationary states but also with the dynamic behavior prior to such a state. In contrast to classical dynamical systems, projected dynamical systems are characterized by a discontinuous right-hand side, with the discontinuity arising due to the constraint set underlying the application in question. Hence, this methodology allows one to model systems dynamically which are subject to limited resources, with a principal constraint in finance being budgetary restrictions. Furthermore, the theory is linked with variational inequality theory in that the set of solutions to a variational inequality problem coincides with the set of stationary points of the appropriate projected dynamical system.

Dong, Zhang, and Nagurney (1996) were the first to apply the methodology of projected dynamical systems to develop a dynamic multi-sector, multi-instrument financial model, whose set of stationary points coincided with the set of solutions to the variational inequality model developed in Nagurney

(1994) and then studied it qualitatively, providing stability analysis results.

Nagurney and Siokos (1996) identified the network structure of the utility maximization problems facing the sectors in different countries out of equilibrium and then showed the evolution through time of the economic networks toward the stationary state, utilizing the methodologies of projected dynamical systems and network theory. This work initiated the use of projected dynamical systems for the formulation, qualitative analysis, and solution of dynamic international financial problems and represented the first instance of the application of this methodology for computational purposes in financial applications.

We now give an overview of the contents of the book. In Part I, we, in addition to this introduction, include a chapter covering the foundations of finance and economics necessary for the understanding and appreciation of the contents of this book. The chapter is included to familiarize the reader with an interest in the subject and this background material.

In Part II, we present an introduction to the methodological underpinnings of the financial models that are developed and studied in Parts III, IV, and V. In the three chapters therein, we present both the qualitative and algorithmic aspects of, respectively, finite-dimensional variational inequality theory, projected dynamical systems theory, and network theory. These methodologies are presented here for completeness. However, since the results are also available elsewhere (for which we provide citations for the reader in the Sources and Notes section following each of the chapters), every effort has been made to simplify the presentation, for example, by excluding theoretical proofs. Moreover, the presentation of the contents of these chapters is designed with the needs of the subsequent chapters.

In Part III, national (single currency) financial multi-sector, multi-instrument models are studied, first from a static perspective with a focus on the equilibrium states, and then from a dynamic perspective with additional emphasis on the disequilibrium behavior. We begin with the study of financial markets that are perfect, that is, those in which there are no transaction costs or policy interventions. We first present the basic models and identify the network structure of an individual sector's portfolio optimization/utility maximization problem as well as the financial network representing the system in equilibrium. We derive variational inequality formulations of the governing equilibrium conditions and also present qualitative properties that are used to establish convergence of the proposed algorithms. In equilibrium, the optimal composition of each sector's portfolio is obtained (equivalently, his utility is maximized), in addition to the equilibrium prices of the instruments.

Subsequently, we extend the basic financial models to allow for hedging through the use of futures and options. The effects of the incorporation of such new instruments are also studied through the network transformations that ensue.

We then turn to the dynamic counterparts of the models, utilizing the theory of projected dynamical systems and the connection between the set of solutions to a variational inequality problem and the set of stationary points to the appropriate projected dynamical system. We study the stability of the financial systems and utilize the stability analysis results in order to establish convergence of discrete time algorithms that serve as approximations to the continuous time adjustment processes proposed for the adjustment of the utilities of the sectors as well as the prices.

We also consider the development of imperfect market models, first, by proposing and analyzing static ones, and then the dynamic ones. In particular, we emphasize the effects on the network structure of such policy interventions as taxes and price floors and ceilings. Furthermore, we explicitly study the effects of transaction costs through the use of arc multipliers.

In Part IV, international, that is, multi-country models are proposed and studied in which each of the sectors in a country has, at least in principle, a multiplicity of financial instruments at his disposal. These instruments, however, can be in distinct currencies. Hence, in such international financial models, one is concerned not only with the prices of the instruments in terms of a basic currency but, also, with the exchange rates. As in Part III, we first present the models in the case of perfect markets, beginning with the equilibrium models through the use of variational inequality theory and then the dynamic counterparts through the use of projected dynamical systems theory.

Hedging in the form of futures and options is then incorporated into the basic international financial models and the resulting new international financial networks identified.

The dynamic model analogues of the static ones are derived and studied both qualitatively, in terms of, for example, stability analysis, and also computationally in the form of discrete time algorithms. The adjustment processes include the dynamic adjustment of the utilities of the sectors as well as those of the instrument prices, in terms of a basic currency, and the exchange rates.

We then study international financial market models in the case of market imperfections, beginning with static models and then deriving the dynamic counterparts. The policy interventions considered here can be viewed as extensions of those proposed in the single country models to the international domain.

The international financial networks developed and studied in Part IV are compared to and contrasted with the financial networks in Part III.

Numerical examples are included throughout the chapters of Parts III and IV for illustration and comprehension purposes.

In Part V, we present network models for the estimation of financial flow of funds accounts. Financial flow of funds accounts provide not only a snapshot of the financial economy but can also be used as a baseline for general equilibrium modeling. Indeed, the networks representing the estimation problems and those corresponding to the perfect market scenario in Part III are intimately related. We also discuss network decomposition algorithms that are dual methods and which decompose the network optimization problems that arise into simpler network subproblems with special structure that can be solved exactly and in closed form. Finally, we apply the algorithms to numerical examples.

In Part VI, we turn to empirical analysis and we show how the theory of financial networks can also be applied in practice.

1.1 Sources and Notes

In this chapter we have provided an introduction and a brief overview of the contents of this book. In particular, we have attempted to frame the contents and the principal topic - that of financial networks - from a historical perspective with an eye towards identifying key conceptual or methodological advances.

Two stepping stones for this book are the earlier books of Nagurney (1993) and Nagurney and Zhang (1996), coupled with our recent papers describing the research on statics and dynamics of financial network systems, the primary ones having been cited in this chapter, with additional ones cited in the appropriate chapter later in the text of this book. The former book includes a chapter on financial equilibrium and variational inequalities, with an exclusive focus on single country models, and an additional section on flows of funds accounts and their estimation, whereas the latter book develops the theory of projected dynamical systems and applications but does not apply this new methodology to financial systems.

One of the goals of this book is to contribute to the arsenal of financial methodologies. The field of numerical methods for finance is broad and growing rapidly and we only claim a small contribution in this direction. Hence, our citations necessarily are focused on the problem at hand. However, due to the critical linkages between numerical methods in economics and those in finance we have also included several fundamental book citations in the references below.

References

Amman, H. M., Kendrick, D. A., and Rust, J., **Handbook of Computational Economics, vol. 1**, Elsevier Science B. V., Amsterdam, The Netherlands, 1996.

Arrow, K. J., "An Extension of the Basic Theorems of Classical Welfare Economics," *Econometrica* **51** (1951) 1305-1323.

Barr, R. S., "The Multinational Cash Management Problem: A Generalized Network Approach," working paper, University of Texas, Austin, Texas (1972).

Charnes, A., and Cooper, W. W., "Nonlinear Network Flows and Convex Programming over Incidence Matrices," *Naval Research Logistics Quarterly* **5** (1958) 231-240.

Charnes, A., and Cooper, W. W., **Management Models and Industrial Applications of Linear Programming**, John Wiley & Sons, Inc., New York, New York, 1961.

Charnes, A., and Cooper, W. W., "Some Network Characterizations for Mathematical Programming and Accounting Approaches to Planning and Control," *The Accounting Review* **42** (1967) 24-52.

Charnes, A., and Miller, M., "Programming and Financial Budgeting," Symposium on Techniques of Industrial Operations Research, Chicago, Illinois, June, 1957.

Christofides, N., Hewins, R. D., and, Salkin, G. R., "Graph Theoretic Approaches to Foreign Exchange Operations," *Journal of Financial and Quantitative Analysis* **14** (1979) 481-500.

Cohen, J., **The Flow of Funds in Theory and Practice**, *Financial and Monetary Studies* **15**, Kluwer Academic Publishers, Dordrecht, The Netherlands, 1987.

Copeland, M. A., **A Study of Moneyflows in the United States**, National Bureau of Economic Research, New York, New York, 1952.

Crum, R. L., "Cash Management in the Multinational Firm: A Constrained Generalized Network Approach," working paper, University of Florida, Gainesville, Florida, 1976.

Crum, R. L., Klingman, D. D., and Tavis, L. A., "Implementation of Large-Scale Financial Planning Models: Solution Efficient Transformations," *Journal of Financial and Quantitative Analysis* **14** (1979) 137-152.

Crum, R. L., Klingman, D. D., and Tavis, L. A., "An Operational Approach to Integrated Working Capital Planning," *Journal of Economics and Business* **35** (1983) 343-378.

Crum, R. L., and Nye, D. J., "A Network Model of Insurance Company Cash Flow Management," *Mathematical Programming Study* **15** (1981) 86-101.

Dantzig, G. B., and Madansky, A., "On the Solution of Two-Stage Linear Programs under Uncertainty," in *Proceedings of the Fourth Berkeley Symposium on Mathematical Statistics and Probability*, **vol. 1**, University of California Press, Berkeley, California, 1961.

Debreu G., "The Coefficient of Resource Utilization," *Econometrica* **19** (1951) 273-292.

Dong, J., Zhang, D., and Nagurney, A., "A Projected Dynamical Systems Model of General Financial Equilibrium with Stability Analysis," *Mathematical and Computer Modelling* **24** (1996) 35-44.

Dupuis, P., and Nagurney, A., "Dynamical Systems and Variational Inequalities," *Annals of Operations Research* **44** (1993) 9-42.

Enke, S., "Equilibrium Among Spatially Separated Markets," *Econometrica* **10** (1951) 40-47.

Fei, J. C. H., "The Study of the Credit System by the Method of Linear Graph," *The Review of Economics and Statistics* **42** (1960) 417-428.

Ferguson, A. R., and Dantzig, G. B., "The Allocation of Aircraft to Routes," *Management Science* **2** (1956) 45-73.

Hughes, M., and Nagurney, A., "A Network Model and Algorithm for the Estimation and Analysis of Financial Flow of Funds," *Computer Science in Economics and Management* **5** (1992) 23-39.

Judd, K., **Numerical Methods in Economics**, MIT Press, Cambridge, Massachusetts, 1997, in press.

Markowitz, H. M., "Portfolio Selection," *The Journal of Finance* **7** (1952) 77-91.

Markowitz, H. M., **Portfolio Selection: Efficient Diversification of Investments**, John Wiley & Sons, Inc., New York, New York, 1959.

Mulvey, J. M., "Nonlinear Networks in Finance," *Advances in Mathematical Programming and Financial Planning* **1** (1987) 253-271.

Mulvey, J. M., and Vladimirou, H., "Stochastic Network Optimization Models for Investment Planning," *Annals of Operations Research* **20** (1989) 187-217.

Mulvey, J. M., and Vladimirou, H., "Solving Multistage Stochastic Networks: An Application of Scenario Aggregation," *Networks* **21** (1991) 619-643.

Nagurney, A., **Network Economics: A Variational Inequality Approach**, Kluwer Academic Publishers, Boston, Massachusetts, 1993.

Nagurney, A., "Variational Inequalities in the Analysis and Computation of Multi-Sector, Multi-Instrument Financial Equilibria," *Journal of Economic Dynamics and Control* **18** (1994) 161-184.

Nagurney, A., Dong, J., and Hughes, M., "Formulation and Computation of General Financial Equilibrium," *Optimization* **26** (1992) 339-354.

Nagurney, A., and Hughes, M., "Financial Flow of Funds Networks," *Networks* **22** (1992) 145-161.

Nagurney, A., and Siokos, S., "Dynamics of International Financial Networks: Modeling, Stability Analysis, and Computation," **Networks and Knowledge in a Dynamic Economy**, M. Beckmann, B. Johansson, F. Snickars, and R. Thord, editors, Springer-Verlag, Berlin, Germany, 1996, in press.

Nagurney, A., and Siokos, S., "Variational Inequalities for International General Financial Equilibrium Modeling and Computation," *Mathematical and Computer Modelling* **25** (1997) 31-49.

Nagurney, A., and Zhang, D., **Projected Dynamical Systems and Variational Inequalities with Applications**, Kluwer Academic Publishers, Boston, Massachusetts, 1996.

Quesnay, F., **Tableau Economique**, 1758, reproduced in facsimile with an introduction by H. Higgs by the British Economic Society, 1895.

Rockafellar, R. T., and Wets, R. J.-B., "Scenarios and Policy in Optimization under Uncertainty," *Mathematics of Operations Research* **16** (1991) 1-29.

Rudd, A., and Rosenberg, B., "Realistic Portfolio Optimization," *TIMS Studies in the Management Sciences* **11** (1979) 21-46.

Rutenberg, D. P., "Maneuvering Liquid Assets in a Multi-National Company: Formulation and Deterministic Solution Procedures," *Management Science* **16** (1970) 671-684.

Samuelson, P. A., "Spatial Price Equilibrium and Linear Programming," *American Economic Review* **42** (1952) 283-303.

Shapiro, A. C., and Rutenberg, D. P., "Managing Exchange Risks in a Floating World," *Financial Management* **16** (1976) 48-58.

Soenen, L. A., **Foreign Exchange Exposure Management: A Portfolio Approach**, Sijthoff and Noordhoff, Germantown, Maryland, 1979.

Srinivasan, V., "A Transshipment Model for Cash Management Decisions," *Management Science* **20** (1974) 1350-1363.

Storoy, S., Thore, S., and Boyer, M., "Equilibrium in Linear Capital Market Networks," *The Journal of Finance* **30** (1975) 1197-1211.

Takayama, T., and Judge, G. G., **Spatial and Temporal Price and Allocation Models**, North-Holland, Inc., Amsterdam, The Netherlands, 1971.

Thore, S., "Credit Networks," *Economica* **36** (1969) 42-57.

Thore, S., "Programming a Credit Network Under Uncertainty," *Journal of Money, Banking, and Finance* **2** (1970) 219-246.

Thore, S., **Programming the Network of Financial Intermediation**, Universitetsforlaget, Oslo, Norway, 1980.

Thore, S., "Spatial Models of the Eurodollar Market," *Journal of Banking and Finance* **8** (1984) 51-65.

Thore, S., and Kydland, F., "Dynamic for Flow-of-Funds Networks," in **Applications of Management Science in Banking and Finance**, pp. 259-276, S. Eilon and T. R. Fowkes, editors, Epping, England, 1972.

Wallace, S., "Solving Stochastic Programs with Network Recourse," *Networks* **16** (1986) 295-317.

Zhang, D., and Nagurney, A., "On the Stability of Projected Dynamical Systems," *Journal of Optimization Theory and Applications* **85** (1995) 97-124.

2 Foundations of Financial Economics

Financial economic theory was founded on several major theoretical breakthroughs in economic theory and has evolved into the tool that governs every financial market worldwide today. It is a unique example of how abstract mathematical theory can explain and extend real applications. Phenomenologically, financial economic theory has become the common language used by all participants in financial markets. Moreover, it provides a solid framework for the study and the development of financial markets and its products.

The theory of financial economics, whose development has been very rapid, is a mixture of many different theories among which the theories of finance and economics, mathematical programming, and utility theory are credited with the biggest contributions. In particular, economic and financial theories offer the theoretical background needed for the accurate representation of problems, whereas mathematical programming is the tool that materializes and solves what the two previous theories suggest, and, lastly, utility theory provides the background needed for handling risk and uncertainty. Obviously, any advance in any of these areas has an immediate effect on financial economics.

In this chapter, we present some principles from both economics and finance that form the foundations of modern financial economics. Rather than presenting a superficial coverage of a wide range of topics, the discussion is concentrated on issues that are directly related to the material in the subsequent chapters.

Section 2.1 provides a brief historical overview, describing the evolution of financial economics during the last forty years so that the reader can understand better its current state and its progression through time. Section 2.2 presents some basic fundamentals of utility theory and risk, which will be used extensively in the subsequent chapters. Section 2.3 provides a detailed look at the behavior of markets, and, more precisely, at the process by which asset allocation and prices are determined, discussing concepts such as market efficiency and equilibrium. We recall that an asset describes anything with tradable value owned by an individual or an institution. Finally, Section 2.4 concentrates on issues related to international economics and finance, where emphasis is given on elements that rarely, if ever, are encountered by single economy applications (e.g., multiple currencies, different tax systems, etc.).

2.1 Historic Overview

The current state of modern financial economic theory is based upon the innovative work of brilliant economists in the decade of the 1950's. The first major breakthrough was by Arrow and Debreu, who, in a series of extraordinary publications (Arrow (1951), Debreu (1951), Arrow (1953), Arrow and Debreu (1954), Debreu (1959)), introduced a simple, but significant, extension to the existing economic theory. Their contributions brought competitive equilibrium theory to a new level and provided the appropriate environment for the birth of modern economic and finance theory.

In particular, Arrow and Debreu, through the use of the techniques of convexity and fixed point theory, showed that the viability and the efficiency of the existing market system were open to analysis, with a model that followed the neoclassical economic foundations of: market clearing, uncertainty, and individual rationality. Subsequently, they derived new fundamental economic properties from these models (e.g., Arrow (1969), Debreu (1970)) and provided significant economic interpretations to the results.

The biggest contribution of the Arrow and Debreu model was to lay out an explicit system of conditions, under which a properly chosen price system must always exist. These conditions realistically defined the way that an economy should behave, in terms of the commodities, the firms, and the consumers and their preferences, in order to have the supply and the demand equally and simultaneously determine a price in equilibrium. It was the first time that precise, detailed assumptions were used to show that the model was consistent.

With the definition of the Arrow-Debreu type economy, standard theorems on the existence, uniqueness, and Pareto optimality (the allocation of goods in a way that no displacement can benefit one consumer unless it harms another (cf. Pareto (1909))) could be reinterpreted. Moreover, for the first time, an efficient allocation of resources became possible under uncertainty. The connection between competitive equilibrium and Pareto optimality was redefined in a more solid way, without the need of strong assumptions. The equivalence between an Arrow-Debreu equilibrium and a Pareto optimum was demonstrated with the first and second theorems of welfare economics that Arrow and Debreu simultaneously published in 1951. Even though some of the ideas that were introduced through their work were perceived much earlier (e.g., the connection between Pareto optimality and competitive equilibrium), most of the ideas were in either a stage of confusion, or not interconnected with each other in a single framework, and, consequently, issues such as the existence and the uniqueness of equilibrium under uncertainty could not be adequately addressed.

Almost simultaneous to the innovative work of Arrow and Debreu, two other major theoretical developments were taking place. The first one was by Modigliani and Miller (1958), who, in a challenging and controversial paper, established that the capital structure of a firm, that is, the financial framework of the firm, usually measured by the debt to equity ratio, does not affect the value of a firm. As a result, there is no optimal mix of securities that a firm can issue to finance its assets; simply stated, there is no optimal debt to equity ratio to characterize the financial structure of a firm. In their work, for the first time, the idea of financial arbitrage was used by stating that any investor can use riskless arbitrage in order to avoid the financial structure of a firm. Their model and approach served as the base for most of the research on capital structure and are considered to be the birth of modern capital structuring.

The other theoretical breakthrough was by Markowitz in 1952, who is credited with the birth of modern portfolio theory. Markowitz determined that one of the principal objectives of investors, besides the maximization of the returns of their portfolios, is to diversify away as much risk as possible. He claimed that investors select assets in such a way that the risk of their portfolio matches their risk preferences. In other words, he suggested that individuals who cannot bear risk will invest in assets with low risk, whereas people more comfortable with risk will accept investments of higher risk. His work also suggested that the tradeoff between risk and return is different for each investor, but the preferences of all people lie upon a fictitious curve (cf. Figure 2.1) which is usually called the "frontier of efficient portfolios." Along this curve lie all the diversified portfolios that have the highest return for a given risk, or the lowest risk for a given return. Markowitz's model was based on mean-variance portfolio selection, where the average and the variability of portfolio returns were determined in terms of the mean and covariance of the corresponding investments. The mean is a measure of an average return and the variance is a measure of the distribution of the returns around the mean return.

More analytically, let n be the total number of securities available in the economy, and let X_i represent the relative amount of capital invested in security i. Let random variable r_i denote the rate of return of security i. Then the rate of return for a portfolio, denoted by r_p, composed of all these securities is given by:

$$r_p = r_1 X_1 + r_2 X_2 \ldots + r_n X_n. \tag{2.1}$$

According to probability theory, the mean of a weighted sum (as in (2.1)) is the weighted sum of the expected values, and, as a result, the expected rate of return of the portfolio, $R = E(r_p)$, is given by:

$$R = \sum_{i=1}^{n} E(r_i) X_i, \tag{2.2}$$

where $E(r_i)$ denotes the expected value of the return on security i.

If we now let μ_i denote the expected value of the return on security i, then equation (2.2) can be simplified to:

$$R = \sum_{i=1}^{n} \mu_i X_i. \tag{2.3}$$

Unfortunately, the variance of a weighted sum is not as simple to derive as is the mean. Again, turning to probability theory, the variance of a weighted sum, and, consequently, the variance on the return of the portfolio, V, is given by:

$$V = \sum_{i=1}^{n} X_i^2 \mathrm{Var}(r_i) + 2 \sum_{i=1}^{n} \sum_{\substack{j=1 \\ j \neq i}}^{n} X_i X_j \sigma_{ij}, \tag{2.4}$$

where $\mathrm{Var}(r_i)$ is the variance of return on security i defined as:

$$\mathrm{Var}(r_i) = E[(r_i - \mu_i)^2], \tag{2.5}$$

and σ_{ij} denotes the covariance between securities i and j, where

$$\sigma_{ij} = E[(r_i - \mu_i)(r_j - \mu_j)]. \tag{2.6}$$

Obviously, $\mathrm{Var}(r_i) = \sigma_{ii}$, and, hence, equation (2.4) can be written as:

$$V = \sum_{i=1}^{n} \sum_{j=1}^{n} X_i X_j \sigma_{ij}. \tag{2.7}$$

In his work, Markowitz suggested that, for a fixed set of expected values μ_i and covariances σ_{ij} of the returns of all assets i and j, every investor can find an (R, V) combination that better fits his taste, solely limited by the constraints of the specific problem. In other words, if we assume that the enclosed area in Figure 2.1 is the set of all possible (R, V) combinations, then the investor must choose a combination that provides the highest return for a given risk, or the lowest risk for a given return. The set of these best combinations, which forms the frontier of efficient portfolios, is depicted in Figure 2.1.

The paper by Markowitz (1952), however, did not provide any specific techniques for determining this set of efficient portfolios although it contained a small illustration of how this set can be determined geometrically. In the original model by Markowitz short sales were excluded, and, thus,

$$X_i \geq 0, \quad i = 1, \ldots, n,$$

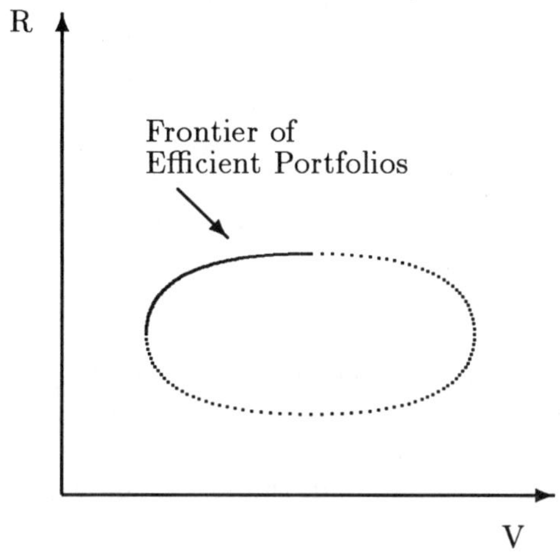

Fig. 2.1. The efficient frontier

and the amount of capital available was limited up to a budget. Hence, the summation over all relative amounts invested in all securities had to be equal to one, that is,

$$\sum_{i=1}^{n} X_i = 1.$$

According to the original work of Markowitz (1952), the efficient frontier had to be identified and then every investor had to select a portfolio through a mean-variance analysis that fitted his preferences. This notion was then extended and presented as a mathematical optimization model by Markowitz (1959), where every investor had to determine his optimal portfolio holdings through the solution of a quadratic programming model similar to:

$$\text{Maximize} \quad \alpha R - (1-\alpha)\, V \tag{2.8}$$

subject to:

$$\sum_{i=1}^{n} X_i = 1$$

$$X_i \geq 0, \quad i = 1, \ldots, n,$$

where α denotes an indicator of how risk-averse a specific investor is, and which will be discussed in Section 2.2.

Many versions and extensions of Markowitz's model have appeared in the literature, a collection of which can be found in Francis and Archer (1979), with $\alpha = 1/2$ being a frequently accepted value.

In the subsequent decade, for the first time, Grubel (1968) documented the gains from internationally diversified portfolios, starting a new era in international macroeconomics which witnessed significant progress in the years that followed. Furthermore, most of the economic and finance literature focused on the extension of the Arrow-Debreu model to financial markets (cf. Hirshleifer (1965)), and on the improvement of the full-covariance model by Markowitz, which required massive calculations in order to determine the efficient frontier and to perform a portfolio analysis.

The first important simplification of Markowitz's model was suggested by Sharpe (1963), through a model known as the *diagonal model,* where "the individual covariances between all securities are assumed to be zero." According to Sharpe's model, the variance-covariance matrix has zeros in all positions other than the diagonal, and, therefore, the variance on the return of a portfolio is given by:

$$V = \begin{pmatrix} X_1 \\ X_2 \\ \vdots \\ X_n \end{pmatrix}^T \begin{pmatrix} \sigma_{11}^2 & 0 & 0 & \dots & 0 \\ 0 & \sigma_{22}^2 & 0 & \dots & 0 \\ \vdots & \ddots & \ddots & \ddots & \vdots \\ 0 & 0 & 0 & \dots & \sigma_{nn}^2 \end{pmatrix} \begin{pmatrix} X_1 \\ X_2 \\ \vdots \\ X_n \end{pmatrix}. \tag{2.9}$$

Obviously, in this model the number of covariances required for portfolio analysis was smaller, and, consequently, the solution process was simplified, requiring less data and less computation time.

The most significant extension of the models by Markowitz (1952) and Sharpe (1963), was the Capital Asset Pricing Model (CAPM), which was based on the work of Sharpe (1964), Lintner (1965), and Mossin (1966). In this model the concept of a risk-free asset and market portfolio were introduced. A risk-free asset is an asset with a positive expected rate of return and a zero standard deviation, with the US Treasury bill being a good example. A market portfolio, on the other hand, is a portfolio on the efficient frontier of the Markowitz model which is considered to be desirable by all investors.

The CAPM assumes that all investors will select a portfolio that will be a linear combination of the risk-free asset and the market portfolio, and, as a result, the equilibrium prices of all assets can be expressed as a linear combination of the risk-free price and the price of the market portfolio. More precisely, the CAPM suggested, for the first time, a simple but, yet, important relationship between the risk and the return of an asset, given by:

$$E(r_j) = r_f + (1 - \alpha)\text{cov}(r_j, \pi) + \alpha\text{cov}(r_j, r_m), \tag{2.10}$$

where $E(r_j)$ denotes the expected nominal rate of return of asset j, r_f is the rate of return of the risk-free asset, r_m denotes the nominal rate of return of

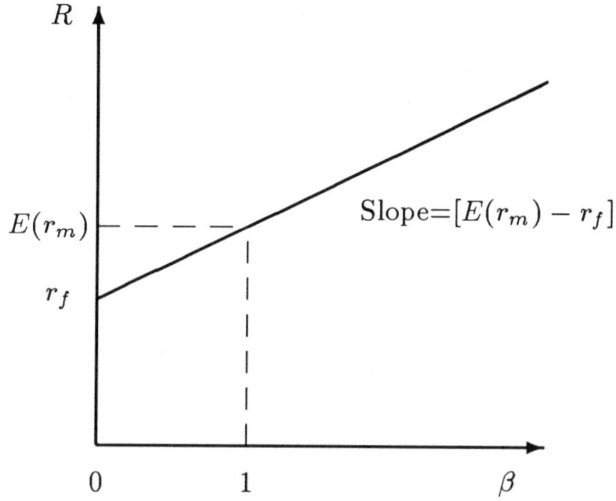

Fig. 2.2. Illustration of risk factor β

the market portfolio, π is the rate of inflation, and α is the market average degree of aversion (and which will be discussed in Section 2.2). It must be pointed out that in equation (2.10) the sum of the coefficient of the covariance with inflation and the coefficient of the covariance with market portfolio is equal to one. Consequently, in the case that investors are risk neutral, that is, when $\alpha = 0$, then all the existing risk is due to inflation.

Another version of the CAPM, which is more commonly used in corporate finance, and which gives the expected rate of return of asset j in a more compact and simple format, without having to deal directly with risk aversion and inflation, is given by:

$$E(r_j) = r_f + \beta_j \left[E(r_m) - r_f\right], \tag{2.11}$$

where $E(r_m)$ denotes the expected rate of return of the market portfolio. β_j represents the correlation of asset j with the overall market and is defined as:

$$\beta_j = \text{Cov}(r_m, r_j)/\text{Var}(r_m), \tag{2.12}$$

where $\text{Cov}(r_m, r_j)$ denotes the covariance between the rate of return of asset j and the rate of return of the market portfolio, and $\text{Var}(r_m)$ represents the variance of the rate of return of the market portfolio. The factor, β_j, denotes how risky an asset j is as compared to the overall market.

As is illustrated in Figure 2.2, if beta (β) is equal to one, then the corresponding asset behaves, on the average, like the entire market, whereas a beta equal to zero represents a risk-free asset.

The assumptions of the CAPM concern the investors, the firms, and the structure of the existing capital market. Investors are assumed to be risk-averse, trying to maximize utility functions that can be expressed in terms of the mean and the variance of the returns. Moreover, returns are assumed to be normally distributed, and investors to be price takers with homogeneous expectations and without any tax obligations. All the firms are equity financed and the market is assumed to be perfect, which means that there are no transaction costs and that the investors cannot influence the price of any product in the economy. Obviously, some of the assumptions governing the CAPM were not realistic and, as a result, the model was extended and improved several times in the years that followed. Everyone, however, is in agreement in that it was one of the major breakthroughs in modern economic and finance theory and forms the basis for most of the financial models that exist in our day.

Most of the major extensions of the CAPM occurred in the decade of the seventies, where a series of papers either relaxed some of its assumptions, or derived empirical results by applying it to a series of problems. Among the most significant contributions of that time were: the extension to a multiperiod economy by Merton (1973), the consumption CAPM by Breeden (1978) (which, however, failed empirically due to the difficulty in observing and computing consumption), and, finally, the inclusion of transaction costs by Milne and Smith (1980). The empirical tests of the CAPM were controversial for quite some time. The first publications documented a reasonable fit between the data and the model's outcome, and, as a result, more practitioners began to favor it. Scientists, in turn, were thoroughly investigating new aspects of testing its validity, and some criticism arose (e.g., Roll (1969), Blume and Friend (1973), Roll (1977)) as to the methodologies that were used for the empirical tests in the preceding years.

The dissatisfaction with the empirical tests of the CAPM led to more advanced models, such as the Arbitrage Pricing Theory (APT) by Ross (1976), which then became the subject of important research. APT's biggest contribution was the inclusion of multiple risk factors and the generalization of the CAPM, which was considered to be a special case of APT with only a single risk factor. According to APT, there is a linear relation among the expected returns of all assets in the economy. In particular, Ross assumed that the rate of return of every security can be expressed as a linear combination of some "basic" risk factors. If we let N denote the total number of such factors, then a security's rate of return satisfies a factor structure given by:

$$r_j = E(r_j) + \sum_{k=1}^{N} f_k \beta_{jk} + e_j \,, \tag{2.13}$$

where the f_k's are common random factors, the β_{jk}'s are coefficients, and the e_j's are the security specific residuals with $E(f) = 0$, $E(e_j) = 0$, and

$E(fe_j) = 0$, where f is the vector with components: $\{f_1, \ldots, f_N\}$.

The factors used in APT are "nondiversifiable" and not preidentified by the model, and, as a result, empirical results were not easily obtainable. Finally, in his paper, Ross showed that, in order to obstruct arbitrage, the expected rates of return of every security must be given by:

$$E(r_j) = r_f + \sum_{k=1}^{N} \beta_{jk} \left[E(f_k) - r_f \right], \tag{2.14}$$

where r_f is the risk-free rate of return.

Another major development was the derivation of an accurate option pricing model by Black and Scholes (1973), which revolutionized the pricing of financial instruments and the entire financial industry. We recall that an option is, in general, the right to trade an asset for a preagreed amount of capital. If the right is not exercised after a predetermined period of time, the option expires and the holder loses the money paid for holding that right. As is to be expected, a large part of the subsequent literature focused on different approaches to, simplifications of, and variations of the Black and Scholes Model (BSM). A significant simplification of the BSM was done by Cox, Ross, and Rubinstein (1979), and an important application was demonstrated by Merton (1974) as to the pricing of corporate debt. The Black and Scholes (1973) model managed to offer a simple but reliable tool for option pricing, where the number of variables that determine an option price is small and the derivation of their value is simple.

At the same time, a series of new models and studies (e.g., Lessard (1973), Solnik (1974)) suggested that international portfolios outperform domestically diversified portfolios. Furthermore, the mean-variance portfolio analysis that was introduced and mathematically formulated by Markowitz (1952, 1959), and later simplified by the diagonal model of Sharpe (1963), was further extended by Pogue (1970) and Francis (1978), with the introduction of variance-covariance matrices for both assets and liabilities, applied to the asset-liability management of banks. Moreover, dynamical programming was used to formulate and solve equilibrium models with asset prices and capital accumulation processes. One of the classic financial models of this ilk is the asset pricing model of Lucas (1978), where special restrictions give the (Arrow-Debreu type) economy a recursive structure.

During the decade of the eighties, most of the aforementioned models and theories were extended and improved. The Arbitrage Pricing Theory of Ross was refined by Chamberlain (1983) and Connor (1984), and the model of Black and Scholes was further explored and significantly generalized (see, e.g., Duffie and Huang (1985), Cox, Ingersoll, and Ross (1985), Duffie (1986)). The type of economy defined by Arrow and Debreu was established as the common ground for both financial modeling and macroeconomics, verifying their parallel evolution.

The theoretical advances of the preceding years, along with the increased volatility of interest and currency exchange rates, led to the increase in the number and the type of financial products. An entirely new financial industry with ever larger sized problems and higher computational demands evolved, and, consequently, there was a need for new advances in economic and finance theory. Among the biggest challenges was the introduction of mathematical tools and frameworks that could capture the complexities of such large-scale problems.

Many techniques, from the entire spectrum of mathematical programming (linear, nonlinear, stochastic, and network programming) were utilized in order to solve a large variety of financial economics problems. In particular, because of the interest that practitioners and monetary authorities demonstrated for the modeling and the computation of solutions to financial applications, a significant part of the literature focused on these topics. Most of the papers, however, studied the problems from either a static or a dynamic perspective without taking advantage of the underlying network structure that many of these problems possessed. In the following chapters we aim to present an integrated mathematical framework that captures both the static and dynamic nature of such problems. More precisely, we combine the theories of variational inequalities and of projected dynamical systems, where, in parallel, we take advantage of the network structure (which, in turn, is often specialized) that characterizes many of the financial problems.

2.2 Utility Theory and Risk Aversion

A large portion of economic and finance theory is based on the assumption that a decision-maker, given a choice of several alternatives, can, and, will be able to, select one of them, depending on his preferences. In this section we will outline some basic concepts of utility theory which form the framework for the preference relationships among different alternatives. We will limit our discussion to the fundamental issues that will be addressed in the subsequent chapters of this book. The concepts of utility and risk can stand alone as the main subject of a book, and, therefore, an exhaustive presentation would not be possible here. The goal of this section is to present, in very general terms, some basics of utility theory in order to familiarize the reader with some important ideas.

Beginning in the nineteenth century, a series of economists, including Jevons (1871) and Walras (1874), were considering utility to be measurable by each consumer. According to them, every consumer had a *cardinal* measure of utility, and, hence, every commodity had a specific number representing the degree of utility that was associated with it. This number was something like a price for each commodity and could be added or compared. For example, commodity X could be "liked" ten times more than commodity Y, and, therefore, commodity X was ten times more *preferable* to commodity Y.

This early interpretation of utility was based on a series of strong as-

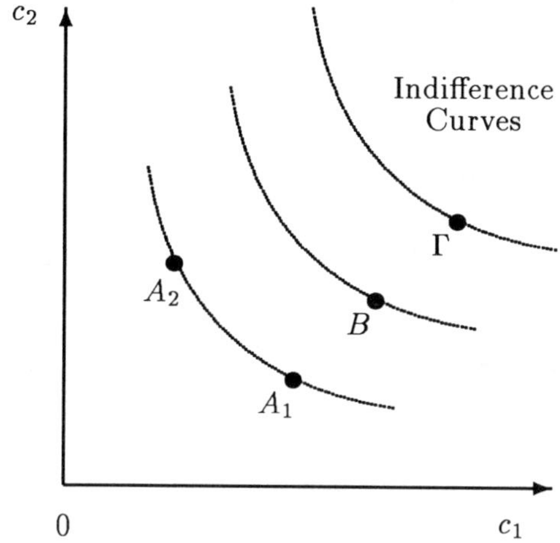

Fig. 2.3. An indifference map

sumptions and theorems. Its flexibility and usefulness, hence, became limited, mostly due to the fact that each commodity had a different number assigned by each consumer and, consequently, the study of a large number of commodities and consumers was prohibitive. Therefore, a new approach to modeling utility was synthesized (cf. Samuelson (1947), Edwards (1992), and Keeney and Raiffa (1993)). According to it, consumers would rank their preferences instead of assigning specific numbers to them. In order to understand this approach to utility theory, let $\mathcal{K}$ be the set of all alternatives that a consumer has, and assume that there are n different alternatives, which are denoted as: $(x_1, x_2, ..., x_n)$. A decision-maker is assumed to be able to rank all the alternatives according to his preferences and we assume that labeling is such that x_1 is less preferred than x_2 and so on. The symbolic representation is then:

$$x_1 \prec x_2 \prec \ldots \prec x_n. \tag{2.15}$$

The real-valued function $u(x)$ that represents the preference relation " $\prec$ " is a utility function, provided that:

$$x_i \prec x_j \Longrightarrow u(x_i) \prec u(x_j). \tag{2.16}$$

Each alternative decision corresponds to a specific combination of commodities, and, consequently, a utility function can also be stated in terms of the quantities that the decision-maker (investor) consumes (invests) from each commodity (asset).

Let c_i represent the quantity that the decision-maker consumes of commodity i, and assume, for simplicity, that the consumer has a choice only between two commodities. Hence, the utility function can be represented as:

$$u = f(c_1, c_2). \tag{2.17}$$

A decision-maker can derive a particular level of satisfaction from a variety of different (c_1, c_2) combinations. The set of all these combinations is called an *indifference curve* and the collection of many indifference curves of different levels of satisfaction is called an *indifference map*. An example of an indifference map is shown in Figure 2.3, where the quantities of c_1 and c_2 are measured along the axes. Points A_1 and A_2 refer to (c_1, c_2) combinations that offer the same level of satisfaction. Obviously, according to the definition, indifference curves never intersect and they correspond to higher levels of satisfaction as one moves further up and to the right as in Figure 2.3. In other words, point Γ is more preferable than point B and points A_1 and A_2 are less preferable than points B and Γ.

In financial economics, satisfaction is measured in terms of wealth and the utility function is assumed to be characterized by several properties (cf. Samuelson (1947), Levy and Sarnat (1977), Henderson and Quandt (1980), Stapleton and Subrahmanyam (1980), Huang and Litzenberger (1988)). The first property is that of *positive marginal utility* of wealth, which states that more wealth is preferred to less wealth. In other words, an investor will always select the portfolio that will increase his wealth, and his preferences will not have any social or emotional input. More wealth in a well functioning economy means that more capital will be spent, so that personal needs and desires can be fulfilled. The second property is that of the *diminishing marginal utility* of wealth, which states that the more a product is consumed, the less satisfaction it brings to the decision-maker. For example, most people who do not have a car will enjoy purchasing one because a car will significantly improve their every day life. For some individuals a second car may even be important and useful for a variety of reasons. An individual may purchase a van, a general utility vehicle, or a sports car because it is needed or simply because one enjoys driving it. A third car becomes less desirable by most individuals, and a fourth is out of the question for almost everyone, and so on. But why do decision-makers behave in this manner? The answer is simple and comes directly out of the diminishing marginal utility of wealth property. At one point, the cost of getting another car exceeds the pleasure that a person receives out of owning it, and, therefore, an individual will not consider purchasing another one.

Now we will introduce and discuss some *qualitative* properties of utility functions. Each of these properties reflects a specific attitude of the corresponding investor. The qualitative properties of a utility function form the basis upon which computational procedures for the solution of problems in financial economics have been developed. Provided that the utility function corresponds to a specific attitude by the investor, then the utility function is limited up to a degree and, hence, it is much easier to analyze and study. Throughout the remainder of this section and, without loss of generality, we will assume that utility functions are continuous, monotonically increasing, and twice continuously differentiable.

It must be pointed out that in many models in the existing literature, additional assumptions such as separability, additivity, and homogeneity of the utility functions are required to hold. For reasons of completeness, we now define these properties for utility functions, and, for simplicity, we follow the same notation as in (2.17). A utility function is said to be *strongly separable* in all of its arguments if it can be written as

$$u = F\left[\sum_{i=1}^{m} f_i(c_i)\right], \tag{2.18}$$

where F and f_i are increasing functions and m is the number of commodities. Similarly, a utility function is said to be *strongly additive* in all of its arguments if it can be written as

$$u = \sum_{i=1}^{m} f_i(c_i), \tag{2.19}$$

where, again, the f_i are increasing functions for all i. Finally, a utility function defined on a feasible set $\mathcal{K}$ is said to be *homogeneous* of degree ϕ, if, for a constant ϕ and any positive number q such that $(qc_1, qc_2, \ldots, qc_m) \in \mathcal{K}$, the following holds:

$$f(qc_1, qc_2, \ldots, qc_m) = q^{\phi} f(c_1, c_2, \ldots, c_m). \tag{2.20}$$

One of the primary functions of financial markets is to transfer risk among different participants of the economy. Every decision in financial economics includes a degree of risk, and, as a consequence, the entire financial industry has been built upon the effort of reducing and controlling risk. This attempt at diminishing risk comes out of the fact that most of the participants in the economy are, in general, risk-averse, or, in other words, conservative towards risk.

Obviously, noone is risk-averse always and in all situations. Most individuals are risk-averse when it comes to money, but they may still pay for a lottery where their chances to win are only one in a million. In practice, however, and in the corresponding literature, decision-makers are considered to be risk-averse. As a result, a clear mathematical description must be given in order to incorporate risk aversion in models of financial economics.

Consider a decision-maker who is facing a lottery with two possible outcomes. Let w_1 be the desired outcome, and let w_2 be the less favorable outcome. Clearly, the expected outcome of the lottery $\bar{w}$ is equal to $(w_1+w_2)/2$.

Assume now that the decision-maker has a choice between getting $\bar{w}$ and playing the lottery. If he decides to stay out of the lottery and get $\bar{w}$, then we say that he is risk-averse. The decision-maker believes that the satisfaction that he will get out of the certainty is higher than the one that he will get out of the lottery. In other words, for a risk-averse decision-maker, the utility of the expected value of the result of an uncertain situation exceeds the expected utility of that result, which can be expressed mathematically as:

$$u\left[E(\bar{w})\right] > E\left[u(\bar{w})\right]. \tag{2.21}$$

Since the notion of risk aversion should be clear, we will now present the way that risk aversion can be estimated, and we will study the relationship between risk aversion and the utility function of a given investor. According to classic utility theory (cf. Von Winterfeldt and Edwards (1986), Keeney and Raiffa (1993)), an investor is risk-averse (prone), if and only if, his utility function is concave (convex). For example, consider the lottery that we presented above and assume that the probability of event w_1 is p_1 and the probability of event w_2 is p_2, so that $p_1 + p_2 = 1$, with $p_1, p_2 \in [0, 1]$. Then the expected outcome of the lottery $\bar{w}$ is:

$$\bar{w} = p_1 w_1 + p_2 w_2. \tag{2.22}$$

If we now combine (2.21) and (2.22), we obtain:

$$u\left[p_1 w_1 + p_2 w_2\right] > p_1 u(w_1) + p_2 u(w_2), \tag{2.23}$$

which satisfies the definition of a concave function. On the other hand, if we consider the same lottery as before, and also assume that the utility function of the decision-maker is concave, then:

$$u\left[\sum_{i=1}^{2} p_i w_i\right] > \sum_{i=1}^{2} p_i u(w_i), \tag{2.24}$$

which is equivalent to (2.21), and, hence, the decision-maker is risk-averse.

Now that a connection between risk and utility functions has been established, we will define two indicators of risk aversion, suggested by Pratt (1964), which can be computed through the utility function of every decision-maker. The first indicator measures absolute risk aversion, and in the case that u is monotonically increasing, and has only the single argument of "wealth," is defined as:

$$\alpha(w) = -\frac{\frac{\partial^2 u(w)}{\partial w^2}}{\frac{\partial u(w)}{\partial w}} = -\frac{\partial}{\partial w}\left[\log \frac{\partial u(w)}{\partial w}\right]. \tag{2.25}$$

Similarly, the second indicator measures relative risk aversion, and is defined as:

$$r(w) = -\frac{\frac{\partial^2 u(w)}{\partial w^2} w}{\frac{\partial u(w)}{\partial w}}. \tag{2.26}$$

Obviously, if wealth w is assumed to be positive, the two indicators are always of the same sign. Moreover, it is easy to prove (see Keeney and Raiffa (1993)) that, if either $\alpha(w)$ or $r(w)$ is positive (negative) for all w, then u is concave (convex), and the decision-maker is risk-averse (prone). In particular, if u is increasing, $\frac{\partial u(w)}{\partial w}$ is positive. If now $\alpha(w)$ or $r(w)$ is also positive, then $\frac{\partial^2 u(w)}{\partial w^2}$ must be negative and, consequently, u is concave. With a similar approach one can verify the convex case.

For completeness, we will illustrate the derivation of the degree of risk aversion for the case of two commonly used utility functions, through the following simple examples.

Example 2.1

Consider the quadratic utility function:

$$u(w) = \eta + \delta w + \gamma w^2, \tag{2.27}$$

where $\delta > 0$, $\gamma > 0$. Then the absolute risk aversion indicator is equal to:

$$\alpha(w) = \frac{2\gamma}{\delta + 2\gamma w} > 0, \tag{2.28}$$

and the relative risk aversion indicator is given by:

$$r(w) = \frac{2w\gamma}{\delta + 2\gamma w} > 0, \tag{2.29}$$

and, therefore, the decision-maker with utility function u given by (2.27) is risk-averse.

Example 2.2

Consider the logarithmic utility function:

$$u(w) = \ln(w). \tag{2.30}$$

Then the absolute risk aversion indicator is given by:

$$\alpha(w) = -\frac{-1/w^2}{1/w} = \frac{1}{w} > 0, \tag{2.31}$$

and the relative risk aversion indicator is equal to:

$$r(w) = -\frac{-(1/w^2)w}{1/w} = 1 > 0, \tag{2.32}$$

and, therefore, the decision-maker with the utility function u given by (2.30) is also risk-averse. Notice that for the logarithmic utility function the degree of relative risk aversion does not depend on wealth and is equal to one.

This feature of a logarithmic utility function makes it a useful tool in some international macroeconomic models, which will be discussed in Section 2.4.

As it has been already pointed out, one of the main characteristics of financial economics is uncertainty. Consequently, the ability to derive the utility function for an investor under uncertainty is crucial. The work of Von Neumann and Morgenstern (1947), Savage (1954), Luce and Raiffa (1957), and Fishburn (1970) made such a task possible by defining the sets of axioms that a utility function must satisfy in order to be derived. These axioms are usually very general, but sufficient enough to imply the existence of the corresponding utility functions.

2.3 Market Equilibrium

Most of the literature in financial economics has been based on the assumption that investors cannot affect the prices at which they buy or sell. Each investor is considered to be an isolated case, who tries to maximize his utility function, subject to the prices that the market provides him. All the participants in the economy, be they buyers or sellers, have as a goal the maximization of their profits and the minimization of their losses. The prices are derived through the market where investors constantly buy and sell commodities. The analysis of market equilibrium tries to determine the prices at which different products will be bought and sold, and also the amount of each product that each participant in the economy will hold in an equilibrium state.

Market equilibrium analysis has its roots in the last half of the nineteenth century. The work of Gossen (1854), Jevons (1871), and Walras (1874) initiated the analysis of equilibrium theory. Subsequently, in the 1930's the study of market equilibrium became more formal and solid. The work of Wald (1935, 1936) and Hicks (1939) provided, for the first time, proofs of different qualitative properties of the equilibrium, along with a detailed study of the conditions under which an equilibrium could be modeled and derived. Furthermore, the innovative work of Arrow (1951) and Debreu (1951) started a new era in equilibrium analysis by bringing uncertainty into equilibrium theory, which led to the current status of market equilibrium theory.

Subsequently, a series of models that combined classical economic theory and equilibrium analysis under uncertainty were developed. A characteristic example of that evolution of equilibrium theory was the innovative work of Tobin (1963, 1969, 1971), who developed a partial equilibrium model under uncertainty for the financial sector of the economy, based on the classical Walrasian (1874) theory. The Tobin-Walras approach is on two levels, with one incorporating the utility functions of the participants, and the other the supply and demand functions of the financial instruments, where econometric techniques can then be applied for their estimation.

The basic assumption that governs most of the existing models that address the theory of market equilibrium is that of *perfect competition*. Perfect competition prohibits any participant in the economy (buyer or seller) from having control over the prices of different products or over the actions of other participants. The price of a product is considered to be a variable, the value of which is determined by the combined actions of all the buyers and sellers. Buyers are, hence, "price takers," in that they modify their holdings of a product according to the price, ignoring the effects that their behavior may have on that price.

Perfect competition assumes that all participants in the economy have perfect information about the products available, the current price, and the bids of a specific product. Moreover, the number of the participants in the economy is assumed to be large enough so that the market activity regarding a specific product will be small compared to the transactions in the overall market. Furthermore, all buyers are identical from the sellers' points of view and all sellers are identical from the buyers' points of view. In other words, sellers (buyers) do not prefer a specific buyer (seller) for any other reason except for the fact that he gives them a better deal. It is also assumed that all participants in the economy have access to all the different transactions that may occur. Since both buyers and sellers are informed about the price of a product, noone can either charge more or pay less than the price that exists in the market.

The mechanism that derives the prices of specific products and the amount that will be bought or sold by a particular investor is governed by the aggregated supply and demand functions of every instrument. Assume that there are n instruments with a typical instrument denoted by i, and m investors with a typical investor denoted by j. The aggregated demand $D_i = D_i(p_i)$ of an instrument i at a given price p_i is the summation of the total demands for that instrument by all investors. The total demand for instrument i is, hence, given by:

$$D_i(p_i) = \sum_{j=1}^{m} d_i^j(p_i), \tag{2.33}$$

where $d_i^j(p_i)$ denotes the demand for instrument i by investor j at price p_i. Similarly, one can define the total supply $S_i = S_i(p_i)$ of instrument i, as:

$$S_i(p_i) = \sum_{j=1}^{m} s_i^j(p_i), \tag{2.34}$$

with $s_i^j(p_i)$ denoting the supply of instrument i by investor j at price p_i.

Equilibrium occurs when the total supply and the total demand are equal (assuming a positive price) for each instrument in the economy. The price at which this equilibrium takes place for each instrument is called the "equilibrium price" of the instrument. As it is, typically, assumed in the literature

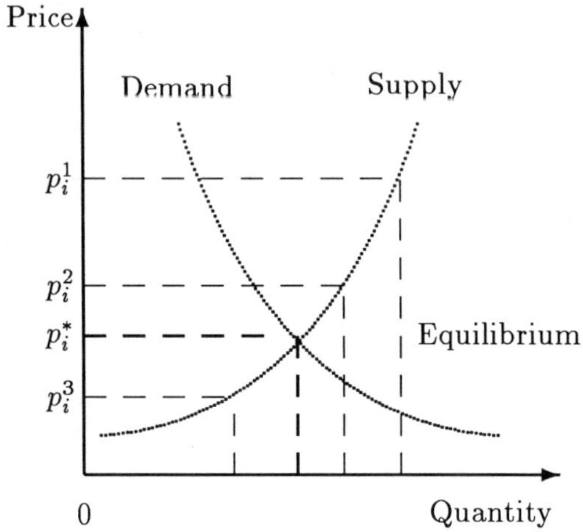

Fig. 2.4. Market equilibrium

and, as is shown in Figure 2.4, we will implicitly consider the demand function D_i for every instrument i to be of negative slope, and the supply function S_i to be of positive slope. (This is made more rigorous in subsequent chapters.) Geometrically, one can say that the point at which the curves of demand and supply intersect is an equilibrium. Market equilibrium theory (under appropriate assumptions) guarantees that the market will force the price to go to its equilibrium state.

For example (cf. Figure 2.4), let us assume that, initially, the market price for instrument i is p_i^1, and that this price is higher than the equilibrium price p_i^*. Because of this situation, at one point investors will decide that it is not worth paying this price for the corresponding instrument i and, as a result, they will stop demanding it. Therefore, the sellers of the instrument will see the buyers' reaction and they will reduce the price to a lower level. If this level is still higher than the equilibrium price, say, at p_i^2, then, even though some people will be willing to buy it, eventually the demand for it will fall again and, consequently, the price will have to be reduced even further. If, on the other hand, the price falls below the equilibrium price, say, to p_i^3, then many buyers will be willing to purchase the product because they will consider the price to be favorable. Some of the buyers, however, will not get as much of the instrument as they would like to, and, in order to make the sellers prefer them, rather than the other consumers, will make a higher bid. Obviously, the sellers will agree with the investors that offer the higher offer and the price will increase. This process will continue until the equilibrium state of instrument i, where $D_i(p_i^*) = S_i(p_i^*)$, is reached, at which the desires of all the participants are satisfied and instrument i will have its equilibrium price p_i^*.

In the equilibrium state, hence, the demand for an instrument is equal to its supply (assuming a positive price), and noone can benefit from buying or selling that instrument. Under the assumption of perfect competition and of nonnegative instrument prices, a significant part of the literature suggests the following economic equilibrium conditions: For each instrument i; $i = 1, \ldots, n$:

$$S_i(p_i^*) - D_i(p_i^*) \begin{cases} = 0, & \text{if } p_i^* > 0 \\ \geq 0, & \text{if } p_i^* = 0. \end{cases} \tag{2.35}$$

Specifically, the system of equalities and inequalities (2.35) states that if the price of a financial instrument is positive in equilibrium, then the market must clear for that instrument and if the price is zero, then either there is an excess supply of that instrument in the economy or the market clears.

In Chapter 3 we will consider a generalization of the above model in which the demand and supply functions d_i^j and s_i^j do not depend solely upon the price of instrument i but may, in general, depend upon the prices of the other instruments, as well.

Of course, certain changes in the market will affect the equilibrium state and, hence, the equilibrium conditions governing the instruments will change. For example, the incorporation of taxes or transaction costs would shift the supply curve, and, as a result, the point of intersection of the demand and the supply curves will be different. If, for example, we assume that the price of an instrument is limited (due to price policy interventions by monctary authorities) and let p_i^F (p_i^C) denote the minimum (maximum) (also known as the floor (ceiling)) price of the instrument, then the economic equilibrium conditions (2.35) are then modified thus: For each instrument i; $i = 1, \ldots, n$:

$$S_i(p_i^*) - D_i(p_i^*) \begin{cases} \leq 0, & \text{if } p_i^* = p_i^C \\ = 0, & \text{if } p_i^F \leq p_i^* \leq p_i^C \\ \geq 0, & \text{if } p_i^* = p_i^F. \end{cases} \tag{2.36}$$

The system of equalities and inequalities (2.36) states that if there is an excess demand of an instrument i in the economy then the price of it is equal to the ceiling price. If the price of a financial instrument i is positive, but not at the ceiling or at the floor, then the market must clear. Finally, if there is an excess supply of that instrument in the economy then the price of it is equal to the floor price.

Moreover, other issues such as the existence, the uniqueness, and the stability of the equilibrium need to be addressed for each specific problem. In Part II of the book we thoroughly examine such topics, providing the theory and the mathematical tools needed for the accurate modeling of financial economics applications.

Market equilibrium theory is divided into two major categories, that of general and that of partial equilibrium. Partial equilibrium considers only a specific part of the economy, while the influences from the rest of the world are considered to be fixed and held constant. On the contrary, in general equilibrium the whole economy is analyzed. Furthermore, partial equilibrium considers only groups of individuals (or sectors) and products from a specific industry (e.g., financial), ignoring the status of other parts of the economy. In the context of this book, we are primarily interested in the derivation and computation of financial equilibrium and, therefore, we mostly perform a partial equilibrium analysis.

Financial equilibrium modeling and analysis provide a useful tool for financial analysts and practitioners since the role of financial equilibrium is of increasing importance in many applications in the real world. One of the major contributions that exposed the practicality of the study of financial equilibrium is the work of Black and Litterman (1992), who suggested that investors could increase the efficiency of their capital allocation processes by combining their personal views on financial products with the information contained in an equilibrium pattern. In particular, they implied that an equilibrium pattern provided a "neutral view" of the market, and that personal views of each investor could then be used to make adjustments to their capital allocation decisions.

According to this approach, equilibrium models can capture the underlying dynamics of the market and provide an accurate, unbiased estimate of the price movements for every financial instrument and currency. Every investor can then combine his personal knowledge and intuition with the information supplied by the equilibrium pattern to construct his optimal portfolio. As a consequence, it is suggested that investors with access to better equilibrium models and better intuition will perform better.

Moreover, one can expect that the degree of deviation from equilibrium will depend on the level of confidence that each investor has in his views. Any price swing from its equilibrium value should then result in a market reaction that would force the prices closer to their equilibrium values. We address such issues rigorously when we study the stability analysis of a variety of dynamic financial adjustment processes in Parts III and IV.

2.4 International Financial Economics

The advantages of investing internationally have been discussed and studied by many authors (cf. Grubel (1968), Levy and Sarnat (1970), Solnik (1974), Lessard (1976), Adler and Dumas (1983)) and, it is a belief now, that international investments offer far more opportunities than domestic ones. Moreover, by diversifying across countries with different economic cycles and market structures, investors can reduce the variability of their returns. The greater the international diversification of funds, the less is the risk that investors hold and, furthermore, the lower are the chances of an extreme return in any country.

In spite of the overwhelming evidence as to the advantages of diversifying internationally, French and Poterba (1991), and Howell and Cozzini (1991) have documented the preference of investors towards domestic assets. Black (1974) and Stulz (1981), among others, suggested that taxation systems and high transaction costs move investors in the direction of domestic assets. Moreover, other authors (e.g., Solnik (1974), Krugman (1981), Adler and Dumas (1983), Branson and Henderson (1985)) have suggested that investors prefer domestic holdings because their consumption preferences are biased towards the market of their country.

Recent developments, however, such as the liberalization of eastern European financial markets and the 1992 Maastricht accord within the fifteen European Union members, with agreements of a common monetary system, common financial laws, regulated inflation levels, and, perhaps, in the near future, a common currency, have created a new environment for all investors. As a result, new studies must be conducted in order to verify if the investors still behave as previously ascertained, or whether investing internationally will become the norm (as intuition suggests now), rather than the exception. In any case, studies from major investment banks have documented that investors do turn to international markets. For example, the investment bank Salomon Brothers estimated that the cross-border equity trading, that is, the amount of stock bought by investors in one country from another country, was approximately 1.6 trillion dollars in 1989 alone (Sesit (1989)).

It is plausible to assume that incorporating multiple countries and currencies increases significantly the complexity of problems. Each country and/or currency has different characteristics and regulations. Investors from different countries do not hold the same expectations and preferences. Assumptions of purely perfect markets, or homogeneous investors cannot hold in an international context. The factors that contribute to this heterogeneity are due not only to the imperfections in the financial markets (due to, for example, transaction costs, taxes, and fees) but, also, due to the differences of purchasing power among investors of different nationalities. Furthermore, the markets are incomplete because investors are restricted from investing in other countries or currencies either by law or by extremely high taxes and transaction costs. For each particular investor-country-currency-security combination a different set of restrictions and regulations applies.

Due to the differences in nationality among investors and the fact that financial markets based on different currencies are not homogeneous, a series of parity conditions have been identified in international macroeconomics. One of the most significant and commonly used conditions is that of Purchasing Power Parity (PPP), which was first stated by the Swedish economist Gustav Cassel (1918). In particular, PPP is a relationship between weighted average price levels, which are counted in terms of some indices used in every country.

Obviously, in order for PPP to hold, all countries must use similar indices, with analogous and accurate ways of computing the consumption preferences of all investors. According to PPP, a unit of any currency worldwide should have the same purchasing power around the world. It must become clear that PPP does not deal with specific securities and instruments in every country, but with an average estimate. On the contrary, the *law of one price* refers to particular goods, and it states that the exchange-adjusted prices of identical securities must be within transaction costs worldwide. In other words, in the absence of market imperfections, the prices of identical assets must be equal worldwide.

The empirical evidence concerning the *law of one price* (Katseli-Papaefstratiou (1979), Isard (1977), Richardson (1978)) documents that violation of the law of one price is rather the rule than the exception. This is mainly due to the fact that goods cannot be purely homogeneous and also because of the differences among the statistical procedures followed by each country. As far as PPP is concerned, empirical results (e.g., Gailliot (1970), Kravis and Lipsey (1978), Roll (1979), Adler and Dumas (1983)) suggest that PPP does not hold in general at a particular point of time or for any time horizon. Therefore, the assumption of homogeneous investors and markets cannot be used in international financial economics.

As can be expected, in an international setting, the definition and the derivation of prices are more complicated than in the simple single country case. The rates of return of all securities must be expressed in terms of the same unit. Hence, a basic currency must be selected and all the rates of return have to be expressed in terms of it. In particular, if we let the random variable $\tilde{r_i}$ represent the rate of return of a specific security in terms of the local currency, and we let e_i denote the rate of appreciation of the local currency against the basic currency, then the rate of return of this security in terms of the basic currency, is given by:

$$r_i = (1 + \tilde{r_i}) \times (1 + e_i) - 1, \tag{2.37}$$

$$r_i = \tilde{r_i} + e_i + \tilde{r_i} \times e_i. \tag{2.38}$$

In a large part of the existing literature (cf. Eun and Resnick (1988)), the product $\tilde{r_i} \times e_i$ is considered to be insignificant in the case of efficient markets, and, therefore, equation (2.38) can be approximated by:

$$r_i \simeq \tilde{r_i} + e_i. \tag{2.39}$$

Based on the approximation (2.39), the variance of the return, in terms of the basic currency, is given by:

$$\mathrm{Var}(r_i) = \mathrm{Var}(\tilde{r_i}) + \mathrm{Var}(e_i) + 2\mathrm{cov}(\tilde{r_i}, e_i). \tag{2.40}$$

Let n be the total number of securities available in the economy, and also let X_i denote the relative amount invested in security i. We can then generalize the previous analysis to a portfolio context, where the variance of portfolio returns, denoted by $\text{Var}(r_p)$, in terms of the basic currency, can be written as:

$$\text{Var}(r_p) = \sum_{i=1}^{n} X_i^2 \text{Var}(r_i) + \sum_{i=1}^{n} \sum_{\substack{j=1 \\ j \neq i}}^{n} X_i X_j \text{cov}(r_i, r_j), \tag{2.41}$$

$$\text{Var}(r_p) = \sum_{i=1}^{n} \sum_{j=1}^{n} X_i X_j \text{cov}(r_i, r_j), \tag{2.42}$$

where $\text{cov}(r_i, r_j)$ represents the covariance between the returns in the markets of currencies i and j, and can be approximated by:

$$\text{cov}(r_i, r_j) \simeq \text{cov}(\tilde{r}_i, \tilde{r}_j) + \text{cov}(e_i, e_j) + 2\text{cov}(\tilde{r}_i, e_j). \tag{2.43}$$

Using equation (2.43), (2.42) can be written as:

$$\text{Var}(r_p) = \sum_{i=1}^{n} \sum_{j=1}^{n} X_i X_j \left[\text{cov}(\tilde{r}_i, \tilde{r}_j) + \text{cov}(e_i, e_j) + 2\text{cov}(\tilde{r}_i, e_j)\right]. \tag{2.44}$$

Grubel (1968) was the first to propose that international investments offer lower return variances, due to the fact that the correlation between market indices from different countries is significantly lower than one. Siegel (1972), in turn, initiated the study of asset pricing among investors of different nationalities. Moreover, Solnik (1974) demonstrated that the variance reduction in international portfolios can be performed even with a small number of securities. He also described the equilibrium holdings of investors from different countries and faced the issue of deriving international equilibrium rates.

In one of the most important surveys in international macroeconomics, Adler and Dumas (1983) presented an international version of the CAPM, following procedures used by Fischer (1975) and Losq (1977). We will present now the fundamentals of this model, which is a natural extension of the single country CAPM presented in Section 2.1. In particular, let r_p^l be the rate of return, in terms of a basic currency, of an optimal portfolio that investors in country l hold, and let π^l be the inflation rate that the investor from country l faces. Let also w^l be the wealth of country l and let $w = \sum_{l=1}^{L} w^l$ be the wealth of the entire world where L is the number of countries. Let α^l be the market average degree of relative risk aversion for investors from country l, as was defined in equation (2.26), and, finally, let $\alpha = \sum_{l=1}^{L} \alpha^l$. Then, according to the international CAPM, the expected nominal rate of return of security j is given by:

$$E(r_j) = r_f + \alpha \sum_{l=1}^{L} \left(\frac{1}{\alpha^l} - 1\right) w^l \frac{\text{cov}(r_j, \pi^l)}{w} + \alpha \text{cov}(r_j, r_m). \tag{2.45}$$

It is easy to observe that, in the case where $\alpha^l = 1$, the second component of equation (2.45) becomes equal to zero. Therefore, the expected return on asset j for investors from country l does not depend on the inflation of their country. Also, due to the fact that the logarithmic utility function has a degree of relative risk aversion equal to one (see Example 2.2), the investor or the group of investors that gets characterized by $\alpha^l - 1$, is called *logarithmic* or *nationless*. In other words, one can say that all the efficient frontiers defined by Markowitz have a common point for all investors in the world.

According to the "separation theorem" of Black (1972), the work of Solnik (1974), and the paper by Sercu (1980), the equilibrium composition of every investor's portfolio is a combination of two different efficient portfolios, with the first one being the universal or the logarithmic portfolio, and the second one being a portfolio that better hedges the home-inflation of every investor. According to Solnik, the part of the portfolio that hedges the risk is entirely devoted to the home currency investments, whereas in subsequent papers, this assumption has been relaxed.

In the case of the model presented by Adler and Dumas, the portfolio holdings in equilibrium were a combination of the logarithmic portfolio with weight $1/\alpha^l$ and of a hedging portfolio with weight $(1 - 1/\alpha^l)$. In particular, if we group the portfolio holdings for investors from country l into the $n \times 1$ vector $\tilde{w}^l$, then the following equation holds:

$$\tilde{w}^l = \frac{1}{\alpha^l} Q^{-1} (\tilde{\mu} - \tilde{r}_f) + \left(1 - \frac{1}{\alpha^l}\right) Q^{-1} q^l, \tag{2.46}$$

where Q is the $n \times n$ variance-covariance matrix of nominal rates of return in terms of the basic currency, that is, element (i, j) of matrix Q, denoted by Q_{ij}, is given by $Q_{ij} = \text{cov}(r_i, r_j)$, with $\tilde{\mu}$ being the $n \times 1$ vector of the nominal expected rates of return, $\tilde{r}_f$ being an $n \times 1$ vector with all of its elements equal to the risk-free rate r_f, and q^l is an $n \times 1$ vector such that $q_j^l = \text{cov}(r_j, \pi^l)$.

The model by Solnik (1974) can be viewed as the precursor to contemporary asset pricing models, whereas the single country CAPM can be considered as a special case of the international CAPM in the case of equities (cf. Adler and Dumas (1983)). As one would expect, a series of different international asset pricing models have appeared in the literature in the last several years, with the vast majority of the models being extensions of the aforementioned CAPM or of the APT by Ross (e.g., Solnik (1983), Levine (1989)). Empirical tests (e.g., Solnik (1977)) have been conducted for most of these models, with the results being controversial with noone being able to claim that one model is much better than another. The fact that most of these models examine partial equilibrium, and, therefore, may only study a part of the whole economy, forces the results to be heterodoxical. Moreover, some of the assumptions that have been used are either unrealistic (such as a common degree of risk aversion among all investors of the same country), or the calculation of some mainly abstract variables cannot be done accurately (as is the case for the risk-free asset, and the holdings in a logarithmic utility portfolio).

It is a common belief, now, that international macroeconomics has experienced significant progress during the last several decades, and that many good ideas and models have been developed. Moreover, almost everyone would also agree that the size and the nature of the problems requires new approaches and new techniques. Therefore, an integrated framework that can unify all the aforementioned ideas, and that can provide a solid and more realistic description of the international economy still needs to be identified and to be developed. We hope to make a contribution in this direction with this volume.

2.5 Sources and Notes

In this chapter we have presented some of the foundations of financial economics. More precisely, we provided a historic overview of the evolution of financial economics, along with some basic single country models from the areas of asset pricing and portfolio optimization. We also discussed the very basic ideas of utility theory, risk management, and market equilibrium, and we concluded by reviewing some of the foundations of international financial economics.

Section 2.1

The goal of Section 2.1 was to provide a brief historical overview of the advances in financial economics during the last forty years. Hence, no models were extensively presented or discussed. The Black and Scholes model, for example, will be presented in a more detailed fashion in an appendix. The books by Duffie (1988) and by Milne (1995) focus on asset pricing, whereas the book edited by Eatwell, Milgate, and Newman (1989) extensively discusses and examines the Arrow-Debreu model and some of its extensions.

Since many of the details in option pricing are beyond the scope of this book, we refer the interested reader to the original papers cited throughout this chapter and to Cox and Huang (1987) and Kolb (1991). For a more detailed analysis of advances in Arbitrage Pricing Theory (due to, among others, Chamberlain (1983) and Connor (1984)), see also the book by Huang and Litzenberger (1988).

For a more complete discussion as to the empirical testing of the CAPM and APT, along with a wide collection of papers on related topics, we refer the reader to Elton and Gruber (1987).

Section 2.2

Section 2.2 deals with the important topic of utility functions and risk. Our purpose was not to give complete details but only a flavor of the basic ideas and characteristics. For an analytical and well-documented study of utility theory, risk, and uncertainty, see the book by Keeney and Raiffa (1993). We must also emphasize that there are many sets of axioms and theorems that indicate the existence of utility functions that are appropriate, accurate, and efficient for the modeling and study of different decision-making processes. Their presentation is beyond the scope of this book, and we direct the reader to the significant work of von Neumann and Morgenstern (1947), Savage (1954), and Luce and Raiffa (1957).

Section 2.3

In Section 2.3, we addressed the issue of market equilibrium. We presented the assumptions that are held in the majority of the literature in financial economics, and we tried to expose the reader to different aspects of equilibrium theory. Even though the material presented in this section is sufficient for the issues that will be covered in the chapters that follow, it is not, by any means, complete in all the pertinent facets of market equilibrium theory. Therefore, we direct the readers interested in this material to the books by Samuelson (1947), Levy and Sarnat (1977), Henderson and Quandt (1980), and to the book edited by Eatwell, Milgate, and Newman (1989).

Section 2.4

Section 2.4 presented some of the foundations of international macroeconomics. The emphasis was on the parity conditions that govern international markets, and on asset pricing in an international context. For a more detailed presentation of these topics, we refer the reader to the work by Solnik (1974), Adler and Dumas (1983), and Dumas (1994). We note that relevant topics such as monetary economics and capital taxation were not presented in this section. These topics are deferred to Parts III and IV of this book where models with market imperfections such as taxes, transaction costs, and policies from monetary authorities will be presented and extensively studied. For a collection of papers in international macroeconomics, see also the book edited by Van der Ploeg (1994).

References

Adler, M., and Dumas, B., "International Portfolio Choice and Corporation Finance: A Synthesis," *Journal of Finance* **38** (1983) 925-984.

Arrow, K. J., "An Extension of the Basic Theorems of Classical Welfare Economics," *Econometrica* **51** (1951) 1305-1323.

Arrow, K. J., "Les Rôle des Valeurs Boursières pour la Répartition la Meilleure des Risques," *Économétrie*, Centre National de la Récherche Scientifique (1953) 41-48.

Arrow, K. J., **Collected Papers of Kenneth Arrow**, Belknap Press, Cambridge, Massachusetts, 1969.

Arrow, K. J., and Debreu, G., "Existence of an Equilibrium for a Competitive Economy," *Econometrica* **22** (1954) 265-290.

Black, F., "Capital Market Equilibrium with Restricted Borrowing," *Journal of Business* **45** (1972) 444-454.

Black, F., "International Capital Market Equilibrium with Investment Barriers," *Journal of Financial Economics* **1** (1974) 337-352.

Black, F., and Litterman, R., "Global Portfolio Optimization," *Financial Analysts Journal* **48** (1992) 28-43.

Black, F., and Scholes, M. "The Pricing of Options and Corporate Liabilities," *Journal of Political Economy* **3** (1973) 637-654.

Blume, M. E., and Friend, I., "A New Look at the CAPM," *Journal of Finance* **28** (1973) 147-162.

Branson, W., and Henderson, D., "The Specification and Influence of Asset Markets," in **Handbook of International Economics**, pp. 749-805, R. W. Jones and P. B. Kenen, editors, North-Holland, Inc., Amsterdam, The Netherlands, 1985.

Breeden, D. T., "An Intertemporal Asset Pricing Model with Stochastic Consumption and Investment Opportunities," *Journal of Financial Economics* **7** (1978) 265-296.

Cassel, G., "Abnormal Deviations in International Exchanges," *Economic Journal* (1918) 413-415.

Chamberlain, G., "Funds, Factors and Diversification in Arbitrage Pricing Models," *Econometrica* **51** (1983) 1305-1323.

Connor, G., "A Unified Beta Pricing Theory," *Journal of Economic Theory* **34** (1984) 13-31.

Cox, J. C., and Huang, C., "Option Pricing Theory and its Applications," in **Frontiers of Financial Theory**, G. Constantinides and S. Bhattacharya, editors, Rowman and Littlefield, Totowa, New Jersey, 1987.

Cox, J. C., Ingersoll, J., and Ross, S. A., "An Intertemporal General Equilibrium Model of Asset Prices," *Econometrica* **53** (1985) 363-384.

Cox, J. C., Ross, S. A., and Rubinstein, M., "Option Pricing: A Simplified Approach," *Journal of Financial Economics* **7** (1979) 229-263.

Debreu, G., "The Coefficient of Resource Utilization," *Econometrica* **19** (1951) 273-292.

Debreu, G., **Theory of Value**, Yale University Press, New Haven, Connecticut, 1959.

Debreu, G., "Economies with a Finite Set of Equilibria," *Econometrica* **38** (1970) 387-392.

Duffie, D., "Stochastic Equilibria: Existence, Spanning Number and the 'No Expected Financial Gain from Trade' Hypothesis," *Econometrica* **54** (1986) 1161-1184.

Duffie, D., **Security Markets. Stochastic Models**, Academic Press, Inc., San Diego, California, 1988.

Duffie, D., and Huang, C., "Implementing Arrow-Debreu Equilibria by Continuous Trading of Few Long-Lived Securities," *Econometrica* **53** (1985) 1337-1356.

Dumas, B., "Partial Equilibrium versus General Equilibrium Models of the International Capital Market," in **The Handbook of International Macroeconomics**, pp. 301-347, F. Van der Ploeg, editor, Blackwell Publishers, Cambridge, Massachusetts, 1994.

Eatwell, J., Milgate, M., Newman, P., editors, **The New Palgrave: General Equilibrium**, W. W. Norton & Company, Inc., New York, New York, 1989.

Edwards, W., editor, **Utility Theories: Measurements and Applications**, Kluwer Academic Publishers, Dordrecht, The Netherlands, 1992.

Elton, E. J., and Gruber, M. J., **Modern Portfolio Theory and Investment Analysis**, John Wiley & Sons, third edition, New York, New York, 1987.

Eun, C., and Resnick, B., "Exchange Rate Uncertainty, Forward Contracts, and International Portfolio Selection," *The Journal of Finance* **43** (1988) 197-215.

Fischer, S., "The Demand for Index Bonds," *Journal of Political Economy* **83** (1975) 529-534.

Fishburn, P., **Utility Theory for Decision Making**, John Wiley & Sons, New York, New York, 1970.

Francis, J. C.,"Portfolio Analysis of Asset and Liability Management in Small-, Medium-, and Large-Sized Banks," *Journal of Monetary Economics* **3** (1978) 112-134.

Francis, J. C., and Archer, S. H., **Portfolio Analysis**, Prentice-Hall, Inc., Englewood Cliffs, New Jersey, 1979.

French, K., and Poterba, J., "Investor Diversification and International Equity Markets," *American Economic Review* **81** (1991) 222-226.

Gailliot, H., "Purchasing Power Parity as an Explanation of Long Term Changes in Exchange Rates," *Journal of Money, Credit, and Banking* **2** (1970) 348-357.

Gossen, H., **Entwicklung der Gesetze des Menschlichen Verkehrs**, Prager, Berlin, Germany, 1854.

Grubel, H. G., "Internationally Diversified Portfolios: Welfare Gains and Capital Flows," *American Economic Review* **58** (1968) 1299-1314.

Henderson, J. M., and Quandt, R. E., **Microeconomic Theory: A Mathematical Approach**, McGraw-Hill, Inc., New York, New York, 1980.

Hicks, J. R., **Value and Capital**, Clarendon Press, Oxford, Great Britain, 1939.

Hirshleifer, J., "Investment Decision under Uncertainty: Choice Theoretic Approaches," *Quarterly Journal of Economics* **79** (1965) 509-536.

Howell, M., and Cozzini, A., **International Equity Flows**, International Equity Research, Salomon Brothers, London, Great Britain, 1991.

Huang, C., and Litzenberger, R. H., **Foundations for Financial Economics**, Prentice-Hall, Inc., Englewood Cliffs, New Jersey, 1988.

Isard, P., "How Far Can We Push The Law of One Price?" *American Economic Review* **67** (1977) 942-948.

Jevons, W., **The Theory of Political Economy**, Macmillan Press, Ltd., London, Great Britain, 1871.

Katseli-Papaefstratiou, L., "The Reemergence of the Purchasing Power Parity Doctrine in the 1970's," *Special Paper in International Economics* **13** (1979).

Keeney, R. L., and Raiffa, H., **Decisions with Multiple Objectives**, Cambridge University Press, New York, New York, 1993.

Kolb, R., **Options An Introduction**, Kolb Publishing Company, Miami, Florida, 1991.

Kravis, I., and Lipsey, R., "Price Behavior in the Light of Balance of Payments Theory," *Journal of International Economics* **8** (1978) 193-246.

Krugman, P., "Consumption Preferences, Assets Demands, and Distribution Effects in International Financial Markets," working paper no. 651, National Bureau of Economic Research, 1981.

Lessard, D., "World Country Industry Relationships in Equity Returns: Implications for Risk Reduction through International Diversification," *Financial Analysts Journal* **32** (1973) 2-8.

Levine, R., "An International Arbitrage Pricing Model with PPP Deviations," *Economic Inquiry* **27** (1989) 587-599.

Levy, H., and Sarnat, M., "International Diversification of Investment Portfolios," *American Economic Review* **60** (1970) 668-675.

Levy, H., and Sarnat, M., editors, **Financial Decision Making Under Uncertainty**, Academic Press, Inc., New York, New York, 1977.

Lintner, J., "The Valuation of Risk Assets and the Selection of Risky Investments in Stock Portfolios and Capital Budgets," *Review of Economic Studies* **47** (1965) 13-37.

Losq, E., "Commodity Price Uncertainty and Capital Market Equilibrium," McGill University Mimeo, Montreal, Canada, 1977.

Lucas, R. E., "Asset Prices in an Exchange Economy," *Econometrica* **46** (1978) 1429-1445.

Luce, R., and Raiffa, H., **Games and Decisions**, John Wiley & Sons, Inc., New York, New York, 1957.

Markowitz, H. M., "Portfolio Selection," *The Journal of Finance* **7** (1952) 77-91.

Markowitz, H. M., **Portfolio Selection: Efficient Diversification of Investments**, John Wiley & Sons, New York, New York, 1959.

Merton, R. C., "An Intertemporal Capital Asset Pricing Model," *Econometrica* **41** (1973) 867-887.

Merton, R. C., "On the Pricing of Corporate Debt: The Risk Structure of Interest Rates," *Journal of Finance* **29** (1974) 449-470.

Milne, F., **Finance Theory and Asset Pricing**, Oxford University Press, Inc., New York, New York, 1995.

Milne, F., and Smith, C., "Capital Asset Pricing with Proportional Transaction Costs," *Journal of Financial and Qualitative Analysis* **15** (1980) 253-265.

Modigliani, F., and Miller, M., "The Cost of Capital, Corporate Finance and the Theory of Corporation Finance," *American Economic Review* **48** (1958) 261-297.

Mossin, J., "Equilibrium in a Capital Asset Market," *Econometrica* **34** (1966) 768-783.

Pareto, V., **Manuel d' Economie Politique**, Giard, Paris, France, 1909.

Pogue, G. A., "An Extension of the Markowitz Portfolio Selection Model to Include Transaction Costs, Short Sales, Leverage Policies, and Taxes," *Journal of Finance* **25** (1970) 1005-1027.

Pratt, J. E., "Risk Aversion in the Small and in the Large," *Econometrica* **32** (1964) 122-136.

Richardson, J., "Some Empirical Evidence on Commodity Arbitrage and the Law of One Price," *Journal of International Economics* **8** (1978) 341-352.

Roll, R., "Bias in Fitting the Sharpe Model to Time Series Data," *Journal of Financial and Quantitative Analysis* **14** (1969) 141-152.

Roll, R., "A Critique of the Asset Pricing Theory's Tests. Part 1: On Past and Potential Testability of the Theory," *Journal of Financial Economics* **4** (1977) 129-176.

Roll, R., "Violations of Purchasing Power Parity and Their Implications for Efficient International Commodity Market," in **International Finance and Trade,** pp. 133-176, M. Sarnat and G. Szego, editors, Ballinger, Cambridge, Massachusetts, 1979.

Ross, S. A., "Arbitrage Theory of Capital Asset Pricing," *Journal of Economic Theory* **13** (1976) 341-360.

Samuelson, P. A., **Foundations of Economic Analysis**, Harvard University Press, Cambridge, Massachusetts, 1947.

Savage, L., **The Foundations of Statistics**, John Wiley & Sons, Inc., New York, New York, 1954.

Sercu, P., "A Generalization of the International Asset Pricing Model," *Revue de l' Association Française de Finance* **1** (1980) 91-135.

Sesit, M., "Foreign Investment Makes a Come Back," *The Wall Street Journal*, September 1, pp. C1 and C14, 1989.

Sharpe, W. F., "A Simplified Model for Portfolio Analysis," *Management Science* **9** (1963) 277-293.

Sharpe, W. F., "Capital Asset Prices: A Theory of Market Equilibrium under Conditions of Risk," *Journal of Finance* **19** (1964) 425-443.

Siegel, J., "Risk, Interest, and Forward Exchange," *Quarterly Journal of Economics* **86** (1972) 303-309.

Solnik, B., "Equilibrium Model of the International Market," *Journal of Economic Theory* **8** (1974) 500-524.

Solnik, B., "Testing International Asset Pricing: Some Pessimistic Views," *Journal of Finance* **32** (1977) 503-511.

Solnik, B., "International Arbitrage Pricing Theory," *Journal of Finance* **38** (1983) 449-457.

Stapleton, R., and Subrahmanyam, M., editors, **Capital Market Equilibrium and Corporate Financial Decisions**, JAI Press, Greenwich, Connecticut, 1980.

Stulz, R., "A Model for International Asset Pricing," *Journal of Financial Economics* **9** (1981) 383-406.

Tobin, J., "Commercial Banks as Creators of Money," in **Banking and Monetary Studies**, D. Carson, editor, Irwin, Homewood, Illinois, 1963.

Tobin, J., "A General Equilibrium Approach to Monetary Theory," *Journal of Money, Credit and Banking* **1** (1969) 15-29.

Tobin, J., **Essays in Macroeconomics**, North-Holland, Inc., Amsterdam, The Netherlands, 1971.

Van der Ploeg, F., editor, **The Handbook of International Macroeconomics**, Blackwell Publishers, Cambridge, Massachusetts, 1994.

Von Neumann, J., and Morgenstern, O., **Theory of Games and Economic Behavior**, Princeton University Press, Princeton, New Jersey, 1947.

Von Winterfeldt, D., and Edwards, W., **Decision Analysis and Behavioral Research**, Cambridge University Press, Cambridge, Great Britain, 1986.

Wald, A., "Über die Eindeutige Positive Losbarkeit der Neuen Productionsgleichungen," *Ergebnisse eines Mathematischen Kolloquiums* **6** (1935) 12-20.

Wald, A., "Über die Productionsgleichungen der Ökonomischen Wertlehre," *Ergebnisse eines Mathematischen Kolloquiums* **7** (1936) 1-6.

Walras, L., **The Eléments d' Economie Politique Pure**, Guillaumin, Paris, France, 1874.

Part II Methodological Foundations

3 Variational Inequalities

Equilibrium is a concept central for the understanding of complex systems in many disciplines, both from a qualitative perspective as well as from a computational standpoint. The importance and pervasiveness of equilibrium problems have stimulated the development of methodological tools for analysis and computation to what are, typically, large-scale problems. One of the proven methodologies for the study of equilibrium problems in economics and in operations research/management science is that of finite-dimensional variational inequality theory. In this book we utilize variational inequality theory for the formulation, qualitative analysis, and computation of financial equilibrium problems. As already noted in Chapter 2, financial equilibrium modeling and analysis provide a useful tool for financial analysts and practitioners since the role of financial equilibrium is of growing importance in many realistic applications today.

The first financial equilibrium model to make use of finite-dimensional variational inequality theory was developed by Nagurney, Dong, and Hughes (1992), who proposed a multi-sector, multi-instrument financial equilibrium model, which yielded the optimal composition of each sector's portfolio in terms of assets and liabilities as well as the equilibrium instrument prices. Their proposed computational procedure decomposed the equilibrium problem into subproblems with special network structure in asset, liability, and price variables, respectively. The network subproblems could then be solved simultaneously and in closed form.

Nagurney and Siokos (1997) subsequently utilized finite-dimensional variational inequality theory to introduce international financial equilibrium models, in which they considered the scenario of imperfect markets. The sectors in the countries were subject to taxes, and price floors and ceilings were imposed on both the instrument prices in distinct currencies and on the exchange rates. Finally, they also incorporated transaction costs.

In this chapter, we provide the foundations of finite-dimensional variational inequality theory at a level that is used for the modeling, analysis, and computation of the static financial equilibrium models in Parts III and

IV. Since the variational inequality problem captures, as special cases, such well-known mathematical programming problems as nonlinear equations, optimization problems, and complementarity problems, it is particularly useful as a unifying framework.

This chapter is organized as follows. In Section 3.1 we discuss some basic problem types occurring in finance and their relationships to the variational inequality problem. We also provide examples. In Section 3.2 we provide some qualitative properties of the variational inequality problem. In Section 3.3 we discuss algorithms and conditions for convergence. Proofs of the theoretical results in this chapter are left out since the results here are now standard and can be found in such books as Kinderlehrer and Stampacchia (1980), Nagurney (1993), and Bertsekas and Tsitsklis (1989).

3.1 The Variational Inequality Problem

In this section we first overview some of the fundamental mathematical problems encountered in financial analysis and practice. In particular, we emphasize problem classes and their relationships to the finite-dimensional variational inequality problem. This presentation is by no means exhaustive but, instead, highlights problems that occur frequently in finance. The goal here is to present unifying concepts in an accessible fashion, in order to establish the foundations upon which the financial modeling, analysis, and computation chapters of Parts III and IV are built.

We begin with systems of equations, which have been used to formulate certain equilibrium problems. We then discuss optimization problems, both unconstrained and constrained. Subsequently, we turn to the variational inequality problem, which is a general problem formulation that encompasses a plethora of mathematical problems, including, among others, nonlinear equations, optimization problems, complementarity problems, and is related to fixed point problems.

Problem Classes

We now briefly review certain problem classes, which appear frequently in finance, and then identify their relationship to the variational inequality problem.

For standardization of notation, let x denote a column vector in R^n and let $F(x)$ be a given continuous function from $\mathcal{K}$ to R^n, where $\mathcal{K}$ is a given closed convex set.

Systems of Equations

Systems of equations are common in finance, in particular, in the setting of defining an economic equilibrium state, reflecting that the demand is equal to the supply of various instruments at the equilibrium price levels. Let $\mathcal{K} = R^n$ and let $F : R^n \mapsto R^n$ be a given function. A vector $x^* \in R^n$ is said to solve a *system of equations* if

$$F(x^*) = 0. \tag{3.1}$$

Example 3.1 (Market Equilibrium with Equalities Only)

As an illustration, we now present an example of a system of equations. As in Section 2.3, we consider m investors, with a typical investor denoted by j, and n financial instruments, with a typical instrument denoted by i. We let p denote the n-dimensional column vector of the instrument prices with components: $\{p_1, \ldots, p_n\}$.

For the sake of generality, (cf. (2.33)), we now assume that the demand for an instrument i may, in general, depend upon the prices of all the instruments, that is,

$$D_i(p) = \sum_{j=1}^{m} d_i^j(p), \tag{3.2}$$

where $d_i^j(p)$ denotes the demand for instrument i by investor j at the price vector p.

Similarly, the supply of an instrument i (cf. (2.34)) may, in general, depend upon the prices of all the instruments, that is,

$$S_i(p) = \sum_{j=1}^{m} s_i^j(p), \tag{3.3}$$

where $s_i^j(p)$ denotes the supply of instrument i of investor j at the price vector p.

We group the aggregate demands for the instruments into the n-dimensional column vector D with components: $\{D_1, \ldots, D_n\}$ and the aggregate supplies of the instruments into the n-dimensional column vector S with components: $\{S_1, \ldots, S_n\}$.

The market equilibrium conditions that require that the supply of each instrument must be equal to the demand for each instrument at the equilibrium price vector p^*, is equivalent to the following system of equations, which we assume, for the sake of generality, to be nonlinear:

$$S(p^*) - D(p^*) = 0. \tag{3.4}$$

Clearly, (3.4) can be put into the standard nonlinear equation form given by (3.1), if we define the vectors $x \equiv p$ and $F(x) \equiv S(p) - D(p)$.

Note, however, that the problem class of nonlinear equations is not sufficiently general to guarantee, for example, that $x^* \geq 0$, which may be desirable in the case where the vector x refers to prices, as in Example 3.1. We come back to this issue when we present, in Example 3.3, a complementarity formulation of the equilibrium conditions (2.35), which consist of not only *equalities* but, also, of *inequalities*.

Optimization Problems

Optimization problems, on the other hand, consider explicitly an objective function to be minimized (or maximized), subject to constraints that may consist of both equalities and inequalities. Let f be a continuously differentiable function where $f : \mathcal{K} \mapsto R$. Mathematically, the statement of an *optimization problem* is:

$$\text{Minimize} \quad f(x) \tag{3.5}$$

subject to:

$$x \in \mathcal{K}.$$

Of course, equivalently, we may substitute "Maximize" for "Minimize" in (3.5), if $-f(x)$ replaces $f(x)$.

Note that, in the special case that $\mathcal{K} = R^n$, then the optimization problem (3.5) is an *unconstrained* problem.

Optimization problems occur frequently in finance (as in economics) in, for example, portfolio optimization problems, asset allocation problems, and in risk management.

Example 3.2 (A Portfolio Optimization Problem)

As an illustration, consider the classical portfolio optimization problem described in Section 2.1, where recall that an investor seeks to determine his optimal composition of his portfolio so that his risk is minimized and his return is maximized, subject to a budget constraint, and assuming no short sales. As before, let X_i denote the relative amount invested in security i, let μ_i denote the expected value of the return on i, and let σ_{ij} denote the covariance between securities i and j. We assume that there are n securities.

Let now Q be the $n \times n$ variance-covariance matrix with element $Q_{ij}=\sigma_{ij}$, and let μ be the n-dimensional column vector with components: $\{\mu_1, \ldots, \mu_n\}$. Finally, let X be the n-dimensional column vector consisting of the securities with components: $\{X_1, \ldots, X_n\}$.

The optimization problem facing the investor is, hence, to minimize his risk and to maximize his return, subject to the constraints, that is,

$$\text{Minimize} \quad X^T Q X - \mu^T X \tag{3.6}$$

subject to:

$$\sum_{i=1}^{n} X_i = 1 \tag{3.7}$$

$$X_i \geq 0, \quad i = 1, \ldots, n. \tag{3.8}$$

Note that here, for simplicity, we have suppressed (cf. (2.8)) the risk parameter α. This is an example of a constrained optimization problem; in fact, a quadratic programming problem, since the objective function given by (3.6) has a quadratic form.

We now put this portfolio optimization problem into the standard form of an optimization problem given by (3.5). We define the vector of variables: $x \equiv X$ and the objective function: $f(x) \equiv X^T QX - \mu^T X$. The feasible set $\mathcal{K}$, in turn, consists of the constraints (3.7) and (3.8).

Complementarity Problems

Let R^n_+ denote the nonnegative orthant in R^n, and let $F : R^n \mapsto R^n$. Then the *nonlinear complementarity problem* over R^n_+ is a system of equations and inequalities stated as:

Find $x^* \geq 0$, such that

$$F(x^*) \geq 0 \quad \text{and} \quad \langle F(x^*)^T, x^* \rangle = 0, \tag{3.9}$$

where $\langle \cdot, \cdot \rangle$ denotes the inner product in R^n, that is, $\langle x^T, x\rangle = x_1 \times x_1 + x_2 \times x_2 + \ldots + x_n \times x_n$.

Whenever the mapping F is affine, that is, whenever $F(x) = Mx + b$, where M is an $n \times n$ matrix and b an n-dimensional column vector, the above problem (3.9) is then known as the *linear complementarity problem*.

Example 3.3 (Market Equilibrium with Equalities and Inequalities)

We now present a nonlinear complementarity formulation of market equilibrium. We return to Example 3.1, where we now assume that the prices must be nonnegative in equilibrium. Hence, we consider the following situation, in which the demand functions are given by (3.2), the supply functions are given by (3.3), but now, instead of the market equilibrium conditions (3.4), we have the following economic equilibrium conditions (cf. (2.35)): For each instrument i; $i = 1, \ldots, n$:

$$S_i(p^*) - D_i(p^*) \begin{cases} = 0, & \text{if } p_i^* > 0 \\ \geq 0, & \text{if } p_i^* = 0. \end{cases} \tag{3.10}$$

Note that equilibrium conditions (3.10) state that if the price of an instrument is positive in equilibrium then the supply of that instrument must be equal to the demand for that instrument. On the other hand, if the price of an instrument at equilibrium is zero, then there may be an excess supply of that instrument at equilibrium, that is, $S_i(p^*) - D_i(p^*) > 0$, or the market clears. Furthermore, (3.10) guarantees that the prices of the instruments do not take on negative values, which may occur in (3.4).

We now demonstrate that the equilibrium conditions (3.10) can be formulated as a nonlinear complementarity problem (3.9).

First, consider instrument i. Then, clearly, (3.10) implies that

$$(S_i(p^*) - D_i(p^*)) \times p_i^* = 0. \tag{3.11}$$

Indeed, if $p_i^* > 0$, then according to (3.10), $S_i(p^*) - D_i(p^*) = 0$ and, hence, (3.11) is satisfied. On the other hand, if $p_i^* = 0$, then, according to (3.10), we must have that $S_i(p^*) - D_i(p^*) \geq 0$ and, again, (3.11) is satisfied.

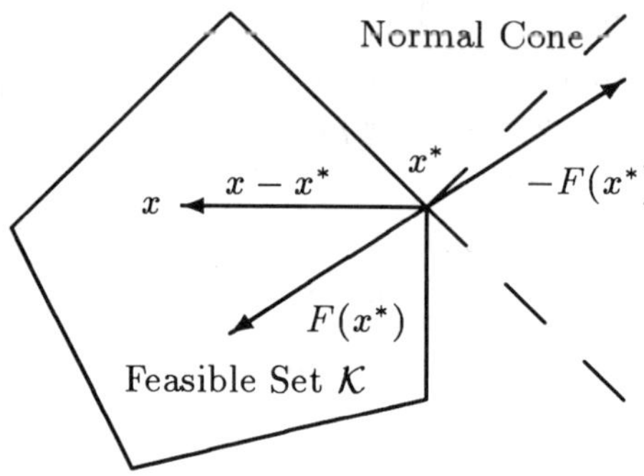

Fig. 3.1. Geometric interpretation of VI$(F, \mathcal{K})$

Since (3.11) holds for each instrument, we can conclude that an equilibrium price vector p^* must satisfy:

$$S(p^*) - D(p^*) \geq 0 \quad \text{and} \quad \langle (S(p^*) - D(p^*))^T, p^* \rangle = 0. \tag{3.12}$$

In order to put (3.12) into standard nonlinear complementarity form (3.9), define the vectors: $x \equiv p$, and $F(x) \equiv S(p) - D(p)$. Note that here the "feasible" set $\mathcal{K} = R^n_+$.

The Variational Inequality Problem

We now present the definition of a variational inequality problem.

Definition 3.1 (The Variational Inequality Problem)
The finite-dimensional variational inequality problem, VI$(F, \mathcal{K})$, *is to determine a vector* $x^* \in \mathcal{K}$, *such that*

$$\langle F(x^*)^T, x - x^* \rangle \geq 0, \quad \forall x \in \mathcal{K}, \tag{3.13}$$

where F is a given continuous function from $\mathcal{K}$ to R^n and $\mathcal{K}$ is a given closed convex set.

Geometric Interpretation of the Variational Inequality Problem

Before presenting an example we provide a geometric depiction of the variational inequality problem (3.13) in Figure 3.1. Note that a necessary and sufficient condition for x^* to be a solution to VI$(F, \mathcal{K})$ is that

$$-F(x^*) \in C(x^*),$$

where $C(x)$ denotes the normal cone of $\mathcal{K}$ at x defined by

$$C(x) \equiv \{y \in R^n : \langle y^T, x' - x \rangle \leq 0, \ \forall x' \in \mathcal{K}\}. \tag{3.14}$$

Analogously, recall that for two vectors $u, v \in R^n$, the inner product $\langle u^T, v \rangle = ||u|| ||v|| \cos\theta$, where θ is the angle between the vectors u and v. Hence, for θ in the range: $0 \leq \theta \leq 90^0$, we have that $\langle u^T, v \rangle \geq 0$. Consequently, one can see from Figure 3.1 that x^* is a solution of VI$(F, \mathcal{K})$ if and only if the angle between the vectors $F(x^*)$ and $x - x^*$, with x and x^* both in $\mathcal{K}$, is less than or equal to 90^0.

Example 3.4 (A Competitive Financial Equilibrium Problem)

Consider the following competitive scenario. Assume that there are m investors and n financial instruments that can be invested in. Each investor is interested in maximizing his utility and in determining the optimal amounts of the instruments that he should obtain for his portfolio, given that his utility is a function not only of how much of the instrument that he holds, but also of the amount that the other investors hold.

Let's assume that investor j's utility is denoted by u^j, and that the amount that he invests in instrument i is denoted by X_i^j. Let X^j denote the n-dimensional column vector with components: $\{X_1^j, \ldots, X_n^j\}$. Let X denote the mn-dimensional column vector consisting of the vectors $\{X^1, \ldots, X^m\}$. Let $\mathcal{K}^j \subset R^n$ denote the constraint set for investor j. Note that this constraint set can include budget constraints, regulatory constraints, etc. We assume that it is closed and convex.

Let's further assume that each investor j is acting in his own self-interest and seeks to select the amounts of the investments $X^j \in \mathcal{K}^j$ that maximize his utility $u^j(X^1, \ldots, X^{j-1}, X^j, X^{j+1} \ldots, X^m)$, given the decisions $(X^k)_{k \neq j}$ of the other investors. In this framework, one then has the following game-theoretic equilibrium concept due to Nash-Cournot (cf. Nash (1950), Cournot (1838)):

Definition 3.2 (Nash-Cournot Equilibrium)

A Nash equilibrium is a vector $X^* = (X^{1^*}, \ldots, X^{m^*}) \in \mathcal{K} = \prod_{j=1}^m \mathcal{K}^j$, *such that*

$$u^j(X^{j^*}, \hat{X}^{j^*}) \geq u^j(X^j, \hat{X}^{j^*}), \quad \forall X^j \in \mathcal{K}^j, \forall j, \tag{3.15}$$

where $\hat{X}^{j^*} = (X^{1^*}, \ldots, X^{j-1^*}, X^{j+1^*}, \ldots, X^{m^*})$.

It has been shown (cf. Gabay and Moulin (1980)) that Nash equilibria satisfy variational inequalities. In the present context, if we assume that each utility function u^j is continuously differentiable on $\mathcal{K}$ and concave with respect to X^j, then we have that $X^* \in \mathcal{K}$ is a Nash equilibrium if and only if it satisfies the variational inequality problem:

$$\sum_{j=1}^{m}\sum_{i=1}^{n} -\frac{\partial u^j}{\partial X_i^j}(X^*) \times (X_i^j - X_i^{j^*}) \geq 0, \quad \forall X \in \mathcal{K}. \tag{3.16}$$

In order to put inequality (3.16) into standard form (3.13) we first need to define the column vectors F and x. Let $F \equiv \{-\nabla_{X^1} u^1, \ldots, -\nabla_{X^m} u^m\}$ and $x \equiv \{X^1, \ldots, X^m\}$, where $\nabla_{X^j} u^j = \{\frac{\partial u^j}{\partial X_1^j}, \ldots, \frac{\partial u^j}{\partial X_m^j}\}$. Inequality (3.16) is now in standard variational inequality form (3.13). (Note, however, that the dimensions of F and x in this problem are mn and mn, respectively.)

Relationship Between the Variational Inequality Problem and Other Problem Classes

We now review the fact that the variational inequality problem contains the above problem classes as special cases and discuss its relationship to the fixed point problem. For rigorous proofs, see the books by Kinderlehrer and Stampacchia (1980) and Nagurney (1993).

For example, a system of equations (3.1) can be formulated as a variational inequality problem. Indeed, a vector $x^* \in R^n$ solves VI(F, R^n) if and only if $F(x^*) = 0$, where $F : R^n \mapsto R^n$.

Similarly, both unconstrained and constrained optimization problems can be formulated as variational inequality problems. Consider the optimization problem (3.5) with x^* as the solution. Then x^* is a solution of the variational inequality problem:

$$\langle \nabla f(x^*)^T, x - x^* \rangle \geq 0, \quad \forall x \in \mathcal{K}, \tag{3.17}$$

where $\nabla f(x^*)$ denotes the gradient of f with respect to x with components: $(\frac{\partial f_1(x^*)}{\partial x_1}, \frac{\partial f_2(x^*)}{\partial x_2}, \ldots, \frac{\partial f_n(x^*)}{\partial x_n})$.

In particular, in the case of the portfolio optimization problem in Example 3.2, we have that if x^* minimizes the risk and maximizes the return, then x^* also solves the variational inequality problem:

$$\langle (2QX^* - \mu)^T, X - X^* \rangle \geq 0, \quad \forall X \in \mathcal{K}, \tag{3.18}$$

where recall that $\mathcal{K}$ was defined as the set of $\{x\}$ satisfying the budget and the nonnegativity constraints.

On the other hand, if $f(x)$ is a convex function (as it is in the case of Example 3.2, if we assume that the symmetric variance-covariance matrix Q is positive semi-definite) and x^* is a solution to VI$(\nabla f, \mathcal{K})$ given by (3.17), then x^* is a solution to the optimization problem (3.5).

If the feasible set $\mathcal{K} = R^n$, then the unconstrained optimization problem is also a variational inequality problem.

Note, however, that the variational inequality problem can be reformulated as a convex optimization problem, only under certain conditions. In particular, if we assume that $F(x)$ is continuously differentiable on $\mathcal{K}$ and that the Jacobian matrix

$$\nabla F(x) = \left\{ \begin{array}{ccc} \frac{\partial F_1}{\partial x_1} & \cdots & \frac{\partial F_1}{\partial x_n} \\ \vdots & & \vdots \\ \frac{\partial F_n}{\partial x_1} & \cdots & \frac{\partial F_n}{\partial x_n} \end{array} \right\} \tag{3.19}$$

is symmetric and positive semi-definite, so that F is convex, then there is a real-valued function $f : \mathcal{K} \mapsto R$ satisfying

$$\nabla f(x) = F(x) \tag{3.20}$$

with x^* the solution of VI$(F, \mathcal{K})$ also being the solution of the optimization problem (3.5).

Hence, although the variational inequality problem encompasses the optimization problem, a variational inequality problem can be reformulated as a convex optimization problem, only when the symmetry condition and the positive semi-definiteness condition hold. The variational inequality problem, therefore, is the more general problem in that it can also handle a function $F(x)$ with an asymmetric Jacobian. It is this characteristic of a variational inequality problem that has made it particularly useful in the study of equilibrium problems (see, e.g., Nagurney (1993)).

The variational inequality problem also contains the complementarity problem (3.9) as a special case. The relationship between the complementarity problem defined on the nonnegative orthant and the variational inequality problem is as follows: VI(F, R^n_+) and the complementarity problem defined above have precisely the same solutions, if any.

We will now further illustrate the above points and relationships through an example. Since a nonlinear complementarity problem is a special case of a variational inequality problem, we may rewrite the nonlinear complementarity formulation of the market equilibrium problem in Example 3.3 as a variational inequality problem:

Determine $p^* \in R^n_+$, such that

$$\langle (S(p^*) - D(p^*))^T, p - p^* \rangle \geq 0, \quad \forall p \in R^n_+. \tag{3.21}$$

Note, first, that in the *special* case of demand functions given by (2.33) and supply functions given by (2.34), the Jacobians (cf. (3.19)) of these functions are symmetric since they are diagonal and given, respectively, by

$$\nabla S(p) = \begin{pmatrix} \frac{\partial S_1}{\partial p_1} & 0 & 0 & \cdots & 0 \\ 0 & \frac{\partial S_2}{\partial p_2} & 0 & \cdots & 0 \\ \vdots & \ddots & \ddots & \ddots & \vdots \\ 0 & 0 & 0 & \cdots & \frac{\partial S_n}{\partial p_n} \end{pmatrix},$$

$$\nabla D(p) = \begin{pmatrix} \frac{\partial D_1}{\partial p_1} & 0 & 0 & \dots & 0 \\ 0 & \frac{\partial D_2}{\partial p_2} & 0 & \dots & 0 \\ \vdots & \ddots & \ddots & \ddots & \vdots \\ 0 & 0 & 0 & \dots & \frac{\partial D_n}{\partial p_n} \end{pmatrix}. \tag{3.22}$$

Indeed, in that model, the supply of an instrument depends only upon the price of that instrument and, similarly, the demand for an instrument depends only upon the price of that instrument.

Hence, in this special case, the price vector p^* that satisfies the equilibrium conditions (2.35) can be obtained, in view of (3.20), by solving the following optimization problem:

$$\text{Minimize} \sum_{i=1}^{n} \int_0^{p_i} S_i(x)dx - \sum_{i=1}^{n} \int_0^{p_i} D_i(y)dy \tag{3.23}$$

subject to:

$$p_i \geq 0, \quad i = 1, \dots, n.$$

Note that one also obtains an optimization reformulation of the equilibrium conditions (3.10), provided that the following symmetry condition holds: $\frac{\partial S_i}{\partial p_k} = \frac{\partial S_k}{\partial p_i}$ and $\frac{\partial D_i}{\partial p_k} = \frac{\partial D_k}{\partial p_i}$ for all instruments i, k. In other words, the price of an instrument k affects the supply of an instrument i in the same way that the price of an instrument i affects the price of an instrument k. A similar situation must hold for the demands for the instruments.

However, such conditions are limiting from the application standpoint and, hence, the appeal of variational inequality problem that enables the formulation and, as we shall see shortly, the computation of equilibria where such restrictive symmetry assumptions on the underlying functions need no longer hold. Indeed, such symmetry assumptions were not imposed in the variational inequality problem (3.21).

Fixed Point Problems

We now turn to a discussion of fixed point problems in conjunction with variational inequality problems. We also provide the geometric interpretation of the variational inequality problem and its relationship to a fixed point problem.

We first define a projection that will be useful throughout this text. For a graphical depiction, see Figure 3.2. As before, let $\mathcal{K}$ be a closed convex set in R^n. Then for each $x \in R^n$, there is a unique point $y \in \mathcal{K}$, such that

$$||x - y|| \leq ||x - z||, \quad \forall z \in \mathcal{K},$$

and y is known as the orthogonal projection of x on the set $\mathcal{K}$ with respect to the Euclidean norm, that is,

$$y = P_{\mathcal{K}}(x) = \arg\min_{z \in \mathcal{K}} ||x - z||. \tag{3.24}$$

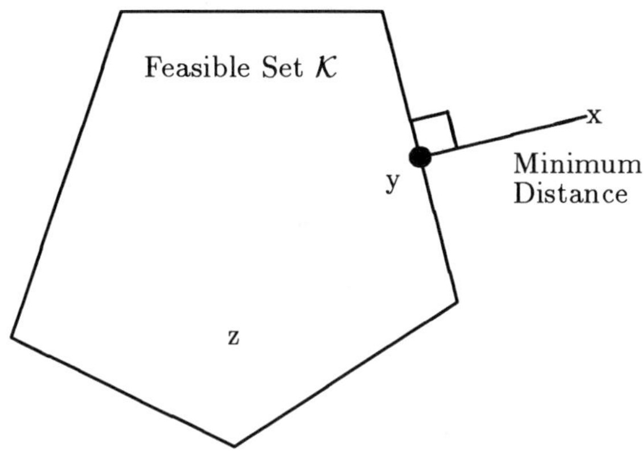

Fig. 3.2. The projection y of x on the set $\mathcal{K}$

In other words, the closest point to x lying in the set $\mathcal{K}$ is given by y.

We now present a property of the projection operator that is useful both in the qualitative analysis of equilibria and in their computation. Let $\mathcal{K}$ again be a closed convex set. Then the projection operator $P_{\mathcal{K}}$ is nonexpansive, that is,

$$||P_{\mathcal{K}}x - P_{\mathcal{K}}x'|| \leq ||x - x'|| \quad \forall x, x' \in R^n.$$

The relationship between a variational inequality and a fixed point problem can now be stated (see Figure 3.3). Assume that $\mathcal{K}$ is closed and convex. Then $x^* \in \mathcal{K}$ is a solution of the variational inequality problem VI$(F, \mathcal{K})$ if and only if x^* is a fixed point of the map: $P_{\mathcal{K}}(I - \gamma F) : \mathcal{K} \mapsto \mathcal{K}$, for $\gamma > 0$, that is,

$$x^* = P_{\mathcal{K}}(x^* - \gamma F(x^*)). \tag{3.25}$$

3.2 Qualitative Properties

In this section, we present certain qualitative results for the variational inequality problem, in particular, existence and uniqueness results in regards to the solution x^*. We also present some basic sensitivity analysis results. In addition, we review certain properties and recall definitions that will be referred to in our discussions of the convergence of algorithms. The interested reader may see Kinderlehrer and Stampacchia (1980) for accompanying results in standard variational inequality theory and for proofs and to Nagurney (1993) for a more recent treatment with a focus on finite-dimensional variational inequality problems and applications.

Existence of a solution to a variational inequality problem follows from the assumption of continuity of the function F entering the variational inequality,

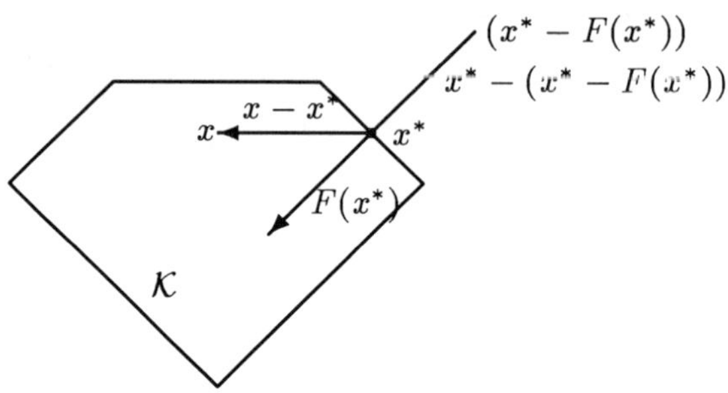

Fig. 3.3. Geometric depiction of the variational inequality problem and its fixed point equivalence (with $\gamma = 1$)

provided that the feasible set $\mathcal{K}$ is compact (that is, closed and bounded, in the case of R^n), as stated in the following theorem.

Theorem 3.1

If $\mathcal{K}$ is a compact convex set and $F(\cdot)$ is continuous on $\mathcal{K}$, then the variational inequality problem VI$(F, \mathcal{K})$ *admits at least one solution x^*.*

In the case that the feasible set $\mathcal{K}$ is unbounded, we have

Theorem 3.2

VI$(F, \mathcal{K})$ *admits a solution if and only if there exists an $R > 0$ and a solution x^*_R of* VI(F, S)*, such that $\|x^*_R\| < R$, where $S = \{x : \|x\| \leq R\}$.*

Under a coercivity condition on the function F, the existence of a solution to the variational inequality problem is stated in the following theorem.

Theorem 3.3

Suppose that $F(x)$ satisfies the coercivity condition

$$\frac{\langle (F(x) - F(x_0))^T, x - x_0 \rangle}{\|x - x_0\|} \to \infty, \tag{3.26}$$

as $\|x\| \to \infty$, for $x \in \mathcal{K}$ and for some $x_0 \in \mathcal{K}$. Then VI$(F, \mathcal{K})$ *always has a solution.*

Consequently, in view of Theorem 3.1, the existence of a Nash-Cournot equilibrum is guaranteed in Example 3.4 under the sole assumption that the marginal utility functions are continuous, provided that the feasible set is compact. If the feasible set is no longer compact and is, for example, unbounded, then one may appeal to Theorem 3.3 and assume coercivity of (minus) the marginal utility functions in order to guarantee existence. This was proposed by Gabay and Moulin (1980) for game theoretic problems, operating under the Nash equilibrium concept, in the framework of oligopolistic market problems.

Qualitative properties of existence and uniqueness of a solution to a variational inequality problem become easily obtainable under certain monotonicity conditions. We first outline the definitions and then present the results. In particular, the local and global concepts of monotonicity of a vector function F are introduced in the following definitions.

Definition 3.3 (Monotonicity)

$F(x)$ is said to be locally monotone at x^1 if there is a neighborhood $N(x^1)$ of x^1 such that

$$\langle (F(x) - F(x^1))^T, x - x^1 \rangle \geq 0, \quad \forall x \in N(x^1). \tag{3.27}$$

$F(x)$ is monotone at x^1 if (3.27) holds true for all $x \in \mathcal{K}$. $F(x)$ is said to be monotone if (3.27) holds for all $x, x^1 \in \mathcal{K}$.

Definition 3.4 (Strict Monotonicity)

$F(x)$ is said to be locally strictly monotone at x^1 if there is a neighborhood $N(x^1)$ of x^1 such that

$$\langle (F(x) - F(x^1))^T, x - x^1 \rangle > 0, \quad \forall x \in N(x^1),\ x \neq x^1. \tag{3.28}$$

$F(x)$ is strictly monotone at x^1 if (3.28) holds true for all $x \in \mathcal{K}$. $F(x)$ is said to be strictly monotone if (3.28) holds for all $x, x^1 \in \mathcal{K}$, $x \neq x^1$.

Definition 3.5 (Strong Monotonicity)

$F(x)$ is said to be locally strongly monotone at x^1 if there is a neighborhood $N(x^1)$ of x^1 and an $\eta > 0$ such that

$$\langle (F(x) - F(x^1))^T, x - x^1 \rangle \geq \eta \|x - x^1\|^2, \quad \forall x \in N(x^1). \tag{3.29}$$

$F(x)$ is strongly monotone at x^1 if (3.29) holds true for all $x \in \mathcal{K}$. $F(x)$ is said to be strongly monotone if (3.29) holds for all $x, x^1 \in \mathcal{K}$.

The monotonicity of a vector function F is closely related to the positive definiteness of its Jacobian matrix as illustrated in the following proposition. Monotonicity plays a role in variational inequality theory similar to that of convexity in optimization theory.

Proposition 3.1

Suppose that $F(x)$ is continuously differentiable on $\mathcal{K}$.

(i). *If the Jacobian matrix $\nabla F(x)$ is positive semi-definite, that is,*

$$z^T \nabla F(x) z \geq 0, \quad \forall z \in R^n, \forall x \in \mathcal{K}, \tag{3.30}$$

then $F(x)$ is monotone on $\mathcal{K}$.
(ii). *If $\nabla F(x)$ is positive definite, that is,*

$$z^T \nabla F(x) z > 0, \quad \forall z \neq 0, z \in R^n, \forall x \in \mathcal{K}, \tag{3.31}$$

then $F(x)$ is strictly monotone on $\mathcal{K}$.
(iii). *If $\nabla F(x)$ is strongly positive definite, that is,*

$$z^T \nabla F(x) z \geq \eta \|z\|^2, \quad \forall z \in R^n, \forall x \in \mathcal{K}, \text{ and some } \eta > 0, \tag{3.32}$$

then $F(x)$ is strongly monotone on $\mathcal{K}$.
(iv). *More generally, when (3.30), (3.31), and (3.32) hold locally for all x in a neighborhood $N(x^1)$ of x^1 (instead of $\mathcal{K}$), then, respectively, $F(x)$ is locally monotone, locally strictly monotone, and locally strongly monotone, on $N(x^1)$.*

One obtains even stronger results in the special case where $F(x)$ is affine. In particular, suppose that $F(x) = Mx + b$, with M an $n \times n$ matrix and b an $n \times 1$ (column) vector. The function F is monotone if and only if M is positive semi-definite; F is strongly monotone if and only if M is positive definite. In the context of the portfolio optimization problem in Example 3.2 it follows then (cf. (3.18)) that $2(QX) - \mu$ is monotone (strongly monotone) if and only if the variance-covariance matrix Q is positive semi-definite (positive definite).

Definition 3.6 (Lipschitz Continuity)
$F : \mathcal{K} \mapsto R^n$ is locally Lipschitz continuous if for every $x \in \mathcal{K}$ there is a neighborhood $N(x)$ and a positive number $L(x) > 0$ such that

$$\|F(x^1) - F(x^2)\| \leq L(x)\|x^1 - x^2\|, \quad \forall x^1, x^2 \in N(x). \tag{3.33}$$

When (3.33) holds uniformly on $\mathcal{K}$ for some constant $L > 0$, that is,

$$\|F(x^1) - F(x^2)\| \leq L\|x^1 - x^2\|, \quad \forall x^1, x^2 \in \mathcal{K}, \tag{3.34}$$

then F is said to be Lipschitz continuous on $\mathcal{K}$.

We remark that any continuously differentiable function F is locally Lipschitz continuous.

We now present the following uniqueness results.

Theorem 3.4
Suppose that $F(x)$ is strictly monotone on $\mathcal{K}$. Then the solution to VI$(F, \mathcal{K})$ *is unique, if one exists.*

Theorem 3.5
Suppose that $F(x)$ is strongly monotone on $\mathcal{K}$. Then there exists precisely one solution x^* to VI$(F, \mathcal{K})$.

Summarizing the above, we see that, in the case of an unbounded feasible set $\mathcal{K}$, strong monotonicity of the function F guarantees both existence and uniqueness of a solution. If the feasible set $\mathcal{K}$ is compact, then existence is guaranteed if F is continuous, and only strict monotonicity of F is needed to provide uniqueness of the solution x^*.

Returning to the examples of Section 3.1, we see that, in the case of Example 3.2, uniqueness of an optimal portfolio is, hence, guaranteed under the assumption that the variance-covariance matrix Q is positive definite. Indeed, then $2QX - \mu$ is strictly monotone and since the feasible set $\mathcal{K}$ there is compact, the result follows from Theorem 3.4. (Since this is a straightforward optimization problem one could have obtained these results directly from convexity theory.) On the other hand, in order to guarantee the existence of a unique solution to the problem in Example 3.4, one needs to assume that minus the Hessian of the utility functions, $-\nabla^2 u(X)$, is uniformly positive definite over the respective feasible set $\mathcal{K}$ (unless $\mathcal{K}$ is compact, in which case positive definiteness will suffice).

Assume now that $F(x)$ is both strongly monotone and Lipschitz continuous. Then the projection $P_{\mathcal{K}}[x - \gamma F(x)]$ is a contraction with respect to x, that is, if we fix $\gamma \leq \frac{\eta}{L^2}$ where η and L are the constants appearing, respectively, in the strong monotonicity and the Lipschitz continuity condition definitions. Then

$$||P_{\mathcal{K}}(x - \gamma F(x)) - P_{\mathcal{K}}(y - \gamma F(y))|| \leq \beta ||x - y|| \tag{3.35}$$

for all $x, y \in \mathcal{K}$, where

$$\beta(1 - \gamma\eta)^{\frac{1}{2}} < 1.$$

It follows from this result and from the Banach fixed point theorem that the operator $P_{\mathcal{K}}(x - \gamma F(x))$ has a unique fixed point x^*.

Another important qualitative issue in the study of equilibrium patterns is the sensitivity of solutions when the problem is subjected to perturbations in the data. We now recall some basic nonparametric sensitivity analysis results for finite-dimensional variational inequality problems. Proofs, as well as parametric sensitivity analysis, can be found in Nagurney (1993). We later in this book adapt these results to financial equilibrium problems for purposes of comparative statics.

The following theorem states that a small change in the function F entering the variational inequality problem (3.13) induces a small change in the resulting solution pattern. Denote the original function by F with solution x to VI($F, \mathcal{K}$) and the perturbed function by F^* with solution x^* to VI($F^*, \mathcal{K}$).

Assume that the strong monotonicity condition (cf. Definition 3.5) on F holds. Then one has

Theorem 3.6

Let η be the positive constant in the definition of strong monotonicity.

Then

$$||x^* - x|| \leq \frac{1}{\eta}||F^*(x^*) - F(x^*)||. \tag{3.36}$$

Sensitivity analysis results are now presented in a global context. No restrictions as to the size or the nature of the perturbations introduced to create F^* from F are imposed. The only assumption is the existence of at least one solution to $\mathrm{VI}(F^*, \mathcal{K})$.

Theorem 3.7

Let $F : \mathcal{K} \subset R^n \mapsto R^n$ be any continuous strictly monotone function over the closed convex set $\mathcal{K}$. Let $F^* : \mathcal{K} \subset R^n \mapsto R^n$ be any other continuous (not necessarily monotone) function on $\mathcal{K}$. Let x and x^* denote solutions to $\mathrm{VI}(F, \mathcal{K})$ and $\mathrm{VI}(F^*, \mathcal{K})$, respectively.

If $x \neq x^*$, then

$$\langle (F^*(x^*) - F(x^*))^T, x^* - x \rangle < 0. \tag{3.37}$$

Theorem 3.8

Let $F : \mathcal{K} \subset R^n \mapsto R^n$ be any strictly monotone function over the convex set $\mathcal{K}$. Let $F^* : \mathcal{K} \subset R^n \mapsto R^n$ be any other continuous (not necessarily monotone) function on $\mathcal{K}$. Let x and x^* denote solutions to $\mathrm{VI}(F, \mathcal{K})$ and to $\mathrm{VI}(F^*, \mathcal{K})$, respectively. Then

$$\langle (F^*(x^*) - F(x))^T, x^* - x \rangle \leq 0. \tag{3.38}$$

3.3 Algorithms

The results in Section 3.2 are useful in establishing convergence of algorithms. In this section we present some of the basic algorithmic schemes for the solution of the above problem classes, with an emphasis on algorithms for finite-dimensional variational inequality problems. In particular, we focus on those algorithms that have been successfully implemented in practice and that have been subject to theoretical analysis. Conditions for convergence are briefly discussed with an aim towards accessibility. References where complete proofs can be obtained are also included. Finally, we present applications of a variety of algorithms for the computation of the financial equilibrium patterns in Parts III and IV of this book.

Many iterative methods for the solution of systems of equations, optimization problems, variational inequality and other problems, have the form

$$x^{\tau+1} = g(x^\tau), \quad \tau = 0, 1, \ldots, \tag{3.39}$$

where x^τ is an n-dimensional vector and g is some function from R^n into itself with components: $\{g_1, g_2, \ldots, g_n\}$. For example, in the case where $g(x) = Ax + b$, where A is of dimension $n \times n$, and b is an n-dimensional column vector, one obtains a linear iterative algorithm.

The principal iterations of the form (3.39) are the

Jacobi iteration:

$$x_i^{\tau+1} = g_i(x_1^\tau, \ldots, x_n^\tau), \quad i = 1, \ldots, n, \tag{3.40}$$

and the

Gauss-Seidel iteration:

$$x_i^{\tau+1} = g_i(x_1^{\tau+1}, \ldots, x_{i-1}^{\tau+1}, x_i^\tau, \ldots, x_n^\tau), \quad i = 1, \ldots, n. \tag{3.41}$$

As is well-known, the Gauss-Seidel algorithm incorporates the information as it becomes available, whereas the Jacobi method updates the iterates simultaneously. Hence, the Jacobi method is a natural parallel method. Indeed, each subproblem i, for the evaluation of $x_i^{\tau+1}$ can be allocated to a distinct processor for simultaneous solution. It is also worth noting that there are different Gauss-Seidel algorithms, depending on the specific order with which the variables are updated.

In our statements of the algorithms, for the sake of brevity, we present only the typical iteration. Of course, each algorithm must be suitably initialized and also convergence must be verified through an appropriate convergence criterion. This latter issue is discussed more fully in terms of the specific applications and numerical examples in Parts III, IV, and V.

In particular, we first present projection methods and then decomposition algorithms for when the variational inequality to be solved is defined over a Cartesian product of sets, as was the case in Example 3.4, and as will be the case in the multi-sector, multi-instrument financial problems under study in this book. We discuss decomposition algorithms of both the Jacobi and Gauss-Seidel type, the former being naturally implementable on parallel computer architectures. We don't present algorithms for complementarity problems, since these are special cases of variational inequality problems, and the theory of variational inequality algorithms is more developed. Moreover, we don't discuss fixed point algorithms since they may not be appropriate for large-scale problems.

Variational inequality algorithms resolve the variational inequality problem (3.13) into simpler variational inequality subproblems, which, typically, are optimization problems. The overall efficiency of a variational inequality algorithm, hence, will depend upon the optimization algorithm used at each iteration. The subproblems under consideration often have a special structure and special-purpose algorithms that exploit that underlying structure can be used to solve the embedded mathematical programming problems to realize further efficiencies. In particular, in Chapter 5, we will discuss special-purpose network algorithms that will be utilized for the solution of a variety of financial subproblems in subsequent chapters. We also defer the presentation of illustrative examples until Chapter 5, where we synthesize variational inequality theory and projected dynamical systems theory with network theory, since it is this synthesis for financial problems that is one of the focal points of this book.

3.3.1 Projection Methods

Projection methods resolve a variational inequality problem (cf. (3.13)), typically, into a series of quadratic programming problems. Projection methods have intuitive appeal due to their exploitation of the geometry of the variational inequality problem, which was highlighted in Section 3.1. Moreover, projection methods have been successfully applied for the computation of a plethora of equilibrium problems (cf. Nagurney (1993)).

Again, we present a typical iteration and provide further details in subsequent chapters where the algorithm is applied to the solution of a particular problem.

Projection Method:

$$x^{\tau+1} = P_{\mathcal{K}}(x^{\tau} - \gamma G^{-1}F(x^{\tau})) \tag{3.42}$$

where G is a symmetric $n \times n$ positive definite matrix, and $\gamma > 0$.

The subproblems, at an iteration τ, induced by (3.42), in view of the definition of the projection operator in (3.24), consist of the solution of the minimum norm problem:

$$\min_{x \in \mathcal{K}} \|x - (x^{\tau} - \gamma G^{-1}F(x^{\tau}))\|, \tag{3.43}$$

or, equivalently, to the solution of the strictly convex quadratic programming problem:

$$\min_{x \in \mathcal{K}} \frac{1}{2} x^T \cdot x - (x^{\tau} - \gamma G^{-1}F(x^{\tau}))^T \cdot x. \tag{3.44}$$

Interestingly, the objective function in (3.44) is precisely of the form of the objective function in (3.6) for the basic portfolio optimization problem, where Q (cf. (3.6)) is simply the $n \times n$ identity matrix in (3.44), and the vector μ in (3.6) corresponds to $(x^{\tau} - \gamma G^{-1}F(x^{\tau}))$ in (3.44).

In the special case where the feasible set $\mathcal{K}$ is the nonnegative orthant, that is, when $\mathcal{K} = R^n_+$, then the projection operation becomes particularly simple. In this case, an iteration of the projection method (3.42), takes on the closed form expression:

$$(x^{\tau+1})_i = \begin{cases} (x^{\tau} - \gamma G^{-1}F(x^{\tau}))_i, & \text{if } (x^{\tau} - \gamma G^{-1}F(x^{\tau}))_i \geq 0, \\ 0, & \text{otherwise,} \end{cases} \tag{3.45}$$

for $i = 1, 2, \cdots, n$.

Hence, in the case that the feasible set $\mathcal{K}$ is the nonnegative orthant, in order to compute the iterate $\{x^{\tau+1}\}$, one need only to apply a simple formula. Also, it is worth noting that the evaluation of each $(x^{\tau+1})_i$; $i = 1, \ldots, n$, can be done independently and simultaneously.

An analogous expression to (3.45) can be constructed in the case that $\mathcal{K}$ consists of "box" type constraints, that is, constraints of the form: $a_i \leq x_i \leq b_i$. We will see such constraints in subsequent chapters when we consider imperfect market financial models in which such bounds correspond to imposed price floors and ceilings.

Convergence of the projection method is guaranteed (cf. Bertsekas and Tsitsiklis (1989)) provided that the function F is strongly monotone (cf. Definition 3.5) and Lipschitz continuous (cf. Definition 3.6), for any $\gamma \in (0, \gamma^0]$, such that the mapping induced by the projection above is a contraction mapping with respect to the norm $\|\cdot\|_G$. The sequence $\{x^\tau\}$ generated by the projection algorithm then converges to the solution x^* of (3.13) geometrically.

In the case where the function F is no longer strongly monotone, but satisfies the less restrictive monotonicity condition (cf. Definition 3.3), and is also Lipschitz continuous, then the modified projection method of Korpelevich (1977) is guaranteed to converge to the solution of the variational inequality problem. If the function F is monotone, rather than strongly monotone, then a unique solution, however, is no longer guaranteed.

We now state the modified projection method. It will play a very important role in subsequent chapters in the computation of financial equilibria. Again, we provide a typical iteration.

Modified Projection Method:

$$x^{\tau+1} = P_{\mathcal{K}}(x^\tau - \gamma F(\bar{x}^\tau)), \tag{3.46}$$

where $\bar{x}^\tau$ is given by

$$\bar{x}^\tau = P_{\mathcal{K}}(x^\tau - \gamma F(x^\tau)) \tag{3.47}$$

and γ is a positive scalar, such that $\gamma \in (0, \frac{1}{L}]$, where L is the Lipschitz constant in Definition 3.6. Note that here (cf. (3.42)) $G^{-1} = I$.

3.3.2 Basic Decomposition Algorithms

In this subsection, we assume that the feasible set $\mathcal{K}$ is a Cartesian product, that is, it is of the form

$$\mathcal{K} = \prod_{i=1}^{z} \mathcal{K}^i \tag{3.48}$$

where each $\mathcal{K}^i \subset R^{n_i}$; $\sum_{i=1}^{z} n_i = n$; and each x_i now denotes a vector in R^{n_i}, with $F_i(x) : \mathcal{K} \mapsto R^{n_i}$ for each i.

Many equilibrium problems are defined over a Cartesian product set and, hence, are amenable to solution via variational inequality decomposition algorithms. For example, a variety of game theory problems fall into this framework, as illustrated in Example 3.4, where each player has his or her own objective function and feasible set, with the feasible set depending upon only the individual's particular strategies, and not on those of the other players. However, the objective function of a particular player may depend not only on his strategies but also on those of the other players. The financial equilibrium models that will be developed in subsequent chapters will also be characterized by feasible sets that are Cartesian products.

The appeal of decomposition algorithms lies in their particular suitability for the solution of large-scale problems. Moreover, parallel decomposition algorithms can be implemented on parallel computer architectures and further efficiencies realized. For additional discussion on this point, see Nagurney (1996).

We emphasize that for any given equilibrium problem there may be several alternative, albeit, equivalent, variational inequality formulations, which may, in turn, suggest distinct, novel, and not immediately apparent, decomposition procedures.

We present the nonlinear decomposition methods and then the linear decomposition methods. For each, we first present the Jacobi version and then the Gauss-Seidel version.

Nonlinear Jacobi Method

The statement of a typical iteration τ of the nonlinear Jacobi method is given by: Determine $x_i^{\tau+1} \in \mathcal{K}^i$; $i = 1, \ldots, z$, where

$$x_i^{\tau+1} = \text{solution of:} \quad \langle F_i(x_1^\tau, \ldots, x_{i-1}^\tau, x_i, x_{i+1}^\tau, \ldots, x_z^\tau)^T, x_i' - x_i \rangle \geq 0, \quad \forall x_i' \in \mathcal{K}^i. \tag{3.49}$$

Nonlinear Gauss-Seidel Method

A typical iteration τ of the nonlinear Gauss-Seidel method is given by: Determine $x_i^{\tau+1} \in \mathcal{K}^i$; $i = 1, \ldots, z$, where

$$x_i^{\tau+1} = \text{solution of:} \quad \langle F_i(x_1^{\tau+1}, \ldots, x_{i-1}^{\tau+1}, x_i, x_{i+1}^{\tau-1}, \ldots, x_z^{\tau-1})^T, x_i' - x_i \rangle \geq 0, \quad \forall x_i' \in \mathcal{K}^i. \tag{3.50}$$

Linear Jacobi Method

The linear Jacobi method, on the other hand, is given by the following expression for an iteration τ: Determine $x_i^{\tau+1} \in \mathcal{K}^i$; $i = 1, \ldots, z$, where

$$x_i^{\tau+1} = \text{solution of: } \quad \left\langle \left[F_i(x^\tau) + A_i(x^\tau) \cdot (x_i - x_i^\tau)\right]^T, x_i' - x_i \right\rangle \geq 0, \quad (3.51)$$

$$\forall x_i' \in \mathcal{K}^i.$$

Linear Gauss-Seidel Method

The linear Gauss-Seidel method has the iteration τ given by: Determine $x_i^{\tau+1} \in \mathcal{K}^i$; $i = 1, \ldots, z$, where

$$x_i^{\tau+1} = \text{solution of: } \quad \left\langle \left[F_i(x_1^{\tau+1}, \ldots, x_{i-1}^{\tau+1}, x_i^\tau, \ldots, x_z^\tau)\right.\right.$$

$$\left.\left. + A_i(x_1^{\tau+1}, \ldots, x_{i-1}^{\tau+1}, x_i^\tau, \ldots, x_z^\tau) \cdot (x_i - x_i^\tau)\right]^T, x_i' - x_i \right\rangle \geq 0, \quad (3.52)$$

$$\forall x_i \in \mathcal{K}^i.$$

We now further discuss the linear decomposition methods. In particular, there exist several possibilities for the choice of $A_i(\cdot)$. If one chooses $A_i(x^\tau) = \nabla_{x_i} F_i(x^\tau)$, then one obtains a Newton's method. If one lets $A_i(x^\tau) = D_i(x^\tau)$, where $D_i(\cdot)$ denotes the diagonal part of $\nabla_{x_i} F_i(\cdot)$, then one has a linearization method. If $A_i(\cdot) = G_i$, where G_i is a fixed, symmetric, and positive definite matrix, then one gets a projection method.

Note that the variational inequality subproblems above should be easier to solve than the original variational inequality problem since they are smaller variational inequality problems, defined over smaller feasible sets. For example, if in the linear methods one was to select $A_i(\cdot)$ to be diagonal and positive definite, for each i, then each of the subproblems would be equivalent to a separable quadratic programming problem with a unique solution (cf. Section 3.2).

The subproblems that must be solved at each iteration of the nonlinear methods, on the other hand, are themselves variational inequality problems. Hence, an algorithm such as the projection method would have to then be applied or the relaxation method. See Dafermos (1983) and Nagurney (1993) for additional discussion of the projection method for variational inequality problems, as well as other algorithms, including the relaxation method.

The linear methods are especially attractive since each variational inequality subproblem may be expected to take on a simpler form for computational purposes than in the case of the nonlinear methods. This is especially true, as already mentioned above, if $A_i(\cdot)$ is selected to be diagonal.

We now present a convergence theorem for the above decomposition algorithms that is due to Bertsekas and Tsitsiklis (1989) (see, also, Nagurney (1993)).

Theorem 3.9

Suppose that the variational inequality problem (3.13) has a solution x^* and that there exist symmetric positive definite matrices G_i and some $\delta > 0$

such that $A_i(x) - \delta G_i$ is nonnegative definite for every i and $x \in \mathcal{K}$, and there exists a $\gamma \in [0,1)$ such that

$$\|G_i^{-1}(F_i(x) - F_i(y) - A_i(y) \cdot (x_i - y_i))\|_i \leq \delta\gamma \max_j \|x_j - y_j\|_j, \; \forall x, y \in \mathcal{K}, \tag{3.53}$$

where $\|x_i\|_i = (x_i^T G_i x_i)^{\frac{1}{2}}$. Then the Jacobi and the Gauss-Seidel linear and nonlinear decomposition algorithms, with $A_i(x)$ being diagonal and positive definite, converge to the solution x^*.

3.4 Sources and Notes

Variational inequalities were introduced in 1966 by Hartman and Stampacchia as a tool in the study of partial differential equations arising from applications drawn from mechanics. Such applications made use of infinite-dimensional variational inequalities. The applicability of variational inequality theory outside the physical and engineering sciences was recognized by Dafermos (1980), who noted that the traffic network equilibrium conditions, as formulated by Smith (1979), satisfied a finite-dimensional variational inequality problem, and then proposed a projection algorithm for the computation of the network equilibrium link flow pattern. Since that contribution, a plethora of equilibrium problems in operations research / management science and in economics have been formulated and studied as variational inequality problems.

For example, in addition to traffic network equilibrium problems occurring in congested urban transportation systems (see also Dafermos (1982), Florian and Hearn (1995), and the references therein), spatial price equilibrium problems, in which the equilibrium levels of production, consumption, and trade are to be determined, in the presence of transportation costs, have been widely studied as variational inequality problems (cf. Florian and Los (1982), Friesz, Harker, and Tobin (1984), Nagurney (1993), and the references therein). Another application, that of oligopolistic markets, in which several firms compete and operate under the Nash-Cournot concept of noncooperative behavior, has also been studied using this methodology (cf. Gabay and Moulin (1980), Dafermos and Nagurney (1987)). Finally, the study of general economic equilibrium problems has benefited from the methodology of variational inequalities (cf. Dafermos (1990), Zhao and Dafermos (1991)).

In this chapter we have provided an overview of finite-dimensional variational inequality theory on a level to be utilized in the subsequent financial modeling and computation chapters. This theory will be utilized for studying statics in the context of financial equilibrium problems. We note that variational inequalities have also been used in financial applications outside the context of equilibrium problems. For example, infinite-dimensional variational inequalities have been used for the pricing of American options by Jaillet, Lamberton, and Lapeyre (1990), whereas stochastic variational inequalities have been used, again, for American option pricing by Gürkan, Özge, and Robinson (1996). Stochastic variational inequalities have also been used by McLean (1993) for the nonlinear portfolio choice problem.

The foundations were laid here for the qualitative study of solutions to finite-dimensional variational inequality problems as well as their computation. Theoretical proofs and additional results and applications can be found in the books by Kinderlehrer and Stampacchia (1980), Bertsekas and Tsitsiklis (1989), and Nagurney (1993). The book by Kinderlehrer and Stampacchia (1980) serves as the standard reference for infinite-dimensional varational inequality problems. The book by Bertsekas and Tsitsiklis (1989) contains serial and parallel algorithms for the solution of optimization problems and finite-dimensional variational inequality problems. For those interested in numerical results for the parallel computation of economic problems, see Nagurney (1996). The book by Nagurney (1993) is a reference for the theory and applications of finite-dimensional variational inequalities.

Section 3.1

This section provides a synthesis of the variational inequality problem and other problem classes with examples drawn from finance.

Section 3.2

This section discussed well-known existence and uniqueness results and presented some useful definitions to be used in both the qualitative analysis of solutions as well as in the proof of convergence of algorithms. For completeness, some basic sensitivity analysis results were also included.

Section 3.3

In this section some basic algorithms for the solution of variational inequality problems were provided. Although the exposition herein was general and can be used for reference purposes, it was been necessarily selective, since we are interested ultimately in the solution of financial problems. We have attempted to include a variety of algorithms in order to also stimulate their application in finance in, as yet, unforeseen ways.

References

Bertsekas, D. P., and Tsitsiklis, J. N., **Parallel and Distributed Computation – Numerical Methods**, Prentice-Hall, Inc., Englewood Cliffs, New Jersey, 1989.

Cournot, A. A., **Researches into the Mathematical Principles of the Theory of Wealth**, 1838, English translation, MacMillan Press, Ltd., London, England, 1897.

Dafermos, S., "Traffic Equilibria and Variational Inequalities," *Transportation Science* **14** (1980) 42-54.

Dafermos, S., "The General Multimodal Network Equilibrium Problem with Elastic Demand," *Networks* **12** (1982) 57-72.

Dafermos, S., "An Iterative Scheme for Variational Inequalities," *Mathematical Programming* **26** (1983) 40-47.

Dafermos, S., "Exchange Price Equilibria and Variational Inequalities," *Mathematical Programming* **46** (1990) 391-402.

Dafermos, S., and Nagurney, A., "Oligopolistic and Competitive Behavior of Spatially Separated Markets," *Regional Science and Urban Economics* **17** (1987) 245-254.

Florian, M., and Hearn, D., "Network Equilibrium Models and Algorithms," in **Handbooks in Operations Research and Management Science, vol. 7**, pp. 485-550, M. O. Ball, T. L. Magnanti, C. L. Monma, and G. L. Nemhauser, editors, Elsevier Science B. V., Amsterdam, The Netherlands, 1995.

Florian, M., and Los, M., "A New Look at Static Spatial Price Equilibrium Models," *Regional Science and Urban Economics* **12** (1982) 579-597.

Friesz, T. L., Harker, P. T., and Tobin, R. L., "Alternative Algorithms for the General Network Spatial Price Equilibrium Problem," *Journal of Regional Science* **24** (1984) 475-507.

Gabay, D., and Moulin, H., "On the Uniqueness and Stability of Nash-Equilibria in Noncooperative Games," in **Applied Stochastic Control in Econometrics and Management Science**, pp. 271-294, A. Bensoussan, P. Kleindorfer, and C. S. Tapiero, editors, North-Holland, Amsterdam, The Netherlands, 1980.

Gürkan, G., Özge, A. Y., and Robinson, S. M., "Sample-Path Solution of Variational Inequalities with Application to Option Pricing," in **Proceedings of the 1996 Winter Simulation Conference**, pp. 337-344, J. M. Charnes, D. J. Morrice, D. T. Brunner, and J. M. Swain, editors, Coronado, California, 1996.

Hartman, P., and Stampacchia, G., "On Some Nonlinear Elliptic Differential Functional Equations," *Acta Mathematica* **115** (1966) 271-310.

Jaillet, P., Lamberton, D., and Lapeyre, B., "Variational Inequalities and the Pricing of American Options," *Acta Applicanda Mathematicae* **21** (1990) 253-289.

Kinderlehrer, D., and Stampacchia, G., **An Introduction to Variational Inequalities and Their Applications**, Academic Press, Inc., New York, New York, 1980.

Korpelevich, G. M., "The Extragradient Method for Finding Saddle Points and Other Problems," *Matekon* **13** (1977) 35-49.

McLean, R. P., "Approximation Theory for Stochastic Variational Inequality and Ky Fan Inequalities in Finite Dimensions," *Annals of Operations Research* **44** (1993) 43-61.

Nagurney, A., **Network Economics: A Variational Inequality Approach**, Kluwer Academic Publishers, Boston, Massachusetts, 1993.

Nagurney, A., "Parallel Computation," in **Handbook of Computational Economics, vol. 1**, pp. 331-400, H. M. Amman, D. A. Kendrick, and J. Rust, editors, Elsevier Science B. V., Amsterdam, The Netherlands, 1996.

Nagurney, A., Dong, J., and Hughes, M., "Formulation and Computation of General Financial Equilibrium," *Optimization* **26** (1992) 339-354.

Nagurney, A., and Siokos, S., "Variational Inequalities for International General Financial Equilibrium Modeling and Computation," *Mathematical and Computer Modelling* **25** (1997) 31-49.

Nash, J., "Equilibrium Points in n-Person Games," *Proceedings of the National Academy of Sciences, USA* **36** (1950) 48-49.

Smith, M. J., "Existence, Uniqueness, and Stability of Traffic Equilibria," *Transportation Research* **13B** (1979) 295-304.

Wilmott, P., Dewynne, J., and Howison, S., **Option Pricing Mathematical Models and Computation**, Oxford Financial Press, Oxford, United Kingdom, 1995.

Zhao, L., and Dafermos, S., "General Economic Equilibrium and Variational Inequalities," *Operations Research Letters* **10** (1991) 369-376.

4 Projected Dynamical Systems

The study of financial systems out of equilibrium and the underlying dynamics is a topic as important as the study of the systems in equilibrium. Central to dynamical systems is the evaluation of the stability of a system in terms of the ability of the system to maintain or restore its equilibrium when acted upon by forces tending to displace it. In addition, the development of algorithms for the computation of solutions to dynamical systems is as relevant as the investigation of qualitative properties of such systems.

In this chapter we describe the recently introduced methodology of projected dynamical systems for the study of dynamical systems in the presence of constraints. This methodology will be utilized in Parts III and IV for the modeling, stability analysis, and computation of solutions to dynamic financial models.

Projected dynamical systems were introduced by Dupuis and Nagurney (1993) and Zhang and Nagurney (1995). This new class of dynamical system was developed in order to provide a theoretical framework for the study of the dynamics of a plethora of complex competitive system problems, such as traffic network equilibrium problems and spatial price equilibrium problems that had, to that point, been studied almost exclusively in the static setting of equilibrium points, using, for the most part, finite-dimensional variational inequality theory.

What is notable about projected dynamical systems theory is that it provides a rigorous foundation for the investigation of a class of dynamical system characterized by a discontinuous right-hand side, a characteristic that arises in numerous applications in which constraints are essential. For example, constraints in financial problems may include budget constraints, government regulations, bounds on investments to be made, and/or a nonnegativity requirement for the instrument prices. In particular, the theory provides conditions for the existence and uniqueness of the solution path, stability analysis results, and computational procedures. Classical dynamical systems, on the other hand, are characterized by continuous right-hand sides and, hence, cannot explicitly handle constraints.

Moreover, it was proven by Dupuis and Nagurney (1993) that the set of solutions to a finite-dimensional variational inequality problem coincides with the set of stationary points of a projected dynamical system. Consequently, a variety of financial problems which had been studied at an equilibrium (or even at an optimum point) could now be addressed from this new dynamic perspective.

The first dynamic financial model to be formulated as a projected dynamical system was proposed by Dong, Zhang, and Nagurney (1996), who focused on the stability analysis of the multi-sector, multi-instrument model. The set of stationary points of this model coincided with the set of solutions to the variational inequality formulation of the equilibrium conditions governing the financial model in Nagurney (1994). Nagurney and Siokos (1996), subsequently, developed a dynamic international financial model, along with stability analysis results and a discrete time algorithm, using the methodology of projected dynamical systems.

To date, this methodology has been utilized to develop dynamic models, to conduct stability analysis, and to establish convergence of discrete time algorithms for: spatial price problems (cf. Nagurney, Takayama, and Zhang (1995a, b), Nagurney and Zhang (1996a)), oligopolistic market problems (cf. Nagurney, Dupuis, and Zhang (1994), Zhang and Nagurney (1996a)), as well as, traffic network problems (cf. Zhang and Nagurney (1996b), Nagurney and Zhang (1996b)). See also the book by Nagurney and Zhang (1996c). One of the goals of this book is to demonstrate the use of this methodology in finance.

This chapter is organized as follows. In Section 4.1, we define a projected dynamical system and show its connection to a variational inequality problem. In Section 4.2, we provide some basic stability analysis results. In Section 4.3, we discuss discrete time algorithms, along with convergence results. For theoretical proofs of the results herein, see Dupuis and Nagurney (1993), Zhang and Nagurney (1995), and Nagurney and Zhang (1996c).

4.1 A Projected Dynamical System

In this section we present the definition of a projected dynamical system (PDS). The relationship between a projected dynamical system and its associated variational inequality problem with the same constraint set is then identified. Finally, fundamental properties such as the existence and uniqueness of the solution to the ordinary differential equation (ODE) that defines such a projected dynamical system are provided.

Throughout this chapter we attempt to emphasize the geometric nature of this dynamical system.

Let $\mathcal{K} \subset R^n$ be closed and convex. Denote the boundary and interior of $\mathcal{K}$, respectively, by $\partial\mathcal{K}$ and $\mathcal{K}^0$. Given $x \in \partial\mathcal{K}$, define the set of inward normals to $\mathcal{K}$ at x by

$$N(x) = \{\gamma : \|\gamma\| = 1, \text{ and } \langle \gamma^T, x - y \rangle \leq 0, \forall y \in \mathcal{K}\}. \tag{4.1}$$

We define $N(x)$ to be $\{\gamma : \|\gamma\| = 1\}$ for x in the interior of $\mathcal{K}$.

When $\mathcal{K}$ is a convex polyhedron (for example, when $\mathcal{K}$ consists of linear constraints, which will be the type of constraints of encountered in the subsequent financial modeling chapters), $\mathcal{K}$ takes the form $\cap_{i=1}^{Z}\mathcal{K}_i$, where each $\mathcal{K}_i$ is a closed half-space with inward normal N_i. Let $P_\mathcal{K}$ be the norm projection, defined in (3.24). Then $P_\mathcal{K}$ projects onto $\mathcal{K}$ "along N," in that if $y \in \mathcal{K}$, then $P(y) = y$, and if $y \notin \mathcal{K}$, then $P(y) \in \partial\mathcal{K}$, and $P(y) - y = \alpha\gamma$ for some $\alpha > 0$ and $\gamma \in N(P(y))$.

Definition 4.1

Given $x \in \mathcal{K}$ and $v \in R^n$, define the projection of the vector v at x (with respect to $\mathcal{K}$) by

$$\Pi_\mathcal{K}(x, v) = \lim_{\delta \to 0} \frac{(P_\mathcal{K}(x + \delta v) - x)}{\delta}. \tag{4.2}$$

Whenever the constraint set $\mathcal{K}$ is clear from the context, we write $\Pi_\mathcal{K}(x, v)$ simply as $\Pi(x, v)$.

The class of ordinary differential equations that are of concern in this book take on the following form:

$$\dot{x} = \Pi_\mathcal{K}(x, -F(x)), \tag{4.3}$$

where $\mathcal{K}$ is a closed convex set, corresponding to the constraint set in a particular application, and $F(x)$ is a vector field defined on $\mathcal{K}$.

We note that the classical dynamical system, in contrast to (4.3), is of the form

$$\dot{x} = -F(x). \tag{4.4}$$

We now present two illustrative examples drawn from finance.

Example 4.1 (A Tatonnement Process for Example 3.3)

We consider the market equilibrium model example given in Example 3.3 and we propose the following adjustment or tatonnement process: For each instrument i; $i = 1, \ldots, n$:

$$\dot{p}_i = \begin{cases} D_i(p) - S_i(p), & \text{if } p_i > 0 \\ \max\{0, D_i(p) - S_i(p)\}, & \text{if } p_i = 0. \end{cases} \tag{4.5}$$

In other words, a price of an instrument will increase if the demand for that instrument exceeds the supply of that instrument; the price will decrease if the demand for that instrument is less than the supply for that instrument.

However, if the price of an instrument is equal to zero, and the supply of that instrument exceeds the demand, then the price will not change since one cannot have negative prices according to equilibrium conditions (3.10).

In vector form, we may express (4.5) as

$$\dot{p} = \Pi_{\mathcal{K}}(p, D(p) - S(p)), \tag{4.6}$$

where $\mathcal{K} = R^n_+$. Note that (4.6) can be put into the form given by (4.3) if we define the column vectors: $x \equiv p$ and $F(x) \equiv S(p) - D(p)$.

On the other hand, if we do not constrain the instrument prices to be nonnegative, then $\mathcal{K} = R^n$, and the above tatonnement process would take the form:

$$\dot{p} = D(p) - S(p). \tag{4.7}$$

This is an example of a classical dynamical system (cf. (4.4)). Note that the dynamical system (4.7) describes a tatonnement process for the market equilibrium model discussed in Example 3.1.

Example 4.2 (A Tatonnement Process in the Case of Price Floors and Ceilings)

We now consider an extension of Example 4.1 to which we impose price floors and ceilings on the instrument prices as in (2.36). We now propose the following tatonnement or adjustment process: For each instrument i: $i = 1, \ldots, n$:

$$\dot{p}_i = \begin{cases} \min\{0, D_i(p) - S_i(p)\}, & \text{if } p_i = p_i^C \\ D_i(p) - S_i(p), & \text{if } p_i^F < p_i < p_i^C \\ \max\{0, D_i(p) - S_i(p)\}, & \text{if } p_i = p_i^F. \end{cases} \tag{4.8}$$

Hence, the price of an instrument follows the laws of supply and demand, provided that the price of an instrument lies within the imposed price floor and ceiling for that instrument. If, however, the demand exceeds the supply and the price of that instrument is at the ceiling, then the price cannot rise above the ceiling. On the other hand, if the supply exceeds the demand for an instrument and the price of the instrument is at the floor, then the price cannot go below the floor. Note that a dynamical system of the form (4.4) could not guarantee that the prices always lay within the floors and ceilings.

Note that if we define the feasible set $\mathcal{K}$ now as $\{p|p^F \leq p \leq p^C\}$, where p^F and p^C denote, respectively, the vectors of price floors and price ceilings, then (4.8) takes the form of (4.6) with the feasible set $\mathcal{K}$ as defined above.

We now provide a geometric interpretation of (4.2) with $v = -F(x)$ (and also of (4.3)), and distinguish between the case that x lies in the interior of the constraint set and when it lies on the boundary. This distinction is critical and is needed to ensure that the dynamic trajectories evolve within the constraint set. Practically speaking, this feature guarantees that the constraints underlying the problem are satisfied (and not violated!). Hence, one can be assured that the asset allocation trajectory, for example, does not wander outside the budgetary restrictions. This desirable feature of a dynamical system has been illustrated in the case of prices in Examples 4.1 and 4.2.

(i). If $x \in \mathcal{K}^0$, then

$$\Pi_{\mathcal{K}}(x, -F(x)) = -F(x). \tag{4.9}$$

(ii). If $x \in \partial\mathcal{K}$, then

$$\Pi_{\mathcal{K}}(x, -F(x)) = -F(x) + \beta(x)N^*(x), \tag{4.10}$$

where

$$N^*(x) = \arg\max_{N \in N(x)} \langle (-F(x))^T, -N \rangle, \tag{4.11}$$

and

$$\beta(x) = \max\{0, \ \langle (-F(x))^T, -N^*(x) \rangle\}. \tag{4.12}$$

Note that since the right-hand side of the ordinary differential equation (4.3) is associated with a projection operator, it is discontinuous on the boundary of $\mathcal{K}$. Therefore, one needs to explicitly state what one means by a solution to an ODE with a discontinuous right-hand side.

Definition 4.2

We say that the function $x : [0, \infty) \mapsto \mathcal{K}$ is a solution to the equation $\dot{x} = \Pi_{\mathcal{K}}(x, -F(x))$ if $x(\cdot)$ is absolutely continuous and $\dot{x}(t) = \Pi_{\mathcal{K}}(x(t), -F(x(t)))$, save on a set of Lebesgue measure zero.

In order to distinguish between the pertinent ODEs (4.3) from the classical ODEs with continuous right-hand sides, we refer to (4.3) as ODE$(F, \mathcal{K})$.

Definition 4.3 (An Initial Value Problem)

For any $x_0 \in \mathcal{K}$ as an initial value, we associate with ODE$(F, \mathcal{K})$ *an initial value problem,* IVP$(F, \mathcal{K}, x_0)$, *defined as:*

$$\dot{x} = \Pi_{\mathcal{K}}(x, -F(x)), \quad x(0) = x_0. \tag{4.13}$$

One sees immediately that if there is a solution $\phi_{x_0}(t)$ to the initial value problem IVP$(F, \mathcal{K}, x_0)$, with $\phi_{x_0}(0) = x_0 \in \mathcal{K}$, then $\phi_{x_0}(t)$ always stays in the constraint set $\mathcal{K}$ for $t \geq 0$.

We now present the definition of a projected dynamical system, governed by such an ODE(F, K), which, correspondingly, will be denoted by PDS(F, K).

Definition 4.4 (The Projected Dynamical System)

Define the projected dynamical system PDS$(F, \mathcal{K})$ *as the map $\Phi : \mathcal{K} \times R \mapsto \mathcal{K}$ where*

$$\Phi(x, t) = \phi_x(t)$$

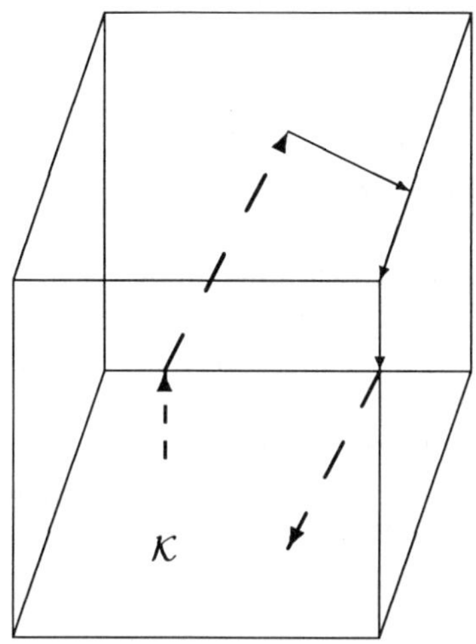

Fig. 4.1. A trajectory of a projected dynamical system that evolves both on the interior and on the boundary of the constraint set $\mathcal{K}$

solves the IVP$(F, \mathcal{K}, x)$, *that is,*

$$\dot{\phi}_x(t) = \Pi_{\mathcal{K}}(\phi_x(t), -F(\phi_x(t))), \quad \phi_x(0) = x. \tag{4.14}$$

The behavior of the dynamical system is now described. One may refer to Figure 4.1 for an illustration of this behavior.

If $x(t) \in \mathcal{K}^0$, then the evolution of the solution is directly given in terms of $F : \dot{x} = -F(x)$. However, if the vector field $-F$ drives x to $\partial\mathcal{K}$ (that is, for some t one has $x(t) \in \partial\mathcal{K}$ and $-F(x(t))$ points "out" of $\mathcal{K}$) the right-hand side of (4.13) becomes the projection of $-F$ onto $\partial\mathcal{K}$. The solution to (4.13) then evolves along a "section" of $\partial\mathcal{K}$, e. g., $\partial\mathcal{K}_i$ for some i. At a later time the solution may re-enter $\mathcal{K}^0$, or it may enter a lower dimensional part of ∂K, e.g., $\partial K_i \cap \partial K_j$. Depending on the particular vector field F, it may then evolve within the set $\partial K_i \cap \partial K_j$, re-enter ∂K_i, enter ∂K_j, etc.

Example 4.3 (A Tatonnement Process for the Competitive Financial Equilibrium Model)

For illustrative purposes, we consider now an adjustment or tatonnement process for the model in Example 3.4. Let $\nabla u(X)$ be the gradient of the utility functions of the investors with respect to the financial instruments.

We propose the following adjustment process which we write as the following projected dynamical system:

$$\dot{X} = \Pi_{\mathcal{K}}(X, \nabla u(X)), \tag{4.15}$$

where recall that $\mathcal{K}$ consists of the Cartesian product of the constraint sets of all the investors.

The dynamical system (4.15) says the following: An investor will increase his investment of an instrument if his marginal utility is increasing for that instrument; he will decrease his investment of an instrument if his marginal utility is decreasing for that instrument. However, if this process drives the level of financial instruments out of the feasible set, then the projection operator $\Pi_{\mathcal{K}}$ will guarantee that the evolution of the financial investments over time takes place within the constraint set.

We now define a stationary or an equilibrium point.

Definition 4.5 (A Stationary Point or an Equilibrium Point)

The vector $x^* \in \mathcal{K}$ is a stationary point or an equilibrium point of the projected dynamical system PDS$(F, \mathcal{K})$ *if*

$$0 = \Pi_{\mathcal{K}}(x^*, -F(x^*)). \tag{4.16}$$

In other words, we say that x^* is a stationary point or an equilibrium point if, once the projected dynamical system is at x^*, it will remain at x^* for all future times.

From Definition 4.5 it is clear that x^* is an equilibrium point of the projected dynamical system PDS$(F, \mathcal{K})$ if the vector field F vanishes at x^*. The contrary, however, is only true when x^* is an interior point of the constraint set $\mathcal{K}$. Indeed, when x^* lies on the boundary of $\mathcal{K}$, we may have $F(x^*) \neq 0$.

Note that for classical dynamical systems, the necessary and sufficient condition for an equilibrium point is that the vector field vanish at that point, that is, that $0 = -F(x)$.

The following theorem makes a fundamental connection between the static world of finite-dimensional variational inequality problems (a common tool for the formulation and analysis of equilibrium problems) and the dynamic world of projected dynamical systems (a new class of dynamical system).

Theorem 4.1

Assume that $\mathcal{K}$ is a convex polyhedron. Then the equilibrium points of the PDS$(F, \mathcal{K})$ *coincide with the solutions of* VI$(F, \mathcal{K})$. *Hence, for $x^* \in \mathcal{K}$ and satisfying*

$$0 = \Pi_{\mathcal{K}}(x^*, -F(x^*))$$

also satisfies

$$\langle F(x^*)^T, x - x^* \rangle \geq 0, \quad \forall x \in \mathcal{K}. \tag{4.17}$$

Theorem 4.1, due to Dupuis and Nagurney (1993), establishes the equivalence between the set of equilibria of a projected dynamical system and the set of solutions of a variational inequality problem. Moreover, it provides a natural underlying dynamics (out of equilibrium) of such systems.

In the context of Example 4.1, we have then that, according to Theorem 4.1, the stationary point of prices, p^*, that is, those prices that satisfy

$$0 = \Pi_{\mathcal{K}}(p^*, D(p^*) - S(p^*)) \tag{4.18}$$

also satisfy the variational inequality problem

$$\langle (S(p^*) - D(p^*))^T, p - p^* \rangle \geq 0, \quad \forall p \in \mathcal{K}. \tag{4.19}$$

Recall that the p^* that solves (4.19), in turn, satisfies the market equilibrium conditions (3.10). Hence, there is a natural underlying dynamics for the prices, and the equilibrium point satisfies the variational inequality problem (4.19); equivalently, is a stationary point of the projected dynamical system (4.6).

Before stating the fundamental theorem about projected dynamical systems, we introduce the following assumption needed for the theorem.

Assumption 4.1

There exists a $B < \infty$ such that the vector field $-F : R^n \mapsto R^n$ satisfies the linear growth condition: $\|F(x)\| \leq B(1 + \|x\|)$ for $x \in \mathcal{K}$, and also

$$\langle (-F(x) + F(y))^T, x - y \rangle \leq B\|x - y\|^2, \quad \forall x, y \in \mathcal{K}. \tag{4.20}$$

Theorem 4.2 (Existence, Uniqueness, and Continuous Dependence)

Assume Assumption 4.1. Then
(i). *For any $x_0 \in \mathcal{K}$, there exists a unique solution $x_0(t)$ to the initial value problem (4.13);*
(ii). *If $x_k \to x_0$ as $k \to \infty$, then $x_k(t)$ converges to $x_0(t)$ uniformly on every compact set of $[0, \infty)$.*

The second statement of Theorem 4.2 is sometimes called the continuous dependence of the solution path to ODE$(F, \mathcal{K})$ on the initial value. By virtue of Theorem 4.2, the PDS$(F, \mathcal{K})$ is well-defined and inhabits $\mathcal{K}$ whenever Assumption 4.1 holds.

Lipschitz continuity (cf. Definition 3.6) implies Assumption 4.1 and is, therefore, a sufficient condition for the fundamental properties of projected dynamical systems stated in Theorem 4.2. For additional discussion, see the book by Nagurney and Zhang (1996c).

4.2 Stability Analysis

Stability analysis of a system is concerned with the qualitative aspects of the behavior of the system relative to an equilibrium point. Basic questions that need to be addressed in the stability analysis of a dynamical system are the following:

(1). If a competitive behavior starts close to an equilibrium, will it remain close to it forever and

(2). Given the current state of the dynamical system, will the competitive behavior asymptotically approach an equilibrium.

We now, for preciseness and easy reference, include the definitions of various stability concepts for projected dynamical systems. These definitions are adaptations of standard stability concepts found in classical dynamical systems theory (cf. Hirsch and Smale (1974)). We adapt them in subsequent chapters to the dynamic financial adjustment processes under study therein.

We require first the following notation. The notation $x \cdot t$ and $x(t)$ denote the solution path of the IVP $(F, \mathcal{K}, x)$ (cf. (4.13)) that passes through x at time $t = 0$, that is, $x \cdot 0 = x(0) = x$. We will use the notation $B(x, r)$ to denote the open ball with radius r and center x.

Definition 4.6 (Stable (and Unstable) Equilibrium Point)

An equilibrium point x^* is stable if for any $\epsilon > 0$, there exists a $\delta > 0$ such that for all $x \in B(x^*, \delta)$ and $t \geq 0$

$$x \cdot t \in B(x^*, \epsilon).$$

The equilibrium point x^* is unstable if it is not stable.

In Figures 4.2 and 4.3, respectively, stable and an unstable equilibrium points are depicted.

Definition 4.7 (An Asymptotically Stable Equilibrium Point)

An equilibrium point x^* is asymptotically stable if it is stable and there exists a $\delta > 0$ such that for all $x \in B(x^*, \delta)$

$$\lim_{t \to \infty} x \cdot t \longrightarrow x^*. \tag{4.21}$$

In Figure 4.4 an asymptotically stable equilibrium point is depicted.

Definition 4.8 (An Exponentially Stable Equilibrium Point)

An equilibrium point x^* is exponentially stable if there exists a $\delta > 0$ and constants $B > 0$ and $\mu > 0$ such that

$$\|x \cdot t - x^*\| \leq B\|x - x^*\| \exp(-\mu t), \quad \forall t \geq 0, \, \forall x \in B(x^*, \delta); \tag{4.22}$$

x^* is globally exponentially stable, if (4.22) holds true for all $x \in \mathcal{K}$.

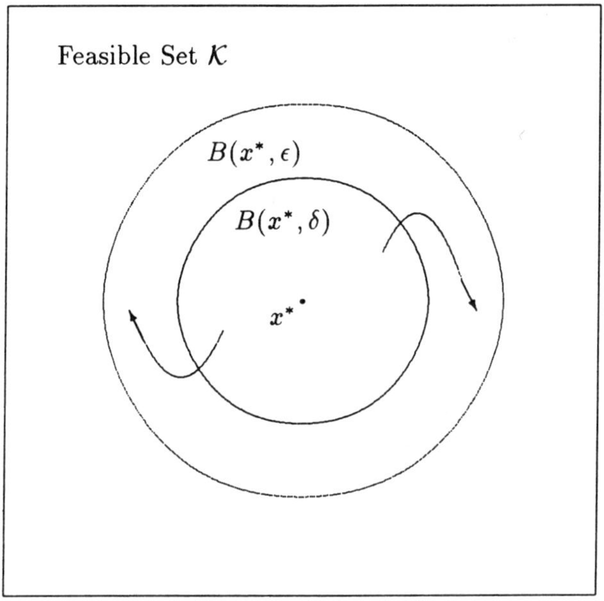

Fig. 4.2. A stable equilibrium point

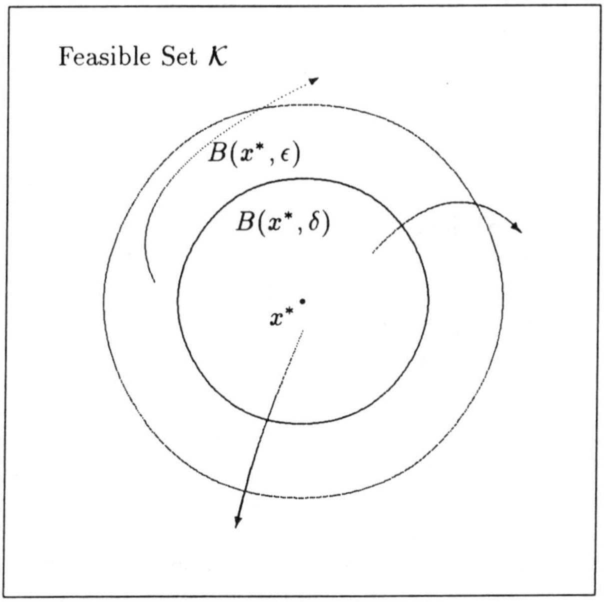

Fig. 4.3. An unstable equilibrium point

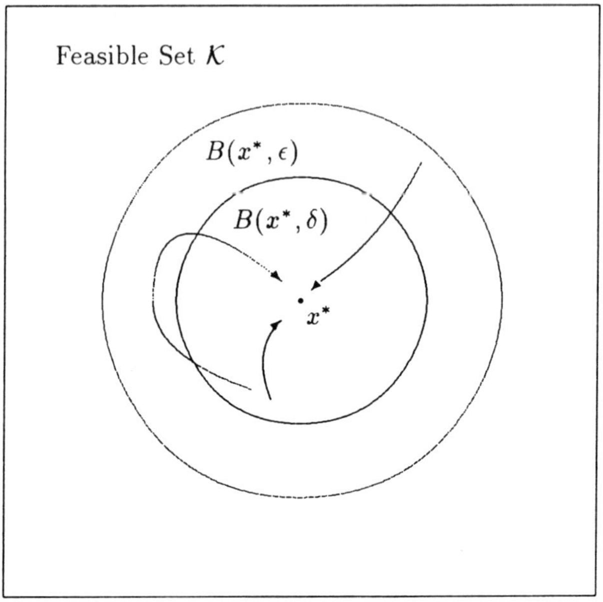

Fig. 4.4. An asymptotically stable equilibrium point

Definition 4.9 (A Monotone Attractor)

An equilibrium point x^* is a monotone attractor if there exists a $\delta > 0$ such that for all $x \in B(x^*, \delta)$

$$d(x,t) = \|x \cdot t - x^*\| \tag{4.23}$$

is a nonincreasing function of t; x^* is a global monotone attractor if $d(x,t)$ is nonincreasing in t for all $x \in \mathcal{K}$.

Definition 4.10 (A Strictly Monotone Attractor)

An equilibrium point x^* is a strictly monotone attractor if there exists a $\delta > 0$ such that for all $x \in B(x^*, \delta)$, $d(x,t)$ is monotonically decreasing to zero in t; x^* is a strictly global monotone attractor if $d(x,t)$ is monotonically decreasing to zero in t for all $x \in \mathcal{K}$.

The remainder of this section is devoted to studying local and global stability directly under various monotonicity conditions. Recall now the definitions of monotonicity at x^* given in Definition 3.2 (monotonicity), Definition 3.3 (strict monotonicity), and Definition 3.4 (strong monotonicity) in order from weak to strong. In what follows, we will state their correspondence to the stability at x^* in the same order. Namely, monotonicity implies a monotone attractor at x^*, strict monotonicity implies a strictly monotone attractor at x^*, and strong monotonicity implies that x^* is exponentially stable. The proofs of the subsequent theorems can be found in Zhang and Nagurney (1995).

We begin with the following

Theorem 4.3

Suppose that x^* solves VI$(F, \mathcal{K})$. *If $F(x)$ is locally monotone at x^*, then x^* is a monotone attractor for the* PDS$(F, \mathcal{K})$; *if $F(x)$ is monotone, then x^* is a global monotone attractor.*

Next we state

Theorem 4.4

Suppose that x^* solves VI$(F, \mathcal{K})$. *If $F(x)$ is locally strictly monotone at x^*, then x^* is a strictly monotone attractor; if $F(x)$ is strictly monotone at x^*, then x^* is a strictly global monotone attractor.*

Under strong monotonicity, we have

Theorem 4.5

Suppose that x^* solves VI$(F, \mathcal{K})$. *If $F(x)$ is locally strongly monotone at x^*, then x^* is exponentially stable; if $F(x)$ is strongly monotone at x^*, then x^* is globally exponentially stable.*

Let us now briefly illustrate some of the concepts set forth in Theorems 4.3 through 4.5. We return to the tatonnement process (4.6). We can then conclude from these theorems the following results. If $S(p) - D(p)$ (the excess supply vector) is monotone (or, equivalently, its Jacobian is positive semi-definite over R^n_+), then p^* satisfying (4.19), equivalently, (4.18), is a global monotone attractor. If $S(p) - D(p)$ is strictly monotone at p^* (cf. Proposition 3.1), then p^* is a strictly global monotone attractor. Finally, if $S(p) - D(p)$ is strongly monotone at p^* (cf. Proposition 3.1), then p^* is globally exponentially stable.

4.3 Algorithms

Although the dynamical system (4.3) provides a continuous adjustment process, a discrete time process is needed for actual computational purposes. Towards this end, in this section, we first review a general iterative scheme introduced in Dupuis and Nagurney (1993), which induces a variety of numerical procedures, all of which, in turn, are designed to trace the trajectory of the projected dynamical system from the initial state and to estimate solutions to the variational inequality problem (4.17), equivalently, to determine stationary points of the projected dynamical system (cf. (4.18)). We then present several schemes induced by the general iterative scheme.

The proposed algorithms for obtaining a stationary point (cf. (4.16)) of the projected dynamical system (4.3) all take the form

$$x^{\tau+1} = P_{\mathcal{K}}(x^{\tau} - a_{\tau} F_{\tau}(x^{\tau})), \tag{4.24}$$

where, without loss of generality, the "τ" denotes an iteration (or time period), $\{a_\tau, \tau \in T\}$ is a sequence of positive scalars, and the sequence of vector fields $\{F_\tau(\cdot), \tau \in T\}$ "approximates" $F(\cdot)$.

We now present the Euler-type method, which is the simplest algorithm induced by the above general iterative scheme.

Euler-Type Method:

In this case we have that

$$F_\tau(x) = F(x) \tag{4.25}$$

for all $\tau \in T$ and $x \in \mathcal{K}$. This would correspond to the basic Euler scheme in the numerical approximation of standard ODEs.

Another method is

Heun-Type Method:

In this case we have that

$$F_\tau(x) = \frac{1}{2}\left[F(x) + F(P_{\mathcal{K}}(x - a_\tau F(x)))\right]. \tag{4.26}$$

Finally, if the function F is defined in a sufficiently large neighborhood of $\mathcal{K}$, another method is

Alternative Heun-Type Method:

In this case we set

$$F_\tau(x) = \frac{1}{2}\left[F(x) + F(x - a_\tau F(x))\right]. \tag{4.27}$$

Other methods, which are induced by this general iterative scheme, include Runge-Kutta type algorithms.

The discrete time algorithms induced by the general iterative scheme (4.24), solve at iteration τ, the minimum norm problem:

$$\min_{x \in \mathcal{K}} \|x - (x^\tau - a_\tau F_\tau(x^\tau))\|, \tag{4.28}$$

or, equivalently, the strictly convex quadratic programming problem:

$$\min_{x \in \mathcal{K}} \frac{1}{2} x^T \cdot x - (x^\tau - a_\tau F_\tau(x^\tau))^T \cdot x. \tag{4.29}$$

In the case where the feasible set $\mathcal{K}$ is the nonnegative orthant, that is, when $\mathcal{K} = R^n_+$, then the projection operation becomes particularly simple. In this special case, an iteration of the general iterative scheme (4.24), given by (4.28) or (4.29), takes on the closed form expression:

$$(x^{\tau+1})_i = \begin{cases} (x^\tau - a_\tau F_\tau(x^\tau))_i, & \text{if } (x^\tau - a_\tau F_\tau(x^\tau))_i \geq 0, \\ 0, & \text{otherwise}, \end{cases} \tag{4.30}$$

for $i = 1, 2, \cdots, n$.

Hence, in the case that the feasible set $\mathcal{K}$ is the nonnegative orthant, in order to compute the iterate $\{x^{\tau+1}\}$, one need only to apply a simple formula. Also, it is worth noting that the evaluation of each $(x^{\tau+1})_i$; $i = 1, \ldots, n$, can be done independently and simultaneously. This feature opens up the possibility of parallel computation for the determination of the iterates.

In the case where the feasible set is no longer the nonnegative orthant, there are, nevertheless, many efficient algorithms to solve quadratic programming problems of the form (4.29), some of which exploit the underlying special structure of a problem, such as a network structure, if it exists. Indeed, this will be exactly the case in many of the financial models that will be studied in this text, which will be characterized by a constraint set that is a Cartesian product, consisting of networks.

In particular, the financial subproblems in the asset variables (as well as in the liability variables) facing a sector will be characterized by a special network structure which will enable an explicit solution in closed form using exact equilibration which will be discussed in Chapter 5. In addition, the price subproblems, as we shall show in subsequent chapters, will be computable using the straightforward formula (4.30).

It is worth comparing the general iterative scheme (4.24) and the projection method (3.24). Note, first, that the general iterative scheme allows for a varying "step size" a_τ, with each iteration τ, whereas the projection method has a fixed step size γ. Also, the general iterative scheme allows for different approximations $F_\tau(\cdot)$ to $F(\cdot)$, whereas the projection method does not. However, if, in the projection method, we set the matrix $G = I$, the $n \times n$ identity matrix, then the Euler method given by $F_\tau(\cdot) = F(\cdot)$ (cf. (4.25)) can be interpreted as a projection method with a varying step size a_τ. Of course, if one fixes the step size a_τ in (4.25) to be γ, then one obtains the projection method (3.24) with G set equal to I.

It is also worth mentioning that the projection method focuses on the solution of the variational inequality problem, whereas the general iterative scheme also induces alternative discrete time approximation schemes for the continuous time projected dynamical system.

Before giving the precise conditions for the general convergence theorem, we include the following definition.

Definition 4.11

For any subset A of R^n, the ω-limit set of A is defined by

$$\omega(A) = \{y : \exists x^k \in A, t^k \to \infty, \text{ such that } x^k \cdot t^k \to y, \text{ as } k \to \infty\}.$$

Assumption 4.2

Fix an initial condition $x^0 \in \mathcal{K}$ and define the sequence $\{x^\tau, \tau \in T\}$ by (4.24). Assume the following conditions:

1. $\sum_{\tau=0}^{\infty} a_\tau = \infty, \quad a_\tau > 0, \quad a_\tau \to 0, \text{ as } \quad \tau \to \infty.$
2. $d(F_\tau(x), \bar{F}(x)) \to 0$ *uniformly on compact subsets of* $\mathcal{K}$ *as* $\tau \to \infty$, *where* $d(x, A) = \inf\{\|x - y\|, y \in A\}$, *and the overline indicates closure.*
3. Define ϕ_y *to be the unique solution to* $\dot{x} = \Pi_{\mathcal{K}}(x, -F(x))$ *that satisfies* $\phi_y(0) = y \in \mathcal{K}$. *The* $\omega-$*limit set*

$$\cup_{y\in\mathcal{K}} \cap_{t\geq 0} \overline{\cup_{s\geq t} \{\phi_y(s)\}}$$

is contained in the set of stationary points of $\dot{x} = \Pi_{\mathcal{K}}(x, -F(x))$.
4. The sequence $\{x^\tau, \tau \in T\}$ *is bounded.*
5. The solutions to $\dot{x} = \Pi_{\mathcal{K}}(x, -F(x))$ *are stable in the sense that given any compact set* $\mathcal{K}_1$ *there exists a compact set* $\mathcal{K}_2$ *such that* $\cup_{y\in\mathcal{K}\cap\mathcal{K}_1} \cup_{t\geq 0} \{\phi_y(t)\} \subset \mathcal{K}_2$.

The assumptions are stated as above since they describe more or less what is needed for convergence, and because there are a number of rather different sets of conditions that imply the assumptions.

Theorem 4.6

Let S *denote the solutions to variational inequality (4.17), and assume Assumptions 4.1 and 4.2. Suppose that* $\{x^\tau, \tau \in T\}$ *is the scheme generated by (4.24). Then* $d(x^\tau, S) \to 0$ *as* $\tau \to \infty$.

Corollary 4.1

Assume the conditions of Theorem 4.6, and also that S *consists of a finite set of points. Then* $\lim_{\tau\to\infty} x^\tau$ *exists and equals a solution to the variational inequality (4.17).*

We now provide an interpretation of Assumption 4.2.1. Note that τ may be viewed as a stage or period. The requirement that $a_\tau \to \infty$, as $\tau \to \infty$, in a sense, suggests that the possibility of error accumulation should be reduced to reflect learning over time. The requirement that $\sum_{\tau=0}^{\infty} a_\tau = \infty$, in turn, suggests that the forces behind (4.24) should be given enough time to evolve. Both of these conditions imply that the system will react more strongly at the beginning and its responsiveness will decrease later on.

The following two propositions are due to Nagurney and Zhang (1996c). They are useful in simplifying parts of the Assumption 4.2.

Proposition 4.1

If the vector field $F(x)$ *is strictly monotone at some solution* x^* *to (4.17), then Assumption 4.2.3 holds true.*

Proposition 4.2

If the vector field $F(x)$ *is monotone at some solution* x^* *to (4.17), then Assumption 4.2.5 holds true.*

4.4 Sources and Notes

In this chapter we have provided the fundamentals of projected dynamical systems in terms of qualitative analysis and computational procedures. What is important to realize is that, although projected dynamical systems are nonclassical in that the right-hand side of the ordinary differential equation is discontinuous, one can now obtain results that are as strong as those obtained in classical dynamical systems. Standard references for classical dynamical systems are the books by: LaSalle and Lefschetz (1961), Hirsch and Smale (1974), and Perko (1991). Proofs and additional source material as well as applications of projected dynamical systems can be found in the book by Nagurney and Zhang (1996c).

Section 4.1

The theoretical results in this section are taken from Dupuis and Nagurney (1993), who initiated the study and development of projected dynamical systems. The presentation here follows that of Nagurney and Zhang (1996c). The examples are new and have been constructed with the topic of this book which is financial applications. It is worth emphasizing that others have proposed tatonnement processes similar to those in the examples (cf. Arrow, Hurwicz, and Uzawa (1958), Arrow and Hurwicz (1977), and Okuguchi and Szidarovsky (1990)). However, the projected dynamical systems methodology allows for the relaxation of conditions that need to be imposed to obtain qualitative results. Hence, assumptions can be considerably relaxed.

Section 4.2

Zhang and Nagurney (1995) initiated the stability analysis theory for projected dynamical systems using two distinct approaches: the "monotonicity approach" and the "regularity approach." The former approach has been discussed in this section. For applications of the regularity approach, we refer the interested reader to the book by Nagurney and Zhang (1996c). The presentation here follows that in Nagurney and Zhang (1996c).

Section 4.3

There are many books on the topic of the numerical solution of ordinary differential equations, for example, the books by: Henrici (1962), Gear (1971), Lambert (1973), and Conte and de Boor (1980). In this section we have described a general iterative scheme proposed by Dupuis and Nagurney (1993) for the solution of projected dynamical systems. Proofs of convergence of the scheme can also be found therein. Note that numerical methods for the solution of classical dynamical systems do not make use of the projection operator as the general iterative scheme does. This is needed to handle the constraints underlying the applications and to guarantee that the iterates satisfy the constraints.

As noted in this section, the Euler method defined by (4.25) can be viewed as a projection method with a varying step size. Various step-size rules have been proposed in the literature, along with other assumptions on the function $F(\cdot)$, in order to establish convergence of the projection method (see, e.g., Bakusinskii and Polyak (1974), Alber (1979), Fukushima (1986), and Flam (1992)). Among these assumptions, Assumption 4.1.1 is usually one of the weakest conditions, imposed typically with the assumption of strong monotonicity of F to guarantee convergence. Other research that should be recognized on the study of step-size rules for the gradient projection method (for the solution of optimization problems) includes the work of Goldstein (1964), Armijo (1966), and Bertsekas (1976).

References

Alber, Y. I., "On the Solution of Equations and Variational Inequalities with Maximal Monotone Operators," *Soviet Mathematics Doklady* **20** (1979) 871-876.

Armijo, L., "Minimization of Functions Having Continuous Partial Derivatives," *Pacific Journal of Mathematics* **16** (1966) 1-3.

Arrow, K. J., and Hurwicz, L., **Studies in Resource Allocation Processes**, Cambridge University Press, New York, New York, 1977.

Arrow, K. J., Hurwicz, L., and Uzawa, H., **Studies in Linear and Nonlinear Programming**, Stanford University Press, Stanford, California, 1958.

Bakusinskii, A. B., and Polyak, B. T., "On the Solution of Variational Inequalities," *Soviet Mathematics Doklady* **15** (1974) 1705-1710.

Bertsekas, D. P., "On the Goldstein-Levitin-Polyak Gradient Projection Method," *IEEE Transactions on Automatic Control* **21** (1976) 174-184.

Conte, S. D., and de Boor, C., **Elementary Numerical Analysis: An Algorithmic Approach**, third edition, McGraw-Hill, Inc., New York, New York, 1980.

Dong, J., Zhang, D., and Nagurney, A., "A Projected Dynamical Systems Model of General Financial Equilibrium with Stability Analysis," *Mathematical and Computer Modelling* **24** (1996) 35-44.

Dupuis, P., and Nagurney, A., "Dynamical Systems and Variational Inequalities," *Annals of Operations Research* **44** (1993) 9-42.

Flam, S. D., "On Finite Convergence and Constraint Identification of Subgradient Projection Methods," *Mathematical Programming* **57** (1992) 427-437.

Fukushima, M., "A Relaxed Projection Method for Variational Inequalities," *Mathematical Programming* **35** (1986) 58-70.

Gear, C. W., **Numerical Initial Value Problems in Ordinary Differential Equations**, Prentice-Hall, Inc., Englewood Cliffs, New Jersey, 1971.

Goldstein, A. A., "Convex Programming in Hilbert Space," *Bulletin of the American Mathematical Society* **70** (1964) 709-710.

Henrici, P., **Discrete Variable Methods in Ordinary Differential Equations**, John Wiley & Sons, Inc., New York, New York, 1962.

Hirsch, M. W., and Smale, S., **Differential Equations, Dynamical Systems, and Linear Algebra**, Academic Press, Inc., New York, New York, 1974.

Lambert, J. D., **Computational Methods in Ordinary Differential Equations**, John Wiley & Sons, Inc., New York, New York, 1973.

LaSalle, J., and Lefschetz, S., **Stability by Liapunov's Direct Method with Applications**, Academic Press, Inc., New York, New York, 1961.

Nagurney, A., **Network Economics: A Variational Inequality Approach**, Kluwer Academic Publishers, Boston, Massachusetts, 1993.

Nagurney, A, "Variational Inequalities in the Analysis and Computation of Multi-Sector, Multi-Instrument Financial Equilibria," *Journal of Economic Dynamics and Control* **18** (1994) 161-184.

Nagurney, A., "Parallel Computation," in **Handbook of Computational Economics, vol. 1**, pp. 331-400, H. M. Amman, D. A. Kendrick, and J. Rust, editors, Elsevier Science B. V., Amsterdam, The Netherlands, 1996.

Nagurney, A., Dupuis, P., and Zhang, D., "A Dynamical Systems Approach for Network Oligopolies and Variational Inequalities," *Annals of Regional Science* **28** (1994) 26-283.

Nagurney, A., and Siokos, S., "Dynamics of International Financial Networks: Modeling, Stability Analysis, and Computation," **Networks and Knowledge in a Dynamic Economy**, M. Beckmann, B. Johansson, F. Snickars, and R. Thord, editors, Springer-Verlag, Berlin, Germany, 1996, in press.

Nagurney, A., Takayama, T., and Zhang, D., "Massively Parallel Computation of Spatial Price Equilibrium Problems as Dynamical Systems," *Journal of Economic Dynamics and Control* **18** (1995a) 3-37.

Nagurney, A., Takayama, T., and Zhang, D., " Projected Dynamical Systems Modeling and Computation of Spatial Network Equilibria," *Networks* **26** (1995b) 69-85.

Nagurney, A., and Zhang, D., "On the Stability of Spatial Price Equilibria Modeled as a Projected Dynamical System," *Journal of Economic Dynamics and Control* **20** (1996a) 43-63.

Nagurney, A., and Zhang, D., "Projected Dynamical Systems in the Modeling, Stability Analysis, and Computation of Fixed Demand Traffic Network Equilibria," (1996b), to appear in *Transportation Science*.

Nagurney, A., and Zhang, D., **Projected Dynamical Systems and Variational Inequalities with Applications**, Kluwer Academic Publishers, Boston, Massachusetts, 1996c.

Okuguchi, K., and Szidarovszky, F., **The Theory of Oligopoly with Multi-Product Firms**, *Lecture Notes in Economics and Mathematical Systems* **342**, Springer-Verlag, Berlin, Germany, 1990.

Perko, L., **Differential Equations, Dynamical Systems, and Linear Algebra**, Academic Press, Inc., New York, New York, 1974.

Zhang, D., and Nagurney, A., "On the Stability of Projected Dynamical Systems, *Journal of Optimization Theory and Applications* **85** (1995) 97-124.

Zhang, D., and Nagurney, A., "Stability Analysis of an Adjustment Process for Oligopolistic Market Equilibrium Modeled as a Projected Dynamical System," *Optimization* **36** (1996a) 263-285.

Zhang, D., and Nagurney, A., "On the Local and Global Stability of a Travel Route Choice Adjustment Process," *Transportation Research* **30B** (1996b) 245-262.

5 Nonlinear Networks

Although Quesnay in 1758 conceptualized the financial flows in an economy as a network, the formal study of network flow problems dates to Kantorovich (1939), with the first applications being drawn from production and transportation/logistics problems (see also Hitchcock (1941) and Koopmans (1947)). Interestingly, such studies even preceded the development of linear programming with the work of Dantzig (1948) on the simplex method. The first network models were linear in that the costs on the links were assumed to be linear functions of the flows on the links.

Since those seminal contributions, linear as well as nonlinear, network models have been used to study a plethora of applications in many diverse fields, including transportation, communications, and energy. More obvious are network systems that are physical, such as in transportation and communication systems. Other settings in which network problems arise are more subtle, such as in economics and in finance. Nevertheless, the role that network theory can play therein is substantial in terms of both the visualization that such a tool provides as well as the algorithmic methods.

In finance, nonlinear network models are capable of handling risk through the construction of the appropriate nonlinear link cost functions. Hence, this book is exclusively concerned with nonlinear networks. In particular, we distinguish between network optimization problems, network equilibrium problems formulated as variational inequality problems, and dynamic network problems formulated as projected dynamical systems.

A network optimization problem is characterized by a single objective function to be optimized whereas in a network equilibrium problem no such optimization formulation may exist. Consequently, one may view a network optimization problem as consisting of a single agent who seeks to determine an optimal solution, whereas in a network equilibrium problem there are typically many agents, each with his own objective function, who compete on a network. In the latter problem, the equilibrium conditions play a paramount role whereas in the former it is the optimality conditions that are pivotal. Consequently, optimization theory plays a major role in network optimization problems whereas variational inequality theory is the primary methodology for the study of network equilibrium problems. In addition, we now have available projected dynamical systems theory to enable the dynamic modeling and computation of network-structured, decision-making problems over time, whose stationary points coincide with the solutions to the variational inequality formulation of the governing network equilibrium conditions.

This chapter is organized as follows. In Section 5.1 we present the foundations of nonlinear network optimization problems and include network optimization problems with special structure that occur in financial applications. In Section 5.2 we provide algorithms to compute solutions to the nonlinear network optimization problems contained in Section 5.1. Section 5.3 describes network equilibrium problems and makes linkages to Chapter 3. Section 5.4 discusses algorithms for the computation of solutions to network equilibrium problems. Finally, Section 5.5 discusses dynamic network problems in the framework of projected dynamical systems and makes connections to Chapter 4.

5.1 Network Optimization Problems

In this section we present some of the basic network notation and terminology as well as the general nonlinear network optimization problem. We also highlight certain specially structured network problems that are special cases of the general nonlinear network optimization problem. Such specially structured network optimization problems will be featured in the financial modeling chapters to follow.

The Nonlinear Network Optimization Problem

We consider a network consisting of a graph $\mathcal{G} = (\mathcal{N}, \mathcal{L})$ where $\mathcal{N}$ denotes the set of nodes and $\mathcal{L}$ denotes the set of links or arcs. Assume that the number of nodes in the network is equal to m and the number of links in the network is equal to n.

We assume that the links of the network are *directed* with each link represented by an arrow pointing from a tail node to a head node. A link of the network is denoted by the pair (i, j) with i representing the tail node of the link and j representing the head node of the link. We let x_{ij} denote the flow on arc (i, j) and we group the link flows in lexicographic order into the column vector $x \in R^n$.

We also assume that one seeks to minimize the total cost in a network represented by an objective function $f(x)$, where $f : R^n \mapsto R$, and is assumed to be a convex and twice continuously differentiable function.

The general nonlinear network optimization problem can be stated as:

$$\text{Minimize} \quad f(x) \tag{5.1}$$

subject to:

$$Ax = b \tag{5.2}$$

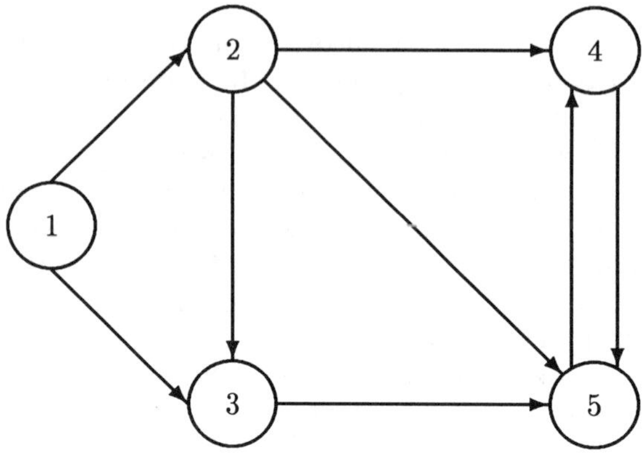

Fig. 5.1. A pure network example

$$l \le x \le u, \tag{5.3}$$

where A is an $m \times n$ node-arc incidence matrix, $b \in R^m$, $l \in R^n$, and $u \in R^n$ are given column vectors. The vector b is sometimes referred to as the "right-hand" side and its components sum to zero, that is, $\sum_{i=1}^{m} b_i = 0$. If component $b_i > 0$, then node i is called a supply node; if $b_i < 0$, then node i is called a demand node, and if $b_i = 0$, then node i is called a transshipment node. The vectors l and u represent, respectively, the vectors of lower and upper bounds on the flows on the arcs.

Note that the nonlinear network optimization problem is a special case of an optimization problem (3.5) in which the feasible set $\mathcal{K}$ consists of the constraints (5.2) and (5.3), which are a defining characteristic of network problems with A representing, in effect, the network topology on which the optimization problem takes place.

It is important to make a distinction between two basic network optimization problems – *pure* network optimization problems and *generalized* network optimization problems. In the former, each column of the node-arc matrix A has two non-zero entries: a '+1' and a '-1.'

Example 5.1 (A Pure Network Example)

In Figure 5.1 we present a small pure network example consisting of 5 nodes and 8 arcs.

The objective function is given by:

$$\text{Minimize} \quad 10x_{12}^2 + 5x_{13}^2 + 4x_{23}^2 + x_{24}^2$$

$$+8x_{25}^2 + 5x_{35}^2 + 6x_{45}^2 + 2x_{54}^2$$

subject to:

$$Ax = b,$$

$$x \ge 0,$$

with the node-arc-incidence matrix A (cf. Figure 5.1) given by

$$\begin{array}{c} \\ (1) \\ (2) \\ (3) \\ (4) \\ (5) \end{array} \begin{array}{c} \begin{array}{cccccccc} (1,2) & (1,3) & (2,3) & (2,4) & (2,5) & (3,5) & (4,5) & (5,4) \end{array} \\ \left(\begin{array}{cccccccc} 1 & 1 & 0 & 0 & 0 & 0 & 0 & 0 \\ -1 & 0 & 1 & 1 & 1 & 0 & 0 & 0 \\ 0 & -1 & -1 & 0 & 0 & 1 & 0 & 0 \\ 0 & 0 & 0 & -1 & 0 & 0 & 1 & -1 \\ 0 & 0 & 0 & 0 & -1 & -1 & -1 & 1 \end{array} \right) \end{array}.$$

The right-hand side vector $b = (10, 0, 0, -5, -5)^T$ and the vector $x = (x_{12}, x_{13}, x_{23}, x_{24}, x_{25}, x_{35}, x_{45}, x_{54})^T$.

Generalized networks, on the other hand, can also be represented by an A matrix with two non-zero entries in each column: a '+1' and a real number $-m_{ij}$ that denotes minus the multiplier on the arc. Typically, in financial applications, the multiplier for an arc (i, j), m_{ij}, lies in the range: $(0, 2]$, with a value less than 1 representing a "loss" in the financial flow as the arc is traversed and a value greater than 1 representing a "gain" or increase in the financial flow.

Note that for a given x_{ij}, we have that i is the row of the corresponding column of the constraint matrix A with the entry '+1', whereas j is the row with entry '-1' in the case of pure networks and a $-m_{ij}$ in the case of generalized networks. In fact, the flow passing across an arc in a generalized network is acted upon by a nonzero multiplier. Therefore, in contrast to pure networks, on an arc with a multiplier (not equal to 1) the amount of the flow that starts at the tail node of an arc is not equal to the amount that arrives at the head node of that arc. Hence, in generalized networks, the total supply may not be equal to the total demand, whereas, in pure networks they should always be equal.

In general, there are two different ways in which multipliers may act in a generalized network: they can either modify the amount of flow of a particular commodity, or transform the flow from one type to another. In an example of the former case, multipliers could represent interest rates, whereas in an example of the latter case multipliers could model currency exchange rates.

For example, we can consider a generalized network to model a currency translation procedure, originally developed by Soenen (1979), and later formulated as a network optimization problem by Mulvey (1987). We will now present a version of that problem for managing international cash flows through a single period, two-currency (dollars, and British pounds) translation model.

Example 5.2 (A Currency Translation Problem)

We depict the generalized network for the specific currency translation problem in Figure 5.2.

Assuming that there is a fixed total demand for cash at the end of the currency translation procedure, the primary objective of a manager that deals

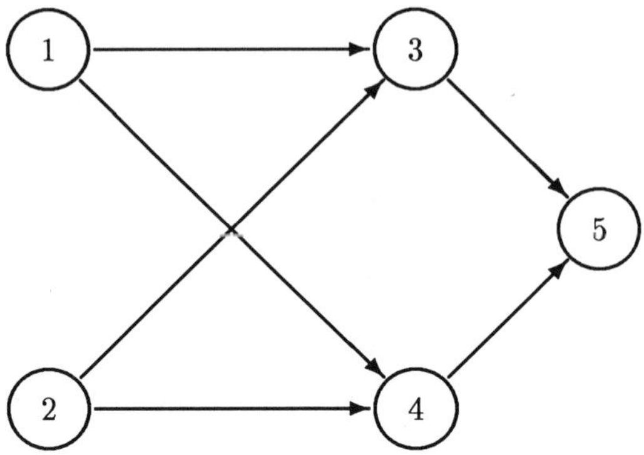

Fig. 5.2. A two-currency translation network model

with such an application is to minimize the corresponding risk which is assumed to be measured through a variance-covariance matrix.

We denote the cash flowing from node i to node j by x_{ij}, with nodes 1 and 3 referring to dollars, and nodes 2 and 4 referring to British pounds. The cash moving from one node to the other is exposed to some translation factors which we denote by m_{ij}, and we translate both currencies in terms of a basic currency denoted by node 5. Moreover, we let b_1 denote the cash supply in dollars and we let b_2 denote the cash supply in British pounds. Notice that there is no cash collector node since both currencies are translated in a pairwise fashion.

Consider now the following numerical example, with the translation factors having the following values:

$$m_{13} = 1.0, \quad m_{14} = 0.62, \quad m_{23} = 1.59,$$

$$m_{24} = 1.0, \quad m_{35} = 0.75, \quad m_{45} = 1.3.$$

Let the currency cash supply and demand values be equal to:

$$b_1 = 5.0, \quad b_2 = 8.0. \quad b_5 = -14.0,$$

with $b_3 = b_4 = 0$. Lastly, assume that all lower bounds on the cash flows are zero, and that there are no upper bounds.

The variance-covariance matrix for this example is given by:

$$Q = \begin{pmatrix} 1.0 & 0.3 & 0 & 0 & 0 & 0 \\ 0.3 & 1.0 & 0 & 0 & 0 & 0 \\ 0 & 0 & 1.0 & 0.5 & 0 & 0 \\ 0 & 0 & 0.5 & 1.0 & 0 & 0 \\ 0 & 0 & 0 & 0 & 1.0 & .15 \\ 0 & 0 & 0 & 0 & .15 & 1.0 \end{pmatrix}.$$

Then the currency translation model for this example is given by:

$$\text{Minimize} \quad \begin{pmatrix} x_{13} \\ x_{14} \\ x_{23} \\ x_{24} \\ x_{35} \\ x_{45} \end{pmatrix}^T Q \begin{pmatrix} x_{13} \\ x_{14} \\ x_{23} \\ x_{24} \\ x_{35} \\ x_{45} \end{pmatrix}$$

subject to:

$$\begin{array}{lllllll}
+1.0x_{13} & +1.0x_{14} & & & & & = 5 \\
 & & +1.0x_{23} & +1.0x_{24} & & & = 8 \\
-1.0x_{13} & & -1.59x_{23} & & +1.0x_{35} & & = 0 \\
 & -0.62x_{14} & & -1.0x_{24} & & +1.0x_{45} & = 0 \\
 & & & & -0.75x_{35} & -1.3x_{45} & = -14
\end{array}$$

$$x_{13},\ x_{14},\ x_{23},\ x_{24},\ x_{35},\ x_{45} \geq 0.$$

We now highlight certain *special* cases of the general nonlinear network optimization problem. The "specialness" may be due to: **(1).** the form of the objective function $f(x)$, **(2).** the network topology itself, as represented by the constraint matrix A, or to **(3).** a combination of both (1) and (2). Such special cases are important since they suggest features of the network problem that may then, in turn, be exploited algorithmically (and computationally), as we shall show in the next section.

In addition, we also describe **(4).** a special case of the nonlinear optimization problem (3.5), in which a subset of the constraints has a network structure. Such a problem may be amenable to solution via a primal-dual decomposition algorithm which we will also present in Section 5.2.

5.1.1 Special Objective Functions

In this subsection we discuss special cases of the above general nonlinear network optimization problem in which the form of the constraints is as in (5.2) and (5.3) but the form of the objective function (5.1) is specialized.

A Separable Network Optimization Problem

In the first special case of the general nonlinear network optimization problem that we can consider, the objective function (5.1) is separable, that is, of the form

$$f(x) = \sum_{(i,j)\in\mathcal{L}} f_{ij}(x_{ij}), \tag{5.4}$$

where the cost on a link (i,j) depends solely upon the flow on the link. This problem, subject to (5.2) and (5.3), is commonly referred to as a *separable* nonlinear network optimization problem. If one further assumes that the cost on a link is linear, that is, given by $c_{ij}x_{ij}$, where c_{ij} is assumed to be positive, then one obtains a *linear* minimum network cost flow problem.

A Quadratic Network Optimization Problem

Another common network problem that occurs in finance is the network optimization problem in which the objective function given by (5.1) takes on a quadratic form, for example, to represent risk to be minimized (and return to be maximized).

In this case, we have that (5.1) is replaced by:

$$\text{Minimize} \quad x^T Q x + c^T x, \tag{5.5}$$

with Q being an $n \times n$ matrix and c being an n-dimensional column vector.

Note that quadratic programming formulation of the portfolio optimization problem in (2.8) is precisely of this form. In addition, the currency translation problem in Example 5.2 is also of this form. In Chapter 14 we will formulate an estimation problem encountered in financial flow of funds accounts that is also a separable quadratic network optimization problem.

Of course, if the matrix Q is diagonal, then one obtains a separable quadratic network optimization problem. Note that Example 5.1 is a separable quadratic network optimization problem in which the vector c, in this case, consists of all zero elements. Moreover, Sharpe's model with the quadratic form given by (2.9) is also a quadratic network optimization problem with a separable objective function since the variance/covariance matrix in this case is assumed to be diagonal.

5.1.2 Special Network Topology

We now present special cases of the general nonlinear network optimization problem in which the objective function (5.1) is retained but the network topology constraints (5.2) have a special structure.

Bipartite Network Topology

A network topology in which the network is as depicted in Figure 5.3, where the network consists of only two groups of nodes that can either be an origin or a destination node is termed *bipartite*.

In this special case, the network $\mathcal{G}$ is bipartite and consists of the M origin nodes and N destination nodes. Let s denote the vector of supplies associated with the origin nodes and let d denote the vector of demands associated with the demand nodes. Then the nonlinear network optimization problem on a bipartite network is given by objective function (5.1), subject to:

$$\sum_{j=1}^{N} x_{ij} = s_i, \quad i = 1, \ldots, M \tag{5.6}$$

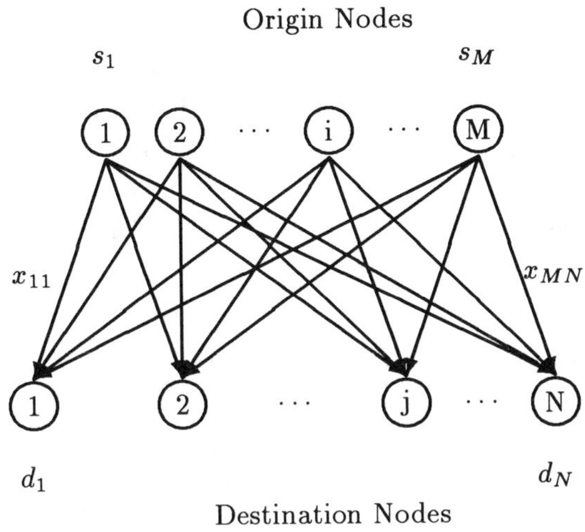

Fig. 5.3. A bipartite network

$$\sum_{i=1}^{M} x_{ij} = d_j, \quad j = 1, \ldots, N \tag{5.7}$$

$$l_{ij} \leq x_{ij} \leq u_{ij}, \quad i = 1, \ldots, M; \; j = 1, \ldots, N, \tag{5.8}$$

where l_{ij} and u_{ij} denote, respectively, the lower and the upper bounds on the flow on link (i, j). In this formulation, with constraints expressed as (5.6) and (5.7), it is assumed that $s_i > 0$ and $d_j > 0$ for all nodes i and j.

This network topology, although quite specialized, interestingly, arises frequently in practice in many different types of applications. For example, when the objective function is linear and separable and constraints are of the form (5.6) and (5.7), one obtains then the classical Hitchcock-Koopmans linear transportation problem.

A Single Pair of Nodes Network Topology

In this special case, the network consists of only n links as depicted in Figure 5.4. Note that if we label an "origin" node O and a destination node D, then one may transform the network, as depicted in Figure 5.4, into a single origin/destination (O/D) pair of nodes network. Without any loss in generality, we may relabel the links as $\{1, 2, \ldots, n\}$ as in Figure 5.4.

Due to the simplicity of this network, one may suppress the subscript j

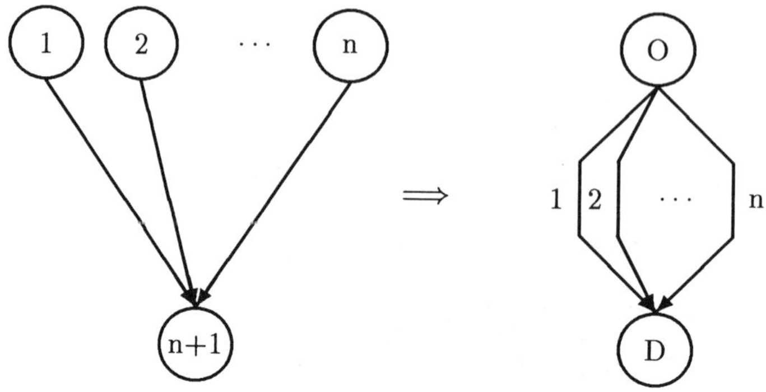

Fig. 5.4. A two node, n link network

in the variable x_{ij}, and the index j in d_j and simply write the constraints as:

$$\sum_{i=1}^{n} x_i = d \tag{5.9}$$

$$x_i \geq 0, \quad i = 1, \ldots, n. \tag{5.10}$$

Note that the objective function would be reduced and simplified accordingly.

Of course, this network model may be viewed, in turn, as a special case of the bipartite network model in which we collapse the n origin nodes into a single origin node and retain the single destination node, as was depicted in Figure 5.4.

5.1.3 Special Objective Functions and Topologies

In this subsection we present nonlinear network optimization models in which both the objective functions and the network topologies are specialized. These types of network optimization problems have been subjected to much algorithmic research with a great deal of success since they have features that are clearly exploitable for the development of efficient special-purpose algorithms. Judiciously, they are also frequently encountered in financial practice. The listing of special cases is by no means exhaustive; rather, it is simply representative of the types of special network subproblems that will arise in subsequent chapters in this text.

Separable Quadratic Objective Function, Bipartite Network

The formulation of this special case quadratic problem (cf. Figure 5.3) is given by:

$$\text{Minimize} \quad \sum_{(i,j)\in\mathcal{L}} q_{ij}x_{ij}^2 + c_{ij}x_{ij} \tag{5.11}$$

subject to: (5.6), (5.7), and (5.8), with (5.8), oftentimes, simplified to:

$$x_{ij} \geq 0, \quad \forall (i,j) \in \mathcal{L}. \tag{5.12}$$

In some applications (cf. Nagurney and Robinson (1992)), one may have constraints such as (5.6)–(5.8), but with a full quadratic matrix Q as in (5.5). One then obtains a nonseparable quadratic problem on a bipartite network. Such problems arise frequently and are often referred to as *constrained matrix problems* (see, e. g., Nagurney and Eydeland (1992) and the references therein).

Nonseparable Quadratic Objective Function, Two Node Network

In this special case, the objective function is quadratic, of the form given by (5.5), whereas the constraints are given by (5.9) and (5.10). The network topology is as depicted in Figure 5.4. It is easy to see that the Markowitz model (1959) given in (2.8) is precisely a nonlinear network optimization problem with this special network structure and this quadratic objective function and constraints.

Separable Quadratic Objective Function, Two Node Network

If one further specializes the preceding special case and assumes that the quadratic objective function has a Q matrix that is diagonal, in which case, one obtains a separable objective function, and, consequently, a nonlinear network optimization problem with a separable quadratic objective function, subject to constraints (5.9) and (5.10). The network topology is, again, depicted by Figure 5.4.

Note that this special case is precisely the network optimization equivalent of the Sharpe (1963) diagonal portfolio optimization model (cf. Section 2.1).

The above network problems are just some of the network optimization problems that are encountered in finance. Others, including those with special structure not discussed above, will be identified as they are needed and utilized in the subsequent chapters. The special cases outlined above are, nevertheless, fundamental and will be encountered in a variety of settings in this book.

5.1.4 Separable Nonlinear Optimization Problem

In this subsection we consider a special case of the nonlinear optimization problem (3.5), in which both the objective function $f(x)$ and the constraint set $\mathcal{K}$ take on special forms. In particular, the objective function is now separable in the sense that f_i is now a function only of the vector x_i with components $\{x_{i1}, \dots, x_{in_i}\}$. Hence, $f_i(x_i) : S_i \mapsto R^{n_i}$, for each i; $i = 1, \dots, z$, where $S_i \subset R^{n_i}$ and $\sum_{i=1}^{z} n_i = n$. In addition to the constraint set S_i for each i, there are certain "complicating" constraints that include terms that are not only a function of x_i. For example, each S_i may have a network structure, whereas the complicating constraints may not. On the other hand, even if the entire feasible set is that of a network one may wish to partition the feasible set in such a way so that the sets S_i; $i = 1, \dots, z$, have a particularly simple network form for computational purposes.

This problem takes on the formulation:

$$\text{Minimize} \quad \sum_{i=1}^{z} f_i(x_i) \tag{5.13}$$

subject to:

$$g_j(x) = \sum_{i=1}^{z} g_{ji}(x_i) \leq b_j, \quad j = 1, \ldots, m \tag{5.14}$$

$$x_i \in S_i, \quad i = 1, \ldots, z. \tag{5.15}$$

5.2 Network Optimization Algorithms

In this section we present algorithms for the solution of convex nonlinear network optimization problems. In particular, we consider both a general-purpose algorithm, the primal truncated Newton method (cf. Dembo and Steihaug (1983)), as well as special-purpose algorithms. In terms of special-purpose algorithms, we present the Splitting Equilibration Algorithm developed and theoretically analyzed by Nagurney and Eydeland (1992), which is a dual method, as well as an exact equilibration algorithm due to Dafermos and Sparrow (1969) for the solution of specially-structured network problems that have been presented in Section 5.1. In addition, we present a primal-dual decomposition method, which enables the exploitation of an underlying network structure of a problem, if such a structure exists. The primal-dual decomposition method (cf. Lasdon (1970)) is not a network optimization algorithm, per se, but may be used to exploit an underlying network structure.

5.2.1 The Primal Truncated Newton Method

The primal truncated Newton method (cf. Dembo and Steihaug (1983)), when implemented within the active set framework (cf. Murtagh and Saunders (1978)), is one of the most effective algorithms for the solution of the nonlinear network optimization problem (5.1), subject to (5.2) and (5.3). It is especially suitable for the solution of large-scale network problems. Dembo (1987) describes the combination of both techniques for pure networks, whereas Ahlfeld, Dembo, Mulvey, and Zenios (1987) describe the synthesis for generalized networks. Mulvey (1987) discussed the application of this algorithm to a variety of financial network optimization problems. The presentation of the primal truncated Newton method below is done in two parts, with the first part presenting Newton's algorithm for unconstrained optimization problems and the second part describing how the active set method reduces a constrained optimization problem (cf. (3.5)) into a sequence of unconstrained (locally) problems in lower dimensions. The presentation below follows that in Bertsekas, Castanon, Eckstein, and Zenios (1995). For additional discussion, see Gill, Murray, and Wright (1981), Mulvey (1987), and Bertsekas, Castanon, Eckstein, and Zenios (1995).

As in most nonlinear programming algorithms, the primal truncated Newton method consists of two basic stages: **(1).** a search direction determination stage and **(2).** a step length determination stage. The direction must be a direction of descent since we are interested in minimizing $f(x)$. Also, the step size, roughly speaking, tells us how far in the direction one can move.

Part I: A Truncated Newton Algorithm for Unconstrained Optimization

Assume that $f(x)$ is convex and twice continuously differentiable and consider the unconstrained optimization problem

$$\text{Minimize} \quad f(x) \tag{5.16}$$

subject to:

$$x \in R^n.$$

The primal truncated Newton method begins with an initial feasible point $x^0 \in R^n$ and generates a sequence $\{x^\tau\}$, $\tau = 1, 2, \ldots$, such that

$$\lim_{\tau \to \infty} x^\tau = x^*, \tag{5.17}$$

where x^* lies in the set of optimal solutions to (5.16).

An iterative step is given by:

$$x^{\tau+1} = x^\tau + \alpha_\tau d^\tau, \tag{5.18}$$

where $\{\alpha_\tau\}$ is a sequence of step sizes and $\{d^\tau\}$ is a sequence of descent directions.

In particular, the sequence of descent directions is computed by solving the system of Newton's equations, given by:

$$\nabla^2 f(x^\tau) d^\tau = -\nabla f(x^\tau). \tag{5.19}$$

The system (5.19), however, is not solved exactly and, hence, the term "truncated" in the name of the algorithm. Instead, d^τ is obtained so that it satisfies:

$$\|\nabla^2 f(x^\tau) d^\tau + \nabla f(x^\tau)\|_\infty \leq \epsilon^\tau, \tag{5.20}$$

with ϵ^τ being a preset positive tolerance.

A measure of the residual error, at iteration τ, e^τ, in turn, is given by:

$$e^\tau = \frac{\|\nabla^2 f(x^{\tau-1}) d^\tau + \nabla f(x^{\tau-1})\|}{\|\nabla f(x^{\tau-1})\|}. \tag{5.21}$$

The step direction d^τ is determined from (5.19) so that the condition $e^\tau \leq \epsilon^\tau$ is satisfied, with the sequence $\{\epsilon^\tau\} \to 0$, as $\tau \to \infty$.

The sequence of step sizes $\{a_\tau\}$ is determined as follows with step size α_τ being the step size that minimizes, at iteration τ, the function $f(x)$ along the direction d^τ, beginning from the point x^τ. It is computed by solving, at iteration τ:

$$\alpha_\tau = \text{argmin}_{\alpha>0}\{f(x^\tau + \alpha d^\tau)\}. \tag{5.22}$$

Note that it may be computationally expensive to compute α_τ according to (5.22) at each iteration and, hence, one may appeal to an inexact linesearch method. More discussion of this point can be found in Bertsekas (1982).

Part II: An Active Set Method for Constrained Optimization

We now describe the second part of the primal truncated Newton method that involves the transformation of the nonlinear network optimization problem (5.1), subject to (5.2) and (5.3), into a locally *unconstrained* problem. Following Murtagh and Saunders (1978), partition the matrix A as follows:

$$A = [B|S|N], \tag{5.23}$$

where B is a non-singular matrix of dimension $m \times m$, whose columns form a basis, S is a matrix of dimension $m \times r$, and corresponds to the superbasic variables, that is, those variables at their lower bound with negative reduced gradient, variables at their upper bound with positive reduced gradient, or free variables, and N is a matrix of dimension $m\times(n-m-r)$, and corresponds to the non-basic variables. Non-basic variables are those variables that have a positive reduced gradient and are at their lower bound, or have a negative reduced gradient and are at their upper bound.

At iteration τ, we partition the vector x^τ as follows:

$$x^\tau = [x_B^\tau|x_S^\tau|x_N^\tau], \tag{5.24}$$

where x_B^τ are the basic variables, x_S^τ are the superbasic variables, and x_N^τ are the non-basic variables. We note that non-basic variables, for a specific partitioning (5.23)–(5.24), are kept fixed to one of their bounds. Similarly, we can partition the step direction according to:

$$d^\tau = [d_B^\tau|d_S^\tau|d_N^\tau]. \tag{5.25}$$

Note that the non-basic variables remain fixed, so we must have that $d_N^\tau = 0$. Moreover, d^τ must satisfy $Ad^\tau = 0$ in order to insure that d^τ is a feasible direction. Consequently, d^τ must satisfy

$$Bd_B^\tau + Sd_S^\tau = 0 \tag{5.26}$$

or, equivalently,

$$d_B^\tau = -(B^{-1}S)d_S^\tau. \tag{5.27}$$

If the superbasic variables are strictly between the bounds and the basis matrix B is maximal in that a non-zero step in the basic variables x_B is possible for any direction $(d_B^\tau|d_S^\tau|0)$ (cf. Dembo and Klincewicz (1985)), then the problem is a locally unconstrained problem with respect to the superbasic variables. Consequently, a descent direction for d_S^T can be obtained by solving the *projected* Newton's equations given by:

$$(X^T \nabla^2 f(x^\tau) X) d_S^\tau = -X^T \nabla f(x^\tau) + \epsilon^\tau \tilde{\epsilon}, \tag{5.28}$$

where X is a basis for the nullspace of A defined as:

$$X = \begin{bmatrix} -B^{-1}S \\ I \\ 0 \end{bmatrix}. \tag{5.29}$$

More discussion of (5.28) and, in particular, the term $\epsilon^\tau \tilde{e}$, in regards to, for example, the precision of the computer used, can be found in Dembo (1987).

The most computationally expensive step of the algorithm lies in solving the system of equations (5.28). This system is usually solved using a conjugate gradient method.

5.2.2 The Splitting Equilibration Algorithm

In this subsection we describe a special-purpose algorithm, the Splitting Equilibration Algorithm, for the solution of the separable, quadratic objective function, bipartite network problem presented in Subsection 5.1.3. In Chapter 14, we describe extensions of this algorithm for the estimation of financial flow of funds accounts. The Splitting Equilibration Algorithm was introduced by Nagurney and Eydeland (1992) for the solution of quadratic programming problems with constraints of the form (5.6) and (5.7) on bipartite networks. It is a dual method and its convergence analysis and complexity analysis can be found therein. In particular, it consists of two basic steps: Row Equilibration and Column Equilibration. The algorithm, roughly speaking, can be described as follows: First, one modifies the objective function $f(x)$ and considers only the supply constraints; then one updates the objective function and considers only the demand constraints. Due to the simplicity of the supply (and of the demand) constraints, the resulting network subproblems can be solved exactly and in closed form using an "exact" equilibration algorithm which we will present in Section 5.2.3.

Without any loss of generality, we assume that there are now M origin or supply nodes and N destination or demand nodes. The network topology is as depicted in Figure 5.3. The objective function is quadratic and separable. For easy reference, we now state the problem as:

$$\text{Minimize} \quad f(x) = \sum_{i=1}^{M} \sum_{j=1}^{N} q_{ij} x_{ij}^2 + c_{ij} x_{ij} \tag{5.30}$$

subject to:

$$\sum_{j=1}^{N} x_{ij} = s_i, \quad i = 1, \ldots, M \tag{5.31}$$

$$\sum_{i=1}^{M} x_{ij} = d_j, \quad j = 1, \ldots, N \tag{5.32}$$

$$x_{ij} \geq 0, \quad i = 1, \ldots, M; \quad j = 1, \ldots, N. \tag{5.33}$$

It is assumed, in view of the constraints (5.31) and (5.32), that $s_i > 0$ and $d_j > 0$ for all i and j.

The statement of the algorithm is as follows:

Step 0: Initialization Step

Let $\mu^1 \in R^N = 0$. Set $\tau := 1$.

Step 1: Row Equilibration

Find $(X(\mu^\tau))$, which is the optimal vector x satisfying

$$X(\mu^\tau) \to \min_x f(x) - \sum_{j=1}^{N} \mu_j^\tau (\sum_{i=1}^{M} x_{ij} - d_j) \tag{5.34}$$

subject to:

$$\sum_{j=1}^{N} x_{ij} = s_i, \quad i = 1, \ldots, M \tag{5.35}$$

$$x_{ij} \geq 0, \quad \text{for all} \quad i, j.$$

Compute the corresponding Lagrange multipliers $\lambda_i^{\tau+1}$; $i = 1, \ldots, M$, according to: $\lambda_i^{\tau+1} = 2q_{ij}X_{ij}(\mu^\tau) + c_{ij} - \mu_j^\tau$, and use them in Step 2.

Step 2: Column Equilibration

Find $X(\lambda^{\tau+1})$, which is the optimal x satisfying

$$(X(\lambda^{\tau+1})) \to \min_x f(x) - \sum_{i=1}^{M} \lambda_i^{\tau+1} (\sum_{j=1}^{N} x_{ij} - d_j) \tag{5.36}$$

subject to:

$$\sum_{i=1}^{M} x_{ij} = d_j, \quad j = 1, \ldots, N \tag{5.37}$$

$$x_{ij} \geq 0, \quad \text{for all} \quad i, j.$$

Compute the corresponding Lagrange multipliers $\mu_j^{\tau+1}$; $j = 1, \ldots, N$, according to $\mu_j^{\tau+1}$=$2q_{ij}X_{ij}(\lambda^{\tau+1})$+$c_{ij}$ $-$ $\lambda_i^{\tau+1}$ and use them in Step 1.

Step 3: Convergence Verification

If $|X_{ij}(\lambda^{\tau+1}) - s_i| \leq \epsilon$, for all i, then terminate; otherwise, set $\tau := \tau + 1$, and go to Step 1.

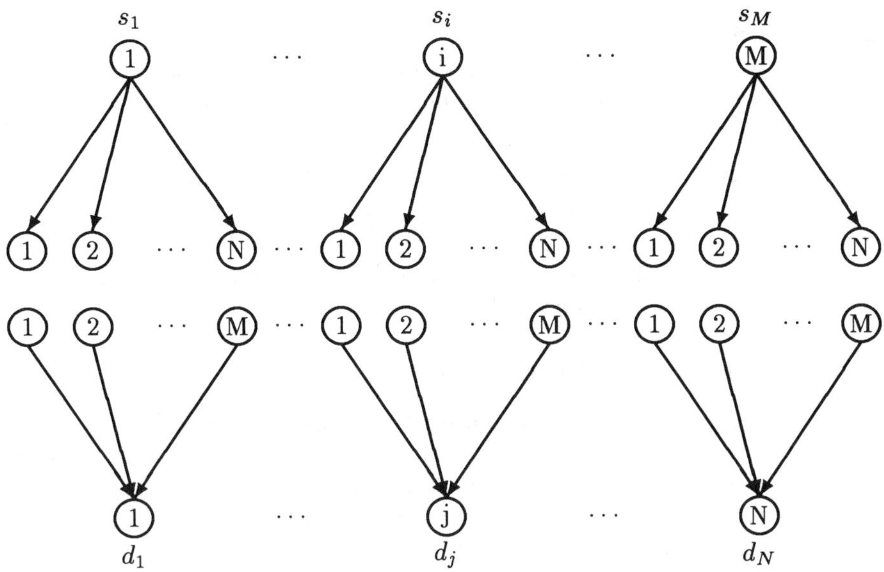

Fig. 5.5. Network structure of row and column equilibration subproblems

We would like to emphasize that each of the row and column equilibration problems above has a characteristic special network structure (cf. Figure 5.5) that enables parallel computation. Indeed, each network subproblem is, in fact, of the special form of the network depicted in Figure 5.4.

An exact equilibration scheme, which will be described in the subsequent subsection, can be used for the computation of the subproblems.

We now present a dual interpretation of the Splitting Equilibration Algorithm. We define the Lagrangian $L(x, \lambda, \mu)$ and the function ζ as:

$$L(x, \lambda, \mu) = f(x) - \sum_{i=1}^{M} \lambda_i (\sum_{j=1}^{N} x_{ij} - s_i) - \sum_{j=1}^{N} \mu_j (\sum_{i=1}^{M} x_{ij} - d_j) \tag{5.38}$$

$$\zeta(\lambda, \mu) = \min_{x \geq 0} L(x, \lambda, \mu). \tag{5.39}$$

Note that this algorithm is a dual method and can be expressed as:

$$\lambda^{\tau+1} \to \max \zeta(\lambda, \mu^{\tau}) \tag{5.40a}$$

$$\mu^{\tau+1} \to \max \zeta(\lambda^{t+1}, \mu) \tag{5.40b}$$

where $\mu^1 \in R^N = 0$.

Proof of the following convergence theorem can be found in Nagurney and Eydeland (1992) (see also Nagurney (1993)).

Theorem 5.1

The Splitting Equilibration Algorithm given by (5.40a) and (5.40b) is convergent with the convergence criterion: $||\zeta(\lambda, \mu)|| \leq \epsilon$*, for some preset tolerance* $\epsilon > 0$.

In the case that the quadratic objective function is no longer separable, then one may, nevertheless, embed the above scheme in a projection method (cf. (3.42)), for example. For details on the solution of quadratic programming problems on bipartite networks, see Nagurney and Robinson (1992) and Nagurney, Kim, and Robinson (1990).

5.2.3 An Exact Equilibration Algorithm

Dafermos and Sparrow (1969) proposed "equilibration" algorithms for the solution of both system-optimized and user-optimized transportation networks. These algorithms are network optimization algorithms applied to a class of network problems, commonly referred to as "symmetric" network equilibrium problems since they can be reformulated as optimization problems. The first equilibration algorithms assumed that the demand associated with an origin/destination (O/D) pair was known and fixed. For networks of special structure, specifically, those with linear and separable "user" cost functions, equivalently, cost functions on the links that were quadratic and separable, and paths connecting an O/D pair having no links in common (as in Figure 5.4), a special-purpose algorithm could be used to compute an O/D pair's "equilibrium" path flows and associated link flows exactly and in closed form; this approach is sometimes referred to as "exact equilibration".

Later, the algorithms were generalized to the case where the demand is unknown and has to be computed, as well (cf. Dafermos and Nagurney (1989)). For simplicity, we present an exact "demand" market equilibration algorithm that can be used to determine the solution of a single O/D pair problem. This algorithm can be applied to compute the solution to the special case network optimization problem described in Section 5.1.3 consisting of a separable, quadratic objective function, 2 nodes, and n links. Hence, this algorithm can be used to compute the solution to the Sharpe (1963) portfolio model. For completeness, and easy reference, we state the full problem (cf. Figure 5.4):

$$\text{Minimize} \quad \sum_{i=1}^{n} q_i x_i^2 + c_i x_i \tag{5.41}$$

subject to:

$$\sum_{i=1}^{n} x_i = d \tag{5.42}$$

$$x_i \geq 0, \quad i = 1, \ldots, n. \tag{5.43}$$

We assume that the $q_i > 0$ for all i in (5.41) and that $d > 0$ in (5.42).

It is easy to verify that the Kuhn-Tucker conditions (see appendix A) for this nonlinear network optimization problem take on the form: For each i; $i = 1, \ldots, n$:

$$2q_i x_i^* + c_i \begin{cases} = \lambda, & \text{if} \quad x_i^* > 0 \\ \geq \lambda, & \text{if} \quad x_i^* = 0, \end{cases} \tag{5.44}$$

where λ denotes the Lagrange multiplier associated with the linear constraint (5.42).

The algorithm for the solution of this problem is now presented. It is a finite algorithm, in that the problem is solved in a finite number of steps and is very easy to implement.

Exact Equilibration Algorithm

Step 0: Sort

Sort the c_i's in nondescending order and relabel the c_i's accordingly. We assume, henceforth, that they are relabeled. Define $c_{n+1} \equiv \infty$. Set $v := 1$.

Step 1: Computation

Compute

$$\lambda^v = \frac{\sum_{i=1}^{v} \frac{c_i}{2q_i} + d}{\sum_{i=1}^{v} \frac{1}{2q_i}}. \tag{5.45}$$

Step 2: Evaluation

If $c_v < \lambda^v \leq c_{v+1}$, then stop, set $s' = v$, and go to Step 3. Otherwise, let $v := v + 1$, and go to Step 1.

Step 3: Update

Set

$$x_i^* = \frac{\lambda^{s'} - c_i}{2q_i}, \quad i = 1, \ldots, s' \tag{5.46}$$

$$x_i^* = 0, \quad i = s' + 1, \ldots, n.$$

Example 5.3

We now present an example to which we apply the above exact equilibration algorithm. Let $n = 3$, and let the data be as follows:

$$q_1 = .5, \quad q_2 = 1, \quad q_3 = .5$$

$$c_1 = 5, \quad c_2 = 10, \quad c_3 = 2$$

with $d = 10$, then the optimization problem (5.41)–(5.43) for the specific data is:

$$\text{Minimize} \quad 0.5x_1^2 + 1x_2^2 + 0.5x_3^2 + 5x_1 + 10x_2 + 2x_3$$

subject to:

$$x_1 + x_2 + x_3 = 10$$

$$x_1,\ x_2,\ x_3 \geq 0.$$

Applying the exact equilibration yields the following optimal solution:

$$x_1^* = 3.5, \quad x_2^* = 0, \quad x_3^* = 6.5.$$

Note that here only links 1 and 3 are used or have positive flow on them, with

$$2q_1x_1^* + c_1 = 2q_3x_3^* + c_3 = 8.5 = \lambda \leq 2q_2x_2^* + c_2 = 10.$$

Hence, the solution satisfies the optimality condition (5.44).

Later in the text, in Section 9.4, we provide an adaptation of the exact equilibration algorithm in the case of multipliers on the arcs of the network that model transaction costs.

The importance of the above procedure lies not only in its simplicity, but also in its applicability to the computation of a wide-range of economic equilibrium problems. In particular, we will see in the chapters of Parts III, IV, and V how often exact equilibration can be applied to solve subproblems that arise in the solution of financial systems. Later in the text we describe an "elastic" version of the exact equilibration algorithm applied to the quadratic separable two node network optimization problem when the right-hand side d value (cf. (5.42)) is not known, but, needs to be determined as well and, hence, appears as a variable also in an expanded objective function.

In Section 5.4, we describe a general equilibration algorithm for separable quadratic objective functions. This equilibration algorithm is referred to as a "general" equilibration algorithm since the network topology need not take the special structure as in Figure 5.4. Later, in Section 6.4.2, we provide an extended equilibration algorithm in the case that the quadratic functions are no longer separable that can be used to compute the solution to the Markowitz (1959) model in which the matrix Q is not assumed to be diagonal.

5.2.4 A Primal-Dual Decomposition Method

We now present an algorithm for the solution of problem (5.13), subject to (5.14) and (5.15). As in any decomposition method, it resolves a "harder" and, typically, "larger" problem into simpler and smaller subproblems. The algorithm is reported in Lasdon (1970).

We assume that the objective function $f(x)$, of the form (5.13) is strictly convex, continuous, and continuously differentiable, and that (cf. (5.14)) the $g_j(x)$; $j = 1, \ldots, m$, are continuous over the feasible set and convex. We also assume that the feasible set $\mathcal{K}$ defined by (5.14) and (5.15) is a closed and bounded subset of R^n. Convergence results, as well as, implementation suggestions, can be found in Lasdon (1970).

A Primal-Dual Decomposition Method

Step 0: Initialization

Select an initial Lagrange multiplier vector $\lambda^0 \in R^m_+$, associated with the constraints (5.14). Set $\tau := 0$.

Step 1: Solve the Lagrangian Problem

Solve the Lagrangian problem for $i = 1, \ldots, z$:

$$\text{Minimize} \quad \tilde{f}_i(x_i, \lambda^\tau) = f_i(x_i) + \sum_{j=1}^{m} \lambda_j^\tau g_{ji}(x_i), \tag{5.47}$$

subject to:

$$x_i \in S_i. \tag{5.48}$$

Step 2: Search Direction and Step Size Determination

Define a direction of search, d^τ according to: For $j = 1, \ldots, m$:

$$d_j^\tau = \begin{cases} \sum_{i=1}^{z} g_{ji}(x_i(\lambda^\tau)) - b_j, & \text{if} \quad \lambda_j^\tau > 0 \\ \max\{0, \sum_{i=1}^{z} g_{ji}(x_i(\lambda^\tau)) - b_j\}, & \text{if} \quad \lambda_j^\tau = 0. \end{cases} \tag{5.49}$$

Select a new vector $\lambda^{\tau+1}$ according to:

$$\lambda^{\tau+1} = \lambda^\tau + \alpha_\tau d^\tau. \tag{5.50}$$

The step size α_τ must be selected so that

$$\sum_{i=1}^{z} \tilde{f}_i(x_i(\lambda^{\tau+1}), \lambda^{\tau+1}) > \sum_{i=1}^{z} \tilde{f}_i(x_i(\lambda^\tau), \lambda^\tau). \tag{5.51}$$

Step 3: Convergence Verification

If $\alpha_\tau \leq \epsilon$, with $\epsilon > 0$, a prespecified tolerance, then stop; else, set $\tau := \tau + 1$, and go to Step 1.

5.3 Network Equilibrium Problems

Equilibrium is a concept fundamental in the study of complex, interacting systems, not only in the physical sciences, but also in the economic sciences. Underlying a competitive equilibrium problem is the behavioral mechanism of the agents as well as the system itself in which the interactions take place. Different competitive mechanisms and systems have given rise to different equilibrium concepts.

In this section we are concerned with network systems on which agents compete, driven, via a competitive mechanism, to an equilibrium state. As in the case of network optimization problems, the networks may be physical, for example, as in transportation systems or they may be more abstract, as in certain economic networks, where one needs to make an identification between the nodes, links, and flows in the network, as well as the network topology, and the corresponding economic system components.

The study of network equilibrium problems in a rigorous fashion dates to Beckmann, McGuire, and Winsten (1956), who formalized the study of traffic network equilibrium problems. They proved that the Wardrop (1952) user-optimized (or equilibrium) solution, which stated that all travelers between an origin/destination pair of travel could not reduce their cost of travel by altering their routes unilaterally, could be reformulated, under certain "symmetry" assumptions on the link user cost functions, as an equivalent optimization problem, with the Kuhn-Tucker conditions coinciding with the Wardropian conditions.

Samuelson (1952), in turn, proved that spatial price equilibrium conditions could be reformulated, again, under certain "symmetry" assumptions, as the solution to an equivalent optimization problem. Spatial price equilibrium conditions state that there will be trade between a pair of supply and demand markets if the supply price plus transaction cost is equal to the demand price; if the supply price plus transaction cost exceeds the demand price, then there will be no trade (or flow) between that market pair. Samuelson also recognized the network structure of the basic spatial price equilibrium problem, which is bipartite as in Figure 5.3. Takayama and Judge (1971) subsequently developed many extensions of the basic spatial price equilibrium model.

The symmetry assumption (cf. (3.19) and (3.20)) allowed for the reformulation and solution of such equilibrium problems as optimization problems. However, the assumption was restrictive and did not allow for the adequate modeling of, for example, multiple modes of transportation, different commodities, as well as other behaviors leading to, for example, a Nash-Cournot equilibrium (cf. (3.15)) arising in oligopolistic markets, both spatial and aspatial.

In 1980, Dafermos, recognized that the traffic network equilibrium conditions, as stated by Smith (1979), satisfied a finite-dimensional variational inequality problem. One could, hence, apply and extend the methodology of variational inequalities (originally developed by Hartman and Stampacchia (1966) for the study of partial differential equations, with applications drawn principally from mechanics) to other application domains. Since that identification, a plethora of equilibrium problems ranging from spatial price equilibrium problems to general economic equilibrium problems had been formulated and studied using this methodology (cf. Nagurney (1993) and the references therein).

In this section we define a network equilibrium problem and then give several illustrative applications. We first present the necessary notation and relate it to the network optimization problem in Section 5.1. It is the feasible set that gives the network equilibrium problem a characteristic structure and helps to define it, in addition, to the governing equilibrium conditions. Indeed, in a network equilibrium problem it is routes or paths, typically, that get selected, rather than arcs (as in an optimization problem).

Towards that end, we first describe the *node-arc* formulation of the feasible set underlying the network equilibrium problem (in the case of fixed demands). We then give the *arc-route* formulation of the feasible set. It is the latter that is frequently used in network equilibrium applications and which we will adopt herein.

Node-Arc Formulation of Feasible Set

As in the case of the general network optimization problem, we let $\mathcal{G} = (\mathcal{N}, \mathcal{L})$ be a network with $\mathcal{N}$ denoting the set of nodes, and $\mathcal{L}$ the set of links. As before, we assume that there are m nodes in the network and n arcs. Let W denote the set of "commodities" that "flow" on the network. Associated with each commodity w, there is now a (known and fixed) demand vector b^w, of dimension m, with component i, b_i^w, denoting the demand for commodity w at node i. Also, as in network optimization problems, we assume that the entries of each vector b^w sum to zero. We let x^w denote the commodity flow vector for commodity w, with component (i,j) given by x_{ij}^w, and we denote the sum of all commodity flow vectors by the arc flow vector x, which is a column vector of dimension n. The constraints defining the feasible link flows can be expressed as:

$$x = \sum_w x^w \tag{5.52}$$

$$Ax^w = b^w, \quad \forall w \in W \tag{5.53}$$

$$x^w \geq 0, \quad \forall w, \tag{5.54}$$

where A is the node-arc incidence matrix defined in Section 5.1.

Note that if we have only a single commodity, then clearly, (5.52)– (5.54) are of the form for the feasible set for the general nonlinear network optimization problem, given by (5.2) and (5.3), where the lower bound vector $l = 0$ and the upper bound vector in this case is set to ∞.

Arc-Route Formulation of the Feasible Set

We now describe the often-used arc-route (or arc-path) formulation of the feasible set underlying network equilibrium problems (in the case of fixed demands). This formulation has the following demand pattern, which is more restrictive than the one described above. We assume that each "commodity" is of the single origin/single destination (O/D) type. In particular, if we have an origin/destination pair of nodes $w = (O, D)$ with O denoting an origin node and D a destination node, with demand $d_w > 0$, then the demand vector $b^w = d_w(e_O - e_D)$, where e_j denotes the m-dimensional vector with a

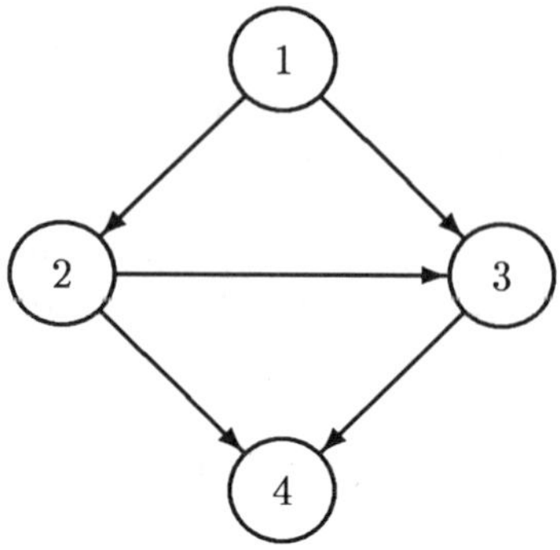

Fig. 5.6. A network example

"1" in the j-th location and, "0" elements, elsewhere. We group the demands into a vector d of dimension J, where J is the number of O/D pairs.

Let P_w denote the set of paths, assumed to be acyclic, joining O/D pair w, where a path consists of a sequence of (directed) links, and let P denote the set of all paths connecting all the O/D pairs. We assume that the number of paths in the set P is N_P. Let X_p denote the flow on path p and group the path flows into a vector X. The constraints defining the feasible path flows and link loads in this formulation are:

$$\tilde{A}X = x \tag{5.55}$$

$$BX = d \tag{5.56}$$

$$X \geq 0, \tag{5.57}$$

where $\tilde{A}$ is the arc-route (or arc-path) incidence matrix, with component $((i,j),p)$ equal to 1, if arc (i,j) is contained in path p, and 0, otherwise, and B is the O/D pair-path incidence matrix with component (w,p)=1, if path p is contained in the set of paths P_w, and 0, otherwise. The arc-route incidence matrix is of dimension $n \times N_P$, whereas the O/D pair-path incidence matrix is of dimension $J \times N_P$.

Example 5.4 (Incidence Matrices)

For illustrative purposes, we now present a network example and give both its arc-route incidence matrix $\tilde{A}$ and its O/D pair incidence matrix B. Consider the network depicted in Figure 5.6, consisting of 4 nodes and 5 links: (1,2), (1,3), (2,3), (2,4), and (3,4). Assume that there are two O/D pairs: $w_1 = (1,4)$ and $w_2 = (1,3)$. There are, hence, 5 paths in the network, where

$$P_{w_1} = \{p_1, p_2, p_3\}$$

with

$$p_1 = (1,2),(2,4), \quad p_2 = (1,2),(2,3),(3,4), \quad p_3 = (1,3),(3,4),$$

and

$$P_{w_2} = \{p_4, p_5\}$$

with

$$p_4 = (1,2), (2,3), \quad p_5 = (1,3).$$

The arc-route incidence matrix is depicted below.

$$\begin{array}{c} \\ (1,2) \\ (1,3) \\ (2,3) \\ (2,4) \\ (3,4) \end{array} \begin{array}{c} \begin{array}{ccccc} p_1 & p_2 & p_3 & p_4 & p_5 \end{array} \\ \begin{pmatrix} 1 & 1 & 0 & 1 & 0 \\ 0 & 0 & 1 & 0 & 1 \\ 0 & 1 & 0 & 1 & 0 \\ 1 & 0 & 0 & 0 & 0 \\ 0 & 1 & 1 & 0 & 0 \end{pmatrix} \end{array}.$$

The O/D pair incidence matrix for the above network problem is as given below.

$$\begin{array}{c} \\ w_1 \\ w_2 \end{array} \begin{array}{c} \begin{array}{ccccc} p_1 & p_2 & p_3 & p_4 & p_5 \end{array} \\ \begin{pmatrix} 1 & 1 & 1 & 0 & 0 \\ 0 & 0 & 0 & 1 & 1 \end{pmatrix} \end{array}.$$

In the presentation that follows, we focus on the arc-route formulation. Specifically, we present two alternative formulations of network equilibrium problems, the path flow formulation, as well as the link flow (or load) formulation. For the sake of generality, we state the network equilibrium problem as a variational inequality problem defined over a feasible set of the arc-route form above. We first consider fixed demand problems and then elastic demand problems.

Fixed Demand Network Equilibrium Problem – Path Flow Formulation

We say that a fixed demand problem is a *fixed demand network equilibrium problem* with a *path flow formulation* if its solution can be expressed as:

Determine $X^* \in \mathcal{K}^1$, such that

$$\langle F^1(X^*)^T, X - X^* \rangle \geq 0, \quad \forall X \in \mathcal{K}^1, \tag{5.58}$$

where

$$\mathcal{K}^1 \equiv \{X | X \text{ satisfies } (5.56) \text{ and } (5.57).\}$$

Fixed Demand Network Equilibrium Problem – Link Load Formulation

We say that a fixed demand problem is a *fixed demand network equilibrium problem* with a *link load formulation* if its solution can be expressed as:

Determine $x^* \in \mathcal{K}^2$, such that

$$\langle F^2(x^*)^T, x - x^* \rangle \geq 0, \quad \forall x \in \mathcal{K}^2, \tag{5.59}$$

where

$$\mathcal{K}^2 \equiv \{x | \text{there exists an } X \text{ such that } (5.55), (5.56), (5.57) \text{ hold}\}.$$

Clearly, for both (5.58) and (5.59), one needs to construct the appropriate $F^1(X)$ and $F^2(x)$ for the application in question. We will show how this can be done in several subsequent example applications. Note that both inequalities (5.58) and (5.59) are variational inequalities as in (3.13).

The above network equilibrium problems are *fixed demand* problems in that the vector of demands d is assumed known and given. The *elastic demand* problem arises when d in (5.56) is a vector of variables. Indeed, we now construct the elastic demand counterparts of both formulations given above.

Elastic Demand Network Equilibrium Problem – Path Flow Formulation

We say that an elastic demand problem is an *elastic demand network equilibrium problem* with a *path flow formulation* if its solution can be formulated as:

Determine $(X^*, d^*) \in \mathcal{K}^3$, such that

$$\langle F^1(X^*)^T, X - X^* \rangle - \langle G^1(d^*)^T, d - d^* \rangle \geq 0, \quad \forall (X, d) \in \mathcal{K}^3, \tag{5.60}$$

where

$$\mathcal{K}^3 \equiv \{(X, d) | \text{such that } (5.56) \text{ and } (5.57) \text{ hold.}\}$$

Elastic Demand Network Equilibrium Problem – Link Load Formulation

We say that an elastic demand problem is an *elastic demand network equilibrium problem* with a *link load formulation* if its solution can be formulated as:

Determine $(x^*, d^*) \in \mathcal{K}^4$, such that

$$\langle F^2(x^*)^T, x - x^* \rangle - \langle G^2(d^*)^T, d - d^* \rangle \geq 0, \quad \forall (x, d) \in \mathcal{K}^4, \tag{5.61}$$

where

$$\mathcal{K}^4 \equiv \{(x, d) | \text{ there exists an } X \text{ satisfying } (5.55), (5.56), \text{ and } (5.57)\}.$$

We note that the above variational inequality formulations of network equilibrium problems are the fundamental ones. All of these are in *flow* variables, whether in path or link flow variables. There also exist variational inequality formulations of network equilibrium problems in flow and in price variables (rather than demand variables, for example). For such models, we refer the reader to Nagurney (1993) and the references therein.

We now illustrate the above network equilibrium problems through several applications.

Application 5.1 – Flow of Funds Network Equilibrium with Fixed Demands

We consider a flow of funds network similar to what was suggested by Thore (1980), but we extend it to a network equilibrium framework. We assume that the available positive net worth of the creditors becomes available to the debtors in the economy through the financial markets. Thore (1980) suggested a directed flow (from the top to the bottom) network, where the top nodes represent the sources of funds in the economy (creditors) and the bottom nodes represent the potential uses of these funds (debtors). In addition, we assume that there is a supersource node (cf. Figure 5.7) that represents an abstraction of the source of all funds in the economy. Between the sources and the uses of funds nodes there are three intermediate levels of nodes, denoting, respectively, the primary financial markets, the financial intermediaries, and the final financial markets. A primary market is a market from which funds from all possible sources (creditors) flow into the market, whereas, the final markets are the ones from which funds flow out to all possible uses (debtors) of funds. Furthermore, financial intermediaries are the mechanisms that tap flow from the primary markets and route them to the final markets. Eventually, all funds from all the available sources will be directed to the uses of funds. Such a flow of funds network is depicted in Figure 5.7 with the nodes being enumerated therein.

One can easily notice that the nodes that represent the sources of funds could also reflect the asset side of the portfolio of all participants in the economy, and, similarly, the bottom nodes that denote the final uses of funds could also represent the liability side of the portfolio of each participant. For simplicity, and, without loss of generality, we can further assume that all financial intermediaries have no other inflow or outflow channels except the ones flowing in from the primary markets and flowing out to the final financial markets.

We consider the supersource node of the most upper level to be the origin node of funds, whereas any node in the lowest level, corresponding to a use of the funds, can be a destination node for funds. Hence, according to Figure 5.7, there are $(N_U - N_{FF+1}) + 1$ O/D pairs in this financial network.

Therefore, there exist $(N_U - N_{FF+1}) + 1$ origin/destination pairs connecting the supersource of funds with the nodes that correspond to the potential uses of funds, where a typical O/D pair is denoted by w. We consider a path in the network to be any sequence of directed links connecting an origin/destination pair, and we denote the demand for potential funds flowing between a particular O/D pair w, by d_w, which is equal to the sum of the flow of funds on all the paths joining that particular O/D pair. We assume that the demands are given and fixed. Finally, we denote the demand price for funds flowing between the O/D pair w by λ_w.

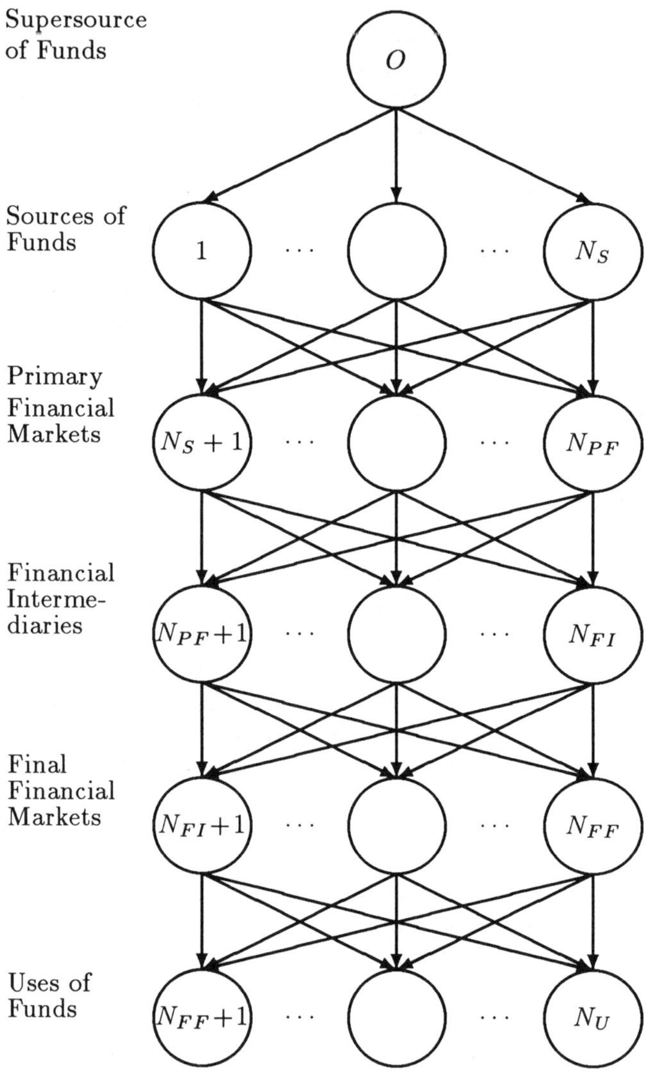

Fig. 5.7. A financial network equilibrium problem

Moreover, we assume that there are no fixed supplies but, instead, that we have a supply price function associated with the sources of funds which is represented by a cost function associated with each of the arcs leading from the supersource node to the arcs on the next level.

We also assume that the cost (e. g., taxes, fees, transaction costs) on a link (i,j) for a unit of fund flowing through this link is denoted by c_{ij}, and we assume that, in general, the cost on a link can depend upon the flows of funds on all links in the network, denoted by the vector x, that is,

$$c_{ij} = c_{ij}(x), \tag{5.62}$$

or, in vector form,

$$c = c(x), \tag{5.63}$$

where c is the n-dimensional column vector of arc costs.

The cost on a path p is denoted by C_p, and is equal to the sum of the costs on the links that comprise that path, that is,

$$C_p = \sum_{(i,j)\in\mathcal{L}} c_{ij}(x)\delta_{(i,j)p}, \quad \forall p, \tag{5.64}$$

where $\delta_{(i,j)p} = 1$, if arc (i,j) is contained in path p, and 0, otherwise.

Grouping the path costs into an $N_{\mathcal{P}}$-dimensional column vector, where $N_{\mathcal{P}}$ denotes the number of paths, we may write (5.64) in vector form as:

$$C^T = c^T(x)\tilde{A}. \tag{5.65}$$

Flow of Funds Network Equilibrium Conditions

The flow of funds network equilibrium conditions are similar to transportation network equilibrium conditions (cf. Wardrop (1952), Beckmann, McGuire, and Winsten (1956), Dafermos and Sparrow (1969), Smith (1979), and Dafermos (1980)), and which state that, a path flow pattern, $(X^*) \in \mathcal{K}^1$, is in equilibrium if it satisfies the following equilibrium conditions: For each O/D pair w, and each path $p \in P_w$:

$$C_p(X^*) \begin{cases} = \lambda_w, & \text{if} \quad X_p^* > 0 \\ \geq \lambda_w, & \text{if} \quad X_p^* = 0. \end{cases} \tag{5.66}$$

In other words, in equilibrium, all used paths connecting an O/D pair have equal and minimal costs, where the minimal cost for an O/D pair is equal to λ_w. Hence, the cost of a transaction is equal to the sum of the costs (assumed to be unit or average costs) of all the transactions that take place from the originating node of the funds to the use node of the funds. Moreover, in equilibrium, only those sequences of transactions will take place that have minimal cost and the costs on those transaction paths are equal for a particular source and destination pair.

As shown in Dafermos (1980) (see also Smith (1979)), the path flow pattern (X^*) is a network equilibrium pattern, that is, satisfies (5.66), if and only if $(X^*) \in \mathcal{K}^1$, and satisfies the following variational inequality problem in path flows:

$$\langle C(X^*)^T, X - X^* \rangle \geq 0, \quad \forall X \in \mathcal{K}^1, \tag{5.67}$$

or, equivalently, the link load pattern x^*, induced by a path flow pattern X^* is an equilibrium pattern if and only if $x^* \in \mathcal{K}^2$ and satisfies the following variational inequality problem in link loads:

$$\langle c(x^*)^T, x - x^* \rangle \geq 0, \quad \forall x \in \mathcal{K}^2. \tag{5.68}$$

Clearly, (5.67) is of the form (5.58), whereas (5.68) is of the form (5.59). Indeed, to make the equivalence we need only to define the column vectors $F^1 \equiv C$ and $F^2 \equiv c$.

Note that in the special case where the Jacobian of the link cost functions, $c(x)$, is symmetric, that is, $\frac{\partial c_{ij}}{\partial x_{kl}} = \frac{\partial c_{kl}}{\partial x_{ij}}$, for all links (i,j), $(k,l) \in \mathcal{L}$, then by Green's Lemma, the vector $c(x)$ can be interpreted as the gradient of the line integral $\int_0^x c(y)dy$. Moreover, monotonicity of c implies that $\nabla c(x)$ is positive semi-definite. Consequently, $\int_0^x c(y)dy$ is a convex function. It follows then (cf. (3.20) and the preceding discussion) that x^*, in this special case, solves the convex optimization problem:

$$\text{Minimize} \quad \int_0^x c(y)dy$$

subject to: $(x) \in \mathcal{K}^2$, if and only if it solves the variational inequality problem (5.68). This problem can, hence, be solved using convex programming algorithms. In Section 5.3, we provide an equilibration algorithm for the solution of this problem in the case that the link costs are linear and separable, that is, the cost on a link depends only upon the flow on a link. In Section 5.4.1, in turn, we provide the projection method for the solution of (5.68), for which an equivalent optimization reformulation is not assumed to exist.

Application 5.2 – Walrasian Price Equilibrium

We now show that the Walrasian price equilibrium problem or pure exchange equilibrium problem is, in fact, a network equilibrium problem with a fixed demand. This problem has been extensively studied in the economic literature dating to Walras (1874) (see also Wald (1951), Debreu (1959), and Mas-Colell (1985)). In particular, we return to Example 3.3, and we assume that the excess supply function, $S(p) - D(p)$ is homogeneous of degree zero in p, that is, $S(\gamma p) - D(\gamma p) = S(p) - D(p)$, for all $p \in C$, where C here denotes a subcone of R^n_+ and $\gamma > 0$.

We assume that $S(p) - D(p)$ satisfies Walras' law, that is,

$$\langle (S(p) - D(p))^T, p \rangle = 0$$

on C. Because of homogeneity, we may normalize the prices so that they take on values in the unit simplex:

$$S^n = \{p | p \in R^n_+, \sum_{i=1}^{n} p_i = 1\} \tag{5.69}$$

and, consequently, we may restrict the aggregate excess supply function to the intersection E on S^n with C.

The definition of a Walrasian equilibrium is now stated (cf. (3.10)).

Walrasian Price Equilibrium Conditions

A price vector $p^* \in R^n_+$ is a Walrasian equilibrium price vector if

$$S(p^*) - D(p^*) \geq 0. \tag{5.70}$$

We now make the identification between Walrasian price equilibria and network equilibria. Consider now the network topology given in Figure 5.4, which consists of a single O/D pair and n links. Let a link i correspond to instrument i (or to commodity i) and let the "flow" on link i be equal to the price p_i. The cost on link i is given by the excess supply $S_i(p) - D_i(p)$. It is clear that constraint (5.69) can be represented on this network topology with "flow" on link i is equal to p_i, for $i = 1, \ldots, n$, and the demand $d = 1$.

As shown in Dafermos (1990), equilibrium conditions (5.70) can be formulated as the solution to the variational inequality problem:

Determine $p^* \in E$ such that:

$$\langle (S(p^*) - D(p^*))^T, p - p^* \rangle \geq 0, \quad \forall p \in S^n. \tag{5.71}$$

Note that in this problem a path consists of a single link. Clearly, (5.71) is a network equilibrium problem with fixed demand as in (5.58) with $\mathcal{K}^1$ given by S^n.

Application 5.3 – Flow of Funds Network Equilibrium with Elastic Demands for Funds

This application will correspond to a flow of funds network equilibrium problem with elastic demands. Hence, the notation and discussion follows the presentation in Application 5.1. However, now we associate with each O/D pair w a flow of funds demand price function λ_w and we assume that, in general, the flow of funds demand price λ_w may depend upon the demands of funds for all the O/D pairs, that is,

$$\lambda_w = \lambda_w(d), \tag{5.72}$$

where d is the vector of demands for the funds, or, in vector form,

$$\lambda = \lambda(d). \tag{5.73}$$

Note that, unlike the fixed demand problem in Application 5.1, the demands for funds d are now variables. The price corresponds to how much the consumers are willing to pay for a particular use of the funds.

Flow of Funds Elastic Demand Network Equilibrium Conditions

The flow of funds network equilibrium conditions (5.66) now are modified as follows: We say that $(X^*, d^*) \in \mathcal{K}^3$ is an equilibrium path flow and demand pattern, if for each O/D pair w, and every path $p \in P_w$:

$$C_p(X^*) \begin{cases} = \lambda_w(d^*), & \text{if } X_p^* > 0 \\ \geq \lambda_w(d^*), & \text{if } X_p^* = 0. \end{cases} \tag{5.74}$$

As shown in Dafermos (1982), the network equilibrium conditions (5.74) can be formulated as the following variational inequality problem in path flows:

Determine $(X^*, d^*) \in \mathcal{K}^3$ satisfying:

$$\langle C(X^*)^T, X - X^* \rangle - \langle \lambda(d^*)^T, d - d^* \rangle \geq 0, \quad \forall (X, d) \in \mathcal{K}^3, \tag{5.75}$$

or, equivalently, as the following variational inequality problem in link loads:

Determine $(x^*, d^*) \in \mathcal{K}^4$ satisfying:

$$\langle c(x^*)^T, x - x^* \rangle - \langle \lambda(d^*)^T, d - d^* \rangle \geq 0, \quad \forall (x, d) \in \mathcal{K}^4. \tag{5.76}$$

Note that the inequalities (5.75) and (5.76) are, respectively, precisely of the form (5.60) and (5.61).

If the Jacobians of the link transaction cost functions and the flow of funds demand price functions are symmetric, that is, $\frac{\partial c_{ij}}{\partial x_{kl}} = \frac{\partial c_{kl}}{\partial x_{ij}}$ for all links (i, j), $(k, l) \in \mathcal{L}$, and $\frac{\partial \lambda_w}{\partial d_\omega} = \frac{\partial \lambda_\omega}{\partial d_w}$ for all O/D pairs w and ω, and if the Jacobian of the link transaction cost functions is positive semi-definite, whereas minus the Jacobian of the flow of funds demand price functions is positive definite, then, as in the case of fixed demands for funds, we can reformulate the financial network equilibrium conditions (5.74) as the solution to a convex optimization problem, which here takes the form:

$$\text{Minimize} \quad \int_0^x c(y)dy - \int_0^d \lambda(z)dz$$

subject to: $(x, d) \in \mathcal{K}^4$.

This problem can be solved using standard convex programming algorithms, in particular, a convex network programming algorithm.

Application 5.4 – Spatial Price Equilibrium Problem

We now present a spatial price equilibrium model for loanable funds due to Moore and Nagurney (1989). For additional background on such problems, see Samuelson (1952), Takayama and Judge (1971), and Nagurney (1993) and the references therein. For a spatial price equilibrium model applied to the Eurodollar market, see Thore (1984).

Consider M supply markets and N demand markets involved the lending and consumption of loanable funds. Denote a typical supply market by i and a typical demand market by j. Let s_i denote the supply of the funds associated with supply market i and let π_i denote the supply price of the financial funds associated with supply market i. Let d_j denote the demand associated with demand market j and let ρ_j denote the demand price associated with demand market j. Group the supplies and supply prices, respectively, into a column vector $s \in R^M$ and a column vector $\pi \in R^M$. Similarly, group the demands and the demand prices, respectively, into a column vector $d \in R^N$ and a column vector $\rho \in R^N$.

Let Q_{ij} denote the nonnegative funds shipment between the supply and demand market pair (i, j) and let c_{ij} denote the nonnegative unit transaction cost associated with trading the loanable funds between (i, j). Group then the loanable fund transfers into a column vector $Q \in R^{MN}_+$ and the transaction costs into a column vector $c \in R^{MN}$.

The following feasibility conditions must hold for every i and j:

$$s_i = \sum_{j=1}^{N} Q_{ij} \tag{5.77}$$

and

$$d_j = \sum_{i=1}^{M} Q_{ij}. \tag{5.78}$$

(5.77) and (5.78) state that the supply at the supply market is equal to the sum of the loanable funds flows to all the demand markets. Also, the demand at a demand market must be satisfied by the sum of the loanable funds flows from all the supply markets. Let $\mathcal{K}$ denote the closed convex set where $\mathcal{K} \equiv \{(s, Q, d) | (5.77) \text{ and } (5.78) \text{ hold}\}$.

The supply price, demand price, and transaction cost structure is now discussed. Assume that the supply price associated with any supply market may depend upon the supply of the loanable funds at every supply market, that is,

$$\pi = \pi(s) \tag{5.79}$$

where π is a known smooth function.

Similarly, the demand price associated with a demand market may depend upon, in general, the demand for the loanable funds at every demand market, that is,

$$\rho = \rho(d) \tag{5.80}$$

where ρ is a known smooth function.

The transaction cost between a pair of supply and demand markets may, in general, depend upon the shipments or transfers of the loanable funds

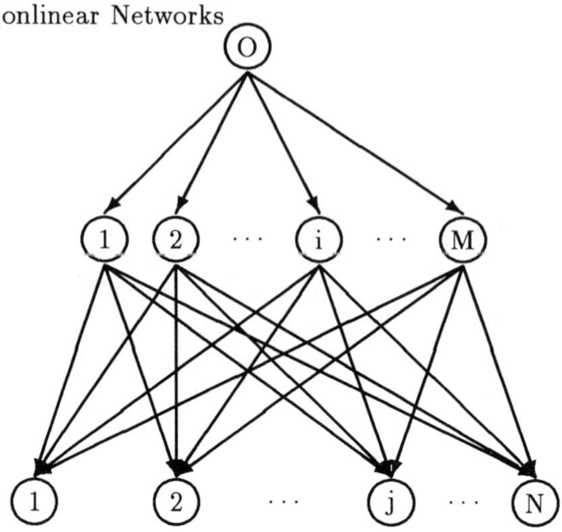

Fig. 5.8. Network equilibrium representation of spatial price equilibrium

between every pair of markets, that is,

$$c = c(Q) \tag{5.81}$$

where c is a known smooth function.

Spatial Price Equilibrium Conditions

The market equilibrium conditions, due to Samuelson (1952), Takayama and Judge (1971), under the assumption of perfect competition, take the following form: A supply, transfer, and demand pattern $(s^*, Q^*, d^*) \in \mathcal{K}$, is said to be an equilibrium pattern if: For all pairs of supply and demand markets $(i, j) : i = 1, \dots, M; j = 1, \dots, N$:

$$\pi_i(s^*) + c_{ij}(Q^*_{ij}) \begin{cases} = \rho_j(d^*), & \text{if} \quad Q^*_{ij} > 0 \\ \geq \rho_j(d^*), & \text{if} \quad Q^*_{ij} = 0. \end{cases} \tag{5.82}$$

The condition (5.82) states that if there is trade in loanable funds between a market pair (i, j), then the supply price at supply market i plus the transaction cost between the pair of markets must be equal to the demand price at demand market j in equilibrium; if the supply price plus the transaction cost exceeds the demand price, then there will be no transfer of loanable funds between the supply and demand market pair.

We now present the variational inequality formulation of the equilibrium conditions (5.82), due to Florian and Los (1982).

In particular, we have that a supply, transfer, and demand pattern $(s^*, Q^*, d^*) \in \mathcal{K}$ is a spatial price equilibrium if and only if it satisfies the variational inequality problem:

$$\langle \pi(s^*)^T, s - s^* \rangle + \langle c(Q^*)^T, Q - Q^* \rangle - \langle \rho(d^*)^T, d - d^* \rangle \geq 0, \quad \forall (s, Q, d) \in \mathcal{K}. \tag{5.83}$$

At first glance, one may think that the network equilibrium problem underlying the spatial price equilibrium problem takes place on the bipartite network depicted in Figure 5.4. Indeed, it may be viewed thus, with the proviso, that the supplies and demand are now variables, rather than fixed. However, the network underlying the network equilibrium representation is actually the one given in Figure 5.8, with an O/D pair w_j consisting of the origin node O and the destination node (demand market j). Clearly, the spatial price equilibrium problem is a network equilibrium problem of the form (5.60) where a flow on a path from origin node O to destination node j through supply market node i is given by Q_{ij}. Note that this is an elastic demand network equilibrium problem. The complete identification can be found in Dafermos and Nagurney (1985).

5.4 Network Equilibrium Algorithms

As discussed in Section 5.3, network equilibrium problems are variational inequality problems in which the feasible set has a network structure with an arc-route form. Hence, such problems are best solved as variational inequality problems in which, typically, at each iteration, one applies a network-based algorithm to solve the embedded mathematical programming problems. Indeed, if one applies, for example, either the projection method (cf. (3.42)) (in the case of a strongly monotone and Lipschitz continuous $F(\cdot)$) or the modified projection method (cf. (3.46) and (3.47)) (in the case of a monotone and Lipschitz continuous $F(\cdot)$), then one obtains a sequence of quadratic programming problems (diagonal in the case of the modified projection method and in the case of the projection method if G in (3.42) is selected to be diagonal). These quadratic programming problems are network optimization problems in which the feasible set has a characteristic network structure. Hence, such variational inequality algorithms applied to network equilibrium problems solve a sequence of symmetric network equilibrium problems of the form presented in Applications 5.1 and 5.3.

Note that, in the case of decomposition algorithms, as in the linear Jacobi method (cf. (3.51)) and the linear Gauss-Seidel method (cf. (3.52)), one, depending upon the selection of the $A_i(\cdot)$ function, for all i, may also obtain separable, that is, diagonal, (or nonseparable) quadratic programming problems over networks. However, both in the case of the nonlinear Jacobi method (3.49) and the nonlinear Gauss-Seidel method (3.50) (as with the use of alternative selections of A_i in the linear methods), one obtains a variational inequality problem of a similar form to that in the original problem. Hence, here one would then have to go further and resolve the resulting problems into mathematical programming problems which need not be quadratic programming problems. This is also the case in the relaxation method (cf. Dafermos (1983)).

Hence, all of the algorithms given in Section 3.3 for the solution of finite-dimensional variational inequality problems can, at least in principle, be applied for the computation of network equilibria, provided that the conditions for convergence are satisfied by the problem under study.

5.4.1 The Projection Method

Since the projection method is one of the "classical" methods for the solution of network equilibrium problems, in order to fix ideas, we present this algorithm in the context of the flow of funds network equilibrium problem with elastic demands (cf. Application 5.3) and then we specialize it to the flow of funds network equilibrium problem with fixed demands (cf. Application 5.1). In both cases, we utilize the link load formulations given, respectively, by (5.76) and (5.68).

The Projection Method for Elastic Demand Flow of Funds Network Equilibrium Problem

Here we present the projection method for the solution of variational inequality (5.76) governing the link load formulation of the elastic demand network equilibrium problem. The method is due to Dafermos (1982). We subsequently adapt it for the solution of variational inequality (5.68) governing the link load formulation of the fixed demand network equilibrium problem (cf. Dafermos (1980)).

Step 0: Initialization

Select an initial feasible link load and demand for funds pattern $(x^0, d^0) \in \mathcal{K}^4$. Also, select symmetric, positive definite matrices G and $-M$ of dimensions $n \times n$ and $J \times J$, respectively. Select a contraction parameter γ. Set $\tau := 1$.

Step 1: Construction and Computation

Construct

$$h^{\tau} = \gamma c(x^{\tau-1}) - Gx^{\tau-1} \tag{5.84}$$

and

$$t^{\tau} = \gamma \lambda(d^{\tau-1}) - Md^{\tau-1}. \tag{5.85}$$

Compute the new link and demand pattern $(x^{\tau}, d^{\tau}) \in \mathcal{K}^4$, corresponding to the link transfer cost and O/D pair flow of funds disutility functions of the special form:

$$\tilde{c}^{\tau}(x) = Gx + h^{\tau} \tag{5.86}$$

and

$$\tilde{\lambda}^{\tau}(d) = Md + t^{\tau}, \tag{5.87}$$

that is, solve:

$$\text{Minimize} \quad \int_0^x (Gy + h^{\tau})dy - \int_0^d (Mz + t^{\tau})dz \tag{5.88}$$

subject to: $(x, d) \in \mathcal{K}^4$.

Step 2: Convergence Verification

If $|x^\tau - x^{\tau-1}| \leq \epsilon$, with ϵ a prespecified tolerance, stop; otherwise, set $\tau := \tau + 1$, and go to Step 1.

In the case of fixed demands for funds, the steps above are modified as follows. In Step 0, we select $x^0 \in \mathcal{K}^2$; in Step 1, we need only to construct h^τ in (5.84) and $\tilde{c}^\tau$ in (5.86) and to then compute $x^\tau \in \mathcal{K}^2$ with these new user cost functions, that is, to solve the following optimization problem:

$$\text{Minimize} \quad \int_0^x (Gy + h^\tau)dy \tag{5.89}$$

subject to: $x \in \mathcal{K}^2$.

Step 2 remains as above.

Consequently, the overall efficiency of the projection method for the computation of network equilibria depends on the efficiency and effectiveness of the utilized network-based algorithm for the solution of the embedded mathematical programming problems, that is, how effectively, for example, one can solve problems (5.88) or (5.89).

Towards that end, we present now a general equilibration algorithm for the solution of problem (5.89) in the case when the G matrix is selected to be diagonal. The algorithm is due to Dafermos and Sparrow (1969). In contrast to the exact equilibration algorithm described in Section 5.2.3, this algorithm is applicable to any network topology. The equilibration algorithm is a path equilibration algorithm for the solution of the symmetric and separable flow of funds network equilibrium problem in the case of linear user costs on the links.

5.4.2 A General Equilibration Algorithm for Separable Link Cost Functions

We now present an equilibration algorithm for the solution of problem (5.89), where the user cost on a link (cf. (5.62)) is given by

$$c_{ij} = g_{ij}x_{ij} + h_{ij},$$

where we assume that q_{ij} and h_{ij} are positive for all (i, j). Explicitly, the problem that is solved is:

$$\text{Minimize} \quad \sum_{(i,j)\in\mathcal{L}} \frac{1}{2} g_{ij} x_{ij}^2 + h_{ij} x_{ij}$$

subject to: $x \in \mathcal{K}^2$.

The algorithm is called an equilibration algorithm since it utilizes the network equilibrium conditions (5.66), which in this case, are equivalent to the Kuhn-Tucker conditions of problem (5.89), for its motivation. We first present the Single O/D Pair Equilibration Algorithm, and then two alternative Multiple O/D Pair Equilibration Algorithms, which utilize the single/pair equilibration algorithm.

The single pair equilibration algorithm proceeds as follows. One selects the most costly *used* path connecting the O/D pair and the cheapest path. One then distributes the flow from the most expensive used path to the cheapest path using an explicit formula which is actually obtained by solving a minimization problem over a reduced feasible set. One continues in this fashion until the equilibrium conditions (5.66) hold within a prespecified tolerance. For further details, and proof of convergence, see Dafermos and Sparrow (1969).

Single O/D Pair Equilibration

Step 0: Initialization

Construct an initial feasible link load pattern induced by a feasible path flow pattern, such that $x^0 \in \mathcal{K}^2$. Set $k := 1$.

Step 1: Selection and Convergence Verification

Determine

$$r = \{p | \max_p C_p \quad \text{and} \quad X_p^{k-1} > 0\}$$

$$q = \{p | \min_p C_p\}.$$

If $|C_r - C_q| \leq \epsilon$, with $\epsilon > 0$, a prespecified tolerance, then stop; else, go to Step 2.

Step 2: Computation

Compute

$$\Delta' = \frac{[C_r - C_q]}{\sum_{(i,j) \in \mathcal{L}} g_{ij} (\delta_{(i,j)q} - \delta_{(i,j)r})^2} \tag{5.90}$$

$$\Delta = \min\{\Delta', X_r^{k-1}\}. \tag{5.91}$$

Set

$$X_r^k = X_r^{k-1} - \Delta$$

$$X_q^k = X_q^{k-1} + \Delta$$

$$X_p^k = X_p^{k-1}, \quad \forall p \neq q \cup r.$$

Let $k := k + 1$, and go to Step 1.

In the case that a tie exists for the selection of path r and/or q, then any such selection is appropriate.

We now present a small example to which we apply this algorithm.

Example 5.5

Consider the network depicted in Figure 5.6. This is, in fact, the well-known Braess (1968) network. Assume that the user costs on the links are:

$$c_{12}(x_{12}) = 10x_{12}, \quad c_{13}(x_{13}) = x_{13} + 50,$$

$$c_{23}(x_{23}) = x_{23} + 10, \quad c_{24}(x_{24}) = x_{24} + 50, \quad c_{34}(x_{34}) = 10x_{34}.$$

Assume that there is a now only single O/D pair $w_1 = (1,4)$ with demand equal to 6.

The set of paths $P_{w_1} = \{p_1, p_2, p_3\}$, where

$$p_1 = (1,2),(2,4), \quad p_2 = (1,2),(2,3),(3,4), \quad p_3 = (1,3),(3,4).$$

Assume that the initial path flow pattern is:

$$X^0_{p_1} = 4, \quad X^0_{p_2} = 0, \quad X^0_{p_3} = 2,$$

which induces the link load pattern:

$$x^0_{12} = 4, \quad x^0_{13} = 2, \quad x^0_{23} = 0, \quad x^0_{24} = 4, \quad x^0_{34} = 2.$$

Under this link load and path flow pattern, the link costs are:

$$c_{12} = 40, \quad c_{13} = 52, \quad c_{23} = 10, \quad c_{24} = 54, \quad c_{34} = 20,$$

and the path costs are:

$$C_{p_1} = 94, \quad C_{p_2} = 70, \quad C_{p_3} = 72.$$

Clearly, the most expensive used path is path p_1 and, hence, $r = p_1$, whereas the cheapest path is path p_2 and, consequently, $q = p_2$.

Applying formula (5.90), we obtain $\frac{94-70}{1+1+10} = 2$, and, hence, according to (5.91), $\Delta = 2$.

The new feasible path flow pattern is given by:

$$X^1_{p_1} = X^0_{p_1} - 2 = 2, \quad X^1_{p_2} = X^0_{p_2} + 2 = 2, \quad X^1_{p_3} = X^0_{p_3} = 2.$$

This path flow pattern, in turn, induces the link load pattern:

$$x^1_{12} = 4, \quad x^1_{13} = 2, \quad x^1_{23} = 2, \quad x^1_{24} = 2, \quad x^1_{34} = 4,$$

with associated user link costs given by:

$$c_{12} = 40, \quad c_{13} = 52, \quad c_{23} = 12, \quad c_{24} = 52, \quad c_{34} = 20,$$

with path costs:

$$C_{p_1} = C_{p_2} = C_{p_3} = 92.$$

Note that this solution satisfies conditions (5.66) and, hence, the algorithm has computed an equilibrium solution.

On a network in which there are now J O/D pairs, the above single O/D pair equilibration procedure is applicable, as well.

We term Step 1 (without the convergence check) and Step 2 of the above equilibration operator E_{w_i}. Now two possibilities for equilibration present themselves. In Equilibration Algorithm I one equilibrates the costs on the most expensive and cheapest paths for the first O/D pair, then does the same for the second O/D pair, and so on, until the J-th O/D pair. One then verifies convergence; if the algorithm has not converged, one continues in the same manner. In Equilibration Algorithm II, one keeps on equilibrating the most expensive and the cheapest paths for the first O/D pair, until optimality has been reached for this O/D pair. One then does the same for the second O/D pair, and so on through the J-th O/D pair. If convergence has not been reached for all O/D pairs, then one proceeds as above again for all O/D pairs.

Multiple O/D Pair Equilibration Algorithm I

Let $E^1 \equiv E_{w_J} \circ \ldots \circ E_{w_1}$.

Step 0: Initialization

Construct an initial feasible flow pattern which induces a feasible link load pattern. Set $k := 1$.

Step 1: Equilibration

Apply E^1.

Step 2: Convergence Verification

If convergence holds, stop; else, set $k := k + 1$, and go to Step 1.

Multiple O/D Pair Equilibration Algorithm II

Let $E^2 = (E_{w_J} \circ (\ldots \circ (E_{w_J}))) \circ \ldots \circ (E_{w_1} \circ (\ldots \circ (E_{w_1})))$.

Step 0: Initialization: (as above).

Step 1: Equilibration:

Apply E^2.

Step 2: Convergence Verification: (as above).

The difference between E^1 and E^2 is as follows. E^1 equilibrates only one pair of paths for an O/D pair before proceeding to the next O/D pair, and so on, whereas, E^2 equilibrates the costs on all the paths connecting an O/D pair using the 2-path procedure above, before proceeding to the next O/D pair, and so on.

Note that to solve the embedded elastic demand flow of funds network equilibrium problem induced by the projection method in Step 1 above, one can either convert the elastic demand problem to a fixed demand problem as discussed in Gartner (1980) or apply an elastic demand equilibration algorithm given in Nagurney (1988).

5.5 Dynamic Network Problems

Dynamic network problems involve decision-making over time. In this section we present dynamic counterparts of the network equilibrium problems (in path flows) given in Section 5.3. The methodology that we utilize is that of projected dynamical systems. Necessarily, hence, this section will make use of the results of Chapter 4.

Since the selection of "routes" or paths, rather than arcs or links, is basic to the study of network equilibrium, we first provide dynamic counterparts of (5.58) and (5.60).

5.5.1 Tatonnement Processes for Network Equilibrium Problems

We first propose an adjustment process for the fixed demand network equilibrium problem and then an adjustment process for the elastic demand network equilibrium problem. Both of these adjustment processes are projected dynamical systems.

A Tatonnement Process for the Fixed Demand Problem

We turn back to the problem given by (5.58), and we propose the following adjustment process for the fixed demand network equilibrium problem. We provide its motivation in the context of the flow of funds network equilibrium problem with fixed demands (cf. Application 5.1). The funds flowing between an O/D pair will switch from more costly routes to less costly routes connecting this O/D pair. However, this dynamic adjustment cannot violate the feasibility condition that the path flows must be nonnegative and must sum up to demand for funds for each O/D pair. Mathematically, this route adjustment process takes the following form:

$$\dot{X} = \Pi_{\mathcal{K}^1}(X, -F^1(X)) \tag{5.92}$$

Due to Theorem 4.1, we know that X^* that satisfies variational inequality problem (5.58) also satisfies:

$$0 = \Pi_{\mathcal{K}^1}(X^*, -F^1(X^*)). \tag{5.93}$$

In the context of the flow of funds network equilibrium model with fixed demands (cf. (5.67)), (5.92) becomes

$$\dot{X} = \Pi_{\mathcal{K}^1}(X, -C(X)). \tag{5.94}$$

Hence, the funds flowing on the paths change at a rate that is equal to the projection of minus the path costs onto the constraint set $\mathcal{K}^1$.

The stationary point of (5.94), in turn, coincides with the solution of the variational inequality problem (5.67).

A Tatonnement Process for the Elastic Demand Problem

Analogously, for the network equilibrium problem with elastic demands (cf. (5.60)), we can also construct a tatonnement process. In view of constraint (5.56), we can define $\tilde{G}^1(X) \equiv B^T G^1(BX) = B^T G^1(d)$. We may then write a variational inequality equivalent to (5.60): Determine $X^* \in R_+^{N_P}$, such that

$$\langle F^1(X^*)^T, X - X^* \rangle - \langle \tilde{G}^1(X^*)^T, X - X^* \rangle \geq 0, \quad \forall X \in R_+^{N_P}. \tag{5.95}$$

The projected dynamical system, whose set of stationary points coincides with the set of solutions to (5.95), is given by:

$$\dot{X} = \Pi_{R_+^{N_P}}(X, -F^1(X) + \tilde{G}^1(X)). \tag{5.96}$$

We now illustrate (5.96) in the context of the flow of funds network equilibrium model with elastic demands discussed in Application 5.3. Let $\tilde{\lambda}(X) \equiv B^T \lambda(BX) = B^T \lambda(d)$. Then we have the following adjustment process:

$$\dot{X} = \Pi_{R_+^{n_P}}(X, -C(X) + \tilde{\lambda}(X)), \tag{5.97}$$

which states that the funds flow on a path p connecting an O/D pair w will change at a rate that is equal to the difference between the demand price λ_w and the path cost C_p. When the demand price exceeds the path cost, that is, $\lambda_w > C_p$, the path flow X_p will increase; when $\lambda_w < C_p$, then X_p will decrease. Hence, the flows of funds continuously switch from more costly routes to less costly routes, relative to the demand prices at a rate $\lambda_w - C_p$. However, in order to maintain feasibility (which in this application amounts to ensuring that the path flows remain nonnegative), the projection operation guarantees that this, indeed, holds true.

5.5.2 Discrete Time Algorithms

Although the adjustment processes given by (5.94) and (5.97) are, in fact, continuous time computational procedures, for practical purposes, one needs discrete time approximation schemes for the computation of the stationary points, equivalently, for the solution of the (corresponding) variational inequality problems.

We now provide theorems that provide convergence results for discrete time algorithms that are special cases of the general iterative scheme given by (4.24). We first consider the solution of the fixed demand flow of funds network equilibrium problem and then the elastic demand flow of funds network equilibrium problem. Theorem 5.2 is due to Nagurney and Zhang (1996b) whereas Theorem 5.3 is due to Nagurney and Zhang (1996a), where proofs can also be found.

Theorem 5.2

Suppose that the link costs c are strictly monotone increasing (cf. Definition 3.4). Let $\{a_\tau\}$ *be a sequence of positive numbers that satisfies*

$$\lim_{\tau \to \infty} a_\tau = 0 \tag{5.98}$$

and

$$\sum_{\tau=0}^{\infty} a_\tau = \infty. \tag{5.99}$$

Then the Euler method given by

$$X^{\tau+1} = P_{\mathcal{K}^2}(X^\tau - a_\tau C(X^\tau)), \tag{5.100}$$

converges to some flow of funds network equilibrium satisfying (5.67) (and (5.66)).

Theorem 5.3

Suppose that the link cost function c is regular, that is, for every link (i, j), *we have that*

$$c_{ij}(x) \rightarrow \infty, \quad as \quad x_{ij} \rightarrow \infty, \tag{5.101}$$

holds uniformly true for all link load patterns, and that the link cost function c is strictly monotone increasing and the flow of funds demand price function is strictly monotone decreasing. Let $\{a_\tau\}$ *be a sequence of positive real numbers that satisfies (5.98) and (5.99). Then the Euler method given by*

$$X^{\tau+1} = P_{R_+^{N_P}}(X^\tau - a_\tau(C(X^\tau) - \tilde{\lambda}(X^\tau))) \tag{5.102}$$

converges to some flow of funds network equilibrium pattern satisfying (5.74) (and (5.75)).

It is worth emphasizing the simplicity of the basic iterative steps (5.100) and (5.102).

In particular, (5.100) is a projection in path flows for each O/D pair and is equivalent to the solution of:

$$\text{Minimize} \quad \frac{1}{2} X^T \cdot X - (X^\tau - a_\tau C(X^\tau))^T) \cdot X, \tag{5.103}$$

subject to: $X \in \mathcal{K}^1$, which, in turn, is equivalent to the solution of: For each O/D pair w, compute:

$$\text{Minimize} \quad \frac{1}{2} \sum_{p \in P_w} x_p^2 + \sum_{p \in P_w} h_p^\tau X_p \tag{5.104}$$

subject to:

$$\sum_{p \in P_w} X_p = d_w \tag{5.105}$$

$$X_p \geq 0, \quad \forall p \in P_w, \tag{5.106}$$

where

$$h_p^\tau = a_\tau C_p(X^\tau) - X_p^\tau. \tag{5.107}$$

Hence, one solves (5.104) for each O/D pair in the network at an iteration τ. These may be done simultaneously. Moreover, these subproblems can be solved exactly and in closed form using exact equilibration (cf. Section 5.2.3).

For the elastic demand problem, the iterative step (5.102) takes on the following closed form expression: For each path p on the network, compute the path flow $X_p^{\tau+1}$ according to:

$$X_p^{\tau+1} = \max\{0, X_p^\tau + a_\tau(\lambda_w(d^\tau) - C_p(X^\tau))\}. \tag{5.108}$$

Hence, in the case of elastic demands, at each iteration, the updated financial path flows can also be solved exactly and in closed form, but now using a simple formula given by (5.108).

5.6 Sources and Notes

The topic of network flows is vast and constantly evolving due to its wide applicability in today's modern, competitive world in such domains as production/distribution systems, communication systems, and, more recently, in financial and economic networks. Models, applications, and algorithms abound and in this chapter, as well as, in this text we focus primarily on those network models and algorithms of interest to us in terms of financial economic networks.

Recent fundamental references to network flows (which also include many useful and important citations) are: the book by Ahuja, Magnanti, and Orlin (1993), which includes numerous applications and algorithms with an emphasis on linear network flow problems, the handbooks on network models and network routing edited by Ball, Magnanti, Monma, and Nemhauser (1995a, b), with the latter containing a survey of network equilibrium models, applications, and algorithms written by Florian and Hearn (1995), and the book by Nagurney (1993), which focuses on network equilibrium problems in economics and includes a chapter on finance.

Section 5.1

In this section we presented the nonlinear network optimization problem and highlighted certain special cases. We also overviewed incidence matrices that are common in network theory.

Section 5.2

In this section we presented an algorithm, the primal truncated Newton method, following Bertsekas, Castanon, Eckstein, and Zenios (1995), for the solution of the nonlinear network optimization problem as well as special-purpose algorithms, such as the Splitting Equilibration Algorithm of Nagurney and Eydeland (1992) and the exact equilibration algorithm of Dafermos and Sparrow (1969) for the solution of networks with special structure (that is, topology) and special objective functions. These algorithms can also be embedded in other algorithms, including variational inequality algorithms, to exploit special network structure that arises in applications.

Section 5.3

In Section 5.3 we discussed a variety of network equilibrium problems, in particular, those with elastic demands and those with fixed demands and we provided variational inequality formulations of both path flow and link load formulations. We then described a equilibrium problems that are network equilibrium problems, notably, Walrasian price equilibrium problems and spatial price equilibrium problems, in addition to flow of funds network equilibrium problems. We made a distinction between asymmetric network equilibrium problems that need to be formulated as variational inequality problems and symmetric network equilibrium problems that can be reformulated as optimization problems. Additional background on such problems, qualitative analysis, and numerical results can be found in Nagurney (1993).

Section 5.4

In this section we discussed the application of variational inequality algorithms described in Section 3.3, along with equilibration algorithms for the solution of the embedded mathematical programming problems over networks. In particular, we discussed the projection method of Dafermos (1980, 1982) for the solution of asymmetric network equilibrium problems and the path equilibration algorithm of Dafermos and Sparrow (1969) for the solution of symmetric network equilibrium problems with linear user cost functions. Other algorithms that are suitable for the solution of the asymmetric network equilibrium problem include: the relaxation method, the dual cutting plane method, and simplicial decomposition. Algorithms that have been applied for the computation of symmetric network equilibria include, in addition to path equilibration algorithms, linear approximation methods, and its variants, and restricted decomposition, as well as dual ascent. See Florian and Hearn (1995) for a discussion of these algorithms, along with additional references.

Section 5.5

In this section we focused on dynamic network problems modeled as projected dynamical systems. Additional background on dynamic network flow problems, within an optimization framework, and numerous applications, can be found in the survey by Aronson (1989).

References

Ahlfeld, D. P., Dembo, R, S., Mulvey, J. M., and Zenios, S. A., "Nonlinear Programming on Generalized Networks," *ACM Transactions on Mathematical Software* **13** (1987) 350-368.

Ahuja, R. K., Magnanti, T. L., and Orlin, J. B., **Network Flows Theory, Algorithms, and Applications**, Prentice-Hall, Inc., Upper Saddle River, New Jersey, 1993.

Aronson, J. E., "A Survey of Dynamic Network Flows," *Annals of Operations Research* **20** (1989) 1-66.

Ball, M. O., Magnanti, T. L., Monma, C. L., and Nemhauser, G. L., editors, **Network Models, Handbooks in Operations Research and Management Science, vol. 7**, Elsevier Science B. V., Amsterdam, The Netherlands, 1995a.

Ball, M. O., Magnanti, T. L., Monma, C. L., and Nemhauser, G. L., editors, **Network Routing, Handbooks in Operations Research and Management Science, vol. 8**, Elsevier Science B. V., Amsterdam, The Netherlands, 1995b.

Beckmann, M. J., McGuire, C. B., and Winsten, C. B., **Studies in the Economics of Transportation**, Yale University Press, New Haven, Connecticut, 1956.

Bertsekas, D. P., **Constrained Optimization and Lagrange Multiplier Methods**, Academic Press, Inc., New York, New York, 1982.

Bertsekas, D., Castanon, D., Eckstein, J., and Zenios, S., "Parallel Computing in Network Optimization," **Network Models, Handbooks in Operations Research and Management Science, vol. 7**, pp. 331-399, M. O. Ball, Magnanti, T. L., Monma, C. L., and Nemhauser, G. L., editors, Elsevier Science, B. V., Amsterdam. The Netherlands, 1995.

Braess, D., "Uber ein Paradoxon der Verkehrsplanung," *Unternehmenforschung* **12** (1968) 258-268.

Dafermos, S., "Traffic Equilibrium and Variational Inequalities," *Transportation Science* **14** (1980) 42-54.

Dafermos, S., "The General Multimodal Network Equilibrium Problem with Elastic Demand," *Networks* **12** (1982) 57-72.

Dafermos, S., "An Iterative Scheme for Variational Inequalities," *Mathematical Programming* **26** (1983) 40-47.

Dafermos, S., "Exchange Price Equilibria and Variational Inequalities," *Mathematical Programming* **46** (1990) 391-402.

Dafermos, S., and Nagurney, A., "Isomorphism Between Spatial Price and Traffic Network Equilibrium Problems," LCDS #85-17, Lefschetz Center for Dynamical Systems, Brown University, Providence, Rhode Island, 1985.

Dafermos, S., and Nagurney, A., "Supply and Demand Equilibration Algorithms for a Class of Market Equilibrium Problems," *Transportation Science* **23** (1989) 118-124.

Dafermos, S. C., and Sparrow, F. T., "The Traffic Assignment Problem for a General Network," *Journal of Research of the National Bureau of Standards* **75B** (1969) 91-117.

Dantzig, G. B., "Programming in a Linear Structure," in **Comptroller,** United States Air Force, Washington D.C., February 1948.

Debreu, G., **Theory of Value**, Yale University Press, New Haven, Connecticut.

Dembo, R. S., "A Primal Truncated Newton Algorithm for Large-Scale Nonlinear Network Optimization," *Mathematical Programming Study* **31** (1987) 43-72.

Dembo, R. S., and Klincewicz, J. G., "Dealing with Degeneracy in Reduced Gradient Algorithms," *Mathematical Programming* **31** (1985) 357-363.

Dembo, R. S., and Steihaug, T., "Truncated-Newton Algorithms for Large-Scale Unconstrained Optimization," *Mathematical Programming* **26** (1983) 357-363.

Florian, M., and Hearn, D., "Network Equilibrium Models and Algorithms," in **Network Routing, Handbooks in Operations Research and Management Science, vol. 8**, pp. 485-550, M. O. Ball, T. L. Magnanti, Monma, C. L., Nemhauser, G. L., editors, Elsevier Science B. V., Amsterdam, The Netherlands, 1995.

Florian, M., and Los, M., "A New Look at Static Spatial Price Equilibrium Models," *Regional Science and Urban Economics* **12** (1982) 579-597.

Gartner, N. H., "Optimal Traffic Assignment with Elastic Demands: A Review Part II: Algorithmic Approaches," *Transportation Science* **14** (1980) 192-208.

Gill, P. E., Murray, W., and Wright, M. H., **Practical Optimization**, Academic Press, Inc., London, England, 1981.

Hartman, P., and Stampacchia, G. "On some Nonlinear Elliptic Differential Functional Equations," *Acta Mathematica* **115** (1966) 271-310.

Hitchcock, F. L., "The Distribution of a Product from Several Sources to Numerous Facilities," *Journal of Mathematical Physics* **20** (1941) 224-230.

Kantorovich, L. V., "Mathematical Methods in the Organization and Planning of Production," Publication House of Leningrad University, Leningrad, USSR, 1939, translated in *Management Science* **6** (1960) 366-422.

Koopmans, T. C., "Optimum Utilization of the Transportation Systems," **Proceedings of the International Statistical Conference**, Washington, DC, 1947.

Lasdon, L. S., **Optimization Theory for Large Systems**, The MacMillan Company, New York, New York, 1970.

Markowitz, H. M., **Portfolio Selection: Efficient Diversification of Investments**, John Wiley & Sons, Inc., New York, New York, 1959.

Mas-Colell, A., **The Theory of General Economic Equilibrium: A Differentiable Approach**, *Econometric Society Monographs* **9**, Cambridge University Press, Cambridge, United Kingdom, 1985.

Moore, C., and Nagurney, A., "A General Equilibrium Model of Interregional Monetary Flows," *Environment and Planning A* (1989) 397-404.

Mulvey, J. M., "Nonlinear Networks in Finance," *Advances in Mathematical Programming and Financial Planning* **1** (1987) 253-271.

Murtagh, B., and Saunders, M., "Large-Scale Linearly Constrained Optimization," *Mathematical Programming* **14** (1978) 41-72.

Nagurney, A., "An Equilibration Scheme for the Traffic Assignment Problem with Elastic Demand," *Transportation Research* **22B** (1988) 73-79.

Nagurney, A., **Network Economics: A Variational Inequality Approach**, Kluwer Academic Publishers, Boston, Massachusetts, 1993.

Nagurney, A., and Eydeland, A., "A Splitting Equilibration Algorithm for the Computation of Large-Scale Constrained Matrix Problems: Theoretical Analysis and Application," **Computational Economics and Econometrics** *Advanced Studies in Theoretical and Applied Econometrics* **22**, pp. 65-105, H. M. Amman, D. Belsley, and L. Pau, editors, 1992.

Nagurney, A., Kim, D. S., and Robinson, A. G., "Serial and Parallel Equilibration of Large-Scale Constrained Matrix Problems with Application to the Social and Economic Sciences," *The International Journal of Supercomputer Applications* **4.1** (1990) 49-71.

Nagurney, A., and Robinson, A. G., "Algorithms for Quadratic Constrained Matrix Problems," *Mathematical and Computer Modelling* **16** (1992) 53-65.

Nagurney A., and Zhang, D., **Projected Dynamical Systems and Variational Inequalities with Applications**, Kluwer Academic Publishers, Boston, Massachusetts, 1996a.

Nagurney, A., and Zhang, D., "Projected Dynamical Systems in the Formulation, Stability Analysis, and Computation of Fixed Demand Traffic Network Equilibria," (1996b), to appear in *Transportation Science*.

Quesnay, F., **Tableau Economique**, 1758, reproduced in facsimile with an introduction by H. Higgs by the British Economic Society, 1895.

Samuelson, P. A., "Spatial Price Equilibrium and Linear Programming," *American Economic Review* **42** (1952) 283-303.

Sharpe, W. F., "A Simplified Model for Portfolio Analysis," *Management Science* **9** (1963) 277-293.

Smith, M. J., "Existence, Uniqueness, and and Stability of Traffic Equilibria," *Transportation Research* **13B** (1979) 259-304.

Soenen, L. A., **Foreign Exchange Exposure Management: A Portfolio Approach**, Sijthoff and Noordhoff, Germantown, Maryland, 1979.

Takayama, T., and Judge, G. G., **Spatial and Temporal Price and Allocation Models**, North-Holland, Amsterdam, The Netherlands, 1971.

Thore, S., **Programming the Network of Financial Intermediation**, Universitetsforlaget, Oslo, Norway, 1980.

Thore, S., "Spatial Models of the Eurodollar Market," *Journal of Banking and Finance* **8** (1984) 51-65.

Wald, A., "On Some Systems of Equations in Mathematical Economics," *Econometrica* **19** (1951) 368-403.

Walras, L., **Elements d'Economique Politique Pure**, Corbaz, Lausanne, Switzerland, 1874.

Wardrop, J. G., "Some Theoretical Aspects of Road Traffic Research," in **Proceedings of the Institute of Civil Engineers**, Part II, pp. 25-378, 1952.

Part III Single Country Models

6 Static Single Country Models

In this chapter we present the first of a series of financial models that will be studied in this book. These models are static, single country financial equilibrium models and, although they are the simplest marcroeconomic models that are presented in this text, they form the foundation upon which all the subsequent models in this book rest.

In particular, the models that we develop in this chapter assume a perfect market in which there are no transaction costs and no policy interventions. We consider a single country economy, with multiple sectors and multiple instruments. Recall that a sector consists of any particular group of individual investors, institutions, and/or corporations that share similar interests in a specific part of the economy in which they perform the majority of their transactions. For example, all the participants in the country's economy that own, manage, or operate banking institutions, form the banking sector of that country. Similarly, one can define a series of other sectors such as, for example, the agricultural and the technological sectors. On the other hand, an instrument is any standardized medium of transferring capital and risk (e.g., cash, bonds, stocks, etc.) among the participants in the economy. As such, the instruments are priced at relative prices to one another with the prices being determined through the interaction between the supplies of and demands for the instruments by the sectors, in conjunction with the corresponding opportunities and risk perceptions held by the sectors. Hence, the price of every instrument demonstrates to all the sectors of the country the reactions of the economy as to the total allocation of assets and liabilities of each instrument.

Throughout this chapter, the assumption of free disposal holds and, hence, the instrument prices must be either positive or zero.

The modeling approach presented in this chapter relaxes the CAPM assumptions of homogeneous expectations (cf. Sharpe (1964), Lintner (1965), and Mossin (1966)), without imposing restrictions as to the nature of different sectors (e.g., Gonedes (1976)). Moreover, the models under consideration here are not based on the existence of either a risk-free rate of return or a market portfolio as were those financial models that were reviewed in Chapter 2.

The mathematical framework that is utilized to develop and qualitatively analyze the multi-sector, multi-instrument financial equilibrium models, as well as, to study the computational properties of the proposed algorithmic schemes is finite-dimensional variational inequality theory. For an introduction to this methodology, we refer the reader to Chapter 3 as well as to the books by Kinderlehrer and Stampacchia (1980) and Nagurney (1993).

The methodology of finite-dimensional variational inequalities was first suggested for the modeling, analysis, and computation of multi-sector, multi-instrument financial equilibrium problems by Nagurney, Dong, and Hughes (1992) and was further explored by Nagurney (1994).

6.1 A General Utility Function Model

Consider a single country economy with multiple instruments and with multiple sectors. The segmentation of the single country economy into different sectors will vary from case to case, but the total number of sectors in the economy, as well as, the way in which the sectors are segmented and defined do not have to be fixed a priori. The modeling approach presented here, hence, is open to any partitioning of the economy required by the application under consideration. Note that throughout this chapter, for simplicity, the meaning of word "economy" is used in the general setting of a single country economy.

We let i denote a typical instrument, with the total number of instruments available in the economy, denoted by I. We let j denote a typical sector in the economy, with the number of sectors denoted by J. As in the case of sectors, the total number of instruments under consideration is application-specific and need not be fixed a priori.

Let r_i denote the (nonnegative) price of instrument i, and group the prices of all the instruments into the column vector $r \in R^I_+$.

Denote the volume of instrument i that sector j holds as an asset, by X^j_i, and group the (nonnegative) assets in the portfolio of sector j into the column vector $X^j \in R^I_+$. Further, group the assets of all sectors in the economy into the column vector $X \in R^{JI}_+$. Similarly, denote the volume of instrument i that sector j holds as a liability, by Y^j_i, and group the (nonnegative) liabilities in the portfolio of sector j into the column vector $Y^j \in R^I_+$. Finally, group the liabilities of all sectors in the economy into the column vector $Y \in R^{JI}_+$.

Throughout this chapter, we assume that the total volume of each balance sheet side of each sector is exogenous. Recall that a balance sheet is a financial report that demonstrates the status of a company's assets, liabilities, and the owner's equity at a specific point of time. The left-hand side of a balance sheet contains the assets that a sector holds at a particular point of time, whereas the right-hand side accommodates the liabilities and owner's equity held by that sector at the same point of time. According to accounting principles, the sum of all assets is equal to the sum of all the liabilities and the owner's equity. In this book, the term "liabilities" is used in its general form and, hence, also includes the owner's equity.

Moreover, we assume that the sectors under consideration act in a perfectly competitive environment. Recall from Section 2.3, that perfect competition does not allow any sector to have control over the prices of different instruments or over the actions of the other sectors. The price of an instrument is considered to be a variable, the value of which is determined by the combined actions of all the sectors. Therefore, sectors that buy an instrument are "price takers," in that they modify their holdings of an instrument according to the price, ignoring the effects that their behavior may have on that price. We recall from Chapter 2 that perfect competition assumes that all sectors have perfect information about all the available instruments, the current prices, and the corresponding bids.

In addition, the number of the sectors in the economy is assumed to be large enough so that the market activity regarding a specific instrument will be small as compared to the transactions in the overall market. Furthermore, all sectors that purchase an instrument are viewed as being identical from the perspectives of the buying sectors of that instrument. Similarly, all selling sectors are viewed as being identical from the buying sectors' points of view. In other words, a sector will prefer to trade with another sector solely because he offers a better price.

Throughout this chapter we also assume that all sectors have access to the entire set of different transactions that may occur, and that there are no limitations in terms of resources, liquidity, and availability (as defined by their feasible sets which represent their constraints). Since all sectors are informed of the price of a product, noone can either charge more or pay less than the price that exists in the market.

Since each sector's expectations are formed by reference to current market activity, a sector's expected utility maximization can be written in terms of optimizing the current portfolio. Sectors may trade, issue, or liquidate holdings in order to optimize their portfolio compositions.

We assume that each sector j tries to maximize his utility function, which we denote as $U^j(X^j, Y^j, r)$. We also assume that the utility function of every sector is concave, continuous, and twice continuously differentiable. Furthermore, the accounts of each sector must balance. We denote the total financial volume held by sector j by S^j. Therefore, the optimization problem that each sector j faces is given by:

$$\text{Maximize } U^j(X^j, Y^j, r) \tag{6.1}$$

subject to:

$$\sum_{i=1}^{I} X_i^j = S^j \tag{6.2a}$$

$$\sum_{i=1}^{I} Y_i^j = S^j \tag{6.2b}$$

$$X_i^j \geq 0, \; Y_i^j \geq 0, \quad i = 1, 2, \ldots, I, \tag{6.3}$$

where the price vector r is an exogenous vector in the optimization problem of every sector j; $j = 1, \ldots, J$. In Figure 6.1, we represent the network structure of the individual sectors' optimization problems (out of equilibrium), where the uppermost and lowermost nodes correspond to the sectors, and the assets and the liabilities of the sectors are denoted by the links of the network. The flows on the asset links correspond to the assets, whereas the flows on the liability links correspond to the liabilities. The supplies at the sectoral nodes are given by the sector volumes.

An important special case of the utility function $U^j(X^j, Y^j, r)$ is the following:

$$U^j(X^j, Y^j, r) = u^j(X^j, Y^j) + r^T \cdot (X^j - Y^j), \tag{6.4}$$

which will be of interest to us theoretically in this (and subsequent chapters). Note that the utility function in (6.4) consists of two parts: with the first part representing the utility obtained from the composition of the portfolio (and which is not dependent upon the prices) and with the second part representing the total return on the portfolio.

We now discuss the feasible set (cf. (6.2a), (6.2b), and (6.3)) of the sectors. For each sector j; $j = 1, \ldots, J$, we let

$$\tilde{X}^j \equiv \{X^j \in R_+^I : \sum_{i=1}^{I} X_i^j = S^j\} \tag{6.5}$$

denote the constraint set of his assets. Similarly, we let

$$\tilde{Y}^j \equiv \{Y^j \in R_+^I : \sum_{i=1}^{I} Y_i^j = S^j\} \tag{6.6}$$

denote the constraint set for his liabilities. Then, the feasible set for a sector j is a Cartesian product, denoted by κ^j, where

$$\kappa^j \equiv \{\tilde{X}^j \times \tilde{Y}^j\}. \tag{6.7}$$

Let $\tilde{X}$ denote the feasible set for the assets of all the sectors, where:

$$\tilde{X} \equiv \tilde{X}^1 \times \ldots \times \tilde{X}^j \times \ldots \times \tilde{X}^J. \tag{6.8}$$

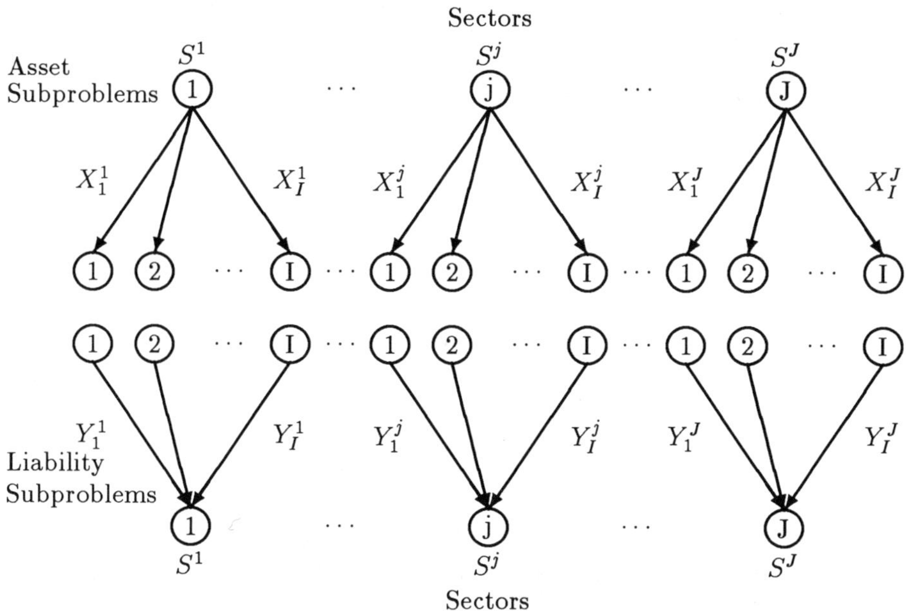

Fig. 6.1. Network structure of the sectors' optimization problems

Similarly, for the liabilities, let $\tilde{Y}$ denote the feasible set of the liabilities of all the sectors, that is,

$$\tilde{Y} \equiv \tilde{Y}^1 \times \ldots \times \tilde{Y}^j \times \ldots \times \tilde{Y}^J. \tag{6.9}$$

Also, define $\kappa \equiv \{\tilde{X} \times \tilde{Y}\}$.

We now derive the optimality conditions for a sector's utility maximization problem, given by (6.1), subject to: (6.2)–(6.3). We then give the economic conditions determining the instrument prices (in equilibrium).

Optimality Conditions

The necessary and sufficient conditions (see Appendix A) for an optimal portfolio for sector j are that the vector of assets and liabilities, $(X^{j^*}, Y^{j^*}) \in \kappa^j$, satisfies the following system of equalities and inequalities: For each instrument i; $i = 1, \ldots, I$, we must have the following Kuhn-Tucker conditions being satisfied, at an equilibrium price vector r^*:

$$\begin{aligned}
-\frac{\partial U^j(X^{j^*}, Y^{j^*}, r^*)}{\partial X_i^j} - \mu_j^1 &\geq 0, \\
-\frac{\partial U^j(X^{j^*}, Y^{j^*}, r^*)}{\partial Y_i^j} - \mu_j^2 &\geq 0, \\
X_i^{j^*}\left(-\frac{\partial U^j(X^{j^*}, Y^{j^*}, r^*)}{\partial X_i^j} - \mu_j^1\right) &= 0, \\
Y_i^{j^*}\left(-\frac{\partial U^j(X^{j^*}, Y^{j^*}, r^*)}{\partial Y_i^j} - \mu_j^2\right) &= 0,
\end{aligned} \tag{6.10}$$

where μ_j^1, μ_j^2 are the Lagrange multipliers associated with constraints (6.2a) and (6.2b). Obviously, a similar set of equalities and inequalities holds for every other sector in the single country economy.

Economic System Conditions

Moreover, the economic system conditions that ensure market clearance at a positive instrument price (and a possible excess supply of the instrument at a zero price) are:

For each instrument $i; i = 1, \ldots, I$, we must have that:

$$\sum_{j=1}^{J}(X_i^{j^*} - Y_i^{j^*})\begin{cases} = 0, & \text{if } r_i^* > 0 \\ \geq 0, & \text{if } r_i^* = 0. \end{cases} \tag{6.11}$$

The system of equalities and inequalities (6.11) states that if the price of a financial instrument is positive, then the market must clear for that instrument and if the price is zero, then either there is an excess supply of that instrument in the economy or the market clears.

Let $\mathcal{K}$ be the feasible set for all the asset and liability holdings of all the sectors, and all the prices of all the instruments where $\mathcal{K} \equiv \{\kappa \times R^I_+\}$.

Combining (6.11), along with conditions (6.10), we present the following definition of equilibrium.

Definition 6.1 (Perfect Market Equilibrium)

A vector $(X^*, Y^*, r^*) \in \mathcal{K}$ is an equilibrium of the single country, multi-sector, multi-instrument financial model if and only if it satisfies the system of equalities and inequalities (6.10) and (6.11), for all sectors j; $j = 1, \ldots, J$, and for all instruments i; $i = 1, \ldots, I$, simultaneously.

The necessary and sufficient conditions (6.10), along with the economic conditions for the instrument prices (6.11), are now utilized to derive the variational inequality formulation of the financial equilibrium conditions.

Theorem 6.1 (Variational Inequality Formulation)

A vector of assets and liabilities of the sectors, and instrument prices, $(X^*, Y^*, r^*) \in \mathcal{K}$, is a perfect market financial equilibrium if and only if it satisfies the variational inequality problem:

$$\sum_{j=1}^{J}\sum_{i=1}^{I}\left[-\frac{\partial U^j(X^{j*}, Y^{j*}, r^*)}{\partial X_i^j}\right] \times \left[X_i^j - X_i^{j*}\right]$$

$$+\sum_{j=1}^{J}\sum_{i=1}^{I}\left[-\frac{\partial U^j(X^{j*}, Y^{j*}, r^*)}{\partial Y_i^j}\right] \times \left[Y_i^j - Y_i^{j*}\right]$$

$$+\sum_{i=1}^{I}\sum_{j=1}^{J}\left[X_i^{j*} - Y_i^{j*}\right] \times \left[r_i - r_i^*\right] \geq 0, \quad \forall (X, Y, r) \in \mathcal{K}, \tag{6.12a}$$

which in the case of utility functions (6.4), takes the form

$$\sum_{j=1}^{J}\sum_{i=1}^{I}\left[-\frac{\partial u^j(X^{j*}, Y^{j*})}{\partial X_i^j} - r_i^*\right] \times \left[X_i^j - X_i^{j*}\right]$$

$$+\sum_{j=1}^{J}\sum_{i=1}^{I}\left[-\frac{\partial u^j(X^{j*}, Y^{j*})}{\partial Y_i^j} + r_i^*\right] \times \left[Y_i^j - Y_i^{j*}\right]$$

$$+\sum_{i=1}^{I}\sum_{j=1}^{J}\left[X_i^{j*} - Y_i^{j*}\right] \times \left[r_i - r_i^*\right] \geq 0, \quad \forall (X, Y, r) \in \mathcal{K}. \tag{6.12b}$$

Proof: Assume that $(X^*, Y^*, r^*) \in \mathcal{K}$ is an equilibrium point of the multi-sector, multi-instrument financial model, that is, it satisfies Definition 6.1.

Then inequalities (6.10) and (6.11) hold for all sectors j and for all instruments i. The system of equalities and inequalities (6.10) implies that, for a fixed instrument i, we must have that

$$\left[-\frac{\partial U^j(X^{j^*}, Y^{j^*}, r^*)}{\partial X_i^j} - \mu_j^1\right] \times \left[X_i^j - X_i^{j^*}\right] > 0. \qquad (6.13a)$$

Indeed, if $X_i^{j^*} > 0$, then the second term in (6.13a) can be (for a given X_i^j) greater than zero, less than zero, or equal to zero, but since the first term of (6.13a) is equal to zero, due to the optimality condition (6.10), we have that the product of these two terms is equal to zero and, thus, (6.13a) holds true. On the other hand, if $X_i^{j^*} = 0$, then the second term in (6.13a) is greater than equal to zero, as is the first term (from the optimality condition), and, consequently, (6.13a) also holds true. Since (6.13a) is independent of the instrument i, we may sum over all the instruments to obtain

$$\sum_{i=1}^{I}\left[-\frac{\partial U^j(X^{j^*}, Y^{j^*}, r^*)}{\partial X_i^j} - \mu_j^1\right] \times \left[X_i^j - X_i^{j^*}\right] \geq 0. \qquad (6.13b)$$

Applying now equation (6.2a), the Lagrange multiplier in (6.13b), μ_j^1, vanishes, and we obtain:

$$\sum_{i=1}^{I}\left[-\frac{\partial U^j(X^{j^*}, Y^{j^*}, r^*)}{\partial X_i^j}\right] \times \left[X_i^j - X_i^{j^*}\right] \geq 0. \qquad (6.14)$$

Since (X^*, Y^*, r^*) is an equilibrium point, inequality (6.14) must hold for all sectors j. Hence, summing (6.14) over all sectors j yields:

$$\sum_{j=1}^{J}\sum_{i=1}^{I}\left[-\frac{\partial U^j(X^{j^*}, Y^{j^*}, r^*)}{\partial X_i^j}\right] \times \left[X_i^j - X_i^{j^*}\right] \geq 0. \qquad (6.15)$$

Similarly, for the liabilities, using analogous arguments to those above, we obtain:

$$\sum_{j=1}^{J}\sum_{i=1}^{I}\left[-\frac{\partial U^j(X^{j^*}, Y^{j^*}, r^*)}{\partial Y_i^j}\right] \times \left[Y_i^j - Y_i^{j^*}\right] \geq 0. \qquad (6.16)$$

Also, since $(X^*, Y^*, r^*) \in \mathcal{K}$ is an equilibrium point, the system of equalities and inequalities (6.11) holds, which is equivalent to the following inequality, for a fixed instrument i:

$$\sum_{j=1}^{J}\left[X_i^{j^*} - Y_i^{j^*}\right] \times \left[r_i - r_i^*\right] \geq 0, \quad \forall r_i \geq 0. \qquad (6.17)$$

But (6.17) must hold for all instruments i, and, hence, the summation of (6.17) over all instruments, yields:

$$\sum_{i=1}^{I}\sum_{j=1}^{J}\left[X_i^{j^*}-Y_i^{j^*}\right]\times\left[r_i-r_i^*\right]\geq 0, \quad \forall r\in R_+^I. \tag{6.18}$$

Summing now inequalities (6.15), (6.16), and (6.18), we obtain the variational inequality (6.12a). The variational inequality (6.12b) follows by noting (6.4), and taking the partial derivatives of the utility function for each sector with respect to his asset holdings of an instrument and the liability holdings of an instrument.

We will now prove that if $(X^*, Y^*, r^*) \in \mathcal{K}$ is a solution to variational inequality (6.12a), then it will also satisfy the equilibrium conditions (6.10) and (6.11).

In particular, if we let $(X^*, Y^*, r^*) \in \mathcal{K}$ be a solution to variational inequality (6.12a), and we let $X^j = X^{j^*}$, $Y^j = Y^{j^*}$, for all sectors j, then substitution into variational inequality (6.12a) yields:

$$\sum_{i=1}^{I}\sum_{j=1}^{J}\left[X_i^{j^*}-Y_i^{j^*}\right]\times\left[r_i-r_i^*\right]\geq 0, \quad \forall r\in R_+^I, \tag{6.19}$$

which implies the system economic conditions (6.11).

If we now let $r_i = r_i^*$ for all instruments i and substitute the resultants into inequality (6.12a), we obtain:

$$\sum_{j=1}^{J}\sum_{i=1}^{I}\left[-\frac{\partial U^j(X^{j^*},Y^{j^*},r^*)}{\partial X_i^j}\right]\times\left[X_i^j-X_i^{j^*}\right]$$

$$+\sum_{j=1}^{J}\sum_{i=1}^{I}\left[-\frac{\partial U^j(X^{j^*},Y^{j^*},r^*)}{\partial X_i^j}\right]\times\left[Y_i^j-Y_i^{j^*}\right]\geq 0, \tag{6.20}$$

which implies the optimality conditions (6.10). The variational inequality (6.12b) is a special case of (6.12a) with utility functions given by (6.4); hence, the conclusion also follows in this case. □

We will now put variational inequality (6.12a) into standard form given by (3.13). We first define the J-dimensional column vector U with components: $\{U^1, \ldots, U^J\}$ and let $\nabla_X U$ denote the JI-dimensional vector with components: $\{\nabla_{X^1}U^1, \ldots, \nabla_{X^J}U^J\}$ with $\nabla_{X^j}U^j$ denoting the gradient of U^j with respect to the vector X^j. The expression $\nabla_Y U$ is defined accordingly. We let $n = 2JI + I$. We define the n-dimensional column vector $x \equiv (X, Y, r) \in \mathcal{K}$, and the n-dimensional column vector $F(x)$ with components:

$$F(x) = \begin{bmatrix} F_1(x) \\ \vdots \\ F_b(x) \\ \vdots \\ F_n(x) \end{bmatrix} = \begin{bmatrix} -\nabla_X U(X,Y,r) \\ -\nabla_Y U(X,Y,r) \\ \sum_{j=1}^J \left(X_1^j - Y_1^j\right) \\ \vdots \\ \sum_{j=1}^J \left(X_I^j - Y_I^j\right) \end{bmatrix}_{n\times 1} \tag{6.21}$$

Consequently, (6.12a) (and (6.12b)) can be written as:
Determine $x^* \in \mathcal{K}$ satisfying:

$$\langle F(x^*)^T, x - x^* \rangle \geq 0, \quad \forall x \in \mathcal{K}. \tag{6.22}$$

6.1.1 Quadratic Utility Functions

In this subsection we consider a special case of the utility function (6.4). In particular, we recall the classical mean-variance portfolio optimization model presented in Section 2.1 and in Example 3.2, which is based on the pioneering work of Markowitz (1959). Here, the optimization problem facing each sector is to maximize the return and, at the same time, to minimize the risk of his portfolio, subject to the balance accounting and nonnegativity constraints. We recall that in the mean-variance approach for portfolio optimization, the minimization of a portfolio's risk is performed through the use of the variance-covariance matrix. As a result, the portfolio optimization problem for each sector j is the following:

$$\text{Minimize} \quad \begin{pmatrix} X^j \\ Y^j \end{pmatrix}^T Q^j \begin{pmatrix} X^j \\ Y^j \end{pmatrix} - \sum_{i=1}^I r_i \left(X_i^j - Y_i^j\right) \tag{6.23}$$

subject to:

$$\sum_{i=1}^I X_i^j = S^j \tag{6.24a}$$

$$\sum_{i=1}^I Y_i^j = S^j \tag{6.24b}$$

$$X_i^j \geq 0, \; Y_i^j \geq 0, \quad i = 1, 2, \ldots, I, \tag{6.25}$$

where Q^j is a symmetric $2I \times 2I$ variance-covariance matrix associated with the assets and liabilities of sector j. Moreover, since Q^j is a variance-covariance matrix, we can also assume that it is positive definite and, as a result, the objective function of each sector's portfolio optimization problem, given by (6.23), is strictly convex.

We now partition (see Appendix A) the symmetric matrix Q^j, as

$$Q^j = \begin{pmatrix} Q^j_{11} & Q^j_{12} \\ Q^j_{21} & Q^j_{22} \end{pmatrix}, \tag{6.26}$$

where Q^j_{11} and Q^j_{22} are the variance-covariance matrices for only the assets and only the liabilities, respectively, of sector j. These submatrices are each of dimension $I \times I$. The submatrices Q^j_{12} and Q^j_{21}, in turn, are identical since Q^j is symmetric. They are also of dimension $I \times I$. These submatrices are, in fact, the symmetric variance-covariance matrices between the asset and the liabilities of sector j.

We denote the i-th column of matrix $Q^j_{(\alpha\beta)}$, by $Q^j_{(\alpha\beta)i}$, where α and β can take on the values of 1 and/or 2.

The necessary and sufficient conditions for an optimal portfolio for sector j (similar to those given in (6.10)), are that the vector of assets and liabilities, $(X^{j^*}, Y^{j^*}) \in \kappa^j$, satisfies the following system of equalities and inequalities: For each instrument $i; i = 1, \ldots, I$, we must have that:

$$\begin{aligned} 2(Q^j_{(11)i})^T \cdot X^{j^*} + 2(Q^j_{(21)i})^T \cdot Y^{j^*} - r^*_i - \mu^1_j \geq 0, \\ 2(Q^j_{(22)i})^T \cdot Y^{j^*} + 2(Q^j_{(12)i})^T \cdot X^{j^*} + r^*_i - \mu^2_j \geq 0, \\ X^{j^*}_i \left[2(Q^j_{(11)i})^T \cdot X^{j^*} + 2(Q^j_{(21)i})^T \cdot Y^{j^*} - r^*_i - \mu^1_j\right] = 0, \\ Y^{j^*}_i \left[2(Q^j_{(22)i})^T \cdot Y^{j^*} + 2(Q^j_{(12)i})^T \cdot X^{j^*} + r^*_i - \mu^j_2\right] = 0, \end{aligned} \tag{6.27}$$

where μ^1_j and μ^2_j are the Lagrange multipliers associated with constraints (6.24a) and (6.24b), respectively.

Moreover, the economic system conditions are identical to those given by (6.11), that is: For each instrument $i; i = 1, \ldots, I$, an equilibrium asset, liability, and price pattern, $(X^*, Y^*, r^*) \in \mathcal{K}$, must satisfy:

$$\sum_{j=1}^{J} (X^{j^*}_i - Y^{j^*}_i) \begin{cases} = 0, & \text{if } r^*_i > 0 \\ \geq 0, & \text{if } r^*_i = 0. \end{cases} \tag{6.28}$$

The variational inequality formulation of the equilibrium conditions (cf. Definition 6.1), governing the financial model in the case of quadratic utility functions is immediate from Theorem 6.1.

Corollary 6.1 (Variational Inequality Formulation for the Quadratic Model)

A vector of assets and liabilities of the sectors, and instrument prices, $(X^*, Y^*, r^*) \in \mathcal{K}$, is a financial equilibrium if and only if it satisfies the variational inequality problem:

$$\sum_{j=1}^{J} \sum_{i=1}^{I} \left[2(Q^j_{(11)i})^T \cdot X^{j^*} + 2(Q^j_{(21)i})^T \cdot Y^{j^*} - r^*_i\right] \times \left[X^j_i - X^{j^*}_i\right]$$

$$+\sum_{j=1}^{J}\sum_{i=1}^{I}\left[2(Q^j_{(22)i})^T\cdot Y^{j^*}+2(Q^j_{(12)i})^T\cdot X^{j^*}+r_i^*\right]\times\left[Y_i^j-Y_i^{j^*}\right]$$

$$+\sum_{i=1}^{I}\sum_{j=1}^{J}\left[X_i^{j^*}-Y_i^{j^*}\right]\times[r_i-r_i^*]\geq 0,\quad \forall(X,Y,r)\in\mathcal{K}. \tag{6.29}$$

For simplicity, and in order to maintain a compact mathematical formulation, we will now present the standard form of variational inequality (6.29). As before, we define the n-dimensional column vector $x\equiv(X,Y,r)\in\mathcal{K}$, and the n-dimensional column vector $F(x)$ such that:

$$F(x)\equiv D\begin{pmatrix}X\\Y\\r\end{pmatrix} \tag{6.30}$$

where D is given by:

$$D=\begin{pmatrix}2Q & B\\ -B^T & 0\end{pmatrix}, \tag{6.31}$$

and

$$Q=\begin{pmatrix}Q^1_{11} & & & Q^1_{21} & & \\ & \ddots & & & \ddots & \\ & & Q^J_{11} & & & Q^J_{21}\\ Q^1_{12} & & & Q^1_{22} & & \\ & \ddots & & & \ddots & \\ & & Q^J_{12} & & & Q^J_{22}\end{pmatrix}_{2JI\times 2JI}, \tag{6.32}$$

with B^T denoting the $I\times JI$ matrix such that:

$$B^T=\begin{pmatrix}-\mathcal{I} & \dots & -\mathcal{I} & \mathcal{I} & \dots & \mathcal{I}\end{pmatrix}_{I\times JI} \tag{6.33}$$

where $\mathcal{I}$ is the $I\times I$-dimensional identity matrix.

Therefore, if we take into consideration the notation of (6.30)–(6.33), it is clear that (6.29) can be put into standard variational inequality form:

Determine $x^*\in\mathcal{K}$, satisfying:

$$\langle F(x^*)^T, x-x^*\rangle\geq 0,\ \forall x\in\mathcal{K}.$$

6.2 Qualitative Properties

In this section we present some of the qualitative properties for the model(s) presented in Section 6.1. In particular, we address the questions of existence and uniqueness of the equilibrium pattern. Moreover, through the theory presented in this section we will illustrate variational inequality theory as a tool for the qualitative study of financial equilibrium problems in a static setting. Obviously, identical qualitative properties hold for the quadratic utility function model, since it is a special case of the more general model.

All of the qualitative properties, along with their proofs, presented in this section are due to Nagurney, Dong, and Hughes (1992), Dong (1994), and Nagurney (1994). We believe that a collective representation of all these theoretical points will be instructive, and that it will help the reader better understand the models that will be presented in the subsequent chapters.

First, we investigate the existence of an equilibrium asset, liability, and price pattern for the model with utility functions of the form (6.4). Then we establish the uniqueness of the asset and liability equilibrium pattern for the general utility function model, which, of course, includes, as a special case, the quadratic utility function model.

Theorem 6.2 (Existence)

Assume that the utility function for each sector is as given by (6.4). If $(X^*, Y^*, r^*) \in \mathcal{K}$ *is an equilibrium pattern and, therefore, a solution to variational inequality (6.12b), then* (X^*, Y^*) *is a solution of the variational inequality:*

$$\sum_{j=1}^{J}\sum_{i=1}^{I}\left[-\frac{\partial u^j(X^{j^*}, Y^{j^*})}{\partial X_i^j}\right] \times \left[X_i^j - X_i^{j^*}\right]$$

$$+\sum_{j=1}^{J}\sum_{i=1}^{I}\left[-\frac{\partial u^j(X^{j^*}, Y^{j^*})}{\partial Y_i^j}\right] \times \left[Y_i^j - Y_i^{j^*}\right] \geq 0, \ \forall (X, Y) \in S, \tag{6.34}$$

where S *is a non-empty set such that:*

$$S \equiv \{(X, Y) : \ (X, Y) \in \kappa; \ \sum_{j=1}^{J}(X_i^j - Y_i^j) \geq 0; \ i = 1, \ldots, I\}.$$

If, on the other hand, (X^*, Y^*) *is a solution of variational inequality (6.34), then there exists an* I*-dimensional vector of Lagrange multipliers,* r^**, associated with the constraints:* $\sum_{j=1}^{J}(X_i^j - Y_i^j) \geq 0; \ i = 1, \ldots, I$*, such that* (X^*, Y^*, r^*) *is an equilibrium pattern, and, therefore, a solution to variational inequality (6.12b).*

Proof: Assume that (X^*, Y^*, r^*) is a financial equilibrium and, therefore, it satisfies variational inequality (6.12b). If we now let $(X^j, Y^j) = (X^{j^*}, Y^{j^*})$, for all sectors j, and $r_i = 0$, for all instruments i, then, by substitution into (6.12b), we obtain:

$$-\sum_{i=1}^{I}\left[\sum_{j=1}^{J} X_i^{j^*} - Y_i^{j^*}\right] r_i^* \geq 0. \tag{6.35}$$

Similarly, if we let $r_i = r_i^*$, for all instruments i, and substitute these values into (6.12b), yields:

$$\sum_{j=1}^{J}\sum_{i=1}^{I}\left[-\frac{\partial u^j(X^{j*},Y^{j*})}{\partial X_i^j} - r_i^*\right] \times \left[X_i^j - X_i^{j*}\right]$$

$$+\sum_{j=1}^{J}\sum_{i=1}^{I}\left[-\frac{\partial u^j(X^{j*},Y^{j*})}{\partial Y_i^j} + r_i^*\right] \times \left[Y_i^j - Y_i^{j*}\right] \geq 0, \tag{6.36}$$

or, equivalently,

$$\sum_{j=1}^{J}\sum_{i=1}^{I}\left[-\frac{\partial u^j(X^{j*},Y^{j*})}{\partial X_i^j}\right] \times \left[X_i^j - X_i^{j*}\right]$$

$$+\sum_{j=1}^{J}\sum_{i=1}^{I}\left[-\frac{\partial u^j(X^{j*},Y^{j*})}{\partial Y_i^j}\right] \times \left[Y_i^j - Y_i^{j*}\right]$$

$$\geq \sum_{i=1}^{I} r_i^*\left[\sum_{j=1}^{J}(X_i^j - Y_i^j) - \sum_{j=1}^{J}(X_i^{j*} - Y_i^{j*})\right]. \tag{6.37}$$

By taking into consideration (6.35), and the constraint set S, one can easily observe that the right-hand side of (6.37) is greater than or equal to zero, and, therefore, if (X^*, Y^*) satisfies (6.12b), it must also satisfy (6.34).

Since the constraint set S is compact, it follows from Theorem 3.1, that there exists an asset and liability equilibrium pattern (X^*, Y^*) that satisfies (6.34). Furthermore, if we apply the Lagrange Multiplier Theorem (see Appendix A), then there exists a vector of Lagrange multipliers, $r^* \in R^I$, associated with the constraints: $\sum_{j=1}^{J}(X_i^j - Y_i^j) \geq 0$; $i = 1, \ldots, I$, with r_i^* corresponding to constraint i. Consequently, for every (X^*, Y^*, r^*), variational inequality (6.12b) holds. □

We will now address the issue of the uniqueness of the equilibrium asset and liability pattern. The following theorem is for general utility functions.

Theorem 6.3 (Uniqueness)

Under the assumption that the utility functions $U^j(X^j, Y^j, r)$ are strictly concave in X^j and in Y^j for each sector j, the equilibrium pattern of assets and liabilities, (X^*, Y^*), is unique.

Proof: Assume that we have an equilibrium price vector r^*. Since the utility functions U^j are strictly concave for each sector j, then according to the definition of a strictly concave function (see Appendix A), we must have that: For every $(X^{j^1}, Y^{j^1}) \neq (X^{j^2}, Y^{j^2}) \in \kappa^j$, and for all sectors j:

$$-\sum_{j=1}^{J}\left[\nabla_{X^j} U^j(X^{j^1}, Y^{j^1}, r^*) - \nabla_{X^j} U^j(X^{j^2}, Y^{j^2}, r^*)\right]^T \cdot \left[X^{j^1} - X^{j^2}\right]$$

$$-\sum_{j=1}^{J}\left[\nabla_{Y^j}U^j(X^{j^1},Y^{j^1},r^*)-\nabla_{Y^j}U^j(X^{j^2},Y^{j^2},r^*)\right]^T\cdot\left[Y^{j^1}-Y^{j^2}\right]>0. \tag{6.38}$$

Suppose now that we have two distinct equilibrium asset and liability patterns. Denote these two equilibrium patterns, respectively, by (X^1, Y^1, r^*) and (X^2, Y^2, r^*). Hence, each of these patterns must satisfy variational inequality (6.12a), that is,

$$-\sum_{j=1}^{J}\left[\nabla_{X^j}U^j(X^{j^1},Y^{j^1},r^*)\right]^T\cdot\left[X^j-X^{j^1}\right]$$

$$-\sum_{j=1}^{J}\left[\nabla_{Y^j}U^j(X^{j^1},Y^{j^1},r^*)\right]^T\cdot\left[Y^j-Y^{j^1}\right]$$

$$+\sum_{i=1}^{I}\left[\sum_{j=1}^{J}X_i^{j^1}-\sum_{j=1}^{J}Y_i^{j^1}\right]\times[r_i-r_i^*]\geq 0,\quad\forall(X,Y,r)\in\mathcal{K}. \tag{6.39}$$

Similarly,

$$-\sum_{j=1}^{J}\left[\nabla_{X^j}U^j(X^{j^2},Y^{j^2},r^*)\right]^T\cdot\left[X^j-X^{j^2}\right]$$

$$-\sum_{j=1}^{J}\left[\nabla_{Y^j}U^j(X^{j^2},Y^{j^2},r^*)\right]^T\cdot\left[Y^j-Y^{j^2}\right]$$

$$+\sum_{i=1}^{I}\left[\sum_{j=1}^{J}X_i^{j^2}-\sum_{j=1}^{J}Y_i^{j^2}\right]\times[r_i-r_i^*]\geq 0,\quad\forall(X,Y,r)\in\mathcal{K}. \tag{6.40}$$

If we now let $(X^j, Y^j, r) = (X^{j^1}, Y^{j^1}, r^*)$ and substitute these values into (6.40), and we let $(X^j, Y^j, r) = (X^{j^2}, Y^{j^2}, r^*)$ and substitute these values into (6.39), and add the results, we obtain:

$$-\sum_{j=1}^{J}\left[\nabla_{X^j}U^j(X^{j^1},Y^{j^1},r^*)-\nabla_{X^j}U^j(X^{j^2},Y^{j^2},r^*)\right]^T\cdot\left[X^{j^2}-X^{j^1}\right]$$

$$-\sum_{j=1}^{J}\left[\nabla_{Y^j}U^j(X^{j^1},Y^{j^1},r^*)-\nabla_{Y^j}U^j(X^{j^2},Y^{j^2},r^*)\right]^T\cdot\left[Y^{j^2}-Y^{j^1}\right]\geq 0, \tag{6.41}$$

which is in contradiction to (6.38). Hence, the equilibrium asset and liability pattern must be unique. □

We now state a lemma that will be used in establishing the monotonicity of F (cf. (6.21)).

Lemma 6.1

If a matrix A is nonsingular and w^T and z are two vectors, with 0 denoting the scalar zero, and $|B|$ denoting the determinant of B, then

$$\left|\begin{pmatrix} A & z \\ w^T & 0 \end{pmatrix}\right| = (-w^T A^{-1} z)|A|. \tag{6.42}$$

Proof: Since A is nonsingular, we have that

$$\begin{pmatrix} I & 0 \\ -w^T A^{-1} & 1 \end{pmatrix}\begin{pmatrix} A & z \\ w^T & 0 \end{pmatrix} = \begin{pmatrix} A & z \\ 0 & -w^T A^{-1} z \end{pmatrix}.$$

Hence,

$$\left|\begin{pmatrix} I & 0 \\ -w^T A^{-1} & 1 \end{pmatrix}\begin{pmatrix} A & z \\ w^T & 0 \end{pmatrix}\right|$$

$$= \left|\begin{pmatrix} A & z \\ 0 & -w^T A^{-1} z \end{pmatrix}\right| = |A|(-w^T A^{-1} z). \tag{6.43}$$

Theorem 6.4

Under the assumption that the utility functions are strictly concave and twice continuously differentiable, $F(x)$ defined in (6.21) is monotone, that is, $\langle (F(x^1) - F(x^2))^T, x^1 - x^2 \rangle \geq 0$, $\forall x^1, x^2 \in \mathcal{K}$.

Proof: To establish that $F(x)$ is monotone, it is sufficient to show, according to Proposition 3.1, that the Jacobian of F, $\nabla F(x)$, is positive semi-definite over the feasible set $\mathcal{K}$.

Here $\nabla F(\cdot)$ is of the form:

$$\nabla F(\cdot) = \begin{pmatrix} -\nabla^2 U & C \\ -B^T & 0 \end{pmatrix}, \tag{6.44}$$

where

$$C = \begin{pmatrix} -\nabla_{xr} U \\ \\ -\nabla_{yr} U \end{pmatrix},$$

with B^T as in (6.33).

Note that

$$\begin{pmatrix} -\nabla^2 U & C \\ -B^T & 0 \end{pmatrix} = \begin{pmatrix} -\nabla^2 U & 2(-B+C) \\ -(-B^T + C^T) & 0 \end{pmatrix}$$

$$+ \begin{pmatrix} 0 & -(-2B+C) \\ (-2B^T + C) & 0 \end{pmatrix}. \tag{6.45}$$

Now let's consider the following matrix and show that it is positive semi-definite:

$$E = \begin{pmatrix} -\nabla^2 U & 2(-B+C) \\ -(-B^T + C^T) & 0_{I\times I} \end{pmatrix}_{(2JI+I)\times(2JI+I)}.$$

Consider all the principal minors of E: $|E_1|, |E_2|, \ldots, |E_{2JI}|, |E_{2JI+1}|, \ldots, |E_{2JI+I}|$. Since under the assumption that U is strictly concave, the Hessian $-\nabla^2 U$ is positive definite, it follows that $|E_1|, \ldots, |E_{2JI}|$ are all positive. Now consider $|E_{2JI+1}|$, which is of the form

$$|E_{2JI+1}| = \begin{pmatrix} -\nabla^2 U & z \\ w^T & 0 \end{pmatrix},$$

where, specifically, $w^T = -\frac{1}{2}z^T$.

Applying now Lemma 6.1, we obtain

$$|E_{2JI+1}| = (\frac{1}{2}z^T(-\nabla^2 U)^{-1}z)| - \nabla^2 U| \geq 0.$$

Hence, E_{2JI+1} is positive semi-definite. By induction, we can conclude that $|E_{2JI+2}| \geq 0, \ldots, |E_{2JI+I}| \geq 0$, which implies that E is positive semi-definite.

Clearly,

$$\tilde{E} = \begin{pmatrix} 0 & -(-2B+C) \\ (-2B^T + C) & 0 \end{pmatrix}$$

is positive semi-definite.

Since the sum of two positive semidefinite matrices is also positive semidefinite, we conclude that $\nabla F(\cdot) = E + \tilde{E}$ is positive semidefinite and, hence, monotone. □

Theorem 6.5

The function $F(x)$ defined in (6.21) is Lipschitz continuous (cf. Definition 3.6), under the assumption that the utility function U^j has bounded second order derivatives for all sectors j and for all $x \in \mathcal{K}$.

Proof: Note that

$$\|F(x^1) - F(x^2)\|^2 = \sum_{k=1}^{2JI+I} \left[F_k(x^1) - F_k(x^2)\right]^2$$

$$= \sum_{k=1}^{2JI+I} \left[\nabla F_k(\tilde{x}^k)^T \cdot (x^1 - x^2)\right]^2, \qquad (6.46)$$

since $F(x)$ is differentiable, and since the Mean Value Theorem can then be applied to each component $F_k(x)$ of $F(x)$ where $\tilde{x}^k = \Theta_k(x^1) + (1-\Theta_k)(1-x^2)$, for some Θ_k, such that $0 < \Theta_k < 1$.

Applying then the Schwarz inequality to the right-hand side expression in (6.46), one obtains

$$\sum_{k=1}^{2JI+I} \left[\nabla F_k(\tilde{x}^k)^T \cdot (x^1 - x^2)\right]^2 \leq \sum_{k=1}^{2JI+I} \|\nabla F_k(\tilde{x}^k)\|^2 \times \|x^1 - x^2\|^2. \quad (6.47)$$

But since, by assumption, one has that each U^j has bounded second order derivatives for all $x \in \mathcal{K}$, and since F_k; $k = 2JI+1, \ldots, 2JI$, are linear functions of x, the ∇F_k; $k = 1, \ldots, 2JI + I$, are bounded. Consequently, there exist constants $L_k > 0$; $k = 1, \ldots, 2JI + I$, such that $\|\nabla F_k(x)\| \leq L_k$; $k = 1, \ldots, 2JI + I$, $\forall x \in \mathcal{K}$, and, hence,

$$\sum_{k=1}^{2JI+I} \|\nabla F_k(\tilde{x}^k)\|^2 \times \|x^1 - x^2\|^2 \leq \sum_{k=1}^{2JI+I} L_k^2 \|x^1 - x^2\|^2 \leq L^2 \|x^1 - x^2\|^2,$$

where $L = \max_{1 \leq k \leq 2JI+I}\{L_k\}$. □

Both Theorems 6.4 and 6.5 will be utilized to establish convergence of the modified projection method in Section 6.4.

6.3 Network Optimization Reformulation

In this section we consider the financial equilibrium model in which the sectors possess utility functions of the form given by (6.4), whose variational inequality formulation of the governing equililibrium conditions is given by (6.12b). In particular, we will show that, in this special case, the equilibrium asset, liability, and price pattern can be obtained as the solution to a particular network optimization problem. This is accomplished through several steps: first, we establish that the equilibrium solution is the solution to an optimization problem; second, we prove that, in equilibrium, the market must clear for all instruments, and, third, we then utilize these results to construct the network over which the optimization takes place. Hence, the individual sector's optimization problems, which take place on the networks in Figure 6.1 merge, at equilibrium, into a complete network, which is illustrated in Figure 6.2.

Theorem 6.6

The variational inequality problem of finding $(X^*, Y^*, r^*) \in \mathcal{K}$ satisfying:

$$\sum_{j=1}^{J}\sum_{i=1}^{I}\left[-\frac{\partial u^j(X^{j*}, Y^{j*})}{\partial X_i^j} - r_i^*\right] \times \left[X_i^j - X_i^{j*}\right]$$

$$+\sum_{j=1}^{J}\sum_{i=1}^{I}\left[-\frac{\partial u^j(X^{j*}, Y^{j*})}{\partial Y_i^j} + r_i^*\right] \times \left[Y_i^j - Y_i^{j*}\right]$$

$$+\sum_{i=1}^{I}\sum_{j=1}^{J}\left[X_i^{j^*} - Y_i^{j^*}\right] \times [r_i - r_i^*] \geq 0, \quad \forall (X,Y,r) \in \mathcal{K}, \tag{6.48}$$

is equivalent to the problem:

$$\textit{Maximize} \sum_{j=1}^{J} u^j(X^j, Y^j) \tag{6.49}$$

subject to:

$$\sum_{j=1}^{J}(X_i^j - Y_i^j) \geq 0, \quad i = 1, \ldots, I, \tag{6.50}$$

and

$$(X^j, Y^j) \in \kappa^j, \quad j = 1, \ldots, J, \tag{6.51}$$

where $r_i^* \geq 0$ *corresponds to the Lagrange multiplier associated with the i-th constraint in (6.50).*

Proof: It follows from the standard theory of variational inequalities (see Chapter 3 and Bertsekas and Tsitsiklis (1989)) that the solution to the optimization problem (6.49)–(6.51) coincides with the solution to the variational inequality problem (6.48) since the utility functions u^j are assumed to be concave for each sector j and the feasible sets are closed and convex. □

Lemma 6.2

In equilibrium, the markets clear for each instrument, that is,

$$\sum_{j=1}^{J}(X_i^{j^*} - Y_i^{j^*}) = 0, \quad i = 1, \ldots, I, \tag{6.52}$$

and the prices r_i^* *are strictly positive, for* $i = 1, \ldots, I$.

Proof: One can easily observe that from (6.2a) and (6.2b) that the following expression must hold:

$$\sum_{i=1}^{I}\sum_{j=1}^{J}(X_i^{j^*} - Y_i^{j^*}) = 0. \tag{6.53}$$

If we assume now that for some instrument k we have, that, in equilibrium,

$$\sum_{j=1}^{J}(X_k^{j^*} - Y_k^{j^*}) > 0, \tag{6.54}$$

then, according to (6.53), this would imply that for some other instrument l, we would then have to have that:

$$\sum_{j=1}^{J}(X_l^{j^*} - Y_l^{j^*}) < 0, \tag{6.55}$$

which is in contradiction to equilibrium condition (6.11) being satisfied for every instrument price. Hence, we must have that

$$\sum_{j=1}^{J}(X_i^{j*} - Y_i^{j*}) = 0, \tag{6.56}$$

for every instrument i; $i = 1, \ldots, I$.

Furthermore, from Lagrange multiplier theory, in view of (6.50), the Lagrange multipliers r_i^* must be positive for all instruments i (see Appendix A). □

The subsequent corollary follows immediately from Theorem 6.6 and Lemma 6.2.

Corollary 6.2

The solution to the optimization problem:

$$\text{Maximize} \sum_{j=1}^{J} u^j(X^j, Y^j) \tag{6.57}$$

subject to:

$$\sum_{j=1}^{J}(X_i^j - Y_i^j) = 0, \quad i = 1, \ldots, I \tag{6.58}$$

$$(X^j, Y^j) \in \kappa^j, \quad j = 1, \ldots, J, \tag{6.59}$$

with Lagrange multiplier r_i^* associated with the i-th constraint in (6.58) coincides with the solution to the optimization problem (6.49)–(6.51). Moreover, this solution is an equilibrium solution, that is, it satisfies variational inequality problem (6.12b).

The network structure of the solution to the optimization problem (6.57), subject to (6.58)–(6.59), is presented in Figure 6.2. We now elaborate upon this network structure. The uppermost J nodes and the lowermost J nodes correspond to the sectors. There are also I intermediate nodes. From each uppermost node j there are I arcs emanating, one to each intermediate node. This set of arcs corresponds to the assets of the sectors with the flow on arc (j, i) equal to X_i^j. The second set of arcs, originating in the intermediate nodes and terminating in the lowermost nodes, corresponds to the liabilities of the sectors with the flow on such an arc (i, j) being equal to Y_i^j.

In addition, the supplies at the uppermost nodes $j; j = 1, \ldots, J$, are equal to $S_1, \ldots, S_J$, respectively, with the demands at the lowermost nodes $j; j = 1, \ldots, J$ equal to $S_1, \ldots, S_J$, respectively.

The costs on the arcs, in turn, correspond to the appropriate terms in the objective function (6.57).

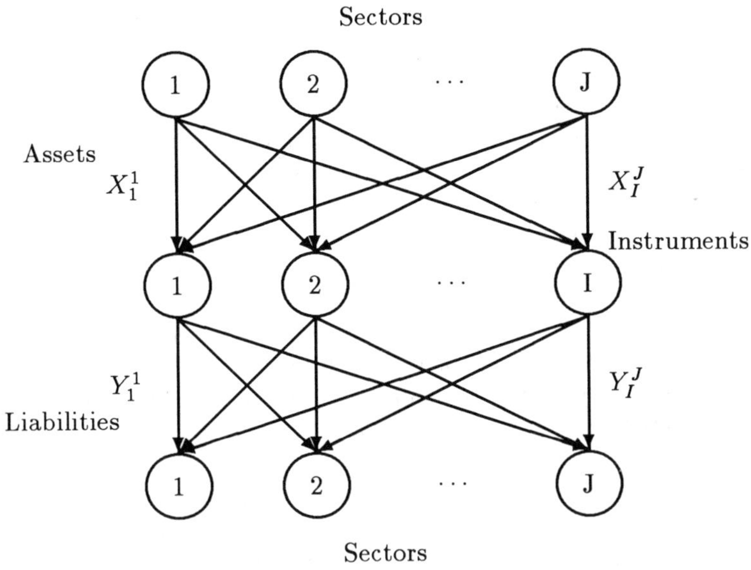

Fig. 6.2. The network structure at equilibrium

It is straightforward to then verify that the network in Figure 6.2 satisfies the constraints (6.58) since these are just the basic conservation of flow equations for the intermediate, that is, transshipment, nodes of the network.

We now discuss further the network optimization reformulation of the financial equilibrium in the case of utility functions of the form (6.4). Objective function (6.57) has the following interpretation: it says that, in the economy, at equilibrium, the total utility over all sectors is maximized, with the total utility being the sum of the (price-independent) parts of the utility function for each sector. This objective is subject to the budget constraints of the sectors and the market clearing conditions. The instrument prices, in turn, correspond to Lagrange multipliers associated with the market clearing constraints.

It is also worth highlighting the similarities between the network in Figure 6.2 and the bipartite network in Figure 5.3. Note that the two networks are identical except for an additional layer of intermediate nodes in the network in Figure 6.2. Finally, we note that the network in Figure 6.2 is a subset of the network in Figure 5.7 in which the primary financial market nodes, the financial intermediary nodes, and the final financial market nodes in Figure 5.7 are collapsed into the instrument nodes in Figure 6.2. Note, also, that in the financial model developed here the sector volumes are assumed to be known and fixed, whereas in the network in Figure 5.7, discussed in Applications 5.1 and 5.3, the supplies are assumed to be elastic whereas the demands are first assumed to be fixed (in Application 5.1) and then to be elastic (in Application 5.3).

The question remains as to how general is the network in Figure 6.2 in capturing the structure of the single country economy in equilibrium? Note that both Theorems 6.6 and Corollary 6.2 assumed that the utility functions for each sector had a special form. Hence, in this special case, one obtained not only an optimization reformulation of variational inequality (6.12b), but, a *network* optimization problem! If one considers now utility functions that are the most general discussed in this chapter, that is, those given by $U^j(X^j, Y^j, r)$ for each sector j, then one can no longer obtain an optimization reformulation of the equilibrium conditions. In other words, one can not reformulate variational inequality (6.12a) as an optimization problem, much less as a network optimization problem.

Nevertheless, Lemma 6.2 holds true even in the case of the general utility function financial equilibrium model, governed by variational inequality (6.12a), since it makes use only of the feasible sets of the sectors and the economic system conditions and these are identical for all the models discussed thus far in this chapter. Consequently, the network in Figure 6.2 also provides a snapshot of the economy in equilibrium in the case of the more general utility functions. However, we now have a network equilibrium problem, and no longer a network optimization problem. Consequently, although the latter is amenable to solution via network optimization algorithms, the former one is not.

Finally, we raise the following question: how applicable are the results presented thus far for financial equilibrium models in which each sector now not only has a general utility function but the feasible set of each sector contains *additional* constraints to those given by (6.2) and (6.3)? Even in this "most" general case, the network structure at equilibrium depicted in Figure 6.2 still must hold. Moreover, the variational inequality formulation (6.12a) is still relevant, with the feasible set $\mathcal{K}$ (assumed to be closed and convex) redefined accordingly to capture the additional constraints. Theorems 6.3, 6.4, and 6.5 hold true in this most general case, as well. Note that if one were to introduce intermediate markets, as in Figure 5.7, then one would have to derive additional equilibrium conditions, but the basic structure would still hold true.

In the next section we discuss the computation of financial equilibria. In particular, we present the modified projection algorithm for the computation of solutions to all of the above models. We also present the primal-dual method for the solution of the model in the case of utility functions (6.4) as a network optimization problem.

6.4 Computation of Financial Equilibria

In this section we discuss algorithms for the computation of solutions to the financial equilibrium problems discussed in the preceding sections of this chapter.

In Section 6.4.1, we present the modified projection method which can be applied for the solution of variational inequality (6.12a) (and (6.12b), of course). In Section 6.4.2, we present the primal-dual algorithm for the solution of the network optimization problem (6.57), subject to constraints (6.58) and (6.59). This optimization algorithm is applicable to the computation of the financial equilibrium problem with utility functions of the special form given by (6.4). Consequently, it can also be applied to compute the equilibrium asset, liability, and price pattern for the quadratic model with variational inequality (6.29). In particular, we will show how the primal-dual algorithm exploits the special network structure of the network at equilibrium depicted in Figure 6.2.

6.4.1 The Modified Projection Method

In this subsection we present an algorithm for the solution of variational inequality (6.12a), governing the single country, multi-sector, multi-instrument, financial equilibrium model. The algorithm that we propose for the computation of the equilibrium patterns is the modified projection method of Korpelevich (1977). The advantage of this method is that the original problem can be decomposed into a series of smaller and simpler subproblems, as described in Section 3.3.1. We will now illustrate the application of the modified projection method for the case of general utility functions.

Recall from Section 3.3.1 (cf. (3.46) and (3.47)), that the modified projection method, can be expressed as:

Step 0: Initialization

Select $x^0 \in \mathcal{K}$. Let $\tau := 0$ and let γ be a scalar such that $0 < \gamma < \frac{1}{L}$, where L is the Lipschitz constant (see (3.34)).

Step 1: Computation

Compute $\bar{x}^\tau$ by solving the variational inequality subproblem:

$$\left[\bar{x}^\tau + \gamma F(x^\tau)^T - x^\tau\right]^T \cdot [x - \bar{x}^\tau] \geq 0, \quad \forall x \in \mathcal{K}. \tag{6.60}$$

Step 2: Adaptation

Compute $x^{\tau+1}$ by solving the variational inequality subproblem:

$$\left[x^{\tau+1} + \gamma F(\bar{x}^\tau)^T - x^\tau\right]^T \cdot \left[x - x^{\tau+1}\right] \geq 0, \quad \forall x \in \mathcal{K}. \tag{6.61}$$

Step 3: Convergence Verification

If $\max |x_b^{\tau+1} - x_b^{\tau}| \leq \epsilon$, for all b, with $\epsilon > 0$, a prespecified tolerance, then stop; else, set $\tau := \tau + 1$, and go to Step 1.

For completeness, we now present the modified projection algorithm in which the function $F(x)$ is in expanded form for our specific model.

The Modified Projection Method

Step 0: Initialization

Set $(X^0, Y^0, r^0) \in \mathcal{K}$. Let $\tau := 0$ and set γ so that $0 < \gamma < \frac{1}{L}$.

Step 1: Computation

Compute $(\bar{X}^\tau, \bar{Y}^\tau, \bar{r}^\tau) \in \mathcal{K}$ by solving the variational inequality subproblem:

$$\sum_{j=1}^{J}\sum_{i=1}^{I}\left[\bar{X}_i^{j^\tau} + \gamma\left(-\frac{\partial U^j(X^{j^\tau}, Y^{j^\tau}, r^\tau)}{\partial X_i^j}\right) - X_i^{j^\tau}\right] \times \left[X_i^j - \bar{X}_i^{j^\tau}\right]$$

$$+\sum_{j=1}^{J}\sum_{i=1}^{I}\left[\bar{Y}_i^{j^\tau} + \gamma\left(-\frac{\partial U^j(X^{j^\tau}, Y^{j^\tau}, r^\tau)}{\partial Y_i^j}\right) - Y_i^{j^\tau}\right] \times \left[Y_i^j - \bar{Y}_i^{j^\tau}\right]$$

$$+\sum_{i=1}^{I}\left[\bar{r}_i^\tau + \gamma\left[\sum_{j=1}^{J}\left(X_i^{j^\tau} - Y_i^{j^\tau}\right)\right] - r_i^\tau\right] \times \left[r_i - \bar{r}_i^\tau\right], \quad \forall (X, Y, r) \in \mathcal{K}. \tag{6.62}$$

Step 2: Adaptation

Compute $(X^{\tau+1}, Y^{\tau+1}, r^{\tau+1}) \in \mathcal{K}$ by solving the variational inequality subproblem:

$$\sum_{j=1}^{J}\sum_{i=1}^{I}\left[X_i^{j^{\tau+1}} + \gamma\left(-\frac{\partial U^j(\bar{X}^{j^\tau}, \bar{Y}^{j^\tau}, \bar{r}^\tau)}{\partial X_i^j}\right) - X_i^{j^\tau}\right] \times \left[X_i^j - X_i^{j^{\tau+1}}\right]$$

$$+\sum_{j=1}^{J}\sum_{i=1}^{I}\left[Y_i^{j^{\tau+1}} + \gamma\left(-\frac{\partial U^j(\bar{X}^{j^\tau}, \bar{Y}^{j^\tau}, \bar{r}^\tau)}{\partial Y_i^j}\right) - Y_i^{j^\tau}\right] \times \left[Y_i^j - Y_i^{j^{\tau+1}}\right]$$

$$\sum_{i=1}^{I}\left[r_i^{\tau+1} + \gamma\left[\sum_{j=1}^{J}\left(\bar{X}_i^{j^\tau} - \bar{Y}_i^{j^\tau}\right)\right] - r_i^\tau\right] \times \left[r_i - r_i^{\tau+1}\right], \quad \forall (X, Y, r) \in \mathcal{K}. \tag{6.63}$$

Step 3: Convergence Verification:

If $\max_{i,j} |X_i^{j^{\tau+1}} - X_i^{j^{\tau}}| \leq \epsilon$; $\max_{i,j} |Y_i^{j^{\tau+1}} - Y_i^{j^{\tau}}| \leq \epsilon$; $\max_i |r_i^{\tau+1} - r_i^{\tau}| \leq \epsilon$, for all $i; i = 1, \ldots, I$, and $j; j = 1, \ldots, J$, with $\epsilon > 0$, a prespecified tolerance, then stop; else, set $\tau := \tau + 1$, and go to Step 1.

In the following theorem we present the assumptions under which the modified projection algorithm is guaranteed to converge to a financial equilibrium.

Theorem 6.7

The modified projection algorithm is guaranteed to converge to an equilibrium asset, liability, and price pattern, satisfying variational inequality (6.12), provided that a solution exists.

Proof: Convergence of the algorithm follows (cf. Korpelevich (1977)), under the assumptions that $F(x)$ is monotone and Lipschitz continuous. The conclusion follows from Theorems 6.4 and 6.5, under the assumptions that the utility functions of the sectors are strictly concave and have bounded second order derivatives over the feasible set. □

Furthermore, as established in Nagurney, Dong and Hughes (1992), if $\frac{1}{\sqrt{2}L} < \gamma < \frac{1}{L}$, then the convergence is guaranteed at the rate of a geometric progression with ratio $(2\gamma^2 L^2 - 1)$.

We now provide an interpretation of the modified projection method as an adjustment process. The interpretation of the algorithm as an adjustment process was given by Nagurney (1993), and it naturally follows the discussion of Section 2.3. In particular, at an iteration, the sectors in the economy receive all the price information on every instrument from the previous iteration. They then allocate their capital according to their preferences. The market reacts on the decisions of the sectors and derives new instrument prices. The sectors then improve upon their positions through the adaptation step, whereas the market also adjusts during the adaptation step. This process continues until noone can improve upon his position, and the equilibrium is reached, that is, variational inequality (6.12a) is satisfied with the computed asset, liability, and price pattern.

The variational inequality subproblems (6.62) and (6.63), in turn, are equivalent to the solution of separable quadratic programming problems. In particular, in view of the feasible set $\mathcal{K}$, given by $\mathcal{K} \equiv \kappa \times R^I_+$, with κ also being a Cartesian product, with κ^j given by (6.7), the subproblems take place on networks of special structure, each of which can be solved simultaneously and explicitly and in closed form. In particular, the network subproblems, in asset variables, in liability variables, and in price variables, are as drawn in Figure 6.3. Note that each sector's asset subproblem at an iteration, as well as his liability subproblem at an iteration has the special network structure depicted in Figure 5.4. Hence, each of the asset and liability subproblems can

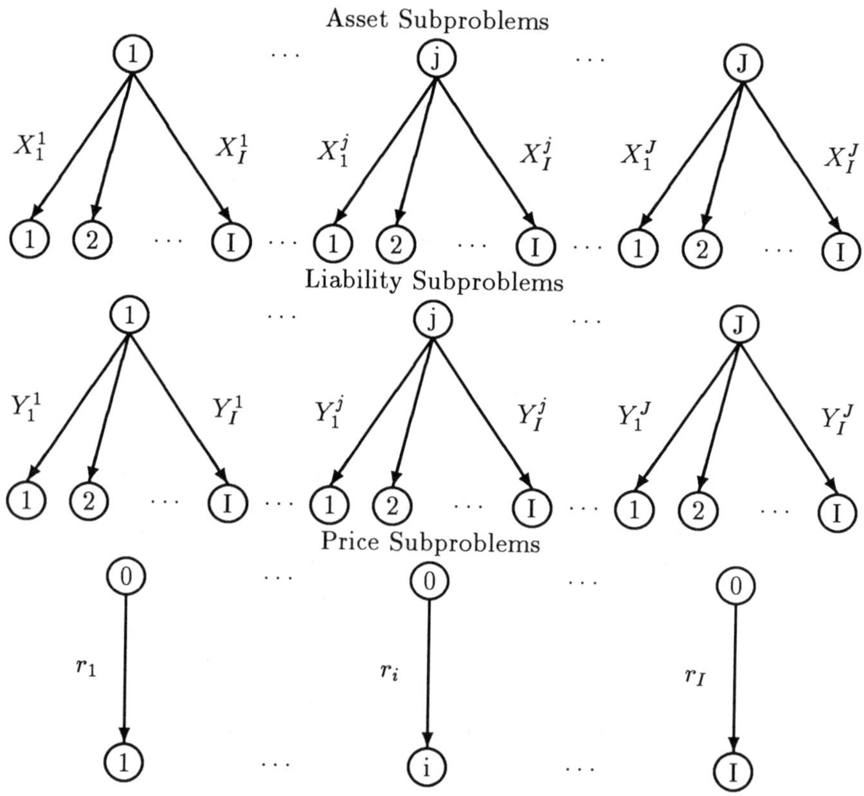

Fig. 6.3. Financial network subproblems induced by the modified projection method

be solved using exact equilibration as given in Section 5.2.3. Finally, each price subproblem can be solved explicitly and in closed form using a simple formula.

Specifically, the financial optimization problem in the computation step (6.62), as well as, the adaptation step (6.63), are equivalent to quadratic programming problems, of the form:

$$\text{Minimize}_{x \in \kappa \times R^I_+} \; x^T x + h^T x,$$

where $h \in R^{2JI+I}$ consists of the fixed linear terms in (6.62) (and (6.63)).

In view of the discussion above, we see that the modified projection method decomposes the large-scale variational inequality problem (6.12a) into a series of network optimization problems, which are separable quadratic programming problems on networks with very simple structure (cf. Figure 6.3). Each of these network subproblems of special structure can then be solved, at an iteration, simultaneously, and exactly in closed form using the exact equilibration algorithm.

We now present a small and simple numerical example for illustrative purposes.

Example 6.1: A Small Numerical Example

We now provide a small numerical example to illustrate the behavior of the model as well as the performance of the modified projection method for the solution of the general financial equilibrium problems. We utilize the exact equilibration algorithm (cf. Section 5.2.3) for solving the embedded asset and liability network subproblems at each iteration, along with an explicit formula, for the determination of the prices.

We assume that there are two sectors in the economy and three financial instruments. Here we assume that the "size" of each sector is given by $S^1 = 1$ and $S^2 = 2$. The variance–covariance matrices of the two sectors are:

$$Q^1 = \begin{pmatrix} 1 & .25 & .3 & 0 & 0 & 0 \\ .25 & 1 & .1 & 0 & 0 & 0 \\ .3 & 1 & 1 & 0 & 0 & 0 \\ 0 & 0 & 0 & 1 & .2 & .3 \\ 0 & 0 & 0 & .2 & 1 & .5 \\ 0 & 0 & 0 & .3 & .5 & 1 \end{pmatrix}$$

and

$$Q^2 = \begin{pmatrix} 1 & 0 & .3 & 0 & 0 & 0 \\ 0 & 1 & .2 & 0 & 0 & 0 \\ .3 & .2 & 1 & 0 & 0 & 0 \\ 0 & 0 & 0 & 1 & .5 & 0 \\ 0 & 0 & 0 & .5 & 1 & .2 \\ 0 & 0 & 0 & 0 & .2 & 1 \end{pmatrix}.$$

The modified projection method was coded in FORTRAN and the numerical runs were done on an IBM SP2. The variables were initialized as follows: $r_i^0 = 1$, for all i, with the financial volume S^j equally distributed among all the assets and among all the liabilities for each sector j. The γ parameter was set to 0.35. The convergence tolerance ε was set to 10^{-3}.

The numerical results for this example were:

Equilibrium Prices:

$$r_1^* = .34039, \quad r_2^* = .23805, \quad r_3^* = .42156,$$

Equilibrium Asset Holdings:

$$X_1^{1*} = .27899, \quad X_2^{1*} = .31803, \quad X_3^{1*} = .40298,$$

$$X_1^{2*} = .79662, \quad X_2^{2*} = .60904, \quad X_3^{2*} = .59434,$$

Equilibrium Liability Holdings:

$$Y_1^{1*} = .37081, \quad Y_2^{1*} = .43993, \quad Y_3^{1*} = .18927,$$

$$Y_1^{2*} = .70579, \quad Y_2^{2*} = .48693, \quad Y_3^{2*} = .80729.$$

The modified projection method converged in 16 iterations and in a negligible amount of CPU time, not including input/output time. The above results show that the algorithm yielded optimal portfolios that were feasible. Moreover, cf. equilibrium conditions (6.11), the market cleared for each instrument, since the price of each instrument was positive. That this would hold true was established in Lemma 6.2.

6.4.2 The Primal-Dual Method

In this section we discuss the application of the primal-dual method, discussed in Section 5.2.4, for the solution of the network optimization reformulation of financial equilibrium, in the case of utility functions of the special form (6.4).

It is easy to see that the network optimization problem given by (6.57), subject to (6.58) and (6.59), over the network depicted in Figure 6.2, is precisely of the form of the separable nonlinear optimization problem discussed in Section 5.1.4, given by (5.13), subject to (5.14) and (5.15). Indeed, each sector's objective function is separable in terms of his asset and liability variables. Moreover, cf (6.59), each sector also has his particular feasible set κ^j, which is of the form (5.15). Finally, the market clearing constraints given by (6.58), can be viewed as the "complicating" constraints, coinciding with (5.14).

We first state the primal-dual decomposition method of Section 5.2.4 for the financial network optimization problem. We then discuss the decomposition method in terms of an adjustment process.

In particular, the primal-dual decomposition algorithm applied to compute the optimal solution on a network of the structure given in Figure 6.2 has the following intuitive foundation: it splits the uppermost nodes with the asset links, as well as, the lowermost nodes with the liability links, from the intermediate nodes. It then solves a modified problem (which prices out this mechanism) over a simpler feasible set on networks with special structure. The Lagrange multipliers associated with the complicating constraints serve as prices to equilibrate the supply and demand for the instruments, that is, they measure how far from the equilibrium (and from the network structure in Figure 6.2) we are at an iteration. A depiction of this process is given in Figure 6.4

The Primal-Dual Decomposition Method

Step 0: Initialization

Select an initial Lagrange multiplier vector $\lambda^0 \in R^I_+$. Set $\tau := 0$.

Step 1: Solve the Lagrangian Problem

Solve the following Lagrangian problem for each sector j; $j = 1, \ldots, J$:

$$\text{Minimize} \quad -\tilde{u}^j(X^j, Y^j, \lambda^\tau) = -u^j(X^j, Y^j) - \sum_{i=1}^{I} \lambda_i^\tau \sum_{j=1}^{J} (X_i^j - Y_i^j), \quad (6.64)$$

subject to:

$$(X^j, Y^j) \in \kappa^j. \quad (6.65)$$

Step 2: Search Direction and Step Size Determination

Define a direction of search, d^τ, according to: For $i = 1, \ldots, I$:

$$d_i^\tau = \begin{cases} -\sum_{i=1}^{I} \sum_{j=1}^{J} (X_i^j(\lambda^\tau) - Y_i^j(\lambda^\tau)), & \text{if} \quad \lambda_i^\tau = 0 \\ \max\{0, -\sum_{i=1}^{I} \sum_{j=1}^{J} (X_i^j(\lambda^\tau) - Y_i^j(\lambda^\tau))\}, & \text{if} \quad \lambda_i^\tau = 0. \end{cases} \quad (6.66)$$

Select a new vector $\lambda^{\tau+1}$ according to:

$$\lambda^{\tau+1} = \lambda^\tau + \alpha_\tau d^\tau. \quad (6.67)$$

The step size α_τ should be selected according to:

$$\sum_{j=1}^{J} -\tilde{u}^j(X^j(\lambda^{\tau+1}), Y^j(\lambda^{\tau+1}), \lambda^{\tau+1}) > \sum_{j=1}^{J} -\tilde{u}^j(X^j(\lambda^\tau), Y^j(\lambda^\tau), \lambda^\tau). \quad (6.68)$$

Step 3: Convergence Verification

If $\max_{j,i} |X_i^{j^{\tau+1}} - X_i^{j^\tau}| \leq \epsilon$; $\max_{j,i} |Y_i^{j^{\tau+1}} - Y_i^{j^\tau}| \leq \epsilon$; and $\max_i |\lambda_i^{\tau+1} - \lambda_i^\tau| \leq \epsilon$, then stop; else, set $\tau := \tau + 1$, and go to Step 1.

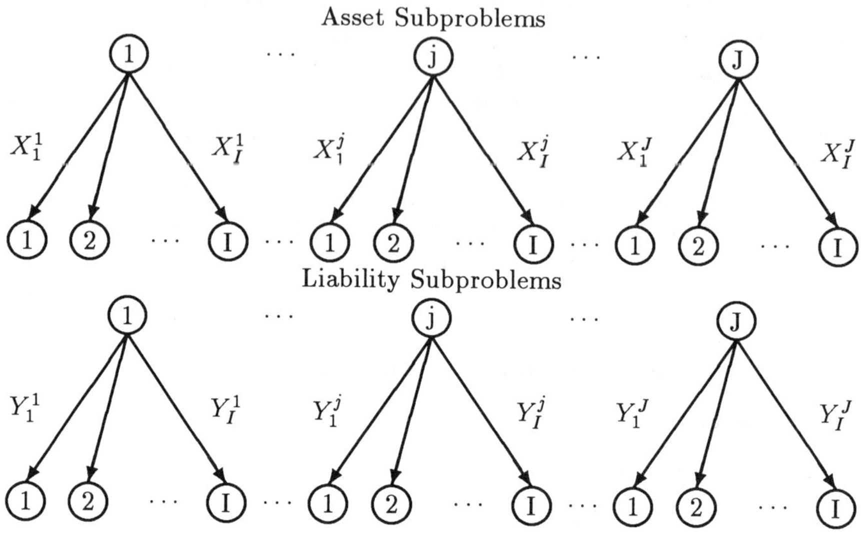

Fig. 6.4. Financial network subproblems induced by the primal-dual method

We now give an interpretation of the primal-dual method as an adjustment process. First, we note that the Lagrange multiplier vector λ coincides with the price vector r. In Step 1, each sector seeks to maximize that part of his utility function which is only a function of his asset and liability holdings, modified by the total return of all the portfolios. The prices then are modified according to the laws of supply and demand.

In view of the feasible set (6.59) and the objective function (6.57), the optimality conditions (at an iteration τ) for each subproblem facing each sector in Step 1, are precisely of the form (6.10) (with the gradients being taken of the utility functions (6.4).

Note that in the case that the utility functions are quadratic, with objective function given by (6.23), the subproblems in the asset and liability variables in Step 1, are quadratic (nonseparable) programming problems, again on networks of the simple structure depicted in Figure 5.4.

We now provide an extended equilibration algorithm that can be used to solve the symmetric, nonseparable quadratic programming problem on each network in Figure 6.4. This algorithm is also due to Dafermos and Sparrow (1969). Specifically, it can be used to solve each sector's subproblem in Step 1 of the primal-dual method, if the utility functions are quadratic, as discussed in Section 6.1.1. We adapt the algorithm for the case of a single O/D pair, since that is what is needed here. This algorithm is also a path equilibration algorithm and as the Single O/D Pair Equilibration Algorithm of Section

5.4.2 (for separable, quadratic functions), it selects the most expensive used path and the cheapest path connecting the O/D pair and redistributes the flow so that the value of the objective function to be minimized decreases. The algorithm may also be used to solve the Markowitz model.

For the sake of generality, the problem that the extended equilibration algorithm solves can be stated as (refer to Sections 5.4.2 and 5.2.3):

$$\text{Minimize} \quad \sum_{i=1}^{n}\sum_{j=1}^{n}\frac{1}{2}g_{ij}x_ix_j + \sum_{i=1}^{n}c_ix_i \tag{6.69}$$

subject to:

$$\sum_{i=1}^{n} x_i = d \tag{6.70}$$

$$x_i \geq 0, \quad i = 1, \ldots, n. \tag{6.71}$$

For simplicity of exposition, define the "cost" on a link i, denoted by C_i, which corresponds to the cost on path i (and which is the marginal cost on a link), since paths in this problem consist of a single link each, as

$$C_i = \sum_{j=1}^{n} g_{ij}x_j + c_i. \tag{6.72}$$

Extended Equilibration Algorithm

Single O/D Pair Equilibration

Step 0: Initialization

Select x^0, satisfying the nonnegativity and demand constraint above. Set $k := 1$.

Step 1: Selection and Convergence Verification

Determine

$$r = \{i | \max_i C_i \quad \text{and} \quad x_i > 0\}$$

$$q = \{i | \min_i C_i\}.$$

If $|C_r - C_q| \leq \epsilon$, with $\epsilon > 0$, a predetermined tolerance, then stop; else, go to Step 2.

Computation

Compute

$$\Delta' = \frac{C_r - C_q}{g_{rr} + g_{qq} - 2g_{qr}} \tag{6.73}$$

$$\Delta = \min\{\Delta', x_r\}. \tag{6.74}$$

Set

$$x_r^k = x_r^{k-1} - \Delta$$

$$x_q^k = x_q^{k-1} + \Delta$$

$$x_i^k = x_i^{k-1}, \quad \forall i \neq q \cup r.$$

Set $k := k + 1$, and go to Step 1.

In the case that a tie exists for the selection of q and/or r, then any such selection is appropriate.

We now present a small example to which we apply this algorithm.

Example 6.2

We consider an example consisting of only two variables. In this case, the extended equilibration algorithm should converge in a single iteration. We assume that the data (cf. (6.69) and (6.70)) is as follows:

$$g_{11} = 2, \quad g_{12} = 1, \quad g_{21} = 1, \quad g_{22} = 2$$

and

$$c_1 = 5, \quad c_2 = 5$$

with $d = 1$. Hence, we can write down (cf. (6.72)) the expressions for the C_i:

$$C_1 = 2x_1 + x_2 + 5, \quad C_2 = x_1 + 2x_2 + 5.$$

Assume that the initial pattern is:

$$x_1^0 = 1, \quad x_2^0 = 0,$$

which gives us the costs:

$$C_1 = 7, \quad C_2 = 6.$$

Clearly, $r = 1$ and $q = 2$. An application of the formula (6.73), hence, yields:

$$\Delta' = \frac{7-6}{2+2-2} = \frac{1}{2},$$

and, hence, (cf. (6.74)) we have that $\Delta = \frac{1}{2}$ so the updated variables are:

$$x_1^1 = \frac{1}{2}, \quad x_2^1 = \frac{1}{2},$$

with

$$C_1 = C_2 = 6\frac{1}{2}.$$

Since these costs are "equilibrated," we are done. The value of the objective function in (6.69) with this pattern is: 5.75.

We now apply the primal-dual method, embedded with the extended equilibration algorithm, to Example 6.1. The algorithm was coded in FORTRAN, and the initialization was the same as for the modified projection method. We selected the step size $a_\tau = .1$ for all τ. The primal-dual method converged in 36 iterations and in a negligible amount of CPU time.

It is worth noting that both the modified projection method and the primal-dual method decompose what are large-scale problems in practice into smaller and simpler subproblems. These subproblems, in turn, are amenable to solution on parallel architectures.

6.5 Sources and Notes

In this chapter we developed and studied, both qualitatively and computationally, several fundamental financial eqilibrium models, and identified their network structure. The models in this chapter were static. The methodologies utilized herein included variational inequality theory and network theory. The chapter provided linkages to the methodological foundation chapters 3 and 5. This chapter laid the groundwork for the subsequent chapters since it is the most basic. Hence, for completeness, the theory was accompanied by proofs.

Section 6.1

The financial equilibrium model with general utility functions of the form (6.4) was developed and studied by Nagurney (1994). Nagurney and Dong (1996) later utilized variational inequality theory for the formulation, analysis, and computation of financial equilibrium problems with the general utility functions, but in the case of imperfect markets.

The model with quadratic utility functions is due to Nagurney, Dong, and Hughes (1992), who introduced finite-dimensional variational inequality theory to this application domain. We also refer the reader to Nagurney (1993), and Dong (1994) for a more detailed analysis of this model and for additional numerical results.

Section 6.2

The qualitative properties of the models were established by Nagurney, Dong, and Hughes (1992) and Nagurney and Dong (1996). They are extracted from these references.

Section 6.3

The network reformulation of financial equilibrium, in the special case of a class of utility functions, was first reported by Nagurney and Siokos (1996) for an international financial equilibrium model with multiple sectors and multiple instruments. The model herein, being a single country one, is a special case of that one. Hence, the theoretical results in this section are primarily drawn and adapted from there. Here, however, we identify this network structure as being the foundation of any such financial equilibrium problem with budget constraints (as well as additional constraints).

Section 6.4

The application of the modified projection method for the computation of financial equilibrium models was first suggested by Nagurney, Dong, and Hughes (1992), in the case of the quadratic model. Here we have the statement and proof of convergence which also applies to the case of general utility functions (as well as closed and convex feasible sets).

The statement and application of the primal-dual method for the computation of financial equilibria, in the case of certain utility functions, is reported here for the first time. Here we, in particular, emphasize the simplicity of the induced network subproblems. We also, for completeness, provide an extended equilibration algorithm (single O/D pair case), adapted from Dafermos and Sparrow (1969) for the solution of the embedded nonseparable quadratic programming problems on networks with special structure.

References

Bertsekas, D. P., and Tsitsiklis, J. N., **Parallel and Distributed Computation - Numerical Methods**, Prentice-Hall, Inc., Englewood Cliffs, New Jersey, 1989.

Dafermos, S. C., and Sparrow, F. T., "The Traffic Assignment Problem for a General Network," *Journal of Research of the National Bureau of Standards* **73B** (1969) 91-118.

Dong, J., "Formulation and Computation of General Financial Equilibrium: A Variational Inequality Approach," Ph.D. Dissertation, University of Massachusetts, Amherst, Massachusetts, 1994.

Gonedes, N. J., "Capital Market Equilibrium for a Class of Heterogeneous Expectations in a Two-Parameter World," *Journal of Finance* **31** (1976) 1-15.

Kinderlehrer, D., and G. Stampacchia, G., **An Introduction to Variational Inequalities and Their Applications**, Academic Press, Inc., New York, New York, 1980.

Korpelevich, G. M., "The Extragradient Method for Finding Saddle Points and other Problems," *Matecon* **13** (1977) 747-756.

Lintner, J., "The Valuation of Risk Assets and the Selection of Risky Investments in Stock Portfolios and Capital Budgets," *Review of Economic Studies* **47** (1965) 13-37.

Markowitz, H. M., **Portfolio Selection: Efficient Diversification of Investments**, John Wiley & Sons, New York, New York, 1959.

Mossin, J., "Equilibrium in a Capital Asset Market," *Econometrica* **34** (1966) 768-783.

Nagurney, A., **Network Economics: A Variational Inequality Approach**, Kluwer Academic Publishers, Boston, Massachusetts, 1993.

Nagurney, A., "Variational Inequalities in the Analysis and Computation of Multi-Sector, Multi-Instrument Financial Equilibria," *Journal of Economic Dynamics and Control* **18** (1994) 161-184.

Nagurney, A., and Dong, J., "General Financial Equilibrium Modeling with Policy Interventions and Transaction Costs," *Computational Economics* **9** (1996) 3-17.

Nagurney, A., Dong, J., and Hughes, M., "Formulation and Computation of General Financial Equilibrium," *Optimization* **26** (1992) 339-354.

Nagurney, A., and Siokos, S., "Dynamics of International Financial Networks: Modeling, Stability Analysis, and Computation," to appear in **Networks and Knowledge in a Dynamic Economy**, M. Beckmann, B. Johansson, F. Snickars, and R. Thord, editors, Springer-Verlag, Berlin, Germany, 1996.

Sharpe, W. F., "Capital Asset Prices: A Theory of Market Equilibrium under Conditions of Risk," *Journal of Finance* **19** (1964) 425-443.

7 Static Single Country Hedging Models

In this chapter we develop extensions of the models in Chapter 6 by allowing the inclusion of hedged financial instruments in addition to the unhedged instruments. We recall that hedging refers to any type of strategy whose primary goal is to offset any investment risk. A perfect hedge reflects the elimination of the possibility of any gains or losses. Obviously, it is difficult, if not impossible, to accomplish perfect hedging.

The goal of a hedger is to reduce or to eliminate the risk associated with the price level of a financial instrument at the time of delivery, so that he will be able to rely on profitability and price calculations with higher certainty.

Clearly, in times of high price volatility, a greater financial exposure can have dramatic results in the financial performance of a firm or of an individual investor, and, therefore, hedging strategies are needed.

The models presented in this chapter focus on hedging interest rate exposure, which is mainly due to floating interest rates. Additional types of financial exposure (e.g., currency exposure), as well as, ways of hedging them will be discussed in a more detailed fashion subsequently in Part IV of this book. For example, uncertainty as to the future price levels can be reflected with both potential gains or losses, and, therefore, full hedging positions do not only eliminate the possibility for dramatic losses but they also incorporate significant opportunity costs. In particular, if an investor has his assets associated with a fixed rate of return, and his liabilities tied to a floating rate, then if at the end of a specific time period the floating rate is larger (smaller) than the fixed, then the investor will experience some type of losses (gains). Similarly, if the liabilities of an investor are based on a fixed rate of return and his assets depend on the floating rate, then if for a particular time-frame the floating rate of return is higher (lower) than the fixed rate of return, the investor will be subject to some type of gains (losses).

The liberalization of interest rate policies in the United States in the

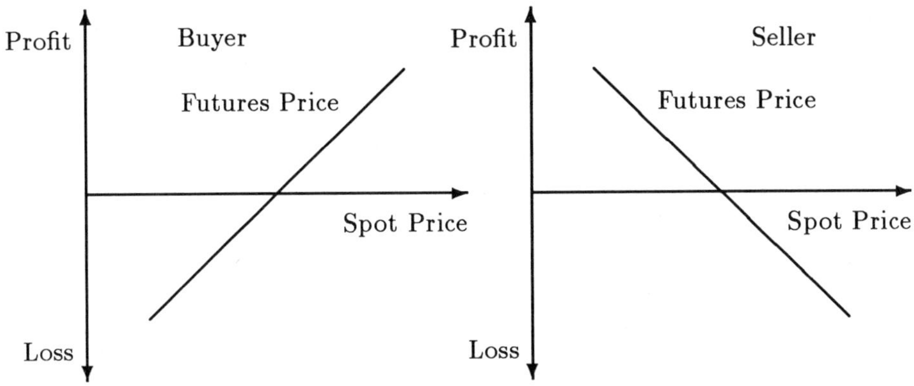

Fig. 7.1. Profits and losses for a futures contract

1970's, led to the development of new financial products that could provide some risk protection. The majority of these financial products were simple adaptations of existing products from the markets for raw materials, where hedging strategies had existed for many years.

The most important and commonly used financial products for hedging financial risk are financial *futures* and *options*. A futures contract is a firm commitment to deliver or receive a specific quantity of a financial instrument (known as an *underlying instrument*) at a predetermined price and at a point in time. On the other hand, an option is the *right*, but not the obligation, to purchase or sell an instrument, at a specified price, before or at a specific point in time.

The first interest rate futures contract appeared at the Chicago Board of Trade (CBOT) in 1975, and it was a futures certificate by the Government National Mortgage Association (GNMA). In the following years new futures markets, along with a variety of products, were introduced worldwide. First, the London International Financial Futures Exchange (LIFFE) was established in 1982, to be followed by financial markets in Frankfurt (DTB), Singapore (SIMEX), and Tokyo (TSE) (see Andersen (1993)).

Investors are interested in financial futures because they can eliminate or reduce the uncertainty as to the price of an instrument at the time of delivery. The price expectations of investors are directly related to their actions on the futures market. More precisely, investors can hedge against increasing prices by selling futures contracts, whereas investors that expect decreasing prices and want to get a fixed price will have to buy a futures contract.

Figure 7.1 depicts the profits and losses for a buyer and a seller of a futures contract, where on the vertical axis the profit is presented, in terms of the market price (spot price) of the underlying instrument at maturity, which is

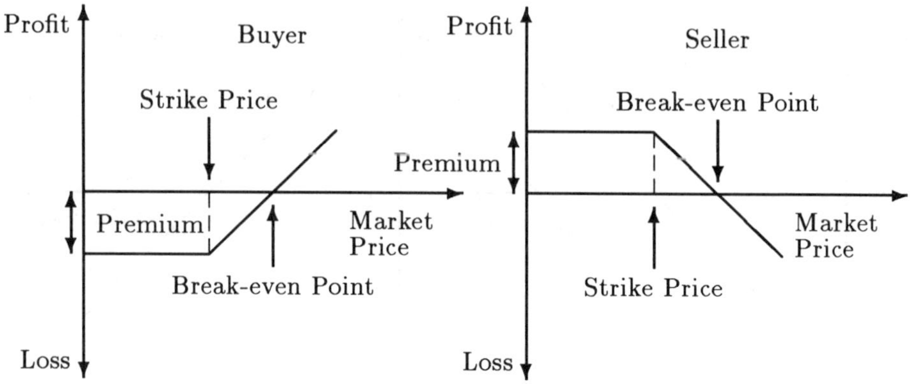

Fig. 7.2. Profits and losses for a call option

measured on the horizontal axis.

On the other hand, options had existed for many years in the financial markets but it was not until 1973 that the first organized market (Chicago Board of Options Exchanges (CBOE)) appeared. Initially, options existed solely for stocks and, hence, the majority of the models and studies on options are based on stock options.

An option contract is characterized by its *expiration date*, that is, the date before which the option can be exercised. If an option is not exercised by the time of its expiration date it has no value. There are two types of options available in the market. First, there is the *put* option which gives the holder the *right to sell* an instrument at the exercise price before the expiration date, and the *call* option which gives the holder the *right to buy* an instrument at the exercise price before the expiration date. Figure 7.2 and Figure 7.3 present the profit and loss profiles both for the writer and the buyer of, respectively, a call and a put option. In this figure, the vertical axis corresponds to the profits or losses, in terms of the market price of the underlying instrument at maturity which is the subject of the horizontal axis. The point at which the investor has neither a profit or a loss, is called the *break-even point.*

The relationship between the instrument's spot market price and the option's strike price determines whether or not an option has an actual value, which is referred to as its *intrinsic value.* The life of the option (its *time value*) is reflected in the current price of an option as the amount in excess of the option's intrinsic value. Time value plays more of a role in *American options*, which can be exercised at any point in time prior to expiration, than in *European options*, where the options can be exercised only at the expiration date. Since an option represents a right and not an obligation its value

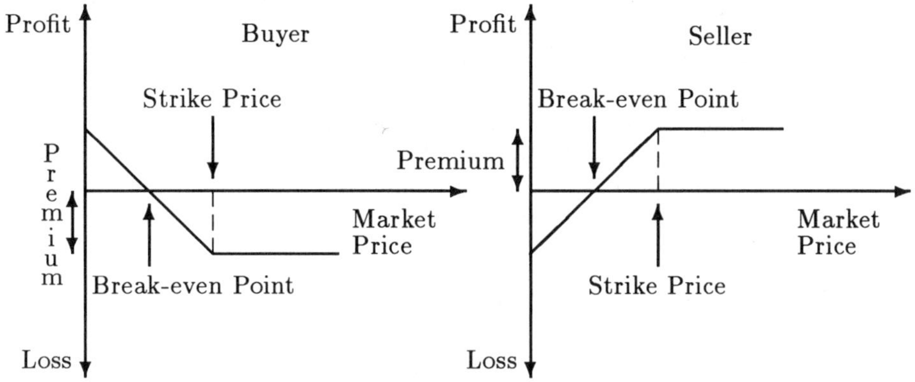

Fig. 7.3. Profits and losses for a put option

can never be negative.

The pricing of options has been extensively studied and many models have been presented and applied (see, e.g., Black and Scholes (1973), Brennan and Schwartz (1977), Karatzas (1988)). The most well-known and widely used model, however, is still the one by Black and Scholes (1973) (see Appendix C), which turns out to be accurate enough in the pricing of options, even though some of its assumptions cannot be completely fulfilled (i.e., interest rates are assumed to be unchanged, price developments are assumed to follow a lognormal distribution, and there are no taxes and transaction costs).

Options investors can either be *long* or *short* on their positions. An investor that is buying an option is opening an options transaction and is said to hold a long position, whereas an investor that writes an option is considered to hold a short position. Obviously, the decision of an investor to be short or long mirrors his expectations of the market. Those who expect to profit with an increase of the underlying instrument price (buy calls or sell puts) are said to be *bullish*, whereas investors who anticipate a decline as to the price of the underlying instrument in order to profit (sell calls or buy puts) are said to be *bearish*.

Furthermore, an option can be *in*, *out of*, or, *at the money*. In particular, an option is said to be at the money if the current market price of the underlying instrument is equal to the exercise price of the contract, and it is out of the money if the exercise price is higher (lower) than the current market price of the underlying instrument for a call (put) option. Finally, a call (put) option is in the money if the current market price of the underlying instrument is below (above) the contract exercise price.

This chapter is organized as follows. In Section 7.1 we present the financial equilibrium models with futures and examine their qualitative properties in

Section 7.2. Section 7.3 then focuses on the network structure of the financial economy in equilibrium. Section 7.4 turns to the computation of financial equilibria in the presence of futures and illustrates the behavior of the model with numerical examples.

Section 7.5 then develops a financial equilibrium model with options. Section 7.6 provides qualitative properties of the equilibrium pattern. Section 7.7 constructs the network underlying the financial economy in the presence of options at the equilibrium state.

7.1 Models with Futures

As in Chapter 6, we consider an economy consisting of J sectors, with a typical sector denoted by j, and with I instruments, with a typical instrument denoted by i.

We denote the volume of instrument i held as an unhedged asset by sector j as X_i^j, and group the unhedged (nonnegative) assets in the portfolio of sector j into the column vector $X^j \in R_+^I$. Similarly, we denote the volume of instrument i that sector j holds as an unhedged liability, by Y_i^j, and group the (nonnegative) unhedged liabilities in the portfolio of sector j into the column vector $Y^j \in R_+^I$.

The volume of instrument i held by sector j as a hedged, through instrument futures contracts, asset, is denoted by Z_i^j. We group the instrument hedged assets of sector j into the column vector $Z^j \in R_+^I$. Similarly, we let Ψ_i^j denote the volume of instrument i held by sector j as a hedged, through instrument futures contracts, liability, and we group the instrument hedged liabilities of sector j into the column vector $\Psi^j \in R_+^I$.

Finally, we group the unhedged and hedged asset vectors (X^j, Z^j) for sector j into the asset column vector $\mathcal{X}^j \in R_+^{2I}$ and the unhedged and hedged liability vectors (Y^j, Ψ^j) into the liability column vector $\mathcal{Y}^j \in R_+^{2I}$. We then group these vectors, respectively, into the vectors $\mathcal{X} \in R_+^{J2I}$ and $\mathcal{Y} \in R_+^{J2I}$. We assume that all these vectors are nonnegative.

Let r_i represent the nonnegative price of instrument i and group the instrument prices into the column vector $r \in R_+^I$. Furthermore, let π_i denote the contracted price of instrument i on the futures market, as entered into by the contract. We group the fixed futures prices into a column vector $\pi \in R^I$. In addition, we denote the shadow price or "opportunity cost" associated with instrument i held as a hedged instrument by λ_i (associated with the market clearing condition, which will be detailed later in this section). We then group the shadow prices into the column vector $\lambda \in R^I$. We assume that there is only one type of futures contract available per instrument, for exposition purposes, and that all contracts call for delivery at the time the contract was entered into.

Each sector j has, as an objective, to determine his optimal composition of instruments held as assets and as liabilities, so as to maximize the value of his hedged and unhedged asset holdings and to minimize the value of his hedged and unhedged liabilities, as well as the risk associated with the portfolio choice. Moreover, we assume that the majority of the assumptions that characterized the models presented in Chapter 6 still hold. In particular, we still assume that sectors act in a "perfectly competitive environment," buyers of instruments are "price takers," the size of the market is big enough with no limitations as to resources (outside of the stated constraints). As previously, we assume that the utility function of every sector is concave with respect to the instrument variables, continuous, and twice continuously differentiable, with each sector taking the prices r and λ as given. We assume that the accounts of each sector must balance, and denote the total financial volume held by sector j by S^j.

The optimization problem that each sector j faces, hence, in the presence of futures, is given by:

$$\text{Maximize } U^j(X^j, Z^j, Y^j, \Psi^j, r, \lambda; \pi) \tag{7.1}$$

subject to:

$$\sum_{i=1}^{I} X_i^j + Z_i^j = S^j, \tag{7.2a}$$

$$\sum_{i=1}^{I} Y_i^j + \Psi_i^j = S^j, \tag{7.2b}$$

$$X_i^j, Y_i^j, Z_i^j, \Psi_i^j \geq 0, \quad i = 1, \ldots, I. \tag{7.3}$$

An important special case of the utility function in (7.1) is given by:

$$U^j = u^j(\mathcal{X}^j, \mathcal{Y}^j) + \sum_{i=1}^{I} r_i \left(X_i^j - Y_i^j\right) + \sum_{i=1}^{I} (\pi_i + \lambda_i) \left(Z_i^j - \Psi_i^j\right), \tag{7.4}$$

where the first term in the utility function in(7.4), $u^j(\mathcal{X}^j, \mathcal{Y}^j)$, reflects the risk associated with the portfolio choice, the second term reflects the total return due to the unhedged part of the portfolio, and the last term represents the return from the hedged part of the portfolio. Note that (7.4) is an extension of the utility function (6.4) to the case of futures.

We will now examine the structure of the feasible set for the asset and liability patterns as defined by constraints (7.2a), (7.2b), and (7.3). More precisely, for each sector j; $j = 1, \ldots, J$, we let

$$\tilde{\mathcal{X}}^j \equiv \{X^j \in R_+^I, Z^j \in R_+^I : \sum_{i=1}^{I} X_i^j + Z_i^j = S^j\} \tag{7.5}$$

denote the constraint set of his assets. Similarly, we let

$$\tilde{\mathcal{Y}}^j \equiv \{Y^j \in R_+^I, \Psi^j \in R_+^I : \sum_{i=1}^{I} Y_i^j + \Psi_i^j = S^j\} \tag{7.6}$$

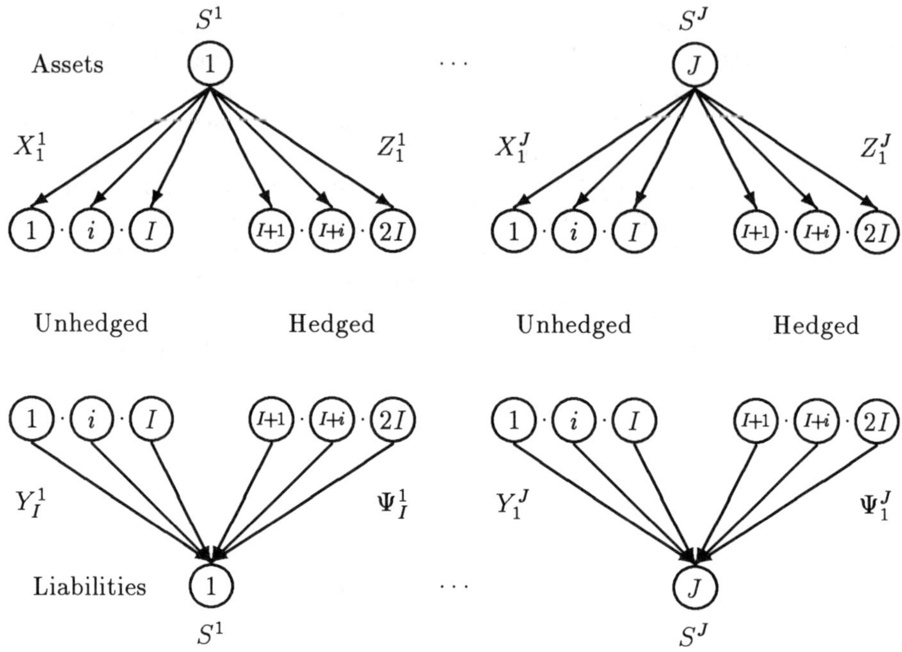

Fig. 7.4. Network structure of the sectors' optimization problems

denote the constraint set for his liabilities. Then, the feasible set for a sector j is a Cartesian product, denoted by $\tilde{\kappa}^j$, where

$$\tilde{\kappa}^j \equiv \{\tilde{\mathcal{X}}^j \times \tilde{\mathcal{Y}}^j\}. \tag{7.7}$$

Let $\tilde{\mathcal{X}}$ denote the feasible set for the assets of all the sectors, where:

$$\tilde{\mathcal{X}} \equiv \tilde{\mathcal{X}}^1 \times \ldots \times \tilde{\mathcal{X}}^j \times \ldots \times \tilde{\mathcal{X}}^J. \tag{7.8}$$

Similarly, for the liabilities, let $\tilde{\mathcal{Y}}$ denote the feasible set of the liabilities of all the sectors, that is,

$$\tilde{\mathcal{Y}} \equiv \tilde{\mathcal{Y}}^1 \times \ldots \times \tilde{\mathcal{Y}}^j \times \ldots \times \tilde{\mathcal{Y}}^J. \tag{7.9}$$

Also, define $\tilde{\kappa} \equiv \{\tilde{\mathcal{X}} \times \tilde{\mathcal{Y}}\}$.

In Figure 7.4, we depict the network structure of the individual sectors' optimization problems, in which the nodes correspond to the sectors and the links to the assets and to the liabilities. Note the special structure of the network subproblems (out of equilibrium), which, in contrast to the network subproblems in Figure 6.1, have double the number of arcs, with the additional arcs representing the hedged instrument choices.

The Equilibrium Conditions

The economy under consideration is governed by market equilibrium conditions, both for the sectors and for the instruments. In the following paragraphs we will present these equilibrium conditions.

Portfolio Optimality

Under the assumption that the utility function for each sector is concave, continuous, and twice continuously differentiable, the necessary and sufficient conditions for an optimal portfolio for a sector j, $(\mathcal{X}^{j^*}, \mathcal{Y}^{j^*}) \in \tilde{\kappa}^j$, is that it satisfies the following inequality:

$$-\nabla_{\mathcal{X}^j} U^j(\mathcal{X}^{j^*}, \mathcal{Y}^{j^*}, r^*, \lambda^*; \pi)^T \cdot (\mathcal{X}^j - \mathcal{X}^{j^*})$$

$$-\nabla_{\mathcal{Y}^j} U^j(\mathcal{X}^{j^*}, \mathcal{Y}^{j^*}, r^*, \lambda^*; \pi)^T \cdot (\mathcal{Y}^j - \mathcal{Y}^{j^*}) \geq 0, \quad \forall (\mathcal{X}^j, \mathcal{Y}^j) \in \tilde{\kappa}^j, \tag{7.10}$$

where ∇_Φ denotes the gradient with respect to the variables in the vector Φ, that is,

$$\nabla_{\mathcal{X}^j} U^j \equiv \left(\frac{\partial U^j}{\partial X_1^j}, \dots, \frac{\partial U^j}{\partial X_i^j}, \dots, \frac{\partial U^j}{\partial X_I^j}, \frac{\partial U^j}{\partial Z_1^j}, \dots, \frac{\partial U^j}{\partial Z_i^j}, \dots, \frac{\partial U^j}{\partial Z_I^j} \right) \tag{7.11}$$

and

$$\nabla_{\mathcal{Y}^j} U^j \equiv \left(\frac{\partial U^j}{\partial Y_1^j}, \dots, \frac{\partial U^j}{\partial Y_i^j}, \dots, \frac{\partial U^j}{\partial Y_I^j}, \frac{\partial U^j}{\partial \Psi_1^j}, \dots, \frac{\partial U^j}{\partial \Psi_i^j}, \dots, \frac{\partial U^j}{\partial \Psi_I^j} \right). \tag{7.12}$$

Obviously, an inequality similar to (7.10) holds for every other sector in the economy.

Furthermore, the economic system conditions for the unhedged instrument prices are:

Unhedged Instrument Market Equilibrium Conditions

For each unhedged instrument $i; i = 1, \dots, I$, we must have that:

$$\sum_{j=1}^{J} (X_i^{j^*} - Y_i^{j^*}) \begin{cases} = 0, & \text{if } r_i^* > 0 \\ \geq 0, & \text{if } r_i^* = 0. \end{cases} \tag{7.13}$$

The system of equalities and inequalities (7.13) states that if the price of a financial instrument is positive, then the market must clear for that instrument and if the price is zero, then either there is an excess supply of that instrument in the economy or the market clears.

Hedged Instrument Market Equilibrium Conditions

Also, for each hedged instrument i, we must have that

$$\sum_{j=1}^{J} (Z_i^{j^*} - \Psi_i^{j^*}) = 0, \tag{7.14}$$

with the shadow price λ_i^* associated with constraint (7.14). In the futures market, the market must clear for each instrument because either there are buyers and sellers at the contract price π_i or there are none. In either of these cases, (7.14) must always hold true. The shadow price λ_i^*, in turn, represents the opportunity cost (in equilibrium) associated with trading the instrument i at the fixed price π_i. It can, hence, be either positive or negative (or zero).

Let $\mathcal{K}$ denote the feasible set for all the hedged and unhedged asset and liability holdings of all the sectors, and all the prices of all the instruments where $\mathcal{K} \equiv \{\tilde{\kappa} \times R_+^I \times R^I\}$.

We now state the following definition of a financial equilibrium with futures.

Definition 7.1 (Financial Equilibrium with Futures)

A vector $(\mathcal{X}^*, \mathcal{Y}^*, r^*, \lambda^*) \in \mathcal{K}$ is an equilibrium point of the single country, multi-sector, multi-instrument financial model with futures if and only if it satisfies the system of equalities and inequalities (7.10), (7.13), and (7.14), for all sectors j, all unhedged instruments i, and all hedged instruments i, simultaneously.

Combining now the system of necessary and sufficient conditions (7.10), along with the economic equilibrium conditions related to the hedged (7.13), as well as, to the unhedged instruments (7.14), we will derive the variational inequality formulation of the governing equilibrium conditions.

Theorem 7.1 (Variational Inequality Formulation with Futures)

A vector of assets and liabilities of the sectors, and instrument prices, $(\mathcal{X}^*, \mathcal{Y}^*, r^*, \lambda^*) \in \mathcal{K}$, is a financial equilibrium with futures if and only if it satisfies the variational inequality problem:

$$-\sum_{j=1}^{J} \nabla_{\mathcal{X}^j} U^j(\mathcal{X}^{j^*}, \mathcal{Y}^{j^*}, r^*, \lambda^*; \pi)^T \cdot (\mathcal{X}^j - \mathcal{X}^{j^*})$$

$$-\sum_{j=1}^{J} \nabla_{\mathcal{Y}^j} U^j(\mathcal{X}^{j^*}, \mathcal{Y}^{j^*}, r^*, \lambda^*; \pi)^T \cdot (\mathcal{Y}^j - \mathcal{Y}^{j^*})$$

$$+\sum_{i=1}^{I}\sum_{j=1}^{J}\left[X_i^{j^*} - Y_i^{j^*}\right] \times [r_i - r_i^*] + \sum_{i=1}^{I}\sum_{j=1}^{J}\left[Z_i^{j^*} - \Psi_i^{j^*}\right] \times [\lambda_i - \lambda_i^*] \geq 0,$$

$$\forall (\mathcal{X}, \mathcal{Y}, r, \lambda) \in \mathcal{K}, \tag{7.15a}$$

which, in the case of utility functions given by (7.4), takes the form:

$$\sum_{j=1}^{J}\sum_{i=1}^{I}\left[-\frac{\partial u^j(\mathcal{X}^{j^*}, \mathcal{Y}^{j^*})}{\partial X_i^j} - r_i^*\right] \times \left[X_i^j - X_i^{j^*}\right]$$

$$+\sum_{j=1}^{J}\sum_{i=1}^{I}\left[-\frac{\partial u^j(\mathcal{X}^{j^*},\mathcal{Y}^{j^*})}{\partial Z_i^j}-(\pi_i+\lambda_i^*)\right]\times\left[Z_i^j-Z_i^{j^*}\right]$$

$$+\sum_{j=1}^{J}\sum_{i=1}^{I}\left[-\frac{\partial u^j(\mathcal{X}^{j^*},\mathcal{Y}^{j^*})}{\partial Y_i^j}+r_i^*\right]\times\left[Y_i^j-Y_i^{j^*}\right]$$

$$+\sum_{j=1}^{J}\sum_{i=1}^{I}\left[-\frac{\partial u^j(\mathcal{X}^{j^*},\mathcal{Y}^{j^*})}{\partial \Psi_i^j}+(\pi_i+\lambda_i^*)\right]\times\left[\Psi_i^j-\Psi_i^{j^*}\right]$$

$$+\sum_{i=1}^{I}\sum_{j=1}^{J}\left[X_i^{j^*}-Y_i^{j^*}\right]\times[r_i-r_i^*]$$

$$+\sum_{i=1}^{I}\sum_{j=1}^{J}\left[Z_i^{j^*}-\Psi_i^{j^*}\right]\times[\lambda_i-\lambda_i^*]\geq 0,\quad \forall(\mathcal{X},\mathcal{Y},r,\lambda)\in\mathcal{K}. \qquad (7.15b)$$

Proof: We will present now a proof for (7.15a), and since variational inequality (7.15b) is a special case of (7.15a) with utility functions given by (7.4), the conclusion also follows in this case.

Assume that $(\mathcal{X}^*,\mathcal{Y}^*,r^*,\lambda^*)\in\mathcal{K}$ is an equilibrium point of the multi-sector, multi-instrument financial model with futures, that is, it satisfies Definition 7.1. Therefore, the system of equalities and inequalities (7.10), (7.13), and (7.14) hold for all sectors j, all unhedged instruments i, and all hedged instruments i. Summing now (7.10) over all sectors j, we obtain

$$-\sum_{j=1}^{J}\nabla_{\mathcal{X}^j}U^j(\mathcal{X}^{j^*},\mathcal{Y}^{j^*},r^*,\lambda^*;\pi)^T\cdot(\mathcal{X}^j-\mathcal{X}^{j^*})$$

$$-\sum_{j=1}^{J}\nabla_{\mathcal{Y}^j}U^j(\mathcal{X}^{j^*},\mathcal{Y}^{j^*},r^*,\lambda^*;\pi)^T\cdot(\mathcal{Y}^j-\mathcal{Y}^{j^*})\geq 0,\quad\forall(\mathcal{X},\mathcal{Y})\in\tilde{\kappa}. \qquad (7.16)$$

Similarly, by using analogous arguments for the system of equalities and inequalities that represent the economic system conditions (7.13) for the unhedged instruments, we have that, for a fixed unhedged instrument i:

$$\sum_{j=1}^{J}\left[X_i^{j^*}-Y_i^{j^*}\right]\times[r_i-r_i^*]\geq 0,\quad\forall r_i\geq 0, \qquad (7.17)$$

which must hold for all unhedged instruments. As a result, the summation of (7.17) over all unhedged instruments, yields:

$$\sum_{i=1}^{I}\sum_{j=1}^{J}\left[X_i^{j^*}-Y_i^{j^*}\right]\times[r_i-r_i^*]\geq 0,\quad\forall r\in R_+^I. \qquad (7.18)$$

Finally, since the system of equalities (7.14) holds for each hedged instrument i, summation over all hedged instruments yields:

$$\sum_{i=1}^{I}\sum_{j=1}^{J}\left[Z_i^{j^*}-\Psi_i^{j^*}\right]\times[\lambda_i-\lambda_i^*]=0, \quad \forall\lambda\in R^I. \tag{7.19}$$

If we now sum inequalities (7.17), (7.18), and equality (7.19) we obtain variational inequality (7.15a). In the special case where the utility function is of the form (7.4), then the variational inequality (7.15a) takes the form of (7.15b).

We will now prove that if $(\mathcal{X}^*,\mathcal{Y}^*,r^*,\lambda^*)\in\mathcal{K}$ is a solution to variational inequality (7.15a) then it also satisfies the equilibrium conditions (7.10), (7.13), and (7.14). In particular, if we let $\mathcal{X}^j=\mathcal{X}^{j^*}$, $\mathcal{Y}^j=\mathcal{Y}^{j^*}$, for all sectors j, and $\lambda_i=\lambda_i^*$ for all hedged instruments i, then substitution into variational inequality (7.15a) yields:

$$\sum_{i=1}^{I}\sum_{j=1}^{J}\left[X_i^{j^*}-Y_i^{j^*}\right]\times[r_i-r_i^*]\geq 0, \quad \forall r\in R_+^I, \tag{7.20}$$

which implies the system economic conditions (7.13).

If we now let $r_i=r_i^*$ for all unhedged instruments i, and $\lambda_i=\lambda_i^*$ for all hedged instruments i, and substitute the resultants into inequality (7.15a) we obtain:

$$-\sum_{j=1}^{J}\nabla_{\mathcal{X}^j}U^j(\mathcal{X}^{j^*},\mathcal{Y}^{j^*},r^*,\lambda^*;\pi)^T\cdot(\mathcal{X}^j-\mathcal{X}^{j^*})$$

$$-\sum_{j=1}^{J}\nabla_{\mathcal{Y}^j}U^j(\mathcal{X}^{j^*},\mathcal{Y}^{j^*},r^*,\lambda^*;\pi)^T\cdot(\mathcal{Y}^j-\mathcal{Y}^{j^*})\geq 0, \quad \forall(\mathcal{X},\mathcal{Y})\in\tilde{\kappa}, \tag{7.21}$$

which implies the optimality conditions (7.10).

Moreover, if we let $\mathcal{X}^j=\mathcal{X}^{j^*}$, $\mathcal{Y}^j=\mathcal{Y}^{j^*}$, for all sectors j, and $r_i=r_i^*$ for all unhedged instruments i, then substitution into variational inequality (7.15a) yields:

$$\sum_{i=1}^{I}\sum_{j=1}^{J}\left[Z_i^{j^*}-\Psi_i^{j^*}\right]\times[\lambda_i-\lambda_i^*]\geq 0, \quad \forall\lambda\in R^I,$$

which can only hold as an equality for each i, since λ_i^* can be of either sign. □

For simplicity, and in order to maintain compact mathematical notation, we introduce the following: Let $n=4JI+2I$. We define the J-dimensional column vector U with components: $\{U^1,\dots,U^J\}$ and we let $\nabla_{\mathcal{X}}$ denote the

$2JI$-dimensional vector with components given by $\{\nabla_{\mathcal{X}^1}, \ldots, \nabla_{\mathcal{X}^J} U^J\}$ with $\nabla_{\mathcal{Y}} U$ defined accordingly. We define the n-dimensional column vector $x \equiv (\mathcal{X}, \mathcal{Y}, r, \lambda) \in \mathcal{K}$, and the n-dimensional column vector $F(x)$ with components:

$$F(x) = \begin{bmatrix} F_1(x) \\ \vdots \\ F_b(x) \\ \vdots \\ F_n(x) \end{bmatrix} = \begin{bmatrix} -\nabla_{\mathcal{X}} U(\mathcal{X}, \mathcal{Y}, r, \lambda; \pi) \\ -\nabla_{\mathcal{Y}} U(\mathcal{X}, \mathcal{Y}, r, \lambda; \pi) \\ \sum_{j=1}^J \left(X_1^j - Y_1^j\right) \\ \vdots \\ \sum_{j=1}^J \left(X_I^j - Y_I^j\right) \\ \sum_{j=1}^J \left(Z_1^j - \Psi_1^j\right) \\ \vdots \\ \sum_{j=1}^J \left(Z_I^j - \Psi_I^j\right) \end{bmatrix}_{n \times 1} . \tag{7.22}$$

Therefore, (7.15a) as well as, (7.15b) can be written as:
Determine $x^* \in \mathcal{K}$ satisfying:

$$\langle F(x^*)^T, x - x^* \rangle \geq 0, \quad \forall x \in \mathcal{K}. \tag{7.23}$$

7.1.1 Quadratic Utility Functions

We will now present a special case of the model(s) presented in the previous section. In particular, we consider a special case of the utility function (7.4), which is quadratic. We assume that the main goal of every sector in the economy remains the minimization of his risk, as well as, the maximization of the return of his portfolio, but, in this special case, the term $u^j(\mathcal{X}^j, \mathcal{Y}^j)$, which reflects the risk associated with the portfolio choice is based on a variance-covariance matrix. More precisely, the portfolio optimization problem for each sector j is the following:

$$\text{Minimize} \begin{pmatrix} \mathcal{X}^j \\ \mathcal{Y}^j \end{pmatrix}^T Q^j \begin{pmatrix} \mathcal{X}^j \\ \mathcal{Y}^j \end{pmatrix} - \sum_{i=1}^I r_i \left(X_i^j - Y_i^j\right) - \sum_{i=1}^I (\pi_i + \lambda_i) \left(Z_i^j - \Psi_i^j\right) \tag{7.24}$$

subject to:

$$\sum_{i=1}^I \left(X_i^j + Z_i^j\right) = S^j \tag{7.25a}$$

$$\sum_{i=1}^I \left(Y_i^j + \Psi_i^j\right) = S^j \tag{7.25b}$$

$$X_i^j \geq 0, \; Y_i^j \geq 0, Z_i^j \geq 0, \; \Psi_i^j \geq 0, \quad i = 1, 2, \ldots, I, \tag{7.26}$$

where Q^j is a symmetric $4I \times 4I$ variance-covariance matrix.

Note that this model is an extension of the model in Section 6.1.1 to the case of futures.

Clearly, the economic conditions that govern the instrument prices as well as the opportunity costs associated with the futures contracts remain the same as in the preceding section, given, respectively, by (7.13) and (7.14). Therefore, the variational inequality formulation of the model with the quadratic utility function is simply a special case of (7.15b).

7.2 Qualitative Properties

In this section we address the issues of existence and uniqueness of the equilibrium pattern for the model(s) presented in the previous sections, as well as, some qualitative properties for the function $F(x)$ (cf. (7.22) that enters the variational inequality problem (7.23).

First, we present the existence proof for the financial equilibrium model with futures with utility functions of the form (7.4).

Theorem 7.2 (Existence)

Assume that the utility function for each sector is as given by (7.4). If $(\mathcal{X}^*, \mathcal{Y}^*, r^*, \lambda^*) \in \mathcal{K}$ is an equilibrium pattern and, therefore, a solution to variational inequality (7.15b), then $(\mathcal{X}^*, \mathcal{Y}^*)$ is a solution of the variational inequality

$$\sum_{j=1}^{J}\sum_{i=1}^{I}\left[-\frac{\partial u^j(\mathcal{X}^{j*}, \mathcal{Y}^{j*})}{\partial X_i^j}\right] \times \left[X_i^j - X_i^{j*}\right]$$

$$+\sum_{j=1}^{J}\sum_{i=1}^{I}\left[-\frac{\partial u^j(\mathcal{X}^{j*}, \mathcal{Y}^{j*})}{\partial Z_i^j} - \pi_i\right] \times \left[Z_i^j - Z_i^{j*}\right]$$

$$+\sum_{j=1}^{J}\sum_{i=1}^{I}\left[-\frac{\partial u^j(\mathcal{X}^{j*}, \mathcal{Y}^{j*})}{\partial Y_i^j}\right] \times \left[Y_i^j - Y_i^{j*}\right]$$

$$+\sum_{j=1}^{J}\sum_{i=1}^{I}\left[-\frac{\partial u^j(\mathcal{X}^{j*}, \mathcal{Y}^{j*})}{\partial \Psi_i^j} + \pi_i\right] \times \left[\Psi_i^j - \Psi_i^{j*}\right] \geq 0, \quad \forall (\mathcal{X}, \mathcal{Y}) \in \tilde{S}, \tag{7.27}$$

where $\tilde{S}$ is a non-empty set such that:

$$\tilde{S} \equiv \{(\mathcal{X}, \mathcal{Y}) \in \tilde{\kappa};\ \sum_{j=1}^{J}(X_i^j - Y_i^j) \geq 0; \sum_{j=1}^{J}(Z_i^j - \Psi_i^j) = 0;\ i = 1, \ldots, I\}. \tag{7.28}$$

If, on the other hand, $(\mathcal{X}^*, \mathcal{Y}^*)$ is a solution of variational inequality (7.27), then there exist I-dimensional vectors of Lagrange multipliers associated, respectively, with the constraints: $\sum_{j=1}^{J}(X_i^j - Y_i^j) \geq 0$, and $\sum_{j=1}^{J}(Z_i^j -$

$\Psi_i^j) = 0$, for $i = 1, \ldots, I$, such that $(\mathcal{X}^*, \mathcal{Y}^*, r^*, \lambda^*)$ is a solution to variational inequality (7.15b) and, hence, is an equilibrium pattern.

Proof: Assume that $(\mathcal{X}^*, \mathcal{Y}^*, r^*, \lambda^*)$ is an equilibrium and, therefore, satisfies variational inequality (7.15b). If we now let $(\mathcal{X}^j, \mathcal{Y}^j) = (\mathcal{X}^{j^*}, \mathcal{Y}^{j^*})$ for all sectors j; $\lambda_i = \lambda_i^*$, and $r_i = 0$, for all instruments i, and substitute these values into (7.15b), we obtain:

$$-\sum_{i=1}^{I}\left[\sum_{j=1}^{J} X_i^{j^*} - Y_i^{j^*}\right] r_i^* \geq 0. \tag{7.29}$$

Similarly, if we make the same substitutions again for $\mathcal{X}$ and for $\mathcal{Y}$, but now let $r_i = r_i^*$ and $\lambda_i = 0$, for all i, and substitute these values into (7.15b), we obtain:

$$-\sum_{i=1}^{I}\left[\sum_{j=1}^{J} Z_i^{j^*} - \Psi_i^{j^*}\right] \lambda_i^* \geq 0. \tag{7.30}$$

Now, if we let $r_i = r_i^*$ and $\lambda_i = \lambda_i^*$ for all i, and substitute the resultants into (7.15b), yields

$$\sum_{j=1}^{J}\sum_{i=1}^{I}\left[-\frac{\partial u^j(\mathcal{X}^{j^*}, \mathcal{Y}^{j^*})}{\partial X_i^j} - r_i^*\right] \times \left[X_i^j - X_i^{j^*}\right]$$

$$+\sum_{j=1}^{J}\sum_{i=1}^{I}\left[-\frac{\partial u^j(\mathcal{X}^{j^*}, \mathcal{Y}^{j^*})}{\partial Z_i^j} - (\pi_i + \lambda_i^*)\right] \times \left[Z_i^j - Z_i^{j^*}\right]$$

$$+\sum_{j=1}^{J}\sum_{i=1}^{I}\left[-\frac{\partial u^j(\mathcal{X}^{j^*}, \mathcal{Y}^{j^*})}{\partial Y_i^j} + r_i^*\right] \times \left[Y_i^j - Y_i^{j^*}\right]$$

$$+\sum_{j=1}^{J}\sum_{i=1}^{I}\left[-\frac{\partial u^j(\mathcal{X}^{j^*}, \mathcal{Y}^{j^*})}{\partial \Psi_i^j} + (\pi_i + \lambda_i^*)\right] \times \left[\Psi_i^j - \Psi_i^{j^*}\right] \geq 0, \tag{7.31}$$

or, equivalently,

$$\sum_{j=1}^{J}\sum_{i=1}^{I}\left[-\frac{\partial u^j(\mathcal{X}^{j^*}, \mathcal{Y}^{j^*})}{\partial X_i^j}\right] \times \left[X_i^j - X_i^{j^*}\right]$$

$$+\sum_{j=1}^{J}\sum_{i=1}^{I}\left[-\frac{\partial u^j(\mathcal{X}^{j^*}, \mathcal{Y}^{j^*})}{\partial Z_i^j} - \pi_i\right] \times \left[Z_i^j - Z_i^{j^*}\right]$$

$$+\sum_{j=1}^{J}\sum_{i=1}^{I}\left[-\frac{\partial u^j(\mathcal{X}^{j^*}, \mathcal{Y}^{j^*})}{\partial Y_i^j}\right] \times \left[Y_i^j - Y_i^{j^*}\right]$$

$$+\sum_{j=1}^{J}\sum_{i=1}^{I}\left[-\frac{\partial u^j(\mathcal{X}^{j*},\mathcal{Y}^{j*})}{\partial \Psi_i^j}+\pi_i\right]\times\left[\Psi_i^j-\Psi_i^{j*}\right]$$

$$\geq \sum_{i=1}^{I} r_i^*\left[\sum_{j=1}^{J}(X_i^j-Y_i^j)-\sum_{j=1}^{J}(X_i^{j*}-Y_i^{j*})\right]$$

$$+\sum_{i=1}^{I}\lambda_i^*\left[\sum_{j=1}^{J}(Z_i^j-\Psi_i^j)-\sum_{j=1}^{J}(Z_i^{j*}-\Psi_i^{j*})\right]. \tag{7.32}$$

By taking into consideration (7.29) and (7.30), and the constraint set $\tilde{S}$, one can easily see that the right-hand side of (7.32) is greater than equal to zero and, therefore, if $(\mathcal{X}^*,\mathcal{Y}^*)$ satisfies (7.15b) it must also satisfy (7.27).

Since the constraint set $\tilde{S}$ is compact, it follows from Theorem 3.1, that there exists an asset and liability pattern $(\mathcal{X}^*,\mathcal{Y}^*)$ that satisfies (7.27). Also, it follows from the Lagrange Multiplier Theorem, that there exists a vector of Lagrange multipliers $r^* \in R_+^I$ associated with the constraints: $\sum_{j=1}^{J}(X_i^{j*}-Y_i^{j*}) \geq 0$, for all i; $i=1,\ldots,I$, and a vector of Lagrange multipliers $\lambda^* \in R^I$ associated with the constraints: $\sum_{j=1}^{J}(Z_i^{j*}-\Psi_i^{j*})=0$, for all i; $i=1,\ldots,I$, and, moreover, for every such constructed $(\mathcal{X}^*,\mathcal{Y}^*,r^*,\lambda^*)$, variational inequality (7.15b) holds. □

We will now address the issue of the uniqueness of the equilibrium asset and liability pattern. The following theorem is for general utility functions given in (7.1).

Theorem 7.3 (Uniqueness)

Under the assumption that the utility functions U^j are strictly concave in $(\mathcal{X}^j,\mathcal{Y}^j)$ for each sector j, the equilibrium pattern of assets and liabilities, $(\mathcal{X}^*,\mathcal{Y}^*)$, is unique.

Proof: Follows using the same arguments as in the proof of Theorem 6.3. □

Furthermore, the following theorems present some of the properties of function $F(x)$ that enters variational inequality (7.23). The proofs of these theorems are left out due to the fact that they are adaptations of Theorems 6.4 and 6.5.

Theorem 7.4

Under the assumption that the utility function U^j is strictly concave, for each sector j, and twice continuously differentiable, $F(x)$ defined in (7.22) is monotone.

Theorem 7.5

The function $F(x)$ defined in (7.22) is Lipschitz continuous, under the assumption that the utility function U^j has bounded second order derivatives for all sectors j and for all $x \in \mathcal{K}$.

7.3 Network Optimization Reformulation

In this section we establish that the equilibrium solution coincides with the solution to a network optimization problem in the case of utility functions of the form (7.4). In particular, in Theorem 7.6, we establish that the equilibrium solution is a solution to an optimization problem, and then through an application of Lemma 7.1 we prove that the markets clear for all hedged and unhedged instruments. We also construct the network over which the optimization takes place.

Theorem 7.6

The variational inequality problem of finding $(\mathcal{X}^*, \mathcal{Y}^*, r^*, \lambda^*) \in \mathcal{K}$ *satisfying:*

$$\sum_{j=1}^{J}\sum_{i=1}^{I}\left[-\frac{\partial u^j(\mathcal{X}^{j*}, \mathcal{Y}^{j*})}{\partial X_i^j} - r_i^*\right] \times \left[X_i^j - X_i^{j*}\right]$$

$$+\sum_{j=1}^{J}\sum_{i=1}^{I}\left[-\frac{\partial u^j(\mathcal{X}^{j*}, \mathcal{Y}^{j*})}{\partial Z_i^j} - (\pi_i + \lambda_i^*)\right] \times \left[Z_i^j - Z_i^{j*}\right]$$

$$+\sum_{j=1}^{J}\sum_{i=1}^{I}\left[-\frac{\partial u^j(\mathcal{X}^{j*}, \mathcal{Y}^{j*})}{\partial Y_i^j} + r_i^*\right] \times \left[Y_i^j - Y_i^{j*}\right]$$

$$+\sum_{j=1}^{J}\sum_{i=1}^{I}\left[-\frac{\partial u^j(\mathcal{X}^{j*}, \mathcal{Y}^{j*})}{\partial \Psi_i^j} + (\pi_i + \lambda_i^*)\right] \times \left[\Psi_i^j - \Psi_i^{j*}\right]$$

$$+\sum_{i=1}^{I}\sum_{j=1}^{J}\left[X_i^{j*} - Y_i^{j*}\right] \times [r_i - r_i^*] + \sum_{i=1}^{I}\sum_{j=1}^{J}\left[Z_i^{j*} - \Psi_i^{j*}\right] \times [\lambda_i - \lambda_i^*] \geq 0,$$

$$\forall (\mathcal{X}, \mathcal{Y}, r, \lambda) \in \mathcal{K}, \tag{7.33}$$

is equivalent to the problem:

$$\text{Maximize} \quad \sum_{j=1}^{J} u^j(\mathcal{X}^j, \mathcal{Y}^j) + \sum_{j=1}^{J}\sum_{i=1}^{I} \pi_i (Z_i^j - \Psi_i^j) \tag{7.34}$$

subject to:

$$\sum_{j=1}^{J}(X_i^j - Y_i^j) \geq 0, \quad i = 1, \ldots, I \tag{7.35}$$

$$\sum_{j=1}^{J}(Z_i^j - \Psi_i^j) = 0, \quad i = 1, \ldots, I \tag{7.36}$$

and

$$(\mathcal{X}^j, \mathcal{Y}^j) \in \tilde{\kappa}^j, \quad j = 1, \ldots, J, \tag{7.37}$$

where $r_i^* \geq 0$ corresponds to the Lagrange multiplier associated with the i-th constraint in (7.35), and λ_i^* corresponds to the Lagrange multiplier associated with the i-th constraint in (7.36).

Proof: It follows from the standard theory of variational inequalities (cf. Bertsekas and Tsitsiklis (1989)) that the solution to the optimization problem (7.34)–(7.37) coincides with the solution to the variational inequality problem given by (7.33) since the utility function u^j are assumed to be concave for each sector j and the feasible sets are closed and convex. □

Lemma 7.1

In equilibrium, the markets clear for all unhedged instruments and for all hedged instruments, that is,

$$\sum_{j=1}^{J}(X_i^{j^*} - Y_i^{j^*}) = 0, \quad i = 1, \ldots, I \tag{7.38}$$

and

$$\sum_{j=1}^{J}(Z_i^{j^*} - \Psi_i^{j^*}) = 0, \quad i = 1, \ldots, I. \tag{7.39}$$

Furthermore, for all instruments i: the prices r_i^* are strictly positive, whereas the shadow prices λ_i^* can be positive, negative, or zero.

Proof: Clearly, (7.39) is identical to the hedged instrument market equilibrium condition (7.14), which further implies that

$$\sum_{i=1}^{I}\sum_{j=1}^{J}(Z_i^{j^*} - \Psi_i^{j^*}) = 0. \tag{7.40}$$

Note now that the feasibility conditions (7.2a) and (7.2b) imply that

$$\sum_{i=1}^{I}\sum_{j=1}^{J}\left[(X_i^{j^*} + Z_i^{j^*}) - (Y_i^{j^*} + \Psi_i^{j^*})\right] = 0. \tag{7.41}$$

Hence, it follows from (7.40) and (7.41) that

$$\sum_{i=1}^{I}\sum_{j=1}^{J}(X_i^{j^*} - Y_i^{j^*}) = 0. \tag{7.42}$$

Assume now that for some instrument k

$$\sum_{j=1}^{J}(X_k^{j^*} - Y_k^{j^*}) > 0. \tag{7.43}$$

Then, according to (7.42), this would imply that for some l, we would then have

$$\sum_{j=1}^{J}(X_l^{j^*} - Y_l^{j^*}) < 0, \tag{7.44}$$

which is in contradiction to equilibrium condition (7.13) for unhedged instruments. Hence, we must have that

$$\sum_{j=1}^{J}(X_i^{j^*} - Y_i^{j^*}) = 0, \tag{7.45}$$

for all instruments i.

Furthermore, from Lagrange multiplier theory, the Lagrange multipliers r_i^* must be positive for all i, whereas the multipliers λ_i^*; $i = 1, \ldots, I$, can take on negative, positive, or zero values. □

The following corollary is immediate from Theorem 7.6 and Lemma 7.1.

Corollary 7.1

The solution to the optimization problem:

$$\text{Maximize} \quad \sum_{j=1}^{J} u^j(\mathcal{X}^j, \mathcal{Y}^j) + \sum_{j=1}^{J}\sum_{i=1}^{I} \pi_i(Z_i^j - \Psi_i^j) \tag{7.46}$$

subject to:

$$\sum_{j=1}^{J}(X_i^j - Y_i^j) = 0, \quad i = 1, \ldots, I \tag{7.47}$$

$$\sum_{j=1}^{J}(Z_i^j - \Psi_i^j) = 0, \quad i = 1, \ldots, I \tag{7.48}$$

$$(\mathcal{X}^j, \mathcal{Y}^j) \in \tilde{\kappa}^j, \quad j = 1, \ldots, J, \tag{7.49}$$

with Lagrange multiplier r_i^* for constraint i in (7.47) and λ_i^* for constraint i in (7.48) coincides with the solution to problem (7.34)–(7.37). Moreover, this solution is an equilibrium solution, that is, it satisfies variational inequality problem (7.33).

The network structure of the solution to problem (7.46), subject to (7.47)–(7.49), is immediate and is depicted in Figure 7.5. We now highlight some of the details in the construction of the network. First, as in the network in Figure 7.4, the uppermost J nodes and the lowermost J nodes correspond to the sectors. There are also $2I$ intermediate nodes. From each uppermost node j there are $2I$ arcs emanating, with an individual such arc terminating in the intermediate node i, with the flow on arc (j, i) equal to X_i^j for i;

$i = 1, \ldots, I$ and to Z_i^j for i; $i = I+1, \ldots, 2I$. This set of arcs corresponds to the assets. Analogously, the second set of arcs, originating in the intermediate nodes and terminating in the lowermost nodes, correspond to the liabilities with the flow on such an arc (i, j) being equal to Y_i^j, for i; $i = 1, \ldots, I$, and to Ψ_i^j for i; $i = I+1, \ldots, 2I$.

In addition, the supplies at the uppermost nodes j; $j = 1, \ldots, J$, are equal to $S^1, \ldots, S^J$, respectively, with the demands at the lowermost nodes j; $j = 1, \ldots, J$, equal to $S^1, \ldots, S^J$, respectively.

The costs on the arcs, in turn, correspond to the appropriate terms in the objective function (7.46).

It is straightforward to then verify that the network in Figure 7.5 satisfies the constraints (7.47)–(7.49) since these are just basic conservation of flow equations.

Moreover, due to the preceding theoretical results the solution to the network optimization problem coincides with the solution to the variational inequality problem (7.15b).

Note that the individual networks in Figure 7.4, representing the optimization problems of the individual sectors, merge to yield the complete synthesized network of Figure 7.5, corresponding to a single optimization problem representing the equilibrium state. Interestingly, if one is concerned in solely the computation of the financial equilibrium pattern, then one may solve problem (7.46), subject to (7.47)–(7.49). This can be accomplished, for example, by applying the primal-dual method.

The network structure at equilibrium depicted in Figure 7.5 also holds for the general utility function model with futures given by (7.1)–(7.3), (7.13), and (7.14), with the variational inequality formulation (7.15a). Indeed, (7.47) through (7.49) which represent the conservation of flow equations on the network in Figure 7.5 are independent of the form of the utility function, and only dependent on the budget constraints of the sectors and the economic conditions for hedged and unhedged instruments. Note that this was also the case for the financial equilibrium model studied in Chapter 6, which, of course, did not include hedged instruments. The network in Figure 7.5, however, has twice as many links as the network underlying the financial equilibrium depicted in Figure 6.2. In the case of general utility functions, however, one can no longer reformulate the solution to the variational inequality problem (7.15a) as the solution to a convex optimization problem.

Finally, we emphasize that the network structure drawn in Figure 7.5, also holds when the feasible set facing each sector includes additional constraints to those given by the budget constraints (7.2a) and (7.2b).

7.4 Computation of Equilibria with Futures

In this section we focus on the computation of financial equilibria in the presence of futures. In particular, we present the modified projection method,

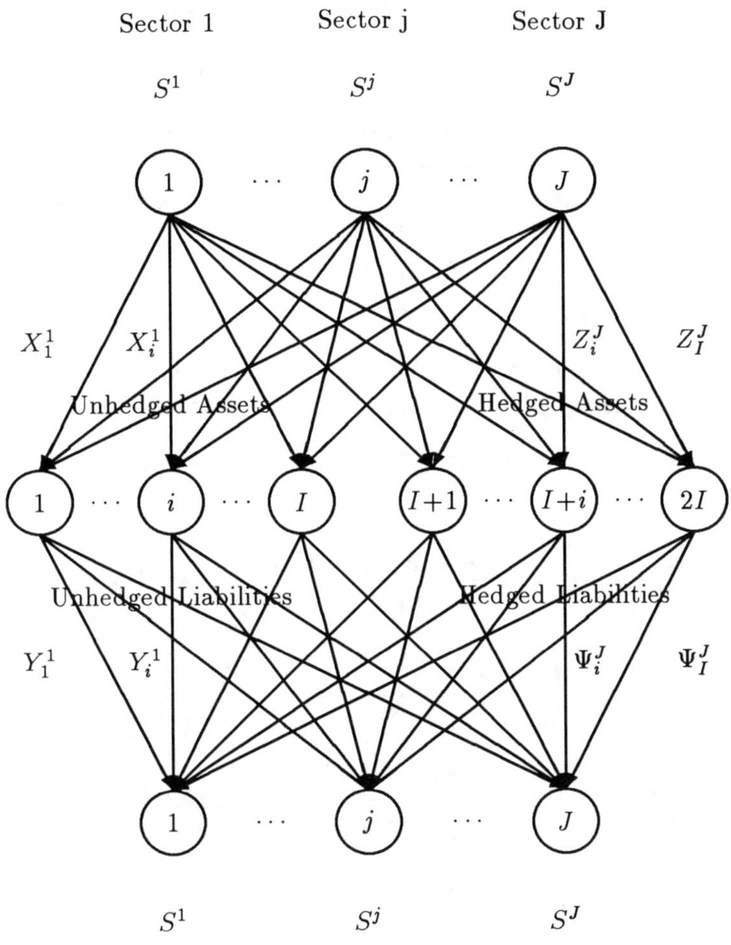

Fig. 7.5. The network structure at equilibrium

along with numerical examples. Of course, the primal-dual method can be applied for the solution of the network optimization problem in the case of utility functions of the form given by (7.4).

We now discuss the application of the modified projection method for the computation of the financial equilibrium pattern, in the presence of futures. We recall that the advantage of this method (cf. Section 3.3.1) is that, in the context of the financial applications studied here, which are defined over Cartesian products of sets, the original problem decomposes into a series of smaller and easier to solve subproblems, which have specialized network structure.

We will now illustrate the application of the modified projection method for the general utility function model of Section 7.1. In particular, we now present the modified projection algorithm in which the function $F(x)$ is in expanded form for our specific model.

The Modified Projection Method

Step 0: Initialization

Set $(\mathcal{X}^0, \mathcal{Y}^0, r^0, \lambda^0) \in \mathcal{K}$. Let $\tau := 0$ and set γ so that $0 < \gamma < \frac{1}{L}$.

Step 1: Computation

Compute $(\bar{X}^\tau, \bar{Y}^\tau, \bar{r}^\tau, \bar{\lambda}^\tau) \in \mathcal{K}$ by solving the variational inequality subproblem:

$$\sum_{j=1}^{J}\sum_{i=1}^{I}\left[\bar{X}_i^{j^\tau} + \gamma\left(\frac{-\partial U^j(\mathcal{X}^{j^\tau}, \mathcal{Y}^{j^\tau}, r^\tau, \lambda^\tau; \pi)}{\partial X_i^j}\right) - X_i^{j^\tau}\right] \times \left[X_i^j - \bar{X}_i^{j^\tau}\right]$$

$$+\sum_{j=1}^{J}\sum_{i=1}^{I}\left[\bar{Y}_i^{j^\tau} + \gamma\left(-\frac{\partial U^j(\mathcal{X}^{j^\tau}, \mathcal{Y}^{j^\tau}, r^\tau, \lambda^\tau; \pi)}{\partial Y_i^j}\right) - Y_i^{j^\tau}\right] \times \left[Y_i^j - \bar{Y}_i^{j^\tau}\right]$$

$$+\sum_{j=1}^{J}\sum_{i=1}^{I}\left[\bar{Z}_i^{j^\tau} + \gamma\left(-\frac{\partial U^j(\mathcal{X}^{j^\tau}, \mathcal{Y}^{j^\tau}, r^\tau, \lambda^\tau; \pi)}{\partial Z_i^j}\right) - Z_i^{j^\tau}\right] \times \left[Z_i^j - \bar{Z}_i^{j^\tau}\right]$$

$$+\sum_{j=1}^{J}\sum_{i=1}^{I}\left[\bar{\Psi}_i^{j^\tau} + \gamma\left(-\frac{\partial U^j(\mathcal{X}^{j^\tau}, \mathcal{Y}^{j^\tau}, r^\tau, \lambda^\tau; \pi)}{\partial \Psi_i^j}\right) - \Psi_i^{j^\tau}\right] \times \left[\Psi_i^j - \bar{\Psi}_i^{j^\tau}\right]$$

$$+\sum_{i=1}^{I}\left[\bar{r}_i^\tau + \gamma\left[\sum_{j=1}^{J}\left(X_i^{j^\tau} - Y_i^{j^\tau}\right)\right] - r_i^\tau\right] \times \left[r_i - \bar{r}_i^\tau\right]$$

$$+\sum_{i=1}^{I}\left[\bar{\lambda}_i^\tau + \gamma\left[\sum_{j=1}^{J}\left(Z_i^{j^\tau} - \Psi_i^{j^\tau}\right)\right] - \lambda_i^\tau\right] \times \left[\lambda_i - \bar{\lambda}_i^\tau\right],$$

$$\forall (\mathcal{X}, \mathcal{Y}, r, \lambda) \in \mathcal{K}. \tag{7.50}$$

Step 2: Adaptation

Compute $(X^{\tau+1}, Y^{\tau+1}, r^{\tau+1}, \lambda^{\tau+1}) \in \mathcal{K}$ by solving the variational inequality subproblem:

$$\sum_{j=1}^{J}\sum_{i=1}^{I}\left[X_i^{j^{\tau+1}} + \gamma\left(-\frac{\partial U^j(\bar{\mathcal{X}}^{j^\tau}, \bar{\mathcal{Y}}^{j^\tau}, \bar{r}^\tau, \bar{\lambda}^\tau; \pi)}{\partial X_i^j}\right) - X_i^{j^\tau}\right] \times \left[X_i^j - X_i^{j^{\tau+1}}\right]$$

$$+\sum_{j=1}^{J}\sum_{i=1}^{I}\left[Y_i^{j^{\tau+1}} + \gamma\left(-\frac{\partial U^j(\bar{\mathcal{X}}^{j^\tau}, \bar{\mathcal{Y}}^{j^\tau}, \bar{r}^\tau, \bar{\lambda}^\tau; \pi)}{\partial Y_i^j}\right) - Y_i^{j^\tau}\right] \times \left[Y_i^j - Y_i^{j^{\tau+1}}\right]$$

$$+\sum_{j=1}^{J}\sum_{i=1}^{I}\left[Z_i^{j^{\tau+1}} + \gamma\left(-\frac{\partial U^j(\bar{\mathcal{X}}^{j^\tau}, \bar{\mathcal{Y}}^{j^\tau}, \bar{r}^\tau, \bar{\lambda}^\tau; \pi)}{\partial Z_i^j}\right) - Z_i^{j^\tau}\right] \times \left[Z_i^j - Z_i^{j^{\tau+1}}\right]$$

$$+\sum_{j=1}^{J}\sum_{i=1}^{I}\left[\Psi_i^{j^{\tau+1}} + \gamma\left(-\frac{\partial U^j(\bar{\mathcal{X}}^{j^\tau}, \bar{\mathcal{Y}}^{j^\tau}, \bar{r}^\tau, \bar{\lambda}^\tau; \pi)}{\partial \Psi_i^j}\right) - \Psi_i^{j^\tau}\right] \times \left[\Psi_i^j - \Psi_i^{j^{\tau+1}}\right]$$

$$+\sum_{i=1}^{I}\left[r_i^{\tau+1} + \gamma\left[\sum_{j=1}^{J}\left(\bar{X}_i^{j^\tau} - \bar{Y}_i^{j^\tau}\right)\right] - r_i^\tau\right] \times \left[r_i - r_i^{\tau+1}\right]$$

$$+\sum_{i=1}^{I}\left[\lambda_i^{\tau+1} + \gamma\left[\sum_{j=1}^{J}\left(\bar{Z}_i^{j^\tau} - \bar{\Psi}_i^{j^\tau}\right)\right] - \lambda_i^\tau\right] \times \left[\lambda_i - \lambda_i^{\tau+1}\right],$$

$$\forall (\mathcal{X}, \mathcal{Y}, r, \lambda) \in \mathcal{K}. \tag{7.51}$$

Step 3: Convergence Verification:

If $\max_{i,j} |X_i^{j^{\tau+1}} - X_i^{j^\tau}| \leq \epsilon$; $\max_{i,j} |Y_i^{j^{\tau+1}} - Y_i^{j^\tau}| \leq \epsilon$; $\max_{i,j} |Z_i^{j^{\tau+1}} - Z_i^{j^\tau}| \leq \epsilon$; $\max_{i,j} |\Psi_i^{j^{\tau+1}} - \Psi_i^{j^\tau}| \leq \epsilon$; $\max_i |r_i^{\tau+1} - r_i^\tau| \leq \epsilon$, and $\max_i |\lambda_i^{\tau+1} - \lambda_i^\tau| \leq \epsilon$, for all $i; i = 1, \ldots, I$, and $j; j = 1, \ldots, J$, with $\epsilon > 0$, a prespecified tolerance, then stop; else, set $\tau := \tau + 1$, and go to Step 1.

The convergence of the algorithm is guaranteed following Theorems 7.4 and 7.5. Hence, we can state the following theorem.

Theorem 7.7

The modified projection algorithm is guaranteed to converge to an equilibrium asset, liability, and price pattern, satisfying variational inequality (7.15a) (and (7.15b)), provided that a solution exists.

In view of the feasible set $\mathcal{K}$, which is a Cartesian product and which consists of simple linear and nonnegativity constraints, and the projection operation, the variational inequality problems (7.50), as well as (7.51), decompose into quadratic programming subproblems that can be solved explicitly and in closed form (cf. Figure 7.6).

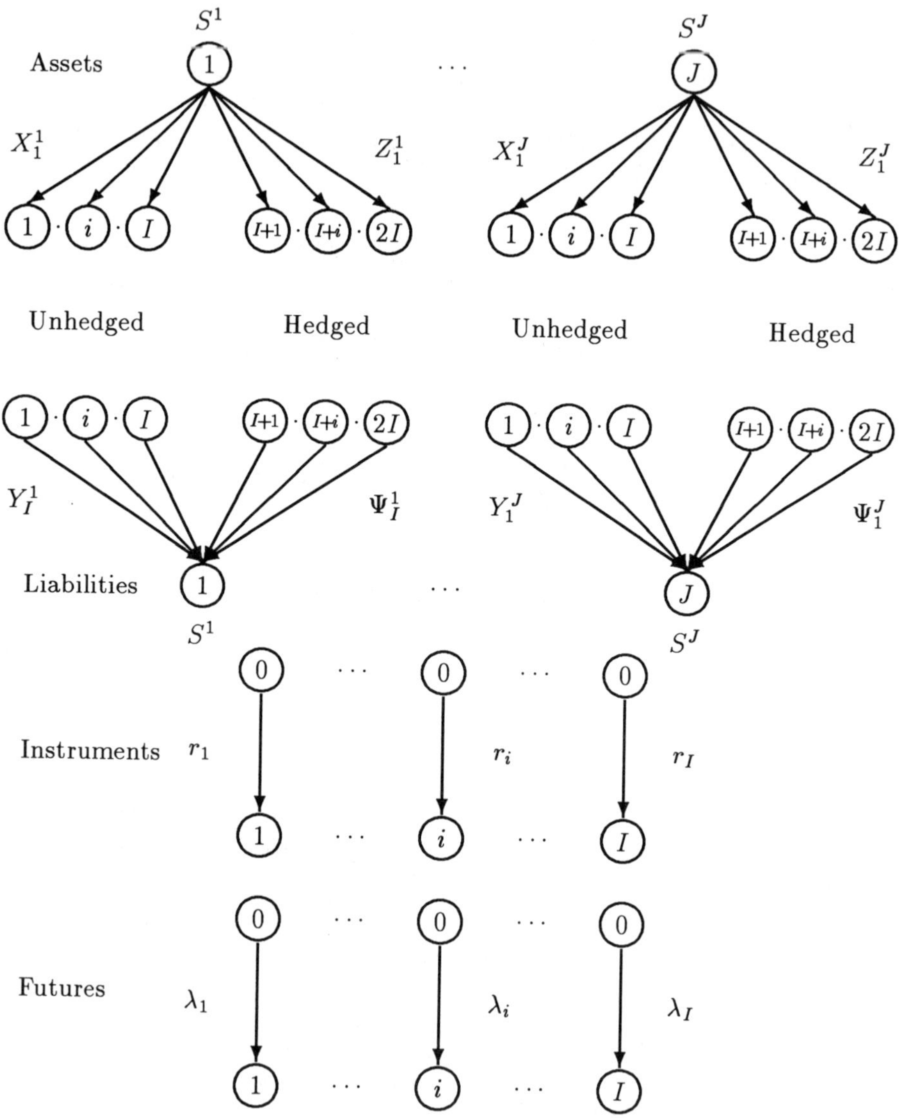

Fig. 7.6. The network structure of financial subproblems induced by the modified projection method

In particular, variational inequality subproblems (7.50) and (7.51) can decompose into variational inequality subproblems in the asset, liability, and price variables, respectively. The first variational inequality subproblem, consisting of the first and third terms in (7.50) and (7.51), in turn, further decomposes into J subproblems in the asset variables. Similarly, the second variational subproblem, consisting of the second and fourth terms in (7.50) and (7.51), decomposes into J subproblems in the liability variables. The third subproblem, consisting of the subsequent term in (7.50) and (7.51), decomposes into I instrument price subproblems. Finally, the last term in (7.50) and (7.51) decomposes into I shadow price subproblems. Note that all of these subproblems can be solved simultaneously.

Specifically, each asset subproblem for a sector is a separable quadratic programming problem with a single linear constraint and the nonnegativity assumption on the asset variables; the same holds for each liability subproblem for a sector. These can, hence, be solved via exact equilibration (cf. Section 5.2.3). Each subproblem in an instrument price, in turn, consists of a single variable (quadratic and separable) minimization problem subject to only a nonnegativity assumption on the variable, which can be computed using a closed form expression. Finally, each subproblem in shadow price also consists of a single variable (quadratic and separable) optimization problem but, unlike the instrument price subproblem, the variable is unconstrained. The network structure of the individual subproblems are illustrated in Figure 7.6.

7.4.1 Numerical Examples

In this section we present numerical examples to illustrate the behavior of the model. Note that these examples can be solved using the modified projection method or the primal-dual method. Moreover, they are amenable to solution via the Euler method as will be discussed in Chapter 8.

More precisely, we consider utility functions which are quadratic (cf. (7.24)–(7.27)), and we present some numerical examples of increasing complexity.

Example 7.1: 2 Sectors, 2 Unhedged Instruments, 2 Hedged Instruments

We first present an example consisting of two sectors trading in two unhedged financial instruments and two hedged financial instruments. The variance-covariance matrices for each of the sectors were as follows:

For sector 1:

$$Q^1 = \begin{pmatrix} 1.0 & 0.2 & 0 & 0 & -0.2 & -0.3 & 0 & 0 \\ 0.2 & 1.0 & 0 & 0 & -0.1 & -0.2 & 0 & 0 \\ 0 & 0 & 1.0 & 0 & 0 & 0 & -0.1 & 0 \\ 0 & 0 & 0 & 1.0 & 0 & 0 & -0.1 & 0 \\ -0.2 & -0.1 & 0 & 0 & 1.0 & 0.4 & 0 & 0 \\ -0.3 & -0.2 & 0 & 0 & 0.4 & 1.0 & 0 & 0 \\ 0 & 0 & -0.1 & -0.1 & 0 & 0 & 1.0 & 0 \\ 0 & 0 & 0 & 0 & 0 & 0 & 0 & 1.0 \end{pmatrix}$$

For sector 2:

$$Q^2 = \begin{pmatrix} 1.0 & 0.3 & 0.2 & 0 & 0 & 0 & -0.1 & -0.2 \\ 0.3 & 1.0 & 0 & 0 & 0 & -0.15 & 0 & 0 \\ 0.2 & 0 & 1.0 & 0.5 & -0.1 & 0 & 0 & 0 \\ 0 & 0 & 0.5 & 1.0 & 0 & -0.3 & 0 & 0 \\ 0 & 0 & -0.1 & 0 & 1.0 & 0 & 0.2 & 0 \\ 0 & -0.15 & 0 & -0.3 & 0 & 1.0 & 0.3 & 0 \\ -0.1 & 0 & 0 & 0 & 0.2 & 0.3 & 1.0 & 0 \\ -0.2 & 0 & 0 & 0 & 0 & 0 & 0 & 1.0 \end{pmatrix}.$$

We set all the financial volumes S^j equal to 1. We set the contracted futures prices thus: $\pi_1 = 1.7$ and $\pi_2 = .3$.

The computed equilibrium solution is:

Instrument Prices:

$$r_1^* = 1.436, \quad r_2^* = 1.558,$$

Shadow Prices:

$$\lambda_1^* = -.166, \quad \lambda_2^* = 1.173,$$

Asset and Liability Pattern:

$$X_1^{1*} = .253, \quad X_2^{1*} = .262, \quad Z_1^{1*} = .255, \quad Z_2^{1*} = .230,$$

$$X_1^{2*} = .229, \quad X_2^{2*} = .312, \quad Z_2^{1*} = .128, \quad Z_2^{2*} = .331,$$

$$Y_1^{1*} = .245, \quad Y_2^{1*} = .239, \quad \Psi_1^{1*} = .269, \quad \Psi_2^{1*} = .246,$$

$$Y_1^{2*} = .230, \quad Y_2^{2*} = .340, \quad \Psi_1^{2*} = .117, \quad \Psi_2^{2*} = .314.$$

As established in Lemma 7.1, we note that the unhedged markets cleared for each instrument and, hence, the instrument prices were positive. The hedged instruments also cleared and, as expected, satisfied the equilibrium conditions. Note that λ_1^* was negative, which reflects that the shadow price for hedged instrument 1 was negative. Indeed, the contracted futures price π_1

exceeded the equilibrium price r_1^*. On the other hand, in the case of hedged instrument 2, the equilibrium price r_2^* was greater than the contracted futures price π_2 and λ_2^* was positive.

Example 7.2: 4 Sectors, 2 Unhedged Instruments, 2 Hedged Instruments

The second example consisted of four sectors and two hedged and two unhedged financial instruments.

The variance-covariance matrices for the first two sectors were as in Example 7.1. The variance-covariance matrices for the third and fourth sectors were as follows:

For sector 3:

$$Q^3 = \begin{pmatrix} 1.0 & 0 & 0.3 & 0 & -0.1 & -0.1 & 0 & 0 \\ 0 & 1.0 & 0.1 & 0 & 0 & 0 & -0.2 & 0 \\ 0.3 & 0.1 & 1.0 & 0 & -0.3 & 0 & 0 & 0 \\ 0 & 0 & 0 & 1.0 & -0.4 & 0 & 0 & 0 \\ -0.1 & 0 & -0.3 & -0.4 & 1.0 & 0 & 0 & 0 \\ -0.1 & 0 & 0 & 0 & 0 & 1.0 & 0.5 & 0 \\ 0 & -0.2 & 0 & 0 & 0 & 0.5 & 1.0 & 0.1 \\ 0 & 0 & 0 & 0 & 0 & 0 & 0.1 & 1.0 \end{pmatrix}$$

For sector 4:

$$Q^4 = \begin{pmatrix} 1.0 & 0.4 & 0 & 0 & -0.2 & 0 & 0 & 0 \\ 0.4 & 1.0 & 0 & 0 & 0 & -0.1 & 0 & 0 \\ 0 & 0 & 1.0 & 0 & -0.3 & 0 & 0 & 0 \\ 0 & 0 & 0 & 1.0 & 0 & 0 & -0.4 & 0 \\ -0.2 & 0 & -0.3 & 0 & 1.0 & 0 & 0 & 0 \\ 0 & -0.1 & 0 & 0 & 0 & 1.0 & 0.3 & 0 \\ 0 & 0 & 0 & -0.4 & 0 & 0.3 & 1.0 & 0.1 \\ 0 & 0 & 0 & 0 & 0 & 0 & 0.1 & 1.0 \end{pmatrix}.$$

Here we lowered the futures price π_1 and set it equal to 1.3 and increased the futures price π_2 and set it to .7, and the sector volumes for these sectors were also set equal to 1.

The equilibrium solution is given by:

Instrument Prices:

$$r_1^* = 1.559, \quad r_2^* = 1.530,$$

Shadow Prices:

$$\lambda_1^* = .203, \quad \lambda_2^* = .708,$$

Asset and Liability Pattern:

$$X_1^{1^*} = .318, \quad X_2^{1^*} = .243, \quad Z_1^{1^*} = .239, \quad Z_2^{1^*} = .200,$$

$$X_1^{2^*} = .320, \quad X_2^{2^*} = .273, \quad Z_1^{2^*} = .102, \quad Z_2^{2^*} = .306,$$
$$X_1^{3^*} = .218, \quad X_2^{3^*} = .230, \quad Z_1^{3^*} = .230, \quad Z_2^{3^*} = .322,$$
$$X_1^{4^*} = .258, \quad X_2^{4^*} = .143, \quad Z_1^{4^*} = .313, \quad Z_2^{4^*} = .286,$$
$$Y_1^{1^*} = .168, \quad Y_2^{1^*} = .288, \quad \Psi_1^{1^*} = .275, \quad \Psi_2^{1^*} = .269,$$
$$Y_1^{2^*} = .190, \quad Y_2^{2^*} = .313, \quad \Psi_1^{2^*} = .147, \quad \Psi_2^{2^*} = .349,$$
$$Y_1^{3^*} = .418, \quad Y_2^{3^*} = .142, \quad \Psi_1^{3^*} = .184, \quad \Psi_2^{3^*} = .255,$$
$$Y_1^{4^*} = .340, \quad Y_2^{4^*} = .139, \quad \Psi_1^{4^*} = .280, \quad \Psi_2^{4^*} = .241.$$

In this example, as expected, the markets also cleared for each unhedged instrument and for each hedged instrument. Both shadow prices λ_1^* and λ_2^* were now positive.

Example 7.3: 6 Sectors, 2 Unhedged Instruments, 2 Hedged Instruments

This example consisted of six sectors with the data for the first four sectors as in the preceding example. The variance/covariance matrices for the fifth and sixth sectors were given by:

For sector 5:

$$Q^5 = \begin{pmatrix} 1.0 & 0.1 & 0 & 0 & 0 & 0 & 0 & -0.1 \\ 0.1 & 1.0 & 0.2 & 0 & -0.2 & 0 & 0 & 0 \\ 0 & 0.2 & 1.0 & 0 & 0 & -0.3 & 0 & 0 \\ 0 & 0 & 0 & 1.0 & 0 & 0 & 0 & 0 \\ 0 & -0.2 & 0 & 0 & 1.0 & 0.5 & 0 & 0 \\ 0 & 0 & -0.3 & 0 & 0.5 & 1.0 & 0 & 0 \\ 0 & 0 & 0 & 0 & 0 & 0 & 1.0 & 0.4 \\ -0.1 & 0 & 0 & 0 & 0 & 0 & 0.4 & 1.0 \end{pmatrix}$$

For sector 6:

$$Q^6 = \begin{pmatrix} 1.0 & 0 & 0.2 & 0 & -0.1 & -0.2 & 0 & 0 \\ 0 & 1.0 & 0.3 & 0 & 0 & -0.4 & 0 & 0 \\ 0.2 & 0.3 & 1.0 & 0 & 0 & 0 & -0.1 & 0 \\ 0 & 0 & 0 & 1.0 & 0 & 0 & 0 & 0 \\ -0.1 & 0 & 0 & 0 & 1.0 & 0.4 & 0 & 0 \\ -0.2 & -0.4 & 0 & 0 & 0.4 & 1.0 & 0 & 0 \\ 0 & 0 & -0.1 & 0 & 0 & 0 & 1.0 & 0.6 \\ 0 & 0 & 0 & 0 & 0 & 0 & 0.6 & 1.0 \end{pmatrix}.$$

We set $S^5 = S^6 = 2$ with the other sector volumes as in the preceding examples. We reset the futures prices to the same values as in Example 7.1, i.e., $\pi_1 = 1.7$ and $\pi_2 = .3$.

The computed equilibrium solution is:

Instrument Prices:

$$r_1^* = 1.492, \quad r_2^* = 1.563,$$

Shadow Prices:

$$\lambda_1^* = -.201, \quad \lambda_2^* = 1.149,$$

Asset and Liability Pattern:

$$X_1^{1*} = .282, \quad X_2^{1*} = .258, \quad Z_1^{1*} = .249, \quad Z_2^{1*} = .211,$$

$$X_1^{2*} = .265, \quad X_2^{2*} = .300, \quad Z_1^{2*} = .132, \quad Z_2^{2*} = .303,$$

$$X_1^{3*} = .169, \quad X_2^{3*} = .226, \quad Z_1^{3*} = .262, \quad Z_2^{3*} = .343,$$

$$X_1^{4*} = .219, \quad X_2^{4*} = .165, \quad Z_1^{4*} = .329, \quad Z_2^{4*} = .288,$$

$$X_1^{5*} = .254, \quad X_2^{5*} = .241, \quad Z_1^{5*} = .286, \quad Z_2^{5*} = .218,$$

$$X_1^{6*} = .641, \quad X_2^{6*} = .806, \quad Z_1^{6*} = .128, \quad Z_2^{6*} = .425,$$

$$Y_1^{1*} = .212, \quad Y_2^{1*} = .256, \quad \Psi_1^{1*} = .271, \quad \Psi_2^{1*} = .262,$$

$$Y_1^{2*} = .235, \quad Y_2^{2*} = .316, \quad \Psi_1^{2*} = .121, \quad \Psi_2^{2*} = .328,$$

$$Y_1^{3*} = .459, \quad Y_2^{3*} = .129, \quad \Psi_1^{3*} = .174, \quad \Psi_2^{3*} = .238,$$

$$Y_1^{4*} = .369, \quad Y_2^{4*} = .134, \quad \Psi_1^{4*} = .268, \quad \Psi_2^{4*} = .229,$$

$$Y_1^{5*} = .241, \quad Y_2^{5*} = .262, \quad \Psi_1^{5*} = .195, \quad \Psi_2^{5*} = .302,$$

$$Y_1^{6*} = .309, \quad Y_2^{6*} = .907, \quad \Psi_1^{6*} = .358, \quad \Psi_2^{6*} = .425.$$

In this example, the markets cleared for each unhedged and hedged financial instrument.

Note that, as in Example 7.1, the shadow price for instrument 1 was negative since the equilibrium price was lower than the futures price.

7.5 Models with Options

In this section we develop a single country multi-sector, multi-instrument financial model with options, and we regard options as financial instruments that can either provide a fixed rate of return in the case that they are exercised, or provide the rate of return from the spot market in the case that they are not exercised. In either case, the holder of the option has to pay a premium for having the right to exercise the option.

We assume that we only have European options (and we are interested in the intrinsic value), which can be exercised only at maturity and that they are *limited* type options, which are the same as *true* options, but where the premium is payable on the maturity date. As in the classical Black and

Scholes (1973) model, we consider an economy without taxes and transaction costs. Finally, we assume that the exercise prices of the options contracts along with the premiums are known constants.

The mathematical framework that we utilize for the development and study of financial equilibrium models in the presence of options, is, again, the theory of variational inequalities, which has already being used for options pricing (e. g., Jaillet, Lamberton, and Lapeyre (1990)). We assume that all the assumptions about the economy under consideration are the same as those imposed in Section 7.1. Pricing of options and study of different hedging strategies with the use of options, however, is beyond the scope of this book.

We consider an economy consisting of J sectors, with a typical sector denoted by j, and with I instruments, with a typical instrument denoted by i. Moreover, we denote the volume of instrument i held as an unhedged asset by sector j as X_i^j, and group the unhedged assets of the sector into the column vector $X^j \in R_+^I$. Similarly, Y_i^j denotes the volume of instrument i held as an unhedged liability by sector j. The unhedged liabilities of each sector are grouped into the column vector $Y^j \in R_+^I$.

We let W_i^j denote the volume of capital that sector j holds as an asset on a European option contract on instrument i where the option will not be exercised. Similarly, we denote the volume of capital that sector j holds as an asset on a European option contract on instrument i where the option will be exercised by Z_i^j. We group the instrument hedged assets of sector j into the column vectors $W^j \in R_+^I$ and $Z^j \in R_+^I$. We also let Φ_i^j denote the volume of capital that sector j holds as a liability on a European option contract on instrument i where the option will not be exercised, and we let Ψ_i^j denote the volume of capital that sector j holds as a liability on a European option contract on instrument i, where the option will be exercised. Note that in the case of W_i^j, in contrast to X_i^j, there is an associated premium that incorporates the right to be in the options market.

Finally, we group the unhedged and hedged asset vectors (X^j, W^j, Z^j) for sector j into the asset column vector $\mathcal{X}^j \in R_+^{3I}$ and the unhedged and hedged liability vectors (Y^j, Φ^j, Ψ^j) into the liability column vector $\mathcal{Y}^j \in R_+^{3I}$. We then group these vectors, respectively, into the vectors $\mathcal{X} \in R_+^{3JI}$ and $\mathcal{Y} \in R_+^{3JI}$.

Let r_i represent the price of instrument i and group the instrument prices into the column vector $r \in R_+^I$. Furthermore, let π_i represent the exercise price of a European option on instrument i and group the exercise prices into an I-dimensional column vector π. Finally, let θ_i denote the premium paid for obtaining the right to exercise a European option on instrument i and group these premiums into an I-dimensional column vector θ. In addition, we denote the shadow price or "opportunity cost" associated with an exercised European option on instrument i by λ_i (analogous to the opportunity cost in the case of futures in Section 7.1). We also group the shadow prices into the column vector λ. For exposition purposes and, without loss of generality, we assume that there is only one type of European options contract available per instrument, and that all contracts call for delivery at the time the contract was entered into.

The utility function for sector j is denoted by $U^j(\mathcal{X}^j, \mathcal{Y}^j, r, \lambda; \theta, \pi)$ and is assumed to be concave in the instrument variables, continuous, and twice continuously differentiable, with each sector taking the prices r and λ as given and with π and θ assumed to be known constants. Moreover, we assume that the accounts of each sector of the country must balance, and, as before, we denote the total financial volume held by sector j by S^j. Here we consider a specific form of the utility function which is a generalization to the case of options of the special utility function (7.4) in the case of futures.

The portfolio optimization problem of sector j can then be expressed as:

$$\text{Maximize } U^j(\mathcal{X}^j, \mathcal{Y}^j, r, \lambda; \theta, \pi) =$$

$$u^j(\mathcal{X}^j, \mathcal{Y}^j) + \sum_{i=1}^{I} r_i(X_i^j - Y_i^j) + \sum_{i=1}^{I}(\pi_i - \theta_i + \lambda_i)(Z_i^j - \Psi_i^j) + \sum_{i=1}^{I}(r_i - \theta_i)(W_i^j - \Phi_i^j) \tag{7.52}$$

subject to:

$$\sum_{i=1}^{I} X_i^j + W_i^j + Z_i^j = S^j, \tag{7.53a}$$

$$\sum_{i=1}^{I} Y_i^j + \Phi_i^j + \Psi_i^j = S^j, \tag{7.53b}$$

$$X_i^j, Y_i^j, W_i^j, \Phi_i^j, Z_i^j, \Psi_i^j \geq 0, \quad i = 1, \ldots, I. \tag{7.54}$$

Note that, as in the models with futures presented the Section 7.1, the term $u^j(\mathcal{X}^j, \mathcal{Y}^j)$ in the objective function (7.52) reflects the risk associated with the particular portfolio choice. The second term reflects (as in (6.4)) the total return due to the unhedged part of the portfolio. Here, for the sake of flexibility, we allow a sector to exercise an option (at a certain volume) and to simultaneously not exercise it (but at a certain volume). Hence, the third term in (7.52) represents the total return from the hedged but not exercised portion of the portfolio, whereas the fourth term represents the total return from the hedged and exercised part of the portfolio.

For each sector j we let:

$$\bar{\mathcal{X}}^j = \{X^j \in R_+^I, W^j \in R_+^I, Z^j \in R_+^I : \sum_{i=1}^{I} X_i^j + W_i^j + Z_i^j = S^j\} \tag{7.55}$$

denote the constraint set for the assets, and, similarly, we let

$$\bar{\mathcal{Y}}^j = \{Y^j \in R_+^I, \Phi^j \in R_+^I, \Psi^j \in R_+^I : \sum_{i=1}^{I} Y_i^j + \Phi_i^j + \Psi_i^j = S^j\} \tag{7.56}$$

denote the constraint set for the liabilities. Then the feasible set for the assets and the liabilities of each sector is a Cartesian product denoted by $\bar{\kappa}^j$, where

$$\bar{\kappa}^j \equiv \{\bar{\mathcal{X}}^j \times \bar{\mathcal{Y}}^j\}. \tag{7.57}$$

We then define the feasible set for the assets of all sectors $\bar{X}$ as:

$$\bar{X} \equiv \bar{X}^1 \times \ldots \times \bar{X}^j \times \ldots \times \bar{X}^J, \tag{7.58}$$

and, similarly, for the liabilities:

$$\bar{Y} \equiv \bar{Y}^1 \times \ldots \times \bar{Y}^j \times \ldots \times \bar{Y}^J, \tag{7.59}$$

with $\bar{\kappa} \equiv \{\bar{X} \times \bar{Y}\}$.

Furthermore, the feasible set for all hedged and unhedged assets and liabilities of all sectors, and all prices of all the instruments, is denoted as $\mathcal{K}$ and is given by: $\mathcal{K} \equiv \{\bar{\kappa} \times R^I_+ \times R^I\}$.

The Equilibrium Conditions

We are now ready to state the equilibrium conditions.

Portfolio Optimality

Since for each sector j, we have assumed that the utility function U^j is concave, continuous, and twice continuously differentiable, the necessary and sufficient conditions for an optimal portfolio of sector j, $(\mathcal{X}^{j*}, \mathcal{Y}^{j*}) \in \bar{\kappa}^j$, can be expressed as:

$$-\nabla_{\mathcal{X}^j} U^j(\mathcal{X}^{j*}, \mathcal{Y}^{j*}, r^*, \lambda^*; \theta, \pi)^T \cdot (\mathcal{X}^j - \mathcal{X}^{j*})$$
$$-\nabla_{\mathcal{Y}^j} U^j(\mathcal{X}^{j*}, \mathcal{Y}^{j*}, r^*, \lambda^*; \theta, \pi)^T \cdot (\mathcal{Y}^j - \mathcal{Y}^{j*}) \geq 0, \quad \forall (\mathcal{X}^j, \mathcal{Y}^j) \in \bar{\kappa}^j, \tag{7.60}$$

where ∇_Ω denotes the gradient with respect to the variables in the vector Ω, that is,

$$\nabla_{\mathcal{X}^j} U^j \equiv \left(\frac{\partial U^j}{\partial X^j_1}, \ldots, \frac{\partial U^j}{\partial X^j_I}, \frac{\partial U^j}{\partial W^j_1}, \ldots, \frac{\partial U^j}{\partial W^j_I}, \frac{\partial U^j}{\partial Z^j_1}, \ldots, \frac{\partial U^j}{\partial Z^j_I} \right) \tag{7.61}$$

and

$$\nabla_{\mathcal{Y}^j} U^j \equiv \left(\frac{\partial U^j}{\partial Y^j_1}, \ldots, \frac{\partial U^j}{\partial Y^j_I}, \frac{\partial U^j}{\partial \Phi^j_1}, \ldots, \frac{\partial U^j}{\partial \Phi^j_I}, \frac{\partial U^j}{\partial \Psi^j_1}, \ldots, \frac{\partial U^j}{\partial \Psi^j_I} \right). \tag{7.62}$$

Furthermore, the economic system conditions for the unhedged instrument prices are:

Unhedged Instrument Market Equilibrium Conditions

For each unhedged instrument j; $j = 1, \dots, J$, we must have that:

$$\sum_{j=1}^{J} \left[\left(X_i^{j*} + W_i^{j*} \right) - \left(Y_i^{j*} + \Phi_i^{j*} \right) \right] \begin{cases} = 0, & \text{if } r_i^* > 0 \\ \geq 0, & \text{if } r_i^* = 0. \end{cases} \tag{7.63}$$

The system of equalities and inequalities (7.63) states that if the price of a financial instrument is positive, then the market must clear for that instrument, and if the price is zero, then either there is an excess supply of that instrument in the economy or the market clears.

Hedged Instrument Market Equilibrium Conditions

Similarly, the assets and the liabilities for an option contract on instrument i; $i = 1, \dots, I$, that will be exercised, must satisfy:

$$\sum_{j=1}^{J} \left(Z_i^{j*} - \Psi_i^{j*} \right) = 0, \tag{7.64}$$

The shadow price λ_i^*, associated with the constraint (7.64), represents the opportunity cost associated with exercising an option on instrument i. Since the constraint is an equality, λ_i^* can be positive, negative, or zero.

Definition 7.2

A vector $(\mathcal{X}^*, \mathcal{Y}^*, r^*, \lambda^*) \in \mathcal{K}$ is an equilibrium point of the single country, multi-sector, multi-instrument financial model with options if and only if it satisfies the system of equalities and inequalities (7.60), (7.63), and (7.64), for all sectors j, all unhedged instruments i, and all hedged instruments i, simultaneously.

We now present Theorem 7.8, which demonstrates the variational inequality formulation of the equilibrium conditions for the financial model with options.

Theorem 7.8 (Variational Inequality Formulation with Options)

A vector of assets and liabilities of the sectors, and instrument prices, $(\mathcal{X}^*, \mathcal{Y}^*, r^*, \lambda^*) \in \mathcal{K}$, is a financial equilibrium if and only if it satisfies the variational inequality problem:

$$\sum_{j=1}^{J} \sum_{i=1}^{I} \left[-\frac{\partial u^j(\mathcal{X}^{j*}, \mathcal{Y}^{j*})}{\partial X_i^j} - r_i^* \right] \times \left[X_i^j - X_i^{j*} \right]$$

$$+ \sum_{j=1}^{J} \sum_{i=1}^{I} \left[-\frac{\partial u^j(\mathcal{X}^{j*}, \mathcal{Y}^{j*})}{\partial Z_i^j} - (\pi_i - \theta_i + \lambda_i^*) \right] \times \left[Z_i^j - Z_i^{j*} \right]$$

$$+\sum_{j=1}^{J}\sum_{i=1}^{I}\left[-\frac{\partial u^j(\mathcal{X}^{j*},\mathcal{Y}^{j*})}{\partial W_i^j}-(r_i^*-\theta_i)\right]\times\left[W_i^j-W_i^{j*}\right]$$

$$+\sum_{j=1}^{J}\sum_{i=1}^{I}\left[-\frac{\partial u^j(\mathcal{X}^{j*},\mathcal{Y}^{j*})}{\partial Y_i^j}+r_i^*\right]\times\left[Y_i^j-Y_i^{j*}\right]$$

$$+\sum_{j=1}^{J}\sum_{i=1}^{I}\left[-\frac{\partial u^j(\mathcal{X}^{j*},\mathcal{Y}^{j*})}{\partial \Psi_i^j}+(\pi_i-\theta_i+\lambda_i^*)\right]\times\left[\Psi_i^j-\Psi_i^{j*}\right]$$

$$+\sum_{j=1}^{J}\sum_{i=1}^{I}\left[-\frac{\partial u^j(\mathcal{X}^{j*},\mathcal{Y}^{j*})}{\partial \Phi_i^j}+(r_i^*-\theta_i)\right]\times\left[\Phi_i^j-\Phi_i^{j*}\right]$$

$$+\sum_{i=1}^{I}\sum_{j=1}^{J}\left[\left(X_i^{j*}+W_i^{j*}\right)-\left(Y_i^{j*}+\Phi_i^{j*}\right)\right]\times\left[r_i-r_i^*\right]$$

$$+\sum_{i=1}^{I}\sum_{j=1}^{J}\left[Z_i^{j*}-\Psi_i^{j*}\right]\times\left[\lambda_i-\lambda_i^*\right]\geq 0,\quad \forall(\mathcal{X},\mathcal{Y},r,\lambda)\in\mathcal{K}, \tag{7.65}$$

Proof: Follows using similar argument as the proof of Theorem 7.1. □

We now present variational inequality (7.65) in standard form. Let $n = 6JI + 2I$. Define the J-dimensional column vector U with components: $\{U^1, \ldots, U^J\}$. Define the n-dimensional column vector $x \equiv (\mathcal{X}, \mathcal{Y}, r, \lambda) \in \mathcal{K}$, and the n-dimensional column vector $F(x)$ with components:

$$F(x)=\begin{bmatrix} F_1(x)\\ \vdots \\ F_b(x) \\ \vdots \\ F_n(x)\end{bmatrix}=\begin{bmatrix} -\nabla_{\mathcal{X}}U(\mathcal{X},\mathcal{Y},r,\lambda;\theta,\pi)\\ -\nabla_{\mathcal{Y}}U(\mathcal{X},\mathcal{Y},r,\lambda;\theta,\pi)\\ \sum_{j=1}^{J}\left[(X_1^j+W_1^j)-(Y_1^j+\Phi_1^j)\right]\\ \vdots\\ \sum_{j=1}^{J}\left[(X_I^j+W_I^j)-(Y_I^j+\Phi_I^j)\right]\\ \sum_{j=1}^{J}(Z_1^j-\Psi_1^j)\\ \vdots\\ \sum_{j=1}^{J}(Z_I^j-\Psi_I^j)\end{bmatrix}_{n\times 1} \tag{7.66}$$

Therefore, (7.65) can be written as:
Determine $x^* \in \mathcal{K}$ satisfying:

$$\langle F(x^*)^T, x-x^*\rangle \geq 0, \quad \forall x\in\mathcal{K}. \tag{7.67}$$

7.6 Qualitative Properties

In this section we present qualitative properties for the financial equilibrium model with options developed in Section 7.5. In order to illustrate the flexibility of the methodology of variational inequality theory (as well as network optimization theory), we provide alternative existence and monotonicity proofs to those given in Theorems 7.2 and 7.4. Theorem 7.3, the uniqueness result, holds true for the options model under the identical assumptions, as does Theorem 7.5, as does Lipschitz continuity of the function that enters the variational inequality problem (where $F(x)$ is now altered accordingly). In addition, we illustrate qualitatively, some economic properties of the options model.

The existence result is deferred until Section 7.7, where we take advantage of the network optimization reformulation of the governing equilibrium conditions.

Theorem 7.9 (Monotonicity)

Under the assumption that the utility function U^j given in (7.52) is strictly concave for each sector j, and twice continuously differentiable, the function F defined in (7.66) is monotone.

Proof: Assume that x^1 and x^2 lie in $\mathcal{K}$. Writing

$$\langle (F(x^1) - F(x^2))^T, x^1 - x^2 \rangle, \tag{7.68}$$

and making algebraic simplifications, yields:

$$-\sum_{j=1}^{J} \left[\nabla_{\mathcal{X}^j} U^j(\mathcal{X}^{j^1}, \mathcal{Y}^{j^1}, r^1, \lambda^1; \theta, \pi) - \nabla_{\mathcal{X}^j} U^j(\mathcal{X}^{j^2}, \mathcal{Y}^{j^2}, r^2, \lambda^2; \theta, \pi) \right]^T$$
$$\cdot \left[\mathcal{X}^{j^1} - \mathcal{X}^{j^2} \right]$$
$$-\sum_{j=1}^{J} \left[\nabla_{\mathcal{Y}^j} U^j(\mathcal{X}^{j^1}, \mathcal{Y}^{j^1}, r^1, \lambda^1; \theta, \pi) - \nabla_{\mathcal{Y}^j} U^j(\mathcal{X}^{j^2}, \mathcal{Y}^{j^2}, r^2, \lambda^2; \theta, \pi) \right]^T$$
$$\cdot \left[\mathcal{Y}^{j^1} - \mathcal{Y}^{j^2} \right]. \tag{7.69}$$

But under the assumption that the utility functions are strictly concave for each sector j, (7.69) must be nonnegative, and, hence, $F(x)$ must be monotone. □

We now utilize the variational inequality (7.65) to investigate some economic tradeoffs.

Corollary 7.2

Assume that, in equilibrium, $\frac{\partial u^j}{\partial Z_i^j} = \frac{\partial u^j}{\partial W_i^j}$ for all sectors j and all instruments i.

If, in equilibrium, we have that for a given sector j and an instrument i, $W_i^{j*} > 0$, *that is, a certain volume of instrument i is not exercised by sector j as an option held as an asset, then*

$$r_i^* \geq (\pi_i + \lambda_i^*). \tag{7.70}$$

On the other hand, if, in equilibrium, we have that for a given sector j and an instrument i, $Z_i^{j*} > 0$, *that is, a certain volume of instrument i is exercised as an option held as an asset by sector j, then*

$$(\pi_i + \lambda_i^*) \geq r_i^*. \tag{7.71}$$

Finally, if, in equilibrium, both $W_i^{j*} > 0$ *and* $Z_i^{j*} > 0$, *then*

$$r_i^* = (\pi_i + \lambda_i^*). \tag{7.72}$$

Proof: Into variational inequality (7.65) we make the following substitutions: $X_i^j = X_i^{j*}$, $Y_i^j = Y_i^{j*}$, $\Psi_i^j = \Psi_i^{j*}$, $\Phi_i^j = \Phi_i^{j*}$, and $r_i = r_i^*$, $\lambda_i = \lambda_i^*$, for all i and j. Moreover, we set $Z_k^l = Z_k^{l*}$, for all $k \neq i$, and $l \neq j$. Similarly, we set $W_k^l = W_k^{l*}$, for all $k \neq i$, and $l \neq j$. We select a small $\delta > 0$ and next we construct, since $W_i^{j*} > 0$, the following: $W_i^j = W_i^{j*} - \delta$, and $Z_i^j = Z_i^{j*} + \delta$. Clearly, such a pattern is still feasible. A simple calculation yields, under the assumption of equal partial derivatives, that

$$r_i^* \geq (\pi_i + \lambda_i^*),$$

which is (7.70).

If, on the other hand, $Z_i^{j*} > 0$, then we can construct an analogous feasible pattern to the one above, with the exception that δ is now subtracted from Z_i^{j*} to construct Z_i^j and added to W_i^{j*} to obtain W_i^j. Simple substitution of these values into (7.65) (under the same assumption of equal partial derivatives at equilibrium), yields

$$(\pi_i + \lambda_i^*) \geq r_i^*,$$

which is (7.71).

Finally, if both W_i^{j*} and Z_i^{j*} are positive at equilibrium, then constructing the inequalities as above yields both (7.71) and (7.72) and, hence, they must hold with equality. □

Making an analogous construction but for the hedged liabilities yields:

Corollary 7.3

Assume that, in equilibrium, $\frac{\partial u^j}{\partial \Psi_i^j} = \frac{\partial u^j}{\partial \Phi_i^j}$ *for all sectors j and all instruments i.*

If, in equilibrium, we have that, for a given sector j and instrument i, $\Psi_i^{j*} > 0$, that is, a certain volume of instrument i is not exercised by j as a liability option, then

$$(\pi_i + \lambda_i^*) \geq r_i^*. \tag{7.73}$$

On the other hand, if, in equilibrium, we have that for a sector j and instrument i, $\Psi_i^{j*} > 0$, that is, a certain volume of i is exercised by sector j as a liability option, then

$$r_i^* \geq (\pi_i + \lambda_i^*). \tag{7.74}$$

Finally, if, in equilibrium, both $\Psi_i^{j*} > 0$ and $\Phi_i^{j*} > 0$, then

$$r_i^* = (\pi_i + \lambda_i^*). \tag{7.75}$$

Note that the above corollaries have the following interpretation: If the marginal utilities (associated with the risk), at equilibrium, for a sector of exercising or not exercising an option on an instrument as an asset (or an a liability) are equal, then a sector will or will not exercise a volume of the instrument, depending on the difference between the rate of return or price at equilibrium and the fixed price plus the shadow price.

7.7 Network Optimization Reformulation

In this section we provide results, analogous to those obtained in Section 7.3 for the options model of Section 7.5. The proofs herein are omitted since they are straightforward adaptations of the corresponding results in Section 7.3.

Theorem 7.10

The variational inequality problem of finding $(\mathcal{X}^*, \mathcal{Y}^*, r^*, \lambda^*) \in \mathcal{K}$ satisfying:

$$\sum_{j=1}^{J}\sum_{i=1}^{I}\left[-\frac{\partial u^j(\mathcal{X}^{j*}, \mathcal{Y}^{j*})}{\partial X_i^j} - r_i^*\right] \times \left[X_i^j - X_i^{j*}\right]$$

$$+\sum_{j=1}^{J}\sum_{i=1}^{I}\left[-\frac{\partial u^j(\mathcal{X}^{j*}, \mathcal{Y}^{j*})}{\partial Z_i^j} - (\pi_i - \theta_i + \lambda_i^*)\right] \times \left[Z_i^j - Z_i^{j*}\right]$$

$$+\sum_{j=1}^{J}\sum_{i=1}^{I}\left[-\frac{\partial u^j(\mathcal{X}^{j*}, \mathcal{Y}^{j*})}{\partial W_i^j} - (r_i^* - \theta_i)\right] \times \left[W_i^j - W_i^{j*}\right]$$

$$+\sum_{j=1}^{J}\sum_{i=1}^{I}\left[-\frac{\partial u^j(\mathcal{X}^{j*}, \mathcal{Y}^{j*})}{\partial Y_i^j} + r_i^*\right] \times \left[Y_i^j - Y_i^{j*}\right]$$

$$+\sum_{j=1}^{J}\sum_{i=1}^{I}\left[-\frac{\partial u^j(\mathcal{X}^{j*},\mathcal{Y}^{j*})}{\partial \Psi_i^j}+(\pi_i-\theta_i+\lambda_i^*)\right]\times\left[\Psi_i^j-\Psi_i^{j*}\right]$$

$$+\sum_{j=1}^{J}\sum_{i=1}^{I}\left[-\frac{\partial u^j(\mathcal{X}^{j*},\mathcal{Y}^{j*})}{\partial \Phi_i^j}+(r_i^*-\theta_i)\right]\times\left[\Phi_i^j-\Phi_i^{j*}\right]$$

$$+\sum_{i=1}^{I}\sum_{j=1}^{J}\left[\left(X_i^{j*}+W_i^{j*}\right)-\left(Y_i^{j*}+\Phi_i^{j*}\right)\right]\times\left[r_i-r_i^*\right]$$

$$+\sum_{i=1}^{I}\sum_{j=1}^{J}\left[Z_i^{j*}-\Psi_i^{j*}\right]\times\left[\lambda_i-\lambda_i^*\right]\geq 0,\quad \forall(\mathcal{X},\mathcal{Y},r,\lambda)\in\mathcal{K}, \tag{7.76}$$

is equivalent to the problem:

$$\text{Maximize}\ \sum_{j=1}^{J}u^j(\mathcal{X}^j,\mathcal{Y}^j)+\sum_{j=1}^{J}\sum_{i=1}^{I}(\pi_i-\theta_i)(Z_i^j-\Psi_i^j)+\sum_{j=1}^{J}\sum_{i=1}^{I}(-\theta_i)(W_i^j-\Phi_i^j) \tag{7.77}$$

subject to:

$$\sum_{j=1}^{J}\left[\left(X_i^j+W_i^j\right)-\left(Y_i^j+\Phi_i^j\right)\right]\geq 0,\quad i=1,\ldots,I \tag{7.78}$$

$$\sum_{j=1}^{J}(Z_i^j-\Psi_i^j)=0,\quad i=1,\ldots,I \tag{7.79}$$

and

$$(\mathcal{X}^j,\mathcal{Y}^j)\in\bar{\kappa}^j,\quad j=1,\ldots,J, \tag{7.80}$$

where $r_i^*\geq 0$ corresponds to the Lagrange multiplier associated with the i-th constraint in (7.78), and λ_i^* corresponds to the Lagrange multiplier associated with the i-th constraint in (7.79).

Lemma 7.2

In equilibrium, the markets clear for all unhedged instruments and for all hedged instruments, that is,

$$\sum_{j=1}^{J}\left[\left(X_i^{j*}+W_i^{j*}\right)-\left(Y_i^{j*}+\Phi_i^{j*}\right)\right]=0,\quad i=1,\ldots,I \tag{7.81}$$

and

$$\sum_{j=1}^{J}(Z_i^{j*}-\Psi_i^{j*})=0,\quad i=1,\ldots,I. \tag{7.82}$$

Furthermore, the prices r_i^* are strictly positive, whereas the shadow prices λ_i^* can be positive, negative, or zero, for all instruments i.

Corollary 7.4

The solution to the optimization problem:

$$\text{Maximize} \sum_{j=1}^{J} u^j(\mathcal{X}^j, \mathcal{Y}^j) + \sum_{j=1}^{J}\sum_{i=1}^{I}(\pi_i - \theta_i)(Z_i^j - \Psi_i^j) + \sum_{j=1}^{J}\sum_{i=1}^{I}(-\theta_i)(W_i^j - \Phi_i^j) \tag{7.83}$$

subject to:

$$\sum_{j=1}^{J}\left[\left(X_i^j + W_i^j\right) - \left(Y_i^j + \Phi_i^j\right)\right] = 0, \quad i = 1, \ldots, I \tag{7.84}$$

$$\sum_{j=1}^{J}(Z_i^j - \Psi_i^j) = 0, \quad i = 1, \ldots, I \tag{7.85}$$

$$(\mathcal{X}^j, \mathcal{Y}^j) \in \bar{\kappa}^j, \quad j = 1, \ldots, J, \tag{7.86}$$

with Lagrange multiplier r_i^* for the i-th constraint in (7.84) and λ_i^* for the i-th constraint in (7.85) coincides with the solution to problem (7.77)–(7.80). Moreover, this solution is an equilibrium solution, that is, it satisfies variational inequality problem (7.76).

The network structure for problem (7.83), subject to: (7.84) – (7.86) will now be identified. It is depicted in Figure 7.7.

First, as in the network in Figure 7.5, corresponding to the network for financial equilibrium with futures, the uppermost J nodes correspond to the sectors, as do the J lowermost nodes. Again, there are $2I$ intermediate nodes. But now from each uppermost node j there are $3I$ arcs emanating, where for each intermediate node i; $i = 1, \ldots, I$, there are now two arcs joining node j to node i with one arc having flow X_i^j on it, and the neighboring arc having flow W_i^j. The flow on arc (j, i), with $i = I + 1, \ldots, 2I$, in turn, is equal to Z_i^j. This set of arcs corresponds to the assets. Analogously, the second set of arcs, originating in the intermediate nodes and terminating in the lowermost nodes, corresponds to the liabilities. There are two arcs from each such node i; $i = 1, \ldots, I$, going to a lowermost node j, with the one such arc having flow Y_i^j on it and its neighboring arc having flow Φ_i^j. An arc i; $i = I + 1, \ldots, 2I$, on the other hand, has flow Ψ_i^j.

It is easy to see from Figure 7.7 that the conservation of flow equations (7.84), (7.85), and (7.86) are satisfied on this network. The costs on the links, in turn, are obtained from the corresponding terms in the objective function in (7.83), where recall that maximizing the objective function is equivalent to minimizing minus the function.

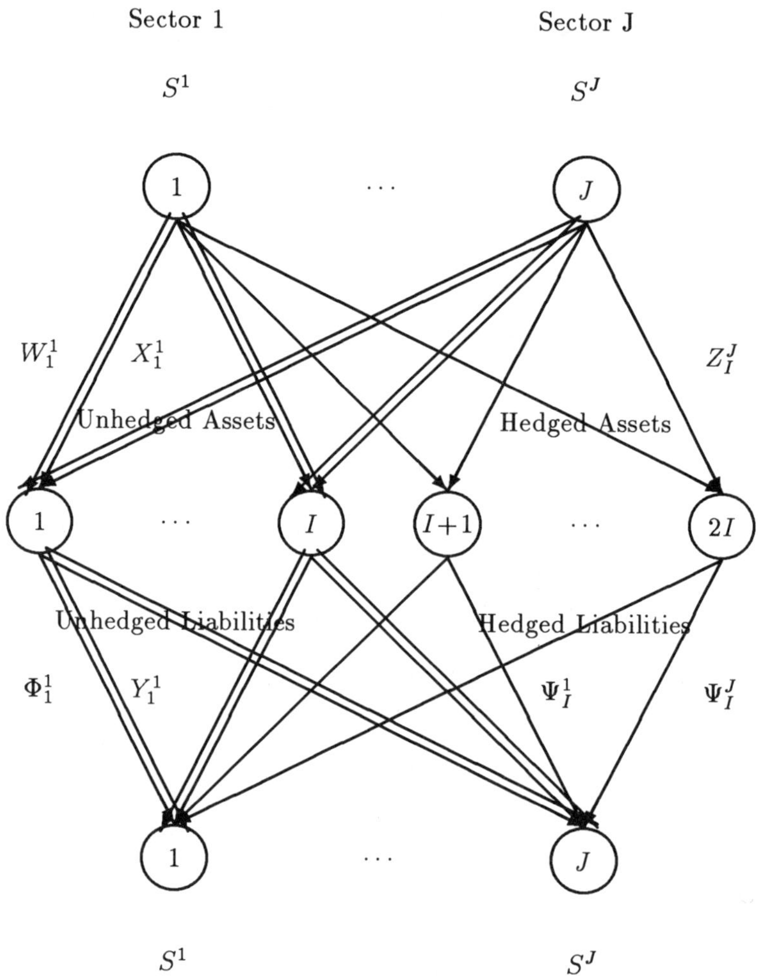

Fig. 7.7. The network structure of financial equilibrium with options

Note that the network in Figure 7.7 has $2I$ more links than the network in Figure 7.5, since one now has the option of exercising or not.

We now present the existence result.

Theorem 7.11

An equilibrium solution $(\mathcal{X}^*, \mathcal{Y}^*, r^*, \lambda^*) \in \mathcal{K}$ *is guaranteed to exist.*

Proof: Since the feasible set defined by (7.84)–(7.86) is compact, there is clearly a solution $(\mathcal{X}^*, \mathcal{Y}^*)$ to the optimization problem (7.83), subject to (7.84)-(7.86). Moreover, from the Lagrange Multiplier Theorem, we know that there exist the vectors of Lagrange multipliers r^* and λ^* associated with the constraints (7.84) and (7.85). Finally, from Corollary 7.4 one has that a solution to this network optimization problem also satisfies variational inequality (7.76) and is, hence, an equilibrium. □

Clearly, this model can be solved using the primal-dual method or the modified projection method.

7.8 Sources and Notes

This chapter focused on the development and study of financial equilibrium models in the presence of such financial products as financial futures and options. We presented a series of static single country, multi-sector, multi-instrument models with futures, and, subsequently, with options. We also identified their network structure both out of equilibrium and in equilibrium. As in Chapter 6, the mathematical framework that was used for the qualitative analysis of the models, as well as, the computation of the equilibrium patterns, was variational inequality theory in conjunction with network theory.

Clearly, models incorporating both futures and options could be easily synthesized through the separate models presented for futures and options.

It is beyond the scope of this book to present a detailed analysis of the theory and the practices of financial futures and options, along with all the possible ways in which one can hedge. For a detailed analysis of futures markets we refer the reader to: Schwarz, Hill, and Schneeweis (1986), Chicago Board of Trade (1989), and Teweles and Jones (1987).

For a better understanding of hedging we suggest the papers by Frankcle (1980) and Stulz (1984) and the publication of the Chicago Board of Trade (1984).

Similarly, for a detailed analysis of options and the strategies that could be used we suggest the work of Welch (1982), Cox and Rubinstein (1985), and McMillan (1986).

Finally, for general information on futures, options, and hedging we suggest the books by Duffie (1989), Kolb (1991), Andersen (1993), Hull (1993), and Winstone (1995).

Section 7.1

The special case of the financial equilibrium model with futures, with utility functions of the form (7.4), along with the study of its qualitative properties and its underlying network structure, is an adaptation of the work reported in Nagurney and Siokos (1996). The financial equilibrium model with futures and general utility functions is reported here for the first time. The models herein can be generalized even further with the inclusion of different futures contracts per underlying instrument. We skip the presentation of such models since they are straightforward extensions of the models presented.

Section 7.2

The qualitative analysis of the financial equilibrium models with futures using variational inequality theory is reported here for the first time. The results of this analysis form the basis for the computational methodologies suggested in Section 7.4.

Section 7.3

This section contains results that were presented in Nagurney and Siokos (1996).

Section 7.4

This is the first time that the modified projection method has been proposed for the solution of financial equilibria in the presence of futures. The numerical examples are taken from Nagurney and Siokos (1996).

Section 7.5

The options model developed here is presented for the first time. It can be seen as an extension of the futures model. However, the options model incorporates the possibility of exercising or not.

Section 7.6

The qualitative properties developed here are novel and have not been reported elsewhere. The qualitative analysis presented in this section defines the range of algorithms that can be utilized for the computation of an equilibrium pattern. Obviously, the primal-dual, as well as the modified projection algorithm, could be utilized for the computation of an equilibrium pattern with options.

Section 7.7

The network structure of the financial economy in equilibrium in the presence of options is constructed here for the first time. It is a natural extension of the network presented for the futures model, where the choice of exercising is added.

References

Andersen, T. J., **Currency and Interest Hedging,** New York Institute of Finance, New York, New York, 1993.

Bertsekas, D. P., and Tsitsiklis, J. N., **Parallel Distributed Computation – Numerical Methods**, Prentice-Hall, Inc., Englewood Cliffs, New Jersey, 1989.

Black, F., and Scholes, M., "The Pricing of Options and Corporate Liabilities," *Journal of Political Economy* **81** (1973) 637-659.

Brennan, M. J., and Schwartz, E. S., "The Valuation American Put Option," *Journal of Finance* **32** (1977) 449-462.

Chicago Board of Trade, **Introduction to Hedging**, Chicago, Illinois, 1984.

Chicago Board of Trade, **Commodity Trading Manual**, Chicago, Illinois, 1989.

Cox, J. C., and Rubinstein, M., **Options Markets,** Prentice-Hall Inc., Englewood Cliffs, New Jersey, 1985.

Duffie, D., **Futures Markets**, Prentice-Hall Inc., Englewood Cliffs, New Jersey, 1989.

Frankcle, C. T., "The Hedging Performance of the New Futures Market: Comment," *Journal of Finance* **35** (1980) 1273-1279.

Hull, J., **Options, Futures, and Other Derivatives,** Prentice-Hall Inc., Englewood Cliffs, New Jersey, 1993.

Jaillet, P., Lamberton, D., and Lapeyre, B., "Variational Inequalities and the Pricing of American Options," *Acta Applicandae Mathematicae* **21** (1990) 263-289.

Karatzas, I., "On the Pricing of American Options," *Applied Mathematical Optimization* **17** (1988) 37-60.

Kolb, R., **Understanding Futures Markets,** New York Institute of Finance, New York, New York, 1991.

McMillan, L. G., **Options as a Strategic Investment,** New York Institute of Finance, New York, New York, 1986.

Nagurney, A., and Siokos, S., "Dynamic Multi-Sector, Multi-Instrument Financial Networks with Futures: Modeling and Computation," University of Massachusetts, Amherst, Massachusetts, 1996.

Schwarz, E. W., Hill, J. M., and Schneeweis, T., **Financial Futures: Fundamentals, Strategies, and Applications**, Irwin, Homewood, Illinois, 1986.

Stulz, R. M., "Optimal Hedging Policies," *Journal of Financial and Qualitative Analysis* **19** (1984) 127-140.

Teweles, R. J., and Jones, F. J., **The Futures Game,** McGraw Hill Inc., New York, New York, 1987.

Welch, W. W., **Strategies for Put and Call Option Trading**, Winthrop, Cambridge, Massachusetts, 1982.

Winstone, D., **Financial Derivatives: Hedging with Futures, Forwards, Options and Swaps**, Chapman and Hall, London, Great Britain, 1995.

8 Dynamic Single Country Models

In this chapter we begin the dynamic modeling of single country, multi-sector, multi-instrument financial problems. We utilize, as the basis, the models of Chapters 6 and 7, but we develop their dynamic counterparts. The methodology that we utilize in this chapter is now that of projected dynamical systems (cf. Chapter 4). In this chapter we are interested in the dynamic modeling of such financial systems, their stability analysis, as well as computational procedures. The financial models of the preceding two chapters are important since the sets of stationary points of the projected dynamical systems that we will present here will coincide with the sets of solutions to the corresponding variational inequality problem derived earlier.

In this chapter we make the same assumptions as those imposed on the models in Chapters 6 and 7. In particular, we are dealing here with perfect markets in which there are no transaction costs and no policy interventions. We will relax these assumptions in Chapters 9 and 10 where we focus on imperfect market financial models, static and dynamic, respectively.

The first work on the use of projected dynamical systems in the study of financial systems was by Dong, Zhang, and Nagurney (1996), who proposed a multi-sector, multi-instrument dynamic financial adjustment process, gave its projected dynamical systems formulation, and then obtained stability analysis results. Nagurney and Siokos (1996a) then used the methodology not only for stability analysis but also for computational purposes in the case of a financial adjustment process in the presence of futures. Nagurney and Siokos (1996b), in turn, applied this methodology to international finance.

Although Smale (1976a, b) recognized the importance of dynamic questions of stability in problems of general economic equilibrium, this is the first such study, in addition to the aforementioned ones, to address such questions in multi-sector, multi-instrument financial equilibrium problems. This chapter is organized as follows. Section 8.1 introduces the dynamic models without and with hedging. In particular, it develops three distinct dynamic, single country financial models by deriving the financial adjustment processes and their projected dynamical systems formulation. Section 8.1.1 develops the dynamic counterpart of the financial model introduced in Section 6.1. Section 8.1.2 introduces a dynamic financial model with futures, whose static counterpart is given in Section 7.1. Section 8.1.3 then develops the dynamic counterpart of the financial model with options provided in Section 7.5.

Section 8.2 subsequently presents the stability analysis results for the dynamic financial models without hedging. Analogous results can be obtained for the dynamic models with hedging using the arguments set forth herein.

Section 8.3 describes the Euler method, which is a dicrete time approximation to the continuous time adjustment processes, for the computation of the stationary points, along with convergence results. Numerical examples are also given.

8.1 Dynamic Perfect Market Financial Models

In this section we develop three distinct dynamic financial models, which are counterparts of the static, perfect market models presented, respectively, in Sections 6.1, 7.1, and 7.5. Hence, throughout this chapter we rely heavily on both the economics and financial assumptions made, and the notation used, in Chapters 6 and 7. Moreover, as in those chapters, we assume that the utility function facing each sector, which is spelled out for each model, is concave with respect to the instrument variables, continuous, and twice continuously differentiable.

We first present a proposition that is needed in developing the projected dynamical systems formulations of the dynamic financial adjustment processes.

The following proposition states that the projection operator $\Pi_{\mathcal{K}}$ (cf. (4.2)) is decomposable over a Cartesian product. A Cartesian product structure of the underlying feasible set is the case in all of the multi-sector, multi-instrument financial models under study in this text.

Proposition 8.1

Let $\mathcal{K}^l$ be a closed convex subset of R^{n_l}, and $x_l \in \mathcal{K}^l, v_l \in R^{n_l}$. Denote $\mathcal{K} = \mathcal{K}^1 \times \mathcal{K}^2 \times \cdots \times \mathcal{K}^k \subset R^{\sum_{l=1}^k n_l}$, $v = (v_1, v_2, \cdots, v_k) \in R^{\sum_{l=1}^k n_l}$, and $x = (x_1, x_2, \cdots, x_k) \in \mathcal{K}$. Then we have

$$\Pi_{\mathcal{K}}(x, v) = (\Pi_{\mathcal{K}^1}(x_1, v_1), \cdots, \Pi_{\mathcal{K}^k}(x_k, v_k)). \tag{8.1}$$

Proof: We claim that

$$P_{\mathcal{K}}[x_1 + \delta v_1, \cdots, x_k + \delta v_k]$$
$$= [P_{\mathcal{K}^1}(x_1 + \delta v_1), \cdots, P_{\mathcal{K}^k}(x_k + \delta v_k)] \in \mathcal{K}^1 \times \mathcal{K}^2 \times \cdots \times \mathcal{K}^k. \tag{8.2}$$

In fact, let $y=(y_1,\cdots,y_k)=P_{\mathcal{K}}[x_1+\delta v_1,\cdots,x_k+\delta v_k]$. Then $y_l\in\mathcal{K}^l$ and

$$\sum_{l=1}^{k}\|y_l-(x_l+\delta v_l)\|^2=\|y-(x_1+\delta v_1,\cdots,x_k+\delta v_k)\|^2$$

$$=\min_{y'\in\mathcal{K}}\|y'-(x_1+\delta v_1,\cdots,x_k+\delta v_k)\|^2\geq\sum_{l=1}^{k}\|P_{\mathcal{K}^l}(x_l+\delta v_l)-(x_l+\delta v_l)\|^2. \quad (8.3)$$

Therefore, the claim is true.

Now it follows directly from the definition (cf. (4.2)) that

$$\Pi_{\mathcal{K}}(x,v)=\lim_{\delta\to 0}\frac{P_{\mathcal{K}}(x+\delta v)-x}{\delta}$$

$$=\lim_{\delta\to 0}\frac{[P_{\mathcal{K}^1}(x_1+\delta v_1),\cdots,P_{\mathcal{K}^k}(x_k+\delta v_k)]-[x_1,\cdots x_k]}{\delta}$$

$$=[\Pi_{\mathcal{K}^1}(x_1,v_1),\cdots,\Pi_{\mathcal{K}^k}(x_k,v_k)]. \quad \square \quad (8.4)$$

In the following subsections we develop the dynamic financial models and provide their projected dynamical systems formulations.

8.1.1 A Dynamic General Utility Function Model

In this section we present the dynamic counterpart to the general utility function model of Section 6.1. Hence, that section is a companion to this one.

As in Chapter 6, we consider an economy consisting of J sectors, with a typical sector denoted by j, and with I instruments, with a typical instrument denoted by i. As before, we let X_i^j denote the volume of instrument i held by sector j as an asset and we let Y_i^j denote the volume of instrument i held by sector j as a liability. We group the assets held by sector j into the column vector $X^j\in R_+^I$ and the liabilities into the column vector $Y^j\in R_+^I$. Finally, we group the assets held by all the sectors into the column vector $X\in R_+^{JI}$ and the liabilities held by all the sectors into the column vector $Y\in R_+^{JI}$.

As previously, we let r_i denote the nonnegative price of instrument i and we group the instrument prices into the column vector $r\in R_+^I$.

In this model, we assume that the total volume of each balance sheet side is exogenous and is given by S^j for sector j. Moreover, under the assumption of perfect competition, each sector will behave as if he has no influence on the instrument prices or on the behavior of the other sectors.

As in Section 6.1, we let $U^j(X^j,Y^j,r)$ denote the utility function of sector j, where, recall that the optimization problem of a sector j (cf. (6.1)–(6.3)), was as follows:

$$\text{Maximize } U^j(X^j,Y^j,r)$$

subject to:

$$\sum_{i=1}^{I} X_i^j = S^j$$

$$\sum_{i=1}^{I} Y_i^j = S^j$$

$$X_i^j \geq 0, \; Y_i^j \geq 0, \quad i = 1, 2, \ldots, I,$$

with the price vector r being an exogenous vector in the optimization problem of every sector j; $j = 1, \ldots, J$.

We now present a financial adjustment process and the projected dynamical system that describes both the dynamic behavior of the financial sectors and that of the instrument prices. We first describe the behavior of the sectors. We then describe the adjustment process underlying the prices of the financial instruments.

The model assumes that each sector j seeks to adjust his asset and liability pattern (X^j, Y^j) in a direction that maximizes his utility, as given above (and in (6.1)), while maintaining the accounting constraints.

Precisely, recall that $\nabla_{X^j} U^j = (\frac{\partial U^j}{\partial X_1^j}, \cdots, \frac{\partial U^j}{\partial X_I^j})$ is the vector of marginal utilities of sector j with respect to his assets, and $\nabla_{Y^j} U^j = (\frac{\partial U^j}{\partial Y_1^j}, \cdots, \frac{\partial U^j}{\partial Y_I^j})$ is the vector of marginal utilities of sector j with respect to his liabilities. Then, $(\nabla_{X^j} U^j, \nabla_{Y^j} U^j)$ constitutes sector j's idealized direction for unconstrained utility maximization. However, this idealized direction needs to be revised in order that the accounting constraints be satisfied, that is,

$$\sum_{i=1}^{I} X_i^j = S^j; \quad \sum_{i=1}^{I} Y_i^j = S^j,$$

as well as the nonnegativity constraints: $X_i^j \geq 0, Y_i^j \geq 0$; $i = 1, \ldots, I$.

Therefore, the best-realizable direction that sector j takes to maximize his utility is the projection of his idealized direction, given by $(\nabla_{X^j} U^j, \nabla_{Y^j} U^j)$, onto his constraint set, given by $\kappa^j \equiv \tilde{X}^j \times \tilde{Y}^j$ (as defined in (6.7)), at his current portfolio (X^j, Y^j). Note that κ^j consists of precisely the accounting and nonnegativity constraints for sector j given above. This best-realizable direction can be mathematically expressed by

$$\Pi_{\tilde{X}^j \times \tilde{Y}^j} \left((X^j, Y^j), (\nabla_{X^j} U^j, \nabla_{Y^j} U^j) \right), \tag{8.5}$$

where, recall that (cf. (4.2)), for any closed convex set $\mathcal{K} \in R^n, x \in \mathcal{K}$, and $v \in R^n$,

$$\Pi_{\mathcal{K}}(x, v) = \lim_{\delta \to 0} \frac{P_{\mathcal{K}}(x + \delta v) - x}{\delta}, \tag{8.6}$$

and $P_{\mathcal{K}}$ (cf. (3.24)) is the norm projection defined by

$$P_{\mathcal{K}}(x) = \text{Argmin}_{z \in \mathcal{K}} \|z - x\|. \tag{8.7}$$

Hence, the asset and liability volumes for sector j are adjusted according to the following processes over time t:

$$\dot{X}^j = \Pi_{\tilde{X}^j}(X^j, \nabla_{X^j} U^j), \quad \dot{Y}^j = \Pi_{\tilde{Y}^j}(Y^j, \nabla_{Y^j} U^j); \quad j = 1, \cdots, J. \tag{8.8}$$

We now turn to describing the adjustment process for the instrument prices. One expects that the price of financial instrument i, r_i, increases when the demand of this instrument exceeds its supply and decreases otherwise, where the difference between the supply of and demand for instrument i, denoted by γ_i, is expressed as:

$$\mu_i = \sum_{j=1}^{J} X_i^j - \sum_{j=1}^{J} Y_i^j, \tag{8.9}$$

where μ denotes the I-dimensional column vector of supply and demand differences. However, since the price of the financial instruments cannot be negative, it is reasonable to assume that the price of the i-th financial instrument, r_i, will remain zero when $r_i = 0$ and $\sum_{j=1}^{J} X_i^j - \sum_{j=1}^{J} Y_i^j < 0$.

Thus, instrument price r_i changes according to:

$$\dot{r}_i = \begin{cases} \max\{0, -(\sum_{j=1}^{J} X_i^j - \sum_{j=1}^{J} Y_i^j)\}, & \text{if } r_i = 0 \\ -(\sum_{j=1}^{J} X_i^j - \sum_{j=1}^{J} Y_i^j), & \text{if } r_i > 0, \end{cases} \tag{8.10}$$

or, equivalently,

$$\dot{r}_i = \Pi_{R_+}(r_i, -\mu_i). \tag{8.11}$$

The Financial Adjustment Process

Combining (8.8) with (8.10), the entire adjustment process of every sector's allocation of assets and liabilities and each financial instrument's price is given by:

$$\begin{cases} \dot{X}^j &= \Pi_{\tilde{X}^j}(X^j, \nabla_{X^j} U^j); \quad j = 1, \cdots, J \\ \dot{Y}^j &= \Pi_{\tilde{Y}^j}(Y^j, \nabla_{Y^j} U^j); \quad j = 1, \cdots, J \\ \dot{r}_i &= \Pi_{R_+}(r_i, -(\sum_{j=1}^{J} X_i^j - \sum_{j=1}^{J} Y_i^j)); \quad i = 1, \cdots, I. \end{cases} \tag{8.12}$$

In view of Proposition 8.1, the financial adjustment process (8.12) can be expressed by the following projected dynamical system in the entire space of assets, liabilities, and prices:

$$\dot{x} = \Pi_{\mathcal{K}}(x, -F(x)), \tag{8.13}$$

where F is defined in (6.21), and recall that $x \equiv (X, Y, r) \in \mathcal{K}$, with $\mathcal{K} \equiv \{\kappa \times R^I_+\}$, where $\kappa = \kappa^1 \times \ldots \times \kappa^J$.

According to Theorem 4.2, we have the following theorem.

Theorem 8.1

(8.13) well-defines a dynamical system, in that there exists a unique solution path to (8.13) for any boundary condition $x(0) = x_0 \in \mathcal{K}$.

The dynamical system defined by (8.13) is nonclassical due to the discontinuity of the projection map $\Pi_{\mathcal{K}}$ at the boundary of $\mathcal{K}$ (cf. Chapter 4) and was termed a *projected dynamical system* (PDS) by Zhang and Nagurney (1995).

The following theorem unveils another important facet of the financial adjustment process given by (8.13). This theorem follows from Theorem 4.1 and Theorem 6.1.

Theorem 8.2

Every financial equilibrium (cf. Definition 6.1) is a stationary point of the adjustment process (8.13) and vice versa. In other words, $x^* = (X^*, Y^*, r^*)$ constitutes a financial equilibrium if and only if

$$\Pi_{\mathcal{K}}(x^*, -F(x^*)) = 0.$$

Consequently, if one obtains a stationary point to (8.13), then that point is a financial equilibrium, that is, it satisfies Definition 6.1 and, equivalently, is a solution to the variational inequality problem (6.12a). Hence, we now have a financial adjustment process that, under reasonable conditions on the utility functions of the sectors, yields well-defined trajectories. Moreover, the stationary point of the dynamical system is a financial equilibrium. Therefore, we have optimality conditions (6.10) being satisfied, once a stationary point is reached, as well as the economic conditions (6.11). Moreover, the above financial adjustment process is meaningful economically and is representative of reasonable behavior on the part of both the sectors and the prices.

We now discuss the network structure underlying the dynamics. Recall that the optimization problem, given by the utility maximization problem above facing each sector, has the network structure as depicted in Figure 6.1. The network structure is identical for each sector. Moreover, in equilibrium (which corresponds to the stationary point of the above dynamic model), the structure of the financial economy is given by the network in Figure 6.2. Hence, the financial adjustment process (8.12), equivalently, (8.13), describes the movement of the individual sectors' network problems towards the equilibrium network. In Section 8.2, we will make these ideas more precise when we address stability analysis questions.

8.1.2 A Dynamic Financial Model with Futures

We now present a dynamic counterpart to the static financial equilibrium model with futures discussed in Section 7.1. Consequently, our notation here is based on that therein.

In contrast to the model in Section 8.1.1, we now have, at our disposal, the possibility of hedging through the investment in assets and liabilities of the instruments held as futures, where recall that Z_i^j denotes the volume of instrument i held by sector j as a hedged, through instrument futures contracts, asset, and Φ_i^j denotes the volume of instrument i held by sector j as a hedged, through instrument futures contracts, liability. The hedged assets of a sector j are grouped into the column vector $Z^j \in R_+^I$, whereas the hedged liabilities are grouped into the column vector $\Phi^j \in R_+^I$. Finally, recall that the asset and liability vectors for a sector j are grouped into the vectors $\mathcal{X}^j \in R_+^I$ and $\mathcal{Y}^j \in R_+^I$, respectively, with $\mathcal{X}$ and $\mathcal{Y}$ denoting the column vectors of the assets and liabilities, respectively, of all the sectors.

The term π_i denotes the contracted price of instrument i on the futures market, with π denoting the I-dimensional vector of all the contracted prices. On the other hand, λ_i denotes the shadow price associated with instrument i with λ denoting the I-dimensional vector of instrument shadow prices.

The utility function for a sector j, in the presence of futures, is given in (7.1), where, for the convenience of the reader, we now present the utility maximization problem facing each sector (cf. (7.1)–(7.3)):

$$\text{Maximize } U^j(X^j, Z^j, Y^j, \Psi^j, r, \lambda; \pi)$$

subject to:

$$\sum_{i=1}^{I} X_i^j + Z_i^j = S^j,$$

$$\sum_{i=1}^{I} Y_i^j + \Psi_i^j = S^j,$$

$$X_i^j, Y_i^j, Z_i^j, \Psi_i^j \geq 0, \quad i = 1, \ldots, I.$$

Recall that the feasible set for a sector j, κ^j, is given by $\kappa^j \equiv \{\tilde{\mathcal{X}}^j \times \tilde{\mathcal{Y}}^j\}$ and is as defined in (7.7), where $\tilde{\mathcal{X}}^j$ represents the constraints of sector j for the assets (consisting of the accounting and nonnegativity constraints) and $\tilde{\mathcal{Y}}^j$ represents the analogous constraints, but for the liabilities, as given above.

We now present a financial adjustment process and the projected dynamical system that describes the dynamic behavior of the financial sectors in the presence of futures. We first describe the behavior of the sectors and then that of the adjustment process underlying the prices of the financial instruments.

The financial model assumes that each sector j seeks to adjust his asset and liability pattern $(\mathcal{X}^j, \mathcal{Y}^j)$ in a direction that maximizes his utility, as given above (and in (7.1)), while maintaining the accounting and the nonnegativity constraints.

Precisely, let $\nabla_{\mathcal{X}^j} U^j$ be as in (7.11), that is, equal to the vector of the marginal utilities of sector j with respect to his assets, and let $\nabla_{\mathcal{Y}^j} U^j$ be as in (7.12), that is, the vector of the marginal utilities of sector j with respect to his liabilities.

Then, $(\nabla_{\mathcal{X}^j} U^j, \nabla_{\mathcal{Y}^j} U^j)$ is sector j's idealized direction for unconstrained utility maximization. However, this idealized direction needs to be revised in order that the accounting constraints be satisfied, which in the case of futures, take the form:

$$\sum_{i=1}^{I} X_i^j + Z_i^j = S^j; \quad \sum_{i=1}^{I} Y_i^j + \Psi_i^j = S^j,$$

as well as the nonnegativity constraints: $X_i^j \geq 0$, $Z_i^j \geq 0, Y_i^j \geq 0, \Psi_i^j \geq 0$; $i = 1, \cdots, I$.

The best-realizable direction that sector j takes to maximize his utility is still the projection of his idealized direction, given by $(\nabla_{\mathcal{X}^j} U^j, \nabla_{\mathcal{Y}^j} U^j)$, onto his constraint set, given by $\tilde{\kappa}^j$ (as defined in (7.7)), at his current portfolio $(\mathcal{X}^j, \mathcal{Y}^j)$. This best-realizable direction can be mathematically expressed by

$$\Pi_{\tilde{\mathcal{X}}^j \times \tilde{\mathcal{Y}}^j} \left((\mathcal{X}^j, \mathcal{Y}^j), (\nabla_{\mathcal{X}^j} U^j, \nabla_{\mathcal{Y}^j} U^j) \right). \tag{8.14}$$

Hence, the (unhedged and hedged) asset and liability volumes for sector j are adjusted according to the following processes over time t.

$$\dot{\mathcal{X}^j} = \Pi_{\tilde{\mathcal{X}}^j}(\mathcal{X}^j, \nabla_{\mathcal{X}^j} U^j), \quad \dot{\mathcal{Y}^j} = \Pi_{\tilde{\mathcal{Y}}^j}(\mathcal{Y}^j, \nabla_{\mathcal{Y}^j} U^j); \quad j = 1, \cdots, J. \tag{8.15}$$

We now turn to describing the adjustment process for the instrument prices and then that of the shadow prices. As in Section 8.1.1, one expects that the price of unhedged instrument i, r_i, increases when the demand for this instrument exceeds its supply and decreases otherwise, where the difference between the supply of and demand for instrument i is (cf. (8.9)):

$$\mu_i = \sum_{j=1}^{J} X_i^j - \sum_{j=1}^{J} Y_i^j. \tag{8.16}$$

As noted earlier, since the price of the unhedged financial instruments cannot be negative, it is reasonable to assume that the price of the i-th unhedged financial instrument, r_i, will remain zero when $r_i = 0$ and $\sum_{j=1}^{J} X_i^j - \sum_{j=1}^{J} Y_i^j < 0$.

Thus, instrument price r_i changes according to:

$$\dot{r}_i = \begin{cases} \max\{0, -(\sum_{j=1}^{J} X_i^j - \sum_{j=1}^{J} Y_i^j)\}, & \text{if } r_i = 0 \\ -(\sum_{j=1}^{J} X_i^j - \sum_{j=1}^{J} Y_i^j), & \text{if } r_i > 0. \end{cases} \tag{8.17}$$

or, equivalently,

$$\dot{r}_i = \Pi_{R_+}(r_i, -\mu_i). \tag{8.18}$$

Finally, we discuss the behavior of the shadow prices associated with the hedged financial instruments. In particular, we note that the shadow price associated with a hedged instrument can be positive, negative, or zero, and, hence, it is reasonable to propose the following:

$$\dot{\lambda}_i = -(\sum_{j=1}^{J} Z_i^j - \sum_{j=1}^{J} \Psi_i^j), \tag{8.19}$$

which, in turn, is equivalent to:

$$\dot{\lambda}_i = \Pi_R(\lambda_i, -(\sum_{j=1}^{J} Z_i^j - \sum_{j=1}^{J} \Psi_i^j). \tag{8.20}$$

The Financial Adjustment Process in the Presence of Futures

Combining (8.15) with (8.18) and (8.20), the entire adjustment process of every sector's allocation of assets and liabilities, each unhedged financial instrument's price, and each hedged instrument's shadow price, is given by:

$$\begin{cases} \dot{\mathcal{X}}^j = \Pi_{\tilde{\mathcal{X}}^j}(\mathcal{X}^j, \nabla_{\mathcal{X}^j} U^j); & j = 1, \cdots, J \\ \dot{\mathcal{Y}}^j = \Pi_{\tilde{\mathcal{Y}}^j}(\mathcal{Y}^j, \nabla_{\mathcal{Y}^j} U^j); & j = 1, \cdots, J \\ \dot{r}_i = \Pi_{R_+}(r_i, -(\sum_{j=1}^J X_i^j - \sum_{j=1}^J Y_i^j)); & i = 1, \cdots, I \\ \dot{\lambda}_i = \Pi_R(\lambda_i, -(\sum_{j=1}^J Z_i^j - \sum_{j=1}^J \Psi_i^j)); & i = 1, \ldots, I. \end{cases} \tag{8.21}$$

In view of Proposition 8.1, the financial adjustment process (8.21) can be expressed by the following projected dynamical system in the entire space of assets, liabilities, and prices:

$$\dot{x} = \Pi_{\mathcal{K}}(x, -F(x)), \tag{8.22}$$

where F is defined in (7.22), and recall that $x \equiv (X, Y, r, \lambda) \in \mathcal{K}$, with $\mathcal{K} \equiv \{\tilde{\kappa} \times R_+^I \times R^I\}$, where $\tilde{\kappa} = \tilde{\kappa}^1 \times \ldots \tilde{\kappa}^J$, with $\tilde{\kappa}^j$ as in (7.7).

According to Theorem 4.2, we have the following theorem (see also Theorem 8.1).

Theorem 8.3

(8.22) well-defines a dynamical system, in that there exists a unique solution path to (8.22) for any boundary condition $x(0) = x_0 \in \mathcal{K}$.

Moreover, due to Theorem 4.1 and Theorem 7.1 we have the following result:

Theorem 8.4

Every financial equilibrium in the presence of futures (cf. Definition 7.1) is a stationary point of the adjustment process (8.22) and vice versa. In other words, $x^* = (X^*, Y^*, r^*, \lambda^*)$ *constitutes a financial equilibrium if and only if*

$$\Pi_{\mathcal{K}}(x^*, -F(x^*)) = 0.$$

Hence, a stationary point of (8.22) is an equilibrium point, that is, it satisfies Definition 7.1, and is also a solution to the variational inequality problem (7.15a).

Note now that the individual sectors' optimization problems have the network structure depicted in Figure 7.4, whereas the structure of the financial economy in the presence of futures in equilibrium is as given in Figure 7.5. As a consequence, the adjustment process (8.22) describes also the movement of the individual networks towards the equilibrium network.

8.1.3 A Dynamic Financial Model with Options

We now develop a financial adjustment process, whose set of stationary points coincides with the set of solutions to the variational inequality problem (7.65) governing the financial equilibrium model with options discussed in Section 7.5.

As in Sections 8.1.1 and 8.1.2, we let X_i^j and Y_i^j denote, respectively, the (unhedged) volume of instrument i held as an asset and as a liability by sector j. Recall that, as in Section 7.5, Z_i^j now denotes the volume of capital that sector j holds as an asset on a European contract on instrument i where the option will be exercised, with Ψ_i^j denoting the liability counterpart. The term W_i^j denotes the volume of capital that sector j holds as an asset on a European option contract on instrument i where the option will not be exercised, with Φ_i^j denoting its liability counterpart. The vector $\mathcal{X}$ consists of the unhedged and hedged asset vectors of all sectors, where now, $\mathcal{X}^j = (X^j, W^j, Z^j)$ for sector j, whereas $\mathcal{Y}$ consists of the unhedged and hedged liability vectors of all sectors, where $\mathcal{Y}^j$ is comprised of the unhedged and hedged liability vectors for sector j with $\mathcal{Y}^j = (Y^j, \Phi^j, \Psi^j)$.

The notation r_i is still utilized to denote the price of instrument i, whereas π_i now denotes the exercise price of a European option on instrument i. Lastly, recall from Section 7.5, that θ_i denotes the premium paid for getting the right to exercise a European option on instrument i. The shadow price associated with the exercised European option on instrument i, in turn, is denoted by λ_i.

The utility maximization problem for a sector j is as given in Section 7.5 (cf. (7.52)–(7.54)), that is:

$$\text{Maximize } U^j(\mathcal{X}^j, \mathcal{Y}^j, r, \lambda; \theta, \pi) =$$

$$u^j(\mathcal{X}^j, \mathcal{Y}^j) + \sum_{i=1}^{I} r_i(X_i^j - Y_i^j) + \sum_{i=1}^{I} (\pi_i - \theta_i + \lambda_i)(Z_i^j - \Psi_i^j) + \sum_{i=1}^{I} (r_i - \theta_i)(W_i^j - \Phi_i^j)$$

subject to:

$$\sum_{i=1}^{I} X_i^j + W_i^j + Z_i^j = S^j$$

$$\sum_{i=1}^{I} Y_i^j + \Phi_i^j + \Psi_i^j = S^j$$

$$X_i^j, Y_i^j, W_i^j, \Phi_i^j, Z_i^j, \Psi_i^j \geq 0, \quad i = 1, \ldots, I.$$

Note that here, unlike the models in Sections 8.1.1 and 8.1.2, the utility function for each sector is assumed to take on a specific form. We first discuss the adjustment behavior of the sectors and then that of the unhedged and hedged instruments, respectively.

The financial model, again, assumes that each sector j seeks to adjust his asset and liability pattern $(\mathcal{X}^j, \mathcal{Y}^j)$ in a direction that maximizes his utility, as given above (and in (7.52)), while maintaining the accounting constraints.

Precisely, let $\nabla_{\mathcal{X}^j} U^j$ be as in (7.61), that is, the vector of marginal utilities of sector j with respect to his assets, and let $\nabla_{\mathcal{Y}^j} U^j$ be as in (7.62), that is, the vector of marginal utilities of sector j with respect to his liabilities.

Then, $(\nabla_{\mathcal{X}^j} U^j, \nabla_{\mathcal{Y}^j} U^j)$ is sector j's idealized direction for unconstrained utility maximization. However, this idealized direction needs to be revised in order that the accounting constraints be satisfied, which in the case of options, take the form:

$$\sum_{i=1}^{I} X_i^j + W_i^j + Z_i^j = S^j; \quad \sum_{i=1}^{I} Y_i^j + \Phi_i^j + \Psi_i^j = S^j,$$

as well as the nonnegativity constraints: $X_i^j \geq 0$, $W_i^j \geq 0$, $Z_i^j \geq 0$, $Y_i^j \geq 0$, $\Phi_i^j \geq 0$, $\Psi_i^j \geq 0$; $i = 1, \cdots, I$.

The best-realizable direction that sector j takes to maximize his utility is, again, the projection of his idealized direction, $(\nabla_{\mathcal{X}^j} U^j, \nabla_{\mathcal{Y}^j} U^j)$, onto his constraint set, given by $\bar{\kappa}^j = \bar{\mathcal{X}}^j \times \bar{\mathcal{Y}}^j$ (as defined in (7.57)), at his current portfolio $(\mathcal{X}^j, \mathcal{Y}^j)$.

This best-realizable direction can be mathematically expressed by

$$\Pi_{\bar{\mathcal{X}}^j \times \bar{\mathcal{Y}}^j}\left((\mathcal{X}^j, \mathcal{Y}^j), (\nabla_{\mathcal{X}^j} U^j, \nabla_{\mathcal{Y}^j} U^j)\right). \tag{8.23}$$

Consequently, the (unhedged and hedged) asset and liability volumes for sector j are adjusted according to the following processes over time t:

$$\dot{\mathcal{X}}^j = \Pi_{\bar{\mathcal{X}}^j}(\mathcal{X}^j, \nabla_{\mathcal{X}^j} U^j), \quad \dot{\mathcal{Y}}^j = \Pi_{\bar{\mathcal{Y}}^j}(\mathcal{Y}^j, \nabla_{\mathcal{Y}^j} U^j); \quad j = 1, \cdots, J. \tag{8.24}$$

We now turn to describing the adjustment process for the instrument prices and then of the shadow prices. One expects that the price of unhedged and unexercised instrument i, r_i, increases when the demand of this instrument exceeds its supply and decreases otherwise, where the difference between the supply of and demand for instrument i, $\bar{\mu}_i$, is

$$\bar{\mu}_i = \sum_{j=1}^{J}(X_i^j + W_i^j) - \sum_{j=1}^{J}(Y_i^j - \Phi_i^j). \tag{8.25}$$

However, since the price of the unhedged financial instruments cannot be negative, it is reasonable to assume that the price of the i-th unhedged financial instrument, r_i, will remain zero when $r_i = 0$ and $\sum_{j=1}^{J}(X_i^j + W_i^j) - \sum_{j=1}^{J}(Y_i^j + \Phi_i^j) < 0$.

Thus, instrument price r_i changes according to:

$$\dot{r}_i = \begin{cases} \max\{0, -(\sum_{j=1}^{J}(X_i^j + W_i^j) - \sum_{j=1}^{J}(Y_i^j + \Phi_i^j))\}, & \text{if } r_i = 0 \\ -(\sum_{j=1}^{J}(X_i^j + W_i^j) - \sum_{j=1}^{J}(Y_i^j + \Phi_i^j)), & \text{if } r_i > 0. \end{cases} \tag{8.26}$$

Finally, we discuss the behavior of the shadow prices associated with the hedged financial instruments. In particular, we note that the shadow price associated with a hedged instrument can be positive, negative, or zero and, hence, it is reasonable to propose the following:

$$\dot{\lambda}_i = -(\sum_{j=1}^{J} Z_i^j - \sum_{j=1}^{J} \Psi_i^j), \tag{8.27}$$

which, in turn, is equivalent to:

$$\dot{\lambda}_i = \Pi_R(\lambda_i, -(\sum_{j=1}^{J} Z_i^j - \sum_{j=1}^{J} \Psi_i^j)). \tag{8.28}$$

The Financial Adjustment Process in the Presence of Options

Combining (8.24) with (8.26) and (8.28), the entire adjustment process of every sector's allocation of assets and liabilities, each unhedged financial instrument's price, and each hedged instrument's shadow price, is given by:

$$\begin{cases} \dot{\mathcal{X}}^j = \Pi_{\bar{\mathcal{X}}^j}(\mathcal{X}^j, \nabla_{\mathcal{X}^j} U^j); \quad j = 1, \cdots, J \\ \dot{\mathcal{Y}}^j = \Pi_{\bar{\mathcal{Y}}^j}(\mathcal{Y}^j, \nabla_{\mathcal{Y}^j} U^j); \quad j = 1, \cdots, J \\ \dot{r}_i = \Pi_{R_+}(r_i, -(\sum_{j=1}^{J}(X_i^j + W_i^j) - \sum_{j=1}^{J}(Y_i^j + \Phi_i^j))); \quad i = 1, \cdots, I \\ \dot{\lambda}_i = \Pi_R(\lambda_i, -(\sum_{j=1}^{J} \Psi_i^j - \sum_{j=1}^{J} Z_i^j)); \quad i = 1, \ldots, I. \end{cases} \tag{8.29}$$

In view of Proposition 8.1, the financial adjustment process (8.29) can be expressed by the following projected dynamical system in the entire space of assets, liabilities, and prices:

$$\dot{x} = \Pi_{\mathcal{K}}(x, -F(x)), \tag{8.30}$$

where F is defined in (7.66), and recall that now $x \equiv (\mathcal{X}, \mathcal{Y}, r, \lambda) \in \mathcal{K}$, with $\mathcal{K} \equiv \{\bar{\kappa} \times R^I_+ \times R^I\}$, with $\bar{\kappa} = \bar{\kappa}^1 \times \ldots \times \bar{\kappa}^J$.

According to Theorem 4.2, we have the following theorem.

Theorem 8.5

(8.30) well-defines a dynamical system, in that there exists a unique solution path to (8.30) for any boundary condition $x(0) = x_0 \in \mathcal{K}$.

In addition, due to Theorem 4.1 and Theorem 7.8, the following theorem holds true.

Theorem 8.6

Every financial equilibrium in the presence of options (cf. Definition 7.2) is a stationary point of the adjustment process (8.30) and vice versa. In other words, $x^* = (\mathcal{X}^*, \mathcal{Y}^*, r^*, \lambda^*)$ constitutes a financial equilibrium if and only if

$$\Pi_{\mathcal{K}}(x^*, -F(x^*)) = 0.$$

Hence, a stationary point of (8.30) is an equilibrium point and, consequently, also a solution to the variational inequality problem (7.65) with utility functions given by (7.52).

Note that the dynamical systems (8.13), (8.22), and (8.30) guarantee that the evolution of the instrument and price trajectories over time lie within the feasible set underlying the particular problem. Thus, the methodology of projected dynamical systems allows one to model financial systems so that constraints and, in particular, budget constraints will not be violated, if that is so desired. Moreover, it guarantees that instrument prices be nonnegative, whereas shadow prices can take on negative values since they represent opportunity costs associated with hedging the instruments.

Also, we emphasize that, as in the case of the static financial equilibrium models studied in Chapters 6 and 7, one can expand the feasible set for each sector to account for additional constraints. The above results are still valid (with the feasible sets redefined accordingly) under the assumptions above and in the case that the new (expanded) feasible sets are convex polyhedrons as required by Theorem 4.1, which established the connection between the set of solutions to a finite-dimensional variational inequality problem and the set of solutions to the corresponding projected dynamical system.

8.2 Stability Analysis

In this section we turn to the stability analysis in regards to the dynamic financial models discussed in Section 8.1. For conciseness, we present the results only in the context of the model of Section 8.1.1 since analogous results can be obtained using the arguments herein for the models with hedged instruments, as well. For completeness, however, we do spell out the proofs of the stability analysis results in detail.

In particular, we will explore the asymptotical behavior of the dynamic financial model presented in Section 8.1.1. A question of interest will be whether a financial disequilibrium state of assets, liabilities, and prices approaches a financial equilibrium state under the adjustment process (8.13) (and, of course, (8.22) and (8.30), as well).

The following definitions facilitate the stability analysis of the financial adjustment process (8.13). These definitions are adapted to financial equilibrium problems from the corresponding definitions in Section 4.2.

Definition 8.1 (Stable Financial Adjustment Process)

The financial adjustment process (8.13) is stable if each financial equilibrium, $x^* = (X^*, Y^*, r^*)$, is a monotone attractor, that is, for any initial asset, liability, and price pattern, (X_0, Y_0, r_0), the distance,

$$\|(X(t), Y(t), r(t)) - (X^*, Y^*, r^*)\|,$$

is nonincreasing in time t, where $(X(t), Y(t), r(t))$ satisfy (8.12).

Definition 8.2 (Asymptotically Stable Financial Adjustment Process)

The financial adjustment process is asymptotically stable if it is stable, and for any initial asset, liability, and price pattern, (X_0, Y_0, r_0), the financial adjustment process starting with (X_0, Y_0, r_0) converges to some equilibrium pattern (X^*, Y^*, r^*); namely,

$$(X_0(t), Y_0(t), r_0(t)) \longrightarrow (X^*, Y^*, r^*), \quad \text{as } t \longrightarrow \infty. \tag{8.31}$$

We see from the above definitions that if a financial adjustment process is stable, then any state of financial disequilibrium will stay close to an equilibrium forever; if a financial adjustment process is asymptotically stable, then any financial disequilibrium state will eventually approach an equilibrium.

We will now present the stability results of the financial adjustment process. We will see that each financial sector's behavior and his risk attitude assumption determine the stability of the financial equilibrium. First, Theorem 8.7 below illustrates that the financial adjustment process is stable under the broadest condition - the concavity of the utility functions of the financial sectors, which assumes that each financial sector is risk-averse. We now consider utility functions of the special form given by (6.4).

Theorem 8.7 (Stability of the Financial Adjustment Process) *Suppose that each sector's utility function U^j; $j = 1, \ldots, J$, is continuous, twice continuously differentiable, and concave in X^j and Y^j, and that the utility functions are of the form:*

$$U^j(X^j, Y^j, r) = u^j(X^j, Y^j) + r^T(X^j - Y^j)$$

Then the financial adjustment process (8.13) is stable.

Proof: Let $x^* = (X^*, Y^*, r^*)$ be any financial equilibrium pattern of assets, liabilities, and prices satisfying Definition 6.1. For any initial pattern, $x_0 = (X_0, Y_0, r_0)$, let $x_0(t) = (X_0(t), Y_0(t), r_0(t))$ be the financial distribution at time t under the financial adjustment process starting with (X_0, Y_0, r_0). Define

$$D(x_0, x^*, t) := \frac{1}{2}\|x_0(t) - x^*\|^2. \tag{8.32}$$

Then

$$\dot{D}(x_0, x^*, t) = \langle (x_0(t) - x^*)^T, \Pi_{\mathcal{K}}(x(t), -F(x(t))) \rangle. \tag{8.33}$$

Recall from Section 4.1 (cf. (4.10)), that

$$\Pi_{\mathcal{K}}(x(t), -F(x(t))) = -F(x_0(t)) + \eta(x_0(t))N^*(x_0(t)),$$

where $N^*(x(t))$ is an inward normal to $\mathcal{K}$ at $x(t)$, and $\eta(x(t))$ is a nonnegative real number. Then we have an upper bound for (8.33), i.e.,

$$\dot{D}(x_0, x^*, t) \leq \langle (x_0(t) - x^*)^T, -F(x_0(t)) \rangle$$

$$= \langle (X_0(t) - X^*)^T, \nabla_X U \rangle + \langle (Y_0(t) - Y^*)^T, \nabla_Y U \rangle + \langle (r_0(t) - r^*)^T, -\mu \rangle$$

$$= \sum_{j=1}^{J}\sum_{i=1}^{I} \left(X_0(t)_i^j - X_i^{j*}\right)\left[\frac{\partial}{\partial X_i^j} u^j(X_0(t), Y_0(t), r_0(t)) + r_0(t)_i\right]$$

$$+ \sum_{j=1}^{J}\sum_{i=1}^{I} \left(Y_0(t)_i^j - Y_i^{j*}\right)\left[\frac{\partial}{\partial Y_i^j} u^j(X_0(t), Y_0(t), r_0(t)) - r_0(t)_i\right]$$

$$- \sum_{i=1}^{I} (r_0(t)_i - r_i^*) \sum_{j=1}^{J} \left(X_0(t)_i^j - Y_0(t)_i^j\right)$$

$$= \sum_{j=1}^{J} \left(X_0(t)^j - X^{j*}, Y_0(t)^j - Y^{j*}\right)^T$$

$$\cdot \nabla^2 u^j(X_0(t), Y_0(t), r_0(t)) \cdot \left(X_0(t)^j - X^{j*}, Y_0(t)^j - Y^{j*}\right). \tag{8.34}$$

Since each U^j is concave with respect to X^j and Y^j, the right-hand side of (8.34) is nonpositive. This implies that $\|x_0(t) - x^*\|$ is monotone nonincreasing in time t, and, by definition, x^* is a monotone attractor. □

We now consider the case that some of the utility functions are strictly concave while the others are just concave, which implies that some financial sectors are strictly risk-averse, while the others are just risk-averse. In such cases, the asset-liability-price pattern of the sectors with strictly concave utilities converges to some unique equilibrium pattern, independent of the starting pattern of the financial adjustment process.

Theorem 8.8

Assume the conditions of Theorem 8.7. Assume also that there is a subset of the financial sectors, $\tilde{J} \subset \{1, 2, \cdots, J\}$, such that for each $j \in \tilde{J}$, the utility function U^j is strictly concave with respect to X^j and Y^j. Then, all financial equilibria are comprised of unique asset and liability patterns, X^{j^*} and Y^{j^*}, for $j \in \tilde{J}$, and, in addition, the financial adjustment process is stable, that is,

$$X_0(t)^j \longrightarrow X^{j^*}, \quad Y_0(t)^j \longrightarrow Y^{j^*}, \quad as\ t \longrightarrow \infty, \quad \forall j \in \tilde{J}, \tag{8.35}$$

regardless as to the initial distribution (X_0, Y_0, r_0).

Proof: Let $x^* = (X^*, Y^*, r^*)$ be any financial equilibrium pattern. Then for any initial pattern, $x_0 = (X_0, Y_0, r_0)$, according to Theorem 8.7,

$$D(x_0, x^*, t) = \frac{1}{2}\|x_0(t) - x^*\|^2$$

is a nonincreasing function of time t. Therefore, for each

$$j \in \tilde{J}, \quad \{(X_0(t)^j, Y_0(t)^j) |\ t \geq 0\}$$

is bounded. To complete the proof, we only need to show that

$$\{(X_0(t)^j, Y_0(t)^j) |\ t \geq 0\}, \quad \forall j \in J,$$

does not have any other limit point except (X^{j^*}, Y^{j^*}).

Suppose, on the contrary, that there exists a $j \in J$ and some time sequence $\{t_k\}$, such that

$$X_0(t_k)^j \longrightarrow \bar{X}^j, \quad Y_0(t_k)^j \longrightarrow \bar{Y}^j, \text{ as } k \longrightarrow \infty \tag{8.36}$$

and

$$(\bar{X}^j, \bar{Y}^j) \neq (X^{j^*}, Y^{j^*}).$$

Let

$$d = \frac{1}{4}\|(\bar{X}^j, \bar{Y}^j) - (X^{j^*}, Y^{j^*})\| \tag{8.37}$$

and

$$G^j(X^j, Y^j) = (X^j - X^{j^*}, Y^j - Y^{j^*})^T \nabla^2 u^j(X^j, Y^j)(X^j - X^{j^*}, Y^j - Y^{j^*}). \tag{8.38}$$

Because of the strict concavity of u^j, $G^j(X^j, Y^j)$, as a continuous function of (X^j, Y^j), is negative everywhere except at $(X^j, Y^j) = (X^{j^*}, Y^{j^*})$, which attains, on the set $\mathcal{B}((\bar{X}^j, \bar{Y}^j), 2d)$, which is compact, its maximum, say, $-w^j$. Namely, we have

$$G^j(X^j, Y^j) \leq -w^j < 0, \quad \forall (X^j, Y^j) \in \mathcal{B}((\bar{X}^j, \bar{Y}^j), 2d), \tag{8.39}$$

where $\mathcal{B}((\bar{X}^j, \bar{Y}^j), 2d)$ is the closed ball centered at $(\bar{X}^j, \bar{Y}^j)$ with radius $2d$. In view of (8.39), one has

$$\dot{D}(z_0, z^*, t) \leq G^j(X^j(t), Y^j(t)) \leq -w^j, \tag{8.40}$$

where $(X^j(t), Y^j(t)) \in \mathcal{B}((\bar{X}^j, \bar{Y}^j), 2d)$.

Since $D(x_0, x^*, t) = \frac{1}{2}||x_0(t) - x^*||^2$ is nonnegative, (8.40) implies that

$$T = \{t \geq 0 : \ (X^j(t), Y^j(t)) \in \mathcal{B}((\bar{X}^j, \bar{Y}^j), 2d)\} \tag{8.41}$$

must have finite Lebesque measure.

Combining this fact with (8.36), one asserts the existence of two sequences $\{t_v\}$ and $\{s_v\}$ with

$$t_v < t_v + s_v < t_{v+1}, \quad v = 0, 1, \cdots,$$

such that

$$(X^j(t), Y^j(t)) \in \mathcal{B}\left((\bar{X}^j, \bar{Y}^j), d\right) \tag{8.42}$$

and

$$s_v = \ \text{Sup}\ \{\delta \geq 0 : \ (X^j(t), Y^j(t)) \in \mathcal{B}\left((\bar{X}^j, \bar{Y}^j), 2d\right), \forall \tau \in [t_v, t_v + s_v]\}, \tag{8.43}$$

which implies that

$$||\left(X^j(t_v + s_v), Y^j(t_v + s_v)\right) - (\bar{X}^j, \bar{Y}^j)|| = 2d. \tag{8.44}$$

In fact, $\{t_v\}$ can be extracted as a subsequence from $\{t_k\}$ in (8.36). Since $||x_0(t) - x^*||$ is nonincreasing in t, $\{x_0(t) : t \geq 0\}$ is contained in the compact set $\mathcal{B}_2 = \mathcal{B}(x^*, ||x_0 - x^*||)$. Hence, $F(x)$ defined in (6.21) attains its maximal norm on $\mathcal{B}_2$. Let

$$M = \max_{x \in \mathcal{B}_2} ||F(x)||. \tag{8.45}$$

Then, it follows from $||\Pi_{\mathcal{K}}(x, -F(x))|| \leq ||F(x)||$, that

$$||\Pi_{\mathcal{K}}(x(t), -F(x(t)))|| \leq M, \quad \forall t \geq 0. \tag{8.46}$$

Therefore,

$$||x(t_v + s_v) - x(t_v)|| \leq \int_{t_v}^{t_v + s_v} ||\Pi_{\mathcal{K}}\left(x\left(\tau\right), -F\left(x\left(\tau\right)\right)\right)||d\tau \leq M s_v. \tag{8.47}$$

On the other hand, with notice to (8.42) and (8.44), one has

$$||x(t_v + s_v) - x(t_v)|| \geq d. \tag{8.48}$$

Therefore,

$$s_v \geq \frac{d}{M}, \quad v = 0, 1, \cdots, \tag{8.49}$$

which yields

$$m\left(\bigcup_{v=0}^{\infty} (t_v, t_v + s_v)\right) = \sum_{v=0}^{\infty} s_v = \infty. \tag{8.50}$$

However, (8.50) is in contradiction to the earlier observation that T has finite measure because

$$\bigcup_{v=0}^{\infty} (t_v, t_v + s_v) \subset T.$$

The contradiction we produced shows that the early assumption cannot be true. Therefore, for every j in J,

$$(X_0(t)^j, Y_0(t)^j) \longrightarrow (X^{j^*}, Y^{j^*}), \text{ as } t \longrightarrow \infty. \qquad \square$$

Finally, Theorem 8.9 below establishes the asymptotical stability of the financial adjustment process, provided that each financial sector has a strictly concave utility function.

Theorem 8.9 (Asymptotical Stability)

Suppose that each sector's utility function is continuous, twice continuously differentiable, and strictly concave with respect to its asset and liability pattern. Then the financial adjustment process (8.13) is asymptotically stable.

Proof: Following Theorem 8.8, the financial adjustment process,

$$x_0(t) = (X_0(t), Y_0(t), r_0(t)),$$

initialized at any initial financial pattern, (X_0, Y_0, r_0), converges to some unique equilibrium pattern of assets and liabilities, that is,

$$X_0(t) \longrightarrow X^*, \quad Y_0(t) \longrightarrow Y^*, \text{ as } t \longrightarrow \infty. \tag{8.51}$$

Since $x_0(t)$ is bounded, $\{r_0(t), t \geq 0\}$ has a convergent sequence, say,

$$r_0(t_k) \longrightarrow r^*, \text{ as } k \longrightarrow \infty. \tag{8.52}$$

In what follows, we are going to show that $x^* = (X^*, Y^*, r^*)$ is, indeed, a financial equilibrium pattern and

$$(X_0(t), Y_0(t), r_0(t)) \longrightarrow (X^*, Y^*, r^*), \text{ as } t \longrightarrow \infty. \tag{8.53}$$

Since (X^*, Y^*) is an equilibrium asset and liability pattern, one has

$$\sigma_i := \sum_{j=1}^{J} (X_i^{j^*} - Y_i^{j^*}) \geq 0, \quad \forall i = 1, 2, \cdots, I. \tag{8.54}$$

However, for those i with $\sigma_i > 0$, (8.51) implies that

$$\sum_{j=1}^{J}(X_0(t)_i^j - Y_0(t)_i^j) > \frac{\sigma_i}{2} > 0 \tag{8.55}$$

for t sufficiently large.

Therefore, for those i with $\sigma_i > 0$, one has

$$\lim_{t\to\infty} r_0(t)_i = 0, \tag{8.56}$$

which yields

$$r_i^* = 0, \quad \text{if } \sigma_i > 0. \tag{8.57}$$

Bearing in mind (8.54) and that r_i^* is nonnegative, one concludes from (8.57) that for $i = 1, \ldots, I$:

$$\sum_{j=1}^{J}(X_i^{j*} - Y_i^{j*}) \begin{cases} = 0 & \text{if } r_i^* > 0 \\ \geq 0 & \text{if } r_i^* = 0. \end{cases} \tag{8.58}$$

Notice that (8.58) is nothing else but the equilibrium condition (6.11). According to Theorem 8.7, the financial equilibrium (X^*, Y^*, r^*) is a monotone attractor. Therefore, in light of (8.51) and (8.52), we know that

$$(X_0(t), Y_0(t), r_0(t)) \longrightarrow (X^*, Y^*, r^*), \text{ as } t \longrightarrow \infty. \qquad \square$$

Theorems 8.7 and 8.9 have the following interpretations in terms of network structure. In the case of utility functions of the specified form, we are guaranteed that if the utility functions are also concave (and twice continuously differentiable), that any disequilibrium state will stay close to the (corresponding) equilibrium network. Furthermore, if the utility functions are not just concave, but, strictly concave, then the individual networks representing all the sectors optimization problems will eventually merge to that equilibrium network.

8.3 A Discrete Time Algorithm

In this section we present a discrete time algorithm, the Euler method, for the computation of the financial equilibrium patterns. This algorithm may be viewed as a discrete time approximation or dicrete time adjustment process for the continuous time models given by (8.13), (8.22), and (8.30). The Euler method, defined by (4.24) and (4.52), is a special case of the general iterative scheme devised in Dupuis and Nagurney (1993), which was presented in Section 4.3. We now recall the Euler method and then show its realization in the context of the three dynamical financial models of Section 8.1. In particular, at each iteration τ, one must compute:

$$x^{\tau+1} = P_{\mathcal{K}}(x^{\tau} - a_{\tau} F(x^{\tau})), \tag{8.59}$$

where $\{a_\tau\}$ is a positive sequence, to be discussed later, and $P_{\mathcal{K}}$ is the projection operator defined in (3.24).

Note that (8.59) is equivalent to the solution of the variational inequality problem:

Determine $x^{\tau+1} \in \mathcal{K}$, satisfying:

$$\langle (x^{\tau+1} + a_{\tau} F(x^{\tau}) - x^{\tau})^T, x - x^{\tau+1} \rangle \geq 0, \quad \forall x \in \mathcal{K}. \tag{8.60}$$

We will now write down the Euler method for each of the dynamic models explicitly, following (8.60), with $F(x)$ and x being spelled out for each model. For the convergence analysis, we will assume that the utility functions are of special form, given, respectively, by (6.4), (7.4), and (7.52).

8.3.1 Euler Method for the Section 8.1.1 Model

We now present the Euler method for the dynamic financial adjustment process given in Section 8.1.1. This method traces the trajectories of the projected dynamical system (8.13) and yields a stationary point. Hence, it also computes a financial equilibrium satisfying Definition 6.1 and, equivalently, determines a solution to variational inequality (6.12a).

Step 0: Initialization

Set $(X^0, Y^0, r^0) \in \mathcal{K}$. Let $\tau := 0$.

Step 1: Computation

Compute $(X^{\tau+1}, Y^{\tau+1}, r^{\tau+1}) \in \mathcal{K}$ by solving the variational inequality subproblem:

$$\sum_{j=1}^{J}\sum_{i=1}^{I}\left[X_i^{j^{\tau+1}} + a_\tau\left(-\frac{\partial U^j(X^{j^\tau}, Y^{j^\tau}, r^\tau)}{\partial X_i^j}\right) - X_i^{j^\tau}\right] \times \left[X_i^j - X_i^{j^{\tau+1}}\right]$$

$$+\sum_{j=1}^{J}\sum_{i=1}^{I}\left[Y_i^{j^{\tau+1}} + a_\tau\left(-\frac{\partial U^j(X^{j^\tau}, Y^{j^\tau}, r^\tau)}{\partial Y_i^j}\right) - Y_i^{j^\tau}\right] \times \left[Y_i^j - Y_i^{j^{\tau+1}}\right]$$

$$+\sum_{i=1}^{I}\left[r_i^{\tau+1} + a_\tau\left[\sum_{j=1}^{J}\left(X_i^{j^\tau} - Y_i^{j^\tau}\right)\right] - r_i^\tau\right] \times \left[r_i - r_i^{\tau+1}\right] \geq 0,$$

$$\forall (X, Y, r) \in \mathcal{K}. \tag{8.61}$$

Step 2: Convergence Verification

If $\max_{i,j} |X_i^{j\,\tau+1} - X_i^{j\,\tau}| \leq \epsilon$; $\max_{i,j} |Y_i^{j\,\tau+1} - Y_i^{j\,\tau}| \leq \epsilon$; $\max_i |r_i^{\tau+1} - r_i^{\tau}| \leq \epsilon$, for all $i; i = 1, \ldots, I$, and $j; j = 1, \ldots, J$, with $\epsilon > 0$, a prespecified tolerance, then stop; else, set $\tau := \tau + 1$, and go to Step 1.

Note the similarity between the iterative step (8.61) above and that of a typical iterative step (6.62) and (6.63) of the modified projection method. Indeed, they are of the identical structure except that in the Euler method one has a varying parameter a_τ for each iteration τ, whereas in the modified projection method one has a fixed parameter γ.

Hence, the structure of problem (8.61) is precisely that of the network subproblems depicted in Figure 6.3 in view of the underlying feasible set. Moreover, the subproblems are quadratic programming problems and can be solved exactly and in closed form using exact equilibration, as discussed following Theorem 6.7.

8.3.2 Euler Method for the Section 8.1.2 Model

We now present the Euler method for the discrete time approximation of the trajectories of the projected dynamical system (8.22). The Euler method also computes a stationary point of this system and, hence, an equilibrium point satisfying variational inequality (7.15a).

Step 0: Initialization

Set $(\mathcal{X}^0, \mathcal{Y}^0, r^0, \lambda^0) \in \mathcal{K}$. Let $\tau := 0$.

Step 1: Computation

Compute $(X^{\tau+1}, Y^{\tau+1}, r^{\tau+1}, \lambda^{\tau+1}) \in \mathcal{K}$ by solving the variational inequality subproblem:

$$\sum_{j=1}^{J}\sum_{i=1}^{I}\left[X_i^{j\,\tau+1} + a_\tau\left(-\frac{\partial U^j(\mathcal{X}^{j\,\tau}, \mathcal{Y}^{j\,\tau}, r^\tau, \lambda^\tau; \pi)}{\partial X_i^j}\right) - X_i^{j\,\tau}\right] \times \left[X_i^j - X_i^{j\,\tau+1}\right]$$

$$+\sum_{j=1}^{J}\sum_{i=1}^{I}\left[Y_i^{j\,\tau+1} + a_\tau\left(-\frac{\partial U^j(\mathcal{X}^{j\,\tau}, \mathcal{Y}^{j\,\tau}, r^\tau, \lambda^\tau; \pi)}{\partial Y_i^j}\right) - Y_i^{j\,\tau}\right] \times \left[Y_i^j - Y_i^{j\,\tau+1}\right]$$

$$+\sum_{j=1}^{J}\sum_{i=1}^{I}\left[Z_i^{j\,\tau+1} + a_\tau\left(-\frac{\partial U^j(\mathcal{X}^{j\,\tau}, \mathcal{Y}^{j\,\tau}, r^\tau, \lambda^\tau; \pi)}{\partial Z_i^j}\right) - Z_i^{j\,\tau}\right] \times \left[Z_i^j - Z_i^{j\,\tau+1}\right]$$

$$+\sum_{j=1}^{J}\sum_{i=1}^{I}\left[\Psi_i^{j\,\tau+1} + a_\tau\left(-\frac{\partial U^j(\mathcal{X}^{j\,\tau}, \mathcal{Y}^{j\,\tau}, r^\tau, \lambda^\tau; \pi)}{\partial \Psi_i^j}\right) - \Psi_i^{j\,\tau}\right] \times \left[\Psi_i^j - \Psi_i^{j\,\tau+1}\right]$$

$$+\sum_{i=1}^{I}\left[r_i^{\tau+1} + a_\tau\left[\sum_{j=1}^{J}\left(X_i^{j\,\tau} - Y_i^{j\,\tau}\right)\right] - r_i^\tau\right] \times \left[r_i - r_i^{\tau+1}\right]$$

$$+\sum_{i=1}^{I}\left[\lambda_i^{\tau+1}+a_\tau\left[\sum_{j=1}^{J}\left(Z_i^{j^\tau}-\Psi_i^{j^\tau}\right)\right]-\lambda_i^\tau\right]\times\left[\lambda_i-\lambda_i^{\tau+1}\right]\geq 0,$$

$$\forall(\mathcal{X},\mathcal{Y},r,\lambda)\in\mathcal{K}. \tag{8.62}$$

Step 2: Convergence Verification

If $\max_{i,j}|X_i^{j^{\tau+1}}-X_i^{j^\tau}|\leq\epsilon$; $\max_{i,j}|Y_i^{j^{\tau+1}}-Y_i^{j^\tau}|\leq\epsilon$; $\max_{i,j}|Z_i^{j^{\tau+1}}-Z_i^{j^\tau}|\leq\epsilon$; $\max_{i,j}|\Psi_i^{j^{\tau+1}}-\Psi_i^{j^\tau}|\leq\epsilon$; $\max_i|r_i^{\tau+1}-r_i^\tau|\leq\epsilon$, and $\max_i|\lambda_i^{\tau+1}-\lambda_i^\tau|\leq\epsilon$, for all $i; i=1,\ldots,I$, and $j; j=1,\ldots,J$, with $\epsilon>0$, a prespecified tolerance, then stop; else, set $\tau:=\tau+1$, and go to Step 1.

Note now the typical iterative step (8.62) as compared to the typical iterative steps (7.50) and (7.51) of the modified projection method applied for the computation of financial equilibria in the presence of futures. The variational inequality subproblems have the identical structure, again, except for the varying parameter a_τ versus the fixed parameter γ. Consequently, the subproblem (8.62) decomposes into quadratic programming problems with network structure as depicted in Figure 7.6. Hence, these subproblems are also amenable to solution via exact equilibration.

8.3.3 Euler Method for the Section 8.1.3 Model

Here we present the Euler method for the discrete time approximation of the projected dynamical system (8.30) describing the financial adjustment process in the case of options. The method also computes an equilibrium satisfying the variational inequality problem (7.65).

Step 0: Initialization

Set $(\mathcal{X}^0,\mathcal{Y}^0,r^0,\lambda^0)\in\mathcal{K}$. Let $\tau:=0$.

Step 1: Computation

Compute $(X^{\tau+1},Z^{\tau+1},W^{\tau+1},Y^{\tau+1},\Psi^{\tau+1},\Phi^{\tau+1},r^{\tau+1})\in\mathcal{K}$ by solving the variational inequality subproblem:

$$\sum_{j=1}^{J}\sum_{i=1}^{I}\left[X_i^{j^{\tau+1}}+a_\tau\left[-\frac{\partial u^j(\mathcal{X}^{j^\tau},\mathcal{Y}^{j^\tau})}{\partial X_i^j}-r_i^\tau\right]-X_i^{j^\tau}\right]\times\left[X_i^j-X_i^{j^{\tau+1}}\right]$$

$$+\sum_{j=1}^{J}\sum_{i=1}^{I}\left[Z_i^{j^{\tau+1}}+a_\tau\left[-\frac{\partial u^j(\mathcal{X}^{j^\tau},\mathcal{Y}^{j^\tau})}{\partial Z_i^j}-(\pi_i-\theta_i+\lambda_i^\tau)\right]-Z_i^{j^\tau}\right]$$

$$\times\left[Z_i^j-Z_i^{j^{\tau+1}}\right]$$

$$+\sum_{j=1}^{J}\sum_{i=1}^{I}\left[W_i^{j^{\tau+1}}+a_\tau\left[-\frac{\partial u^j(\mathcal{X}^{j^\tau},\mathcal{Y}^{j^\tau})}{\partial W_i^j}-(r_i^\tau-\theta_i)\right]-W_i^{j^\tau}\right]$$
$$\times\left[W_i^j-W_i^{j^{\tau+1}}\right]$$
$$+\sum_{j=1}^{J}\sum_{i=1}^{I}\left[Y_i^{j^{\tau+1}}+a_\tau\left[-\frac{\partial u^j(\mathcal{X}^{j^\tau},\mathcal{Y}^{j^\tau})}{\partial Y_i^j}+r_i^\tau\right]-Y_i^{j^\tau}\right]\times\left[Y_i^j-Y_i^{j^{\tau+1}}\right]$$
$$+\sum_{j=1}^{J}\sum_{i=1}^{I}\left[\Psi_i^{j^{\tau+1}}+a_\tau\left[-\frac{\partial u^j(\mathcal{X}^{j^\tau},\mathcal{Y}^{j^\tau})}{\partial \Psi_i^j}+(\pi_i-\theta_i+\lambda_i^\tau)\right]-\Psi_i^{j^\tau}\right]$$
$$\times\left[\Psi_i^j-\Psi_i^{j^{\tau+1}}\right]$$
$$+\sum_{j=1}^{J}\sum_{i=1}^{I}\left[\Phi_i^{j^{\tau+1}}+a_\tau\left[-\frac{\partial u^j(\mathcal{X}^{j^\tau},\mathcal{Y}^{j^\tau})}{\partial \Phi_i^j}+(r_i^\tau-\theta_i)\right]-\Phi_i^{j^\tau}\right]$$
$$\times\left[\Phi_i^j-\Phi_i^{j^{\tau+1}}\right]$$
$$+\sum_{i=1}^{I}\left[r_i^{\tau+1}+a_\tau\sum_{j=1}^{J}\left[\left(X_i^{j^\tau}+W_i^{j^\tau}\right)-\left(Y_i^{j^\tau}-r_i^\tau\right)\right]+\Psi_i^{j^\tau}\right]\times\left[r_i-r_i^{\tau+1}\right]$$
$$+\sum_{i=1}^{I}\left[\lambda_i^{\tau+1}+a_\tau\sum_{j=1}^{J}\left[Z_i^{j^\tau}-\Psi_i^{j^\tau}\right]-\lambda_i^\tau\right]\times\left[\lambda_i-\lambda_i^{\tau+1}\right]\geq 0,$$
$$\forall(\mathcal{X},\mathcal{Y},r,\lambda)\in\mathcal{K}. \tag{8.63}$$

Step 2: Convergence Verification

If $\max_{i,j}|X_i^{j^{\tau+1}}-X_i^{j^\tau}|\leq\epsilon$; $\max_{i,j}|Y_i^{j^{\tau+1}}-Y_i^{j^\tau}|\leq\epsilon$; $\max_{i,j}|Z_i^{j^{\tau+1}}-Z_i^{j^\tau}|\leq\epsilon$; $\max_{i,j}|\Psi_i^{j^{\tau+1}}-\Psi_i^{j^\tau}|\leq\epsilon$; $\max_{i,j}|W_i^{j^{\tau+1}}-W_i^{j^\tau}|\leq\epsilon$; $|\Phi_i^{j^{\tau+1}}-\Phi_i^{j^\tau}|\leq\epsilon$; $\max_i|r_i^{\tau+1}-r_i^\tau|\leq\epsilon$, and $\max_i|\lambda_i^{\tau+1}-\lambda_i^\tau|\leq\epsilon$, for all $i; i=1,\ldots,I$, and $j; j=1,\ldots,J$, with $\epsilon>0$, a prespecified tolerance, then stop; else, set $\tau:=\tau+1$, and go to Step 1.

Note that the Euler method above can easily be adapted to construct the modified projection method for the computation of financial equilibria in the case of options. The latter was not presented in Section 7.7, for the sake of brevity. The subproblems induced by (8.63) have the special network structure as depicted in Figure 7.8 and, consequently, are also amenable to solution via exact equilibration.

We now present the convergence result. It is stated in a general fashion and holds under the given assumptions for the three realizations of the Euler method above.

Theorem 8.10

Suppose that the utility functions U^j are strictly concave with respect to the instrument variables, continuous, twice and continuously differentiable, and are of the form (6.4), (7.4), or as in (7.52), for all sectors j for the dynamic financial model in question. Suppose also that the utility functions are strictly monotone at any equilibrium pattern. Let $\{a_\tau\}$ be a sequence of positive real numbers that satisfies

$$\lim_{\tau \to \infty} a_\tau = 0 \tag{8.64}$$

and

$$\sum_{\tau=0}^{\infty} a_\tau = \infty. \tag{8.65}$$

Then the Euler method given by (8.59), which takes, for an iteration τ, the explicit form (8.61), (8.62), or (8.63), respectively, converges to some financial equilibrium pattern satisfying, respectively, Definition 6.1, Definition 7.1, or Definition 7.2.

Proof: According to Theorem 4.6 and Corollary 4.1, the sequence generated by (8.59), converges to some stationary point of the corresponding projected dynamical system provided that Assumption 4.2 is satisfied. Consequently, by taking advantage, respectively, of Theorems 8.2, 8.4, and 8.6, it converges to the (corresponding) financial equilibrium pattern.

Condition 4.2.1 is satisfied by our selection of the sequence $\{a_\tau\}$ according to (8.64) and (8.65). Condition 4.2.2 of the assumption, in turn, is met since $F(x)$ is continuous in each of the models and $F_\tau = F$ in the case of the Euler method. Since $F(x)$ is assumed to be strictly monotone at any equilibrium pattern, condition 4.2.3 holds true according to Proposition 4.1. Condition 4.2.4 becomes trivial since the accounting and nonnegativity constraints underlying each dynamic financial model yield a compact set. Finally, condition 4.2.5 of the assumption holds true since under the assumption of strict concavity of the utility functions, $F(x)$ is monotone and this condition holds true following Proposition 4.2.2. □

It is worth comparing the conditions for convergence of the modified projection method, as discussed in Section 6.4.1 in Theorem 6.7, with the conditions for convergence of the Euler method. Indeed, either method can be used to compute an equilibrium pattern, provided that certain assumptions are satisfied. In the case of the modified projection method, the function F that enters the variational inequality problem must be both Lipschitz continuous and monotone. These conditions were shown to hold in the case of the (static) financial model in Theorem 6.5 and Theorem 6.4, respectively, provided that the utility functions have bounded second order derivatives (for Lipschitz continuity to hold) and are strictly concave (for monotonicity to hold). Note that, under the identical conditions, as revealed in the proof of Theorem 8.10 above (and recalling Theorem 4.2), convergence of the Euler method is also guaranteed. However, according to Propositions 4.1 and 4.2, which provide conditions on F that guarantee, respectively, that Assumption 4.2.3 and 4.2.5 hold true, only strict monotonicity, respectively, monotonicity at some solution x^* is required, rather than over the entire feasible set. Clearly, the latter condition is a looser condition than monotonicity over the entire feasible set, whereas the former is always satisfied if the utility functions are strictly concave.

As discussed following Theorem 6.7, the modified projection method is guaranteed to converge at the rate of a geometric progression, whereas no analogous such rate has been yet obtained for the Euler method above. However, this rate only holds provided that γ (cf. (6.60) and (6.61)) lies in a certain range, whereas one has more flexibility in selecting the sequence $\{a_\tau\}$ (cf. (8.64) and (8.65)) in the case of the Euler method.

In terms of implementation issues, the Euler method (cf. (8.60)) only requires a single computation step, whereas the modified projection method (cf. (6.60) and (6.61)) requires also an adaptation step, which is, nevertheless, of the same order of complexity, structure, and size as the first computation step. Hence, for a given iteration, the modified projection method solves, essentially, two closely related problems, whereas the Euler method only solves one. Consequently, the Euler method is easier to implement. Furthermore, one would expect any given iteration of the modified projection method to take approximatley twice as long in terms of CPU time as the Euler method. However, it is also reasonable to expect that the modified projection method may take fewer iterations than the Euler method for a given problem and, as a result, the total CPU time may be comparable to that for the Euler method. Further research into the numerical analysis of the sequence $\{a_\tau\}$ in expediting convergence of the Euler method, in particular, and the general iterative scheme, in general, may yield sequences that result in even faster convergence.

Finally, it is worth emphasizing that the Euler method, unlike the modified projection method, provides a discrete time approximation to the (corresponding) continuous time adjustment process. Moreover, as noted in Chapter 4, the sequence $\{a_\tau\}$ which must satisfy (8.64) and (8.65) has the interpretation that the financial system will react more strongly at the beginning and its responsiveness will decrease later on.

8.3.4 Numerical Examples

In this subsection we provide a variety of numerical examples which are solved via the Euler method(s) given above. First, for completeness, we provide information as to the application of the Euler method to datasets that have been used earlier in Chapters 6 and 7. We then present additional numerical examples. We embedded the exact equilibration algorithms in the Euler method for the closed form solution of the quadratic programming problems on the networks.

The Euler method was coded in FORTRAN for each of the three realizations above. We used the IBM SP2 for all the numerical experiments. The CPU time is reported (exclusive of the input/output time) in addition to the number of iterations. In all the examples we assumed that the utility functions were quadratic corresponding to the variance/covariance matrices. The sequence $\{a_\mathcal{T}\}$ used was: $\{a_\mathcal{T}\}=\{1, \frac{1}{2}, \frac{1}{2}, \frac{1}{3}, \frac{1}{3}, \frac{1}{3}, \ldots\}$ for all the examples. The convergence tolerance ϵ was set to .001.

Example 8.1 (see Example 6.1)

The first example that we solved had the identical data as Example 6.1, which had been solved earlier in Chapter 6 using the modified projection method. As reported therein, the example consisted of two sectors and three financial instruments. The utility functions of the sectors were quadratic with the variance/covariance matrices as detailed therein. Hence, here an iteration of the Euler method was as in (8.61) above.

The Euler method converged in 52 iterations and in a negligible amount of CPU time to the equilibrium solution (cf. Example 6.1). Note that the modified projection method converged in 16 iterations.

The subsequent three examples are examples with futures. Hence, the typical iterative step of the Euler method was as given in (8.62).

Example 8.2 (see Example 7.1)

The second example that we solved using the Euler method had identical data to that of Example 7.1. The Euler method converged to the equilibrium solution as reported therein in 60 iterations and .01 seconds of CPU time.

Example 8.3 (see Example 7.2)

The third example that we solved using the Euler method had data identical that that of Example 7.2. The Euler method converged in 117 iterations and in .03 seconds of CPU time.

Example 8.4 (see Example 7.3)

The fourth example had data as in Example 7.3. The Euler method converged to the equilibrium in 194 iterations and .09 seconds of CPU time.

Example 8.5: 4 Sectors, 4 Instruments

We now present an example of the dynamic financial model in Section 8.1.1 that is larger than Example 8.1. It consists of four sectors trading in four financial instruments. The variance-covariance matrices for each of the sectors are as follows:

For sector 1:

$$Q^1 = \begin{pmatrix} 1.0 & 0.15 & 0 & 0 & -0.2 & -0.3 & 0 & 0 \\ 0.15 & 1.0 & 0 & 0 & -0.1 & -0.2 & 0 & 0 \\ 0 & 0 & 1.0 & 0 & 0 & 0 & -0.1 & 0 \\ 0 & 0 & 0 & 1.0 & 0 & 0 & -0.1 & 0 \\ -0.2 & -0.1 & 0 & 0 & 1.0 & 0.4 & 0 & 0 \\ -0.3 & -0.2 & 0 & 0 & 0.4 & 1.0 & 0 & 0 \\ 0 & 0 & -0.1 & -0.1 & 0 & 0 & 1.0 & 0 \\ 0 & 0 & 0 & 0 & 0 & 0 & 0 & 1.0 \end{pmatrix}$$

For sector 2:

$$Q^2 = \begin{pmatrix} 1.0 & 0.2 & 0.2 & 0 & 0 & 0 & -0.1 & -0.2 \\ 0.2 & 1.0 & 0 & 0 & 0 & -0.15 & 0 & 0 \\ 0.2 & 0 & 1.0 & 0.5 & -0.1 & 0 & 0 & 0 \\ 0 & 0 & 0.5 & 1.0 & 0 & -0.3 & 0 & 0 \\ 0 & 0 & -0.1 & 0 & 1.0 & 0 & 0.2 & 0 \\ 0 & -0.15 & 0 & -0.3 & 0 & 1.0 & 0.3 & 0 \\ -0.1 & 0 & 0 & 0 & 0.2 & 0.3 & 1.0 & 0 \\ -0.2 & 0 & 0 & 0 & 0 & 0 & 0 & 1.0 \end{pmatrix}$$

For sector 3:

$$Q^3 = \begin{pmatrix} 1.0 & 0 & 0.3 & 0 & -0.1 & -0.1 & 0 & 0 \\ 0 & 1.0 & 0.1 & 0 & 0 & 0 & -0.2 & 0 \\ 0.3 & 0.1 & 1.0 & 0 & -0.3 & 0 & 0 & 0 \\ 0 & 0 & 0 & 1.0 & -0.4 & 0 & 0 & 0 \\ -0.1 & 0 & -0.3 & -0.4 & 1.0 & 0 & 0 & 0 \\ -0.1 & 0 & 0 & 0 & 0 & 1.0 & 0.5 & 0 \\ 0 & -0.2 & 0 & 0 & 0 & 0.5 & 1.0 & 0.1 \\ 0 & 0 & 0 & 0 & 0 & 0 & 0.1 & 1.0 \end{pmatrix}$$

For sector 4:

$$Q^4 = \begin{pmatrix} 1.0 & 0.4 & 0 & 0 & -0.2 & 0 & 0 & 0 \\ 0.4 & 1.0 & 0 & 0 & 0 & -0.1 & 0 & 0 \\ 0 & 0 & 1.0 & 0 & -0.3 & 0 & 0 & 0 \\ 0 & 0 & 0 & 1.0 & 0 & 0 & -0.4 & 0 \\ -0.2 & 0 & -0.3 & 0 & 1.0 & 0 & 0 & 0 \\ 0 & -0.1 & 0 & 0 & 0 & 1.0 & 0.3 & 0 \\ 0 & 0 & 0 & -0.4 & 0 & 0.3 & 1.0 & 0.1 \\ 0 & 0 & 0 & 0 & 0 & 0 & 0.1 & 1.0 \end{pmatrix}.$$

The sector volumes for all the sectors were set equal to 1.
The computed equilibrium solution via the Euler method is given by:

Instrument Prices:

$$r_1^* = 1.072, \quad r_2^* = 1.021, \quad r_3^* = .990, \quad r_4^* = .917,$$

Asset and Liability Pattern:

$$X_1^{1*} = .323, \quad X_2^{1*} = .249, \quad X_3^{1*} = .233, \quad X_4^{1*} = .195,$$

$$X_1^{2*} = .328, \quad X_2^{2*} = .284, \quad X_3^{2*} = .092, \quad X_2^{4*} = .297,$$

$$X_1^{3*} = .215, \quad X_2^{3*} = .223, \quad X_3^{3*} = .236, \quad X_4^{3*} = .327,$$

$$X_1^{4*} = .258, \quad X_2^{4*} = .140, \quad X_3^{4*} = .316, \quad X_4^{4*} = .285,$$

$$Y_1^{1*} = .169, \quad Y_2^{1*} = .291, \quad Y_3^{1*} = .272, \quad Y_4^{1*} = .267,$$

$$Y_1^{2*} = .192, \quad Y_2^{2*} = .318, \quad Y_3^{2*} = .143, \quad Y_4^{2*} = .347,$$

$$Y_1^{3*} = .421, \quad Y_2^{3*} = .149, \quad Y_3^{3*} = .178, \quad Y_4^{3*} = .252,$$

$$Y_1^{4*} = .341, \quad Y_2^{4*} = .144, \quad Y_3^{4*} = .276, \quad Y_4^{4*} = .239.$$

In this example, as established theoretically in Section 6.3, the markets cleared for each instrument.

The Euler method (cf. (8.61)) converged in 91 iterations and in .03 seconds of CPU time to this solution.

We then proceeded to do the following simulation in the subsequent two examples. We retained the variance/covariance matrices of Example 8.5, but assumed that there were no longer 4 unhedged instruments but, rather two unhedged, and two hedged instruments. We first, in Example 8.6, set the contracted prices of the two unhedged instruments lower than the equilibrium prices obtained in Example 8.5 for instruments 3 and 4. We then, in Example 8.7, raised the contracted prices of the two unhedged instruments above the equilibrium values that had been obtained for the prices of instruments 3 and 4 in Example 8.5.

Example 8.6

This example had variance/covariance matrices identical to those in the preceding example but now they had distinct interpretations since we assume that there were two unhedged and two hedged financial instruments. The remainder of the data was identical to that in Example 8.5.

In particular, we set $\pi_1 = .8$ and $\pi_2 = .8$. The Euler method converged in 115 iterations and .03 seconds of CPU time to the following equilibrium solution:

Instrument Prices:

$$r_1^* = 1.455, \quad r_2^* = 1.426,$$

Shadow Prices:

$$\lambda_1^* = .603, \quad \lambda_2^* = .516,$$

Asset and Liability Pattern:

$$X_1^{1*} = .322, \quad X_2^{1*} = .250, \quad Z_1^{1*} = .233, \quad Z_2^{1*} = .196,$$

$$X_1^{2*} = .328, \quad X_2^{2*} = .284, \quad Z_1^{2*} = .088, \quad Z_2^{2*} = .299,$$
$$X_1^{3*} = .215, \quad X_2^{3*} = .226, \quad Z_1^{3*} = .233, \quad Z_2^{3*} = .326,$$
$$X_1^{4*} = .257, \quad X_2^{4*} = .141, \quad Z_1^{4*} = .314, \quad Z_2^{4*} = .287,$$
$$Y_1^{1*} = .170, \quad Y_2^{1*} = .291, \quad \Psi_1^{1*} = .272, \quad \Psi_2^{1*} = .266,$$
$$Y_1^{2*} = .192, \quad Y_2^{2*} = .316, \quad \Psi_1^{2*} = .145, \quad \Psi_2^{2*} = .348,$$
$$Y_1^{3*} = .422, \quad Y_2^{3*} = .146, \quad \Psi_1^{3*} = .180, \quad \Psi_2^{3*} = .252,$$
$$Y_1^{4*} = .342, \quad Y_2^{4*} = .142, \quad \Psi_1^{4*} = .278, \quad \Psi_2^{4*} = .238.$$

Example 8.7

As discussed earlier, we then proceeded to raise the contracted prices for the two hedged financial instruments. In particular, we set $\pi_1 = 3$ and $\pi_2 = 3$. The remainder of the data was identical to that in Example 8.6.

The Euler method converged to the following solution in .04 CPU seconds and 107 iterations:

Instrument Prices:

$$r_1^* = 2.564, \quad r_2^* = 2.534,$$

Shadow Prices:

$$\lambda_1^* = -.524, \quad \lambda_2^* = -.575,$$

Asset and Liability Pattern:

$$X_1^{1*} = .325, \quad X_2^{1*} = .250, \quad Z_1^{1*} = .229, \quad Z_2^{1*} = .196,$$
$$X_1^{2*} = .329, \quad X_2^{2*} = .285, \quad Z_1^{2*} = .088, \quad Z_2^{2*} = .298,$$
$$X_1^{3*} = .216, \quad X_2^{3*} = .224, \quad Z_1^{3*} = .232, \quad Z_2^{3*} = .327,$$
$$X_1^{4*} = .261, \quad X_2^{4*} = .141, \quad Z_1^{4*} = .312, \quad Z_2^{4*} = .286,$$
$$Y_1^{1*} = .167, \quad Y_2^{1*} = .291, \quad \Psi_1^{1*} = .275, \quad \Psi_2^{1*} = .266,$$
$$Y_1^{2*} = .191, \quad Y_2^{2*} = .316, \quad \Psi_1^{2*} = .147, \quad \Psi_2^{2*} = .347,$$
$$Y_1^{3*} = .420, \quad Y_2^{3*} = .149, \quad \Psi_1^{3*} = .180, \quad \Psi_2^{3*} = .251,$$
$$Y_1^{4*} = .341, \quad Y_2^{4*} = .143, \quad \Psi_1^{4*} = .278, \quad \Psi_2^{4*} = .238.$$

Note that in Example 8.6, the shadow prices associated with both hedged instruments were positive since the contracted prices were lower than the equilibrium prices of the unhedged instruments. On the other hand, in Example 8.7, the shadow prices were both negative since the contracted prices were higher than the equilibrium prices of the unhedged instruments.

Moreover, one can easily notice that the increase of the contracted prices for the futures forces the prices of the underlying instruments to higher levels, since it sets new standards for the available returns, and, therefore, the dynamics of the economy are changed. Interestingly enough, the change in prices takes place with no significant changes in the pattern that sectors allocate their capital. This is due to the fact the utility functions for each sector remain unchanged for all examples and since we allow for perfect hedging for all sectors in the economy. Notice also that when hedging is allowed (cf. Examples 8.6 and 8.7), the variation among prices of different instruments are smaller (see Example 8.5), and no instrument offers significant profits or losses as compared to the others.

8.4 Sources and Notes

This chapter developed dynamic financial models that were counterparts to the static multi-sector, multi-instrument models of Chapters 6 and 7. We presented both models that did not allow for hedging as well as models with hedging in the form of futures or options. The methodology used here was that of projected dynamical systems. Qualitative properties of the dynamic models were investigated, in particular, in terms of stability analysis, as well as computational procedures, accompanied by convergence results and numerical examples. Note that in the dynamic models when we speak of existence and uniqueness questions, we are primarily interested in the context of existence and uniqueness of trajectories, whereas in discussions of existence and uniqueness in static models, we are exploring these questions as they apply to the equilibrium pattern itself.

The theory of dynamical systems has been used for the study of many different phenomena, in a plethora of different fields (e. g., economics, biology, chemistry, engineering, etc.), and, as a consequence, the fundamentals, as well as, the innovations in an particular area are a product of many heterogeneous contributions. Therefore, a global understanding of the subject would require an extensive study of different source materials. Our suggestions to the reader who wishes to explore further the theory of dynamic systems is biased by the economics literature since that is our viewpoint. In particular, in addition to the books cited in Chapter 4, we recommend the books by Samuelson (1947), Luenberger (1979), and Batten (1985), as well as the work by Grandmont and Malgrange (1986) for a solid initiation to the subject of dynamic systems and their applications. For an introduction to projected dynamical systems, we refer the reader to the book by Nagurney and Zhang (1996).

Section 8.1

In this section we presented three distinct dynamic financial models. The model in Section 8.1.1 was proposed by Dong, Zhang, and Nagurney (1996).

The model with futures in Section 8.1.2 was proposed by Nagurney and Siokos (1996a). The dynamic model with options in Section 8.1.3 is new and is presented here for the first time.

Section 8.2

The stability analysis results are due to Dong, Zhang, and Nagurney (1996).

Section 8.3

The Euler method for the model with futures was proposed by Nagurney and Siokos (1996a). The convergence results are also taken from that reference. The adaptations of the Euler method for the dynamic models in Sections 8.1.1 and 8.1.3 is given here for the first time. The former realization can be viewed as a special case of the Euler method for dynamic international financial problems which was conceived by Nagurney and Siokos (1996b) and which will be studied in Chapter 13. Numerical examples 8.2–8.4 are taken from Nagurney and Siokos (1996a). The other examples are new.

References

Batten, D., **New Mathematical Advances in Economic Dynamics: Introduction,** New York University Press, New York, New York, 1985.

Dong, J., Zhang, D., and Nagurney, A., "A Projected Dynamical Systems Model of General Financial Equilibrium with Stability Analysis," *Mathematical and Computer Modelling* **24** (1996) 35-44.

Dupuis, P., and Nagurney, A., "Dynamical Systems and Variational Inequalities," *Annals of Operations Research* **44** (1993) 9-42.

Grandmont, J. M., and Malgrange, P., "Nonlinear Economic Dynamics: Introduction," *Journal of Economic Theory* **40(1)** (1986) 3-12.

Luenberger, D. G., **Introduction to Dynamic Systems: Theory, Models, and Applications**, John Wiley & Sons, Inc., New York, New York, 1979.

Nagurney, A., and Siokos, S., "Dynamic Multi-Sector, Multi-Instrument Financial Networks with Futures: Modeling and Computation," University of Massachusetts, Amherst, Massachusetts, Amherst, Massachusetts, 1996a.

Nagurney, A., and Siokos, S., "Dynamics of International Financial Networks: Modeling, Stability Analysis, and Computation," **Networks and Knowledge in a Dynamic Economy**, M. Beckmann, B. Johansson, F. Snickars, and R. Thord, editors, Springer-Verlag, Berlin, Germany, 1996b, in press.

Nagurney, A., and Zhang, D., **Projected Dynamical Systems and Variational Inequalities with Applications**, Kluwer Academic Publishers, Boston, Massachusetts, 1996.

Samuelson, P. A., **Foundations of Economic Analysis**, Harvard University Press, Cambridge, Massachusetts, 1947.

Smale, S., "Dynamics in General Equilibrium Theory," *American Economic Review* **66** (1976a) 288-294.

Smale, S., "A Convergence Process of Price Adjustment and Global Newton Methods," *Journal of Mathematical Economics* **3** (1976b) 107-120.

Zhang, D., and Nagurney, A., "On the Stability of Projected Dynamical Systems," *Journal of Optimization Theory and Applications* **85** (1995) 97-124.

9 Static Imperfect Market Models

The study of financial equilibrium is concerned with the formulation, qualitative analysis, and computation of solutions to problems that consist of multiple sectors in an economy, each of which can hold multiple financial instruments and seeks to determine his optimal portfolio. In addition, the sectors are often subject to a variety of government regulations and policy interventions, and encounter costs of transacting. An appropriate mathematical framework should be sufficiently general to enable the incorporation of alternative policy interventions for evaluation purposes, be theoretically justified, and, at the same time, be computationally tractable. Finally, the theoretical framework should allow for eventual empirical testing.

In this chapter we turn our attention away from perfect markets, which was the environment of the models of Chapters 6 through 8, to imperfect markets. We introduce a financial equilibrium model that allows for multiple sectors and multiple financial instruments, but each sector, while still seeking to maximize his utility, is now subject to the imposed taxes. In addition, there are now also policy interventions present in the form of price controls. Finally, transaction costs are included.

The model(s) developed and studied here extend the models of Chapter 6 to include taxes, transaction costs, and policy interventions. The methodology utilized for these financial equilibrium problem is, again, finite-dimensional variational inequality theory.

In the capital asset pricing model (CAPM), on the other hand, as formulated by Sharpe (1964), Lintner (1965), and Mossin (1966), which represents the general extension of the basic Markowitz (1959) mean variance portfolio selection model, the market system is perfect in the sense that there are no costs and no taxes associated with trading in all markets. Moreover, it is assumed that investors have homogeneous expectations of each security's probability distribution and can borrow or lend an unlimited amount at a riskless rate of interest. However, because of transaction costs and because of inherent differences in information between financial agents, capital markets are bound to be imperfect. Efforts have, nevertheless, been made in studying the imperfection of the markets. For example, Leland (1974), Mukherjee and Zabel (1974), Goldsmith (1976), Levy (1978) and Mayshar (1979, 1981) discuss single period models with fixed transaction costs. Constantinides (1986) studied a two–asset intertemporal portfolio selection model incorporating proportional transaction costs. Pogue (1970) earlier extended the Markowitz model to include variable transaction costs and taxes. However, that paper is still based on the homogeneous expectation assumption and does not provide any computational procedures.

Lintner (1969), on the other hand, examined the relaxation of the assumption of homogeneity by imposing some special conditions on the investors' utility functions other than the homogeneous expectation assumption. Later, Sharpe (1970) and Fama (1971) also studied heterogeneous expectations in the asset pricing model. Jarrow (1980), in turn, determined the effect of restricting short sales on equilibrium asset prices under heterogeneous expectations. Recently, Smith (1993) examined the properties of asset prices with heterogeneous assessments of the expected return. However, all of the above researchers assumed that there is a risk-free asset which can be borrowed and lent without limit. In reality, it is clear that there is no asset without risk.

Consequently, the framework introduced here can also be viewed as relaxing the perfectness assumption of the capital asset pricing model, where no taxes and no transaction costs are assumed. In addition, we consider the nonhomogeneous situation which assumes that each financial sector in the economy has his own perception of the future and, hence, is characterized by his own utility function. This is to be contrasted with much of the financial literature which assumes a single representative agent or sector.

The chapter is organized as follows. Section 9.1 develops the financial equilibrium model with policy interventions and transaction costs, which yields the equilibrium asset and liability holdings of each sector, as well as the equilibrium prices of all financial instruments. The equilibrium pattern is shown to satisfy a variational inequality. The model is then related to other models that have appeared earlier in this book.

Section 9.2 then turns to the study of the qualitative properties of the equilibrium pattern. In particular, it is shown that a solution is always guaranteed to exist, under some continuity assumptions on the utility functions. Moreover, provided that the utility function of each sector is strictly concave, uniqueness of the equilibrium asset and liability patterns is also guaranteed. Section 9.3 then proves that in a special case of the general model presented in Section 9.1, in which there are taxes, but no transaction costs, and no price policy interventions, plus the utility functions are of a special form, one can obtain a network optimization reformulation of the imperfect market equilibrium conditions.

Section 9.4 then shows that the modified projection method of Korpelevich (1977) can also be applied to imperfect financial market equilibrium models for the computation of the equilibrium holdings and the instrument prices. Convergence results are provided along with several numerical examples. Finally, we present the primal-dual method for the computation of the equilibrium pattern to the network model of Section 9.3.

9.1 A General Imperfect Market Model

As in Chapter 6, we consider a single country economy with multiple instruments and with multiple sectors.

We let i denote a typical instrument, with the total number of instruments available in the economy, denoted by I. We let j denote a typical sector in the economy, with the number of sectors denoted by J. As before, we let r_i denote the (nonnegative) price of instrument i, and we group the prices of all the instruments into the column vector $r \in R^I_+$. We let r_i^F denote the nonnegative price floor imposed on instrument i and we let r_i^C denote the positive price ceiling imposed on instrument i. Clearly, $r_i^F < r_i^C$, for all instruments i. We group the price floors into the column vector $r^F \in R^I_+$ and the price ceilings into the column vector $r^C \in R^I_+$.

We denote the tax rate levied on sector j's net yield on instrument i as $\mathcal{T}_i^j$, and we assume that $0 \leq \mathcal{T}_i^j < 1$. We group the tax rates into the column vector $\mathcal{T} \in R^{JI}_+$. Consequently, the government in this model has the flexibility of levying a distinct tax rate across both sectors and instruments.

We associate with each instrument i held as an asset a positive coefficient α_i, and with instrument i held as a liability a positive coefficient β_i, which we assume incorporates the unit transaction costs c_i^x and c_i^y. For example, we may have that: $\alpha_i = 1 + c_i^x$ and $\beta_i = 1 - c_i^y$.

As previously, denote the volume of instrument i that sector j holds as an asset, by X_i^j, and group the (nonnegative) assets in the portfolio of sector j into the column vector $X^j \in R^I_+$. Further, group the assets of all sectors in the economy into the column vector $X \in R^{JI}_+$. Similarly, denote the volume of instrument i that sector j holds as a liability, by Y_i^j, and group the (nonnegative) liabilities in the portfolio of sector j into the column vector $Y^j \in R^I_+$. Finally, group the liabilities of all sectors in the economy into the column vector $Y \in R^{JI}_+$.

Throughout this chapter, we assume that the total volume of each balance sheet side of each sector is exogenous. We also retain the assumption that the sectors under consideration act in a perfectly competitive environment.

We assume that each sector j tries to maximize his utility function, in the presence of taxes, which we denote as $U^j(X^j, Y^j, r; \mathcal{T})$. We also assume, as before, that the utility function of every sector is concave with respect to the instrument variables, is continuous, and twice continuously differentiable. Furthermore, the accounts of each sector must balance, but now they are modified from those in (6.2) in order to incorporate the transaction costs explicitly. Hence, the assets and liabilities will decrease/increase accordingly. We denote the total financial volume held by sector j by S^j.

Therefore, the optimization problem that each sector j faces is given by:

$$\text{Maximize } U^j(X^j, Y^j, r; \mathcal{T}) \tag{9.1}$$

subject to:

$$\sum_{i=1}^{I} \alpha_i X_i^j = S^j \tag{9.2a}$$

$$\sum_{i=1}^{I} \beta_i Y_i^j = S^j \tag{9.2b}$$

$$X_i^j \geq 0,\ Y_i^j \geq 0, \quad i = 1, 2, \ldots, I, \tag{9.3}$$

where, as in the previous perfect market models, the price vector r is an exogenous vector in the optimization problem of every sector j; $j = 1, \ldots, J$.

In Figure 9.1, we represent the network structure of the individual sectors' optimization problems (out of equilibrium), where every node corresponds to a specific sector, and the assets and the liabilities are denoted by the links of the network. The flows on the asset links correspond to the assets, whereas the flows on the liability links correspond to the liabilities. The supplies at the sectoral nodes are given by the sector volumes. Note that now we have arc multipliers on the arcs given by α_i for each asset link (j, i) and by β_i for each liability link (i, j) for all instruments i and all sectors j.

An important special case of the utility function $U^j(X^j, Y^j, r; \mathcal{T})$ is the following:

$$U^j(X^j, Y^j, r; \mathcal{T}) = u^j(X^j, Y^j) + \sum_{i=1}^{I}(1 - \mathcal{T}_i^j) r_i (X_i^j - Y_i^j), \tag{9.4}$$

where the last term in (9.4) reflects the value of the portfolio of sector j after taxes, and, as in (6.4), the first term represents the utility obtained from the composition of the portfolio. This term can reflect the risk.

We now discuss the feasible set (cf. (9.2a), (9.2b), and (9.3)) of the sectors. For each sector j; $j = 1, \ldots, J$, we let

$$\tilde{X}^j \equiv \{X^j \in R_+^I : \sum_{i=1}^{I} \alpha_i X_i^j = S^j\} \tag{9.5}$$

denote the constraint set of his assets. Similarly, we let

$$\tilde{Y}^j \equiv \{Y^j \in R_+^I : \sum_{i=1}^{I} \beta_i Y_i^j = S^j\} \tag{9.6}$$

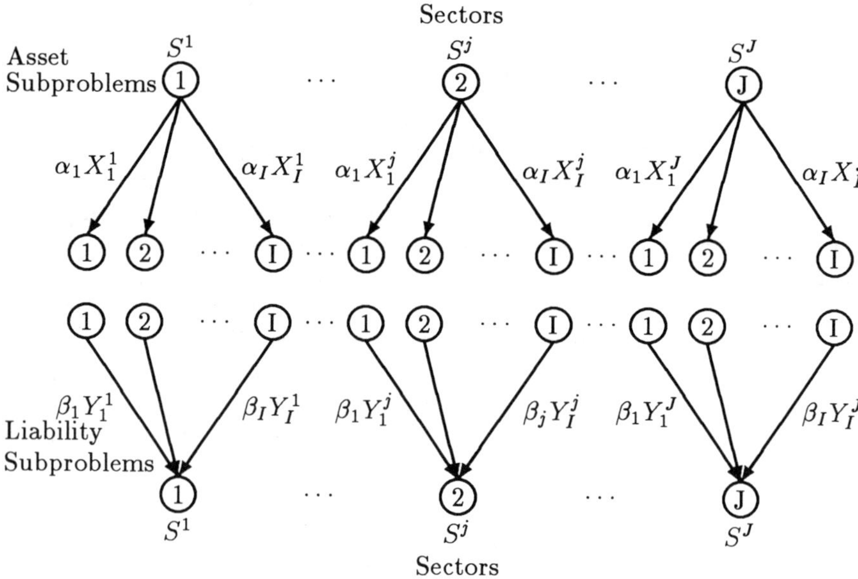

Fig. 9.1. Network structure of the sectors' optimization problems

denote the constraint set for his liabilities. The feasible set for a sector j is a Cartesian product, which is now denoted by $\tilde{\kappa}^j$, to differentiate between this feasible set and the one underlying the models in Chapter 6. We have that

$$\tilde{\kappa}^j \equiv \{\tilde{X}^j \times \tilde{Y}^j\}. \tag{9.7}$$

Let $\tilde{X}$ denote the feasible set for the assets of all the sectors, where:

$$\tilde{X} \equiv \tilde{X}^1 \times \ldots \times \tilde{X}^j \times \ldots \times \tilde{X}^J. \tag{9.8}$$

Similarly, for the liabilities, let $\tilde{Y}$ denote the feasible set of the liabilities of all the sectors, that is,

$$\tilde{Y} \equiv \tilde{Y}^1 \times \ldots \times \tilde{Y}^j \times \ldots \times \tilde{Y}^J. \tag{9.9}$$

Also, define $\tilde{\kappa} \equiv \{\tilde{X} \times \tilde{Y}\}$.

We now present the optimality conditions for a sector's utility maximization problem, given by (9.1), subject to: (9.2)–(9.3). We then give the economic conditions determining the instrument prices (in equilibrium). However, unlike in Section 6.1, which was more expository, we present the optimality conditions directly, making use of the connection between an optimization problem and a variational inequality problem (cf. (3.17)).

Optimality Conditions

The necessary and sufficient condition for an optimal portfolio for sector j, under the above imposed assumptions on the utility functions, is that the vector of assets and liabilities, $(X^{j^*}, Y^{j^*}) \in \tilde{\kappa}^j$, satisfies the following inequality: For each instrument $i; i = 1, \ldots, I$, we must have that, given an (equilibrium) price vector r^*:

$$-\nabla_{X^j} U^j(X^j, Y^j, r^*; T)^T \cdot (X^j - X^{j^*})$$

$$-\nabla_{Y^j} U^j(X^j, Y^j, r^*, T)^T \cdot (Y^j - Y^{j^*}) \geq 0, \quad \forall (X^j, Y^j) \in \tilde{\kappa}^j. \tag{9.10}$$

Obviously, a similar inequality holds for every other sector in this imperfect market single country economy.

Note that, in contrast to writing the optimality conditions explicitly as in (6.10), we have immediately formulated them as a variational inequality problem, which is a more compact formulation.

We now describe the equalities and inequalities governing the instrument prices in the economy. These are now modified from those in Section 6.1, (cf. (6.11)), governing the perfect market economy, in order to incorporate the taxes and policy interventions.

Economic System Conditions

The economic system conditions are now given by: For each instrument $i; i = 1, \ldots, I$, we must have that:

$$\sum_{j=1}^{J}(1 - T_i^j)(\alpha_i X_i^{j^*} - \beta_i Y_i^{j^*}) \begin{cases} \leq 0, & \text{if} \quad r_i^* = r_i^C \\ = 0, & \text{if} \quad r_i^F < r_i^* < r_i^C \\ \geq 0, & \text{if} \quad r_i^* = r_i^F. \end{cases} \tag{9.11}$$

In other words, if the price of an instrument lies between the price floor and the price ceiling imposed on that instrument, then the market must clear for that instrument. However, if the price at equilibrium is at the ceiling, then there may be an excess demand for that instrument. On the other hand, if the price is at the floor, then there may be an excess supply of that instrument at equilibrium.

Let $\mathcal{K}$ be the feasible set for all the asset and liability holdings of all the sectors, and all the prices of all the instruments where $\mathcal{K}\equiv\{\tilde{\kappa} \times \mathcal{S}\}$, where $\mathcal{S}\equiv\{r | r^F \leq r \leq r^C\}$.

Combining (9.11), along with conditions (9.10), we present the following definition of imperfect market equilibrium.

Definition 9.1 (Imperfect Market Equilibrium)

A vector $(X^*, Y^*, r^*) \in \mathcal{K}$ is an equilibrium of the imperfect market, single country, multi-sector, multi-instrument financial model if and only if it satisfies the system of inequalities (9.10) and the system of equalities and inequalities (9.11), for all sectors j; $j = 1, \ldots, J$, and for all instruments i; $i = 1, \ldots, I$, simultaneously.

The necessary and sufficient conditions (9.10), along with the economic conditions for the instrument prices (9.11), are now utilized to derive the variational inequality formulation of the financial equilibrium conditions in the case of market imperfections.

Theorem 9.1 (Variational Inequality Formulation)

A vector of assets and liabilities of the sectors, and instrument prices, $(X^*, Y^*, r^*) \in \mathcal{K}$, is an imperfect market financial equilibrium if and only if it satisfies the variational inequality problem:

$$\sum_{j=1}^{J}\sum_{i=1}^{I}\left[-\frac{\partial U^j(X^{j^*}, Y^{j^*}, r^*; T)}{\partial X_i^j}\right] \times \left[X_i^j - X_i^{j^*}\right]$$

$$+\sum_{j=1}^{J}\sum_{i=1}^{I}\left[-\frac{\partial U^j(X^{j^*}, Y^{j^*}, r^*; T)}{\partial Y_i^j}\right] \times \left[Y_i^j - Y_i^{j^*}\right]$$

$$+\sum_{j=1}^{J}\left[\sum_{i=1}^{I}(1 - T_i^j)(\alpha_i X_i^{j^*} - \beta_i Y_i^{j^*})\right] \times [r_i - r_i^*] \geq 0, \quad \forall (X, Y, r) \in \mathcal{K}, \tag{9.12a}$$

which in the case of utility functions (9.4), takes the form

$$\sum_{j=1}^{J}\sum_{i=1}^{I}\left[-\frac{\partial u^j(X^{j^*},Y^{j^*})}{\partial X_i^j}-(1-\mathcal{T}_i^j)r_i^*\right]\times\left[X_i^j-X_i^{j^*}\right]$$

$$+\sum_{j=1}^{J}\sum_{i=1}^{I}\left[-\frac{\partial u^j(X^{j^*},Y^{j^*})}{\partial Y_i^j}+(1-\mathcal{T}_i^j)r_i^*\right]\times\left[Y_i^j-Y_i^{j^*}\right]$$

$$+\sum_{i=1}^{I}\left[\sum_{j=1}^{J}(1-\mathcal{T}_i^j)(\alpha_i X_i^{j^*}-\beta_i Y_i^{j^*})\right]\times[r_i-r_i^*]\geq 0,\quad \forall (X,Y,r)\in\mathcal{K}. \tag{9.12b}$$

Proof: Assume that $(X^*, Y^*, r^*) \in \mathcal{K}$ is an equilibrium point of the imperfect market, multi-sector, multi-instrument financial model, that is, it satisfies Definition 9.1. Then inequalities (9.10) and (9.11) hold for all sectors j and for all instruments i. Summing (9.10) over all sectors j yields:

$$-\sum_{j=1}^{J}\nabla_{X^j}U^j(X^{j^*},Y^{j^*},r^*;\mathcal{T})^T\cdot(X^j-X^{j^*})$$

$$-\sum_{j=1}^{J}\nabla_{Y^j}U^j(X^{j^*},Y^{j^*},r^*;\mathcal{T})^T\cdot(Y^j-Y^{j^*})\geq 0,\quad \forall (X,Y)\in\tilde{\kappa}. \tag{9.13}$$

Also, from the system of equalities and inequalities (9.11), we can concude that, for a fixed instrument i:

$$\sum_{j=1}^{J}(1-\mathcal{T}_i^j)(\alpha_i X_i^{j^*}-\beta_i Y_i^{j^*})\times[r_i-r_i^*]\geq 0,\quad \forall r_i | r_i^F\leq r_i\leq r_i^C. \tag{9.14}$$

But (9.14) must hold for all instruments i, and, hence, the summation of (9.14) over all instruments, yields:

$$\sum_{i=1}^{I}\left[\sum_{j=1}^{J}(1-\mathcal{T}_i^J)(\alpha_i X_i^{j^*}-\beta_i Y_i^{j^*})\right]\times[r_i-r_i^*]\geq 0,\quad \forall r\in\mathcal{S}. \tag{9.15}$$

Summing now inequalities (9.13) and (9.15), we obtain the variational inequality (9.12a). The variational inequality (9.12b) follows by noting (9.4), and taking the partial derivatives of the utility function for each sector with respect to his asset holdings of an instrument and the liability holdings of an instrument, in the presence of taxes.

We will now prove that if $(X^*, Y^*, r^*) \in \mathcal{K}$ is a solution to variational inequality (9.12a), then it will also satisfy the equilibrium conditions (9.10) and (9.11).

In particular, if we let $(X^*, Y^*, r^*) \in \mathcal{K}$ be a solution to variational inequality (9.12a), and we let $X^j = X^{j^*}$, $Y^j = Y^{j^*}$, for all sectors j, then substitution into variational inequality (9.12a) yields:

$$\sum_{i=1}^{I}\left[\sum_{j=1}^{J}\left((1-T_i^j)(\alpha_i X_i^{j^*} - \beta_i Y_i^{j^*})\right)\right] \times [r_i - r_i^*] \geq 0, \quad \forall r \in \mathcal{S}, \tag{9.16}$$

which implies the system economic conditions (9.11).

If we now let $r_i = r_i^*$ for all instruments i and substitute the resultants into inequality (9.12a), we obtain:

$$-\sum_{j=1}^{J} \nabla_{X^j} U^j(X^{j^*}, Y^{j^*}, r^*; T)^T \cdot (X^j - X^{j^*})$$

$$-\sum_{j=1}^{J} \nabla_{Y^j} U^j(X^{j^*}, Y^{j^*}, r^*; T)^T \cdot (Y^j - Y^{j^*}) \geq 0, \quad \forall (X, Y) \in \tilde{\kappa}, \tag{9.17}$$

which is equivalent to the optimality conditions (9.10). The variational inequality (9.12b) is a special case of (9.12a) with utility functions given by (9.4); hence, the conclusion also follows in this case. □

We will now put variational inequality (9.12a) into standard form given by (3.13). We let $n = 2JI + I$. We define the column vector $U \in R^J$ with components: $\{U^1, \ldots, U^j\}$. We also define the n-dimensional column vector $x \equiv (X, Y, r) \in \mathcal{K}$, and the n-dimensional column vector $F(x)$ with components:

$$F(x) = \begin{bmatrix} F_1(x) \\ \vdots \\ F_b(x) \\ \vdots \\ F_n(x) \end{bmatrix} = \begin{bmatrix} -\nabla_X U(X, Y, r; T) \\ -\nabla_Y U(X, Y, r; T) \\ \sum_{j=1}^{J}(1-T_1^j)\left(\alpha_1 X_1^j - \beta_1 Y_1^j\right) \\ \vdots \\ \sum_{j=1}^{J}(1-T_I^j)\left(\alpha_I X_I^j - \beta_I Y_I^j\right) \end{bmatrix}_{n\times 1}. \tag{9.18}$$

Consequently, (9.12a) (and (9.12b)) can be written as:
Determine $x^* \in \mathcal{K}$ satisfying:

$$\langle F(x^*)^T, x - x^* \rangle \geq 0, \quad \forall x \in \mathcal{K}. \tag{9.19}$$

9.1.1 Quadratic Utility Functions

In this subsection we consider a special case of the utility function (9.4). As in the quadratic model in Section 6.1.2, the optimization problem facing each sector is to maximize the return and, at the same time, to minimize the risk of his portfolio, but now there are taxes present, as well as transaction costs. As a result, the portfolio optimization problem for each sector j is the following:

$$\text{Minimize} \quad \begin{pmatrix} X^j \\ Y^j \end{pmatrix}^T Q^j \begin{pmatrix} X^j \\ Y^j \end{pmatrix} - \sum_{i=1}^{I}(1-\mathcal{T}_i^j) r_i \left(X_i^j - Y_i^j\right) \tag{9.20}$$

subject to:

$$\sum_{i=1}^{I} \alpha_i X_i^j = S^j \tag{9.21a}$$

$$\sum_{i=1}^{I} \beta_i Y_i^j = S^j \tag{9.21b}$$

$$X_i^j \geq 0, \; Y_i^j \geq 0, \quad i = 1, 2, \ldots, I, \tag{9.22}$$

where Q^j is a symmetric $2I \times 2I$ variance-covariance matrix, as defined in Section 6.1.2.

The optimality conditions as well as the economic system conditions are identical to those in the preceding section, with the variational inequality formulation being immediate from Theorem 9.1, adapted to this special case.

Corollary 9.1 (Variational Inequality Formulation for the Imperfect Market, Quadratic Model)

A vector of assets and liabilities of the sectors, and instrument prices, $(X^*, Y^*, r^*) \in \mathcal{K}$, is a financial equilibrium if and only if it satisfies the variational inequality problem:

$$\sum_{j=1}^{J}\sum_{i=1}^{I}\left[2(Q^j_{(11)i})^T \cdot X^{j^*} + 2(Q^j_{(21)i})^T \cdot Y^{j^*} - (1-\mathcal{T}_i^j) r_i^*\right] \times \left[X_i^j - X_i^{j^*}\right]$$

$$+\sum_{j=1}^{J}\sum_{i=1}^{I}\left[2(Q^j_{(22)i})^T \cdot Y^{j^*} + 2(Q^j_{(12)i})^T \cdot X^{j^*} + (1-\mathcal{T}_i^j) r_i^*\right] \times \left[Y_i^j - Y_i^{j^*}\right]$$

$$+\sum_{i=1}^{I}\left[\sum_{j=1}^{J}(1-\mathcal{T}_i^j)(\alpha_i X_i^{j^*} - \beta_i Y_i^{j^*})\right] \times [r_i - r_i^*] \geq 0, \quad \forall (X, Y, r) \in \mathcal{K}. \tag{9.23}$$

9.2 Qualitative Properties

In this section we present some of the qualitative properties for the model(s) presented in Section 9.1. In particular, we address the questions of existence and uniqueness of the equilibrium pattern. Interestingly, the existence proof is now direct, as compared to the existence results in Section 6.2, although the imperfect market models in Section 9.1 are clearly more complex than the perfect market models presented in Section 6.1.

Theorem 9.2 (Existence)

The equilibrium asset, liability, and price pattern satisfying variational inequality (9.12a) (or (9.12b)) is guaranteed to exist.

Proof: Existence of a solution follows from the standard theory of variational inequalities, cf. Theorem 3.1, since the utility functions are assumed to be continuously differentiable and the feasible set is compact and convex. □

We will now address the issue of the uniqueness of the equilibrium asset and liability pattern.

Theorem 9.3 (Uniqueness)

Under the assumption that the utility functions $U^j(X^j, Y^j, r; \mathcal{T})$ are strictly concave in the instrument variables for each sector j, the equilibrium pattern of assets and liabilities, (X^*, Y^*), is unique.

Proof: Follows using the same arguments as in the proof of Theorem 6.3. □

Moreover, we have the following theorems which follow using the same arguments as those in the proofs of Theorems 6.4 and 6.5, respectively. These proofs are due to Nagurney and Dong (1996a).

Theorem 9.4

Under the assumption that the utility functions are strictly concave and twice continuously differentiable, $F(x)$ defined in (9.18) is monotone.

Theorem 9.5

The function $F(x)$ defined in (9.18) is Lipschitz continuous, under the assumption that the utility function U^j has bounded second order derivatives for all sectors j and for all $x \in \mathcal{K}$.

9.3 Network Optimization in a Special Case

In Section 6.3, we were able to establish that, in the case of perfect markets, and for utility functions of the form (6.4), there exists a network optimization reformulation of the equilibrium conditions. Moreover, even in the case of the "most" general utility functions and expanded feasible sets facing each sector (which we assumed to include the budget constraints), the network structure of the economy at equilibrium prevailed.

In the case of imperfect markets, a network reformulation of the equilibrium conditions is only possible in a special case of the model developed in Section 9.1, in which the utility functions facing a sector are given by (9.4), but now there are no transaction costs, that is, $\alpha_i = 1$ and $\beta_i=1$, for all instruments i. Furthermore, the price floors for all instruments are set to zero, whereas the price ceilings are all set to infinity, that is, $r_i^F = 0$, and $r_i^C = \infty$, for all instruments i. Taxes, however, can remain.

Hence, transaction costs and price policy interventions create distortions in the economy which preclude the realization of a network structure in equilibrium. Nevertheless, even in the case of general utility functions and expanded feasible sets for each sector, which are assumed to include the budget constraints in the absence of transaction costs, a network representation of the economy at equilibrium prevails.

However, it is only in this special case imperfect market model that a network optimization reformulation is possible. Consequently, as in the case of perfect markets, one no longer can obtain a network reformulation of the equilibrium conditions in the case of utility functions of the general form as given in the objective function (9.1).

We now rigorously establish the above points. In particular, in this section we are concerned with the following special case of the imperfect market model developed in Section 9.1.

We assume that the optimization problem facing a sector j is given by

$$\text{Maximize} \quad u^j(X^j, Y^j) + \sum_{i=1}^{I}(1 - T_i^j) r_i (X_i^j - Y_i^j) \tag{9.24}$$

subject to:

$$\sum_{i=1}^{I} X_i^j = S^j \tag{9.25a}$$

$$\sum_{i=1}^{I} Y_i^j = S^j \tag{9.25b}$$

$$X_i^j \geq 0, \; Y_i^j \geq 0, \quad i = 1, \ldots, I. \tag{9.26}$$

Note that the feasible set here of a sector j, that is, the set of (X^j, Y^j) satisfying (9.25)–(9.26), is identical to the one in the case of perfect markets as in Section 6.1. Hence, we denote it by κ^j.

The equilibrium conditions (cf. (9.11)), in turn, in the absence of price floors and ceilings (equivalently, setting the price floors to zero and the price ceilings to infinity, for all instruments), and in the absence of transaction costs, take the form:

Economic System Conditions

For each instrument i; $i = 1, \ldots, I$:

$$\sum_{j=1}^{J}(1 - T_i^j)(X_i^{j*} - Y_i^{j*}) \begin{cases} = 0, & \text{if } r_i^* > 0 \\ \geq 0, & \text{if } r_i^* = 0. \end{cases} \tag{9.27}$$

The following corollary is immediate from Theorem 9.1.

Corollary 9.2

A vector of assets and liabilities of the sectors, and instrument prices, $(X^*, Y^*, r^*) \in \mathcal{K}$ (where $\mathcal{K}$ is as in Section 6.1), is an imperfect market equilibrium (in the presence of taxes only) if and only if it satisfies the variational inequality problem:

$$\sum_{j=1}^{J}\sum_{i=1}^{I}\left[-\frac{\partial u^j(X^{j*}, Y^{j*})}{\partial X_i^j} - (1 - T_i^j)r_i^*\right] \times \left[X_i^j - X_i^{j*}\right]$$

$$+\sum_{j=1}^{J}\sum_{i=1}^{I}\left[-\frac{\partial u^j(X^{j*}, Y^{j*})}{\partial Y_i^j} + (1 - T_i^j)r_i^*\right] \times \left[Y_i^j - Y_i^{j*}\right]$$

$$+\sum_{i=1}^{I}\left[\sum_{j=1}^{J}(1 - T_i^j)(X_i^{j*} - Y_i^{j*})\right] \times [r_i - r_i^*] \geq 0, \quad \forall (X, Y, r) \in \mathcal{K}. \tag{9.28}$$

We now show that the solution to variational inequality (9.28) can be obtained by solving an optimization problem.

Theorem 9.6

The variational inequality problem (9.28) is equivalent to the optimization problem:

$$\textit{Maximize} \sum_{j=1}^{J} u^j(X^j, Y^j) \tag{9.29}$$

subject to:

$$\sum_{j=1}^{J}(1 - T_i^j)(X_i^j - Y_i^j) \geq 0, \quad i = 1, \ldots, I, \tag{9.30}$$

and

$$(X^j, Y^j) \in \kappa^j, \quad j = 1, \ldots, J, \tag{9.31}$$

where $r_i^* \geq 0$; $i = 1, \ldots, I$, corresponds to the Lagrange multiplier associated with the i-th constraint in (9.30).

Proof: It follows from the standard theory of variational inequalities (see Chapter 3 and Bertsekas and Tsitsiklis (1989)) that the solution to the optimization problem (9.29)–(9.31) coincides with the solution to the variational inequality problem (9.28) since the utility functions u^j are assumed to be concave for each sector j, continuous, and continuously differentiable, and the feasible sets are closed and convex. □

We now present a lemma that establishes that the equilibrium conditions (9.27) must hold as equalities.

Lemma 9.1

In equilibrium, the markets clear for each instrument (after taxes), that is,

$$\sum_{j=1}^{J}(1-\tau_i^j)(X_i^{j*}-Y_i^{j*})=0, \quad i=1,\ldots,I, \tag{9.32}$$

and the prices r_i^* are strictly positive, for $i=1,\ldots,I$.

Proof: Assume that, on the contrary, for some instrument k, we have that, in equilibrium,

$$\sum_{j=1}^{J}(1-\tau_k^j)(X_k^{j*}-Y_k^{j*})>0. \tag{9.33}$$

Then, it follows from the equilibrium conditions (9.27) that

$$\sum_{i=1}^{I}\left[\sum_{j=1}^{J}(1-\tau_i^j)(X_i^{j*}-Y_i^{j*})\right]>0. \tag{9.34}$$

Furthermore, from the feasible set κ, and Lemma 6.2, we can conclude that, in equilibrium,

$$\sum_{i=1}^{I}\sum_{j=1}^{J}(X_i^{j*}-Y_i^{j*})=0.$$

It then follows from the equilibrium conditions (9.27) that

$$\sum_{i=1}^{I}\sum_{j=1}^{J}-\tau_i^j(X_i^{j*}-Y_i^{j*})\geq 0. \tag{9.35}$$

Rewriting now (9.34) and applying (9.35) yields:

$$\sum_{i=1}^{I}\sum_{j=1}^{J}(X_i^{j*}-Y_i^{j*})>\sum_{i=1}^{I}\sum_{j=1}^{J}-\tau_i^j(X_i^{j*}-Y_i^{j*})\geq 0. \tag{9.36}$$

However, (9.36) is in contradiction to the conclusion of Lemma 6.2 and, hence, we must have that for each instrument k:

$$\sum_{j=1}^{J}(1-\tau_k^j)(X_k^{j*}-Y_k^{j*})=0. \quad \square \tag{9.37}$$

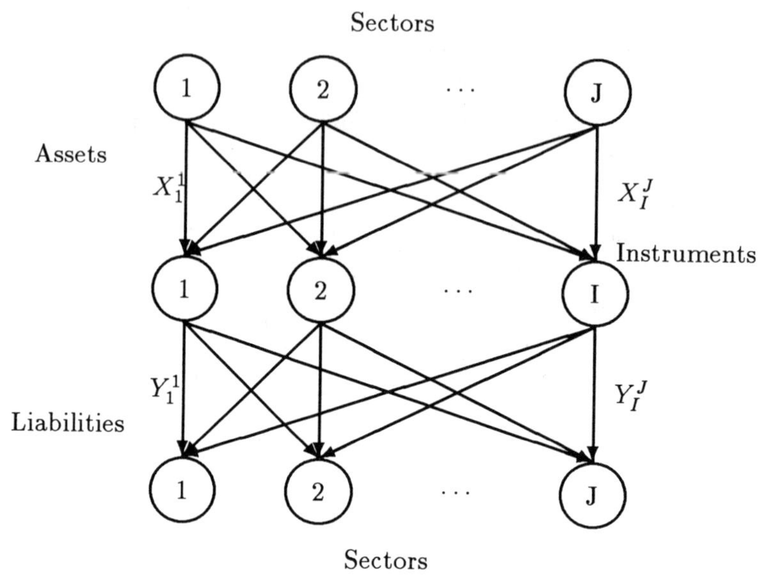

Fig. 9.2. The network structure at equilibrium for a special case

The subsequent corollary follows immediately from Theorem 9.6 and Lemma 9.1.

Corollary 9.3
The solution to the optimization problem:

$$\textit{Maximize} \sum_{j=1}^{J} u^j(X^j, Y^j) \tag{9.38}$$

subject to:

$$\sum_{j=1}^{J} (1 - \mathcal{T}_i^j)(X_i^j - Y_i^j) = 0, \quad i = 1, \ldots, I \tag{9.39}$$

$$(X^j, Y^j) \in \kappa^j, \quad j = 1, \ldots, J, \tag{9.40}$$

with Lagrange multiplier r_i^* associated with the i-th constraint in (9.39) coincides with the solution to the optimization problem (9.29)–(9.31). Moreover, this solution is an equilibrium solution, that is, it satisfies variational inequality problem (9.28).

In Figure 9.2, we depict the network structure of this imperfect market model at equilibrium. Note that now the terms $(1 - \mathcal{T}_i^j)$ are associated with the corresponding asset and liability links and play a role as arc multipliers. The network structure, nevertheless, is identical to the network in Figure

6.2 for the perfect market equilibrium problem. However, in that network problem one does not have arc multipliers.

In the next section we discuss the computation of imperfect market financial equilibria. In particular, we adapt the modified projection algorithm for the computation of solutions to all of the above models. We subsequently adapt the primal-dual method for the solution of the special case market model in Section 9.3.

9.4 Computation of Imperfect Market Equilibria

In this section we adapt the modified projection method for the computation of imperfect market equilibria, that is, for the solution of the models in Section 9.1 (and Section 9.3) and we also present the primal-dual method.

For completeness, we now present the modified projection algorithm in which the function $F(x)$ is in expanded form for our specific model as defined by (9.18).

9.4.1 The Modified Projection Method

Step 0: Initialization

Set $(X^0, Y^0, r^0) \in \mathcal{K}$. Let $\tau := 0$ and set γ so that $0 < \gamma < \frac{1}{L}$, where L is the Lipschitz constant.

Step 1: Computation

Compute $(\bar{X}^\tau, \bar{Y}^\tau, \bar{r}^\tau) \in \mathcal{K}$ by solving the variational inequality subproblem:

$$\sum_{j=1}^{J}\sum_{i=1}^{I}\left[\bar{X}_i^{j^\tau} + \gamma\left(-\frac{\partial U^j(X^{j^\tau}, Y^{j^\tau}, r^\tau; T)}{\partial X_i^j}\right) - X_i^{j^\tau}\right] \times \left[X_i^j - \bar{X}_i^{j^\tau}\right]$$

$$+\sum_{j=1}^{J}\sum_{i=1}^{I}\left[\bar{Y}_i^{j^\tau} + \gamma\left(-\frac{\partial U^j(X^{j^\tau}, Y^{j^\tau}, r^\tau; T)}{\partial Y_i^j}\right) - Y_i^{j^\tau}\right] \times \left[Y_i^j - \bar{Y}_i^{j^\tau}\right]$$

$$+\sum_{i=1}^{I}\left[\bar{r}_i^\tau + \gamma\left[\sum_{j=1}^{J}(1 - T_i^j)\left(\alpha_i X_i^{j^\tau} - \beta_i Y_i^{j^\tau}\right)\right] - r_i^\tau\right] \times [r_i - \bar{r}_i^\tau] \geq 0,$$

$$(X, Y, r) \in \mathcal{K}. \tag{9.41}$$

Step 2: Adaptation

Compute $(X^{\tau+1}, Y^{\tau+1}, r^{\tau+1}) \in \mathcal{K}$ by solving the variational inequality subproblem:

$$\sum_{j=1}^{J}\sum_{i=1}^{I}\left[X_i^{j\,\tau+1} + \gamma\left(-\frac{\partial U^j(\bar{X}^{j^\tau}, \bar{Y}^{j^\tau}, \bar{r}^\tau; \mathcal{T})}{\partial X_i^j}\right) - X_i^{j^\tau}\right] \times \left[X_i^j - X_i^{j\,\tau+1}\right]$$

$$+\sum_{j=1}^{J}\sum_{i=1}^{I}\left[Y_i^{j\,\tau+1} + \gamma\left(-\frac{\partial U^j(\bar{X}^{j^\tau}, \bar{Y}^{j^\tau}, \bar{r}^\tau; \mathcal{T})}{\partial Y_i^j}\right) - Y_i^{j^\tau}\right] \times \left[Y_i^j - Y_i^{j\,\tau+1}\right]$$

$$\sum_{i=1}^{I}\left[r_i^{\tau+1} + \gamma\left[\sum_{j=1}^{J}(1-\mathcal{T}_i^j)\left(\alpha_i \bar{X}_i^{j^\tau} - \beta_i \bar{Y}_i^{j^\tau}\right)\right] - r_i^\tau\right] \times \left[r_i - r_i^{\tau+1}\right] \geq 0,$$

$$\forall (X, Y, r) \in \mathcal{K}. \tag{9.42}$$

Step 3: Convergence Verification:

If $\max_{i,j} |X_i^{j\,\tau+1} - X_i^{j^\tau}| \leq \epsilon$; $\max_{i,j} |Y_i^{j\,\tau+1} - Y_i^{j^\tau}| \leq \epsilon$; $\max_i |r_i^{\tau+1} - r_i^\tau| \leq \epsilon$, for all $i; i = 1, \ldots, I$, and $j; j = 1, \ldots, J$, with $\epsilon > 0$, a prespecified tolerance, then stop; else, set $\tau := \tau + 1$, and go to Step 1.

In the following theorem we present the convergence result.

Theorem 9.7

The modified projection algorithm is guaranteed to converge to an imperfect market equilibrium asset, liability, and price pattern, satisfying variational inequality (9.12).

Proof: Convergence of the algorithm follows (cf. Korpelevich (1977)), under the assumptions that $F(x)$ is monotone and Lipschitz continuous. The conclusion follows from Theorems 9.5 and 9.6. □

The variational inequality subproblems (9.41) and (9.42) are separable quadratic programming problems, which, in view of the feasible set, are decomposable, respectively, in asset variables, liability variables, and price variables.

We now emphasize the special network structure of the decomposed subproblems that enables one to apply efficient special-purpose algorithms. For a graphical depiction, see Figure 9.3. First, we note that the feasible set κ^j corresponding to the constraints of sector j, cf. (9.2) and (9.3)), has a network structure. We also recall that the feasible set governing the variational inequality problem (9.12) is a Cartesian product. Indeed, observe, cf. Figure 9.3, that each variational inequality subproblem decomposes into $2J$ subproblems, corresponding to the asset and liability subproblems facing the sectors, and I subproblems, corresponding to the prices.

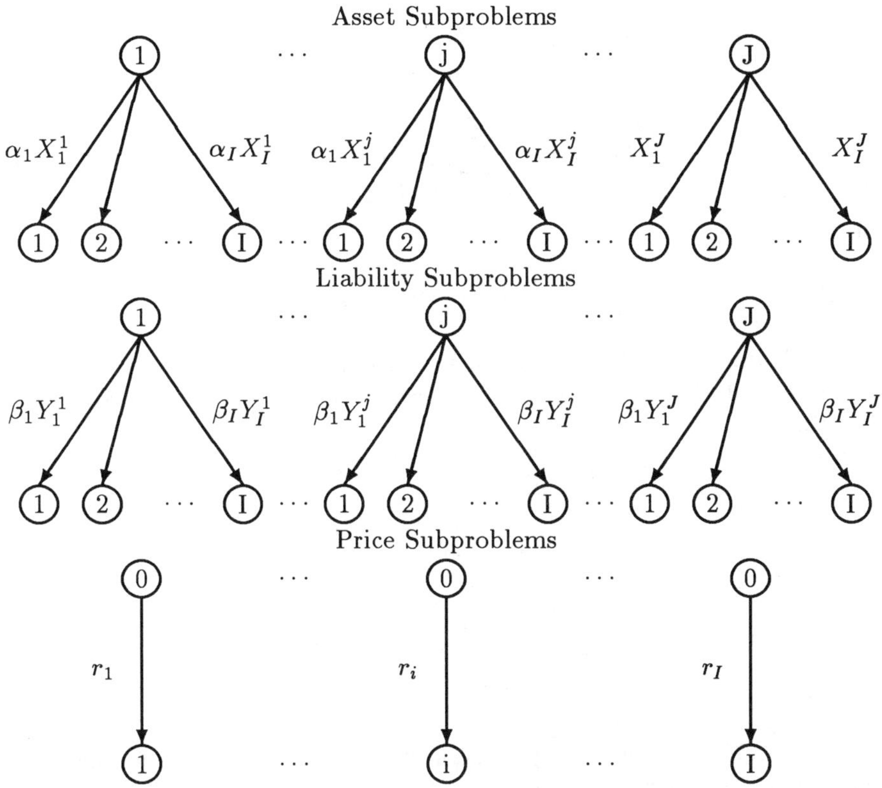

Fig. 9.3. The network structure of financial subproblems induced by the modified projection method

Specifically, the asset subproblem either in (9.41) or (9.42) facing a sector j is of the form:

$$\text{Minimize} \quad \sum_{i=1}^{I}(\frac{1}{2}X_i^{j\,2} + h_{ij}X_i^j) \tag{9.43}$$

subject to:

$$\sum_{i=1}^{I}\alpha_i X_i^j = S^j; \quad X_i^j \geq 0, \quad \forall i. \tag{9.44}$$

If we now define the variables $v_i^j = \alpha_i X_i^j$, for all i, then problem (9.43) subject to (9.44) can be rewritten as:

$$\text{Minimize} \quad \sum_{i=1}^{I}(\frac{1}{2}\frac{1}{\alpha_i^2}v_i^{j\,2} + \frac{h_{ij}}{\alpha_i}v_i^j) \tag{9.45}$$

subject to:

$$\sum_{i=1}^{I} v_i^j = S^j; \quad v_i^j \geq 0, \quad \forall i. \tag{9.46}$$

The Kuhn-Tucker conditions for this problem, in turn, are equivalent to the statement that there exists an ordering: $i_1, \ldots, i_I$, of the instruments, such that:

$$\frac{1}{\alpha_{i_1}^2}v_{i_1}^j + \frac{h_{i_1j}}{\alpha_{i_1}} = \ldots = \frac{1}{\alpha_{i_q}^2}v_{i_q}^j + \frac{h_{i_qj}}{\alpha_{i_q}}$$

$$\leq \frac{1}{\alpha_{i_{q+1}}^2}v_{i_{q+1}}^j + \frac{h_{i_{q+1}j}}{\alpha_{i_{q+1}}} \leq \ldots \frac{1}{\alpha_{i_I}^2}v_{i_I}^j + \frac{h_{i_Ij}}{\alpha_{i_I}}, \tag{9.47}$$

where

$$v_{i_l}^j > 0; \quad l = 1, \ldots, q;$$

$$v_{i_l}^j = 0; \quad l = q+1, \ldots, I.$$

For completeness and easy reference, we now present a modified asset equilibration algorithm to solve (9.47) based on the exact asset equilibration algorithm presented in Chapter 5.

Modified Asset Equilibration Procedure

Step 1: Sort

Set $\frac{h_{I+1j}}{\alpha_{(I+1)}} \equiv \infty$. Sort the components: $\frac{h_{1j}}{\alpha_1}, \ldots, \frac{h_{Ij}}{\alpha_I}$, in nondescending order, and relabel the $v_1^j, \ldots, v_I^j$ and the $\frac{h_{ij}}{\alpha_i}$, accordingly. Assume, henceforth, that they are relabeled. Set $q := 1$.

Step 2: Computation

Define

$$\lambda_j^q = \frac{S^j + \sum_{i=1}^q h_{ij}\alpha_i}{\sum_{i=1}^q \alpha_i^2}.$$

Step 3: Comparison and Update

If $\frac{h_{qj}}{\alpha_q} < \lambda_j^q \leq \frac{h_{(q+1)j}}{\alpha_{q+1}}$, then stop; let

$$v_i^j = \begin{cases} (\lambda_j^q - \frac{h_{ij}}{\alpha_i})\alpha_i^2; & i = 1, \ldots, q \\ 0; & i = q+1, \ldots, I; \end{cases}$$

else, set $q := q + 1$, and go to Step 2.

In a similar manner one can construct a Modified Liability Equilibration Procedure to handle transaction costs.

It is easy to verify that the price network subproblems can also be solved exactly and simultaneously in closed form.

We now present several numerical examples for illustrative purposes.

9.4.2 Numerical Examples

In this subsection we consider both the quadratic imperfect market model discussed in Section 9.1.1 and a model with logarithmic utility functions due to Dong (1994).

We first present several numerical examples in which the utility functions are quadratic and conclude with an example in which the utility functions are logarithmic.

Examples with Quadratic Utility Functions

We assume that there are two sectors in the economy and three financial instruments. The variance-covariance matrices of the two sectors as well as the size of the sectors are as reported in Example 6.1, which serves as a baseline model to which we then add market imperfections.

The modified projection method was coded in FORTRAN and the numerical runs were done on an IBM SP2. For all the examples the variables were initialized as follows: $r_i^0 = 1$, for all i; $X_1^1 = \frac{S^1}{\alpha_1}, X_2^2 = \frac{S^2}{\alpha_2}; Y_1^1 = \frac{S^1}{\beta_1}, Y_2^2 = \frac{S^2}{\beta_2}$; all other variables were set to equal to zero. The γ parameter was set to 0.35. The convergence tolerance ε was set to 10^{-3}. The modified asset and modified liability equilibration algorithms were used to solve the embedded quadratic programming problems with network structure in closed form. The price subproblems were also solved in closed form.

Example 9.1 – Taxes, No Transaction Costs, No Price Ceilings

In this example, all transaction costs were set to zero, that is, $\alpha_i = 1$ and $\beta_i = 1$, for all i. Taxes were distinct for each instrument and each sector:

$\mathcal{T}_1^1 = .15$, $\mathcal{T}_2^1 = .25$, $\mathcal{T}_3^1 = .10$, $\mathcal{T}_1^2 = .30$, $\mathcal{T}_2^2 = .45$, $\mathcal{T}_3^2 = .15$. The price ceilings for each instrument were set infinity, with the price floors set to zero.

The numerical results for this example are:

Equilibrium Prices:

$$r_1^* = 2.28848, \quad r_2^* = 2.59985, \quad r_3^* = 2.12356,$$

Equilibrium Asset Holdings:

$$X_1^{1*} = 0.28326, \quad X_2^{1*} = 0.37695, \quad X_3^{1*} = 0.33979,$$

$$X_1^{2*} = 0.76922, \quad X_2^{2*} = 0.55402, \quad X_3^{2*} = 0.67676,$$

Equilibrium Liability Holdings:

$$Y_1^{1*} = 0.35302, \quad Y_2^{1*} = 0.37764, \quad Y_3^{1*} = 0.26934,$$

$$Y_1^{2*} = 0.68790, \quad Y_2^{2*} = 0.55829, \quad Y_3^{2*} = 0.75385.$$

The modified projection method converged in 844 iterations and required .13 seconds of CPU time for convergence. The results show that the markets for instruments cleared and that the prices were positive.

Example 9.2 – No Taxes, Transaction Costs, No Price Ceilings

In this example, we set $\alpha_1 = 1.5, \alpha_2 = 1.2$ and $\alpha_3 = 1.3$; $\beta_1 = .5$, $\beta_2 = .75$, and $\beta_3 = .9$. Taxes were set to zero and the price ceilings were set to ∞, with the price floors at zero. The numerical results for this example are:

Equilibrium Prices:

$$r_1^* = 0.52324, \quad r_2^* = 1.01982, \quad r_3^* = 1.45694,$$

Equilibrium Asset Holdings:

$$X_1^{1*} = 0.00000, \quad X_2^{1*} = 0.28279, \quad X_3^{1*} = 0.50828,$$

$$X_1^{2*} = 0.31368, \quad X_2^{2*} = 0.53988, \quad X_3^{2*} = 0.67818,$$

Equilibrium Liability Holdings:

$$Y_1^{1*} = 0.38053, \quad Y_2^{1*} = 0.55860, \quad Y_3^{1*} = 0.43421,$$

$$Y_1^{2*} = 0.56324, \quad Y_2^{2*} = 0.75701, \quad Y_3^{2*} = 1.27847.$$

The modified projection method converged in 26 iterations and in a negligible amount of CPU time, not including input/output time.

Example 9.3 – Taxes and Transaction Costs, No Price Ceilings

In this example, we set the tax rates as in Example 9.1 and the transaction costs as in Example 9.2. The algorithm yielded the following solution:

Equilibrium Prices:

$$r_1^* = 1.22830, \quad r_2^* = 2.29035, \quad r_3^* = 2.25456,$$

Equilibrium Asset Holdings:

$$X_1^{1^*} = 0.00000, \quad X_2^{1^*} = 0.33312, \quad X_3^{1^*} = 0.46173,$$

$$X_1^{2^*} = 0.26332, \quad X_2^{2^*} = 0.50233, \quad X_3^{2^*} = 0.77095,$$

Equilibrium Liability Holdings:

$$Y_1^{1^*} = 0.28331, \quad Y_2^{1^*} = 0.48607, \quad Y_3^{1^*} = 0.54866,$$

$$Y_2^{1^*} = 0.45245, \quad Y_2^{2^*} = 0.87464, \quad Y_3^{2^*} = 1.24200.$$

The modified projection method required 570 iterations and required .11 seconds of CPU time for convergence.

Example 9.4 – Taxes, Transaction Costs, and Price Ceilings

In this example, we kept the taxes as in Examples 9.1 and 9.3, and the transaction costs as in Examples 9.2 and 9.3. We then added price ceilings as follows: $r_1^C = 1$, $r_2^C = 2$, and $r_3^C = 2$. The modified projection method yielded the following solution:

Equilibrium Instrument Prices:

$$r_1^* = 1.00000, \quad r_2^* = 2.00000, \quad r_3^* = 2.00000,$$

Equilibrium Asset Holdings:

$$X_1^{1^*} = 0.00000, \quad X_2^{1^*} = 0.32998, \quad X_3^{1^*} = 0.46463,$$

$$X_1^{2^*} = 0.29029, \quad X_2^{2^*} = 0.49611, \quad X_3^{2^*} = 0.74556,$$

Equilibrium Liability Holdings:

$$Y_1^{1^*} = 0.32038, \quad Y_2^{1^*} = 0.49481, \quad Y_3^{1^*} = 0.52078,$$

$$Y_1^{2^*} = 0.48859, \quad Y_2^{2^*} = 0.84554, \quad Y_3^{2^*} = 1.24617.$$

The modified projection method converged in 338 iterations and required .06 seconds of CPU time for convergence.

An Example with Logarithmic Utility Functions

We now present an example with logarithmic utility functions due to Dong (1994) (see also Dong (1993)).

Example 9.5

Here we assumed that each sector has a logarithmic function as a utility function. The portfolio optimization problem for sector j was as follows: For each sector j; $j = 1, \ldots, J$, we assumed that a sector faced the following objective function:

$$\text{Maximize} \quad \sum_{i=1}^{I} a_i^j \log(X_i^j + 1) + \sum_{i=1}^{I} b_i^j \log(Y_i^j + 1) + \sum_{i=1}^{I} (1 - T_i^j) r_i (X_i^j - Y_i^j) \tag{9.48}$$

subject to:

$$\sum_{i=1}^{I} X_i^j = S^j \tag{9.49}$$

$$\sum_{i=1}^{I} Y_i^j = S^j \tag{9.50}$$

$$X_i^j, \; Y_i^j \geq 0, \quad i = 1, \ldots, I, \tag{9.51}$$

where the a_i^j and the b_i^j are positive parameters reflecting the preference of each sector for holding each instrument as an asset or as a liability.

Note that in this example there were taxes but no other transaction costs. We also imposed price ceilings.

We now present an example in which there are two sectors and three financial instruments. We assumed that $S^1 = 1.5$ and $S^2 = 2.5$. We set all the taxes $T_i^j = .35$ for all sectors i and instruments j. Also, we set the price floors to zero but the price ceilings r_i^C=1.1 for all instruments i. Assume here that the preference vectors of each sector for holding each instrument as his assets and liabilities are as follows:

$$\text{Sector } 1 : a^1 = (1.1, 2, .5), \quad b^1 = (1.3, .5, 2.8)$$

$$\text{Sector } 2 : a^2 = (1, 2.5, .5), \quad b^2 = (2, 1.5, 2).$$

The modified projection method was coded by Dong (1994), compiled using the FORTVS compiler, optimization level 3, and the IBM 3090/600J was used for the implementation. The variables were initialized as follows: The prices r_i were set to 1, for all instrument i, and the sector volumes were equally distributed among the instruments held as assets and as liabilities. The γ parameter was set to .35 because the Lipschitz constant could be calculated to be 2.8. The convergence tolerance ϵ was set to 10^{-4}. The numerical results for this example are:

Equilibrium Prices:

$$r_1^* = .64804, \quad r_2^* = 0.00000, \quad r_3^* = 1.10000,$$

Equilibrium Asset Holdings

$$X_1^{1^*} = .54329, \quad X_2^{1^*} = .76357, \quad X_3^{1^*} = .19314,$$
$$X_1^{2^*} = .60101, \quad X_2^{2^*} = 1.38947, \quad X_3^{2^*} = .50952,$$

Equilibrium Liability Holdings:

$$Y_1^{1^*} = .31565, \quad Y_2^{1^*} = 0.00000, \quad Y_3^{1^*} = 1.18435,$$
$$Y_1^{2^*} = .82876, \quad Y_2^{2^*} = 1.22975, \quad Y_3^{2^*} = .44149.$$

As noted by Dong (1994), it is eay to verify that the computed solution satisfies the constraints and the equilibrium conditions. Moreover, it is interesting to note that the price of instrument 2 is zero and that there is an effective excess supply of this instrument. On the other hand, the price of instrument 1 is between 0 and the ceiling price of 1.1, and the market for this instrument clears. Finally, the price of instrument 3 is at the ceiling price of 1.1, and there is an effective excess demand for this instrument.

The modified projection method converged to the above solution in 50 iterations and in a negligible amount of CPU time.

9.4.3 The Primal-Dual Method

In this section we discuss the application of the primal-dual method, discussed in Section 5.2.4, for the solution of the network optimization reformulation of imperfect market financial equilibrium, in the special case in which the utility functions are of the form (9.4) and there are only taxes present. This is the model discussed in Section 9.3, whose equilibrium solution can be obtained by solving a network optimization problem.

We now state the primal-dual decomposition method of Section 5.2.4 for the solution of the imperfect market financial network optimization problem. We then present a numerical example.

The Primal-Dual Decomposition Method

Step 0: Initialization

Select an initial Lagrange multiplier vector $\lambda^0 \in R^I_+$. Set $\tau := 0$.

Step 1: Solve the Lagrangian Problem

Solve the following Lagrangian problem for each sector j; $j = 1, \ldots, J$:

$$\text{Minimize} \quad -\tilde{u}^j(X^j, Y^j, \lambda^\tau) = -u^j(X^j, Y^j) - \sum_{i=1}^{I} \lambda_i^\tau \sum_{j=1}^{J} (1 - \mathcal{T}_i^j)(X_i^j - Y_i^j), \tag{9.52}$$

subject to:

$$(X^j, Y^j) \in \kappa^j. \tag{9.53}$$

Step 2: Search Direction and Step Size Determination

Define a direction of search, d^τ, according to: For $i = 1, \ldots, I$:

$$d_i^\tau = \begin{cases} -\sum_{i=1}^{I} \sum_{j=1}^{J} (1 - \mathcal{T}_i^j)(X_i^j(\lambda^\tau) - Y_i^j(\lambda^\tau)), & \text{if} \quad \lambda_i^\tau = 0 \\ \max\{0, -\sum_{i=1}^{I} \sum_{j=1}^{J} (1 - \mathcal{T}_i^j)(X_i^j(\lambda^\tau) - Y_i^j(\lambda^\tau)), & \text{if} \quad \lambda_i^\tau = 0. \end{cases} \tag{9.54}$$

Select a new vector $\lambda^{\tau+1}$ according to:

$$\lambda^{\tau+1} = \lambda^\tau + \alpha_\tau d^\tau. \tag{9.55}$$

The step size α_τ should be selected according to:

$$\sum_{j=1}^{J} -\tilde{u}^j(X^j(\lambda^{\tau+1}), Y^j(\lambda^{\tau+1}), \lambda^{\tau+1}) > \sum_{j=1}^{J} -\tilde{u}^j(X^j(\lambda^\tau), Y^j(\lambda^\tau), \lambda^\tau). \tag{9.56}$$

Step 3: Convergence Verification

If $\max_{j,i} |X_i^{j\,\tau+1} - X_i^{j\,\tau}| \leq \epsilon$; $\max_{j,i} |Y_i^{j\,\tau+1} - Y_i^{j\,\tau}| \leq \epsilon$; and $\max_i |\lambda_i^{\tau+1} - \lambda_i^\tau| \leq \epsilon$, then stop; else, set $\tau := \tau + 1$, and go to Step 1.

We now apply the primal-dual method, embedded with the extended equilibration algorithm, to Example 9.1. The algorithm was coded in FORTRAN, and the initialization was the same as for the modified projection method. We selected the step size $a_\tau = .1$ for all τ. The primal-dual method converged in 24 iterations and in .01 seconds of CPU time.

9.5 Sources and Notes

Nagurney and Dong (1994) used finite-dimensional variational inequality theory for the first time for the qualitative analysis and computation of imperfect market multi-sector, multi-instrument financial equilibrium problems. The model they developed included both taxes and price ceilings on the instrument prices. The utility functions therein were assumed to be quadratic. In 1995, Nagurney and Dong showed how transaction costs could be incorporated into the budget constraints and emphasized the network structure of the subproblems resulting from an application of the modified projection method whose convergence was then established later in Nagurney and Dong (1996b). Dong (1993) generalized the utility functions from the quadratic case to the form given in (9.4). Finally, Nagurney and Dong (1996a) presented the imperfect market general utility function model, along with the theoretical analysis and algorithm development, which contains the majority of the aforementioned models as special cases. In this chapter we have made a slight generalization of that model by assuming that the price floors imposed on the instruments need not be zero. The models in this chapter are also more general than the imperfect market financial equilibrium models described in the book by Nagurney (1993).

Section 9.1

The general model presented here is a slight extension of the model that was developed by Nagurney and Dong (1996a). Hence, this chapter leans heavily on the theoretical results of that paper.

Section 9.2

The qualitative properties of the model are entirely based on the work of Nagurney and Dong (1996a).

Section 9.3

The results in this section are new and have not been reported elsewhere. They show that in a special case of the imperfect market financial model with general utility functions in which the utility functions are of a special form and in which there are only taxes the equilibrium solution be reformulated as the solution to a network optimization problem. If transaction costs or price ceilings (or positive price floors) are present then this is no longer possible. Moreover, the results demonstrate in a graphical way that the introduction of transaction costs and price ceilings distorts the network structure at equilibrium.

Section 9.4

The modified asset equilibration procedure was presented in Nagurney and Dong (1996b). The numerical examples in this section are new with the exception of the example with logarithmic utility functions which is taken from Dong (1994). Additional numerical examples of the modified projection method applied to imperfect financial market models can be found in Nagurney and Dong (1996a). Additional numerical examples can be found in Nagurney (1993), Dong (1993, 1994), Nagurney and Dong (1994, 1995).

References

Bertsekas, D. P., and Tsitsiklis, J. N., **Parallel and Distributed Computation – Numerical Methods**, Prentice-Hall, Inc., Englewood Cliffs, New Jersey, 1989.

Constantinides, G., "Capital Market Equili brium with Transaction Costs," *Journal of Political Economy* **94** (1986) 842-862.

Davis, M. H. A, and Norman, A. R., "Portfolio Selection with Transaction Costs," *Mathematics of Operations Research* **15** (1990) 676-413.

Dong, J., "General Financial Equilibrium with Policy Interventions: A Variational Incquality Approach," *Annals of Opcrations Rcsearch* **44** (1993) 227-241.

Dong, J., "Formulation and Computation of General Financial Equilibrium: A Variational Inequality Approach," Ph.D. Dissertation, University of Massachusetts, Amherst, Massachusetts, 1994.

Fama, F. M., "Risk, Return, and Equilibrium," *Journal of Political Economy* January (1971) 31-55.

Goldsmith, D., "Transactions Costs and the Theory of Portfolio Selection," *The Journal of Finance* **31** (1976) 1127–1139.

Jarrow, R., "Heterogeneous Expectations, Restrictions on Short Sales, and Equilibrium Asset Prices," *The Journal of Finance* **35** (1980) 1105-1113.

Kinderlehrer, D., and Stampacchia, G., **An Introduction to Variational Inequalities and Their Applications**, Academic Press, Inc., New York, New York, 1980.

Korpelevich, G. M., "The Extragradient Method for Finding Saddle Point and Other Problems," *Matekon* **12** (1977) 747-756.

Leland, H. E., "On Consumption and Portfolio Choices with Transaction Costs," in **Essays on Economic Behavior under Uncertainty**, M. Balch, D. McFadden, and S. Wu, editors, North–Holland, Amsterdam, The Netherlands, 1974.

Levy, H., "Equilibrium in an Imperfect Market: A Constraint on the Number of Securities in the Portfolio," *American Economic Review* **68** (1978) 643-658.

Lintner, J., "Security Prices, Risk, and Maximal Gains from Diversification," *The Journal of Finance* **20** (1965) 587-615.

Lintner, J., "The Aggregation of Investors' Diverse Judgements and Preferences in Purely Competitive Securities Markets," *Journal of Financial and Quantitative Analysis* **4** (1969) 347-400.

Magill, M., and Constantinides, G., "Portfolio Selection with Transaction Costs," *Journal of Economc Theory* **13** (1976) 245-263.

Markowitz, H. M., **Portfolio Selection: Efficient Diversification of Investments**, John Wiley & Sons, Inc., New York, New York, 1959.

Marston, F., and Harris, R. S.,"Risk and Return: A Revisit Using Expected Returns," *The Financial Review* **28** (1993) 117-137.

Mayshar, J., "Transaction Costs in a Model of Capital Market Equilibrium," *Journal of Political Economy* **87** (1979) 673-700.

Mayshar, J., " Transaction Costs and the Pricing of Assets," *The Journal of Finance* **36** (1981) 583-597.

Mossin, J., "Equilibrium in a Capital Asset Market," *Econometrica* **34** (1966) 768-783.

Mukherjee, R. M., and Zabel, E., "Consumption and Portfolio Choices with Transaction Costs," in **Essays on Economic Behavior under Uncertainty**, M.

Balch, D. McFadden, and S. Wu, editors, North-Holland, Amsterdam, The Netherlands, 1974.

Nagurney, A., **Network Economics: A Variational Inequality Approach**, Kluwer Academic Publishers, Boston, Massachusetts, 1993.

Nagurney, A., "Variational Inequalities for the Analysis and Computation of Multi-Sector, Multi-Instrument Financial Equilibria," *Journal of Economic Dynamics and Control* **18** (1994) 161-184.

Nagurney, A., and Dong, J., "Variational Inequalities for the Computation of Financial Equilibria in the Presence of Taxes and Price Controls," in **Computational Techniques for Econometrics and Economic Analysis**, pp. 189-205, D.A. Belsley, editor, Kluwer Academic Publishers, Boston, Massachusetts, 1994.

Nagurney, A., and Dong, J.,"Formulation and Computation of General Financial Equilibrium with Transaction Costs," in **Advances in Mathematical Programming and Financial Planning vol. 4**, pp. 3-24, JAI Press, K. Lawrence, editor, 1995.

Nagurney, A., and Dong, J., "General Financial Equilibrium Modeling with Policy Interventions and Transaction Costs," *Computational Economics* **9** (1996a) 3-17.

Nagurney, A., and Dong, J., "Network Decomposition of General Financial Equilibria with Transaction Costs," *Networks* **28** (1996b) 107-116.

Nagurney, A., Dong, J., and M. Hughes, "Formulation and Computation of General Financial Equilibrium," *Optimization* **26** (1992) 339-354.

Nagurney, A., and Hughes, M.,"Financial Flow of Funds Networks," *Networks* **22** (1992) 145-162.

Pogue, G. A., "An Extension of the Markowitz Portfolio Selection Model to include Variable Transactions' Costs, Short Sales, Leverage Policies and Taxes," *The Journal of Finance* **15** (1970) 1005-1027.

Sharpe, W. F., "Capital Asset Prices: A Theory of Market Equilibrium under Conditions of Risk," *The Journal of Finance* **19** (1964) 425-442.

Sharpe, W. F., **Portfolio Theory and Capital Markets**, McGraw-Hall, Inc., New York, New York, 1970.

Smith, R. T., "Heterogeneous Beliefs and Learning about the Expected Return in a Market for a Short-Lived Asset," *The Financial Review* **28** (1993) 1-24.

10 Dynamic Imperfect Market Models

A large portion of financial theory and modeling neglects the presence of imperfections in financial markets. This is something that one would expect since the inclusion of market imperfections significantly increases the complexity of any model, and qualitatively alters the problem under consideration. The sources for such imperfections are directly connected with the nature of financial trading, and they appear as transaction costs, taxes, and/or price policy interventions. The presence of practically any friction in the market can dramatically change the type of financial modeling that is needed. Nevertheless, practice suggests that imperfections are a source of concern for all participants in the market, and, consequently, realistic models that can incorporate them are needed.

In recent years a significant part of the financial literature has focused on the development of financial models that can incorporate different types of market imperfections, principally, in the form of transaction costs, with the contributions of Merton (1969, 1971, 1973) forming the foundation for their development. The introduction of transaction costs to models by Merton was first done by Magill and Constantinides (1976), in continuous time, and by Constantinides (1979), in discrete time, to be followed by a series of important contributions by Constantinides (1986), Duffie and Sun (1990), Davis and Norman (1990), Dumas and Luciano (1991), and Shreve and Soner (1994).

In this chapter we demonstrate the applicability of the recently introduced mathematical framework of projected dynamical systems (see Chapter 4) to the development of dynamic financial models that incorporate market imperfections. In particular, in this chapter, we propose and study an adjustment process that describes the dynamic behavior of the financial sectors and that of the instrument prices in the market. The adjustment process is formulated as a projected dynamical system. The models presented in this chapter are the dynamic counterparts of the static models discussed in Chapter 9. In addition, we analyze the dynamics under which the individual networks of Figure 9.1, representing the optimization problems of the individual sectors, merge to yield the complete synthesized network of Figure 9.2.

The assumptions that govern the market under consideration here as well as the behavior of all sectors and all instruments are identical to those made in Chapter 9. In particular, we assume that sectors act in a perfectly competitive environment, as was defined in Section 2.3, and that the prices of all instruments follow the supply-demand rule.

The models presented in this chapter give the monetary authorities the ability to apply different types of transaction costs to distinct investors that hold assets or liabilities in different instruments. In addition, they permit the setting of price ceilings and floors on every instrument in the market. We assume that all the transaction costs, as well as the price ceilings and floors, are constants with known values. The transaction costs that we treat include taxes and fees that an investor has to pay for each individual investment. For example, one type of transaction cost that is handled by the models covers costs that are related to the origin and to the identity of both the sectors and the instruments, so that each sector can be charged differently from the others according to his portfolio. This type of transaction cost gives the monetary authorities the ability to apply different fees and taxes to distinct investors. The second type of transaction cost that can be handled is related only to the instrument and currency prices and is a special case of the previous one. This type of transaction cost can be seen as a VAT (value added tax) type of transaction cost.

We will now outline the structure of this chapter. Section 10.1 develops the dynamic counterpart of the model developed in Section 9.1. Section 10.2 presents the stability analysis results for the dynamic models that incorporate market imperfections developed in the preceding section. Finally, in Section 10.3, the Euler method is utilized for the computation of the stationary points, accompanied by convergence results. Numerical examples are also presented.

10.1 The Dynamic Imperfect Financial Model

We consider the same economy as in Chapter 9, that is, one with J sectors, where a typical sector is denoted by j and with I instruments, where a typical instrument is denoted by i. As before, we denote the volume of instrument i that sector j holds as an asset by X_i^j, and, similarly, we let Y_i^j denote the volume of instrument i that sector j holds as a liability. We group the assets and liabilities of sector j, respectively, into the column vectors $X^j \in R_+^I$ and $Y^j \in R_+^I$. We then further group the asset and the liability vectors of all the sectors, respectively, into the column vectors $X \in R_+^{JI}$ and $Y \in R_+^{JI}$. Moreover, we let $\tilde{X}^j$ denote the feasible set for the assets of sector j as was defined in (9.5), and we let $\tilde{Y}^j$ denote the feasible set for the liabilities of sector j as was defined in (9.6). In addition, $\tilde{\kappa}^j$ denotes the feasible set of sector j, where recall that, as discussed in Chapter 9, $\tilde{\kappa}^j = \tilde{X}^j \times \tilde{Y}^j$, and $\tilde{\kappa}$ denotes the Cartesian product of the feasible sets of all the sectors.

As before, we let r_i represent the price of instrument i and we group the instrument prices into the column vector $r \in R^I_+$. From the policy interventions aspect, recall that the price ceiling associated with instrument i is denoted by r_i^C and the price floor associated with instrument i is denoted by r_i^F. Once again, we group the instrument price floors and ceilings, respectively, into the I-dimensional column vectors r^F and r^C. We assume that the price floors are nonnegative and, hence, the ceilings are positive, such that $r_i^C > r_i^F$ for all instruments i.

As in Chapter 9, we let $\mathcal{T}_i^j$ denote the tax rate levied on sector j's net yield on instrument i, and assume that $0 \leq \mathcal{T}_i^j < 1$, with these tax rates being grouped into the column vector $\mathcal{T} \in R^{JI}_+$.

Moreover, every instrument i held as an asset is associated with a positive coefficient α_i, and every instrument i held as a liability is associated with another positive coefficient β_i, which we assume incorporate, respectively, the unit transaction costs c_i^x and c_i^y. For example, we may have that: $\alpha_i = 1 + c_i^x$ and $\beta_i = 1 - c_i^y$.

In addition, we assume that all sectors are risk-averse, with the utility function of each sector j being denoted by $U^j(X^j, Y^j, r; \mathcal{T})$, which is assumed to be continuous, twice continuously differentiable, and strictly concave with respect to the (X^j, Y^j) variables.

The goal of every sector j is to maximize his utility function subject to the constraints that guarantee that the accounts for each sector balance, and that the asset and liabilities holdings are nonnegative.

Therefore, the optimization problem that each sector j faces is given by:

$$\text{Maximize} \quad U^j(X^j, Y^j, r; \mathcal{T}) \tag{10.1}$$

subject to:

$$\sum_{i=1}^{I} \alpha_i X_i^j = S^j \tag{10.2a}$$

$$\sum_{i=1}^{I} \beta_i Y_i^j = S^j \tag{10.2b}$$

$$X_i^j \geq 0, \; Y_i^j \geq 0, \quad i = 1, 2, \ldots, I, \tag{10.3}$$

where S^j denotes the total financial volume held by sector j, and the price vector r is an exogenous vector in the optimization problem of every sector j; $j = 1, \ldots, J$.

The optimization problem for each sector of each country can be interpreted as an effort to adjust his asset and liability pattern in a direction that maximizes his utility function, while maintaining the accounting and nonnegativity constraints.

Obviously, the ideal direction for the maximization of this utility function in the unconstrained case is given by: $(\nabla_{X^j}U^j, \nabla_{Y^j}U^j)$, where:

$$\nabla_{X^j}U^j = (\frac{\partial U^j}{\partial X_1^j}, \ldots, \frac{\partial U^j}{\partial X_i^j}, \ldots, \frac{\partial U^j}{\partial X_I^j}) \tag{10.4}$$

and

$$\nabla_{Y^j}U^j = (\frac{\partial U^j}{\partial Y_1^j}, \ldots, \frac{\partial U^j}{\partial Y_i^j}, \ldots, \frac{\partial U^j}{\partial Y_I^j}), \tag{10.5}$$

where, recall that ∇_{X_j} denotes the gradient with respect to the variables in the vector X^j, with ∇_{Y^j} defined accordingly.

In the absence of any constraints, this direction would be optimal. However, in practice, each sector is faced with the constraints comprising his feasible set and, hence, this "idealized" direction needs to be revised. Consequently, the best-realizable direction of sector j is the projection of the idealized direction $(\nabla_{X^j}U^j, \nabla_{Y^j}U^j)$, onto his constraint set, $\tilde{\kappa}^j$, at his current portfolio (X^j, Y^j).

This best-realizable direction for a sector j can be mathematically expressed as:

$$\Pi_{\tilde{\kappa}^j}\left((X^j, Y^j), (\nabla_{X^j}U^j, \nabla_{Y^j}U^j)\right). \tag{10.6}$$

In view of (10.6), and Proposition 8.1, the asset and liability volumes for sector j are adjusted, equivalently, according to the following process over time:

$$\dot{X}^j = \Pi_{\tilde{X}^j}(X^j, \nabla_{X^j}U^j), \quad \dot{Y}^j = \Pi_{\tilde{Y}^j}(Y^j, \nabla_{Y^j}U^j). \tag{10.7}$$

Moreover, the instrument prices also change through time, adjusting to their supply and demand fluctuations, but subject to the imposed price floors and ceilings.

More precisely, we define ρ_i as:

$$\rho_i \equiv -\sum_{j=1}^{J}(1-\tau_i^j)(\alpha_i X_i^j - \beta_i Y_i^j), \tag{10.8}$$

with the vector $\rho \in R^I$ consisting of the components: $\{\rho_1, \ldots, \rho_I\}$.

The instrument price r_i then changes according to:

$$\dot{r}_i = \begin{cases} \max\{0, \rho_i\}, & \text{if } r_i = r_i^F \\ \rho_i, & \text{if } r_i^F < r_i < r_i^C \\ \min\{0, \rho_i\}, & \text{if } r_i = r_i^C, \end{cases} \tag{10.9}$$

which is equivalent to:

$$\dot{r}_i = \Pi_{[r_i^F, r_i^C]}(r_i, \rho_i). \tag{10.10}$$

The Financial Adjustment Process

In view of (10.7) and (10.9), the financial adjustment process that derives the allocation of assets and liabilities for each sector j, along with the prices of each instrument i, can now be formulated as:

$$\begin{cases} \dot{X}^j &= \Pi_{\tilde{X}^j}(X^j, \nabla_{X^j} U^j); \quad j = 1, \cdots, J \\ \dot{Y}^j &= \Pi_{\tilde{Y}^j}(Y^j, \nabla_{Y^j} U^j); \quad j = 1, \cdots, J \\ \dot{r}_i &= \Pi_{[r_i^F, r_i^C]}(r_i, \rho_i); \quad i = 1, \cdots, I. \end{cases} \tag{10.11}$$

By taking into consideration Proposition 8.1, the financial adjustment process (10.11) can be described by the following projected dynamical system:

$$\dot{x} = \Pi_{\mathcal{K}}(x, -F(x)), \tag{10.12}$$

where, recall from Chapter 9, that $\mathcal{K} \equiv \{\tilde{\kappa} \times \mathcal{S}\}$, where $\mathcal{S} = \{r | r^F \leq r \leq r^C\}$, $x \equiv (X, Y, r, \lambda) \in \mathcal{K}$, and F is as defined in (9.18), that is,

$$F(x) = \begin{bmatrix} F_1(x) \\ \vdots \\ F_b(x) \\ \vdots \\ F_n(x) \end{bmatrix} = \begin{bmatrix} -\nabla_X U(X, Y, r; T) \\ -\nabla_Y U(X, Y, r; T) \\ \sum_{j=1}^J (1 - T_1^j) \left(\alpha_1 X_1^j - \beta_1 Y_1^j \right) \\ \vdots \\ \sum_{j=1}^J (1 - T_I^j) \left(\alpha_I X_I^j - \beta_I Y_I^j \right) \end{bmatrix}_{n \times 1}, \tag{10.13}$$

where $n = 2JI + I$.

The projected dynamical system (10.12) states that the investors will try to expand their holdings on all instruments that increase their marginal utility, while, in parallel, they attempt to reduce their holdings of the instruments that decrease their marginal utility. Clearly, their effort to adjust their holdings constantly changes the price levels of the financial instruments. The projection operation $\Pi_{\mathcal{K}}$ guarantees that the evolution of the capital allocation, as well as, the prices, fall within the predefined constraint set. In particular, the prices of all instruments must be nonnegative and between the price floors and ceilings that the monetary authorities have set, whereas the assets and liabilities must be nonnegative and must satisfy the budget constraints.

Moreover, in view of Theorem 4.2, the following theorem holds.

Theorem 10.1

(10.12) well-defines a dynamical system, in that there exists a unique solution path to (10.10) for any initial condition $x(0) = x_0 \in \mathcal{K}$.

In addition, the following Theorem must also hold true, given Theorem 4.1 and Theorem 9.1.

Theorem 10.2

Every financial equilibrium of the imperfect market, single country, multi-sector, multi-instrument financial model with market imperfections (cf. Definition 9.1) is a stationary point of the adjustment process (10.12) and vice versa. In other words, $x^* = (X^*, Y^*, r^*)$ constitutes a financial equilibrium with market imperfections if and only if

$$\Pi_{\mathcal{K}}(x^*, -F(x^*)) = 0. \tag{10.14}$$

It is worth emphasizing that as long as the utility functions of the sectors follow the general assumptions that we discussed earlier and the feasible set remains a convex polyhedron, a version of the projected dynamical system (10.12) will always prevail. Clearly, this is true even in the case that the monetary authorities and/or the government decide to impose new regulations, in which case more constraints might be added to the model. The incorporation of new regulations and constraints will have an important effect on the trajectories of capital allocation and prices over time. Nevertheless, any new projected dynamical system will guarantee that the prices, as well as the asset and liability holdings of all investors will satisfy the new feasibility conditions.

10.2 Stability Analysis

In this section we address the qualitative aspects of the behavior of the financial adjustment process (10.12) relative to an equilibrium point. We present the conditions under which a disequilibrium pattern of assets, liabilities, and instrument prices will reach a financial equilibrium in the presence of market imperfections.

For easy reference, we present the specific adaptations of the stability definitions from Chapter 4 for the imperfect market financial adjustment process.

Definition 10.1 (Stable Financial Adjustment Process)

The financial adjustment process (10.12) is stable if each financial equilibrium, $x^* = (X^*, Y^*, r^*)$, is a monotone attractor, that is, for any initial asset, liability, and price pattern, (X_0, Y_0, r_0), the distance,

$$\|(X(t), Y(t), r(t)) - (X^*, Y^*, r^*)\|,$$

is nonincreasing in time t, where $(X(t), Y(t), r(t))$ satisfy (10.12).

Definition 10.2 (Asymptotically Stable Financial Adjustment Process)

The financial adjustment process is asymptotically stable if it is stable, and for any initial asset, liability, and price pattern, (X_0, Y_0, r_0)*, the financial adjustment process starting with* (X_0, Y_0, r_0) *converges to some equilibrium pattern* (X^*, Y^*, r^*)*; namely,*

$$(X_0(t), Y_0(t), r_0(t)) \longrightarrow (X^*, Y^*, r^*), \quad as\ t \longrightarrow \infty. \tag{10.15}$$

In Theorem 10.3 we address the issue of stability of the financial adjustment process with market imperfections in the case that every financial sector has a twice continuously differentiable concave utility function in terms of the asset and liability pattern. Moreover, we assume that taxes and price floors and ceilings can be imposed but that other transaction costs are zero; hence, we assume that α_i and β_i are equal to 1 for all instruments $i = 1, \ldots, I$. Recall from Section 9.3, that in order to have a network optimization reformulation of the equilibrium conditions such a condition had to hold as well.

In Theorem 10.4 we expand further the stability analysis discussion for the case that sectors have strictly concave utility functions. The uniqueness of the asset and liability equilibrium pattern is also established under assumptions similar to the ones used for the static case.

Subsequently, in Theorem 10.5, we provide conditions under which any financial disequilibrium state will eventually approach equilibrium, that is, that the financial adjustment process is asymptotically stable.

Theorem 10.3 (Stability of the Financial Adjustment Process)

Assume that α_i *and* β_i *are equal to 1, for all instruments:* $i = 1, \ldots, I$*. Assume also that the utility function* $U^j(X^j, Y^j, r; \mathcal{T})$ *of each sector* j*;* $j = 1, \ldots, J$*, is continuous, twice continuously differentiable, and concave in the vectors* X^j *and* Y^j*, and also of the form:*

$$U^j(X^j, Y^j, r; \mathcal{T}) = u^j(X^j, Y^j) + \sum_{i=1}^{I}(1 - \mathcal{T}_i^j) r_i (X_i^j - Y_i^j), \tag{10.16}$$

with $u^j(X^j, Y^j)$ *representing the risk associated with the portfolio choice of sector* j*. Then the financial adjustment process (10.12) is stable.*

Proof: Let $x^* = (X^*, Y^*, r^*)$ be any financial equilibrium pattern of assets, liabilities, and prices satisfying Definition 9.1. For any initial pattern, $x_0 = (X_0, Y_0, r_0)$, let $x_0(t) = (X_0(t), Y_0(t), r_0(t))$ be the financial distribution at time t under the financial adjustment process starting with (X_0, Y_0, r_0). Define

$$D(x_0, x^*, t) := \frac{1}{2}\|x_0(t) - x^*\|^2. \tag{10.17}$$

Then

$$\dot{D}(x_0, x^*, t) = \langle (x_0(t) - x^*)^T, \Pi_{\mathcal{K}}(x(t), -F(x(t))) \rangle. \tag{10.18}$$

Recall from Section 4.1 (cf. (4.10)), that

$$\Pi_{\mathcal{K}}(x(t), -F(x(t))) = -F(x_0(t)) + \eta(x_0(t)) N^*(x_0(t)),$$

where $N^*(x(t))$ is an inward normal to $\mathcal{K}$ at $x(t)$, and $\eta(x(t))$ is a nonnegative real number. Then we have an upper bound for (10.18), that is,

$$\dot{D}(x_0, x^*, t) \leq \langle (x_0(t) - x^*)^T, -F(x_0(t)) \rangle$$

$$= \langle (X_0(t) - X^*)^T, \nabla_X U \rangle + \langle (Y_0(t) - Y^*)^T, \nabla_Y U \rangle + \langle (r_0(t) - r^*)^T, -\rho \rangle$$

$$= \sum_{j=1}^{J} \sum_{i=1}^{I} \left(X_0(t)_i^j - X_i^{j*} \right) \left[\frac{\partial}{\partial X_i^j} u^j\left(X_0(t), Y_0(t), r_0(t)\right) + r_0(t)_i (1 - \tau_i^j) \right]$$

$$+ \sum_{j=1}^{J} \sum_{i=1}^{I} \left(Y_0(t)_i^j - Y_i^{j*} \right) \left[\frac{\partial}{\partial Y_i^j} u^j\left(X_0(t), Y_0(t), r_0(t)\right) - r_0(t)_i (1 - \tau_i^j) \right]$$

$$- \sum_{i=1}^{I} (r_0(t)_i - r_i^*) \sum_{j=1}^{J} \left(X_0(t)_i^j - Y_0(t)_i^j)(1 - \tau_i^j \right)$$

$$= \sum_{j=1}^{J} (X_0(t)^j - X^{j*}) \left[\nabla_{X^j} u^j (X_0(t)^j, Y_0(t)^j) - \nabla_{X^j} u^j (X^{j*}, Y^{j*}) \right]$$

$$+ \sum_{j=1}^{J} (Y_0(t)^j - Y^{j*}) \left[\nabla_{Y^j} u^j (X_0(t)^j, Y_0(t)^j) - \nabla_{Y^j} u^j (X^{j*}, Y^{j*}) \right]$$

$$= \sum_{j=1}^{J} G^j(X^j, Y^j) + \sum_{j=1}^{J} H^j(X^j, Y^j) \leq 0, \tag{10.19}$$

where

$$G^j(X^j, Y^j) = (X_0(t)^j - X^{j*}) \left[\nabla_{X^j} u^j (X_0(t)^j, Y_0(t)^j) - \nabla_{X^j} u^j (X^{j*}, Y^{j*}) \right],$$

and

$$H^j(X^j, Y^j) = (Y_0(t)^j - Y^{j*}) \left[\nabla_{Y^j} u^j (X_0(t)^j, Y_0(t)^j) - \nabla_{Y^j} u^j (X^{j*}, Y^{j*}) \right].$$

Since each u^j is concave with respect to X^j and Y^j, each G^j and H^j are nonpositive for $j = 1, \ldots, J$. This implies that $\|x_0(t) - x^*\|$ is monotone nonincreasing in time t, and, by definition, x^* is a monotone attractor. □

Note that the sum of the second term on the right-hand side of the equality in (10.16) represents the value of the asset holdings minus the value of the liability holdings. Recall (cf. Section 9.1.1) an important special case of the utility function (10.16) is given by the quadratic utility function:

$$U^j(X^j, Y^j, r; T) = -\begin{pmatrix} X^j \\ Y^j \end{pmatrix}^T Q^j \begin{pmatrix} X^j \\ Y^j \end{pmatrix} + \sum_{i=1}^{I}(1 - T_i^j) r_i (X_i^j - Y_i^j), \tag{10.20}$$

where Q^j is the symmetric $2I \times 2I$ variance/covariance matrix representing the risk associated with the portfolio choice of sector j after taxes. Hence, according to Theorem 10.3, in the case of such quadratic utility functions, the imperfect market financial adjustment process is stable if the variance/covariance matrices are positive semi-definite.

Theorem 10.4

Assume the conditions of Theorem 10.3. Assume also that there is a subset of the financial sectors $\tilde{J}$, such that for each $j \in \tilde{J}$, u^j is strictly concave with respect to X^j and Y^j. Then, all financial equilibria are comprised of unique asset and liability patterns X^{j^*} and Y^{j^*} for $j \in \tilde{J}$, and, in addition, the imperfect market financial adjustment process is asymptotically stable with respect to the assets and liabilities of those financial sectors $j \in \tilde{J}$, that is,

$$X_0(t)^j \to X^{j^*}, \quad Y_0(t)^j \to Y^{j^*}, \quad \text{as } t \to \infty, \ \forall j \in \tilde{J}, \tag{10.21}$$

irregardless of the initial distribution.

Proof: Let $x^* = (X^*, Y^*, r^*)$ be any financial equilibrium pattern. Then for any initial pattern, $x_0 = (X_0, Y_0, r_0)$, according to Theorem 10.3,

$$D(x_0, x^*, t) = \frac{1}{2}\|x_0(t) - x^*\|^2$$

is a nonincreasing function of time t. Therefore, for each

$$j \in \tilde{J}, \quad \{(X_0(t)^j, Y_0(t)^j) |\ t \geq 0\}$$

is bounded. To complete the proof, we only need to show that

$$\{(X_0(t)^j, Y_0(t)^j) |\ t \geq 0\}, \quad \forall j \in \tilde{J},$$

does not have any other limit point except (X^{j^*}, Y^{j^*}).

Suppose, on the contrary, that there exists a $j \in \tilde{J}$ and some time sequence $\{t_k\}$, such that

$$X_0(t_k)^j \longrightarrow \bar{X}^j, \ Y_0(t_k)^j \longrightarrow \bar{Y}^j, \text{ as } k \longrightarrow \infty \tag{10.22}$$

and

$$(\bar{X}^j, \bar{Y}^j) \neq (X^{j^*}, Y^{j^*}).$$

Let

$$d = \frac{1}{4}\|(\bar{X}^j, \bar{Y}^j) - (X^{j^*}, Y^{j^*})\| \tag{10.23}$$

and

$$G^j(X^j, Y^j) = (X^j - X^{j^*})^T \left[\nabla_{X^j} u^j(X^j, Y^j) - \nabla_{X^j} u^j(X^{j^*} - Y^{j^*})\right],$$

$$H^j(X^j, Y^j) = (Y^j - Y^{j^*})^T \left[\nabla_{Y^j} u^j(X^j, Y^j) - \nabla_{Y^j} u^j(X^{j^*} - Y^{j^*})\right]. \tag{10.24}$$

Since u^j is strictly concave in both X^j and Y^j for $j \in \tilde{J}$, $G^j(X^j, Y^j)$ and $H^j(X^j, Y^j)$ are negative everywhere except at (X^{j^*}, Y^{j^*}). Let $-\omega^j$ be the maximum attained by the continuous function $G^j + H^j$ on the compact set $\mathcal{B}((\bar{X}^j, \bar{Y}^j), 2d)$. Namely, we have

$$G^j(X^j, Y^j) + H^j(X^j, Y^j) \leq -\omega^j < 0, \quad \forall (X^j, Y^j) \in \mathcal{B}((\bar{X}^j, \bar{Y}^j), 2d), \tag{10.25}$$

where $\mathcal{B}((\bar{X}^j, \bar{Y}^j), 2d)$ is the closed ball centered at $(\bar{X}^j, \bar{Y}^j)$ with radius $2d$. In view of (10.19), one has

$$\dot{D}(z_0, z^*, t) \leq G^j(X_0^j(t), Y_0^j(t)) + H^j(X_0^j(t), Y_0^j(t)) \leq -\omega^j, \tag{10.26}$$

where $(X^j(t), Y^j(t)) \in \mathcal{B}((\bar{X}^j, \bar{Y}^j), 2d)$.

Since $D(x_0, x^*, t) = \frac{1}{2}\|x_0(t) - x^*\|^2$ is nonnegative, (10.26) implies that

$$T = \{t \geq 0 : \ (X^j(t), Y^j(t)) \in \mathcal{B}((\bar{X}^j, \bar{Y}^j), 2d)\} \tag{10.27}$$

must have finite Lebesque measure.

Combining this fact with (10.22), one asserts the existence of two sequences $\{t_v\}$ and $\{s_v\}$ with

$$t_v < t_v + s_v < t_{v+1}, \quad v = 0, 1, \cdots,$$

such that

$$(X^j(t), Y^j(t)) \in \mathcal{B}\left((\bar{X}^j, \bar{Y}^j), d\right) \tag{10.28}$$

and

$$s_v = \ \mathrm{Sup}\ \{\delta \geq 0 : \ (X^j(t), Y^j(t)) \in \mathcal{B}\left((\bar{X}^j, \bar{Y}^j), 2d\right), \forall \tau \in [t_v, t_v + s_v]\}, \tag{10.29}$$

which implies that

$$\|\left(X^j(t_v + s_v), Y^j(t_v + s_v)\right) - (\bar{X}^j, \bar{Y}^j)\| = 2d. \tag{10.30}$$

In fact, $\{t_v\}$ can be extracted as a subsequence from $\{t_k\}$ in (10.22). Since $\|x_0(t) - x^*\|$ is nonincreasing in t, $\{x_0(t) : \ t \geq 0\}$ is contained in the compact set $\mathcal{B}_2 = \mathcal{B}(x^*, \|x_0 - x^*\|)$. Hence, $F(x)$ defined in (10.13) with utility functions given by (10.16) attains its maximal norm on $\mathcal{B}_2$. Let

$$M = \max_{x \in \mathcal{B}_2} \|F(x)\|. \tag{10.31}$$

Then, it follows from $||\Pi_{\mathcal{K}}(x, -F(x))|| \leq ||F(x)||$, that

$$||\Pi_{\mathcal{K}}(x(t), -F(x(t)))|| \leq M, \ \ \forall t \geq 0. \tag{10.32}$$

Therefore,

$$||x(t_v + s_v) - x(t_v)|| \leq \int_{t_v}^{t_v + s_v} ||\Pi_{\mathcal{K}}\left(x\left(\tau\right), -F\left(x\left(\tau\right)\right)\right)||d\tau \leq M s_v. \tag{10.33}$$

On the other hand, with notice to (10.28) and (10.30), one has

$$||x(t_v + s_v) - x(t_v)|| \geq d. \tag{10.34}$$

Therefore,

$$s_v \geq \frac{d}{M}, \quad v = 0, 1, \cdots, \tag{10.35}$$

which yields

$$m\left(\bigcup_{v=0}^{\infty}(t_v, t_v + s_v)\right) = \sum_{v=0}^{\infty} s_v = \infty. \tag{10.36}$$

However, (10.36) is in contradiction to the earlier observation that T has finite measure because

$$\bigcup_{v=0}^{\infty}(t_v, t_v + s_v) \subset T.$$

The contradiction we produced shows that the early assumption cannot be true. Therefore, for every j in $\tilde{J}$,

$$(X_0(t)^j, Y_0(t)^j) \longrightarrow (X^{j^*}, Y^{j^*}), \text{ as } t \longrightarrow \infty. \qquad \square$$

Theorem 10.5

Assume the conditions of Theorem 10.3 and that each sector's utility function is strictly concave with respect to its asset and liability pattern and that the functions are of the form given in (10.16). Then the financial adjustment process is asymptotically stable.

Proof: Following Theorem 10.4, the financial adjustment process,

$$x_0(t) = (X_0(t), Y_0(t), r_0(t)),$$

initialized at any initial financial pattern, (X_0, Y_0, r_0), converges to some unique equilibrium pattern of assets and liabilities, that is,

$$X_0(t) \longrightarrow X^*, \ \ Y_0(t) \longrightarrow Y^*, \text{ as } t \longrightarrow \infty. \tag{10.37}$$

Since $x_0(t)$ is bounded, $\{r_0(t), t \geq 0\}$ has a convergent sequence, say,

$$r_0(t_k) \longrightarrow r^*, \text{ as } k \longrightarrow \infty. \tag{10.38}$$

In what follows, we are going to show that $x^* = (X^*, Y^*, r^*)$ is, indeed, an imperfect market financial equilibrium pattern and

$$(X_0(t), Y_0(t), r_0(t)) \longrightarrow (X^*, Y^*, r^*), \text{ as } t \longrightarrow \infty. \tag{10.39}$$

Let

$$\sigma_i := \sum_{j=1}^{J} (1 - \mathcal{T}_i^j)(X_i^{j*} - Y_i^{j*}). \tag{10.40}$$

If $\sigma_i > 0$, then for t sufficiently large

$$\sum_{j=1}^{J} (1 - \mathcal{T}_i^j)(X_0(t)_i^j - Y_0(t)_i^j) > \frac{\sigma_i}{2} > 0. \tag{10.41}$$

By definition, we have that $\dot{r}_i(t) < -\frac{\sigma_i}{2}$ for t large unless $r_i(t)=r_i^F$. Thus, $\lim_{t\to\infty} r_i(t)=r_i^F$, which implies that $r_i^* = r_i^F$.

On the other hand, if $\sigma_i < 0$, then, for t large, we have that

$$\sum_{j=1}^{J} (1 - \mathcal{T}_i^j)(X_0(t)_i^j - Y_0(t)_i^j) < \frac{\sigma_i}{2} < 0. \tag{10.42}$$

By definition, we also have that $\dot{r}_i(t) > -\frac{\sigma_i}{2} > 0$, for t large unless $r_i(t) = r_i^C$. Therefore, $\lim_{t\to\infty} r_i(t)=r_i^C$, which implies that $r_i^* = r_i^C$.

In conclusion, if $r_i^* = r_i^F$, we must have that $\sigma_i \geq 0$; if $r_i^* = r_i^C$, we must have that $\sigma_i \leq 0$; if $r_i^F < r_i^* < r_i^C$, we must have that $\sigma_i = 0$. In other words, for each $i = 1, \ldots, I$:

$$\sigma_i = \sum_{j=1}^{J} (1 - \mathcal{T}_i^j)(X_i^{j*} - Y_i^{j*}) \begin{cases} \leq 0, & \text{if } r_i^* = r_i^C \\ = 0 & \text{if } r_i^F < r_i^* < r_i^C \\ \geq 0 & \text{if } r_i^* = r_i^F. \end{cases} \tag{10.43}$$

Notice that (10.43) is nothing else but the equilibrium condition (9.11) with $\alpha_i = \beta_i = 1$. Therefore,

$$(X_0(t), Y_0(t), r_0(t)) \longrightarrow (X^*, Y^*, r^*), \text{ as } t \longrightarrow \infty. \qquad \square$$

10.3 A Discrete Time Algorithm

In this section, we suggest a discrete time algorithm, the Euler method, for the computation of the financial equilibrium pattern in the presence of market imperfections. This algorithm was already utilized in Section 8.3 for the computation of perfect market financial equilibria. The Euler method can be interpreted as a discrete time adjustment process or a discrete time approximation of the continuous time model given by (10.12). The Euler method traces the trajectories of the corresponding projected dynamical system and yields a stationary point (provided certain conditions for convergence are satisfied).

For completeness, and easy reference, we now present the Euler method defined by (4.24) and (4.52), for the solution of the dynamic imperfect market financial model of Section 10.1. We then provide the convergence result. We follow up with numerical examples.

Step 0: Initialization

Set $(X^0, Y^0, r^0) \in \mathcal{K}$. Let $\tau := 0$. Set the sequence $\{a_\tau\}$ according to condition 1 of Assumption 4.2.

Step 1: Computation

Compute $(X^{\tau+1}, Y^{\tau+1}, r^{\tau+1}) \in \mathcal{K}$ by solving the variational inequality subproblem:

$$\sum_{j=1}^{J}\sum_{i=1}^{I}\left[X_i^{j^{\tau+1}} + a_\tau\left[-\frac{\partial U^j(X^{j^\tau}, Y^{j^\tau}; T)}{\partial X_i^j}\right] - X_i^{j^\tau}\right] \times \left[X_i^j - X_i^{j^{\tau+1}}\right]$$

$$+\sum_{j=1}^{J}\sum_{i=1}^{I}\left[Y_i^{j^{\tau+1}} + a_\tau\left[-\frac{\partial U^j(X^{j^\tau}, Y^{j^\tau}; T)}{\partial Y_i^j}\right] - Y_i^{j^\tau}\right] \times \left[Y_i^j - Y_i^{j^{\tau+1}}\right]$$

$$+\sum_{i=1}^{I}\left[r_i^{\tau+1} + a_\tau\left[\sum_{j=1}^{J}\left(\alpha_i X_i^{j^\tau} - \beta_i Y_i^{j^\tau}\right)\right] - r_i^\tau\right] \times \left[r_i - r_i^{\tau+1}\right] \geq 0$$

$$\forall (X, Y, r) \in \mathcal{K}. \qquad (10.44)$$

Step 2: Convergence Verification

If $\max_{i,j} |X_i^{j^{\tau+1}} - X_i^{j^\tau}| \leq \epsilon$; $\max_{i,j} |Y_i^{j^{\tau+1}} - Y_i^{j^\tau}| \leq \epsilon$; $\max_i |r_i^{\tau+1} - r_i^\tau| \leq \epsilon$, for all $i; i = 1, \ldots, I$, and $j; j = 1, \ldots, J$, with $\epsilon > 0$, a prespecified tolerance, then stop; else, set $\tau := \tau + 1$, and go to Step 1.

The projection operation entails the solution of a quadratic programming problem, which, in view of the feasible set, which is a Cartesian product, is further decomposable by sectors in their asset variables, in their liability variables, and, simultaneously, in the prices of the instruments. Hence, the structure of problem (10.44) is precisely that of the network subproblems depicted in Figure 9.3. Moreover, since the constraints are linear and the objective function is quadratic and separable the problems can be solved exactly and in closed form using the modified asset exact equilibration procedure (and the analogous modified liability exact equilibration procedure), as discussed in Section 9.4.1.

The Euler method is guaranteed to converge, provided that the conditions of Assumption 4.2 are satisfied. In Theorem 10.6 we state the convergence result.

Note that, unlike the statement of the corresponding convergence theorem for the dynamic perfect market models studied in Chapter 8, here we assume that Assumption 4.2 is satisfied rather than verifying each of its conditions. Hence, here we do not restrict the utility function to be of the analogous form given by (10.16).

Theorem 10.6

Suppose that the utility functions U^j for each sector j are strictly concave in the instrument variables, continuous, and twice continuously differentiable. Let also $\{a_\tau\}$ be a sequence of positive real numbers that satisfies

$$\lim_{\tau \to \infty} a_\tau = 0 \tag{10.45}$$

and

$$\sum_{\tau=0}^{\infty} a_\tau = \infty, \tag{10.46}$$

and assume that the remaining conditions of Assumption 4.2 hold. Then the Euler method, which here takes the explicit form (10.44), for an iteration τ, converges to some imperfect market financial equilibrium pattern.

10.3.1 Numerical Examples

In this subsection we present numerical examples to illustrate the computational procedure via the Euler method that was described above. In particular, we applied this method to the projected dynamical system that was proposed in Section 10.1.

The Euler method was coded in FORTRAN and we used the IBM SP2 for all the numerical experiments. The Euler method was embedded with the modified asset and liability exact equilibration procedures to allow for closed form solution of the decomposed asset and liability subproblems. The price subproblems were also solved exactly and in closed form. The network structure of the subproblems is as depicted in Figure 9.3. The CPU times are reported (exclusive of the input/output time). In addition, we report the number of iterations. In all the examples we assumed that the utility functions were quadratic, that is, as given by (10.20). The sequence $\{a_\tau\}$ that was used for all the examples was: $\{a_\tau\}=\{1, \frac{1}{2}, \frac{1}{2}, \frac{1}{3}, \frac{1}{3}, \frac{1}{3}, \ldots\}$. The convergence tolerance ϵ was set to .001.

The examples are taken from Section 9.4.2. They all consist of two sectors and three financial instruments and are of increasing complexity. We initialized the Euler method exactly as we had initialized the modified projection method for each corresponding example in Section 9.4.2, to allow for comparisons.

Example 10.1 (see Example 9.1)

The data was identical to that of Example 9.1. This example had taxes but no other transaction costs and no price ceilings. The Euler method converged in only 12 iterations and required a negligible amount of CPU time for convergence.

Example 10.2 (see Example 9.2)

This example had data identical to that of Example 9.2. There were no taxes and no price ceilings, but the transaction costs were as reported therein.

The Euler method converged in 63 iterations and required .01 CPU seconds for convergence.

Example 10.3 (see Example 9.3)

This example was identical to Example 9.3 where recall that in that example there were taxes and transaction costs imposed, but no price ceilings.

The Euler method converged in 52 iterations and in a negligible amount of CPU time.

Example 10.4 (see Example 9.4)

This example was identical to example 9.4 in which there were taxes, transaction costs, as well as price ceilings.

The Euler method, as in the solution of Example 10.3, required 52 iterations for convergence and only a negligible amount of CPU time.

10.4 Sources and Notes

In this chapter we presented single country, multi-sector, multi-instrument, dynamic financial models, where the assumptions of a perfect market with no taxes, no fees, no transaction costs, and no policy interventions were relaxed.

The models presented here were based on the theory of projected dynamical systems. In addition, a connection between the static models discussed in Chapter 9 and the dynamic models of this chapter was established. Stability analysis results were established for an imperfect market dynamic financial adjustment process. Finally, the Euler method was proposed for the computation of the stationary point, along with conditions for convergence. For continuity, we then provided numerical results for the Euler method applied to several examples of increasing complexity, whic had also been solved earlier in Chapter 9 using the modified projection method.

The methodology that we utilized in this chapter is just one of several methodologies that have been used for the dynamic modeling of financial adjustment processes in the presence of market imperfections (mainly transaction costs or taxes). As one would expect, every approach is based on a series of different assumptions. Assumptions that have been made in the literature and which we did not make include: the existence of a risk-free asset, no price interventions, constant prices, etc. Consequently, most of the existing models are application-specific. Although a presentation of all methodologies that can handle financial dynamics and a detailed comparison among them would be insightful and interesting, it is beyond the scope of this book. Nevertheless, we refer the interested reader to the important contributions of Constantinides (1986), Duffie and Sun (1990), and Davis and Norman (1990) for additional reading.

Section 10.1

The general model presented in this section is based on the work by Dong (1996) but extends it to incorporate both transaction costs that are not taxes as well as price floors which need not be zero. The model discussed here also generalizes the model of Dong, Zhang, and Nagurney (1996) through the incorporation of market imperfections. For a more detailed analysis of related issues in the theory of projected dynamical systems, we refer the reader to the book by Nagurney and Zhang (1996).

Section 10.2

The stability results and proofs are due to Dong (1996), with minor adaptations.

Section 10.3

In this section we suggested the Euler method for the dynamic imperfect market financial adjustment process that was presented in Section 10.1.

This is the first time that the Euler method is suggested for the computation of a financial equilibrium in a single country, multi-instrument, multi-sector financial model that incorporate such market imperfections as policy interventions and transaction costs. Obviously, since this is the first time that the Euler method is applied to such a model all the numerical examples presented are new.

References

Constantinides, G. M., "Multiperiod Consumption and Investment Behavior with Convex Transaction Costs," *Management Science* **25** (1979) 1127-1137.

Constantinides, G. M., "Capital Market Equilibrium with Transaction Costs," *Journal of Political Economy* **94** (1986) 842-862.

Davis, M. H. A., and Norman, A., "Portfolio Selection with Transaction Costs," *Mathematics of Operations Research* **15** (1990) 676-713.

Dong, J., "Dynamic Model and Stability Analysis of General Financial Equilibrium with Policy Interventions," presented at the Second International Conference on Computing in Economics and Finance, Geneva, Switzerland, June 1996.

Dong, J., Zhang, D., and Nagurney, A., "A Projected Dynamical Systems Model of General Financial Equilibrium with Stability Analysis," *Mathematical and Computer Modelling* **24** (1996) 35-44.

Duffie, D., and Sun, T., "Transaction Costs and Portfolio Choice in a Discrete-Continuous-Time Setting," *Journal of Economic Dynamics and Control* **14** (1990) 35-51.

Dumas, B., and Luciano, E., "An Exact Solution to a Dynamic Portfolio Choice Problem under Transaction Costs," *The Journal of Finance* **46** (1991) 577-595.

Dupuis, P., and Nagurney, A., "Dynamical Systems and Variational Inequalities," *Annals of Operations Research* **44** (1993) 9-42.

Magill, M. J. P., and Constantinides, G. M., "Portfolio Selection with Transaction Costs," *Journal of Economic Theory* **13** (1976) 245-263.

Merton, R. C., "Lifetime Portfolio Selection Under Uncertainty: The Continuous-Time Case," *Review of Economic Statistics* **51** (1969) 247-257.

Merton, R. C., "Optimum Consumption and Portfolio Rules in a Continuous-Time Case," *Journal of Economic Theory* **3** (1971) 373-413.

Merton, R. C., "An Intertemporal Capital Asset Pricing Model," *Econometrica* **41** (1973) 867-887.

Nagurney, A., and Dong, J., "General Financial Equilibrium Modeling with Policy Interventions and Transaction Costs," *Computational Economics* **9** (1996) 3-17.

Nagurney, A., and Zhang, D., **Projected Dynamical Systems and Variational Inequalities with Applications**, Kluwer Academic Publishers, Boston, Massachusetts, 1996.

Shreve, S. E., and Soner H. M., "Optimal Investment and Consumption with Transaction Costs," *The Annals of Applied Probability* **4** (1994) 609-692.

Part IV International Models

11 International Financial Models

In Part III of this book we explicitly focused on the risk and return of domestically diversified portfolios. With this chapter we begin our discussion of international multi-sector, multi-instrument financial models. Although the same concepts and ideas hold true when we move to the international arena, some important differences are now brought to the fore.

In particular, international investors must now be concerned with the exchange rate risk, which stems from the fact that the exchange prices between currencies change through time, in addition to the risk that they wish to minimize in a single country setting. Moreover, investors from different countries make decisions based on their own nations' different financial environments, and, therefore, they all hold distinct preferences and expectations.

The recent advances in technology, along with the liberalization of international trade and the establishment of international agreements and treaties, have led many investors to diversify their portfolios internationally. Since the late eighties, it has become clear that investing internationally is becoming increasingly common (see, e. g., Sesit (1989)), and new international financial markets have been established that offer a greater variety of new financial products. It is a common belief that the number of investors, as well as, the volume of capital that is involved in international transactions will increase significantly in the future.

Such developments can be significantly accelerated through international agreements, such as the Maastricht treaty (see, e. g., Silva and Sjögren (1990) and Rosenthal and Cafrany (1993)), that suggest, for example, common currencies among countries. The Maastricht treaty, in particular, calls for a common European currency under the name *Euro* for the countries of the European union that fulfill some specific economic requirements. Such developments, however, are still at an experimental stage.

International investments, as discussed in Section 2.4, incorporate the advantage of far more opportunities as compared to solely domestic ones. Consequently, we can readily assume that investors will become less biased towards their home currency products, as new products become available and international transactions become more secure and standardized. We recall from Section 2.4, that until the end of the eighties, investors preferred to allocate their capital in domestic investments, mostly due to fear of the unknown environment of foreign investments (see French and Poterba (1991), Howell and Cozzini (1991)).

In this part of the book, each chapter contains static financial equilibrium models and gives a variational inequality formulation of the governing equilibrium conditions, as well as their dynamic counterparts, based on the methodology of projected dynamical systems. Part III, which was more of a pedagogical nature than this part, established the foundation which makes this synthesis and condensation possible.

In this chapter, hence, we begin the extension of the financial models presented thus far in this book to an international setting. This chapter focuses on international perfect market models, both static and dynamic, whereas Chapter 12 then shows how hedging can be incorporated into the basic models described in this chapter. Finally, Chapter 13, which concludes this part of this book, develops imperfect market models, both static and dynamic.

More precisely, here we present models of international financial equilibrium, with multiple sectors in various countries and with different instruments in multiple currencies. The models under consideration here yield the optimal composition of assets and liabilities in the portfolio of every sector of each country, as well as, the prices of the instruments in each currency, along with the exchange rate prices for each currency in terms of a basic currency. In addition, we provide the financial adjustment process.

We also identify the underlying network structure of the international financial models. Finally, computational techniques are given.

The models presented in this chapter assume a perfect economic environment with no fees, no transaction costs, and no taxes. We also assume that investors compete in a perfectly competitive environment, as was described in the single country models. Obviously, one can argue that this assumption is highly unrealistic in an international setting, which is something that we are in full agreement with and acknowledge. The models in this chapter, however, form the basis upon which the models of subsequent chapters of Part IV are built. Moreover, in the subsequent models we relax most of these assumptions.

We also assume that instrument prices follow the supply/demand rule, in that if the price of a financial instrument is positive, then the market must clear for that instrument, and if the price is zero, then there may be an excess supply of that instrument in the economy or the market clears. Similarly, since currencies are financial assets, and an exchange rate is simply the relative price of two financial assets (one country's asset in terms of another's), currency prices are determined in the same manner as the prices of assets such as stocks, bonds, and gold. According to this view, known as the asset market model of exchange rate determination; for details, see Lacey and Chambers (1993) and Shapiro (1992), the exchange rate between two currencies represents the price that just balances the relative supplies and demands for assets denominated in those currencies.

This chapter is organized as follows. In Section 11.1 we present static international financial models and in Section 11.2 we then use finite-dimensional variational inequality theory to present some qualitative properties, including some comparative static results. Section 11.3 presents the international financial adjustment process and Section 11.4 provides the stability analysis results for the process. Section 11.5 gives conditions under which the international financial equilibrium pattern can be obtained as the solution to a network optimization problem. Section 11.6 follows with algorithmic procedures and numerical examples.

11.1 Static International Financial Models

In this section we present static international financial models operating in a perfectly competitive environment. The dynamic counterparts are given in Section 11.3. These may be viewed, respectively, as extensions of the single country models studied in Chapter 6 and in Chapter 8 (the dynamic model in Section 8.1.1).

We consider an economy consisting of L countries, with a typical country denoted by l. Each country, in turn, has J sectors, with a typical sector denoted by j. We also consider K currencies, with a typical currency denoted by k. In each currency there are I instruments, with a typical instrument denoted by i.

We denote the volume of instrument i in currency k, held as an asset by sector j of country l, by X_{ik}^{jl}, and we group the assets of sector j in country l into the IK-dimensional column vector X^{jl}. Similarly, Y_{ik}^{jl} denotes the volume of instrument k in currency i, held as a liability by sector j of country l. The liabilities of sector j in country l are grouped into an IK-dimensional column vector Y^{jl}. Finally, we group the assets of all sectors of all countries into the column vector $X \in R_+^{JLIK}$ and the liabilities of all sectors of all countries into the column vector $Y \in R_+^{JLIK}$.

Let r_{ik} represent the price of instrument i in currency k and group the instrument prices into the column vector $r \in R_+^{IK}$. Let e_k denote the rate of appreciation of currency k against the basic currency, which can be interpreted as the rate of return earned due to exchange rate fluctuations. These rates are grouped into the column vector $e \in R_+^K$.

Throughout this chapter, we assume that all sectors, independent of country, share the objective of maximizing their specific utility functions, which we assume to be concave, continuous, and twice continuously differentiable. Obviously, every sector j from every country l has a particular utility function, since they do not hold the same levels of risk aversion, expectations, or interests.

If we now denote the utility function of sector j from country l by $U^{jl}(X^{jl}, Y^{jl}, r, e)$, and assume that the accounts of every sector of each country must balance, then the portfolio optimization problem of sector j in country l can be expressed as:

$$\text{Maximize } U^{jl}(X^{jl}, Y^{jl}, r, e) \tag{11.1}$$

subject to:

$$\sum_{i=1}^{I} \sum_{k=1}^{K} X_{ik}^{jl} = S^{jl} \tag{11.2a}$$

$$\sum_{i=1}^{I} \sum_{k=1}^{K} Y_{ik}^{jl} = S^{jl} \tag{11.2b}$$

$$X_{ik}^{jl}, Y_{ik}^{jl} \geq 0, \quad i = 1, \ldots, I; \quad k = 1, \ldots, K, \tag{11.3}$$

where S^{jl} denotes the total volume of capital held by sector j of country l.

Clearly, as was demonstrated in Section 2.4, the rate of return of instrument i in currency k, denoted by R_{ik}, is a function of the rate of return of instrument i in currency k, and of the price fluctuation of currency k. In particular, R_{ik} is given by

$$R_{ik} = (1 + r_{ik}) \times (1 + e_k) - 1, \tag{11.4}$$

or, equivalently,

$$R_{ik} = r_{ik} + e_k + r_{ik} \times e_k, \tag{11.5}$$

where the product $r_{ik} \times e_k$ is considered to be of small magnitude in the case of efficient markets. Hence, (11.5) can be approximated (see Section 2.4) by

$$R_{ik} \simeq r_{ik} + e_k. \tag{11.6}$$

In other words, the rate of return of an instrument i in currency k is equal to the sum of the return of this instrument in terms of the local currency plus the appreciation of the local currency in terms of a basic one (cf. Eun and Resnick (1988) and Rustem (1994)).

For example, under the assumption that every sector j from country l tries to maximize the value of his asset holdings, as well as to minimize the value of his liabilities, then a special case of utility function U^{jl} can be given by:

$$u^{jl}(X^{jl}, Y^{jl}) + \sum_{i=1}^{I} \sum_{k=1}^{K} \left(X_{ik}^{jl} - Y_{ik}^{jl} \right) (R_{ik}) \tag{11.7a}$$

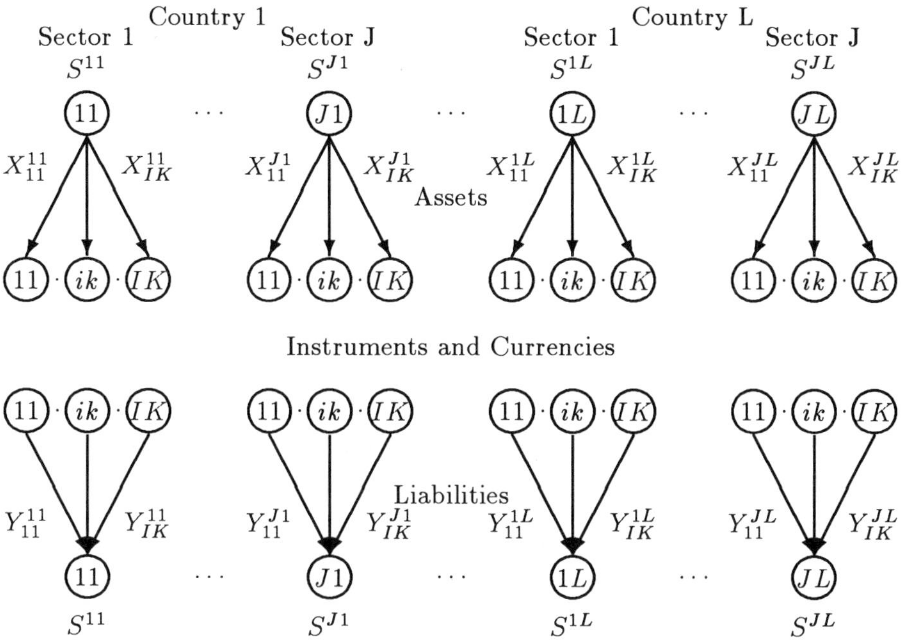

Fig. 11.1. Network structure of the sectors' optimization problems

or, equivalently, as:

$$u^{jl}(X^{jl}, Y^{jl}) + \sum_{i=1}^{I} \sum_{k=1}^{K} \left(X_{ik}^{jl} - Y_{ik}^{jl} \right) (r_{ik} + e_k), \qquad (11.7b)$$

where the term, $u^{jl}(X^{jl}, Y^{jl})$ in (11.7b), reflects the risk associated with a portfolio choice, and the second term in (11.7b) reflects the total return of the portfolio. Vectors r and e are exogenous vectors in the optimization problem of a sector j of a country l and are assumed to be given.

Note that (11.7b) is an extension of the utility function (6.4) for the single country case in which no currency exchange rates were present.

In Figure 11.1, we depict the network structure of the individual sectors' optimization problems. The structure of the network originally (out of equilibrium) is such that the network subproblems in assets and in liabilities are disjoint for each sector in each country. In this chapter, we will later prove that, in equilibrium, the network subproblems unite, to form a synthesized and connected network that also captures market clearance for both instruments and currencies, where all the prices for both instruments and currencies are positive. One can easily observe that Figure 11.1 is a natural extension of Figure 6.1 to an international, multi-currency setting.

The Feasible Set

For each sector $j; j = 1, \ldots, J$, in country l, we let

$$\tilde{X}^{jl} = \{X^{jl} \in R_+^{IK} : \sum_{i=1}^{I} \sum_{k=1}^{K} X_{ik}^{jl} = S^{jl}\} \tag{11.8}$$

denote the constraint set of his assets, and, similarly, we let

$$\tilde{Y}^{jl} = \{Y^{jl} \in R_+^{IK} : \sum_{i=1}^{I} \sum_{k=1}^{K} Y_{ik}^{jl} = S^{jl}\} \tag{11.9}$$

denote the constraint set for his liabilities. Then the feasible set for the assets and the liabilities of each sector j of country l is a Cartesian product denoted by κ^{jl}, where $\kappa^{jl} \equiv \{\tilde{X}^{jl} \times \tilde{Y}^{jl}\}$.

We also define the feasible set for the assets of all sectors from all countries as:

$$\tilde{X} \equiv \tilde{X}^{11} \times \ldots \times \tilde{X}^{jl} \times \ldots \times \tilde{X}^{JL}$$

and, similarly, for the liabilities:

$$\tilde{Y} \equiv \tilde{Y}^{11} \times \ldots \times \tilde{Y}^{jl} \times \ldots \times \tilde{Y}^{JL}.$$

Let κ be the feasible set for all the asset and liability holdings of all the sectors, where $\kappa \equiv \tilde{X} \times \tilde{Y}$.

The Equilibrium Conditions

We now describe the equilibrium conditions that characterize the optimization problem that each sector from every country faces, as well as, the economic conditions that characterize each of the instruments and currencies in the economy under consideration.

Portfolio Optimality

Under the assumption that the utility function for each sector of each country is concave with respect to the instrument variables, continuous, and continuously differentiable, the necessary and sufficient conditions for an optimal portfolio for a sector j of country l, where, $(X^{jl^*}, Y^{jl^*}) \in \kappa^{jl}$, is that it satisfies the following inequality:

$$-\left[\nabla_{X^{jl}} U^{jl}(X^{jl^*}, Y^{jl^*}, r^*, e^*)^T\right] \cdot \left[X^{jl} - X^{jl^*}\right]$$

$$-\left[\nabla_{Y^{jl}} U^{jl}(X^{jl^*}, Y^{jl^*}, r^*, e^*)^T\right] \cdot \left[Y^{jl} - Y^{jl^*}\right] \geq 0, \quad \forall (X^{jl}, Y^{jl}) \in \kappa^{jl}. \tag{11.10}$$

Furthermore, the economic system conditions for the instrument and currency prices are as follows:

Instrument Market Equilibrium Conditions

For each instrument $i; i = 1, \ldots, I$, and currency $k; k = 1, \ldots, K$, we must have that

$$\sum_{j=1}^{J}\sum_{l=1}^{L}(X_{ik}^{jl^*} - Y_{ik}^{jl^*}) \begin{cases} = 0, & \text{if } r_{ik}^* > 0 \\ \geq 0, & \text{if } r_{ik}^* = 0. \end{cases} \tag{11.11}$$

The system of equalities and inequalities (11.11) states that if the price of a financial instrument is positive, then the market must clear for that instrument, and if the price is zero, then either there is an excess supply of that instrument in the economy or the market clears.

Currency Market Equilibrium Conditions

Also, for each currency $k; k = 1, \ldots, K$, we must have that

$$\sum_{j=1}^{J}\sum_{l=1}^{L}\sum_{i=1}^{I}(X_{ik}^{jl^*} - Y_{ik}^{jl^*}) \begin{cases} = 0, & \text{if } e_k^* > 0 \\ \geq 0, & \text{if } e_k^* = 0. \end{cases} \tag{11.12}$$

In other words, if the exchange price of a currency is positive, then the exchange market must clear for that currency; if the exchange price is zero, then either there is an excess supply of that currency in the economy or the market clears.

We now define the feasible set underlying the international financial equilibrium problem and then give the definition of an international financial equilibrium. Let $\mathcal{K} \equiv \{\kappa \times R_+^{IK} \times R_+^K\}$.

Definition 11.1 (A Perfect Market International Financial Equilibrium)

A vector $(X^*, Y^*, r^*, e^*) \in \mathcal{K}$ is an international financial equilibrium if and only if it satisfies the system of equalities and inequalities (11.10), (11.11), and (11.12), for all sectors $j; j = 1, \ldots, J$, all countries $l; l = 1, \ldots, L$, all instruments $i; i = 1, \ldots, I$, and all currencies $k; k = 1, \ldots, K$.

We now derive the variational inequality formulation of the governing equilibrium conditions.

Theorem 11.1 (Variational Inequality Formulation)

A vector of assets and liabilities of the sectors, and instrument prices, $(X^*, Y^*, r^*, e^*) \in \mathcal{K}$, is a perfect market international financial equilibrium if and only if it satisfies the variational inequality problem:

$$\sum_{j=1}^{J}\sum_{l=1}^{L}\left[-\nabla_{X^{jl}} U^{jl}(X^{jl^*}, Y^{jl^*}, r^*, e^*)^T\right] \cdot \left[X^{jl} - X^{jl^*}\right]$$

$$+\sum_{j=1}^{J}\sum_{l=1}^{L}\left[-\nabla_{Y^{jl}}U^{jl}(X^{jl^*},Y^{jl^*},r^*,e^*)^T\right]\cdot\left[Y^{jl}-Y^{jl^*}\right]$$

$$+\sum_{k=1}^{K}\sum_{i=1}^{I}\left[\sum_{j=1}^{J}\sum_{l=1}^{L}X_{ik}^{jl^*}-Y_{ik}^{jl^*}\right]\times\left[r_{ik}-r_{ik}^*\right]$$

$$+\sum_{k=1}^{K}\left[\sum_{i=1}^{I}\sum_{j=1}^{J}\sum_{l=1}^{L}\left(X_{ik}^{jl^*}-Y_{ik}^{jl^*}\right)\right]\times\left[e_k-e_k^*\right]\geq 0,\quad\forall(X,Y,r,e)\in\mathcal{K}, \tag{11.13a}$$

which, in the case of utility functions (11.7b), takes the form

$$\sum_{j=1}^{J}\sum_{l=1}^{L}\sum_{i=1}^{I}\sum_{k=1}^{K}\left[-\frac{\partial u^{jl}(X^{jl^*},Y^{jl^*})}{\partial X_{ik}^{jl}}-r_{ik}^*-e_k^*\right]\times\left[X_{ik}^{jl}-X_{ik}^{jl^*}\right]$$

$$+\sum_{j=1}^{J}\sum_{l=1}^{L}\sum_{i=1}^{I}\sum_{k=1}^{K}\left[-\frac{\partial u^{jl}(X^{jl^*},Y^{jl^*})}{\partial Y_{ik}^{jl}}+r_{ik}^*+e_k^*\right]\times\left[Y_{ik}^{jl}-Y_{ik}^{jl^*}\right]$$

$$+\sum_{k=1}^{K}\sum_{i=1}^{I}\left[\sum_{j=1}^{J}\sum_{l=1}^{L}X_{ik}^{jl^*}-Y_{ik}^{jl^*}\right]\times\left[r_{ik}-r_{ik}^*\right]$$

$$+\sum_{k=1}^{K}\left[\sum_{i=1}^{I}\sum_{j=1}^{J}\sum_{l=1}^{L}\left(X_{ik}^{jl^*}-Y_{ik}^{jl^*}\right)\right]\times\left[e_k-e_k^*\right]\geq 0,\quad\forall(X,Y,r,e)\in\mathcal{K}. \tag{11.13b}$$

Proof: We will only present the proof for the case of variational inequality (11.13a), since the proof for variational inequality (11.13b), which is just a special case of (11.13a), follows immediately.

Assume that $(X^*,Y^*,r^*,e^*)\in\mathcal{K}$ is an equilibrium point of the international financial model, that is, it satisfies Definition 11.1. Then, inequalities (11.10)–(11.12) hold for all sectors j from every country l and for all instruments i and currencies k. If we now sum inequalities (11.10) over all sectors j and countries l, we obtain:

$$\sum_{j=1}^{J}\sum_{l=1}^{L}\left[-\nabla_{X^{jl}}U^{jl}(X^{jl^*},Y^{jl^*},r^*,e^*)^T\right]\cdot\left[X^{jl}-X^{jl^*}\right]$$

$$+\sum_{j=1}^{J}\sum_{l=1}^{L}\left[-\nabla_{Y^{jl}}U^{jl}(X^{jl^*},Y^{jl^*},r^*,e^*)^T\right]\times\left[Y^{jl}-Y^{jl^*}\right]\geq 0,\forall(X,Y)\in\kappa. \tag{11.14}$$

Also, since $(X^*, Y^*, r^*, e^*) \in \mathcal{K}$ is an equilibrium point, the system of equalities and inequalities (11.11), which represents the instrument equilibrium conditions holds, is equivalent to the following inequality, for a fixed instrument i and in currency k:

$$\sum_{j=1}^{J}\sum_{l=1}^{L}\left(X_{ik}^{jl^*} - Y_{ik}^{jl^*}\right) \times [r_{ik} - r_{ik}^*] \geq 0, \quad \forall r_{ik} \geq 0. \tag{11.15}$$

But (11.15) must hold for all instruments i and currencies k, and, therefore, the summation of (11.15) over all instruments and currencies, yields:

$$\sum_{k=1}^{K}\sum_{i=1}^{I}\left[\sum_{j=1}^{J}\sum_{l=1}^{L} X_{ik}^{jl^*} - Y_{ik}^{jl^*}\right] \times [r_{ik} - r_{ik}^*] \geq 0, \quad \forall r \in R_+^{IK}. \tag{11.16}$$

Similarly, since $(X^*, Y^*, r^*, e^*) \in \mathcal{K}$ is an equilibrium point, the system of equalities and inequalities (11.12), which holds for currency k, is equivalent to the following inequality being satisfied:

$$\sum_{i=1}^{I}\sum_{j=1}^{J}\sum_{l=1}^{L}\left(X_{ik}^{jl^*} - Y_{ik}^{jl^*}\right) \times [e_k - e_k^*] \geq 0, \quad \forall e_k \geq 0. \tag{11.17}$$

But (11.17) must hold for all currencies k, and, hence, the summation of (11.17) over all currencies, yields:

$$\sum_{k=1}^{K}\left[\sum_{i=1}^{I}\sum_{j=1}^{J}\sum_{l=1}^{L}\left(X_{ik}^{jl^*} - Y_{ik}^{jl^*}\right)\right] \times [e_k - e_k^*] \geq 0, \quad \forall e \in R_+^{K}. \tag{11.18}$$

Summing now inequalities (11.14), (11.16), and (11.18), we obtain the variational inequality (11.13a).

We will now prove that if $(X^*, Y^*, r^*, e^*) \in \mathcal{K}$ is a solution to variational inequality (11.13a), then it will also satisfy the equilibrium conditions (11.10)–(11.12).

In particular, if we let $(X^*, Y^*, r^*, e^*) \in \mathcal{K}$ be a solution to variational inequality (11.13a), and we let $X^{jl} = X^{jl^*}$, $Y^{jl} = Y^{jl^*}$, and $e_k = e_k^*$ for all sectors j, all countries l, and all currencies k, then substitution into variational inequality (11.13a) yields:

$$\sum_{k=1}^{K}\sum_{i=1}^{I}\left[\sum_{j=1}^{J}\sum_{l=1}^{L} X_{ik}^{jl^*} - Y_{ik}^{jl^*}\right] \times [r_{ik} - r_{ik}^*] \geq 0, \tag{11.19}$$

which implies the instrument economic conditions given by (11.11).

If we now let $X^{jl} = X^{jl^*}$, $Y^{jl} = Y^{jl^*}$ and $r_{ik} = r^*_{ik}$ for all sectors j, all countries l, all currencies k, and, finally, all instruments i, and substitute the resultants into inequality (11.13a), we obtain:

$$\sum_{k=1}^{K}\left[\sum_{i=1}^{I}\sum_{j=1}^{J}\sum_{l=1}^{L}\left(X_{ik}^{jl^*} - Y_{ik}^{jl^*}\right)\right] \times [e_k - e_k^*] \geq 0, \tag{11.20}$$

which implies the urrency equilibrium conditions (11.12).

Lastly, substitution of $r_{ik} = r^*_{ik}$ and $e_k = e^*_k$, for all instruments i and all currencies k, into (11.13a) yields:

$$\sum_{j=1}^{J}\sum_{l=1}^{L}\left[-\nabla_{X^{jl}}U^{jl}(X^{jl^*}, Y^{jl^*}, r^*, e^*)^T\right] \times \left[X^{jl} - X^{jl^*}\right]$$

$$+\sum_{j=1}^{J}\sum_{l=1}^{L}\left[-\nabla_{Y^{jl}}U^{jl}(X^{jl^*}, Y^{jl^*}, r^*, e^*)^T\right] \times \left[Y^{jl} - Y^{jl^*}\right], \tag{11.21}$$

which implies the optimality conditions (11.10). □

For simplicity, and for the sake of compactness, we introduce the following notation: Let $n = 2JLIK + IK + K$, and recall that $\mathcal{K} = \tilde{X} \times \tilde{Y} \times R_+^{IK} \times R_+^I$. Define now the n-dimensional column vector $x \equiv (X, Y, r, e) \in \mathcal{K}$, and the n-dimensional column vector $F(x)$:

$$F(x) = \begin{bmatrix} F_1(x) \\ \vdots \\ F_b(x) \\ \vdots \\ F_n(x) \end{bmatrix}, \tag{11.22}$$

according to:

$$\begin{bmatrix} -\nabla_X U(X, Y, r, e) \\ -\nabla_Y U(X, Y, r, e) \\ \sum_{j=1}^{J}\sum_{l=1}^{L}\left(X_{11}^{jl} - Y_{11}^{jl}\right) \\ \vdots \\ \sum_{j=1}^{J}\sum_{l=1}^{L}\left(X_{IK}^{jl} - Y_{IK}^{jl}\right) \\ \sum_{i=1}^{I}\sum_{j=1}^{J}\sum_{l=1}^{L}\left(X_{i1}^{jl} - Y_{i1}^{jl}\right) \\ \vdots \\ \sum_{i=1}^{I}\sum_{j=1}^{J}\sum_{l=1}^{L}\left(X_{iK}^{jl} - Y_{iK}^{jl}\right) \end{bmatrix}_{n\times 1}. \tag{11.23}$$

Hence, variational inequality (11.13a) can be written in standard form as: Determine $x^* \in \mathcal{K}$ satisfying:

$$\langle F(x^*)^T, x - x^* \rangle \geq 0, \quad \forall x \in \mathcal{K}. \tag{11.24}$$

11.1.1 Quadratic Utility Functions

In this subsection we present an important special case of the utility function U^{jl} for sector j of country l. In particular, we consider the case of a quadratic utility function of the following form:

$$U^{jl}(X^{jl}, Y^{jl}, r, e) = -\begin{pmatrix} X^{jl} \\ Y^{jl} \end{pmatrix}^T Q^{jl} \begin{pmatrix} X^{jl} \\ Y^{jl} \end{pmatrix}$$

$$+\sum_{i=1}^{I}\sum_{k=1}^{K} r_{ik}(X_{ik}^{jl} - Y_{ik}^{jl}) + \sum_{k=1}^{K} e_k \sum_{i=1}^{I}(X_{ik}^{jl} - Y_{ik}^{jl}), \tag{11.25}$$

where Q^{jl} is the symmetric $2IK \times 2IK$ variance-covariance matrix, which is assumed to be symmetric and positive definite, and, as a result, the objective function of each sector's portfolio optimization problem, given by (11.25), is strictly convex.

We now partition the symmetric matrix Q^{jl} as

$$Q^{jl} = \begin{pmatrix} Q_{11}^{jl} & Q_{12}^{jl} \\ Q_{21}^{jl} & Q_{22}^{jl} \end{pmatrix}.$$

Matrices Q_{11}^{jl} and Q_{22}^{jl} are the $IK \times IK$ variance-covariance matrices for only the assets, and only the liabilities, respectively. Submatrices Q_{12}^{jl} and Q_{21}^{jl}, in turn, are identical since Q^{jl} is assumed to be symmetric. These submatrices represent the variance-covariance matrices between the assets and liabilities of sector j from country l for all instruments and currencies.

Therefore, the portfolio optimization problem that sector j from country l faces can be expressed as:

$$\text{Maximize} \quad -\begin{pmatrix} X^{jl} \\ Y^{jl} \end{pmatrix}^T Q^{jl} \begin{pmatrix} X^{jl} \\ Y^{jl} \end{pmatrix}$$

$$+\sum_{i=1}^{I}\sum_{k=1}^{K} r_{ik}(X_{ik}^{jl} - Y_{ik}^{jl}) + \sum_{k=1}^{K} e_k \sum_{i=1}^{I}(X_{ik}^{jl} - Y_{ik}^{jl}) \tag{11.26}$$

subject to:

$$\sum_{i=1}^{I}\sum_{k=1}^{K} X_{ik}^{jl} = S^{jl} \tag{11.27a}$$

$$\sum_{i=1}^{I}\sum_{k=1}^{K} Y_{ik}^{jl} = S^{jl} \tag{11.27b}$$

$$X_{ik}^{jl},\ Y_{ik}^{jl} \geq 0, \quad i=1,\ldots,I,\ k=1,\ldots,K. \tag{11.28}$$

We let z_{ik} denote the z_{ik}-th row of matrix $Q_{\alpha\beta}^{jl}$, where z_{ik} is the pointer defined as $z_{ik}=(k-1)I+i$. Then we can write the variational inequality formulation of the governing international financial equilibrium conditions in the case of quadratic utility functions of the form above immediately as follows:

Corollary 11.1 (Variational Inequality Formulation for the Quadratic Model)

A vector of assets and liabilities of the sectors of the countries, and currency instrument and exchange rate prices, $(X^*,Y^*,r^*,e^*)\in\mathcal{K}$, is an international financial equilibrium in the case of sector portfolio optimization problems given by (11.26)–(11.28) if and only if it satisfies the variational inequality problem:

$$\sum_{j=1}^{J}\sum_{l=1}^{L}\sum_{i=1}^{I}\sum_{k=1}^{K}\left[2\left[\left(Q_{11}^{jl}\right)_{z_{ik}}X^{jl^*}+\left(Q_{12}^{jl}\right)_{z_{ik}}Y^{jl^*}\right]-r_{ik}^*-e_k^*\right]$$
$$\times\left[X_{ik}^{jl}-X_{ik}^{jl^*}\right]$$
$$+\sum_{j=1}^{J}\sum_{l=1}^{L}\sum_{i=1}^{I}\sum_{k=1}^{K}\left[2\left[\left(Q_{22}^{jl}\right)_{z_{ik}}Y^{jl^*}+\left(Q_{21}^{jl}\right)_{z_{ik}}X^{jl^*}\right]+r_{ik}^*+e_k^*\right]$$
$$\times\left[Y_{ik}^{jl}-Y_{ik}^{jl^*}\right]$$
$$+\sum_{i=1}^{I}\sum_{k=1}^{K}\left[\sum_{j=1}^{J}\sum_{l=1}^{L}\left(X_{ik}^{jl^*}-Y_{ik}^{jl^*}\right)\right]\times\left[r_{ik}-r_{ik}^*\right]$$
$$+\sum_{k=1}^{K}\left[\sum_{i=1}^{I}\sum_{j=1}^{J}\sum_{l=1}^{L}\left(X_{ik}^{jl^*}-Y_{ik}^{jl^*}\right)\right]\times\left[e_k-e_k^*\right]\geq 0,\quad \forall (X,Y,r,e)\in\mathcal{K}. \tag{11.29}$$

In the special case where there is only a single country and a single currency, that is, $l=1$ and $k=1$, with the pointer $z_{ik}=i$, then the above variational inequality collapses to variational inequality (6.29) governing the single country financial equilibrium model that was presented in Chapter 6.

11.2 Qualitative Properties

In this section we present certain qualitative results for the equilibrium pattern of the static models discussed in Section 11.1. In particular, we will provide conditions under which existence of a solution is guaranteed. Also, we will give conditions for uniqueness of the asset and liability pattern. Finally, we will give conditions under which the function that enters the variational inequality problem (cf. (11.23)) is monotone and Lipschitz continuous.

Since the proof of the subsequent theorem is a simple adaptation of the uniquenes result in Theorem 6.3, it is left out.

Theorem 11.2 (Uniqueness)

Under the assumption that the utility functions $U^{jl}(X^{jl}, Y^{jl}, r, e)$ are strictly concave in the instrument variables for each sector j of every country l the equilibrium pattern of assets and liabilities, $(X^*, Y^*) \in \kappa$, is unique.

The following theorem, as well as, the two propositions that follow are presented without proof since they are adaptations of the proofs, respectively, of Theorems 6.2, 6.4, and 6.5.

Theorem 11.3 (Existence)

Assume that the utility function for each section is as given by (11.7b). If $(X^*, Y^*, r^*, e^*) \in \mathcal{K}$ is an equilibrium pattern and, therefore, a solution to variational inequality (11.13b), then (X^*, Y^*) is a solution of the variational inequality:

$$\sum_{k=1}^{K}\sum_{i=1}^{I}\sum_{j=1}^{J}\sum_{l=1}^{L}\left[-\frac{\partial u^{jl}(X^{jl^*}, Y^{jl^*})}{\partial X_{ik}^{jl}} - r_{ik}^* - e_k^*\right] \times \left[X_{ik}^{jl} - X_{ik}^{jl^*}\right]$$

$$\sum_{k=1}^{K}\sum_{i=1}^{I}\sum_{j=1}^{J}\sum_{l=1}^{L}\left[-\frac{\partial u^{jl}(X^{jl^*}, Y^{jl^*})}{\partial Y_{ik}^{jl}} + r_{ik}^* + e_k^*\right] \times \left[Y_{ik}^{jl} - Y_{ik}^{jl^*}\right] \geq 0,$$

$$\forall (X, Y) \in S, \tag{11.30}$$

where S is a non-empty set such that:

$$S \equiv \{(X, Y) : (X, Y) \in \kappa;\ \rho_{ik} \geq 0, \forall i, k;\ \epsilon_k \geq 0, \forall k\},$$

with

$$\rho_{ik} \equiv \sum_{j=1}^{J}\sum_{l=1}^{L}(X_{ik}^{jl} - Y_{ik}^{jl})$$

$$\epsilon_k \equiv \sum_{j=1}^{J}\sum_{l=1}^{L}\sum_{i=1}^{I}(X_{ik}^{jl} - Y_{ik}^{jl}).$$

Conversely, if (X, Y) is a solution of variational inequality (11.30), then there exists an $e^* \in R_+^K$ and an $r^* \in R_+^{IK}$ such that (X^*, Y^*, r^*, e^*) is a solution to variational inequality (11.13b) and, thus, (X^*, Y^*, r^*, e^*) is an equilibrium pattern.

Proposition 11.1

Under the assumption that the utility functions are strictly concave and twice continuously differentiable, $F(x)$ defined in (11.23) is monotone, that is,

$$\langle (F(x^1) - F(x^2))^T, x^1 - x^2 \rangle \geq 0, \ \ \forall x^1, x^2 \in \mathcal{K}.$$

Proposition 11.2

Assume that the utility function U^{jl} has bounded second order derivatives for all sectors j and countries l and for all $x \in \mathcal{K}$. Then the function $F(x)$ that enters variational inequality (11.13a) (or (11.13b)) is Lipschitz continuous, that is,

$$\|F(x^1) - F(x^2)\| \leq \mathcal{L}\|x^1 - x^2\|, \quad \forall x^1, x^2 \in \mathcal{K},$$

with Lipschitz constant $\mathcal{L} > 0$.

11.2.1 Comparative Statics

We now present some simple comparative statics results using variational inequality theory which are then applied to the international financial model. The subsequent theory is a specialization of results contained in Theorems 3.7 and 3.8.

Theorem 11.4

Assume that $F(x)$ is monotone. Let $x^* \in \mathcal{K}$ be a solution to VI$(F, \mathcal{K})$, *that is,*

$$\langle F(x^*)^T, x - x^* \rangle \geq 0, \quad \forall x \in \mathcal{K}. \tag{11.31}$$

Consider now a specific perturbation in the data of the following form: a fixed change Δ_b associated with $F_b(\cdot)$ such that $F_b^{**}(\cdot) = F(\cdot) + \Delta_b$, with all other $F_i^{**}(\cdot) = F_i(\cdot)$ for $i \neq b$. Assume that the VI$(F^{**}, \mathcal{K})$ *has a solution x^{**}.*

Then

$$\text{if} \quad \Delta_b > 0 \Longrightarrow x_b^* \geq x_b^{**} \tag{11.32a}$$

$$\text{if} \quad \Delta_b < 0 \Longrightarrow x_b^* \leq x_b^{**}. \tag{11.32b}$$

Proof: We write:

$$\langle F(x^*)^T, x - x^* \rangle \geq 0, \quad \forall x \in \mathcal{K} \tag{11.33}$$

and

$$\langle F^{**}(x^{**})^T, x - x^{**} \rangle \geq 0, \quad \forall x \in \mathcal{K}. \tag{11.34}$$

Substituting x^{**} for x in (11.33) and x^* for x in (11.34), and adding the two resulting inequalities, we obtain

$$\langle (F(x^*) - F^{**}(x^{**}))^T, x^{**} - x^* \rangle \geq 0, \tag{11.35}$$

which can be expressed as

$$\Delta_b(x_b^* - x_b^{**}) \geq \langle (F(x^*) - F(x^{**}))^T, x^* - x^{**} \rangle. \tag{11.36}$$

But the right-hand side of (11.36) must be greater than or equal to zero due to the monotonicity assumption. Consequently, (11.32a) and (11.32b) must hold true. □

We now give an interpretation of Theorem 11.4 in the context of the international financial equilibrium model with variational inequality in standard form given by (11.24) with F as defined in (11.23).

In particular, recognizing that the first $2IK$ terms of $F(\cdot)$ in this model correspond to minus the marginal utility of a particular sector of a particular country with respect to the specific asset or liability of an instrument in a specific currency, we interpret Theorem 11.4 as follows: If we increase the marginal utility by a fixed amount, while keeping all other data fixed, then the volume of that instrument in that currency (held as an asset or as a liability) will not decrease; if we decrease it by a fixed amount, on the other hand, then that volume cannot increase. Note that Theorem 11.4 is also relevant to the single country models in Chapter 6, as well as the other models, with appropriate interpretations.

In the next theorem we consider a change that may come about due, for example, to a change in the feasible set $\mathcal{K}$ to $\mathcal{K}^*$, where $\mathcal{K}^*$ is still a closed and convex subset of R^n. For example, we may wish to investigate a change in the volumes of the sectors in the countries.

Theorem 11.5

Assume that $F(\cdot)$ is as defined in (11.23). Let x^* be the solution to VI$(F, \mathcal{K})$ *and let x^{**} be now the solution to* VI$(F, \mathcal{K}^*)$, *where $\mathcal{K}^*$ is of the form $\mathcal{K}^* \equiv \kappa^{1^*} \times \ldots \times \kappa^{J^*} \times R_+^{IK} \times R_+^{K}$. Then, we can conclude the following: For each instrument i and currency k:*

$$r_{ik}^{**} \geq r_{ik}^* \Longleftrightarrow \sum_{j=1}^{J}\sum_{l=1}^{L}\left[X_{ik}^{jl^*} - Y_{ik}^{jl^*}\right] \geq \sum_{j=1}^{J}\sum_{l=1}^{L}\left[X_{ik}^{jl^{**}} - Y_{ik}^{jl^{**}}\right] \tag{11.37a}$$

$$r_{ik}^{**} \leq r_{ik}^* \Longleftrightarrow \sum_{j=1}^{J}\sum_{l=1}^{L}\left[X_{ik}^{jl^*} - Y_{ik}^{jl^*}\right] \leq \sum_{j=1}^{J}\sum_{l=1}^{L}\left[X_{ik}^{jl^{**}} - Y_{ik}^{jl^{**}}\right] \tag{11.37b}$$

and for each currency k:

$$e_k^{**} \geq e_k^* \Longleftrightarrow \sum_{i=1}^{I}\sum_{j=1}^{J}\sum_{l=1}^{L}\left[X_{ik}^{jl^*} - Y_{ik}^{jl^*}\right] \geq \sum_{i=1}^{I}\sum_{j=1}^{J}\sum_{l=1}^{L}\left[X_{ik}^{jl^{**}} - Y_{ik}^{jl^{**}}\right] \tag{11.38a}$$

$$e_k^{*} \geq e_k^* \Longleftrightarrow \sum_{i=1}^{I}\sum_{j=1}^{J}\sum_{l=1}^{L}\left[X_{ik}^{jl^*} - Y_{ik}^{jl^*}\right] \leq \sum_{i=1}^{I}\sum_{j=1}^{J}\sum_{l=1}^{L}\left[X_{ik}^{jl^{**}} - Y_{ik}^{jl^{**}}\right]. \tag{11.38b}$$

Proof: By assumption, we have that

$$\langle F(x^*)^T, x - x^* \rangle \geq 0, \quad \forall x \in \mathcal{K}, \tag{11.39}$$

and

$$\langle F(x^{**})^T, x - x^{**} \rangle \geq 0, \quad \forall x^{**} \in \mathcal{K}^*. \tag{11.40}$$

We set $x_b = x_b^*$ for all components b of x, except for that component that corresponds to r_{ik}, which we set to r_{ik}^{**}, and substitute the vector x thus constructed into (11.39) (note that such an $x \in \mathcal{K}$). Similarly, we set $x_b = x_b^{**}$, for all components b of x except for that component that, again, corresponds to r_{ik}, which we now set to r_{ik}^*, and substitute such an x into (11.40) (note that such an $x \in \mathcal{K}^*$). Simplification of the two resulting inequalities yields, respectively,

$$\sum_{j=1}^{J} \sum_{l=1}^{L} \left[X_{ik}^{jl*} - Y_{ik}^{jl*} \right] \times [r_{ik}^{**} - r_{ik}^*] \geq 0 \tag{11.41}$$

and

$$\sum_{j=1}^{J} \sum_{l=1}^{L} \left[X_{ik}^{jl**} - Y_{ik}^{jl**} \right] \times [r_{ik}^* - r_{ik}^{**}] \geq 0. \tag{11.42}$$

Summing now (11.41) and (11.42), we obtain

$$\sum_{j=1}^{J} \sum_{l=1}^{L} \left[\left[X_{ik}^{jl*} - Y_{ik}^{jl*} \right] - \left[X_{ik}^{jl**} - Y_{ik}^{jl**} \right] \right] \times [r_{ik}^{**} - r_{ik}^*] \geq 0, \tag{11.43}$$

from which (11.37a) and (11.37b) follows.

Analogous substitutions, but for e_k, can be made to yield (11.38a) and (11.38b). □

Note that Theorem 11.5 says that if a price of an instrument in a currency increases, then the net supply of that instrument in that currency cannot decrease; if the price of an instrument in a currency decreases, then the net supply cannot increase. Analogously, if the net supply increases, then the price cannot increase, and so on. A similar interpretation holds for changes in the currency prices and the net supply of the currency.

11.3 International Financial Adjustment Process

In this section we present the dynamic international financial model formulated as a projected dynamical system. Here, we make immediate and direct use of Definition 4.3 and Theorem 4.1 to obtain the following projected dynamical system, whose set of stationary points coincides with the set of solutions to variational inequality (11.24) with $F(\cdot)$ defined by (11.23):

$$\dot{x} = \Pi_{\mathcal{K}}(x, -F(x)), \tag{11.44}$$

which, in view of Proposition 8.1 can be expressed as:

The International Financial Adjustment Process

The adjustment process of every sector's allocation of assets and liabilities and each financial instrument's price and each currency's price is given by:

$$\begin{cases} \dot{X}^{jl} &= \Pi_{\tilde{X}^{jl}}(X^{jl}, \nabla_{X^{jl}} U^{jl}); \quad j = 1, \cdots, J; l = 1, \ldots, L \\ \dot{Y}^{jl} &= \Pi_{\tilde{Y}^{jl}}(Y^{jl}, \nabla_{Y^{jl}} U^{jl}); \quad j = 1, \ldots, J; l = 1, \ldots, L \\ \dot{r}_{ik} &= \Pi_{R_+}(r_{ik}, -(\sum_{j=1}^{J} \sum_{l=1}^{L} (X_{ik}^{jl} - Y_{ik}^{jl}))); \; i = 1, \cdots, I; \\ & \qquad k = 1, \ldots, K \\ \dot{e}_k &= \Pi_{R_+}(e_k, -(\sum_{i=1}^{I} \sum_{j=1}^{J} \sum_{l=1}^{L} (X_{ik}^{jl} - Y_{ik}^{jl}))); \quad k = 1, \ldots, K. \end{cases} \tag{11.45}$$

Hence, if one obtains a stationary point to (11.44), then that point is an international financial equilibrium, that is, it satisfies Definition 11.1 and, equivalently, is a solution to the variational inequality problem (11.13a). Consequently, we now have a financial adjustment process that, under reasonable conditions on the utility functions of the sectors, yields well-defined trajectories. Moreover, the stationary point of the dynamical system is an international financial equilibrium. Therefore, optimality conditions (11.10) are satisfied, once a stationary point is reached, as well as the economic equilibrium conditions (11.11) and (11.12). The above financial adjustment process is meaningful economically and is representative of reasonable behavior on the part of both the sectors in the countries as well as the instrument and the currency prices.

Finally, according to Theorem 4.2, under the conditions imposed on the utility functions previously, the initial value problem is well-defined.

11.4 Stability Analysis

In this section we provide conditions under which a disequilibrium pattern of assets, liabilities, instrument and currency prices will reach an international financial equilibrium state under the adjustment process (11.44).

For consistency, and in order to simplify the study of the asymptotic behavior of the dynamic international financial model, we present the following definitions, which are adaptations of those found in Chapter 4.

Definition 11.2

The international financial adjustment process is stable if each financial equilibrium, $x^* = (X^*, Y^*, r^*, e^*)$, is a monotone attractor, that is, for any initial asset, liability, and instrument and currency price pattern,

(X_0, Y_0, r_0, e_0), the distance, $\|(X(t), Y(t), r(t), e(t)) - (X^*, Y^*, r^*, e^*)\|$, is nonincreasing in time t, where $(X(t), Y(t), r(t), e(t))$ satisfies the adjustment process (11.44).

In other words, if an international financial adjustment process is stable, then any state of disequilibrium will remain close to an equilibrium pattern forever.

Definition 11.3

The international financial adjustment process is asymptotically stable if it is stable and for any initial asset, liability, and price pattern, (X_0, Y_0, r_0, e_0), the financial adjustment process that starts with (X_0, Y_0, r_0, e_0) converges to some equilibrium pattern (X^*, Y^*, r^*, e^*); i. e.,

$$\lim_{t \to \infty} (X_0(t), Y_0(t), r_0(t), e_0(t)) \to (X^*, Y^*, r^*, e^*). \tag{11.46}$$

Asymptotic stability can then be interpreted as the case that any international financial disequilibrium will eventually approach equilibrium.

Theorem 11.6 (Stability of International Financial Adjustment Process)

If the utility function U^{jl} of each sector j from every country l is continuous, twice continuously differentiable, and concave in X^{jl} and Y^{jl}, and the utility function has the form given by (11.7b), that is,

$$U^{jl}(X^{jl}, Y^{jl}, r, e) = u^{jl}(X^{jl}, Y^{jl}) + \sum_{i=1}^{I} \sum_{k=1}^{K} (X_{ik}^{jl} - Y_{ik}^{jl})(r_{ik} + e_k),$$

then the international financial adjustment process is stable.

Proof: Let $x^* = (X^*, Y^*, r^*, e^*)$ be any financial equilibrium pattern and let $x_0(t) = (X_0(t), Y_0(t), r_0(t), e_0(t))$ be the financial pattern at time t when the international financial adjustment process was initialized at pattern $x_0 = (X_0, Y_0, r_0, e_0)$.

Moreover, we define $\Delta(x_0, x^*, t)$ as:

$$\Delta(x_0, x^*, t) \equiv \frac{1}{2} \|x_0(t) - x^*\|^2$$

and, as a result, it follows that

$$\dot{\Delta}(x_0, x^*, t) = \langle (x_0(t) - x^*)^T, \Pi_{\mathcal{K}}(x(t), -F(x(t))) \rangle. \tag{11.47}$$

Recalling from Chapter 4 that:

$$\Pi_{\mathcal{K}}(x(t), -F(x(t))) = -F(x_0(t)) + N(x_0(t)) N^*(x_0(t)),$$

where $N^*(x(t))$ is an inward normal to $\mathcal{K}$ at $x(t)$ and $N(x(t))$ is a nonnegative real number, we have an upper bound for (11.47) given by

$$\dot{\Delta}(x_0, x^*, t) \leq \langle (x_0(t) - x^*)^T, -F(x_0(t)) \rangle$$

$$= \sum_{j=1}^{J}\sum_{l=1}^{L}\sum_{i=1}^{I}\sum_{k=1}^{K}(X_0(t)_{ik}^{jl} - X_{ik}^{jl*}) \left[\frac{\partial u^{jl}(X_0(t)^{jl}, Y_0(t)^{jl})}{\partial X_{ik}^{jl}} - r_0(t)_{ik} - e_0(t)_k\right]$$

$$+\sum_{j=1}^{J}\sum_{l=1}^{L}\sum_{i=1}^{I}\sum_{k=1}^{K}(Y_0(t)_{ik}^{jl} - Y_{ik}^{jl*}) \left[\frac{\partial u^{jl}(X_0(t)^{jl}, Y_0(t)^{jl})}{\partial Y_{ik}^{jl}} + r_0(t)_{ik} + e_0(t)_k\right]$$

$$+\sum_{i=1}^{I}\sum_{k=1}^{K}(r_0(t)_{ik} - r_{ik}^*)\sum_{j=1}^{J}\sum_{l=1}^{L}\left(X_0(t)_{ik}^{jl} - Y_0(t)_{ik}^{jl}\right)$$

$$+\sum_{k=1}^{K}(e_0(t)_k - e_k^*)\sum_{j=1}^{J}\sum_{l=1}^{L}\sum_{i=1}^{I}\left(X_0(t)_{ik}^{jl} - Y_0(t)_{ik}^{jl}\right)$$

$$= \sum_{j=1}^{J}\sum_{l=1}^{L}(X_0(t)^{jl} - X^{jl^*}, Y_0(t)^{jl} - Y^{jl^*})^T \cdot \nabla^2 u^{jl}(X_0(t), Y_0(t))$$

$$\cdot(X_0(t)^{jl} - X^{jl^*}, Y_0(t)^{jl} - Y^{jl^*}). \tag{11.48}$$

But, since U^{jl} is concave with respect to X^{jl} and Y^{jl}, the right-hand side of (11.48) is nonpositive. This implies that $\| x_0(t) - x^* \|$ is monotone nonincreasing in time t, and, by definition, x^* is a monotone attractor. □

The following theorem is presented without proof since the Theorem is a straightforward extension of Theorem 8.8.

Theorem 11.7

If we assume that all sectors j in all countries l have a strictly concave utility function with respect to their assets and liabilities, then all financial equilibria are comprised of unique asset and liability patterns X^* and Y^*.

The following theorem examines the asymptotical stability of the international financial process under the assumption that each sector l of country l is strictly risk-averse. It is also presented without proof since the proof follows similar arguments as those that can be found in Theorem 8.9.

Theorem 11.8

If we assume that all sectors j in all countries l have a strictly concave utility function with respect to the asset and liability pattern, (X^{jl}, Y^{jl}), the utility functions are continuous and twice continuously differentiable, and of the form (11.46), then the international financial adjustment process is asymptotically stable.

Note that the above stability results hold for utility functions of the form (11.7).

11.5 Network Optimization Reformulation

In this section we prove that, under certain conditions on the utility functions of the sectors of the countries, the international financial equilibrium coincides with the solution to a network optimization problem. In particular, we assume that the utility functions are of the form (11.7b), equivalently, (11.7a).

Theorem 11.9

The variational inequality problem of finding $(X^*, Y^*, r^*, e^*) \in \mathcal{K}$ satisfying:

$$\sum_{j=1}^{J}\sum_{l=1}^{L}\sum_{i=1}^{I}\sum_{k=1}^{K}\left[-\frac{\partial u^{jl}(X^{jl^*}, Y^{jl^*})}{\partial X_{ik}^{jl}} - r_{ik}^* - e_k^*\right] \times \left[X_{ik}^{jl} - X_{ik}^{jl^*}\right]$$

$$+\sum_{j=1}^{J}\sum_{l=1}^{L}\sum_{i=1}^{I}\sum_{k=1}^{K}\left[-\frac{\partial u^{jl}(X^{jl^*}, Y^{jl^*})}{\partial Y_{ik}^{jl}} + r_{ik}^* + e_k^*\right] \times \left[Y_{ik}^{jl} - Y_{ik}^{jl^*}\right]$$

$$+\sum_{i=1}^{I}\sum_{k=1}^{K}\left[\sum_{j=1}^{J}\sum_{l=1}^{L}\left(X_{ik}^{jl^*} - Y_{ik}^{jl^*}\right)\right] \times \left[r_{ik} - r_{ik}^*\right]$$

$$+\sum_{k=1}^{K}\left[\sum_{j=1}^{J}\sum_{l=1}^{L}\sum_{i=1}^{I}\left(X_{ik}^{jl^*} - Y_{ik}^{jl^*}\right)\right] \times \left[e_k - e_k^*\right] \geq 0, \quad \forall (X, Y, r, e) \in \mathcal{K}, \tag{11.49}$$

is equivalent to the problem:

$$\text{Maximize} \sum_{j=1}^{J}\sum_{l=1}^{L} u^{jl}(X^{jl}, Y^{jl}) \tag{11.50}$$

subject to:

$$\sum_{j=1}^{J}\sum_{l=1}^{L}(X_{ik}^{jl} - Y_{ik}^{jl}) \geq 0, \quad i = 1, \ldots, I; \quad k = 1, \ldots, K \tag{11.51}$$

$$\sum_{j=1}^{J}\sum_{l=1}^{L}\sum_{i=1}^{I}(X_{ik}^{jl} - Y_{ik}^{jl}) \geq 0, \quad k = 1, \ldots, K \tag{11.52}$$

and

$$(X^{jl}, Y^{jl}) \in \kappa^{jl}, \quad j = 1, \ldots, J; \quad l = 1, \ldots, L, \tag{11.53}$$

where $r_{ik}^* \geq 0$ corresponds to the Lagrange multiplier associated with the ik-th constraint in (11.51), and $e_k^* \geq 0$ corresponds to the Lagrange multiplier associated with the k-th constraint in (11.52).

Proof: Since the utility function u^{jl} are assumed to be concave for each sector j and country l, and the feasible sets are closed and convex then it follows from the standard theory of variational inequalities (cf. Bertsekas and Tsitsiklis (1989)) that the solution to the optimization problem (11.50)–(11.53) coincides with the solution to the variational inequality problem given by (11.49). □

Lemma 11.1

In equilibrium, the markets clear for all instruments and all currencies, that is,

$$\sum_{j=1}^{J}\sum_{l=1}^{L}(X_{ik}^{jl^*} - Y_{ik}^{jl^*}) = 0, \quad i = 1, \ldots, I; \quad k = 1, \ldots, K \tag{11.54}$$

and

$$\sum_{j=1}^{J}\sum_{l=1}^{L}\sum_{i=1}^{I}(X_{ik}^{jl^*} - Y_{ik}^{jl^*}) = 0, \quad k = 1, \ldots, K, \tag{11.55}$$

that is, (11.51) and (11.52) hold as strict equalities. Furthermore, the prices, r_{ik}^* and e_k^* for all instruments i and currencies k are strictly positive.

Proof: Assume, instead, that for a particular instrument i and currency k, we have that

$$\sum_{j=1}^{J}\sum_{l=1}^{L}(X_{ik}^{jl^*} - Y_{ik}^{jl^*}) > 0. \tag{11.56}$$

Then, it follows that

$$\sum_{j=1}^{J}\sum_{l=1}^{L}\sum_{i=1}^{I}\sum_{k=1}^{K}(X_{ik}^{jl^*} - Y_{ik}^{jl^*}) > 0. \tag{11.57}$$

But, feasibility conditions (11.2a) and (11.2b) imply that:

$$\sum_{j=1}^{J}\sum_{l=1}^{L}\sum_{i=1}^{I}\sum_{k=1}^{K}(X_{ik}^{jl^*} - Y_{ik}^{jl^*}) = 0, \tag{11.58}$$

which is in contradiction to (11.57). Hence,

$$\sum_{j=1}^{J}\sum_{l=1}^{L}(X_{ik}^{jl^*} - Y_{ik}^{jl^*}) = 0, \tag{11.59}$$

and this holds for all instruments i and currencies k. It follows then directly that:

$$\sum_{j=1}^{J}\sum_{l=1}^{L}\sum_{i=1}^{I}(X_{ik}^{jl^*} - Y_{ik}^{jl^*}) = 0, \quad k = 1, \ldots, K. \tag{11.60}$$

Furthermore, from Lagrange multiplier theory, the Lagrange multipliers r^*_{ik} and e^*_k must be positive. □

We will now demonstrate the underlying network structure, by substituting (11.6) into (11.13b) to obtain

$$\sum_{j=1}^{J}\sum_{l=1}^{L}\sum_{i=1}^{I}\sum_{k=1}^{K}\left[-\frac{\partial u^{jl}(X^{jl^*},Y^{jl^*})}{\partial X^{jl}_{ik}} - R^*_{ik}\right] \times \left[X^{jl}_{ik} - X^{jl^*}_{ik}\right]$$
$$+\sum_{j=1}^{J}\sum_{l=1}^{L}\sum_{i=1}^{I}\sum_{k=1}^{K}\left[-\frac{\partial u^{jl}(X^{jl^*},Y^{jl^*})}{\partial Y^{jl}_{ik}} + R^*_{ik}\right] \times \left[Y^{jl}_{ik} - Y^{jl^*}_{ik}\right]$$
$$+\sum_{i=1}^{I}\sum_{k=1}^{K}\sum_{j=1}^{J}\sum_{l=1}^{L}\left[X^{jl^*}_{ik} - Y^{jl^*}_{ik}\right] \times \left[R_{ik} - R^*_{ik}\right] \geq 0,$$
$$\forall (X^*,Y^*,R^*) \in (\tilde{X} \times \tilde{Y} \times R^{IK}_+). \tag{11.61}$$

The following corollary is immediate from Theorem 11.9.

Corollary 11.2

The solution to the optimization problem:

$$\textit{Maximize} \sum_{j=1}^{J}\sum_{l=1}^{L} u^{jl}(X^{jl},Y^{jl}) \tag{11.62}$$

subject to:

$$\sum_{j=1}^{J}\sum_{l=1}^{L}(X^{jl}_{ik} - Y^{jl}_{ik}) \geq 0;\ (X,Y) \in \kappa;\ i = 1,\ldots,I;\ k = 1,\ldots,K, \tag{11.63}$$

with Lagrange multiplier $R^*_{ik} \geq 0$ for constraint ik in (11.62), coincides with the solution to problem (11.50)–(11.53), where $R^*_{ik} \equiv (r^*_{ik} + e^*_k)$ for all ik; $i = 1,\ldots,I$; $k = 1,\ldots,K$.

Moreover, this solution is an equilibrium solution.

Theorem 11.10 below allows us to complete the network optimization reformulation of international financial equilibrium in the case that the utility functions are as given in (11.7a). The theorem follows from Lemma 11.1 and Corollary 11.2.

Theorem 11.10

The international financial equilibrium pattern, $(X^*,Y^*,r^*,e^*) \in \mathcal{K}$, coincides with the solution of the optimization problem:

$$\textit{Maximize} \sum_{j=1}^{J}\sum_{l=1}^{L} u^{jl}(X^{jl},Y^{jl}) \tag{11.64}$$

subject to:

$$\sum_{j=1}^{J}\sum_{l=1}^{L}(X_{ik}^{jl} - Y_{ik}^{jl}) = 0, \ i = 1, \ldots, I; \ k = 1, \ldots, K; \ (X, Y) \in \kappa, \qquad (11.65)$$

with Lagrange multiplier $R_{ik}^* = (r_{ik}^* + e_k^*)$ *for instrument* i *and currency* k *corresponding to the ik-th constraint in (11.65).*

In Figure 11.2, we depict the network structure of the optimization problem in Theorem 11.10. The individual networks in Figure 11.1, representing the problems of the individual sectors in the countries, merge to yield the network of Figure 11.2, representing the structure of the international financial economy in equilibrium. It is worthwhile to compare the structure of the international financial equilibrium network in Figure 11.2 with the structure of the single country financial equilibrium network in Figure 6.2. Note, first, that the basic structure of the two networks is similar, as one would expect, since the latter is a special case of the former. However, in the international case, one now has not only multiple countries, but also instruments in distinct currencies. Hence, the dimension of the international problem is considerably larger than that of the single country problem. Finally, in the international case, prices also correspond to Lagrange multipliers associated with market clearing conditions, but now these include also the currency prices.

Moreover, we note (as was discussed also in the single country case), the network structure of the international financial economy in equilibrium, as depicted in Figure 11.2, is still valid when, in addition to the budget constraints (11.2a) and (11.2b), the feasible set of each sector j in country l, denoted by κ^{jl}, consists also of *other* constraints, provided that the feasible set remains closed and convex. Moreover, this network structure of the international financial economy in equilibrium is retained if the utility functions are of the form given in the objective function (11.1). This is due to the fact that it is the budget constraints, coupled with the instrument and currency equilibrium conditions, that yield such a structure, as established theoretically above.

Obviously, one can compute (in the special case of the utility functions, given by (11.7a)) the international financial equilibrium pattern just by solving (11.64) and (11.65). In the following section we provide alternative ways of computing the equilibrium pattern.

11.6 Computation of International Equilibria

In this section, we address the computation of international financial equilibria. We first present, in Section 11.6.1, the modified projection method. Obviously, the primal-dual method as was outlined in Section 6.4 could also be used for the computation of the international financial equilibrium in the case that the utility functions are of the form (11.7a), in which case one would

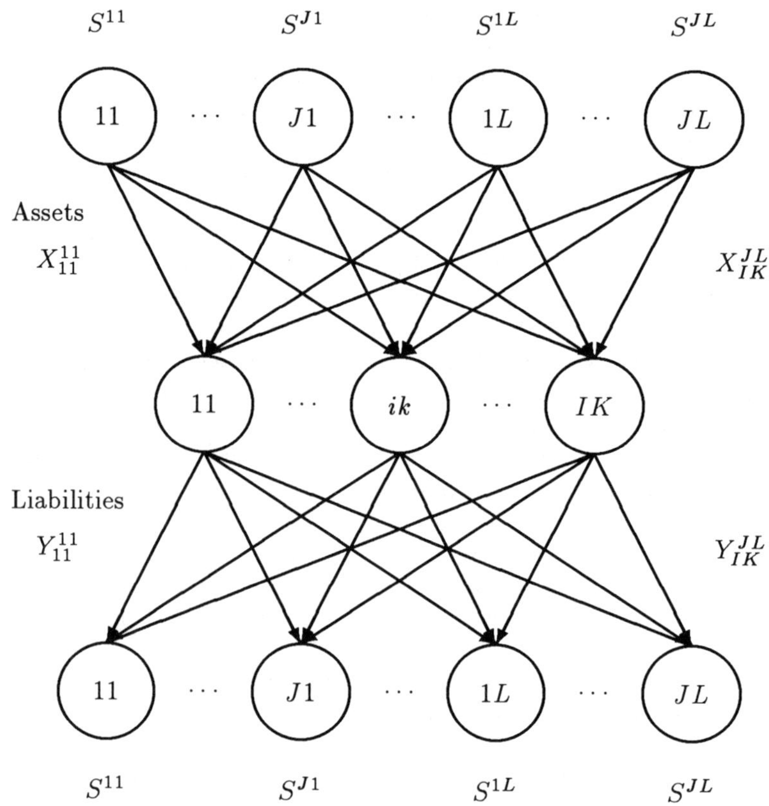

Fig. 11.2. The network structure of international financial equilibrium

be solving the network optimization problem (11.64), subject to (11.65). We then present, in Section 11.6.2, the Euler method, which is a discrete time approximation to the continuous time adjustment process (11.44). In Section 11.6.3, we present numerical examples.

11.6.1 The Modified Projection Method

We will now illustrate the application of the modified projection algorithm for the computation of the international financial equilibrium pattern by expanding the function $F(x)$ (cf. (11.22)), as defined in (11.23). The method computes a solution to variational inequality (11.13a), equivalently, determines an international financial equilibrium, satisfying Definition 11.1. For simplicity of notation, let the vector x^{jl^τ}, be defined as: $(x^{jl^\tau}) \equiv (X^{jl^\tau}, Y^{jl^\tau}, r^\tau, e^\tau)$, where τ represents an iterative step of the modified projection method.

The Modified Projection Method

Step 0: Initialization

Set $(X^0, Y^0, r^0, e^0) \in \mathcal{K}$. Let $\tau := 0$ and set γ so that $0 < \gamma < \frac{1}{\mathcal{L}}$, where $\mathcal{L}$ is the Lipschitz constant.

Step 1: Computation

Compute $(\bar{X}^\tau, \bar{Y}^\tau, \bar{r}^\tau, \bar{e}^\tau) \in \mathcal{K}$ by solving the variational inequality subproblem:

$$\sum_{j=1}^{J}\sum_{l=1}^{L}\sum_{i=1}^{I}\sum_{k=1}^{K}\left[\bar{X}_{ik}^{jl^\tau} + \gamma\left(-\frac{\partial U^{jl}(x^{jl^\tau})}{\partial X_{ik}^{jl}}\right) - X_{ik}^{jl^\tau}\right] \times \left[X_{ik}^{jl} - \bar{X}_{ik}^{jl^\tau}\right]$$

$$+\sum_{j=1}^{J}\sum_{l=1}^{L}\sum_{i=1}^{I}\sum_{k=1}^{K}\left[\bar{Y}_{ik}^{jl^\tau} + \gamma\left(-\frac{\partial U^{jl}(x^{jl^\tau})}{\partial Y_{ik}^{jl}}\right) - Y_{ik}^{jl^\tau}\right] \times \left[Y_{ik}^{jl} - \bar{Y}_{ik}^{jl^\tau}\right]$$

$$+\sum_{i=1}^{I}\sum_{k=1}^{K}\left[\bar{r}_{ik}^\tau + \gamma\left[\sum_{j=1}^{J}\sum_{l=1}^{L}\left(X_{ik}^{jl^\tau} - Y_{ik}^{jl^\tau}\right)\right] - r_{ik}^\tau\right] \times \left[r_{ik} - \bar{r}_{ik}^\tau\right]$$

$$+\sum_{k=1}^{K}\left[\bar{e}_k^\tau + \gamma\left[\sum_{j=1}^{J}\sum_{l=1}^{L}\sum_{i=1}^{I}\left(X_{ik}^{jl^\tau} - Y_{ik}^{jl^\tau}\right)\right] - e_k^\tau\right] \times \left[e_k - \bar{e}_k^\tau\right] \geq 0,$$

$$\forall (X, Y, r, e) \in \mathcal{K}. \tag{11.66}$$

Step 2: Adaptation

Compute $(X^{\tau+1}, Y^{\tau+1}, r^{\tau+1}, e^{\tau+1}) \in \mathcal{K}$ by solving the variational inequality subproblem:

$$\sum_{j=1}^{J}\sum_{l=1}^{L}\sum_{i=1}^{I}\sum_{k=1}^{K}\left[X_{ik}^{jl^{\tau+1}} + \gamma\left(-\frac{\partial U^{jl}(\bar{x}^{jl^\tau})}{\partial X_{ik}^{jl}}\right) - X_{ik}^{jl^\tau}\right] \times \left[X_{ik}^{jl} - X_{ik}^{jl^{\tau+1}}\right]$$

$$+\sum_{j=1}^{J}\sum_{l=1}^{L}\sum_{i=1}^{I}\sum_{k=1}^{K}\left[Y_{ik}^{jl^{\tau+1}}+\gamma\left(-\frac{\partial U^{jl}(\bar{x}^{jl^{\tau}})}{\partial Y_i^j}\right)-Y_{ik}^{jl^{\tau}}\right]\times\left[Y_{ik}^{jl}-Y_{ik}^{jl^{\tau+1}}\right]$$

$$+\sum_{i=1}^{I}\sum_{k=1}^{K}\left[r_{ik}^{\tau+1}+\gamma\left[\sum_{j=1}^{J}\sum_{l=1}^{L}\left(\bar{X}_{ik}^{jl^{\tau}}-\bar{Y}_{ik}^{jl^{\tau}}\right)\right]-r_{ik}^{\tau}\right]\times\left[r_{ik}-r_{ik}^{\tau+1}\right]$$

$$+\sum_{k=1}^{K}\left[e_k^{\tau+1}+\gamma\left[\sum_{j=1}^{J}\sum_{l=1}^{L}\sum_{i=1}^{I}\left(\bar{X}_{ik}^{jl^{\tau}}-\bar{Y}_{ik}^{jl^{\tau}}\right)\right]-e_k^{\tau}\right]\times\left[e_k-e_k^{\tau+1}\right]\geq 0,$$

$$\forall (X,Y,r,e)\in\mathcal{K}. \tag{11.67}$$

Step 3: Convergence Verification:

If $\max_{j,l,i,k}|X_{ik}^{jl^{\tau+1}}-X_{ik}^{jl^{\tau}}|\leq\epsilon$; $\max_{j,l,i,k}|Y_{ik}^{jl^{\tau+1}}-Y_{ik}^{jl^{\tau}}|\leq\epsilon$; $\max_{i,k}|r_{ik}^{\tau+1}-r_{ik}^{\tau}|\leq\epsilon$, $\max_k|e_k^{\tau+1}-e_k^{\tau}|\leq\epsilon$, for all $j;j=1,\ldots,J$, $l;l=1,\ldots,L$, $i;i=1,\ldots,I$, $k;k=1,\ldots,K$, with $\epsilon>0$, a prespecified tolerance, then stop; else, set $\tau:=\tau+1$, and go to Step 1.

Since the function $F(x)$ that enters the variational inequality (11.13a) is monotone (see Proposition 11.1) and Lipschitz continuous (see Proposition 11.2), the modified projection algorithm is guaranteed to converge (see Section 3.3.1) and, as a result, the following theorem holds.

Theorem 11.11 (Convergence)

The modified projection method converges to a perfect market international financial asset, liability, instrument and currency price equilibrium pattern, satisfying variational inequality (11.13a), provided that a solution exists.

In view of the feasible set $\mathcal{K}$, the variational inequality subproblems (11.66) and (11.67) can be further decomposed into simple subproblems, as depicted in Figure 11.3, that can be solved explicitly and in closed form, using exact equilibration. In particular, we note that the feasible set consists solely of simple linear constraints and nonnegativity constraints, where the former constraints correspond to the account balancing constraints of each sector in each country.

Specifically, subproblem (11.66) (as (11.67)) decomposes into smaller and simpler subproblems, respectively, in the (X^{jl}), (Y^{jl}), r_{ik}, and e_k variables for all j,l,i,k. In particular, each asset subproblem for a sector in a country is simply a separable quadratic programming problem subject to a single linear constraint and nonnegativity constraints. This is also the case for each liability subproblem. These subproblems, in turn, can be solved – due to their special structure – explicitly and in closed form using exact equilibration algorithm (cf. Section 5.2.3). The subproblems in the prices, in turn, are also separable quadratic programming problems, respectively, in a single variable each. These can also be solved explicitly and in closed form by using simple formulas.

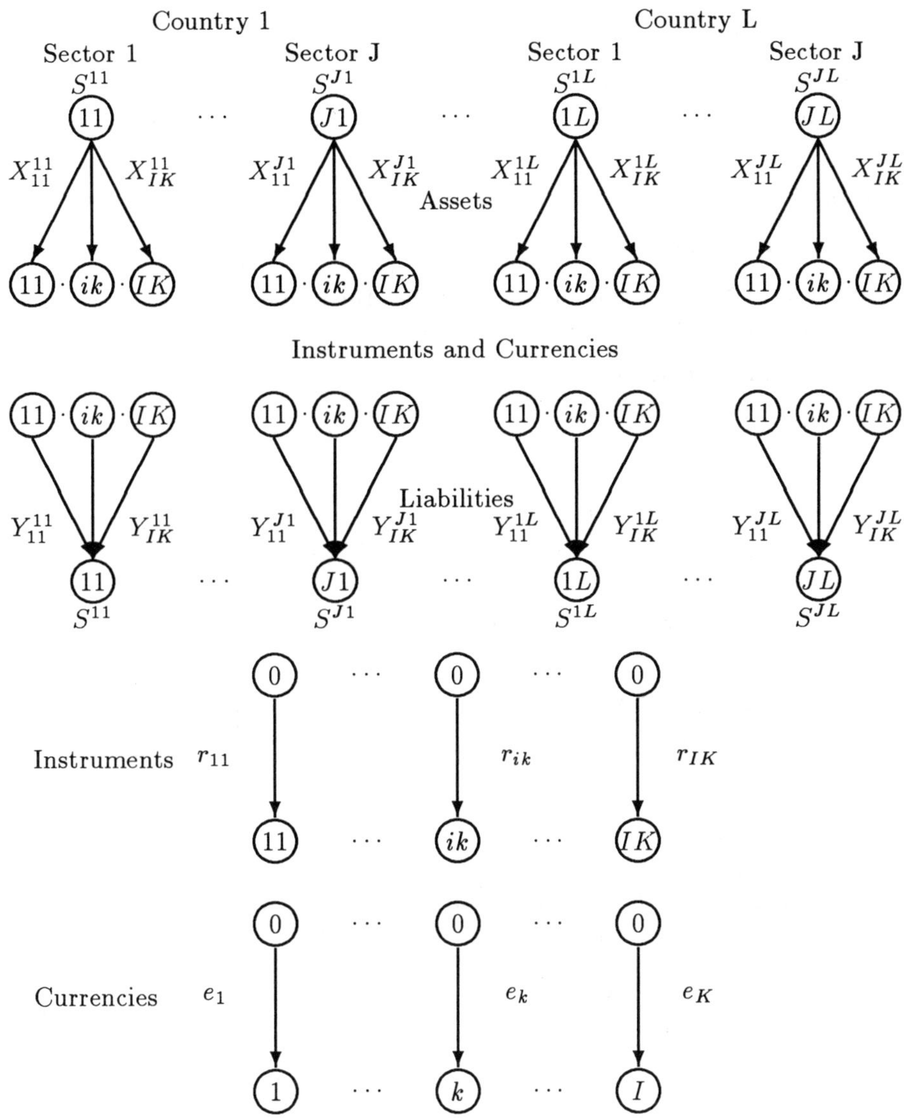

Fig. 11.3. Structure of network subproblems induced by the modified projection method and the Euler method

11.6.2 The Euler Method

In this section, we present a discrete time algorithm, the Euler method, for the computation of the international financial equilibrium pattern. This algorithm may also be viewed as a discrete time approximation or discrete time adjustment process for the continuous time model given by (11.44). The Euler method is a special case of the general iterative scheme (4.24).

We now write down the Euler method (see Chapter 4) explicitly for our problem.

The Euler Method

Step 0: Initialization

Set $(X^0, Y^0, r^0, e^0) \in \mathcal{K}$. Let $\tau := 0$. Set the sequence $\{a_\tau\}$ according to condition 1 of Assumption 4.2.

Step 1: Computation

Compute $(X^{\tau+1}, Y^{\tau+1}, r^{\tau+1}, e^{\tau+1}) \in \mathcal{K}$ by solving the variational inequality problem:

$$\sum_{j=1}^{J}\sum_{l=1}^{L}\sum_{i=1}^{I}\sum_{k=1}^{K}\left[X_{ik}^{jl^{\tau+1}} + a_\tau\left(-\frac{\partial U^{jl}(x^{jl^\tau})}{\partial X_{ik}^{jl}}\right) - X_{ik}^{jl^\tau}\right] \times \left[X_{ik}^{jl} - X_{ik}^{jl^{\tau+1}}\right]$$

$$+\sum_{j=1}^{J}\sum_{l=1}^{L}\sum_{i=1}^{I}\sum_{k=1}^{K}\left[Y_{ik}^{jl^{\tau+1}} + a_\tau\left(-\frac{\partial U^{jl}(x^{jl^\tau})}{\partial Y_{ik}^{jl}}\right) - Y_{ik}^{jl^\tau}\right] \times \left[Y_{ik}^{jl} - Y_{ik}^{jl^{\tau+1}}\right]$$

$$+\sum_{i=1}^{I}\sum_{k=1}^{K}\left[r_{ik}^{\tau+1} + a_\tau\left[\sum_{j=1}^{J}\sum_{l=1}^{L}\left(X_{ik}^{jl^\tau} - Y_{ik}^{jl^\tau}\right)\right] - r_{ik}^\tau\right] \times \left[r_{ik} - r_{ik}^{\tau+1}\right]$$

$$+\sum_{k=1}^{K}\left[e_k^{\tau+1} + a_\tau\left[\sum_{i=1}^{I}\sum_{j=1}^{J}\sum_{l=1}^{L}\left(X_{ik}^{jl^\tau} - Y_{ik}^{jl^\tau}\right)\right] - e_k^\tau\right] \times \left[e_k - e_k^{\tau+1}\right] \geq 0,$$

$$\forall (X, Y, r, e) \in \mathcal{K}. \tag{11.68}$$

Step 3: Convergence Verification:

If $\max_{j,l,i,k} |X_{ik}^{jl^{\tau+1}} - X_{ik}^{jl^\tau}| \leq \epsilon$; $\max_{j,l,i,k} |Y_{ik}^{jl^{\tau+1}} - Y_{ik}^{jl^\tau}| \leq \epsilon$; $\max_{i,k} |r_{ik}^{\tau+1} - r_{ik}^\tau| \leq \epsilon$, $\max_k |e_k^{\tau+1} - e_k^\tau| \leq \epsilon$, for all $j; j = 1, \ldots, J$, $l; l = 1, \ldots, L$, $i; i = 1, \ldots, I$, $k; k = 1, \ldots, K$, with $\epsilon > 0$, a prespecified tolerance, then stop; else, set $\tau := \tau + 1$, and go to Step 1.

Although the focus here is on the Euler method, which is the simplest scheme, we note that it is only one of many computational methods induced by the iterative scheme defined in (4.24). In fact, in addition to the Euler method, we can recover through (4.24) such well-known computational methods in dynamical systems theory as the Heun method and the Runge-Kutta method.

Note that (11.68) is identical in structure to subproblem (11.66) and (11.67) induced by the modified projection method, with the exception that a_τ an vary with each time period τ, whereas ρ in the modified projection method is fixed. Hence, the structure of the induced subproblems in (11.68) is as depicted in Figure 11.3. These are, again quadratic programming problems on networks with simple structure, which can be solved exactly in closed form using exact equilibration.

To conclude this section, the following theorem provides the convergence of the proposed Euler method in the context of the dynamic international financial problem.

Theorem 11.12

Suppose that the utility functions are strictly monotone decreasing and of the form (11.7b). Let $\{a_\tau\}$ be a sequence of positive real numbers that satisfies

$$\lim_{\tau \to \infty} a_\tau = 0 \tag{11.69}$$

and

$$\sum_{\tau=0}^{\infty} a_\tau = \infty. \tag{11.70}$$

Then the Euler method given by

$$x^{\tau+1} = P_{\mathcal{K}}(x^\tau - a_\tau F(x^\tau)), \tag{11.71}$$

where $F(x)$ is the vector defined in (11.22) and (11.23) converges to some international financial equilibrium pattern.

Proof: According to Theorem 4.2, the sequence $\{x^\tau\}$ generated by (11.71) converges to some solution to the variational inequality problem (11.24), equivalently, to a stationary point of the projected dynamical system (11.44)), provided that Assumption 4.2 is satisfied. Consequently, by taking advantage of Theorem Theorem 4.7, it converges to some equilibrium pattern.

Notice that condition 1 of Assumption 4.2 is already met by the chosen sequence according to (11.69) and (11.70). Condition 2 of Assumption 4.2 is also satisfied because $F(x)$ is continuous and $F_\tau = F$. By Theorem 11.8, the international financial adjustment process is asymptotically stable, and, hence, every ω-limit point of the projected dynamical system (11.44) is an equilibrium pattern. This verifies condition 3 of Assumption 4.2. Condition 4 of Assumption 4.2 becomes trivial, with notice to the fact that the feasible set κ is compact. Finally, condition 5 of the assumption holds true because the financial adjustment process (11.44) is asymptotically stable and, therefore, it is bounded. □

11.6.3 Numerical Examples

In this section we present numerical examples to illustrate both the Euler method and the modified projection method applied to international financial equilibrium problems. The numerical examples are of increasing complexity. The utility functions of the sectors of the countries were quadratic, as given by (11.25).

The Euler method, described in Section 11.6.2, was coded in FORTRAN, as was the modified projection method, described in Section 11.6.1, and both algorithms were implemented on an IBM SP2. The CPU time for each example is reported exclusive of input/output times. The asset and liability subproblems were solved using exact equilibration and the prices were solved in closed form.

In all the examples we initialized the algorithms as follows: $X_{ik}^{jl} = \frac{s^{jl}}{IK}$ and $Y_{ik}^{jl} = \frac{s^{jl}}{IK}$ for all jl; $r_{ik} = 1$ for all ik and $e_k = 1$ for all k. The convergence criterion was: $|x_b^{\tau+1} - x_b^{\tau}| \leq .001$, for all $b = 1, \ldots, n$, for both algorithms.

Example 11.1: 1 Country, 2 Sectors, 2 Currencies, 2 Instruments

We first considered an example consisting of a single country with two sectors trading in two currencies and two financial instruments in each currency.

The variance-covariance matrices were as follows:

For sector 1:

$$Q^{11} = \begin{pmatrix} 1.0 & 0.2 & 0 & 0 & -0.2 & -0.3 & 0 & 0 \\ 0.2 & 1.0 & 0 & 0 & -0.1 & -0.2 & 0 & 0 \\ 0 & 0 & 1.0 & 0 & 0 & 0 & -0.1 & 0 \\ 0 & 0 & 0 & 1.0 & 0 & 0 & -0.1 & 0 \\ -0.2 & -0.1 & 0 & 0 & 1.0 & 0.4 & 0 & 0 \\ -0.3 & -0.2 & 0 & 0 & 0.4 & 1.0 & 0 & 0 \\ 0 & 0 & -0.1 & -0.1 & 0 & 0 & 1.0 & 0 \\ 0 & 0 & 0 & 0 & 0 & 0 & 0 & 1.0 \end{pmatrix}$$

For sector 2:

$$Q^{12} = \begin{pmatrix} 1.0 & 0.3 & 0.2 & 0 & 0 & 0 & -0.1 & -0.2 \\ 0.3 & 1.0 & 0 & 0 & 0 & -0.15 & 0 & 0 \\ 0.2 & 0 & 1.0 & 0.5 & -0.1 & 0 & 0 & 0 \\ 0 & 0 & 0.5 & 1.0 & 0 & -0.3 & 0 & 0 \\ 0 & 0 & -0.1 & 0 & 1.0 & 0 & 0.2 & 0 \\ 0 & -0.15 & 0 & -0.3 & 0 & 1.0 & 0.3 & 0 \\ -0.1 & 0 & 0 & 0 & 0.2 & 0.3 & 1.0 & 0 \\ -0.2 & 0 & 0 & 0 & 0 & 0 & 0 & 1.0 \end{pmatrix}.$$

We set all the financial volumes S^{jl} all equal to 1.

We set the sequence $\{a_\tau\}$=1.$\{1, \frac{1}{2}, \frac{1}{2}, \frac{1}{3}, \frac{1}{3}, \frac{1}{3}, \ldots\}$. The Euler method converged in 86 iterations and .01 CPU seconds yielding the following solution:

Instrument Prices:

$$r_{11}^* = .938, \quad r_{12}^* = 1.029, \quad r_{21}^* = 1.054, \quad r_{22}^* = .979,$$

Exchange Rate Prices:

$$e_1^* = .992, \quad e_2^* = 1.008,$$

Asset and Liability Pattern:

$$X_{11}^{11^*} = .251, \quad X_{12}^{11^*} = .255, \quad X_{21}^{11^*} = .264, \quad X_{22}^{11^*} = .230,$$

$$X_{11}^{21^*} = .228, \quad X_{12}^{21^*} = .131, \quad X_{21}^{21^*} = .314, \quad X_{22}^{21^*} = .328,$$

$$Y_{11}^{11^*} = .247, \quad Y_{12}^{11^*} = .269, \quad Y_{21}^{11^*} = .237, \quad Y_{22}^{11^*} = .246,$$

$$Y_{11}^{21^*} = .231, \quad Y_{12}^{21^*} = .118, \quad Y_{21}^{21^*} = .338, \quad Y_{22}^{21^*} = .313.$$

As proven in Lemma 11.1, we note that the markets cleared for each currency and, hence, the exchange rate prices were positive. Also, the markets for the instruments cleared (to within 3 decimal places), and the instrument prices were positive.

The modified projection method, with $\gamma = .35$, in turn, converged in 15 iterations and .01 CPU seconds.

Example 11.2: 2 Countries, 2 Sectors, 2 Currencies, 2 Instruments

The second example consisted of two countries, two sectors in each country trading in two currencies, and two financial instruments in each currency.

The variance-covariance matrices for the sectors in the first country were as in Example 11.1. The variance-covariance matrices for the sectors in the second country were as follows:

For sector 1, country 2:

$$Q^{12} = \begin{pmatrix} 1.0 & 0 & 0.3 & 0 & -0.1 & -0.1 & 0 & 0 \\ 0 & 1.0 & 0.1 & 0 & 0 & 0 & -0.2 & 0 \\ 0.3 & 0.1 & 1.0 & 0 & -0.3 & 0 & 0 & 0 \\ 0 & 0 & 0 & 1.0 & -0.4 & 0 & 0 & 0 \\ -0.1 & 0 & -0.3 & -0.4 & 1.0 & 0 & 0 & 0 \\ -0.1 & 0 & 0 & 0 & 0 & 1.0 & 0.5 & 0 \\ 0 & -0.2 & 0 & 0 & 0 & 0.5 & 1.0 & 0.1 \\ 0 & 0 & 0 & 0 & 0 & 0 & 0.1 & 1.0 \end{pmatrix}$$

For sector 2, country 2:

$$Q^{22} = \begin{pmatrix} 1.0 & 0.4 & 0 & 0 & -0.2 & 0 & 0 & 0 \\ 0.4 & 1.0 & 0 & 0 & 0 & -0.1 & 0 & 0 \\ 0 & 0 & 1.0 & 0 & -0.3 & 0 & 0 & 0 \\ 0 & 0 & 0 & 1.0 & 0 & 0 & -0.4 & 0 \\ -0.2 & 0 & -0.3 & 0 & 1.0 & 0 & 0 & 0 \\ 0 & -0.1 & 0 & 0 & 0 & 1.0 & 0.3 & 0 \\ 0 & 0 & 0 & -0.4 & 0 & 0.3 & 1.0 & 0.1 \\ 0 & 0 & 0 & 0 & 0 & 0 & 0.1 & 1.0 \end{pmatrix}.$$

The sector volumes for the sectors in the second country were set equal to 1.

The Euler method converged in 36 iterations and .01 CPU seconds with the sequence $\{a_\tau\}=.1\{1, \frac{1}{2}, \frac{1}{2}, \frac{1}{3}, \frac{1}{3}, \frac{1}{3}, \ldots\}$, yielding the following solution:

Instrument Prices:

$$r_{11}^* = 1.060, \quad r_{12}^* = 1.001, \quad r_{21}^* = .983, \quad r_{22}^* = .955,$$

Exchange Rate Prices:

$$e_1^* = 1.044, \quad e_2^* = .956,$$

Asset and Liability Pattern:

$$X_{11}^{11^*} = .307, \quad X_{12}^{11^*} = .229, \quad X_{21}^{11^*} = .244, \quad X_{22}^{11^*} = .220,$$

$$X_{11}^{21^*} = .297, \quad X_{12}^{21^*} = .154, \quad X_{21}^{21^*} = .279, \quad X_{22}^{21^*} = .270,$$

$$X_{11}^{12^*} = .235, \quad X_{12}^{12^*} = .213, \quad X_{21}^{12^*} = .243, \quad X_{22}^{22^*} = .309,$$

$$X_{11}^{22^*} = .242, \quad X_{12}^{22^*} = .288, \quad X_{21}^{22^*} = .180, \quad X_{22}^{22^*} = .290,$$

$$Y_{11}^{11^*} = .189, \quad Y_{12}^{11^*} = .288, \quad Y_{21}^{11^*} = .264, \quad Y_{22}^{11^*} = .259,$$

$$Y_{11}^{21^*} = .206, \quad Y_{12}^{21^*} = .184, \quad Y_{21}^{21^*} = .290, \quad Y_{22}^{22^*} = .319,$$

$$Y_{11}^{12^*} = .383, \quad Y_{12}^{12^*} = .200, \quad Y_{21}^{12^*} = .168, \quad Y_{22}^{12} = .249,$$

$$Y_{11}^{22^*} = .312, \quad Y_{12}^{22^*} = .273, \quad Y_{21}^{22^*} = .178, \quad Y_{22}^{22^*} = .237.$$

In this example, as expected, the markets also cleared for each currency and (approximately) cleared for each instrument.

The modified projection method, with $\gamma = .2$, in turn, converged in 19 iterations and .01 seconds of CPU time.

Example 11.3: 3 Countries, 2 Sectors, 2 Currencies, 2 Instruments

This example consisted of three countries, with the data for the first two countries as in the preceding example. The variance/covariance matrix for the third country was given by:

For sector 1, country 3:

$$Q^{13} = \begin{pmatrix} 1.0 & 0.1 & 0 & 0 & 0 & 0 & 0 & -0.1 \\ 0.1 & 1.0 & 0.2 & 0 & -0.2 & 0 & 0 & 0 \\ 0 & 0.2 & 1.0 & 0 & 0 & -0.3 & 0 & 0 \\ 0 & 0 & 0 & 1.0 & 0 & 0 & 0 & 0 \\ 0 & -0.2 & 0 & 0 & 1.0 & 0.5 & 0 & 0 \\ 0 & 0 & -0.3 & 0 & 0.5 & 1.0 & 0 & 0 \\ 0 & 0 & 0 & 0 & 0 & 0 & 1.0 & 0.4 \\ -0.1 & 0 & 0 & 0 & 0 & 0 & 0.4 & 1.0 \end{pmatrix}$$

For sector 2, country 3:

$$Q^{23} = \begin{pmatrix} 1.0 & 0 & 0.2 & 0 & -0.1 & -0.2 & 0 & 0 \\ 0 & 1.0 & 0.3 & 0 & 0 & -0.4 & 0 & 0 \\ 0.2 & 0.3 & 1.0 & 0 & 0 & 0 & -0.1 & 0 \\ 0 & 0 & 0 & 1.0 & 0 & 0 & 0 & 0 \\ -0.1 & 0 & 0 & 0 & 1.0 & 0.4 & 0 & 0 \\ -0.2 & -0.4 & 0 & 0 & 0.4 & 1.0 & 0 & 0 \\ 0 & 0 & -0.1 & 0 & 0 & 0 & 1.0 & 0.6 \\ 0 & 0 & 0 & 0 & 0 & 0 & 0.6 & 1.0 \end{pmatrix}.$$

The Euler method was initialized as in the preceding examples with the exception that $S^{13} = S^{23} = 2$. We utilized the same $\{a_\tau\}$ sequence as in Example 11.2.

The Euler method converged in 76 iterations and .04 seconds of CPU time yielding the following solution:

Instrument Prices:

$$r_{11}^* = 1.002, \quad r_{12}^* = 1.047, \quad r_{21}^* = 1.008, \quad r_{22}^* = .943,$$

Exchange Rate Prices:

$$e_1^* = 1.010, \quad e_2^* = .990,$$

Asset and Liability Pattern:

$$X_{11}^{11*} = .163, \quad X_{12}^{11*} = .288, \quad X_{21}^{11*} = .298, \quad X_{22}^{11*} = .251,$$

$$X_{11}^{21*} = .290, \quad X_{12}^{21*} = .158, \quad X_{21}^{21*} = .276, \quad X_{22}^{21*} = .275,$$

$$X_{11}^{12*} = .215, \quad X_{12}^{12*} = .235, \quad X_{21}^{12*} = .233, \quad X_{22}^{12*} = .317,$$

$$X_{11}^{22*} = .231, \quad X_{12}^{22*} = .316, \quad X_{21}^{22*} = .164, \quad X_{22}^{22*} = .288,$$

$$X_{11}^{13*} = .270, \quad X_{12}^{13*} = .285, \quad X_{21}^{13*} = .226, \quad X_{22}^{13*} = .218,$$

$$X_{11}^{23*} = .618, \quad X_{12}^{23*} = .252, \quad X_{21}^{23*} = .675, \quad X_{22}^{23*} = .455,$$

$$Y_{11}^{11*} = .189, \quad Y_{12}^{11*} = .281, \quad Y_{21}^{11*} = .260, \quad Y_{22}^{11*} = .270,$$

$$Y_{11}^{21*} = .215, \quad Y_{12}^{21*} = .151, \quad Y_{21}^{21*} = .301, \quad Y_{22}^{21*} = .333,$$

$$Y_{11}^{12*} = .413, \quad Y_{12}^{12*} = .175, \quad Y_{21}^{12*} = .160, \quad Y_{22}^{12*} = .251,$$

$$Y_{11}^{22*} = .337, \quad Y_{12}^{22*} = .257, \quad Y_{21}^{22*} = .167, \quad Y_{22}^{22*} = .239,$$

$$Y_{11}^{13*} = .221, \quad Y_{12}^{13*} = .209, \quad Y_{21}^{13*} = .279, \quad Y_{22}^{13*} = .290,$$

$$Y_{11}^{23*} = .391, \quad Y_{12}^{23*} = .408, \quad Y_{21}^{23*} = .790, \quad Y_{22}^{23*} = .410.$$

In this example, the markets cleared (approximately to three decimal points) for each currency and for each financial instrument. The exchange rate prices and instrument prices were, as expected from Lemma 11.1, positive.

The modified projection method converged in 29 iterations and .02 seconds of CPU time with $\gamma = .35$.

11.7 Sources and Notes

In this chapter we have developed international financial equilibrium models with multiple sectors in various countries and with different instruments in multiple currencies. We provide both static models as well as their dynamic counterparts. The models in this chapter may be viewed as extensions to the international domain of the static models in Chapter 6 as well as the dynamic models in Section 8.1.1.

We first modeled the individual behavior of a sector's portfolio optimization problem and showed the underlying network structure. We later verified that the set of equilibrium points coincides with the set of solutions to the variational inequality problem governing the international financial equilibrium conditions.

Moreover, we showed that, in the case of utility functions of a certain form, the international financial equilibrium can be obtained as a solution to a network optimization problem. In fact, the network corresponding to the equilibrium solution is a synthesis of the individual sectors' networks. We also proved that the markets clear providing positive prices for all instruments and currencies. The network representation of the international financial economy is valid even in the case of more general utility functions and constraint sets, provided that the budget constraint is included for each sector of each country.

Section 11.1

The models presented in this section are special (static) cases of the models presented in Nagurney and Siokos (1996) or generalizations, to an international multi-currency setting, of the models presented by Nagurney, Dong, and Hughes (1992) and Nagurney (1994).

Section 11.2

The qualitative properties of existence and uniqueness are generalizations (to an international multi-currency setting) of the qualitative properties that were established for a single country economy and single currency models by Nagurney, Dong, and Hughes (1992) and Nagurney (1994). The comparative statics results are new.

Section 11.4

The stability results are due to Nagurney and Siokos (1996). These results are based on those obtained in Dong, Zhang, and Nagurney (1996), which are recalled in Chapter 8.

Section 11.5

The network reformulation of the model is due to Nagurney and Siokos (1996), along with all the theoretical results.

Section 11.6

In this section we suggested the modified projection method for the computation of the equilibrium pattern, along with convergence results. The discussion presented here is a generalization of the material presented in Section 6.4. The statement of the modified projection method for the computation of the international financial equilibria is reported here for the first time. The Euler method, along with convergence results, for this problem, are due to Siokos and Nagurney (1996). The numerical results for the Euler method were reported therein whereas the results for the modified projection method are new.

References

Bertsekas, D. P., and Tsitsiklis, J. N., **Parallel and Distributed Computation – Numerical Methods**, Prentice-Hall, Inc., Englewood Cliffs, New Jersey, 1989.

Dong, J., Zhang, D., and Nagurney, A., "A Projected Dynamical Systems Model of General Financial Equilibrium with Stability Analysis," *Mathematical and Computer Modelling* **24** (1996) 35-44.

Eun, C., and Resnick, B., "Exchange Rate Uncertainty, Forward Contracts, and International Portfolio Selection," *The Journal of Finance* **43** (1988) 197-215.

French, K., and Poterba, J., "Investor Diversification and International Equity Markets," *American Economic Review* **81** (1991) 222-226.

Howell, M., and Cozzini, A., **International Equity Flows**, International Equity Research Salomon Brothers, London, Great Britain, 1991.

Hufbauer G., and Schott J., **NAFTA: An Assessment,** Institute of International Economics, Washington, DC, 1993.

Lacey, N. and Chambers, D., **Modern Corporate Finance,** Harper Collins College Publishers, New York, New York, 1994.

Nagurney, A., "Variational Inequalities in the Analysis and Computation of Multi-Sector, Multi-Instrument Financial Equilibria," *Journal of Economic Dynamics and Control* **18** (1994) 161-184.

Nagurney, A., Dong, J., and Hughes, M., "Formulation and Computation of General Financial Equilibrium," *Optimization* **26** (1992) 339-354.

Nagurney, A., and Siokos, S., "Dynamics of International Financial Networks: Modeling, Stability Analysis, and Computation," to appear in **Networks and Knowledge in a Dynamic Economy**, M. Beckmann, B. Johansson, F. Snickars, and R. Thord, editors, Springer-Verlag, Berlin, Germany, 1996.

Rosenthal, G., and Cafruny, A., **The State of European Community.The Maastricht Debates and Beyond,** Liener Longman, Boulder, Colorado, 1993.

Rustem B., "Computing Optimal Multi-Currency Mean Variance Portfolios," *Journal of Economic Dynamics and Control* **19** (1995) 901-908.

Sesit M., "Foreign Investment Makes a Come Back," *The Wall Street Journal*, (September 1 1989) pp. C1 and C14.

Shapiro A., **Multinational Financial Management**, Prentice-Hall, Inc., Allyn and Bacon, Needham Heights, Massachusetts, 1992.

Silva M., and Sjörgen, B., **Europe 1992 and the New World Power Game**, John Wiley & Sons, New York, New York, 1990.

12 International Models with Hedging

The first financial hedging instruments on a foreign exchange, which were in the form of currency future contracts, were introduced in 1972 by the Chicago International Monetary Market (IMM), an affiliate of the Chicago Merchandise Exchange (cf. Duffie (1989)). These instruments were introduced in response to the liberalization of foreign exchange rates, which had been kept fixed until 1971, due to the Bretton-Woods agreement in 1994 (cf. Shapiro (1992)). Since that time, market exchange rates have been determined by the corresponding supply and demand for each currency, which is in contrast to the fixed currency parities between individual currencies and the US dollar that had existed earlier (see Andersen (1993)). In 1982, the first currency options contracts, on the Canadian dollar, appeared on the Montreal Exchange, and since then different types of options with an international appeal have been successfully traded throughout Europe, North America, and Asia (see Cox and Rubinstein (1985), Andersen (1993)).

Since the late eighties, hedging strategies have become an important tool for many practitioners, and, consequently, new products as well as standardized combinations of existing strategies have been introduced, and new markets established. The markets for futures and options had initially been dominated by the United States, but in recent years significant advances have taken place in such markets both in Europe (primarily in Great Britain and Germany) and in Asia (mainly in Japan and Singapore).

The vast majority of international markets tend to trade contracts of universal interest such as Eurocurrencies, US treasuries, German or Japanese government bonds, and, finally, strong currencies such as, the Dollar, the Yen, the DM, and the ECU. Moreover, due to innovations in the area of telecommunications, more linkages between markets in different countries and time zones have become possible and, hence, investors can now trade on a 24 hour basis. Indeed, this is an illustration of networks, in the form of telecommunication networks transforming modern society, and working in conjunction with financial networks to establish what may be viewed as composite financial telecommunication networks.

The first such linkage was introduced some years ago between the Singapore International Monetary Exchange (SIMEX) and the IMM. Both of these markets offer currency futures where the SIMEX contracts are almost exact copies of the IMM contracts so that an investor can trade them in either market (cf. Marshall and Barsal (1992)).

In this chapter we extend the international financial models presented thus far to models that incorporate futures and options. Initially, we present general models that include both futures and options contracts, and we then provide some models for specific types of contracts. We analyze and study both the static and the dynamic nature of the models under consideration and we identify their underlying network structure.

The aim of this chapter is to introduce an integrated mathematical framework to the rapidly growing field of computational financial economics in the international domain in the presence of hedging instruments based on the visualization of such systems as networks consisting of nodes and links and the associated flows. Visualizing the modeling and computational methodologies in such a way provides a consistent overall context for understanding the real nature of the underlying financial concepts and their evolution over time.

For simplicity, and without loss of generality, in this chapter, we assume that there is one interest future and/or option contract available per instrument and currency. This assumption does not limit the applicability of the models under consideration. The reader can easily expand them into applications that incorporate more than one type of contract with different types of characteristics, albeit with the simultaneous expansion of notation.

The basic assumptions of the perfect market models presented in previous chapters still hold. For example, we still assume that all sectors are risk-averse, and that all the unhedged instrument prices are determined through the supply/demand rule. In addition, all sectors act in a perfectly competitive environment, and there are contracts available for all currencies and instruments.

This chapter is organized as follows. In Section 12.1 we present the static international hedging models and identify some special cases and variants. In Section 12.2 we then address qualitative properties of the equilibrium pattern. In Section 12.3 we propose the international financial adjustment process in the presence of futures and options. In Section 12.4 we present some stability analysis results. In Section 12.5 we provide conditions under which a network optimization reformulation of the international financial equilibrium exists. In Section 12.6 we turn to the computation of the international financial equilibrium pattern in the presence of futures and options.

12.1 International Hedging Models

As before, we consider an economy consisting of L countries, with a typical country denoted by l, and with J sectors in each country, with a typical sector denoted by j. Moreover, we assume that there are K currencies, with a typical currency represented by k, where in each currency there are I instruments available, with a typical instrument denoted by i.

We assume that every sector of each country can either hedge his assets and liabilities through futures and/or options contracts, or be exposed to the risk incorporated in an internationally diversified unhedged portfolio.

Let r_{ik} be the return of instrument i in currency k, and group all these rates of return into the column vector $r \in R^{IK}_{+}$. Similarly, let e_k represent the rate of appreciation of currency k against the basic currency, and group these rates into the column vector $e \in R^{K}_{+}$.

Once again, we denote the volume of instrument i in currency k, held as an unhedged asset by sector j of country l, by X^{jl}_{ik}, and group the assets of a sector in a country into the column vector $X^{jl} \in R^{IK}_{+}$. Similarly, Y^{jl}_{ik} denotes the volume of instrument i in currency k held as an unhedged liability by sector j of country l. The liabilities of each sector in each country are grouped into the column vector $Y^{jl} \in R^{IK}_{+}$.

Since we have two types of hedging possible, that is, to hedge with futures and/or options, we will now define two different sets of variables for each type of hedging. More precisely, we let Z^{jl}_{ik} denote the volume of instrument i in currency k, held as a hedged asset by sector j of country l through a futures contract, and group the interest hedged assets of a sector j in a country l into the column vector $Z^{jl} \in R^{IK}_{+}$. Analogously, Ψ^{jl}_{ik} represents the volume of instrument i in currency k held as a hedged through futures contracts liability by sector j of country l. The liabilities that are hedged through futures contracts for sector j in country l are grouped into the column vector $\Psi^{jl} \in R^{IK}_{+}$.

In a similar manner, we denote the volume of instrument i in currency k, held as a hedged asset by sector j of country l through a European options contract, where the option will not be exercised, by W^{jl}_{ik}. We denote the volume of instrument i in currency k, held as a hedged liability through a European options contract by sector j of country l, where the option will not be exercised by Φ^{jl}_{ik}. Moreover, Ξ^{jl}_{ik} denotes the volume of capital that sector j of country l holds as an asset on a European option contract on instrument i of currency k where the option will be exercised, and Θ^{jl}_{ik} denotes the volume of capital that sector j of country l holds as a liability on a European option contract on instrument i of currency k where the option will be exercised. We then group the assets and the liabilities of sector j from country l that are hedged through options contracts into the column vectors: W^{jl}, Ξ^{jl}, Φ^{jl}, and Θ^{jl}, respectively. Each of these vectors lies in R^{IK}_{+}.

We also define the column vector $\mathcal{X}^{jl} \equiv (X^{jl}, Z^{jl}, W^{jl}, \Xi^{jl}) \in R^{4IK}_{+}$. In a similar fashion we let $\mathcal{Y}^{jl} \equiv (Y^{jl}, \Psi^{jl}, \Phi^{jl}, \Theta^{jl}) \in R_+^{4IK}$. Finally, we group the asset vectors of all sectors in all countries into the column vector $\mathcal{X} \in R_+^{JL4IK}$, and the liability vectors of all sectors in all countries into the column vector $\mathcal{Y} \in R_+^{JL4IK}$.

In addition, we denote the shadow price or "opportunity cost" associated with the futures contract on instrument i in currency k as λ_{ik} and we group these shadow prices into the column vector $\lambda \in R^{IK}$. Analogously, we denote the shadow price related to the options contract on instrument i of currency k by δ_{ik}, and we group these shadow prices into the column vector $\delta \in R^{IK}$.

Let π_{ik} denote the contracted price for instrument i of currency k through a futures contract, and let μ_{ik} represent the contracted price for instrument i of currency k through an options contract. We then group these fixed prices into the IK-dimensional vectors π, and μ, respectively.

For both types of contracts, we assume that there is a single contract available per instrument and currency, and that all contracts call for delivery at the time the contract was entered into. In addition, for the options contracts, we assume that η_{ik} denotes the premium paid for getting the right to exercise a European option on instrument i of currency k and we group these premiums into the IK-dimensional column vector η. For simplicity, and, without loss of generality, we assume that the premium for a futures contract is the same for all sectors, and, therefore, it is incorporated into the fixed price π_{ik}. Of course, different premiums per sector and contract could easily be incorporated into this model, but with a substantial increase in notation. On the other hand, in the case of the options, the premium cannot be incorporated since it has to be paid even when the option is not exercised.

Furthermore, let $U^{jl}(\mathcal{X}^{jl}, \mathcal{Y}^{jl}, r, e, \lambda, \delta; \pi, \mu, \eta)$ denote the utility function for sector j of country l which is assumed to be strictly concave, continuous, and twice continuously differentiable, with each sector taking the prices r, δ, and λ as given, and with π, μ, and η assumed to be known vectors of constants. Moreover, we assume that the accounts of each sector of the country must balance, and, as before, we denote the total financial volume held by sector j of country l by S^{jl}.

The goal of every sector from every country is still to maximize the return of his international portfolio, as well as to minimize the risk that is associated with his portfolio.

Therefore, the portfolio optimization problem of sector j of country l can be expressed as:

$$\text{Maximize } U^{jl}(\mathcal{X}^{jl}, \mathcal{Y}^{jl}, r, e, \lambda, \delta; \mu, \pi, \eta) \tag{12.1}$$

subject to:

$$\sum_{i=1}^{I}\sum_{k=1}^{K} X_{ik}^{jl} + W_{ik}^{jl} + Z_{ik}^{jl} + \Xi_{ik}^{jl} = S^{jl}, \tag{12.2}$$

$$\sum_{i=1}^{I}\sum_{k=1}^{K} Y_{ik}^{jl} + \Phi_{ik}^{jl} + \Psi_{ik}^{jl} + \Theta_{ik}^{jl} = S^{jl}, \tag{12.3}$$

$$\mathcal{X}^{jl}, \mathcal{Y}^{jl} \geq 0.$$

An important special case of utility function U^{jl} in (12.1) is given by:

$$U^{jl} = u^{jl}(\mathcal{X}^{jl}, \mathcal{Y}^{jl}) + \sum_{i=1}^{I}\sum_{k=1}^{K} (r_{ik} + e_k)(X_{ik}^{jl} - Y_{ik}^{jl})$$

$$+\sum_{i=1}^{I}\sum_{k=1}^{K}(\pi_{ik} + \lambda_{ik})(Z_{ik}^{jl} - \Psi_{ik}^{jl}) + \sum_{i=1}^{I}\sum_{k=1}^{K}(r_{ik} + e_k - \eta_{ik})(W_{ik}^{jl} - \Phi_{ik}^{jl})$$

$$+\sum_{i=1}^{I}\sum_{k=1}^{K}(\delta_{ik} + \mu_{ik} - \eta_{ik})(\Xi_{ik}^{jl} - \Theta_{ik}^{jl}), \tag{12.4}$$

where the term $u^{jl}(\mathcal{X}^{jl}, \mathcal{Y}^{jl})$ mirrors the risk that is associated with the $(\mathcal{X}^{jl}, \mathcal{Y}^{jl})$ portfolio choice. For example, a commonly encountered case assumes a quadratic utility function where u^{jl} is given by:

$$u^{jl}(\mathcal{X}^{jl}, \mathcal{Y}^{jl}) = -\begin{pmatrix} \mathcal{X}^{jl} \\ \mathcal{Y}^{jl} \end{pmatrix}^T Q^{jl} \begin{pmatrix} \mathcal{X}^{jl} \\ \mathcal{Y}^{jl} \end{pmatrix},$$

where Q^{jl} denotes a $8IK \times 8IK$ symmetric variance-covariance matrix, which is also assumed to be positive definite.

The Feasible Set

For each sector j from country l we let:

$$\bar{\mathcal{X}}^{jl} = \{\mathcal{X}^{jl} \in R_+^{4IK} : \sum_{i=1}^{I}\sum_{k=1}^{K} X_{ik}^{jl} + W_{ik}^{jl} + Z_{ik}^{jl} + \Xi_{ik}^{jl} = S^{jl}\} \tag{12.5}$$

denote the constraint set for the assets, and, similarly, we let

$$\bar{\mathcal{Y}}^{jl} = \{\mathcal{Y}^{jl} \in R_+^{4IK} : \sum_{i=1}^{I}\sum_{k=1}^{K} Y_{ik}^{jl} + \Phi_{ik}^{jl} + \Psi_{ik}^{jl} + \Theta_{ik}^{jl} = S^{jl}\} \tag{12.6}$$

denote the constraint set for the liabilities. Then, the overall feasible set for the assets and the liabilities of each sector j in country l is a Cartesian product, denoted by $\bar{\kappa}^{jl}$, where

$$\bar{\kappa}^{jl} \equiv \{\bar{\mathcal{X}}^{jl} \times \bar{\mathcal{Y}}^{jl}\}. \tag{12.7}$$

We then define the feasible set for the assets of all sectors $\bar{X}$ as:

$$\bar{X} \equiv \bar{X}^{11} \times \ldots \times \bar{X}^{jl} \times \ldots \times \bar{X}^{JL}, \tag{12.8}$$

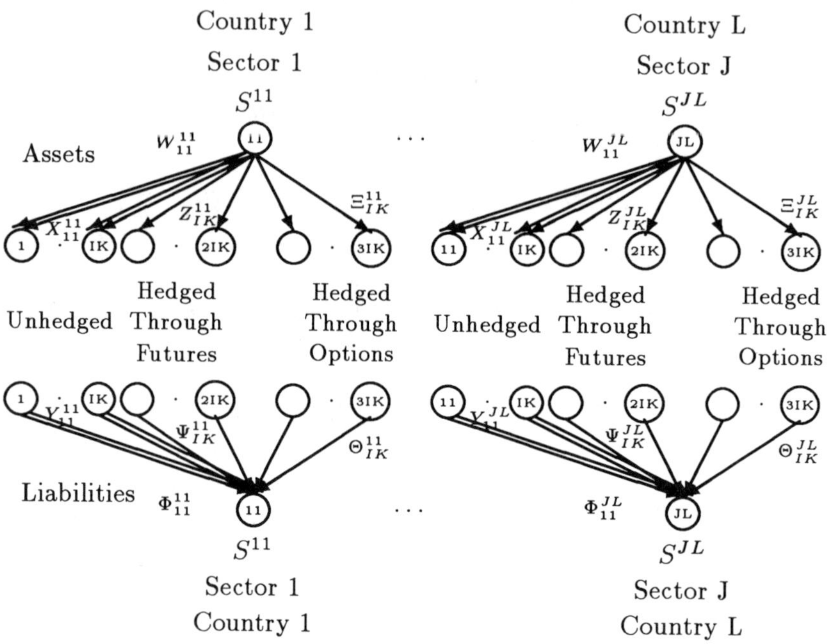

Fig. 12.1. Network structure of the sectors' optimization problems

and, similarly, for the liabilities:

$$\bar{Y} \equiv \bar{Y}^{11} \times \ldots \times \bar{Y}^{jl} \times \ldots \times \bar{Y}^{JL}, \tag{12.9}$$

with $\bar{\kappa} \equiv \{\bar{X} \times \bar{Y}\}$.

Furthermore, the feasible set for all hedged and unhedged assets and liabilities of all sectors, and all prices of all the instruments, is denoted by $\mathcal{K}$ and is given by: $\mathcal{K} \equiv \{\bar{\kappa} \times R_+^{IK} \times R_+^K \times R^{2IK}\}$.

In Figure 12.1, the underlying network structure of the optimization problem of each sector from each country is depicted. The nodes at the highest and at the lowest levels represent the sectors of the countries, the intermediate level nodes stand for the different instruments in different currencies. The uppermost links, in turn, correspond to the assets whereas the lowermost links correspond to the liabilities. Note that since each sector has the possibility of not hedging, of investing in futures and/or options, or not, there are, in fact, three different sets of links originating from the upper sector nodes and, similarly, terminating in the bottom sector nodes.

The Equilibrium Conditions

We now derive the equilibrium conditions governing the international financial model with futures and options.

Portfolio Optimality

Under our assumptions that the utility function of each sector is strictly concave, continuous, and twice continuously differentiable, the necessary and sufficient conditions for an optimal portfolio for a sector j of country l, $(\mathcal{X}^{jl^*}, \mathcal{Y}^{jl^*}) \in \bar{\kappa}^{jl}$, is that it satisfies the following inequality:

$$-\nabla_{\mathcal{X}^{jl}} U^{jl}(\mathcal{X}^{jl^*}, \mathcal{Y}^{jl^*}, r^*, e^*, \lambda^*, \delta^*; \pi, \mu, \eta)^T \cdot (\mathcal{X}^{jl} - \mathcal{X}^{jl^*})$$
$$-\nabla_{\mathcal{Y}^{jl}} U^{jl}(\mathcal{X}^{jl^*}, \mathcal{Y}^{jl^*}, r^*, e^*, \lambda^*, \delta^*; \pi, \mu, \eta)^T \cdot (\mathcal{Y}^{jl} - \mathcal{Y}^{jl^*}) \geq 0,$$
$$\forall (\mathcal{X}^{jl}, \mathcal{Y}^{jl}) \in \bar{\kappa}^{jl}, \tag{12.10}$$

where

$$\nabla_{\mathcal{X}^{jl}} U^{jl} \equiv \left(\frac{\partial U^{jl}}{\partial X_{11}^{jl}}, \ldots, \frac{\partial U^{jl}}{\partial Z_{ik}^{jl}}, \ldots, \frac{\partial U^{jl}}{\partial W_{ik}^{jl}}, \ldots, \frac{\partial U^{jl}}{\partial \Xi_{IK}^{jl}} \right) \tag{12.11}$$

and

$$\nabla_{\mathcal{X}^{jl}} U^{jl} \equiv \left(\frac{\partial U^{jl}}{\partial Y_{11}^{jl}}, \ldots, \frac{\partial U^{jl}}{\partial \Psi_{ik}^{jl}}, \ldots, \frac{\partial U^{jl}}{\partial \Phi_{ik}^{jl}}, \ldots, \frac{\partial U^{jl}}{\partial \Theta_{IK}^{jl}} \right). \tag{12.12}$$

In particular, the portfolio optimality conditions for the special case where the utility function U^{jl} is given by (12.4), are:

$$\sum_{i=1}^{I} \sum_{k=1}^{K} \left[-\frac{\partial u^{jl}(\mathcal{X}^{jl^*}, \mathcal{Y}^{jl^*})}{\partial X_{ik}^{jl}} - (r_{ik}^* + e_k^*) \right] \times \left[X_{ik}^{jl} - X_{ik}^{jl^*} \right]$$
$$+\sum_{i=1}^{I} \sum_{k=1}^{K} \left[-\frac{\partial u^{jl}(\mathcal{X}^{jl^*}, \mathcal{Y}^{jl^*})}{\partial Z_{ik}^{jl}} - (\pi_{ik} + \lambda_{ik}^*) \right] \times \left[Z_{ik}^{jl} - Z_{ik}^{jl^*} \right]$$
$$+\sum_{i=1}^{I} \sum_{k=1}^{K} \left[-\frac{\partial u^{jl}(\mathcal{X}^{jl^*}, \mathcal{Y}^{jl^*})}{\partial W_{ik}^{jl}} - (r_{ik}^* + e_k^* - \eta_{ik}) \right] \times \left[W_{ik}^{jl} - W_{ik}^{jl^*} \right]$$
$$+\sum_{i=1}^{I} \sum_{k=1}^{K} \left[-\frac{\partial u^{jl}(\mathcal{X}^{jl^*}, \mathcal{Y}^{jl^*})}{\partial \Xi_{ik}^{jl}} - (\mu_{ik} + \delta_{ik}^* - \eta_{ik}) \right] \times \left[\Xi_{ik}^{jl} - \Xi_{ik}^{jl^*} \right]$$
$$+\sum_{i=1}^{I} \sum_{k=1}^{K} \left[-\frac{\partial u^{jl}(\mathcal{X}^{jl^*}, \mathcal{Y}^{jl^*})}{\partial Y_{ik}^{jl}} + (r_{ik}^* + e_k^*) \right] \times \left[Y_{ik}^{jl} - Y_{ik}^{jl^*} \right]$$
$$+\sum_{i=1}^{I} \sum_{k=1}^{K} \left[-\frac{\partial u^{jl}(\mathcal{X}^{jl^*}, \mathcal{Y}^{jl^*})}{\partial \Psi_{ik}^{jl}} + (\pi_{ik} + \lambda_{ik}^*) \right] \times \left[\Psi_{ik}^{jl} - \Psi_{ik}^{jl^*} \right]$$

$$+\sum_{i=1}^{I}\sum_{k=1}^{K}\left[-\frac{\partial u^{jl}(\mathcal{X}^{jl^*},\mathcal{Y}^{jl^*})}{\partial \Phi_{ik}^{jl}}+(r_{ik}^*+e_k^*-\eta_{ik})\right]\times\left[\Phi_{ik}^{jl}-\Phi_{ik}^{jl^*}\right]$$

$$+\sum_{i-1}^{I}\sum_{k=1}^{K}\left[-\frac{\partial u^{jl}(\mathcal{X}^{jl^*},\mathcal{Y}^{jl^*})}{\partial \Theta_{ik}^{jl}}+(\mu_{ik}+\delta_{ik}^*-\eta_{ik})\right]\times\left[\Theta_{ik}^{jl}-\Theta_{ik}^{jl^*}\right]\geq 0, \tag{12.13}$$

$$\forall(\mathcal{X}^{jl},\mathcal{Y}^{jl})\in\bar{\kappa}^{jl}.$$

Obviously (in the state of equilibrium), an inequality similar to (12.10) (or (12.13)) must hold for every other sector of every country in the economy.

We now discuss the price equilibrium conditions that govern the market under consideration.

Unhedged Instrument Market Equilibrium Conditions

For each unhedged instrument $i; i = 1,\ldots,I$, in currency $k; k = 1,\ldots,K$, we must have that:

$$\sum_{j=1}^{J}\sum_{l=1}^{L}\left[\left(X_{ik}^{jl^*}+W_{ik}^{jl^*}\right)-\left(Y_{ik}^{jl^*}+\Phi_{ik}^{jl^*}\right)\right]\begin{cases}=0, & \text{if } r_{ik}^*>0\\ \geq 0, & \text{if } r_{ik}^*=0,\end{cases} \tag{12.14}$$

where the system of equalities and inequalities (12.14) states the supply-demand rule that was suggested before, that is, if the price of a financial instrument is positive, then the market must clear for that instrument, and if the price is zero, then either there is an excess supply of that instrument in the economy or the market clears.

In a similar manner, we will now demonstrate the market equilibrium conditions that govern the exchange currency rates.

Unhedged Currency Market Equilibrium Conditions

For each unhedged currency $k; k = 1,\ldots,K$, we must have that:

$$\sum_{j=1}^{J}\sum_{l=1}^{L}\sum_{i=1}^{I}\left[\left(X_{ik}^{jl^*}+W_{ik}^{jl^*}\right)-\left(Y_{ik}^{jl^*}+\Phi_{ik}^{jl^*}\right)\right]\begin{cases}=0, & \text{if } e_k^*>0\\ \geq 0, & \text{if } e_k^*=0.\end{cases} \tag{12.15}$$

The system of equalities and inequalities (12.15) states that if the price of a currency is positive, then the market must clear for that instrument and if the price is zero, then either there is an excess supply of that instrument in the economy or the market clears.

Market Equilibrium Conditions for Futures Contracts

Since the futures market must clear for each instrument because either there is a contract traded at the fixed price π_{ik} or there is none, the following equality must hold for each hedged through futures contracts instrument i in currency k:

$$\sum_{j=1}^{J}\sum_{l=1}^{L}(Z_{ik}^{jl^*} - \Psi_{ik}^{jl^*}) = 0, \tag{12.16}$$

where λ_{ik}^* represents the shadow price that reflects the opportunity cost (in equilibrium) associated with trading the instrument i in currency k at the fixed price π_{ik}. Moreover, since (12.16) is an equality, the associated shadow price, λ_{ik}^*, can be positive, negative, or zero.

Market Equilibrium Conditions for Options Contracts

Similarly, for each hedged instrument i of currency k through options contracts, we must have that:

$$\sum_{j=1}^{J}\sum_{l=1}^{L}(\Xi_{ik}^{jl^*} - \Theta_{ik}^{jl^*}) = 0, \tag{12.17}$$

with the shadow price δ_{ik}^* associated with the equality (12.17) and can take on a positive, negative, or a zero value.

Definition 12.1 (An International Financial Equilibrium with Futures and Options)

A vector $(X^*, Y^*, r^*, e^*, \lambda^*, \delta^*) \in \mathcal{K}$ is an international, multi-sector, multi-instrument, and multi-currency financial equilibrium in the presence of financial futures and options if and only if it satisfies the system of equalities and inequalities (12.10) and (12.14)–(12.17), for all sectors $j; j = 1, \ldots, J$, all countries $l; l = 1, \ldots, L$, all instruments $i; i = 1, \ldots, I$, and all currencies $k; k = 1, \ldots, K$.

We will now present the variational inequality formulation of the governing equilibrium conditions.

Theorem 12.1 (Variational Inequality Formulation)

A vector of assets and liabilities of the sectors, and instrument prices, $(\mathcal{X}^*, \mathcal{Y}^*, r^*, e^*, \lambda^*, \delta^*) \in \mathcal{K}$, is an international financial equilibrium in the presence of financial futures and options if and only if it satisfies the variational inequality problem:

$$-\sum_{j=1}^{J}\sum_{l=1}^{L}\nabla_{\mathcal{X}^{jl}}U^{jl}(\mathcal{X}^{jl^*}, \mathcal{Y}^{jl^*}, r^*, e^*, \lambda^*, \delta^*; \pi, \mu, \eta)^T \cdot (\mathcal{X}^{jl} - \mathcal{X}^{jl^*})$$

$$-\sum_{j=1}^{J}\sum_{l=1}^{L}\nabla_{\mathcal{Y}^{jl}}U^{jl}(\mathcal{X}^{jl^*}, \mathcal{Y}^{jl^*}, r^*, e^*, \lambda^*, \delta^*; \pi, \mu, \eta)^T \cdot (\mathcal{Y}^{jl} - \mathcal{Y}^{jl^*})$$

$$+\sum_{i=1}^{I}\sum_{k=1}^{K}\left[\sum_{j=1}^{J}\sum_{l=1}^{L}\left(X_{ik}^{jl^*}+W_{ik}^{jl^*}\right)-\left(Y_{ik}^{jl^*}+\Phi_{ik}^{jl^*}\right)\right]\times[r_{ik}-r_{ik}^*]$$

$$+\sum_{k=1}^{K}\left[\sum_{i=1}^{I}\sum_{j=1}^{J}\sum_{l=1}^{L}\left(X_{ik}^{jl^*}+W_{ik}^{jl^*}\right)-\left(Y_{ik}^{jl^*}+\Phi_{ik}^{jl^*}\right)\right]\times[e_k-e_k^*]$$

$$+\sum_{i=1}^{I}\sum_{k=1}^{K}\left[\sum_{j=1}^{J}\sum_{l=1}^{L}\left(Z_{ik}^{jl^*}-\Psi_{ik}^{jl^*}\right)\right]\times[\lambda_{ik}-\lambda_{ik}^*]$$

$$+\sum_{i=1}^{I}\sum_{k=1}^{K}\left[\sum_{j=1}^{J}\sum_{l=1}^{L}\left(\Xi_{ik}^{jl^*}-\Theta_{ik}^{jl^*}\right)\right]\times[\delta_{ik}-\delta_{ik}^*]\geq 0, \tag{12.18}$$

$$\forall(\mathcal{X},\mathcal{Y},r,e,\lambda,\delta)\in\mathcal{K}.$$

Proof: Assume that $(\mathcal{X}^*,\mathcal{Y}^*,r^*,e^*,\lambda^*,\delta^*)$ is an equilibrium point of the international multi-currency, multi-sector, and multi-instrument financial model in the presence of futures and options. Hence, it satisfies Definition 12.1. Therefore, (12.10) must hold for all sectors from all countries and, consequently, summation of (12.10) over all sectors and all countries leads to:

$$-\sum_{j=1}^{J}\sum_{l=1}^{L}\nabla_{\mathcal{X}^{jl}}U^{jl}(\mathcal{X}^{jl^*},\mathcal{Y}^{jl^*},r^*,e^*,\lambda^*,\delta^*;\pi,\mu,\eta)^T\cdot(\mathcal{X}^{jl}-\mathcal{X}^{jl^*})$$

$$-\sum_{j=1}^{J}\sum_{l=1}^{L}\nabla_{\mathcal{Y}^{jl}}U^{jl}(\mathcal{X}^{jl^*},\mathcal{Y}^{jl^*},r^*,e^*,\lambda^*,\delta^*;\pi,\mu,\eta)^T\cdot(\mathcal{Y}^{jl}-\mathcal{Y}^{jl^*})\geq 0,$$

$$\forall(\mathcal{X},\mathcal{Y})\in\bar{\kappa}. \tag{12.19}$$

Moreover, (12.14) implies that

$$\sum_{j=1}^{J}\sum_{l=1}^{L}\left[\left(X_{ik}^{jl^*}+W_{ik}^{jl^*}\right)-\left(Y_{ik}^{jl^*}+\Phi_{ik}^{jl^*}\right)\right]\times[r_{ik}-r_{ik}^*]\geq 0,$$

and, hence, summation of this inequality over all instruments and all currencies yields

$$\sum_{i=1}^{I}\sum_{k=1}^{K}\left[\sum_{j=1}^{J}\sum_{l=1}^{L}\left(X_{ik}^{jl^*}+W_{ik}^{jl^*}\right)-\left(Y_{ik}^{jl^*}+\Phi_{ik}^{jl^*}\right)\right]\times[r_{ik}-r_{ik}^*]\geq 0,$$

$$\forall r\in R_+^{IK}. \tag{12.20}$$

Following a similar procedure, we can verify that the equilibrium condition (12.15) leads to the following inequality for all currencies k:

$$\sum_{k=1}^{K}\left[\sum_{i=1}^{I}\sum_{j=1}^{J}\sum_{l=1}^{L}\left(X_{ik}^{jl^*}+W_{ik}^{jl^*}\right)-\left(Y_{ik}^{jl^*}+\Phi_{ik}^{jl^*}\right)\right]\times\left[e_k-e_k^*\right]\geq 0,$$

$$\forall e\in R_+^K. \tag{12.21}$$

Finally, since the systems of equalities (12.16) and (12.17) hold for each instrument i in currency k, the summation of (12.16) as well as of (12.17) over all instruments and currencies leads, respectively, to:

$$\sum_{i=1}^{I}\sum_{k=1}^{K}\left[\sum_{j=1}^{J}\sum_{l=1}^{L}\left(Z_{ik}^{jl^*}-\Psi_{ik}^{jl^*}\right)\right]\times\left[\lambda_{ik}-\lambda_{ik}^*\right]=0,\ \forall\lambda\in R^{IK}, \tag{12.22}$$

and

$$\sum_{i=1}^{I}\sum_{k=1}^{K}\left[\sum_{j=1}^{J}\sum_{l=1}^{L}\left(\Xi_{ik}^{jl^*}-\Theta_{ik}^{jl^*}\right)\right]\times\left[\delta_{ik}-\delta_{ik}^*\right]=0,\ \forall\delta\in R^{IK}. \tag{12.23}$$

If we now sum (12.19)–(12.23) we can easily obtain variational inequality (12.18).

We will now prove that the solution to variational inequality (12.18) is also an international financial equilibrium with futures and options.

If we initially assume that the prices of all instruments and all currencies, hedged and unhedged, as well as all the corresponding shadow prices are equal to their equilibrium prices, then variational inequality (12.18) collapses to:

$$-\sum_{j=1}^{J}\sum_{l=1}^{L}\nabla_{\mathcal{X}^{jl}}U^{jl}(\mathcal{X}^{jl^*},\mathcal{Y}^{jl^*},r^*,e^*,\lambda^*;\pi,\mu)^T\cdot(\mathcal{X}^{jl}-\mathcal{X}^{jl^*})$$

$$-\sum_{j=1}^{J}\sum_{l=1}^{L}\nabla_{\mathcal{Y}^{jl}}U^{jl}(\mathcal{X}^{jl^*},\mathcal{Y}^{jl^*},r^*,e^*,\lambda^*,\delta^*;\pi,\mu)^T\cdot(\mathcal{Y}^{jl}-\mathcal{Y}^{jl^*})\geq 0, \tag{12.24}$$

which suggests economic condition (12.10) for each sector j from every country l.

In addition, if we let $\mathcal{X}^{jl}=\mathcal{X}^{jl^*}$, $\mathcal{Y}^{jl}=\mathcal{Y}^{jl^*}$, for all sectors j, and all countries l, $\lambda_{ik}=\lambda_{ik}^*$ and $\delta_{ik}=\delta_{ik}^*$ for all hedged instruments i and every currency k, along with $e_k=e_k^*$ for every currency k, then substitution into variational inequality (12.18) yields:

$$\sum_{i=1}^{I}\sum_{k=1}^{K}\left[\sum_{j=1}^{J}\sum_{l=1}^{L}\left(X_{ik}^{jl^*}+W_{ik}^{jl^*}\right)-\left(Y_{ik}^{jl^*}+\Phi_{ik}^{jl^*}\right)\right]\times\left[r_{ik}-r_{ik}^*\right]\geq 0, \tag{12.25}$$

which implies the system of equalities and inequalities (12.14).

Similarly, if we let $\mathcal{X}^{jl} = \mathcal{X}^{jl^*}$, $\mathcal{Y}^{jl} = \mathcal{Y}^{jl^*}$, for all sectors j, and all countries l, and $r_{ik} = r^*_{ik}$, along with $\lambda_{ik} = \lambda^*_{ik}$ and $\delta_{ik} = \delta^*_{ik}$, for all instruments i in every currency k, then variational inequality (12.18) reduces to:

$$\sum_{k=1}^{K}\left[\sum_{i=1}^{I}\sum_{j=1}^{J}\sum_{l=1}^{L}\left(X^{jl^*}_{ik}+W^{jl^*}_{ik}\right)-\left(Y^{jl^*}_{ik}+\Phi^{jl^*}_{ik}\right)\right]\times\left[e_k-e^*_k\right]\geq 0, \quad (12.26)$$

which directly leads to (12.15).

Finally, if we let $\mathcal{X}^{jl} = \mathcal{X}^{jl^*}$, $\mathcal{Y}^{jl} = \mathcal{Y}^{jl^*}$, for all sectors j, and all countries l, and $r_{ik} = r^*_{ik}$, for all instruments i in currency k, and $\delta_{ik} = \delta^*_{ik}$ for all instruments i and currencies k, and $e_k = e^*_k$ for all currencies k, then variational inequality (12.18) collapses to:

$$\sum_{i=1}^{I}\sum_{k=1}^{K}\left[\sum_{j=1}^{J}\sum_{l=1}^{L}\left(Z^{jl^*}_{ik}-\Psi^{jl^*}_{ik}\right)\right]\times\left[\lambda_{ik}-\lambda^*_{ik}\right]\geq 0, \quad (12.27)$$

which can only hold as an equality since λ_{ik} can be of either sign or zero, and, hence, it is equivalent to (12.16).

If now, instead of setting $\delta_{ik} = \delta^*_{ik}$ for each instrument i in currency k, we let $\lambda_{ik} = \lambda^*_{ik}$, and make the same substitutions as discussed immediately above, then variational inequality (12.18) reduces to:

$$\sum_{i=1}^{I}\sum_{k=1}^{K}\left[\sum_{j=1}^{J}\sum_{l=1}^{L}\left(\Xi^{jl^*}_{ik}-\Theta^{jl^*}_{ik}\right)\right]\times\left[\delta_{ik}-\delta^*_{ik}\right]\geq 0, \quad (12.28)$$

which leads to the system of equalities (12.17), since δ_{ik} can take both positive or negative or zero values. □

As before, in order to maintain a compact mathematical notation we will present the standard form of variational inequality (12.18), along with some definitions, that will simplify the detailed analysis of the models under consideration. In particular, we let $n = 8JLIK + 3IK + K$ and we define the n-dimensional column vector $x \equiv (\mathcal{X}, \mathcal{Y}, r, e, \lambda, \delta) \in \mathcal{K}$. We also let $F(x)$ be the function that enters variational inequality (12.18), which is of the following form:

$$F(x) = \begin{bmatrix} -\nabla_{\mathcal{X}} U(\mathcal{X}, \mathcal{Y}, r, e, \lambda, \delta; \pi, \mu, \eta) \\ -\nabla_{\mathcal{Y}} U(\mathcal{X}, \mathcal{Y}, r, e, \lambda, \delta; \pi, \mu, \eta) \\ \sum_{j=1}^{J} \sum_{l=1}^{L} \left(X_{11}^{jl} + W_{11}^{jl}\right) - \left(Y_{11}^{jl} + \Phi_{11}^{jl}\right) \\ \vdots \\ \sum_{j=1}^{J} \sum_{l=1}^{L} \left(X_{IK}^{jl} + W_{IK}^{jl}\right) - \left(Y_{IK}^{jl} + \Phi_{IK}^{jl}\right) \\ \sum_{j=1}^{J} \sum_{l=1}^{L} \sum_{i=1}^{I} \left(X_{i1}^{jl} + W_{i1}^{jl}\right) - \left(Y_{i1}^{jl} + \Phi_{i1}^{jl}\right) \\ \vdots \\ \sum_{j=1}^{J} \sum_{l=1}^{L} \sum_{i=1}^{I} \left(X_{iK}^{jl} + W_{iK}^{jl}\right) - \left(Y_{iK}^{jl} + \Phi_{iK}^{jl}\right) \\ \sum_{j=1}^{J} \sum_{l=1}^{L} \left(Z_{11}^{jl} - \Psi_{11}^{jl}\right) \\ \vdots \\ \sum_{j=1}^{J} \sum_{l=1}^{L} \left(Z_{IK}^{jl} - \Psi_{IK}^{jl}\right) \\ \sum_{j=1}^{J} \sum_{l=1}^{L} \left(\Xi_{11}^{jl} - \Theta_{11}^{jl}\right) \\ \vdots \\ \sum_{j=1}^{J} \sum_{l=1}^{L} \left(\Xi_{IK}^{jl} - \Theta_{IK}^{jl}\right) \end{bmatrix}_{n\times 1} . \qquad (12.29)$$

Hence, variational inequality (12.18) can be written as:
Determine $x^* \in \mathcal{K}$ satisfying:

$$\langle F(x^*)^T, (x - x^*)\rangle \geq 0, \quad \forall x \in \mathcal{K}. \qquad (12.30)$$

We will now present several models of specific interest, which are special cases or variants of the above model.

12.1.1 Special Cases and Variants of the International Hedging Model

In this subsection we present special cases and variants of the international hedging model of Section 12.1. Note that the examples presented in this subsection are only a small fragment of the whole spectrum of applications that incorporate financial futures and options. Clearly, there is a large variety of futures and options contracts available in the international markets (e. g., contracts on interest rates, debt instruments, indices, different currencies, etc.), and, ideally, the most general model must include all option and futures contracts available. Such a model, however, would require an immense number of variables, and is beyond the scope of this book. For demonstration purposes, we only present some models that include commonly encountered types of contracts.

In Example 12.1 we consider the special case in which there are futures only, whereas in Example 12.2 we then further assume that there are only interest rate futures. In Example 12.3, on the other hand, we present the special case in which there are only options available whereas in Example 12.4 we then further specialize Example 12.3 to consider fixed exchange rates for the currencies. In the second example, hence, we assume that there are only interest rate futures contracts available and that sectors can only obtain a fixed price on r_{ik} and not on e_k. On the other hand, in the final example, we assume that only currency option contracts are available, and, hence, a sector can obtain a fixed currency exchange rate, which we denote by μ_k, but he cannot hedge the price of a specific instrument.

Example 12.1 (Futures Only)

In this example, we maintain the general notation that was used throughout this section with the difference that there are now no options available. The vectors $\mathcal{X}^{jl}$ and $\mathcal{Y}^{jl}$ now each lie in R_+^{2IK}, whereas the vectors $\mathcal{X}$ and $\mathcal{Y}$ each lie in R_+^{JL2IK}. Moreover, in constraints (12.2) and (12.3), the option variables no longer appear, with the feasible sets $\bar{\mathcal{X}}^{jl}$, $\bar{\mathcal{Y}}^{jl}$, $\bar{\kappa}^{jl}$, $\bar{\kappa}$, and $\mathcal{K}$ begin modified accordingly to incorporate these changes. The structure of the portfolio optimization problem for sector j of country l remains as in (12.1)–(12.3), with the above modifications and with the options constants being excluded.

A special case of the utility function U^{jl}, analogous to (12.4), but adapted to this special case, is the following:

$$U^{jl} = u^{jl}(\mathcal{X}^{jl}, \mathcal{Y}^{jl}) + \sum_{i=1}^{I} \sum_{k=1}^{K} (r_{ik} + e_k)(X_{ik}^{jl} - Y_{ik}^{jl})$$

$$+ \sum_{i=1}^{I} \sum_{k=1}^{K} (\pi_{ik} + \lambda_{ik})(Z_{ik}^{jl} - \Psi_{ik}^{jl}). \tag{12.31}$$

The equilibrium conditions are also presented here for accessibility. In particular, equilibrium condition (12.10) simplifies to:

$$-\nabla_{\mathcal{X}^{jl}} U^{jl}(\mathcal{X}^{jl*}, \mathcal{Y}^{jl*}, r^*, e^*, \lambda^*; \pi)^T \cdot (\mathcal{X}^{jl} - \mathcal{X}^{jl*})$$

$$-\nabla_{\mathcal{Y}^{jl}} U^{jl}(\mathcal{X}^{jl*}, \mathcal{Y}^{jl*}, r^*, e^*, \lambda^*; \pi)^T \cdot (\mathcal{Y}^{jl} - \mathcal{Y}^{jl*}) \geq 0, \; \forall (\mathcal{X}^{jl}, \mathcal{Y}^{jl}) \in \bar{\kappa}^{jl}, \tag{12.32}$$

with the feasible set $\bar{\kappa}^{jl}$ begin simplified to exclude the option variables in the constraints (12.2) and (12.3).

Furthermore, (12.14) is now modified to: For all i and k:

$$\sum_{j=1}^{J} \sum_{l=1}^{L} \left(X_{ik}^{jl*} - Y_{ik}^{jl*} \right) \begin{cases} = 0, & \text{if } r_{ik}^* > 0 \\ \geq 0, & \text{if } r_{ik}^* = 0, \end{cases} \tag{12.33}$$

whereas (12.15) is modified to: For all k:

$$\sum_{j=1}^{J}\sum_{l=1}^{L}\sum_{i=1}^{I}\left(X_{ik}^{jl*}-Y_{ik}^{jl*}\right)\begin{cases}=0, & \text{if } e_k^*>0\\ \geq 0, & \text{if } e_k^*=0.\end{cases} \tag{12.34}$$

The market equilibrium condition for futures contracts (12.16) still holds and remains the same.

Definition 12.2 (An International Financial Equilibrium with Futures Only)

A vector $(X^*, Y^*, r^*, e^*, \lambda^*) \in \mathcal{K}$ is an international, multi-sector, multi-instrument, and multi-currency financial equilibrium in the presence of futures only if and only if it satisfies the system of equalities and inequalities (12.32)–(12.34) and (12.16), for all sectors $j; j = 1, \ldots, J$, all countries $l; l = 1, \ldots, L$, all instruments $i; i = 1, \ldots, I$, and all currencies $k; k = 1, \ldots, K$.

Moreover, the variational inequality formulation of the governing equilibrium conditions is the following.

Corollary 12.1 (Variational Inequality Formulation)

A vector of assets and liabilities of the sectors, and instrument prices, $(\mathcal{X}^*, \mathcal{Y}^*, r^*, e^*, \lambda^*) \in \mathcal{K}$, is an international financial equilibrium in the presence of interest rate futures if and only if it satisfies the variational inequality problem:

$$-\sum_{j=1}^{J}\sum_{l=1}^{L}\nabla_{\mathcal{X}^{jl}}U^{jl}(\mathcal{X}^{jl*},\mathcal{Y}^{jl*},r^*,e^*,\lambda^*;\pi)^T\cdot(\mathcal{X}^{jl}-\mathcal{X}^{jl*})$$

$$-\sum_{j=1}^{J}\sum_{l=1}^{L}\nabla_{\mathcal{Y}^{jl}}U^{jl}(\mathcal{X}^{jl*},\mathcal{Y}^{jl*},r^*,e^*,\lambda^*;\pi)^T\cdot(\mathcal{Y}^{jl}-\mathcal{Y}^{jl*})$$

$$+\sum_{i=1}^{I}\sum_{k=1}^{K}\left[\sum_{j=1}^{J}\sum_{l=1}^{L}\left(X_{ik}^{jl*}-Y_{ik}^{jl*}\right)\right]\times[r_{ik}-r_{ik}^*]$$

$$+\sum_{k=1}^{K}\left[\sum_{i=1}^{I}\sum_{j=1}^{J}\sum_{l=1}^{L}\left(X_{ik}^{jl*}-Y_{ik}^{jl*}\right)\right]\times[e_k-e_k^*]$$

$$+\sum_{i=1}^{I}\sum_{k=1}^{K}\left[\sum_{j=1}^{J}\sum_{l=1}^{L}\left(Z_{ik}^{jl*}-\Psi_{ik}^{jl*}\right)\right]\times[\lambda_{ik}-\lambda_{ik}^*]\geq 0,\forall(\mathcal{X},\mathcal{Y},r,e,\lambda)\in\mathcal{K}. \tag{12.35}$$

In Figure 12.2, the underlying network structure of the sectors' optimization problems, in the case of futures only, is depicted. The nodes at the

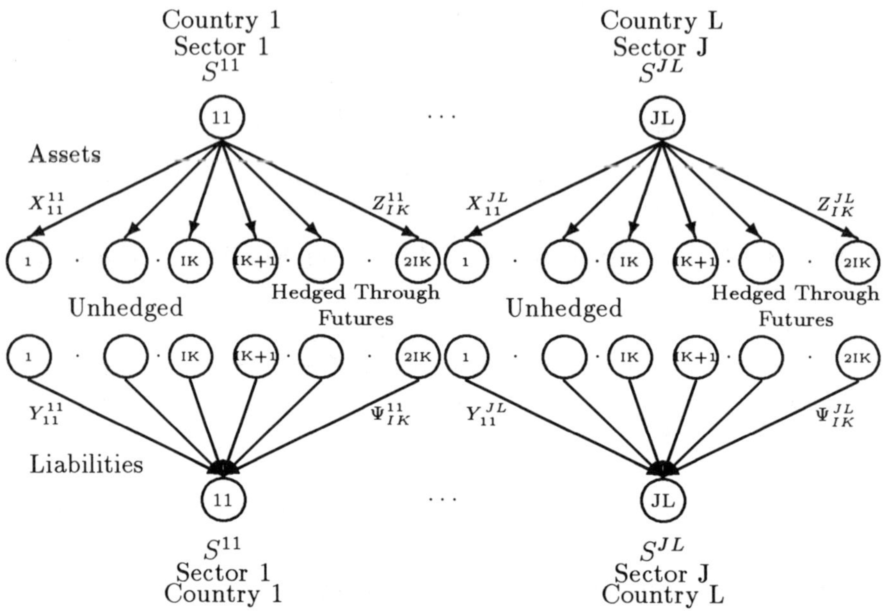

Fig. 12.2. Network structure of the sectors' optimization problems with futures only

highest and the lowest levels represent the sectors of the countries, whereas the intermediate level nodes represent the different types of hedged and unhedged instruments and currencies.

Note that this model generalizes the single country futures model presented in Section 7.1 to the international domain.

Example 12.2 (Interest Rate Futures)

In this example, we maintain the general notation that was used throughout this section and, as in Example 12.1, we assume that there are no options available. Here, however, the fixed price π_{ik} of a futures contract refers only to a fixed interest rate and not to a fixed currency exchange rate. Hence, this model is a variant of the Section 12.1 model in which interest rate futures are incorporated. The portfolio optimization problem for sector j of country l remains as in (12.1)–(12.3), but with the option related variables and constants being excluded.

The special case of the utility function U^{jl}, given by (12.4) (see also (12.31)) in this case is adapted to be the following:

$$U^{jl} = u^{jl}(\mathcal{X}^{jl}, \mathcal{Y}^{jl}) + \sum_{i=1}^{I} \sum_{k=1}^{K} (r_{ik} + e_k)(X_{ik}^{jl} - Y_{ik}^{jl})$$

$$+\sum_{i=1}^{I}\sum_{k=1}^{K}(\pi_{ik}+\lambda_{ik}+e_k)(Z_{ik}^{jl}-\Psi_{ik}^{jl}). \qquad (12.36)$$

Note the difference in the respective third terms on the right-hand sides of the utility function expressions in (12.36) and (12.31). In this model we consider interest rate futures and, consequently, we have the added term $+e_k$ premultiplying the difference between the hedged asset and hedged liability.

Note that the network structure of the sectors' portfolio optimization problems is still as depicted in Figure 12.2.

We now show how the equilibrium conditions need to be modified. Clearly, (12.10) is still appropriate with the utility functions modified and the feasible set modified (as in Example 12.1).

Condition (12.14), as in Example 12.1, takes on the form given in (12.33), whereas (12.15) (rather than taking the form given in (12.34)) is modified to: For all k:

$$\sum_{j=1}^{J}\sum_{l=1}^{L}\sum_{i=1}^{I}\left[\left(X_{ik}^{jl*}+Z_{ik}^{jl*}\right)-\left(Y_{ik}^{jl*}+\Psi_{ik}^{jl*}\right)\right]\begin{cases}=0, & \text{if } e_k^*>0\\ \geq 0, & \text{if } e_k^*=0.\end{cases} \qquad (12.37)$$

The market equilibrium condition for futures contracts (12.16) still holds and remains the same.

Definition 12.3 (An International Financial Equilibrium with Interest Rate Futures Only)

A vector $(X^*,Y^*,r^*,e^*,\lambda^*)\in\mathcal{K}$ is an international, multi-sector, multi-instrument, and multi-currency financial equilibrium in the presence of interest rate futures if and only if it satisfies the system of equalities and inequalities (12.32), (12.33), (12.37), and (12.16), for all sectors $j; j=1,\ldots,J$, all countries $l; l=1,\ldots,L$, all instruments $i; i=1,\ldots,I$, and all currencies $k; k=1,\ldots,K$.

Moreover, the variational inequality formulation of the governing equilibrium conditions is the following.

Corollary 12.2 (Variational Inequality Formulation)

A vector of assets and liabilities of the sectors, and instrument prices, $(\mathcal{X}^*,\mathcal{Y}^*,r^*,e^*,\lambda^*)\in\mathcal{K}$, is an international financial equilibrium in the presence of interest rate futures if and only if it satisfies the variational inequality problem:

$$-\sum_{j=1}^{J}\sum_{l=1}^{L}\nabla_{\mathcal{X}^{jl}}U^{jl}(\mathcal{X}^{jl*},\mathcal{Y}^{jl*},r^*,e^*,\lambda^*;\pi)^T\cdot(\mathcal{X}^{jl}-\mathcal{X}^{jl*})$$

$$-\sum_{j=1}^{J}\sum_{l=1}^{L}\nabla_{\mathcal{Y}^{jl}}U^{jl}(\mathcal{X}^{jl*},\mathcal{Y}^{jl*},r^*,e^*,\lambda^*;\pi)^T\cdot(\mathcal{Y}^{jl}-\mathcal{Y}^{jl*})$$

$$+\sum_{i=1}^{I}\sum_{k=1}^{K}\left[\sum_{j=1}^{J}\sum_{l=1}^{L}\left(X_{ik}^{jl*}-Y_{ik}^{jl*}\right)\right]\times[r_{ik}-r_{ik}^{*}]$$

$$+\sum_{k=1}^{K}\left[\sum_{i=1}^{I}\sum_{j=1}^{J}\sum_{l=1}^{L}\left(X_{ik}^{jl*}+Z_{ik}^{jl*}\right)-\left(Y_{ik}^{jl*}+\Psi_{ik}^{jl*}\right)\right]\times[e_k-e_k^{*}]$$

$$+\sum_{i=1}^{I}\sum_{k=1}^{K}\left[\sum_{j=1}^{J}\sum_{l=1}^{L}\left(Z_{ik}^{jl*}-\Psi_{ik}^{jl*}\right)\right]\times[\lambda_{ik}-\lambda_{ik}^{*}]\geq 0,\forall(\mathcal{X},\mathcal{Y},r,e,\lambda)\in\mathcal{K}. \tag{12.38}$$

Obviously, this basic model can be further extended to more complicated and realistic scenarios where we have multiple futures contracts per instrument and at different fixed prices.

Note that this model is a variation of the general model presented earlier in this section, since here we do not have a fixed price for both the instruments and the currencies, but only for the instruments. In reality, these types of contracts are easier to obtain in the international markets.

Example 12.3 (Options Only)

As in the previous two examples, we maintain the general notation that has been used throughout this section, but now we consider options only. This model is another special case of the model of Section 12.1. Moreover, it is a generalization of the single country options model presented in Section 7.5. Once again, the portfolio optimization problem for sector j of country l remains as in (12.1)–(12.3), but with the futures related variables and constants being excluded. Moreover, the feasible set is simplified to exclude the futures variables as are the utility functions and the asset and liability vectors $\mathcal{X}$ and $\mathcal{Y}$ and their sector subvectors.

A special case of the utility function U^{jl} of sector j from country l, similar to the ones proposed in (12.4), (12.31), and (12.36) is the following:

$$U^{jl}=u^{jl}(\mathcal{X}^{jl},\mathcal{Y}^{jl})+\sum_{i=1}^{I}\sum_{k=1}^{K}(r_{ik}+e_k)(X_{ik}^{jl}-Y_{ik}^{jl})$$

$$+\sum_{i=1}^{I}\sum_{k=1}^{K}(r_{ik}+e_k-\eta_{ik})(W_{ik}^{jl}-\Phi_{ik}^{jl})+\sum_{i=1}^{I}\sum_{k=1}^{K}(\delta_{ik}+\mu_{ik}-\eta_{ik})(\Xi_{ik}^{jl}-\Theta_{ik}^{jl}). \tag{12.39}$$

Clearly, the preceding equilibrium conditions must be modified. In particular, the portfolio optimality conditions (12.10) become in this special case model:

$$-\nabla_{\mathcal{X}^{jl}}U^{jl}(\mathcal{X}^{jl*},\mathcal{Y}^{jl*},r^{*},e^{*},\delta^{*};\mu,\eta)^{T}\cdot(\mathcal{X}^{jl}-\mathcal{X}^{jl*})$$

$$-\nabla_{\mathcal{Y}^{jl}} U^{jl}(\mathcal{X}^{jl^*}, \mathcal{Y}^{jl^*}, r^*, e^*, \delta^*; \mu, \eta)^T \cdot (\mathcal{Y}^{jl} - \mathcal{Y}^{jl^*}) \geq 0, \ \forall (\mathcal{X}^{jl}, \mathcal{Y}^{jl}) \in \bar{\kappa}^{jl}, \tag{12.40}$$

with $\bar{\kappa}^{jl}$ being redefined to exclude the futures variables. Equilibrium conditions (12.14), (12.15), and (12.17) still hold.

Definition 12.4 (An International Financial Equilibrium with Options Only)
A vector $(\mathcal{X}^*, \mathcal{Y}^*, r^*, e^*, \delta^*) \in \mathcal{K}$ is an international, multi-sector, multi-instrument, and multi-currency financial equilibrium in the presence of options only if and only if it satisfies the system of equalities and inequalities (12.40), (12.14), (12.15), and (12.17) for all sectors $j; j = 1, \ldots, J$, all countries $l; l = 1, \ldots, L$, all instruments $i; i = 1, \ldots, I$, and all currencies $k; k = 1, \ldots, K$.

One can easily verify that the variational inequality formulation for this specific model is given by:

Corollary 12.3 (Variational Inequality Formulation)
A vector of assets and liabilities of the sectors, and instrument prices, $(\mathcal{X}^*, \mathcal{Y}^*, r^*, e^*, \delta^*) \in \mathcal{K}$, is an international financial equilibrium in the presence of currency options if and only if it satisfies the variational inequality problem:

$$-\sum_{j=1}^{J}\sum_{l=1}^{L} \nabla_{\mathcal{X}^{jl}} U^{jl}(\mathcal{X}^{jl^*}, \mathcal{Y}^{jl^*}, r^*, e^*, \delta^*; \mu, \eta)^T \cdot (\mathcal{X}^{jl} - \mathcal{X}^{jl^*})$$

$$-\sum_{j=1}^{J}\sum_{l=1}^{L} \nabla_{\mathcal{Y}^{jl}} U^{jl}(\mathcal{X}^{jl^*}, \mathcal{Y}^{jl^*}, r^*, e^*, \delta^*; \mu, \eta)^T \cdot (\mathcal{Y}^{jl} - \mathcal{Y}^{jl^*})$$

$$+\sum_{i=1}^{I}\sum_{k=1}^{K} \left[\sum_{j=1}^{J}\sum_{l=1}^{L} \left[\left(X_{ik}^{jl^*} + W_{ik}^{jl^*} \right) - \left(Y_{ik}^{jl^*} + \Phi_{ik}^{jl^*} \right) \right] \right] \times [r_{ik} - r_{ik}^*]$$

$$+\sum_{k=1}^{K} \left[\sum_{i=1}^{I}\sum_{j=1}^{J}\sum_{l=1}^{L} \left(X_{ik}^{jl^*} - Y_{ik}^{jl^*} \right) \right] \times [e_k - e_k^*]$$

$$+\sum_{i=1}^{I}\sum_{k=1}^{K} \left[\sum_{j=1}^{J}\sum_{l=1}^{L} \left(\Xi_{ik}^{jl^*} - \Theta_{ik}^{jl^*} \right) \right] \times [\delta_{ik} - \delta_{ik}^*] \geq 0, \ \forall (\mathcal{X}, \mathcal{Y}, r, e, \delta) \in \mathcal{K}. \tag{12.41}$$

The network structure of the sectors' optimization problems in this special case model is illustrated in Figure 12.3. The structure is similar to the one depicted in Figure 12.1. Apart from the fact that Figure 12.1 considers future contracts, whereas Figure 12.3 does not, the two figures vary as to the number of nodes that represent the different currencies and instruments,

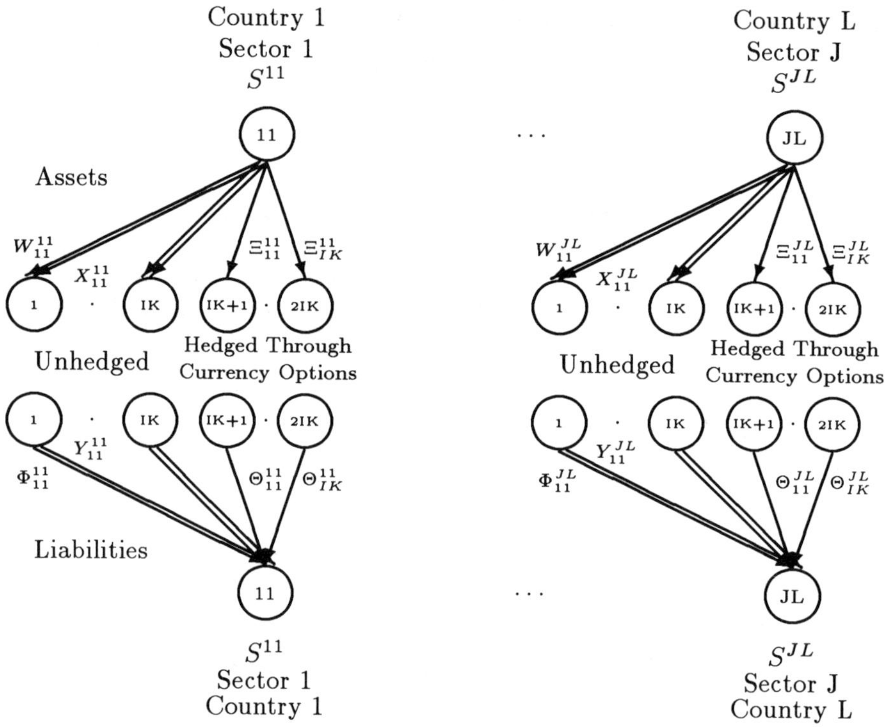

Fig. 12.3. Network structure of the sectors' optimization problems with options only

with the former having hedged instruments and currencies whereas the latter has both hedged and unhedged currencies and unhedged instruments.

In view of the similarities between the two networks, one can easily recognize that the model presented in Example 12.3 is a special case of the general model presented at the beginning of this section.

Example 12.4 (Currency Options Only)

Since there is a large variety of option contracts with international appeal, one can easily obtain many different variations and extensions of the model presented in Example 12.3. For demonstration purposes we will now present a model that incorporates currency option contracts where, for simplicity, and, without loss of generality, we assume that they are the only contracts available.

As in the previous example, we maintain the general notation that has been used throughout this section, but now we denote the fixed exchange rate of currency k that an option contract offers by μ_k (rather than by μ_{ik}), and the premium that is associated with this contract by η_k (rather than η_{ik}). Once again, the portfolio optimization problem for sector j of country l remains the same, as in (12.1)–(12.3), but with the futures related variables and constants being excluded. Moreover, the feasible set is, again, simplified to exclude the futures variables as are the utility functions and the asset and liability vectors $\mathcal{X}$ and $\mathcal{Y}$ and their sector subvectors.

A special case of the utility function U^{jl} of sector j from country l, similar to the ones proposed in (12.4), (12.31), (12.36), and (12.39) is the following:

$$U^{jl} = u^{jl}(\mathcal{X}^{jl}, \mathcal{Y}^{jl}) + \sum_{i=1}^{I}\sum_{k=1}^{K}(r_{ik} + e_k)(X_{ik}^{jl} - Y_{ik}^{jl})$$

$$+\sum_{i=1}^{I}\sum_{k=1}^{K}(\delta_k+\mu_k-\gamma_k)(\Xi_{ik}^{jl}-\Theta_{ik}^{jl})+\sum_{i=1}^{I}\sum_{k=1}^{K}(r_{ik}+e_k-\gamma_k)(W_{ik}^{jl}-\Phi_{ik}^{jl}). \quad (12.42)$$

Clearly, the preceding equilibrium conditions must be modified. The portfolio optimality conditions (12.10) remain as in (12.40).

Equilibrium condition (12.14), however, still holds whereas (12.15) is adjusted to

$$\sum_{j=1}^{J}\sum_{l=1}^{L}\sum_{i=1}^{I}\left(X_{ik}^{jl*} - Y_{ik}^{jl*}\right)\begin{cases} = 0, & \text{if } e_k^* > 0 \\ \geq 0, & \text{if } e_k^* = 0. \end{cases} \quad (12.43)$$

Finally, the equilibrium condition (12.17) for the options contracts is now modified to:

$$\sum_{j=1}^{J}\sum_{l=1}^{L}\sum_{i=1}^{I}(\Xi_{ik}^{jl^*} - \Theta_{ik}^{jl^*}) = 0, \quad (12.44)$$

with δ_k^*, rather than δ_{ik}^* now denoting the shadow price associated with equality (12.44). We now present the definition of an international financial equilibrium in the presence of currency option contracts.

Definition 12.4 (An International Financial Equilibrium with Currency Options Only)
A vector $(\mathcal{X}^*, \mathcal{Y}^*, r^*, e^*, \delta^*) \in \mathcal{K}$ is an international, multi-sector, multi-instrument, and multi-currency financial equilibrium in the presence of currency options if and only if it satisfies the system of equalities and inequalities (12.40), (12.14), (12.43), and (12.44) for all sectors $j; j = 1, \ldots, J$, all countries $l; l = 1, \ldots, L$, all instruments $i; i = 1, \ldots, I$, and all currencies $k; k = 1, \ldots, K$.

One can easily verify that the variational inequality formulation for this specific model is given by:

Corollary 12.4 (Variational Inequality Formulation)
A vector of assets and liabilities of the sectors, and instrument prices, $(\mathcal{X}^*, \mathcal{Y}^*, r^*, e^*, \delta^*) \in \mathcal{K}$, is an international financial equilibrium in the presence of currency options if and only if it satisfies the variational inequality problem:

$$-\sum_{j=1}^{J}\sum_{l=1}^{L} \nabla_{\mathcal{X}^{jl}} U^{jl}(\mathcal{X}^{jl^*}, \mathcal{Y}^{jl^*}, r^*, e^*, \delta^*; \mu, \eta)^T \cdot (\mathcal{X}^{jl} - \mathcal{X}^{jl^*})$$

$$-\sum_{j=1}^{J}\sum_{l=1}^{L} \nabla_{\mathcal{Y}^{jl}} U^{jl}(\mathcal{X}^{jl^*}, \mathcal{Y}^{jl^*}, r^*, e^*, \delta^*; \mu, \eta)^T \cdot (\mathcal{Y}^{jl} - \mathcal{Y}^{jl^*})$$

$$+\sum_{i=1}^{I}\sum_{k=1}^{K} \left[\sum_{j=1}^{J}\sum_{l=1}^{L} \left[\left(X_{ik}^{jl^*} + W_{ik}^{jl^*}\right) - \left(Y_{ik}^{jl^*} + \Phi_{ik}^{jl^*}\right)\right]\right] \times [r_{ik} - r_{ik}^*]$$

$$+\sum_{k=1}^{K} \left[\sum_{i=1}^{I}\sum_{j=1}^{J}\sum_{l=1}^{L} \left(X_{ik}^{jl^*} - Y_{ik}^{jl^*}\right)\right] \times [e_k - e_k^*]$$

$$+\sum_{k=1}^{K} \left[\sum_{j=1}^{J}\sum_{l=1}^{L}\sum_{i=1}^{I} \left(\Xi_{ik}^{jl^*} - \Theta_{ik}^{jl^*}\right)\right] \times [\delta_k - \delta_k^*] \geq 0, \forall (\mathcal{X}, \mathcal{Y}, r, e, \delta) \in \mathcal{K}. \tag{12.45}$$

The network structure of the sectors' optimization problems in this special case model is again as illustrated in Figure 12.3.

As the model in Example 12.2, the model discussed here is a variation of the general model presented earlier in this section, since here we do not have a fixed price for both the instruments and the currencies, but only for the currencies. Currency futures could also be utilized in order to provide fixed exchange rates, with the difference that sectors would not have the option of exercising or not.

12.2 Qualitative Analysis

In this section we address some of the qualitative properties of the models presented in Section 12.1. In particular, we present some results as to the existence and the uniqueness of the equilibrium pattern, so that the reader can also evaluate the boundaries of the computational tools that can be utilized for solving each particular problem.

Theorem 12.2 (Existence)

Assume that the utility functions are of the form given in (12.4). If we assume that $(\mathcal{X}^*, \mathcal{Y}^*, r^*, e^*, \lambda^*, \delta^*) \in \mathcal{K}$ is an equilibrium pattern and, therefore, a solution to variational inequality (12.18), then $(\mathcal{X}^*, \mathcal{Y}^*)$ is a solution of the variational inequality:

$$-\sum_{j=1}^{J}\sum_{l=1}^{L} \nabla_{\mathcal{X}^{jl}} U^{jl}(\mathcal{X}^{jl^*}, \mathcal{Y}^{jl^*}, r^*, e^*, \lambda^*, \delta^*; \pi, \mu, \eta)^T \cdot (\mathcal{X}^{jl} - \mathcal{X}^{jl^*})$$

$$-\sum_{j=1}^{J}\sum_{l=1}^{L} \nabla_{\mathcal{Y}^{jl}} U^{jl}(\mathcal{X}^{jl^*}, \mathcal{Y}^{jl^*}, r^*, e^*, \lambda^*, \delta^*; \pi, \mu, \eta)^T \cdot (\mathcal{Y}^{jl} - \mathcal{Y}^{jl^*}) \geq 0,$$

$$\forall (\mathcal{X}, \mathcal{Y}) \in \tilde{S}, \tag{12.46}$$

where $\tilde{S}$ is a non-empty set such that:

$$\tilde{S} \equiv \{(\mathcal{X}, \mathcal{Y}) \in \kappa;\ \rho_{ik} \geq 0; \sigma_{ik} = 0; h_{ik} = 0; \forall ik\ ; \epsilon_k \geq 0; \forall k\}.$$

where

$$\rho_{ik} \equiv \sum_{j=1}^{J}\sum_{l=1}^{L} \left[\left(X_{ik}^{jl} + W_{ik}^{jl}\right) - \left(Y_{ik}^{jl} + \Phi_{ik}^{jl}\right)\right], \tag{12.47}$$

$$\sigma_{ik} \equiv \sum_{j=1}^{J}\sum_{l=1}^{L} (Z_{ik}^{jl} - \Psi_{ik}^{jl}), \tag{12.48}$$

$$h_{ik} \equiv \sum_{j=1}^{J}\sum_{l=1}^{L} (W_{ik}^{jl} - \Phi_{ik}^{jl}), \tag{12.49}$$

$$\epsilon_k \equiv \sum_{j=1}^{J}\sum_{l=1}^{L}\sum_{i=1}^{I} \left[\left(X_{ik}^{jl} + W_{ik}^{jl}\right) - \left(Y_{ik}^{jl} + \Phi_{ik}^{jl}\right)\right]. \tag{12.50}$$

Conversely, if $(\mathcal{X}^*, \mathcal{Y}^*)$ is an equilibrium solution of variational inequality (12.18), then there exist IK-dimensional vectors of Lagrange multipliers associated, respectively, with the constraints: $\rho_{ik} \geq 0$, $\sigma_{ik} = 0$, and $h_{ik} = 0$, *for $i = 1, \ldots, I$, and $k = 1, \ldots, K$, along with a K-dimensional vector of Lagrange multipliers corresponding to constraint: $\epsilon_k \geq 0$, for $k = 1, \ldots, K$, such that $(\mathcal{X}^*, \mathcal{Y}^*, r^*, e^*, \lambda^*, \delta^*)$ is a solution to variational inequality (12.18) and, hence, is an equilibrium pattern.*

The proof for Theorem 12.2 can be easily obtained as an adaptation of the proof of Theorem 7.2.

The proof of the subsequent proposition can be easily derived utilizing the proof of Theorem 6.3.

Proposition 12.1 (Uniqueness)
If we assume that the utility function U^{jl} is strictly concave for each sector j from every country l, and twice continuously differentiable, then the equilibrium pattern of assets and liabilities, $(\mathcal{X}^*, \mathcal{Y}^*)$, is unique.

We will now present some of the properties that characterize function $F(x)$ that enters variational inequality (12.30). These results will be utilized in later sections of this chapter in order to provide convergence results for computational methodologies that could be utilized for the specific models. We omit the proofs for the two subsequent propositions since they are adaptations, respectively, of the proofs of Theorems 6.4 and 6.5.

Proposition 12.2 (Monotonicity)
If we assume that each sector j from every country l is risk-averse, and, therefore, the utility function U^{jl} is strictly concave, for each j and l, then the function $F(x)$ defined in (12.29) is monotone.

Proposition 12.3 (Lipschitz Continuity)
If we assume that the utility function U^{jl} is continuous with bounded second order derivatives for all sectors j from every country l and for all $x \in \mathcal{K}$ then the function $F(x)$ that enters variational inequality (12.30) is Lipschitz continuous, that is:

$$\| F(x^1) - F(x^2) \| \leq \mathcal{L} \| x^1 - x^2 \|, \quad \forall x^1, x^2 \in \mathcal{K},$$

with Lipschitz constant $\mathcal{L} > 0$.

12.3 International Financial Adjustment Process

In this section we provide the dynamic counterpart of the static international model with futures and options that was discussed in Section 12.1.

Since each sector of every country seeks to determine the direction that maximizes his utility function, the idealized direction for the unconstrained utility maximization problem is equal to $(\nabla_{\mathcal{X}^{jl}} U^{jl}, \nabla_{\mathcal{Y}^{jl}} U^{jl})$, where $(\nabla_{\mathcal{X}^{jl}} U^{jl}$ and $\nabla_{\mathcal{Y}^{jl}} U^{jl})$ are defined in (12.11) and (12.12), respectively.

Since the feasible set is constrained, this idealized direction has to be modified so that the accounting and nonnegativity constraints are not violated.

The best-realizable direction is the projection of the idealized direction onto his constraint set and is denoted as:

$$\Pi_{\bar{\mathcal{X}}^{jl}\times\bar{\mathcal{Y}}^{jl}}\left((\mathcal{X}^{jl},\mathcal{Y}^{jl}),(\nabla_{\mathcal{X}^{jl}}U^{jl},\nabla_{\mathcal{Y}^{jl}}U^{jl})\right), \tag{12.51}$$

and, as a consequence of Proposition 8.1, the asset and liability volumes for sector j of country l are adjusted according to the following processes over time t:

$$\dot{\mathcal{X}}^{jl}=\Pi_{\bar{\mathcal{X}}^{jl}}(\mathcal{X}^{jl},\nabla_{\mathcal{X}^{jl}}U^{jl}),\quad \dot{\mathcal{Y}}^{jl}=\Pi_{\bar{\mathcal{Y}}^{jl}}(\mathcal{Y}^{jl},\nabla_{\mathcal{Y}^{jl}}U^{jl}). \tag{12.52}$$

Moreover, based on the equilibrium condition (12.14), the adjustment process for the price of the unhedged instrument i in currency k is given by:

$$\dot{r}_{ik}=\begin{cases}\max\{0,\ -\rho_{ik}\}, & \text{if } r_{ik}=0\\ -\rho_{ik}, & \text{if } r_{ik}>0,\end{cases} \tag{12.53}$$

or, equivalently,

$$\dot{r}_{ik}=\Pi_{R_+}(r_{ik},-\rho_{ik}), \tag{12.54}$$

where ρ_{ik} is defined in (12.47).

Similarly, the financial adjustment process that characterizes the prices of every currency k is the following:

$$\dot{e}_k=\begin{cases}\max\{0,\ -\epsilon_k\}, & \text{if } e_k=0\\ -\epsilon_k, & \text{if } e_k>0.\end{cases} \tag{12.55}$$

or, equivalently,

$$\dot{e}_k=\Pi_{R_+}(e_k,-\epsilon_k), \tag{12.56}$$

where ϵ_k is defined in (12.50).

If we now take into consideration the fact that the shadow prices associated with a hedged instrument or currency can be of either sign, then the following adjustment processes must hold true for all hedged instruments and currencies.

$$\dot{\lambda}_{ik}=-\left[\sum_{j=1}^{J}\sum_{l=1}^{L}(Z_{ik}^{jl}-\Psi_{ik}^{jl})\right], \tag{12.57}$$

which, in turn, is equivalent to:

$$\dot{\lambda}_{ik}=\Pi_R(\lambda_{ik},-\sigma_{ik}), \tag{12.58}$$

with σ_{ik} being defined in (12.48), and, similarly,

$$\dot{\delta}_{ik}=-\left[\sum_{j=1}^{J}\sum_{l=1}^{L}(\Xi_{ik}^{jl}-\Theta_{ik}^{jl})\right], \tag{12.59}$$

which, in turn, is equivalent to:

$$\dot{\delta}_{ik} = \Pi_R(\delta_{ik}, -h_{ik}), \tag{12.60}$$

where h_{ik} is defined in (12.49).

In view of the structure of the feasible set, and recalling Proposition 8.1 again, the international financial adjustment process with futures and options contracts takes on the following form:

$$\begin{cases} \dot{\mathcal{X}}^{jl} &= \Pi_{\tilde{\mathcal{X}}^{jl}}(\mathcal{X}^{jl}, \nabla_{\mathcal{X}^{jl}} U^{jl}); & j = 1, \cdots, J; l = 1, \ldots, L \\ \dot{\mathcal{Y}}^{jl} &= \Pi_{\tilde{\mathcal{Y}}^{jl}}(\mathcal{Y}^{jl}, \nabla_{\mathcal{Y}^{jl}} U^{jl}); & j = 1, \cdots, J; l = 1, \ldots, L \\ \dot{r}_{ik} &= \Pi_{R_+}(r_{ik}, -\rho_{ik}); & i = 1, \cdots, I; k = 1, \ldots, K \\ \dot{e}_k &= \Pi_{R_+}(e_k, -\epsilon_k); & k = 1, \ldots, K. \\ \dot{\lambda}_{ik} &= \Pi_R(\lambda_{ik}, -\sigma_{ik}); & i = 1, \cdots, I; k = 1, \ldots, K \\ \dot{\delta}_{ik} &= \Pi_R(\delta_{ik}, -h_{ik}); & i = 1, \cdots, I; k = 1, \ldots, K. \end{cases} \tag{12.61}$$

Taking into account the previous definitions, the international financial adjustment process in the presence of futures and options can be expressed in a more compact mathematical form as:

$$\dot{x} = \Pi_{\mathcal{K}}(x, -F(x)), \tag{12.62}$$

where $F(x)$ is as defined in (12.29).

We recall that, according to Theorem 4.1, the set of equilibria of the projected dynamical system (12.62) coincides with the set of solutions to variational inequality (12.18). Also, according to Theorem 4.2, there exists a unique solution path to (12.62) for any boundary condition $x(0) = x_0 \in \mathcal{K}$.

Notice that similar adjustment processes can be derived for the models presented in Examples 12.1 through 12.4.

12.4 Stability Analysis

In this section we present some results on the stability analysis of the adjustment process presented in the previous section, establishing a clear connection between the dynamic and the static counterparts of the model(s) under consideration. In particular, we initially present some definitions, which are adaptations of those found in Chapter 4, which we will use for the stability analysis of the dynamic international financial model in the presence of futures and options, and we then provide the conditions under which a disequilibrium pattern of assets, liabilities, prices and shadow prices related to the futures and options contracts will reach an international financial equilibrium state under the adjustment process (12.62).

Definition 12.5

The international financial adjustment process (12.62) is stable if each financial equilibrium, $x^* = (X^*, Y^*, r^*, e^*, \lambda^*, \delta^*)$, is a monotone attractor, *that is, for any initial asset, liability, instrument and currency price pattern, as well as shadow prices associated with the futures and options contracts* $x_0 = (X_0, Y_0, r_0, e_0, \lambda_0, \delta_0)$, *the distance,* $\|(x(t) - x^*)\|$, *is nonincreasing in time* t, *where* $x(t) = (X(t), Y(t), r(t), e(t), \lambda(t), \delta(t))$, *satisfies the adjustment process (12.62).*

Definition 12.6

The international financial adjustment process with financial futures and options is asymptotically stable if it is stable and for any initial asset, liability, price, and shadow price pattern, x_0, *the financial adjustment process that starts with* x_0 *converges to some equilibrium pattern* x^*; *namely,*

$$\lim_{t \to \infty} x_0(t) \to x^*. \tag{12.63}$$

We recall from Chapter 4, that stability of an adjustment process implies that any state of disequilibrium will remain close to an equilibrium forever. On the other hand, asymptotic stability implies that any disequilibrium pattern will eventually reach an equilibrium.

The following two theorems, which are not accompanied by any proofs, since their proofs are adaptations of Theorems 8.8 and 8.9, respectively, establish conditions under which the international financial adjustment process in the presence of financial futures and options is, respectively, stable and asymptotically stable.

Theorem 12.3 (Stability)

If the utility function U^{jl} *of each sector* j *from every country* l *is twice continuously differentiable and concave in* $\mathcal{X}^{jl}$ *and* $\mathcal{Y}^{jl}$, *and the utility function for each sector has the form given by (12.4), that is,*

$$U^{jl} = u^{jl}(\mathcal{X}^{jl}, \mathcal{Y}^{jl}) + \sum_{i=1}^{I} \sum_{k=1}^{K} (r_{ik} + e_k)(X_{ik}^{jl} - Y_{ik}^{jl})$$

$$+ \sum_{i=1}^{I} \sum_{k=1}^{K} (\pi_{ik} + \lambda_{ik})(Z_{ik}^{jl} - \Psi_{ik}^{jl}) + \sum_{i=1}^{I} \sum_{k=1}^{K} (r_{ik} + e_k - \eta_{ik})(W_{ik}^{jl} - \Phi_{ik}^{jl})$$

$$+ \sum_{i=1}^{I} \sum_{k=1}^{K} (\delta_{ik} + \mu_{ik} - \eta_{ik})(\Xi_{ik}^{jl} - \Theta_{ik}^{jl}), \tag{12.64}$$

then the international financial adjustment process with financial futures and options is stable.

Theorem 12.4 (Asymptotic Stability)

If we assume that all sectors j *in all countries* l *have a strictly concave utility function with respect to the asset and liability pattern,* $(\mathcal{X}^{jl}, \mathcal{Y}^{jl})$, *the utility functions are twice continuously differentiable, and of the form (12.4) (equivalently, (12.64)), then the international financial adjustment process is asymptotically stable.*

Note that the above stability results would also hold for the dynamic adjustment processes underlying the special case financial models presented in Examples 12.1 through 12.4.

12.5 Network Optimization Reformulation

In this section we identify the network optimization problem whose solution coincides with the equilibrium solution in the case that the utility function U^{jl} for each sector j of country l is given by (12.4).

The connection between the equilibrium solution and the solution to a network optimization problem is established in two steps. In the first step, we verify that there is an optimization problem which holds the equilibrium solution as its solution, and, subsequently, in the second step, we establish that the markets clear for all instruments and currencies, hedged and unhedged, allowing us to construct the network over which the optimization takes place.

For simplicity, we let υ^{jl} denote the column vector with components consisting of the asset elements of the left-hand side of inequality (12.13) and let v^{jl} denote the column vector of similar components but consisting of the liability elements, prior to the multiplication signs.

Lemma 12.1

The variational inequality problem of finding $(\mathcal{X}^*, \mathcal{Y}^*, r^*, e^*, \lambda^*, \delta^*) \in \mathcal{K}$ satisfying:

$$\sum_{j=1}^{J}\sum_{l=1}^{L} \upsilon^{jl}(\mathcal{X}^*, \mathcal{Y}^*, r^*, e^*, \lambda^*, \delta^*; \pi, \mu, \eta)^T \cdot (\mathcal{X}^{jl} - \mathcal{X}^{jl*})$$

$$+\sum_{j=1}^{J}\sum_{l=1}^{L} v^{jl}(\mathcal{X}^*, \mathcal{Y}^*, r^*, e^*, \lambda^*, \delta^*; \pi, \mu, \eta)^T \cdot (\mathcal{Y}^{jl} - \mathcal{Y}^{jl*})$$

$$+\sum_{i=1}^{I}\sum_{k=1}^{K}\left[\sum_{j=1}^{J}\sum_{l=1}^{L}\left(X_{ik}^{jl*} + W_{ik}^{jl*}\right) - \left(Y_{ik}^{jl*} + \Phi_{ik}^{jl*}\right)\right] \times [r_{ik} - r_{ik}^*]$$

$$+\sum_{k=1}^{K}\left[\sum_{i=1}^{I}\sum_{j=1}^{J}\sum_{l=1}^{L}\left(X_{ik}^{jl*} + W_{ik}^{jl*}\right) - \left(Y_{ik}^{jl*} + \Phi_{ik}^{jl*}\right)\right] \times [e_k - e_k^*]$$

$$+\sum_{i=1}^{I}\sum_{k=1}^{K}\left[\sum_{j=1}^{J}\sum_{l=1}^{L}\left(Z_{ik}^{jl*} - \Psi_{ik}^{jl*}\right)\right] \times [\lambda_{ik} - \lambda_{ik}^*]$$

$$+\sum_{i=1}^{I}\sum_{k=1}^{K}\left[\sum_{j=1}^{J}\sum_{l=1}^{L}\left(\Xi_{ik}^{jl^*}-\Theta_{ik}^{jl^*}\right)\right]\times[\delta_{ik}-\delta_{ik}^*]\geq 0, \tag{12.65}$$

$$\forall(\mathcal{X},\mathcal{Y},r,e,\lambda,\delta)\in\mathcal{K},$$

is equivalent to the problem:

$$\text{Maximize}\ \sum_{j=1}^{J}\sum_{l=1}^{L}u^{jl}(\mathcal{X}^{jl},\mathcal{Y}^{jl})+\sum_{j=1}^{J}\sum_{l=1}^{L}\sum_{i=1}^{I}\sum_{k=1}^{K}(\pi_{ik})(Z_{ik}^{jl}-\Psi_{ik}^{jl})$$

$$+\sum_{j=1}^{J}\sum_{l=1}^{L}\sum_{i=1}^{I}\sum_{k=1}^{K}(-\eta_{ik})(W_{ik}^{jl}-\Phi_{ik}^{jl})+\sum_{j=1}^{J}\sum_{l=1}^{L}\sum_{i=1}^{I}\sum_{k=1}^{K}(\mu_{ik}-\eta_{ik})(\Xi_{ik}^{jl}-\Theta_{ik}^{jl}) \tag{12.66}$$

subject to:

$$\sum_{j=1}^{J}\sum_{l=1}^{L}\left[\left(X_{ik}^{jl}+W_{ik}^{jl}\right)-\left(Y_{ik}^{jl}+\Phi_{ik}^{jl}\right)\right]\geq 0,\quad i=1,\ldots,I;\quad k=1,\ldots,K \tag{12.67}$$

$$\sum_{j=1}^{J}\sum_{l=1}^{L}\sum_{i=1}^{I}\left[\left(X_{ik}^{jl}+W_{ik}^{jl}\right)-\left(Y_{ik}^{jl}+\Phi_{ik}^{jl}\right)\right]\geq 0,\quad k=1,\ldots,K \tag{12.68}$$

$$\sum_{j=1}^{J}\sum_{l=1}^{L}(Z_{ik}^{jl}-\Psi_{ik}^{jl})=0,\quad i=1,\ldots,I;\quad k=1,\ldots,K \tag{12.69}$$

$$\sum_{j=1}^{J}\sum_{l=1}^{L}(\Xi_{ik}^{jl}-\Theta_{ik}^{jl})=0,\quad i=1,\ldots,I;\quad k=1,\ldots,K \tag{12.70}$$

and

$$(\mathcal{X}^{jl},\mathcal{Y}^{jl})\in\bar{\kappa}^{jl},\quad j=1,\ldots,J;\ l=1,\ldots,L,$$

where $r_{ik}^*\geq 0$ corresponds to the Lagrange multiplier associated with the ik-th constraint in (12.67), $e_k^*\geq 0$ coincides with the Lagrange multiplier associated with the k-th constraint in (12.68), and λ_{ik}^* and δ_{ik}^* correspond to the Lagrange multipliers associated with the ik-th constraint in (12.69) and (12.70), respectively.

Lemma 12.2

In the state of equilibrium, all the markets, both hedged and unhedged, for all instruments and all currencies must clear, that is,

$$\sum_{j=1}^{J}\sum_{l=1}^{L}\left[\left(X_{ik}^{jl^*}+W_{ik}^{jl^*}\right)-\left(Y_{ik}^{jl^*}+\Phi_{ik}^{jl^*}\right)\right]=0,\quad i=1,\ldots,I;\ k=1,\ldots,K \tag{12.71}$$

$$\sum_{j=1}^{J}\sum_{l=1}^{L}\sum_{i=1}^{I}\left[\left(X_{ik}^{jl^*}+W_{ik}^{jl^*}\right)-\left(Y_{ik}^{jl^*}+\Phi_{ik}^{jl^*}\right)\right]=0, \quad k=1,\ldots,K \quad (12.72)$$

$$\sum_{j-1}^{J}\sum_{l-1}^{L}(Z_{ik}^{jl^*}-\Psi_{ik}^{jl^*})=0, \quad i=1,\ldots,I;\ k=1,\ldots,K, \quad (12.73)$$

and

$$\sum_{j=1}^{J}\sum_{l=1}^{L}(\Xi_{ik}^{jl^*}-\Theta_{ik}^{jl^*})=0, \quad i=1,\ldots,I;\ k=1,\ldots,K, \quad (12.74)$$

that is, (12.67) and (12.68) hold as strict equalities. In addition, the prices, r_{ik}^* and e_k^* for all instruments i and for all currencies k are strictly positive, whereas the shadow prices λ_{ik}^* and δ_{ik}^* associated with the futures and option contracts, respectively, can be of either sign (or zero).

Proof: One can easily verify that (12.73) and (12.74) are identical to economic conditions (12.16) and (12.17), respectively.

Furthermore, from (12.73) and (12.74) one can easily obtain that

$$\sum_{j=1}^{J}\sum_{l=1}^{L}\sum_{i=1}^{I}\sum_{k=1}^{K}\left[(Z_{ik}^{jl^*}+\Xi_{ik}^{jl^*})-(\Psi_{ik}^{jl^*}+\Theta_{ik}^{jl^*})\right]=0. \quad (12.75)$$

But, feasibility conditions (12.2) and (12.3) imply that the following must also hold:

$$\sum_{j=1}^{J}\sum_{l=1}^{L}\sum_{i=1}^{I}\sum_{k=1}^{K}(X_{ik}^{jl^*}+Z_{ik}^{jl^*}+W_{ik}^{jl^*}+\Xi_{ik}^{jl^*})-(Y_{ik}^{jl^*}+\Psi_{ik}^{jl^*}+\Phi_{ik}^{jl^*}+\Theta_{ik}^{jl^*})=0. \quad (12.76)$$

If we now combine (12.75) and (12.76) we obtain:

$$\sum_{j=1}^{J}\sum_{l=1}^{L}\sum_{i=1}^{I}\sum_{k=1}^{K}\left[(X_{ik}^{jl^*}+W_{ik}^{jl^*})-(Y_{ik}^{jl^*}+\Phi_{ik}^{jl^*})\right]=0. \quad (12.77)$$

Assume now, that, for a particular currency k, we have that

$$\sum_{j=1}^{J}\sum_{l=1}^{L}\sum_{i=1}^{I}\left[\left(X_{ik}^{jl^*}+W_{ik}^{jl^*}\right)-\left(Y_{ik}^{jl^*}+\Phi_{ik}^{jl^*}\right)\right]>0. \quad (12.78)$$

Then there must exist a currency c such that

$$\sum_{j=1}^{J}\sum_{l=1}^{L}\sum_{i=1}^{I}\left[\left(X_{ic}^{jl^*}+W_{ic}^{jl^*}\right)-\left(Y_{ic}^{jl^*}+\Phi_{ic}^{jl^*}\right)\right]<0, \quad (12.79)$$

which is in contradiction to equilibrium condition (12.15), and, thus, (12.72) must hold.

Assume now that for a specific instrument i in currency k we have that:

$$\sum_{j=1}^{J}\sum_{l=1}^{L}\left[\left(X_{ik}^{jl*}+W_{ik}^{jl*}\right)-\left(Y_{ik}^{jl*}+\Phi_{ik}^{jl*}\right)\right]>0, \tag{12.80}$$

then there must exist an instrument f in currency k such that

$$\sum_{j=1}^{J}\sum_{l=1}^{L}\left[\left(X_{fk}^{jl*}+W_{fk}^{jl*}\right)-\left(Y_{fk}^{jl*}+\Phi_{fk}^{jl*}\right)\right]<0, \tag{12.81}$$

which opposes equilibrium condition (12.14) and, therefore, (12.71) must hold.

Finally, from Lagrange multiplier theory, the Lagrange multipliers r_{ik}^* and e_k^* must be positive, whereas Lagrange multipliers λ_{ik}^* and δ_{ik}^*, can be positive, negative, or zero.

We will now examine the network structure of the models under consideration.

Corollary 12.5

The solution to the optimization problem:

$$\begin{gathered}\text{Maximize}\ \sum_{j=1}^{J}\sum_{l=1}^{L}u^{jl}(\mathcal{X}^{jl},\mathcal{Y}^{jl})+\sum_{j=1}^{J}\sum_{l=1}^{L}\sum_{i=1}^{I}\sum_{k=1}^{K}(\pi_{ik})(Z_{ik}^{jl}-\Psi_{ik}^{jl})\\ +\sum_{j=1}^{J}\sum_{l=1}^{L}\sum_{i=1}^{I}\sum_{k=1}^{K}(-\gamma_{ik})(W_{ik}^{jl}-\Phi_{ik}^{jl})+\sum_{j=1}^{J}\sum_{l=1}^{L}\sum_{i=1}^{I}\sum_{k=1}^{K}(\mu_{ik}-\eta_{ik})(\Xi_{ik}^{jl}-\Theta_{ik}^{jl})\end{gathered} \tag{12.82}$$

subject to:

$$\sum_{j=1}^{J}\sum_{l=1}^{L}\left[\left(X_{ik}^{jl}+W_{ik}^{jl}\right)-\left(Y_{ik}^{jl}+\Phi_{ik}^{jl}\right)\right]=0,\quad i=1,\ldots,I;\ k=1,\ldots,K \tag{12.83}$$

$$\sum_{j=1}^{J}\sum_{l=1}^{L}(Z_{ik}^{jl}-\Psi_{ik}^{jl})=0,\quad i=1,\ldots,I;\ k=1,\ldots,K \tag{12.84}$$

and

$$\sum_{j=1}^{J}\sum_{l=1}^{L}(\Xi_{ik}^{jl}-\Theta_{ik}^{jl})=0,\quad i=1,\ldots,I;\ k=1,\ldots,K \tag{12.85}$$

$$(\mathcal{X}^{jl},\mathcal{Y}^{jl})\in\bar{\kappa}^{jl},\quad j=1,\ldots,J;\ l=1,\ldots,L, \tag{12.86}$$

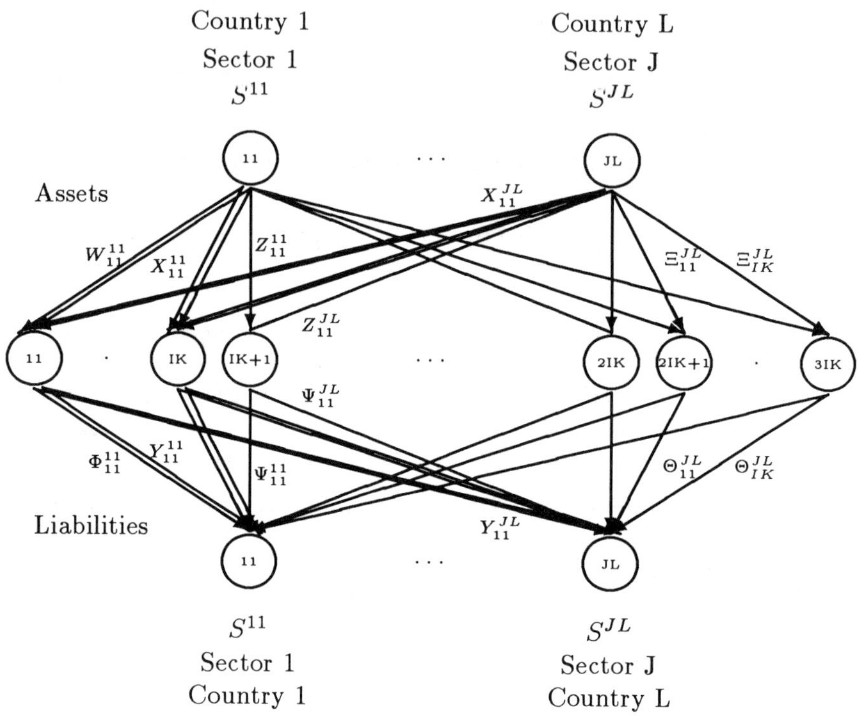

Fig. 12.4. The network structure at equilibrium

with Lagrange multiplier R_{ik}^* for constraint (ik) in (12.83) and Lagrange multipliers λ_{ik}^* and δ_{ik}^* for constraints (12.84) and (12.85), respectively, coincides with the solution to problem (12.66)–(12.70). Furthermore, this solution is an equilibrium solution.

One can easily identify the network structure of the problem in Corollary 12.5 which is depicted in Figure 12.4. As in the single country hedging models presented in Chapter 7, the individual networks of Figure 12.1, which depict the optimization problems of each sector in every country, merge to the single network of Figure 12.4.

12.6 Computational Methods

In this section we provide computational methodologies for the solution of the international hedging models. In Section 12.6.1 we discuss the modified projection method whereas in Section 12.6.2 we discuss the Euler method.

12.6.1 Modified Projection Method

Here we demonstrate the application of the modified projection method for the model of Section 12.1. For simplicity, and in order to maintain a compact notation, we let $U^{jl}(x^{jl^\tau}) \equiv U^{jl}\left(\mathcal{X}^{jl^\tau}, \mathcal{Y}^{jl^\tau}, r^\tau, e^\tau, \lambda^\tau, \delta^\tau; \mu, \pi, \eta\right)$.

Since the function $F(x)$ that enters variational inequality (12.30) is monotone and Lipschitz continuous (see Propositions 12.2 and 12.3), the modified projection method is guaranteed to converge to an equilibrium pattern, provided that a solution exists.

The modified projection method for our specific model is then as follows.

Step 0: Initialization

Set $(\mathcal{X}^0, \mathcal{Y}^0, r^0, e^0, \lambda^0, \delta^0) \in \mathcal{K}$. Let $\tau := 0$ and set γ so that $0 < \gamma < \frac{1}{\mathcal{L}}$, where $\mathcal{L}$ is the Lipschitz constant.

Step 1: Computation

Compute $(\bar{\mathcal{X}}^\tau, \bar{\mathcal{Y}}^\tau, \bar{r}^\tau, \bar{e}^\tau, \bar{\lambda}^\tau, \bar{\delta}^\tau) \in \mathcal{K}$ by solving the variational inequality subproblem:

$$\sum_{j=1}^{J}\sum_{l=1}^{L}\sum_{i=1}^{I}\sum_{k=1}^{K}\left[\bar{X}_{ik}^{jl^\tau} + \gamma\left(-\frac{\partial U^{jl}(x^{jl^\tau})}{\partial X_{ik}^{jl}}\right) - X_{ik}^{jl^\tau}\right] \times \left[X_{ik}^{jl} - \bar{X}_{ik}^{jl^\tau}\right]$$

$$\sum_{j=1}^{J}\sum_{l=1}^{L}\sum_{i=1}^{I}\sum_{k=1}^{K}\left[\bar{Z}_{ik}^{jl^\tau} + \gamma\left(-\frac{\partial U^{jl}(x^{jl^\tau})}{\partial Z_{ik}^{jl}}\right) - Z_{ik}^{jl^\tau}\right] \times \left[Z_{ik}^{jl} - \bar{Z}_{ik}^{jl^\tau}\right]$$

$$\sum_{j=1}^{J}\sum_{l=1}^{L}\sum_{i=1}^{I}\sum_{k=1}^{K}\left[\bar{W}_{ik}^{jl^\tau} + \gamma\left(-\frac{\partial U^{jl}(x^{jl^\tau})}{\partial W_{ik}^{jl}}\right) - W_{ik}^{jl^\tau}\right] \times \left[W_{ik}^{jl} - \bar{W}_{ik}^{jl^\tau}\right]$$

$$\sum_{j=1}^{J}\sum_{l=1}^{L}\sum_{i=1}^{I}\sum_{k=1}^{K}\left[\bar{\Xi}_{ik}^{jl^\tau} + \gamma\left(-\frac{\partial U^{jl}(x^{jl^\tau})}{\partial \Xi_{ik}^{jl}}\right) - \Xi_{ik}^{jl^\tau}\right] \times \left[\Xi_{ik}^{jl} - \bar{\Xi}_{ik}^{jl^\tau}\right]$$

$$+\sum_{j=1}^{J}\sum_{l=1}^{L}\sum_{i=1}^{I}\sum_{k=1}^{K}\left[\bar{Y}_{ik}^{jl^\tau} + \gamma\left(-\frac{\partial U^{jl}(x^{jl^\tau})}{\partial Y_{ik}^{jl}}\right) - Y_{ik}^{jl^\tau}\right] \times \left[Y_{ik}^{jl} - \bar{Y}_{ik}^{jl^\tau}\right]$$

$$+\sum_{j=1}^{J}\sum_{l=1}^{L}\sum_{i=1}^{I}\sum_{k=1}^{K}\left[\bar{\Psi}_{ik}^{jl^\tau} + \gamma\left(-\frac{\partial U^{jl}(x^{jl^\tau})}{\partial \Psi_{ik}^{jl}}\right) - \Psi_{ik}^{jl^\tau}\right] \times \left[\Psi_{ik}^{jl} - \bar{\Psi}_{ik}^{jl^\tau}\right]$$

$$+\sum_{j=1}^{J}\sum_{l=1}^{L}\sum_{i=1}^{I}\sum_{k=1}^{K}\left[\bar{\Phi}_{ik}^{jl^\tau}+\gamma\left(-\frac{\partial U^{jl}(x^{jl^\tau})}{\partial \Phi_{ik}^{jl}}\right)-\Phi_{ik}^{jl^\tau}\right]\times\left[\Phi_{ik}^{jl}-\bar{\Phi}_{ik}^{jl^\tau}\right]$$

$$+\sum_{j=1}^{J}\sum_{l=1}^{L}\sum_{i=1}^{I}\sum_{k=1}^{K}\left[\bar{\Theta}_{ik}^{jl^\tau}+\gamma\left(-\frac{\partial U^{jl}(x^{jl^\tau})}{\partial \Theta_{ik}^{jl}}\right)-\Theta_{ik}^{jl^\tau}\right]\times\left[\Theta_{ik}^{jl}-\bar{\Theta}_{ik}^{jl^\tau}\right]$$

$$+\sum_{i=1}^{I}\sum_{k=1}^{K}\left[\bar{r}_{ik}^{\tau}+\gamma\left[\sum_{j=1}^{J}\sum_{l=1}^{L}\left[\left(X_{ik}^{jl^\tau}+W_{ik}^{jl^\tau}\right)-\left(Y_{ik}^{jl^\tau}+\Phi_{ik}^{jl^\tau}\right)\right]\right.\right.$$
$$\left.-r_{ik}^{\tau}\right]\times\left[r_{ik}-\bar{r}_{ik}^{\tau}\right]$$

$$+\sum_{k=1}^{K}\left[\bar{e}_{k}^{\tau}+\gamma\left[\sum_{j=1}^{J}\sum_{l=1}^{L}\sum_{i=1}^{I}\left[\left(X_{ik}^{jl^\tau}+W_{ik}^{jl^\tau}\right)-\left(Y_{ik}^{jl^\tau}+\Phi_{ik}^{jl^\tau}\right)\right]\right.\right.$$
$$\left.-e_{k}^{\tau}\right]\times\left[e_{k}-\bar{e}_{k}^{\tau}\right]$$

$$+\sum_{i=1}^{I}\sum_{k=1}^{K}\left[\bar{\lambda}_{ik}^{\tau}+\gamma\left[\sum_{j=1}^{J}\sum_{l=1}^{L}\left(Z_{ik}^{jl^\tau}-\Psi_{ik}^{jl^\tau}\right)\right]-\lambda_{ik}^{\tau}\right]\times\left[\lambda_{ik}-\bar{\lambda}_{ik}^{\tau}\right]$$

$$+\sum_{i=1}^{I}\sum_{k=1}^{K}\left[\bar{\delta}_{ik}^{\tau}+\gamma\left[\sum_{j=1}^{J}\sum_{l=1}^{L}\left(\Xi_{ik}^{jl^\tau}-\Theta_{ik}^{jl^\tau}\right)\right]-\delta_{ik}^{\tau}\right]\times\left[\delta_{ik}-\bar{\delta}_{ik}^{\tau}\right]\geq 0,$$

$$\forall(\mathcal{X},\mathcal{Y},r,e,\lambda,\delta)\in\mathcal{K}. \tag{12.87}$$

Step 2: Adaptation

Compute $(\mathcal{X}^{\tau+1},\mathcal{Y}^{\tau+1},r^{\tau+1},e^{\tau+1},\lambda^{\tau+1},\delta^{\tau+1})\in\mathcal{K}$ by solving the variational inequality subproblem:

$$\sum_{j=1}^{J}\sum_{l=1}^{L}\sum_{i=1}^{I}\sum_{k=1}^{K}\left[X_{ik}^{jl^{\tau+1}}+\gamma\left(-\frac{\partial U^{jl}(\bar{x}_{ik}^{jl^\tau})}{\partial X_{ik}^{jl}}\right)-X_{ik}^{jl^\tau}\right]\times\left[X_{ik}^{jl}-X_{ik}^{jl^{\tau+1}}\right]$$

$$\sum_{j=1}^{J}\sum_{l=1}^{L}\sum_{i=1}^{I}\sum_{k=1}^{K}\left[Z_{ik}^{jl^{\tau+1}}+\gamma\left(-\frac{\partial U^{jl}(\bar{x}_{ik}^{jl^\tau})}{\partial Z_{ik}^{jl}}\right)-Z_{ik}^{jl^\tau}\right]\times\left[Z_{ik}^{jl}-Z_{ik}^{jl^{\tau+1}}\right]$$

$$+\sum_{j=1}^{J}\sum_{l=1}^{L}\sum_{i=1}^{I}\sum_{k=1}^{K}\left[W_{ik}^{jl^{\tau+1}}+\gamma\left(-\frac{\partial U^{jl}(\bar{x}_{ik}^{jl^\tau})}{\partial W_{ik}^{jl}}\right)-W_{ik}^{jl^\tau}\right]\times\left[W_{ik}^{jl}-W_{ik}^{jl^{\tau+1}}\right]$$

$$+\sum_{j=1}^{J}\sum_{l=1}^{L}\sum_{i=1}^{I}\sum_{k=1}^{K}\left[\Xi_{ik}^{jl^{\tau+1}}+\gamma\left(-\frac{\partial U^{jl}(\bar{x}_{ik}^{jl^\tau})}{\partial \Xi_{ik}^{jl}}\right)-\Xi_{ik}^{jl^\tau}\right]\times\left[\Xi_{ik}^{jl}-\Xi_{ik}^{jl^{\tau+1}}\right]$$

$$+\sum_{j=1}^{J}\sum_{l=1}^{L}\sum_{i=1}^{I}\sum_{k=1}^{K}\left[Y_{ik}^{jl^{\tau+1}}+\gamma\left(-\frac{\partial U^{jl}(\bar{x}_{ik}^{jl^\tau})}{\partial Y_{ik}^{jl}}\right)-Y_{ik}^{jl^\tau}\right]\times\left[Y_{ik}^{jl}-Y_{ik}^{jl^{\tau+1}}\right]$$

$$+\sum_{j=1}^{J}\sum_{l=1}^{L}\sum_{i=1}^{I}\sum_{k=1}^{K}\left[\Psi_{ik}^{jl^{\tau+1}}+\gamma\left(-\frac{\partial U^{jl}(\bar{x}_{ik}^{jl^{\tau}})}{\partial\Psi_{ik}^{jl}}\right)-\Psi_{ik}^{jl^{\tau}}\right]\times\left[\Psi_{ik}^{jl}-\Psi_{ik}^{jl^{\tau+1}}\right]$$

$$+\sum_{j=1}^{J}\sum_{l=1}^{L}\sum_{i=1}^{I}\sum_{k=1}^{K}\left[\Phi_{ik}^{jl^{\tau+1}}+\gamma\left(-\frac{\partial U^{jl}(\bar{x}_{ik}^{jl^{\tau}})}{\Phi_{ik}^{jl}}\right)-\Phi_{ik}^{jl^{\tau}}\right]\times\left[\Phi_{ik}^{jl}-\Phi_{ik}^{jl^{\tau+1}}\right]$$

$$+\sum_{j=1}^{J}\sum_{l=1}^{L}\sum_{i=1}^{I}\sum_{k=1}^{K}\left[\Theta_{ik}^{jl^{\tau+1}}+\gamma\left(-\frac{\partial U^{jl}(\bar{x}_{ik}^{jl^{\tau}})}{\partial\Theta_{ik}^{jl}}\right)-\Theta_{ik}^{jl^{\tau}}\right]\times\left[\Theta_{ik}^{jl}-\Theta_{ik}^{jl^{\tau+1}}\right]$$

$$+\sum_{i=1}^{I}\sum_{k=1}^{K}\left[r_{ik}^{\tau}+\gamma\left[\sum_{j=1}^{J}\sum_{l=1}^{L}\left[\left(\bar{X}_{ik}^{jl^{\tau+1}}+\bar{W}_{ik}^{jl^{\tau}}\right)-\left(\bar{Y}_{ik}^{jl^{\tau}}+\bar{\Phi}_{ik}^{jl^{\tau}}\right)\right]\right]-r_{ik}^{\tau}\right]$$
$$\times\left[r_{ik}-r_{ik}^{\tau+1}\right]$$

$$+\sum_{k=1}^{K}\left[e_{k}^{\tau+1}+\gamma\left[\sum_{j=1}^{J}\sum_{l=1}^{L}\sum_{i=1}^{I}\left[\left(\bar{X}_{ik}^{jl^{\tau}}+\bar{W}_{ik}^{jl^{\tau}}\right)-\left(\bar{Y}_{ik}^{jl^{\tau}}+\bar{\Phi}_{ik}^{jl^{\tau}}\right)\right]\right]-e_{k}^{\tau}\right]$$
$$\times\left[e_{k}-e_{k}^{\tau+1}\right]$$

$$+\sum_{i=1}^{I}\sum_{k=1}^{K}\left[\lambda_{ik}^{\tau+1}+\gamma\left[\sum_{j=1}^{J}\sum_{l=1}^{L}\left(\bar{Z}_{ik}^{jl^{\tau}}-\bar{\Psi}_{ik}^{jl^{\tau}}\right)\right]-\lambda_{ik}^{\tau}\right]\times\left[\lambda_{ik}-\lambda_{ik}^{\tau+1}\right]$$

$$+\sum_{i=1}^{I}\sum_{k=1}^{K}\left[\delta_{ik}^{\tau+1}+\gamma\left[\sum_{j=1}^{J}\sum_{l=1}^{L}\left(\bar{\Xi}_{ik}^{jl^{\tau}}-\bar{\Theta}_{ik}^{jl^{\tau}}\right)\right]-\delta_{ik}^{\tau}\right]\times\left[\delta_{ik}-\delta_{ik}^{\tau+1}\right]\geq 0,$$

$$\forall(\mathcal{X},\mathcal{Y},r,e,\lambda,\delta)\in\mathcal{K}. \tag{12.88}$$

Step 3: Convergence Verification:

If we have $\max_{ikjl}|X_{ik}^{jl^{\tau+1}}-X_{ik}^{jl^{\tau}}|\leq\epsilon$; $\max_{ikjl}|Y_{ik}^{jl^{\tau+1}}-Y_{ik}^{jl^{\tau}}|\leq\epsilon$; $\max_{ikjl}|Z_{ik}^{jl^{\tau+1}}-Z_{ik}^{jl^{\tau}}|\leq\epsilon$; $\max_{ikjl}|\Psi_{ik}^{jl^{\tau+1}}-\Psi_{ik}^{jl^{\tau}}|\leq\epsilon$; $\max_{ikjl}|W_{ik}^{jl^{\tau+1}}-W_{ik}^{jl^{\tau}}|\leq\epsilon$; $\max_{ikjl}|\Phi_{ik}^{jl^{\tau+1}}-\Phi_{ik}^{jl^{\tau}}|\leq\epsilon$; $\max_{ikjl}|\Xi_{ik}^{jl^{\tau+1}}-\Xi_{ik}^{jl^{\tau}}|\leq\epsilon$; $\max_{ikjl}|\Theta_{ik}^{jl^{\tau+1}}-\Theta_{ik}^{jl^{\tau}}|\leq\epsilon$; $\max_{ik}|r_{ik}^{\tau+1}-r_{ik}^{\tau}|\leq\epsilon$; $\max_{k}|e_{k}^{\tau+1}-e_{k}^{\tau}|\leq\epsilon$; $\max_{ik}|\lambda_{ik}^{\tau+1}-\lambda_{ik}^{\tau}|\leq\epsilon$, and $\max_{ik}|\delta_{ik}^{\tau+1}-\delta_{ik}^{\tau}|\leq\epsilon$, for all $i; i=1,\ldots,I$, $k; k=1,\ldots,K$, $j; j=1,\ldots,J$, and $l; l=1,\ldots,L$, with $\epsilon>0$, a prespecified tolerance, then stop; else, set $\tau:=\tau+1$, and go to Step 1.

Since the feasible set $\mathcal{K}$, consists solely of simple linear constraints and nonnegativity constraints the variational inequality subproblems of the computation and adaptation steps can be further decomposed into subproblems that can be solved explicitly and in closed form.

More precisely, subproblems (12.87) and (12.88) decompose into simple quadratic programming problems with network structure which are illustrated in Figure 12.5.

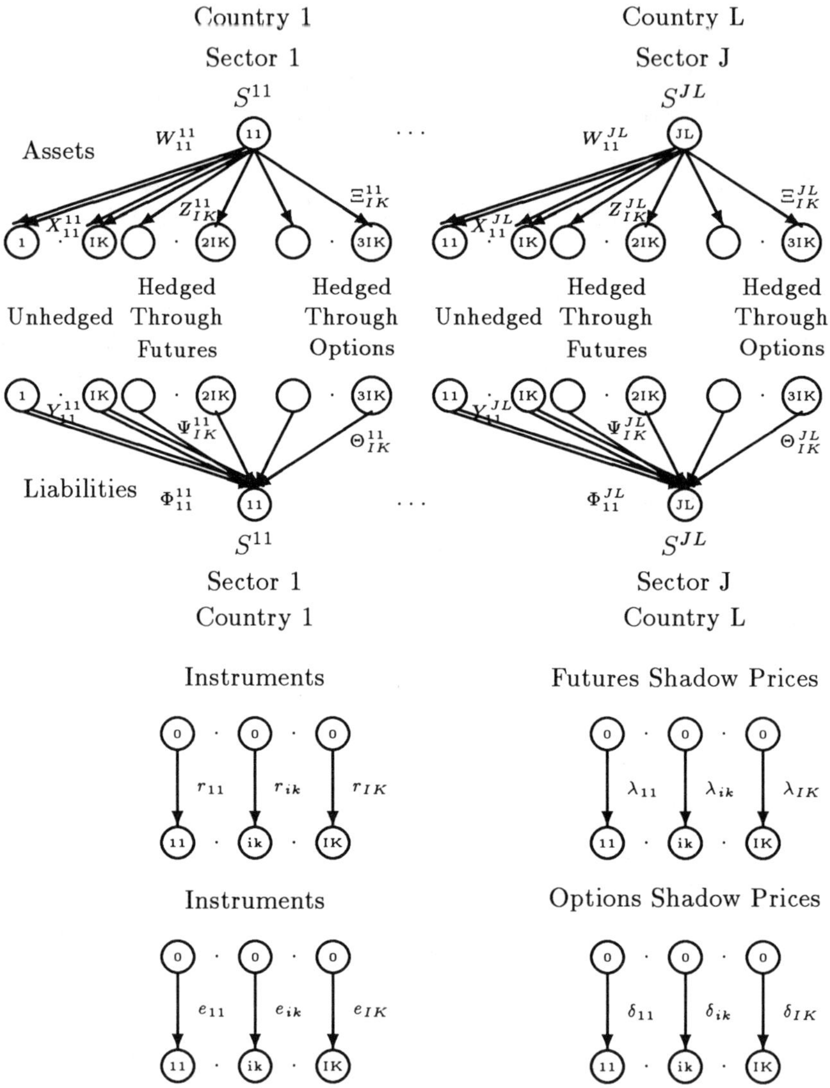

Fig. 12.5. The network structure of financial subproblems

12.6.2 Euler Method for the Adjustment Process of Section 12.3

In this subsection we utilize the Euler method in order to compute the stationary pattern of the international adjustment process with financial futures and options, as well as to approximate the trajectories of the projected dynamical system (12.62).

We recall from Chapter 4, for every iteration τ, of the Euler method we have to compute:

$$x^{\tau+1} = P_{\mathcal{K}}(x^{\tau} - a_{\tau}F(x^{\tau})), \tag{12.89}$$

where $P_{\mathcal{K}}$ is the projection operator defined in (3.24), and $\{a_{\tau}\}$ is a positive sequence with some specific properties, that will be discussed later in this Section.

Step 0: Initialization

Set $(\mathcal{X}^0, \mathcal{Y}^0, r^0, e^0, \lambda^0, \delta^0) \in \mathcal{K}$. Let $\tau := 0$.

Step 1: Computation

Compute $(\mathcal{X}^{\tau+1}, \mathcal{Y}^{\tau+1}, r^{\tau+1}, e^{\tau+1}, \lambda^{\tau+1}, \delta^{\tau+1}) \in \mathcal{K}$ by solving the variational inequality subproblem:

$$\sum_{j=1}^{J}\sum_{l=1}^{L}\sum_{i=1}^{I}\sum_{k=1}^{K}\left[X_{ik}^{jl^{\tau+1}} + a_{\tau}\left(-\frac{\partial U^{jl}(x^{jl^{\tau}})}{\partial X_{ik}^{jl}}\right) - X_{ik}^{jl^{\tau}}\right] \times \left[X_{ik}^{jl} - X_{ik}^{jl^{\tau+1}}\right]$$

$$\sum_{j=1}^{J}\sum_{l=1}^{L}\sum_{i=1}^{I}\sum_{k=1}^{K}\left[Z_{ik}^{jl^{\tau+1}} + a_{\tau}\left(-\frac{\partial U^{jl}(x^{jl^{\tau}})}{\partial Z_{ik}^{jl}}\right) - Z_{ik}^{jl^{\tau}}\right] \times \left[Z_{ik}^{jl} - Z_{ik}^{jl^{\tau+1}}\right]$$

$$\sum_{j=1}^{J}\sum_{l=1}^{L}\sum_{i=1}^{I}\sum_{k=1}^{K}\left[W_{ik}^{jl^{\tau+1}} + a_{\tau}\left(-\frac{\partial U^{jl}(x^{jl^{\tau}})}{\partial W_{ik}^{jl}}\right) - W_{ik}^{jl^{\tau}}\right] \times \left[W_{ik}^{jl} - W_{ik}^{jl^{\tau+1}}\right]$$

$$\sum_{j=1}^{J}\sum_{l=1}^{L}\sum_{i=1}^{I}\sum_{k=1}^{K}\left[\Xi_{ik}^{jl^{\tau+1}} + a_{\tau}\left(-\frac{\partial U^{jl}(x^{jl^{\tau}})}{\Xi_{ik}^{jl}}\right) - \Xi_{ik}^{jl^{\tau}}\right] \times \left[\Xi_{ik}^{jl} - \Xi_{ik}^{jl^{\tau+1}}\right]$$

$$+\sum_{j=1}^{J}\sum_{l=1}^{L}\sum_{i=1}^{I}\sum_{k=1}^{K}\left[Y_{ik}^{jl^{\tau+1}} + a_{\tau}\left(-\frac{\partial U^{jl}(x^{jl^{\tau}})}{\partial Y_{ik}^{jl}}\right) - Y_{ik}^{jl^{\tau}}\right] \times \left[Y_{ik}^{jl} - Y_{ik}^{jl^{\tau+1}}\right]$$

$$\sum_{j=1}^{J}\sum_{l=1}^{L}\sum_{i=1}^{I}\sum_{k=1}^{K}\left[\Psi_{ik}^{jl^{\tau+1}} + a_{\tau}\left(-\frac{\partial U^{jl}(x^{jl^{\tau}})}{\partial \Psi_{ik}^{jl}}\right) - \Psi_{ik}^{jl^{\tau}}\right] \times \left[\Psi_{ik}^{jl} - \Psi_{ik}^{jl^{\tau+1}}\right]$$

$$\sum_{j=1}^{J}\sum_{l=1}^{L}\sum_{i=1}^{I}\sum_{k=1}^{K}\left[\Phi_{ik}^{jl^{\tau+1}} + a_{\tau}\left(-\frac{\partial U^{jl}(x^{jl^{\tau}})}{\partial \Phi_{ik}^{jl}}\right) - \Phi_{ik}^{jl^{\tau}}\right] \times \left[\Phi_{ik}^{jl} - \Phi_{ik}^{jl^{\tau+1}}\right]$$

$$\sum_{j=1}^{J}\sum_{l=1}^{L}\sum_{i=1}^{I}\sum_{k=1}^{K}\left[\Theta_{ik}^{jl^{\tau+1}} + a_{\tau}\left(-\frac{\partial U^{jl}(x^{jl^{\tau}})}{\partial \Theta_{ik}^{jl}}\right) - \Theta_{ik}^{jl^{\tau}}\right] \times \left[\Theta_{ik}^{jl} - \Theta_{ik}^{jl^{\tau+1}}\right]$$

$$+\sum_{i=1}^{I}\sum_{k=1}^{K}\left[r_{ik}^{\tau+1}+a_\tau\left[\sum_{j=1}^{J}\sum_{l=1}^{L}\left[\left(X_{ik}^{jl^\tau}+W_{ik}^{jl^\tau}\right)-\left(Y_{ik}^{jl^\tau}+\Phi_{ik}^{jl^\tau}\right)\right]\right]-r_{ik}^\tau\right]$$

$$\times\left[r_{ik}-r_{ik}^{\tau+1}\right]$$

$$+\sum_{k=1}^{K}\left[e_k^{\tau+1}+a_\tau\left[\sum_{j=1}^{J}\sum_{l=1}^{L}\sum_{i=1}^{I}\left[\left(X_{ik}^{jl^\tau}+W_{ik}^{jl^\tau}\right)-\left(Y_{ik}^{jl^\tau}+\Phi_{ik}^{jl^\tau}\right)\right]\right]-e_k^\tau\right]$$

$$\times\left[e_k-e_k^{\tau+1}\right]$$

$$+\sum_{i=1}^{I}\sum_{k=1}^{K}\left[\lambda_{ik}^{\tau+1}+a_\tau\left[\sum_{j=1}^{J}\sum_{l=1}^{L}\left(Z_{ik}^{jl^\tau}-\Psi_{ik}^{jl^\tau}\right)\right]-\lambda_{ik}^\tau\right]\times\left[\lambda_{ik}-\lambda_{ik}^{\tau+1}\right]$$

$$+\sum_{i=1}^{I}\sum_{k=1}^{K}\left[\delta_{ik}^{\tau+1}+a_\tau\left[\sum_{j=1}^{J}\sum_{l=1}^{L}\left(\Xi_{ik}^{jl^\tau}-\Theta_{ik}^{jl^\tau}\right)\right]-\delta_{ik}^\tau\right]\times\left[\delta_{ik}-\delta_{ik}^{\tau+1}\right]\geq 0,$$

$$\forall(\mathcal{X},\mathcal{Y},r,e,\lambda,\delta)\in\mathcal{K}. \tag{12.90}$$

Step 2: Convergence Verification

If we have $\max_{ikjl}|X_{ik}^{jl^{\tau+1}}-X_{ik}^{jl^\tau}|\leq\epsilon$; $\max_{ikjl}|Y_{ik}^{jl^{\tau+1}}-Y_{ik}^{jl^\tau}|\leq\epsilon$; $\max_{ikjl}|Z_{ik}^{jl^{\tau+1}}-Z_{ik}^{jl^\tau}|\leq\epsilon$; $\max_{ikjl}|\Psi_{ik}^{jl^{\tau+1}}-\Psi_{ik}^{jl^\tau}|\leq\epsilon$; $\max_{ikjl}|W_{ik}^{jl^{\tau+1}}-W_{ik}^{jl^\tau}|\leq\epsilon$; $\max_{ikjl}|\Phi_{ik}^{jl^{\tau+1}}-\Phi_{ik}^{jl^\tau}|\leq\epsilon$; $\max_{ikjl}|\Xi_{ik}^{jl^{\tau+1}}-\Xi_{ik}^{jl^\tau}|\leq\epsilon$; $\max_{ikjl}|\Theta_{ik}^{jl^{\tau+1}}-\Theta_{ik}^{jl^\tau}|\leq\epsilon$; $\max_{ik}|r_{ik}^{\tau+1}-r_{ik}^\tau|\leq\epsilon$; $\max_k|e_k^{\tau+1}-e_k^\tau|\leq\epsilon$; $\max_{ik}|\lambda_{ik}^{\tau+1}-\lambda_{ik}^\tau|\leq\epsilon$; and $\max_{ik}|\delta_{ik}^{\tau+1}-\delta_{ik}^\tau|\leq\epsilon$, for all $i; i=1,\ldots,I$, $k; k=1,\ldots,K$, $j; j=1,\ldots,J$, and $l; l=1,\ldots,L$, with $\epsilon>0$, a prespecified tolerance, then stop; else, set $\tau:=\tau+1$, and go to Step 1.

We will now establish through Theorem 12.5, that the Euler method described above converges to a financial equilibrium pattern.

Theorem 12.5

If we assume that the utility functions U^{jl} are strictly concave and of the form (12.1), for every sector j of country l for the particular financial dynamic model, and we also let $\{a_\tau\}$ be a sequence of positive real numbers satisfying:

$$\lim_{\tau\to\infty}a_\tau=0, \tag{12.91}$$

and

$$\sum_{\tau=0}^{\infty}a_\tau=\infty, \tag{12.92}$$

then the Euler method given by (12.89), converges to some financial equilibrium pattern satisfying, Definition 12.1.

Proof: The proof for this theorem strongly depends on the discussion and the results presented in Chapter 4.

In particular, we will initially verify that all the conditions of Assumption 4.2 hold true, and then based on Theorem 4.6 and Corollary 4.1, we will prove that (12.89) converges to the corresponding financial equilibrium pattern.

Since (12.91) and (12.92) hold true, then the first condition of Assumption 4.2 is clearly met. Similarly, in view of the feasible set which solely consists of accounting and nonnegativity constraints, condition 4.2.4 of Assumption 4.2 is also fulfilled.

If we now take into consideration the fact that $F_\tau = F$ with $F(x)$ being continuous, and we also recall that the financial adjustment process (12.62) is asymptotically stable (Theorem 12.4), and, therefore, bounded, Condition 4.2.2 as well as 4.2.5 are also met. Furthermore, since all sectors from every country are assumed to be risk-averse, and, therefore, they hold strictly concave utility functions, the function $F(x)$ that enters (12.62) is strictly monotone, and, consequently, based on Proposition 4.1, we can easily verify that Condition 4.2.3 is also satisfied.

Once Assumption 4.2 is fulfilled, then Theorem 4.6 and Corollary 4.1 suggest that the sequence produced by (12.89) converges to some equilibrium pattern of the projected dynamical system (12.62).

In addition, Theorem 4.1 also implies that (12.89) must converge to the corresponding financial equilibrium pattern. □

Note that the variational inequality subproblems for both the modified projection method and the Euler method have similar formats, with the Euler method using parameter a_τ, whereas the modified projection method applies the fixed parameter γ. An advantage of the modified projection method is that it usually needs fewer iterations (although each iteration takes typically twice as long since it solves two sets of subproblems). On the other hand, the Euler method has the significant advantage of providing information as to the evolution of the adjustment process through time.

Since variational inequality (12.89) has a similar format to the variational inequality subproblems of both the computation step (12.87) and the adaptation step (12.88), one can easily conclude that the iterative step of the Euler method for the specific utility functions decompose to quadratic programming problems similar in structure to those encountered in the modified projection method. Hence, the network structure of the subproblems induced by the Euler method is, once again, as depicted in Figure 12.5.

12.7 Sources and Notes

This chapter presents and analyzes financial models that incorporate financial futures and options in an international setting. Options and futures contracts are treated as financial products that can provide a fixed price on a given instrument or currency. We recall that the major difference between options and futures is the fact that the former incorporate the right of the holder to accept this predetermined price, whereas in the latter the holder of the contract is forced to accept the fixed price.

The models presented here provide a new approach to equilibrium price determination and asset allocation, in the presence of futures and options. Clearly, these models are open for further extension and study, which can provide insightful and interesting results. The connection of these models with future and options pricing models, along with the inclusion of different types of contracts and the generalization of hedging strategies, are definitely some of the directions for future research.

The scope of this chapter is to provide a solid general mathematical framework that could capture both the static and the dynamic nature of its application. The material presented in this chapter is only a small demonstration of the direction that international financial modeling could follow.

We further recall, from Chapter 7, that the books by Cox and Rubinstein (1985), Duffie (1989), Kolb (1991), Andersen (1993), Hull (1993), and Winstone (1995) form excellent references to options and futures contracts and they extensively explain the way that the corresponding markets operate. Hence, we suggest these books for a detailed analysis and for additional background material on financial hedging, options, and futures. In addition, for a detailed discussion on interest rate futures contracts, we suggest the work by Kolb (1982) and Gay, Kolb, and Chiang (1983), and for additional information on currency options we recommend the work by Garman and Kohlagen (1983) and Biger and Hull (1983).

All of the results presented in this chapter have been presented earlier in Nagurney and Siokos (1997). The models developed here are extensions of the work by Nagurney and Siokos (1996a, b), and are generalizations of the work presented in Chapters 7, 8, 9, and 11.

Obviously, the models presented in this chapter can be further explored and generalized. For example, the incorporation of different types of contracts for each instrument and currency, the inclusion of contracts with different expiration dates and exercise prices, the connection with existing futures and options pricing models, and, finally, the performance evaluation of different portfolios and hedging strategies in terms of different single or customized benchmarks are possible subjects for future research.

References

Andersen, T. J., **Currency and Interest Hedging,** New York Institute of Finance, New York, New York, 1993.

Biger, N., and Hull, J., "The Valuation of Currency Options," *Financial Management* **12** (1983) 24-28.

Cox, J. C., and Rubinstein, M., **Options Markets,** Prentice-Hall Inc., Englewood Cliffs, New Jersey, 1985.

Duffie, D., **Futures Markets,** Prentice-Hall Inc., Englewood Cliffs, New Jersey, 1989.

Garman, M. B., and Kohlhagen, S. W., "Foreign Currency Option Values," *Journal of International Finance* **2** (1983) 231-237.

Gay, G. D., Kolb, R. W., and Chiang, R., "Interest Rate Hedging: An Empirical Test of Alternative Strategies," *Journal of Financial Research* **6** (1983) 187-197.

Hull, J., **Options, Futures, and Other Derivatives**, Prentice-Hall Inc., Englewood Cliffs, New Jersey, 1993.

Kolb, R. W., **Interest Rate Futures: A Comprehensive Introduction,** R. F. Dame, Richmond, Virginia, 1982.

Kolb, R. W., **Understanding Futures Markets,** New York Institute of Finance, New York, New York, 1991.

Marshal, J., and Bansal, V., **Financial Engineering. A Complete Guide to Financial Innovations**, Allyn and Bacon, Inc., New York, New York, 1992.

Nagurney, A., Dong, J., and Hughes, M., "Formulation and Computation of General Financial Equilibrium," *Optimization* **26** (1992) 339-354.

Nagurney, A., and Siokos, S., "Dynamic Multi-Sector, Multi-Instrument Financial Networks with Futures: Modeling and Computation," School of Management, University of Massachusetts, Amherst, Massachusetts, 1996a.

Nagurney, A., and Siokos, S., "Dynamics of International Financial Networks: Modeling, Stability Analysis, and Computation," **Networks and Knowledge in a Dynamic Economy**, M. Beckmann, B. Johansson, F. Snickars, and R. Thord, editors, Springer-Verlag, Berlin, Germany, 1996b, in press.

Nagurney, A., and Siokos, S., "Network Modeling of International Financial Equilibria with Hedging: Statics and Dynamics," School of Management, University of Massachusetts, Amherst, Massachusetts, 1997.

Parel, C., and McElrarey J., "Globalization in the Financial Services Industry," *Economic Perspectives,* Federal Reserve Bank of Chicago, **14**, 1990.

Shapiro, A., **Multinational Financial Management**, Allyn and Bacon, Inc., Needham Heights, Massachusetts, 1992.

Winstone, D., **Financial Derivatives: Hedging with Futures, Forwards, Options and Swaps**, Chapman and Hall, London, Great Britain, 1995.

13 Imperfect Market Models

In this chapter we turn to the development, analysis, and computation of international financial models, both static and dynamic, in the case of market imperfections. This chapter constructs models that are extensions, respectively, of the static single country imperfect market models studied in Chapter 9 and their dynamic counterparts that were developed in Chapter 10. Moreover, here we no longer assume that the feasible set underlying each sector of each country contains only the budget constraints. Consequently, the models in this chapter can also be viewed as extensions of the financial models in preceding chapters that assumed more specialized feasible sets. We conclude this chapter with a discussion of how the models can be even further extended to a noncooperative game scenario.

The structure of this chapter is similar to that of Chapter 11 in that we first present the static international financial equilibrium models and formulate the governing equilibrium conditions as variational inequality problems. We then follow by deriving the international financial adjustment process in the presence of market imperfections using the methodology of projected dynamical systems and the connection of such systems with variational inequality problems.

As already mentioned earlier in this text, the existing literature lacks in the development of general international financial equilibrium models that can handle the reality of such market imperfections as taxes, transaction costs, and policy interventions. Indeed, either the existing literature deals with a small number of countries and instruments (see, e.g., Eun and Janakiramanan (1986)) without deriving currency or instrument prices or it proposes mathematical models that apply only to perfect markets. This is not surprising since it is well-known that the inclusion of market imperfections creates complexities even in single country models (see Constantinides (1986), Davis and Norman (1990), Grauer, Litzenberger, and Stehle (1976), Leape

(1987), and Stulz (1981)). Most of the aforementioned difficulties arise because there is a lack of an integrated mathematical framework that can efficiently formulate, analyze, and solve an international financial equilibrium model with multiple sectors and instruments.

In this chapter, we attempt to fill this void by presenting both static and dynamic modeling approaches for imperfect market, international financial equilibrium. The models presented in this chapter provide the optimal composition of assets and liabilities in the portfolio of every sector of each country. In addition, the prices of each instrument in each currency, as well as the exchange rate prices of each currency, in terms of a basic currency, are also obtained. In this chapter we relax the perfect market assumption made in Chapters 11 and 12 and we take transaction costs and policy interventions into consideration. The suggested models have the flexibility of containing as many countries, currencies, sectors, and financial instruments as mandated by the application in question, with the theoretical limit being bounded solely by the memory of the computer utilized for solution.

The transaction costs that we treat include taxes and fees that an investor has to pay for each individual international investment. For example, one type of transaction cost that is handled by the models covers costs that are related to the origin and to the identity of both the sectors and the instruments, so that each sector can be charged differently from the others according to his portfolio. This type of transaction cost gives the monetary authorities the ability to apply different fees and taxes to investors in distinct countries. The second type of transaction cost that can be handled is related only to the instrument and currency prices and is a special case of the previous one. This type of transaction cost can be seen as a VAT (value added tax) type of transaction cost. There are some papers in the existing literature that look at a similar environment in which the transaction costs (e. g., taxation) are uniform across investors, but are differentiated among the particular type of instrument, that is, between stocks and bonds, as in Miller (1977). However, the proposed models, thus far, provide limited information as to the equilibrium patterns.

The price policy interventions that the models incorporate include price floors and ceilings, for both instruments and currencies, imposed by the governments. We assume that all the transaction costs, as well as the price ceilings and floors, are constants with known values.

This chapter is organized as follows. In Section 13.1, we present the imperfect market international financial equilibrium model, with a general utility function for each sector of each country. In this model we include policy interventions in the form of price floors and ceilings and transaction costs. The variational inequality formulation of the governing equilibrium conditions is also derived in this section. We also relate this model to several other models in the literature.

Section 13.2 then presents a qualitative analysis of the equilibrium pattern for the model developed in Section 13.1. In particular, it is shown that an equilibrium exists for this model and that, under reasonable assumptions on the utility function of each sector in each country, the equilibrium asset and liability patterns are also unique.

Section 13.3 then provides an international financial adjustment process modeled as a projected dynamical system, with stability analysis results in Section 13.4. Section 13.5 proves that, under certain conditions, the imperfect market financial equilibrium pattern can be obtained as the solution to a network optimization problem. Finally, algorithmic procedures are described in Section 13.6. We conclude with an addendum in Section 13.7 that discusses how this framework can be modified to incorporate imperfect competition in the presence of noncooperative behavior leading to a Nash-Cournot equilibrium.

13.1 International Financial Equilibrium Models

As in Chapters 11 and 12, we consider an economy consisting of L countries with a typical country denoted by l. Each country, in turn, has J sectors with a typical sector denoted by j. We also consider K currencies with a typical currency denoted by k. In each currency there are I instruments with a typical instrument denoted by i.

As previously, we denote the volume of instrument i in currency k, held as an asset by sector j of country l, by X_{ik}^{jl}, and group the assets of a sector in a country into the column vector $X^{jl} \in R_+^{IK}$. Similarly, we denote the volume of instrument i in currency k, held as a liability by sector j of country l, by Y_{ik}^{jl}, and group the liabilities of each sector in each country into the column vector $Y^{jl} \in R_+^{IK}$. Finally, we group the asset vectors into the column vector $X \in R_+^{JLIK}$ and the liability vectors into the column vextor $Y \in R_+^{JLIK}$.

Again, r_{ik} denotes the price of instrument i in currency k with the instrument prices grouped into the column vector $r \in R_+^{IK}$. We let e_k denote the rate of appreciation of currency k against the basic currency with $e \in R_+^K$ being the column vector of the currency prices.

Furthermore, from the policy interventions aspect, we denote the price ceiling associated with instrument i in currency k as r_{ik}^C and the exchange rate price ceiling associated with currency k as e_k^C. Similarly, we denote the price floor associated with instrument i in currency k as r_{ik}^F and the price floor associated with currency k as e_k^F. We group the instrument and currency price floors and ceilings, respectively, into the IK-dimensional column vectors r^F and r^C. Also, we group the exchange rate price floors and ceilings, respectively, into the K-dimensional column vectors e^F and e^C. We assume that the price floors are nonnegative and, hence, the price ceilings are positive. We further assume that each sector will behave as if he has no influence on the prices of the instruments and the exchange rates, or on the behavior of the other sectors. The assumption here, hence, is, again, one of perfect competition.

Finally, we denote the given tax rate levied on the net yield of sector j in country l on financial instrument i of currency k as $\mathcal{T}_{ik}^{jl}$ and we group the tax rates into an $JLIK$-dimensional column vector $\mathcal{T}$.

We assume that all the transaction costs $\mathcal{T}_{ik}^{jl}$ (or taxes) are constants with known values and lie in the interval [0,1). These costs depend both on the sector and the country that holds liabilities or assets in this instrument or currency. The model, hence, gives the local governments the flexibility to apply distinct tax rates across instruments in their area of authorization. Note that the model includes, as a special case, VAT type taxes, which only depend on the instrument and the currency. For example, a VAT tax on instrument k and currency i can be handled in our framework by setting $\mathcal{T}_{ik}^{jl} = \mathcal{T}_{ik}$, for all j and l.

We associate now with each asset held in instrument i in currency k a positive coefficient α_{ik}, and with each liability a positive coefficient β_{ik}, which are assumed to incorporate the unit transaction costs c_{ik}^x and c_{ik}^y, respectively, and which, in turn, are assumed to lie in the interval [0,1). For example, one possible form of α_{ik} is: $\alpha_{ik} \equiv 1 + c_{ik}^x$ and of β_{ik} is: $\beta_{ik} \equiv 1 - c_{ik}^y$.

We assume that each sector j of every country l seeks to maximize his utility, where the utility function is denoted by $U^{jl}(X^{jl}, Y^{jl}, r, e; \mathcal{T})$. The portfolio optimization problem of each sector in each country can then be expressed as:

$$\text{Maximize}_{(X^{jl},Y^{jl})\in\tilde{\kappa}^{jl}} \quad U^{jl}(X^{jl}, Y^{jl}, r, e; \mathcal{T}), \tag{13.1}$$

where $\tilde{\kappa}^{jl}$ is a closed, convex and polyhedral, non-empty, and bounded subset of R_+^{2IK}, denoting the feasible set of asset and liability choices. One can in this format, for example, model other transaction costs through the appropriate definition of the feasible set $\tilde{\kappa}^{jl}$, which may include, for example, the constraints given by:

$$\sum_{i=1}^{I}\sum_{k=1}^{K} \alpha_{ik} X_{ik}^{jl} = S^{jl} \tag{13.2a}$$

$$\sum_{i=1}^{I}\sum_{k=1}^{K} \beta_{ik} Y_{ik}^{jl} = S^{jl}, \tag{13.2b}$$

where S^{jl}, as previously, denotes the total financial volume held by sector j of country l. Constraints (13.2a) and (13.2b) represent the account balancing constraints and are generalizations of the single country model constraints (9.2a) and (9.2b).

Note that, in the framework of network theory (cf. Chapter 5), the terms α_{ik} and β_{ik} would correspond to arc multipliers and the constraints (13.2a) and (13.2b), along with the nonnegativity assumption on the flows, to generalized network-type constraints on networks as depicted in Figure 13.1.

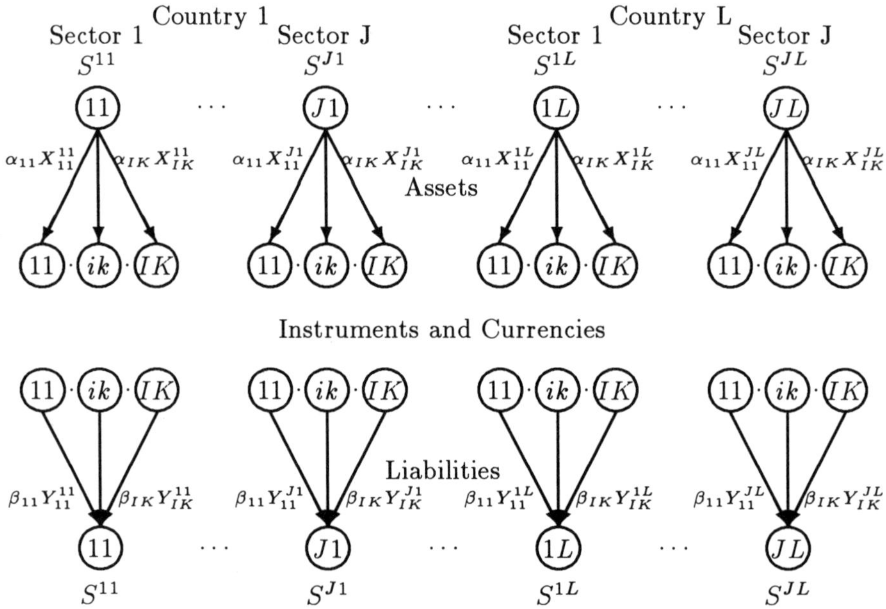

Fig. 13.1. Generalized structure of the sectors' portfolio optimization subproblems in the case of particular transaction costs

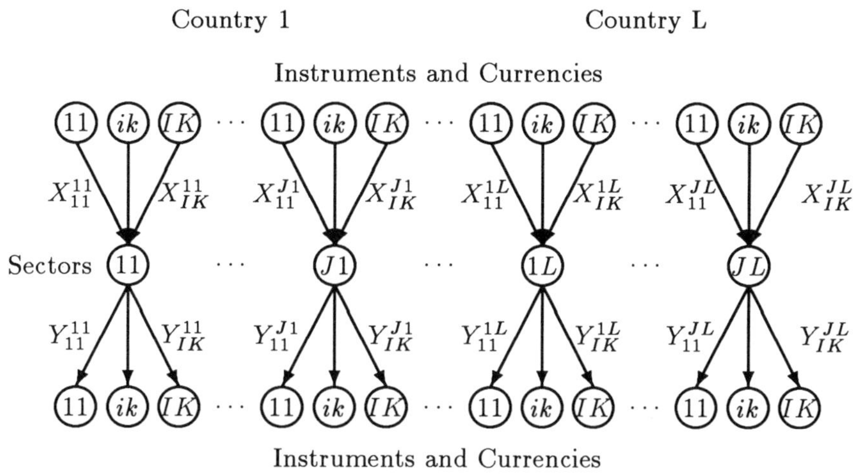

Fig. 13.2. Network structure of individual sectors' optimization problems in the case of net worth constraints

Observe that the feasible set, $\tilde{\kappa}^{jl}$ of a sector in a country is not necessarily a Cartesian product of two sets in the X^{jl} and the Y^{jl} vectors, respectively, as was the case in the models in Chapter 9 and 10. Hence, one can model, for example, a constraint of the form:

$$\sum_{i=1}^{I}\sum_{k=1}^{K} X_{ik}^{jl} - Y_{ik}^{jl} = NW^{jl} \tag{13.2c}$$

to replace (13.2a) and (13.2b), where NW^{jl} denotes the net worth of sector j in country l. Note that such a feasible set is not bounded since, for example, the asset variables and liability variables may go out to infinity and, hence, one may wish also to impose upper bounds on the instrument variables as discussed in Section 5.1.

One can, of course, include the transaction costs α_{ik} and β_{ik} into constrint (13.2c) as multipliers preceding X_{ik}^{jl} and Y_{ik}^{jl}, respectively.

In Figure 13.2 the network structure of the individual sectors' portfolio optimization problems, in the case of net worth constraints of the form (13.2c) is depicted. Interestingly, here, in contrast to the network in Figure 13.1, the instrument and currency nodes are at the uppermost and at the lowermost levels, whereas the sector nodes comprise the middle level of the nodes.

Another possibility for the feasible set $\tilde{\kappa}^{jl}$ would be to incorporate constraints of the form:

$$B\begin{pmatrix} X^{jl} \\ Y^{jl} \end{pmatrix} \leq \bar{b}, \tag{13.2d}$$

where B is an $m \times 2IK$ matrix and $\bar{b}$ is an $(m \times 1)$ vector. Such constraints are further discussed in the book by Thore (1980).

We define the feasible set $\tilde{\kappa}$ as the Cartesian product of all the feasible sets $\tilde{\kappa}^{jl}$ for all j and l. Note that here, in contrast to the feasible set underlying the single country model in Section 9.1, we explicitly allow for constraints in addition to the budget and nonnegativity constraints. We do this for the sake of generality.

The Equilibrium Conditions

We now present the equilibrium conditions governing the imperfect market international financial equilibrium model.

Portfolio Optimality

Under the assumption that each sector is risk-averse, the utility function $U^{jl}(X^{jl}, Y^{jl}, r, e; \mathcal{T})$ is a strictly concave function with respect to (X^{jl}, Y^{jl}), which we assume to be the case, henceforth. We further assume that this function is continuous and twice continuously differentiable.

The necessary and sufficient conditions for an optimal portfolio of sector j of contry l, $(X^{jl^*}, Y^{jl^*}) \in \tilde{\kappa}^{jl}$, is that it satisfies the following inequality:

$$-\nabla_{X^{jl}} U^{jl}(X^{jl^*}, Y^{jl^*}, r^*, e^*; \mathcal{T})^T \cdot (X^{jl} - X^{jl})$$
$$-\nabla_{Y^{jl}} U^{jl}(X^{jl^*}, Y^{jl^*}, r^*, e^*; \mathcal{T})^T \cdot (Y^{jl} - Y^{jl^*}) \geq 0, \quad \forall (X^{jl}, Y^{jl}) \in \tilde{\kappa}^{jl}, \tag{13.3}$$

where, as previously, $\nabla_{X^{jl}}$ denotes the gradient with respect to the variables in the vector X^{jl}; $\nabla_{Y^{jl}}$ is defined accordingly.

Instrument Market Equilibrium Conditions

The economic system conditions for the instrument prices are as follows: For each instrument i; $i = 1, \ldots, I$, and currency k; $k = 1, \ldots, K$, we must have that:

$$\sum_{j=1}^{J} \sum_{l=1}^{L} \left(1 - \mathcal{T}_{ik}^{jl}\right) \left(\alpha_{ik} X_{ik}^{jl^*} - \beta_{ik} Y_{ik}^{jl^*}\right) \begin{cases} \leq 0, & \text{if } r_{ik}^* = r_{ik}^C \\ = 0, & \text{if } r_{ik}^F < r_{ik}^* < r_{ik}^C \\ \geq 0, & \text{if } r_{ik}^* = r_{ik}^F. \end{cases} \tag{13.4}$$

The system of equalities and inequalities (13.4) states that if there is an excess demand of an instrument in a currency in the economy then the price of it is equal to the ceiling price. If the price of a financial instrument in a currency is positive, but not at the ceiling or at the floor, then the market must clear. Finally, if there is an excess supply of that instrument in that currency in the economy then the price of it is equal to the floor price.

Currency Market Equilibrium Conditions

Also, for each currency k; $k = 1, \ldots, K$, we must have that

$$\sum_{j=1}^{J}\sum_{l=1}^{L}\sum_{i=1}^{I}\left(1-\mathcal{T}_{ik}^{jl}\right)\left(\alpha_{ik}X_{ik}^{jl^*}-\beta_{ik}Y_{ik}^{jl^*}\right)\begin{cases}\leq 0, & \text{if } e_k^* = e_k^C\\ = 0, & \text{if } e_k^F < e_k^* < e_k^C\\ \geq 0, & \text{if } e_k^* = e_k^F.\end{cases} \tag{13.5}$$

In other words, if there is an excess demand for a currency in the economy, then the price of it is equal to the ceiling price. If the price of a currency is positive, but not at the ceiling or at the floor, the market must clear. Finally, if there is an excess supply of a currency in the economy then the price of it is equal to the floor price.

We now define the feasible set $\mathcal{K}$ as follows. Let $S^r \equiv \{r | r^F \leq r \leq r^C\}$, $S^e \equiv \{e | e^F \leq e \leq e^C\}$. Then, $\mathcal{K} \equiv \tilde{\kappa} \times S^r \times S^e$.

Combining the above sector and market inequalities and equalities we obtain the following definition.

Definition 13.1 (Imperfect Market International Financial Equilibrium

A vector $(X^*, Y^*, r^*, e^*) \in \mathcal{K}$ is an equilibrium of the imperfect market international financial model if and only if it satisfies the system of equalities and inequalities (13.3), (13.4), and (13.5), for all sectors j; $j = 1, \ldots, J$, all countries l; $l = 1, \ldots, L$, all instruments i; $i = 1, \ldots, I$, and all currencies k; $k = 1, \ldots, K$.

We are now ready to derive the variational inequality formulation of the equilibrium conditions governing the international financial equilibrium model with transaction costs and price policies.

Theorem 13.1 (Variational Inequality Formulation)

A vector of assets and liabilities of the sectors of the countries, and currency instrument and exchange rate prices, $(X^*, Y^*, r^*, e^*) \in \mathcal{K}$, is an imperfect market international financial equilibrium if and only if it satisfies the variational inequality problem:

$$-\sum_{j=1}^{J}\sum_{l=1}^{L}\left[\nabla_{X^{jl}}U^{jl}(X^{jl^*}, Y^{jl^*}, r^*, e^*; \mathcal{T})^T\right]\cdot\left[X^{jl}-X^{jl^*}\right]$$

$$-\sum_{j=1}^{J}\sum_{l=1}^{L}\left[\nabla_{Y^{jl}}U^{jl}(X^{jl^*}, Y^{jl^*}, r^*, e^*; \mathcal{T})^T\right]\cdot\left[Y^{jl}-Y^{jl^*}\right]$$

$$+\sum_{i=1}^{I}\sum_{k=1}^{K}\left[\sum_{j=1}^{J}\sum_{l=1}^{L}\left(1-\mathcal{T}_{ik}^{jl}\right)\left(\alpha_{ik}X_{ik}^{jl^*}-\beta_{ik}Y_{ik}^{jl^*}\right)\right]\times\left[r_{ik}-r_{ik}^*\right]$$

$$+\sum_{k=1}^{K}\left[\sum_{i=1}^{I}\sum_{j=1}^{J}\sum_{l=1}^{L}\left(1-\mathcal{T}_{ik}^{jl}\right)\left(\alpha_{ik}X_{ik}^{jl^*}-\beta_{ik}Y_{ik}^{jl^*}\right)\right]\times\left[e_k-e_k^*\right]\geq 0,$$

$$\forall\,(X,Y,r,e)\in\mathcal{K}. \tag{13.6}$$

Proof: Assume that $(X^*, Y^*, r^*, e^*) \in \mathcal{K}$ is an equilibrium of the imperfect market international financial model. Then inequalities (13.3), (13.4), and (13.5) hold for all j, l, i, k. Hence, summing (13.3) over all countries l and sectors j yields:

$$-\sum_{j=1}^{J}\sum_{l=1}^{L}\left[\nabla_{X^{jl}}U^{jl}(X^{jl^*},Y^{jl^*},r^*,e^*;\mathcal{T})^T\right]\cdot\left[X^{jl}-X^{jl^*}\right]$$

$$-\sum_{j=1}^{J}\sum_{l=1}^{L}\left[\nabla_{Y^{jl}}U^{jl}(X^{jl^*},Y^{jl^*},r^*,e^*;\mathcal{T})^T\right]\cdot\left[Y^{jl}-Y^{jl^*}\right]\geq 0,\ \forall(X,Y)\in\tilde{\kappa}. \tag{13.7}$$

Also, since (X^*, Y^*, r^*, e^*) is an equilibrium, the system of equalities and inequalities (13.4) holds, and we can conclude that $r_{ik}^* \in \left[r_{ik}^F, r_{ik}^C\right]$ must satisfy:

$$\sum_{j=1}^{J}\sum_{l=1}^{L}\left(1-\mathcal{T}_{ik}^{jl}\right)\left(\alpha_{ik}X_{ik}^{jl^*}-\beta_{ik}Y_{ik}^{jl^*}\right)\times\left[r_{ik}-r_{ik}^*\right]\geq 0,$$

$$\forall r_{ik}\in\left[r_{ik}^F,r_{ik}^C\right]. \tag{13.8}$$

But (13.8) must hold for all i and k, and, hence, the summation of (13.8) over all currencies k and instruments i, implies that for $r \in S^r$:

$$\sum_{i=1}^{I}\sum_{k=1}^{K}\left[\sum_{j=1}^{J}\sum_{l=1}^{L}\left(1-\mathcal{T}_{ik}^{jl}\right)\left(\alpha_{ik}X_{ik}^{jl^*}-\beta_{ik}Y_{ik}^{jl^*}\right)\right]\times\left[r_{ik}-r_{ik}^*\right]\geq 0,\ \forall r\in S^r. \tag{13.9}$$

Finally, since (X^*, Y^*, r^*, e^*) is an equilibrium, the system of equalities and inequalities (13.5) holds, for currency k; $k = 1, \ldots, K$, which is equivalent to the fact that $e_k^* \in \left[e_k^F, e_k^C\right]$ must satisfy:

$$\sum_{i=1}^{I}\sum_{j=1}^{J}\sum_{l=1}^{L}\left(1-\mathcal{T}_{ik}^{jl}\right)\left(\alpha_{ik}X_{ik}^{jl^*}-\beta_{ik}Y_{ik}^{jl^*}\right)\times\left[e_k-e_k^*\right]\geq 0,$$

$$\forall e_k\in\left[e_k^F,e_k^C\right]. \tag{13.10}$$

Since (13.10) holds for each currency, summation of (13.10) over all currencies yields that $e \in S^e$ must satisfy:

$$\sum_{k=1}^{K}\left[\sum_{i=1}^{I}\sum_{j=1}^{J}\sum_{l=1}^{L}\left(1-\mathcal{T}_{ik}^{jl}\right)\left(\alpha_{ik}X_{ik}^{jl^*}-\beta_{ik}Y_{ik}^{jl^*}\right)\right]\times\left[e_k-e_k^*\right]\geq 0,\ \forall e\in S^e. \tag{13.11}$$

Summing now inequalities (13.7), (13.9), and (13.11), we obtain variational inequality (13.6).

We now establish that a solution to variational inequality (13.6) also satisfies equilibrium conditions (13.3), (13.4), and (13.5).

If $(X^*,Y^*,r^*,e^*)\in\mathcal{K}$ is a solution to variational inequality (13.6) and we let $r_{ik}=r_{ik}^*$ and $e_k=e_k^*$, for all i and k, then substitution into variational inequality (13.6) yields:

$$-\sum_{j=1}^{J}\sum_{l=1}^{L}\left[\nabla_{X^{jl}}U^{jl}(X^{jl^*},Y^{jl^*},r^*,e^*;\mathcal{T})^T\right]\cdot\left[X^{jl}-X^{jl^*}\right]$$

$$-\sum_{j=1}^{J}\sum_{l=1}^{L}\left[\nabla_{Y^{jl}}U^{jl}(X^{jl^*},Y^{jl^*},r^*,e^*;\mathcal{T})^T\right]\cdot\left[Y^{jl}-Y^{jl^*}\right]\geq 0,\ (X,Y)\in\tilde{\kappa}, \tag{13.12}$$

which implies that (13.3) must hold.

If we now let $X_{ik}^{jl}=X_{ik}^{jl^*}$, $Y_{ik}^{jl}=Y_{ik}^{jl^*}$, and $e_k=e_k^*$, for all i,k,j,l, and substitute the resultants into inequality (13.6), we obtain:

$$\sum_{i=1}^{I}\sum_{k=1}^{K}\left[\sum_{j=1}^{J}\sum_{l=1}^{L}\left(1-\mathcal{T}_{ik}^{jl}\right)\left(\alpha_{ik}X_{ik}^{jl^*}-\beta_{ik}Y_{ik}^{jl^*}\right)\right]\times\left[r_{ik}-r_{ik}^*\right]\geq 0,\ \forall r\in S^r, \tag{13.13}$$

which implies system (13.4).

Finally, if we let $X_{ik}^{jl}=X_{ik}^{jl^*}$, $Y_{ik}^{jl}=Y_{ik}^{jl^*}$, and $r_{ik}=r_{ik}^*$ for all i,k,j,l, and substitute the resultants into inequality (13.6), we obtain:

$$\sum_{k=1}^{K}\left[\sum_{i=1}^{I}\sum_{j=1}^{J}\sum_{l=1}^{L}\left(1-\mathcal{T}_{ik}^{jl}\right)\left(\alpha_{ik}X_{ik}^{jl^*}-\beta_{ik}Y_{ik}^{jl^*}\right)\right]\times\left[e_k-e_k^*\right]\geq 0,\ \forall e\in S^e, \tag{13.14}$$

which implies system (13.5). □

We now turn our attention to special cases of the above model that have have been discussed earlier in this book.

If one assumes that there is only a single country and a single currency, that is, $l=1$ and $k=1$, then the above model collapses to the single country model with price policies and transaction costs studied in Chapter 9, in the case that the feasible set $\tilde{\kappa}^{jl}$ takes on the form given by (13.2a) and (13.2b). In this special case, there are no economic conditions for exchange rates. If one further assumes that there are no transaction costs, that is, $\mathcal{T}_{ik}^{jl} = 0$ for all i, k, j, l and α_{ik} and $\beta_{ik} = 1$ for all i, k, and no price ceilings, with the price floors set to zero, then the above model collapses to the perfect market model presented in Chapter 11, in which the feasible sets are, again assumed to take on a special form.

We now present an important special case that we will utilize for numerical purposes later in this chapter.

13.1.1 Quadratic Utility Functions

In this subsection we study a special case of the above model in which the utility functions are quadratic and in which the feasible set is given by (13.2a) and (13.2b). We, again, assume that each sector j; $j = 1, \ldots, J$, of country l; $l = 1, \ldots, L$, has as an objective to determine his optimal composition of instruments held as assets and as liabilities, so as to maximize the value of his asset holdings and to minimize the value of his liabilities, as well as the risk associated with his portfolio choice.

The objective of maximizing the expected net yield of the portfolio in the presence of transaction costs, for sector j of country l, can be approximated by:

$$\text{Maximize} \sum_{i=1}^{I} \sum_{k=1}^{K} \left(X_{ik}^{jl} - Y_{ik}^{jl}\right)\left(1 - \mathcal{T}_{ik}^{jl}\right)(r_{ik} + e_k). \tag{13.15}$$

We assume that each sector's assessment of risk is based on a variance-covariance matrix denoting the sector's assessment of the standard deviation of prices for each instrument and currency. The symmetric $2IK \times 2IK$ variance-covariance matrix associated with sector j's of country l holdings is denoted by Q^{jl}.

The utility function, U^{jl}, facing each sector j of country l is, thus, assumed to be given by:

$$U^{jl}(X^{jl}, Y^{jl}, r, e; \mathcal{T}) = \sum_{i=1}^{I} \sum_{k=1}^{K} \left(X_{ik}^{jl} - Y_{ik}^{jl}\right)\left(1 - \mathcal{T}_{ik}^{jl}\right)(r_{ik} + e_k)$$
$$- \begin{pmatrix} X^{jl} \\ Y^{jl} \end{pmatrix}^T Q^{jl} \begin{pmatrix} X^{jl} \\ Y^{jl} \end{pmatrix}. \tag{13.16}$$

Then the portfolio optimization for a sector j of country l is given by:

$$\text{Minimize} \begin{pmatrix} X^{jl} \\ Y^{jl} \end{pmatrix}^T Q^{jl} \begin{pmatrix} X^{jl} \\ Y^{jl} \end{pmatrix}$$
$$- \sum_{i=1}^{I} \sum_{k=1}^{K} \left(X_{ik}^{jl} - Y_{ik}^{jl}\right)\left(1 - \mathcal{T}_{ik}^{jl}\right)(r_{ik} + e_k) \tag{13.17}$$

subject to:

$$\sum_{i=1}^{I}\sum_{k=1}^{K}\alpha_{ik}X_{ik}^{jl}=S^{jl}, \tag{13.18a}$$

$$\sum_{i=1}^{I}\sum_{k=1}^{K}\beta_{ik}Y_{ik}^{jl}=S^{jl}, \tag{13.18b}$$

$$X_{ik}^{jl},\ Y_{ik}^{jl}\geq 0,\quad i,\ldots,I;\ k=1,\ldots,K. \tag{13.19}$$

Since Q^{jl} is a variance-covariance matrix we can assume that it is positive definite, and, hence, the objective function (13.17) for sector j of country l is strictly convex. Furthermore, Q^{jl} can be partitioned, as discussed in Section 11.1.1, as:

$$Q^{jl}=\begin{pmatrix} Q_{11}^{jl} & Q_{12}^{jl}\\ Q_{21}^{jl} & Q_{22}^{jl}\end{pmatrix}$$

with z_{ik} being a pointer defined as $z_{ik}\equiv(i-1)K+k$.

Lastly, we assume that the economic system conditions for the instrument and exchange prices are the same as in (13.4) and (13.5). We can now define the feasible set $\mathcal{K}$ for the specific case that we are studying.

Let $S^r\equiv\{r|r^F\leq r\leq r^C\}$, $S^e\equiv\{e|e^F\leq e\leq e^C\}$, and also let $\tilde{\kappa}\equiv\{(X,Y)\in R_+^{2JLIK}|\,(13.18)\text{ and }(13.19)\text{ hold},\forall jl\}$. Then, $\mathcal{K}\equiv S^r\times S^e\times\tilde{\kappa}$.

The variational inequality formulation of the equilibrium conditions of the model with quadratic utility functions can be easily derived from Theorem 13.1.

Corollary 13.1

A vector of assets and liabilities of the sectors of the countries, and currency instrument and exchange rate prices, $(X^*,Y^*,r^*,e^*)\in\mathcal{K}$, is an imperfect market international financial equilibrium, in the case of utility functions of the form (13.16), if and only if it satisfies the variational inequality problem:

$$\sum_{j=1}^{J}\sum_{l=1}^{L}\sum_{i=1}^{I}\sum_{k=1}^{K}\left[2\left[\left(Q_{11}^{jl}\right)_{z_{ik}}X^{jl^*}+\left(Q_{12}^{jl}\right)_{z_{ik}}Y^{jl^*}\right]-\left(1-\tau_{ik}^{jl}\right)\left(r_{ik}+e_k\right)\right]$$
$$\times\left[X_{ik}^{jl}-X_{ik}^{jl^*}\right]$$
$$+\sum_{j=1}^{J}\sum_{l=1}^{L}\sum_{i=1}^{I}\sum_{k=1}^{K}\left[2\left[\left(Q_{22}^{jl}\right)_{z_{ik}}Y^{jl^*}+\left(Q_{21}^{jl}\right)_{z_{ik}}X^{jl^*}\right]+\left(1-\tau_{ik}^{jl}\right)\left(r_{ik}^*+e_k^*\right)\right]$$
$$\times\left[Y_{ik}^{jl}-Y_{ik}^{jl^*}\right]$$
$$+\sum_{i=1}^{I}\sum_{k=1}^{K}\left[\sum_{j=1}^{J}\sum_{l=1}^{L}\left(1-\tau_{ik}^{jl}\right)\left(\alpha_{ik}X_{ik}^{jl^*}-\beta_{ik}Y_{ik}^{jl^*}\right)\right]\times\left[r_{ik}-r_{ik}^*\right]$$

$$+\sum_{k=1}^{K}\left[\sum_{i=1}^{I}\sum_{j=1}^{J}\sum_{l=1}^{L}\left(1-\mathcal{T}_{ik}^{jl}\right)\left(\alpha_{ik}X_{ik}^{jl*}-\beta_{ik}Y_{ik}^{jl*}\right)\right]\times\left[e_k-e_k^*\right]\geq 0,$$

$$\forall (X,Y,r,e)\in\mathcal{K}. \tag{13.20}$$

13.2 Qualitative Properties

In this section we present some qualitative properties of the imperfect market international financial equilibrium model presented in Section 13.1. In particular, we examine the questions of existence and uniqueness of the equilibrium pattern and then present additional properties. For simplicity, we first introduce some notation and then put variational inequality (13.6) into standard form.

Let $n = 2JLIK + IK + K$ and define the n-dimensional column vector $x \equiv (X, Y, r, e) \in \mathcal{K}$, and the column vector $F(x)$:

$$F(x) = \begin{bmatrix} F_1(x) \\ \vdots \\ F_b(x) \\ \vdots \\ F_n(x) \end{bmatrix}_{n\times 1}, \tag{13.21}$$

which is equal to:

$$\begin{bmatrix} -\nabla_X U(X,Y,r,e;\mathcal{T}) \\ -\nabla_Y U(X,Y,r,e;\mathcal{T}) \\ \sum_{j=1}^{J}\sum_{l=1}^{L}\left(1-\mathcal{T}_{11}^{jl}\right)\left(\alpha_{11}X_{11}^{jl}-\beta_{11}Y_{11}^{jl}\right) \\ \vdots \\ \sum_{j=1}^{J}\sum_{l=1}^{L}\left(1-\mathcal{T}_{IK}^{jl}\right)\left(\alpha_{IK}X_{IK}^{jl}-\beta_{IK}Y_{IK}^{jl}\right) \\ \sum_{i=1}^{I}\sum_{j=1}^{J}\sum_{l=1}^{L}\left(1-\mathcal{T}_{i1}^{jl}\right)\left(\alpha_{i1}X_{i1}^{jl}-\beta_{i1}Y_{i1}^{jl}\right) \\ \vdots \\ \sum_{i=1}^{I}\sum_{j=1}^{J}\sum_{l=1}^{L}\left(1-\mathcal{T}_{iK}^{jl}\right)\left(\alpha_{iK}X_{iK}^{jl}-\beta_{iK}Y_{iK}^{jl}\right) \end{bmatrix}_{n\times 1}. \tag{13.22}$$

The variational inequality (13.6) is then equivalent to the variational inequality problem:

Determine $x^* \in \mathcal{K}$, such that

$$F(x^*)^T \cdot (x - x^*) \geq 0, \quad \forall x \in \mathcal{K}. \tag{13.23}$$

We are now ready to present some qualitative properties.

Theorem 13.2 (Existence)
A solution $x^* = (X^*, Y^*, r^*, e^*) \in \mathcal{K}$ *to (13.23), equivalently, to (13.6) is guaranteed to exist.*

Proof: Since, under the imposed assumptions, the feasible set $\mathcal{K}$ is compact, and the function $F(x)$ is continuous on this set, it follows from the standard theory of variational inequalities (cf. Theorem 3.1) that a solution x^* exists, that is, we are guaranteed an equilibrium pattern $x^* = (X^*, Y^*, r^*, e^*)$ satisfying (13.6) and (13.23). □

We now present the uniqueness result. The proof is left out since it is similar to earlier uniqueness proofs presented earlier in this book

Theorem 13.3 (Uniqueness)
For any equilibrium instrument and currency price vector (r^*, e^*) *the equilibrium asset and liability pattern* (X^*, Y^*) *is unique, under the assumption that the utility function of each sector in each country is strictly concave with respect to its instrument variables and twice continuously differentiable.*

The following propositions are also presented without proof since they are adaptations of the proofs of Theorems 6.4 and 6.5, respectively.

Proposition 13.1 (Monotonicity)
$F(x)$ *is monotone, that is,*

$$\left[F(x^1) - F(x^2)\right]^T \cdot \left[x^1 - x^2\right] \geq 0, \quad \forall x^1, x^2 \in \mathcal{K},$$

under the same assumptions on F *as made in Theorem 13.3.*

Proposition 13.2 (Lipschitz Continuity)
$F(x)$ *satisfies the Lipschitz condition:*

$$\| F(x^1) - F(x^2) \| \leq \mathcal{L} \| x^1 - x^2 \|, \quad \forall x^1, x^2 \in \mathcal{K},$$

with Lipschitz constant $\mathcal{L} > 0$, *under the assumption that the utility function* U^{jl} *is strictly concave and has bounded second order derivatives for all countries* l *and all sectors* j *in the feasible set.*

13.3 International Financial Adjustment Process

In this section we present the dynamic international financial adjustment process in the case of market imperfections in the form of transaction costs, price policy floors and ceilings, and taxes. The adjustment process is modeled as a projected dynamical system.

The Imperfect Market International Financial Adjustment Process

Here, as in Chapter 11, we make use of Definition 4.3 and Theorem 4.1 to obtain the following projected dynamical system, whose stationary points coincide with the set of solutions to variational inequality (13.6), equivalently, variational inequality (13.23), with $F(\cdot)$ defined in (13.22):

$$\dot{x} = \Pi_{\mathcal{K}}(x, -F(x)). \tag{13.24}$$

The International Financial Adjustment Process

We define the column vector $(z^{jl}) \equiv (X^{jl}, Y^{jl})$ for each sector j and country l. In view of Proposition 8.1, the financial adjustment process that derives the allocation of assets and liabilities for each sector j of every country l along with the prices of each instrument and each currency can also be stated as:

$$\begin{cases} \dot{z}^{jl} = \Pi_{\bar{\mathcal{K}}^{jl}}(z^{jl}, \nabla_{z^{jl}} U^{jl}); & j = 1, \ldots, J; l = 1, \ldots, L \\ \dot{r}_{ik} = \Pi_{[r^F_{ik}, r^C_{ik}]}(r_{ik}, \tilde{\rho}_{ik}); & i = 1, \ldots, I; k = 1, \ldots, K \\ \dot{e}_k = \Pi_{[e^F_k, e^C_k]}(e_k, \tilde{\epsilon}_k); & k = 1, \ldots, K, \end{cases} \tag{13.25}$$

where $\tilde{\rho}_{ik}$ is defined as

$$\tilde{\rho}_{ik} = -\sum_{j=1}^{J}\sum_{l=1}^{L}(1 - \tau^{jl}_{ik})\left(\alpha_{ik} X^{jl}_{ik} - \beta_{ik} Y^{jl}_{ik}\right)$$

and $\tilde{\epsilon}_k$ is defined as

$$\tilde{\epsilon}_k = -\sum_{i=1}^{I}\sum_{j=1}^{J}\sum_{l=1}^{L}(1 - \tau^{jl}_{ik})\left(\alpha_{ik} X^{jl}_{ik} - \beta_{ik} Y^{jl}_{ik}\right).$$

Consequently, if one obtains a stationary point of the dynamical system (13.24), equivalently, (13.25), then that point is an imperfect market international financial equilibrium, that is, it satisfies Definition 13.1. Also (cf. Theorem 4.2), under reasonable assumptions on the utility functions of the sectors of the countries, one can obtain well-defined trajectories of the assets and liabilities, as well as the prices.

Clearly, the international financial adjustment process (13.25) is meaningful economically, since the prices respond according to the laws of supply and demand, and the sectors as utility maximizers. Again, the projection is needed in (13.24) and (13.25) to ensure that the constraints are not violated, that is, that the asset and liability pattern satisfy the constraints as defined by the feasible sets and the prices lie within the imposed price floors and ceilings.

13.4 Stability Analysis

In this section we provide conditions under which a disequilibrium pattern of assets, liabilities, instrument and currency prices will reach an imperfect market international financial equilibrium state under the adjustment process (13.24). For consistency, and in order to simplify the study of the asymptotic behavior of the dynamic international financial model, we present the following definitions. The theorems are presented without proofs since they are adaptations of stability theorems found in preceding chapters of this book. Note that the corresponding proofs depend on the form of the utility functions and assume that the feasible set is of the form (13.2a) and (13.2b) with $\alpha_{ik} = 1$ and $\beta_{ik} = 1$, for all instruments i and currencies k.

Definition 13.2 (A Stable Imperfect Market International Financial Adjustment Process)

The imperfect market international financial adjustment process defined by (13.24) is stable if each financial equilibrium, $x^* = (X^*, Y^*, r^*, e^*)$, is a monotone attractor, that is, for any initial asset, liability, and instrument and currency price pattern (X_0, Y_0, r_0, e_0), $\|(X(t), Y(t), r(t), e(t)) - (X^*, Y^*, r^*, e^*)\|$, is nonincreasing in time t, with $(X(t), Y(t), r(t), e(t))$ satisfying the adjustment process (13.24).

Definition 13.3 (An Asymptotically Stable Imperfect Market International Financial Adjustment Process)

The international financial adjustment process (13.24) is asymptotically stable if it is stable and for any initial asset, liability, and price pattern (X_0, Y_0, r_0, e_0) the financial adjustment process starting with that pattern converges to some equilibrium pattern (X^*, Y^*, r^*, e^*); that is,

$$\lim_{t\to\infty} (X_0(t), Y_0(t), r_0(t), e_0(t)) \rightarrow (X^*, Y^*, r^*, e^*). \tag{13.26}$$

In the subsequent stability theorems it is assumed that the feasible set is as given by (13.2a) and (13.2b) with $\alpha_{ik} = 1$ and $\beta_{ik} = 1$ for all i and k.

Theorem 13.4 (Stability of the Imperfect Market International Financial Adjustment Process)

If the utility function U^{jl} of each sector j from every country l is continuous, twice continuously differentiable, and concave in X^{jl} and Y^{jl}, and the utility function has the following form:

$$U^{jl}(X^{jl}, Y^{jl}, r, e; \mathcal{T}) = u^{jl}(X^{jl}, Y^{jl}) + \sum_{i=1}^{I} \sum_{k=1}^{K} (1 - \mathcal{T}_{ik}^{jl})(r_{ik} + e_k)(X_{ik}^{jl} - Y_{ik}^{jl}) \tag{13.27}$$

then the international financial adjustment process is stable.

Theorem 13.5 (Asymptotical Stability of the Imperfect Market International Financial Adjustment Process)

If we assume that all sectors j in countries l have a strictly concave utility function with respect to the asset and liability pattern (X^{jl}, Y^{jl}) the utility functions are twice continuously differentiable, and of the form (13.27), then the financial adjustment process is asymptotically stable.

13.5 Network Optimization in a Special Case

In this section we present the international analogue of the single country model studied in Section 9.3 and show that for this imperfect market international financial equilibrium model there exists a network optimization reformulation of the governing equilibrium conditions, as well. As in the model of Section 9.3, we assume that the utility functions are of a special form, specifically, as given by (13.27). Furthermore, we assume that the feasible set consists of the constraints (13.2a) and (13.2b). Moreover, we assume that there are no transaction costs, that is, $\alpha_{ik} = 1$ and $\beta_{ik} = 1$ for all instruments i and all currencies k. In addition, we assume that all price floors are set to zero and all price ceilings are set to infinity, that is, $r_{ik}^F = 0$, $e_k^F = 0$, and $r_{ik}^C = \infty$, $e_k^C = \infty$, for all i and k. Taxes, however, can remain.

The optimization problem facing a sector j of country l is given by

$$\text{Maximize} \quad u^{jl}(X^{jl}, Y^{jl}) + \sum_{i=1}^{I} \sum_{k=1}^{K} (1 - \tau_{ik}^{jl})(r_{ik} + e_k)(X_{ik}^{jl} - Y_{ik}^{jl}) \quad (13.28)$$

subject to:

$$\sum_{i=1}^{I} \sum_{k=1}^{K} X_{ik}^{jl} = S^{jl} \quad (13.29a)$$

$$\sum_{i=1}^{I} \sum_{k=1}^{K} Y_{ik}^{jl} = S^{jl} \quad (13.29b)$$

$$X_{ik}^{jl} \geq 0, \; Y_{ik}^{jl} \geq 0, \quad i = 1, \ldots, I; \; k = 1, \ldots, K. \quad (13.30)$$

We call the feasible set comprised of constraints (13.29)–(13.30) by κ^{jl} and we denote the Cartesian product of all such feasible sets of all the sectors in all the countries by κ.

We note that the optimality conditions (13.3) are still valid, with the gradients taken of the utility functions (13.27). The equilibrium conditions (13.4) and (13.5), take, in the absence of price ceilings and with price floors set to zero, the following form:

Instrument Market Equilibrium Conditions

The economic system conditions for the instrument prices are as follows: For each instrument i; $i = 1, \ldots, I$, and currency k; $k = 1, \ldots, K$, we must have that:

$$\sum_{j=1}^{J} \sum_{l=1}^{L} \left(1 - \tau_{ik}^{jl}\right) \left(X_{ik}^{jl^*} - Y_{ik}^{jl^*}\right) \begin{cases} = 0, & \text{if } r_{ik}^* > 0 \\ \geq 0, & \text{if } r_{ik}^* = 0. \end{cases} \quad (13.31)$$

Currency Market Equilibrium Conditions

Also, for each currency k; $k = 1, \ldots, K$, we must have that

$$\sum_{j=1}^{J}\sum_{l=1}^{L}\sum_{i=1}^{I}\left(1-\mathcal{T}_{ik}^{jl}\right)\left(X_{ik}^{jl*}-Y_{ik}^{jl*}\right)\begin{cases} =0, & \text{if } e_k^*>0 \\ \geq 0, & \text{if } e_k^*=0. \end{cases} \tag{13.32}$$

We now define the feasible set $\mathcal{K}$ as follows. Let $\mathcal{K} \equiv \kappa \times R_+^{IK} \times R_+^K$. The following corollary follows from Theorem 13.1.

Corollary 13.2

A vector of assets, liabilities, instrument and exchange rate prices, $(X^*, Y^*, r^*, e^*) \in \mathcal{K}$, is an imperfect market equilibrium (in the presence of taxes only) with utility functions of the form (13.27) if and only if it satisfies the variational inequality problem:

$$\sum_{j=1}^{J}\sum_{l=1}^{L}\sum_{i=1}^{I}\sum_{k=1}^{K}\left[-\frac{\partial u^{jl}(X^{jl*},Y^{jl*})}{\partial X_{ik}^{jl}}-\left(1-\mathcal{T}_{ik}^{jl}\right)(r_{ik}+e_k)\right]$$
$$\times\left[X_{ik}^{jl}-X_{ik}^{jl*}\right]$$
$$+\sum_{j=1}^{J}\sum_{l=1}^{L}\sum_{i=1}^{I}\sum_{k=1}^{K}\left[-\frac{\partial u^{jl}(X^{jl*},Y^{jl*})}{\partial Y_{ik}^{jl}}+\left(1-\mathcal{T}_{ik}^{jl}\right)(r_{ik}^*+e_k^*)\right]$$
$$\times\left[Y_{ik}^{jl}-Y_{ik}^{jl*}\right]$$
$$+\sum_{i=1}^{I}\sum_{k=1}^{K}\left[\sum_{j=1}^{J}\sum_{l=1}^{L}\left(1-\mathcal{T}_{ik}^{jl}\right)\left(X_{ik}^{jl*}-Y_{ik}^{jl*}\right)\right]\times\left[r_{ik}-r_{ik}^*\right]$$
$$+\sum_{k=1}^{K}\left[\sum_{i=1}^{I}\sum_{j=1}^{J}\sum_{l=1}^{L}\left(1-\mathcal{T}_{ik}^{jl}\right)\left(X_{ik}^{jl*}-Y_{ik}^{jl*}\right)\right]\times\left[e_k-e_k^*\right]\geq 0,$$
$$\forall (X,Y,r,e)\in\mathcal{K}. \tag{13.33}$$

Using arguments analogous to those in the proof of Theorem 9.6, but extended to the international domain, yields:

Theorem 13.6

The variational inequality problem of finding $(X^*, Y^*, r^*, e^*) \in \mathcal{K}$ satisfying (13.33) is equivalent to the problem:

$$\text{Maximize} \quad \sum_{j=1}^{J}\sum_{l=1}^{L} u^{jl}(X^{jl}, Y^{jl}) \tag{13.34}$$

subject to:

$$\sum_{j=1}^{J}\sum_{l=1}^{L}(1-\mathcal{T}_{ij}^{kl})(X_{ik}^{jl}-Y_{ik}^{jl})\geq 0, \quad i=1,\ldots,I; \quad k=1,\ldots,K \tag{13.35}$$

$$\sum_{j=1}^{J}\sum_{l=1}^{L}\sum_{i=1}^{I}(1-\mathcal{T}_{ij}^{kl})(X_{ik}^{jl}-Y_{ik}^{jl})\geq 0, \quad k=1,\ldots,K \tag{13.36}$$

and

$$(X^{jl},Y^{jl})\in\kappa^{jl}, \quad j=1,\ldots,J; \quad l=1,\ldots,L, \tag{13.37}$$

where $r_{ik}^*\geq 0$ corresponds to the Lagrange multiplier associated with the ik-th constraint in (13.35), and $e_k^*\geq 0$ corresponds to the Lagrange multiplier associated with the k-th constraint in (13.36).

The following corollary is immediate from Theorem 13.6.

Corollary 13.3
The solution to the optimization problem:

$$\text{Maximize} \sum_{j=1}^{J}\sum_{l=1}^{L}u^{jl}(X^{jl},Y^{jl}) \tag{13.38}$$

subject to:

$$\sum_{j=1}^{J}\sum_{l=1}^{L}(1-\mathcal{T}_{ik}^{jl})(X_{ik}^{jl}-Y_{ik}^{jl})\geq 0; \; i=1,\ldots,I; \; k=1,\ldots,K; \; (X,Y)\in\kappa, \tag{13.39}$$

with Lagrange multiplier $R_{ik}^*\geq 0$ for the ik-th constraint in (13.39), coincides with the solution to problem (13.34)–(13.37), where $R_{ik}^*\equiv(r_{ik}^*+e_k^*)$ for all ik; $i=1,\ldots,I$; $k=1,\ldots,K$.

Moreover, this solution is an equilibrium solution.

The following lemma is obvious using arguments as in the proofs of Lemma 9.1 and Lemma 11.1.

Lemma 13.1
In equilibrium, the markets clear for all instruments and all currencies, that is,

$$\sum_{j=1}^{J}\sum_{l=1}^{L}(1-\mathcal{T}_{ik}^{jl})(X_{ik}^{jl^*}-Y_{ik}^{jl^*})=0, \quad i=1,\ldots,I; \quad k=1,\ldots,K \tag{13.40}$$

and

$$\sum_{j=1}^{J}\sum_{l=1}^{L}\sum_{i=1}^{I}(1-\mathcal{T}_{ik}^{jl})(X_{ik}^{jl^*}-Y_{ik}^{jl^*})=0, \quad k=1,\ldots,K, \tag{13.41}$$

that is, (13.35) and (13.36) hold as strict equalities. Furthermore, the prices, r^*_{ik} and e^*_k for all instruments i and currencies k are strictly positive.

Theorem 13.7 below allows us to complete the network optimization reformulation of international financial equilibrium in the case that the utility functions are as given in (13.27). The theorem follows from Lemma 13.1 and Corollary 13.3.

Theorem 13.7

The imperfect market international financial equilibrium pattern given by $(X^*, Y^*, r^*, e^*) \in \mathcal{K}$ coincides with the solution of the optimization problem:

$$\text{Maximize} \quad \sum_{j=1}^{J} \sum_{l=1}^{L} u^{jl}(X^{jl}, Y^{jl}) \tag{13.42}$$

subject to:

$$\sum_{j=1}^{J} \sum_{l=1}^{L} (1 - \tau^{jl}_{ik})(X^{jl}_{ik} - Y^{jl}_{ik}) = 0, \quad i = 1, \ldots, I; \; k = 1, \ldots, K; \; (X, Y) \in \kappa, \tag{13.43}$$

with Lagrange multiplier $R^*_{ik} = (r^*_{ik} + e^*_k)$ for instrument i and currency k corresponding to the ik-th constraint in (13.43).

In Figure 13.3, we depict the network structure of the optimization problem in Theorem 13.7. The individual networks in Figure 13.1, representing the problems of the individual sectors in the countries, where the α_{ik} and β_{ik} terms are assumed to take on the values 1 for all instruments i and currencies k, merge to yield the network of Figure 13.3, representing the structure of the international imperfect market financial economy in equilibrium in the case of utility functions of the form (13.27). Note that on the links we now have arc multipliers that include the tax rates. This was also the case in the single country network model depicted in Figure 9.2.

13.6 Computation of International Equilibria

In this section, we address the computation of imperfect market international financial equilibria. We first present, in Section 13.6.1, the modified projection method. Obviously, the primal-dual method, as was outlined in Section 6.4, could also be used for the computation of the special case of the imperfect market international financial equilibrium in the case that the utility functions are of the form (13.27), in which case one would be solving the network optimization problem (13.42), subject to (13.43). We then present, in Section 13.6.2, the Euler method, which is a discrete time approximation to the continuous time adjustment process (13.24). In Section 13.6.3, we present a numerical example.

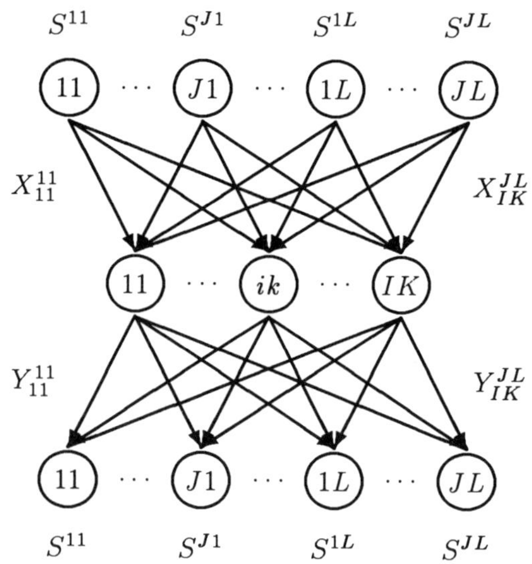

Fig. 13.3. The network structure of imperfect market international financial equilibrium in the absence of particular transaction costs

13.6.1 The Modified Projection Method

We will now illustrate the application of the modified projection algorithm for the computation of the international financial equilibrium pattern by expanding the function $F(x)$ (cf. (13.21)), as defined in (13.22). The method computes a solution to variational inequality (13.6), equivalently, determines an imperfect market international financial equilibrium, satisfying Definition 13.1. For simplicity of notation, let the vector $(x^{j,l^{\tau}})$ be defined as: $(x^{j,l^{\tau}}) \equiv (X^{j,l^{\tau}}, Y^{j,l^{\tau}}, r^{\tau}, e^{\tau})$, where τ represents an iterative step of the modified projection method.

The Modified Projection Method

Step 0: Initialization

Set $(X^0, Y^0, r^0, e^0) \in \mathcal{K}$. Let $\tau := 0$ and set γ so that $0 < \gamma < \frac{1}{\mathcal{L}}$, where $\mathcal{L}$ is the Lipschitz constant.

Step 1: Computation

Compute $(\bar{X}^{\tau}, \bar{Y}^{\tau}, \bar{r}^{\tau}, \bar{e}^{\tau}) \in \mathcal{K}$ by solving the variational inequality subproblem:

$$\sum_{j=1}^{J}\sum_{l=1}^{L}\sum_{i=1}^{I}\sum_{k=1}^{K}\left[\bar{X}_{ik}^{jl^{\tau}} + \gamma\left(-\frac{\partial U^{jl}(x^{jl^{\tau}};\mathcal{T})}{\partial X_{ik}^{jl}}\right) - X_{ik}^{jl^{\tau}}\right] \times \left[X_{ik}^{jl} - \bar{X}_{ik}^{jl^{\tau}}\right]$$

$$+\sum_{j=1}^{J}\sum_{l=1}^{L}\sum_{i=1}^{I}\sum_{k=1}^{K}\left[\bar{Y}_{ik}^{jl^{\tau}} + \gamma\left(-\frac{\partial U^{jl}(x^{jl^{\tau}};\mathcal{T})}{\partial Y_{ik}^{jl}}\right) - Y_{ik}^{jl^{\tau}}\right] \times \left[Y_{ik}^{jl} - \bar{Y}_{ik}^{jl^{\tau}}\right]$$

$$+\sum_{i=1}^{I}\sum_{k=1}^{K}\left[\bar{r}_{ik}^{\tau} + \gamma\left[\sum_{j=1}^{J}\sum_{l=1}^{L}\left(\alpha_{ik}X_{ik}^{jl^{\tau}} - \beta_{ik}Y_{ik}^{jl^{\tau}}\right)\right] - r_{ik}^{\tau}\right] \times \left[r_{ik} - \bar{r}_{ik}^{\tau}\right]$$

$$+\sum_{k=1}^{K}\left[\bar{e}_{k}^{\tau} + \gamma\left[\sum_{j=1}^{J}\sum_{l=1}^{L}\sum_{i=1}^{I}\left(\alpha_{ik}X_{ik}^{jl^{\tau}} - \beta_{ik}Y_{ik}^{jl^{\tau}}\right)\right] - e_{k}^{\tau}\right] \times \left[e_{k} - \bar{e}_{k}^{\tau}\right] \geq 0,$$

$$\forall (X, Y, r, e) \in \mathcal{K}. \tag{13.44}$$

Step 2: Adaptation

Compute $(X^{\tau+1}, Y^{\tau+1}, r^{\tau+1}, e^{\tau+1}) \in \mathcal{K}$ by solving the variational inequality subproblem:

$$\sum_{j=1}^{J}\sum_{l=1}^{L}\sum_{i=1}^{I}\sum_{k=1}^{K}\left[X_{ik}^{jl^{\tau+1}} + \gamma\left(-\frac{\partial U^{jl}(\bar{x}^{jl^{\tau}};\mathcal{T})}{\partial X_{ik}^{jl}}\right) - X_{ik}^{jl^{\tau}}\right] \times \left[X_{ik}^{jl} - X_{ik}^{jl^{\tau+1}}\right]$$

$$+\sum_{j=1}^{J}\sum_{l=1}^{L}\sum_{i=1}^{I}\sum_{k=1}^{K}\left[Y_{ik}^{jl^{\tau+1}} + \gamma\left(-\frac{\partial U^{jl}(\bar{x}^{jl^{\tau}};\mathcal{T})}{\partial Y_{ik}^{jl}}\right) - Y_{ik}^{jl^{\tau}}\right] \times \left[Y_{ik}^{jl} - Y_{ik}^{jl^{\tau}}\right]$$

$$+\sum_{i=1}^{I}\sum_{k=1}^{K}\left[r_{ik}^{\tau+1}+\gamma\left[\sum_{j=1}^{J}\sum_{l=1}^{L}\left(\alpha_{ik}\bar{X}_{ik}^{jl^{\tau}}-\beta_{ik}\bar{Y}_{ik}^{jl^{\tau}}\right)\right]-r_{ik}^{\tau}\right]\times\left[r_{ik}-r_{ik}^{\tau+1}\right]$$

$$+\sum_{k=1}^{K}\left[e_{k}^{\tau}+\gamma\left[\sum_{j=1}^{J}\sum_{l=1}^{L}\sum_{i=1}^{I}\left(\alpha_{ik}\bar{X}_{ik}^{jl^{\tau}}-\beta_{ik}\bar{Y}_{ik}^{jl^{\tau}}\right)\right]-e_{k}^{\tau}\right]\times\left[e_{k}-e_{k}^{\tau+1}\right]\geq 0,$$

$$\forall (X,Y,r,e)\in\mathcal{K}. \tag{13.45}$$

Step 3: Convergence Verification:

If $\max_{j,l,i,k}|X_{ik}^{jl^{\tau+1}}-X_{ik}^{jl^{\tau}}|\leq\epsilon$; $\max_{j,l,i,k}|Y_{ik}^{jl^{\tau+1}}-Y_{ik}^{jl^{\tau}}|\leq\epsilon$; $\max_{i,k}|r_{ik}^{\tau+1}-r_{ik}^{\tau}|\leq\epsilon$, $\max_{k}|e_{k}^{\tau+1}-e_{k}^{\tau}|\leq\epsilon$, for all $j; j=1,\ldots,J$, $l; l=1,\ldots,L$, $i; i=1,\ldots,I$, $k; k=1,\ldots,K$, with $\epsilon>0$, a prespecified tolerance, then stop; else, set $\tau:=\tau+1$, and go to Step 1.

Since the function $F(x)$ (cf. (13.22)) that enters the variational inequality (13.23) is monotone (see Proposition 13.1) and Lipschitz continuous (see Proposition 13.2), the modified projection algorithm is guaranteed to converge (see Section 3.3.1) and, as a result, the following theorem holds.

Theorem 13.8 (Convergence)

The modified projection method converges to an imperfect market international financial asset, liability, instrument and currency price equilibrium pattern, satisfying variational inequality (13.6).

Note that the subproblems induced by (13.44) and (13.45) are still quadratic programming problems. Moreover, recall that the feasible set $\mathcal{K}=\tilde{\kappa}\times R_{+}^{IK}\times R_{+}^{K}$, where $\tilde{\kappa}$ is the Cartesian product of all the sectors' feasible sets of all the countries. Hence, the quadratic programming problems are further decomposable over these feasible sets. Note that we did not assume here that the feasible set of a sector of a country included a budget constraint and, consequently, there may not exist an underlying network structure. Hence, one may have to appeal to another quadratic programming algorithm rather than to a network optimization algorithm or to equilibration to solve the embedded quadratic programming problems. However, the subproblems in price variables are still solvable in closed form. Of course, if the feasible set of each sector of each country consists of the budget constraints given by (13.2a) and (13.2b) then the subproblems in asset and in liability variables may be solved exactly and in closed form using the asset (and liability) exact equilibration algorithm detailed in Section 9.3.

Moreover, if the net worth constraints comprise the feasible set, then one can apply a network optimization algorithm (cf. Chapter 5) to solve the induced network subproblems for the sectors in the countries.

13.6.2 The Euler Method

In this section, we present a discrete time algorithm, the Euler method, for the computation of the imperfect market international financial equilibrium pattern. Recall that this algorithm may also be viewed as a discrete time approximation or discrete time adjustment process for the continuous time model given by (13.24). The Euler method is a special case of the general iterative scheme (4.24).

We now write down the Euler method (see Chapter 4) explicitly for our problem. As in the modified projection method, we use the notation $(x^{jl}) = (X^{jl}, Y^{jl})$.

The Euler Method

Step 0: Initialization

Set $(X^0, Y^0, r^0, e^0) \in \mathcal{K}$. Let $\tau := 0$. Set the sequence $\{a_\tau\}$ according to Condition 1 of Assumption 4.2.

Step 1: Computation

Compute $(X^{\tau+1}, Y^{\tau+1}, r^{\tau+1}, e^{\tau+1}) \in \mathcal{K}$ by solving the variational inequality problem:

$$\sum_{j=1}^{J}\sum_{l=1}^{L}\sum_{i=1}^{I}\sum_{k=1}^{K}\left[X_{ik}^{jl^{\tau+1}} + a_\tau\left(-\frac{\partial U^{jl}(x^{jl^{\tau}}; T)}{\partial X_{ik}^{jl}}\right) - X_{ik}^{jl^{\tau}}\right] \times \left[X_{ik}^{jl} - X_{ik}^{jl^{\tau+1}}\right]$$

$$+\sum_{j=1}^{J}\sum_{l=1}^{L}\sum_{i=1}^{I}\sum_{k=1}^{K}\left[Y_{ik}^{jl^{\tau+1}} + a_\tau\left(-\frac{\partial U^{jl}(x^{jl^{\tau}}; T)}{\partial Y_{ik}^{jl}}\right) - Y_{ik}^{jl^{\tau}}\right] \times \left[Y_{ik}^{jl} - Y_{ik}^{jl^{\tau+1}}\right]$$

$$+\sum_{i=1}^{I}\sum_{k=1}^{K}\left[r_{ik}^{\tau+1} + a_\tau\left[\sum_{j=1}^{J}\sum_{l=1}^{L}\left(\alpha_{ik}X_{ik}^{jl^{\tau}} - \beta_{ik}Y_{ik}^{jl^{\tau}}\right)\right] - r_{ik}^{\tau}\right] \times \left[r_{ik} - r_{ik}^{\tau+1}\right]$$

$$+\sum_{k=1}^{K}\left[e_k^{\tau+1} + a_\tau\left[\sum_{i=1}^{I}\sum_{j=1}^{J}\sum_{l=1}^{L}\left(\alpha_{ik}X_{ik}^{jl^{\tau}} - \beta_{ik}Y_{ik}^{jl^{\tau}}\right)\right] - e_k^{\tau}\right] \times \left[e_k - e_k^{\tau+1}\right] \geq 0,$$

$$\forall (X, Y, r, e) \in \mathcal{K}. \tag{13.46}$$

Step 3: Convergence Verification:

If $\max_{j,l,i,k} |X_{ik}^{jl^{\tau+1}} - X_{ik}^{jl^{\tau}}| \leq \epsilon$; $\max_{j,l,i,k} |Y_{ik}^{jl^{\tau+1}} - Y_{ik}^{jl^{\tau}}| \leq \epsilon$; $\max_{i,k} |r_{ik}^{\tau+1} - r_{ik}^{\tau}| \leq \epsilon$, $\max_k |e_k^{\tau+1} - e_k^{\tau}| \leq \epsilon$, for all $j; j = 1, \ldots, J$, $l; l =$

$1, \ldots, L$, $i; i = 1, \ldots, I$, $k; k = 1, \ldots, K$, with $\epsilon > 0$, a prespecified tolerance, then stop; else, set $\tau := \tau + 1$, and go to Step 1.

To conclude this section, the following theorem provides the convergence of the proposed Euler method in the context of the dynamic imperfect market international financial problem. It is presented without proof since it follows using similar arguments as the proof of Theorem 11.12

Theorem 13.9

Suppose that the utility functions u are strictly monotone decreasing and of the form (13.27) and that $\alpha_{ik} = 1$ and $\beta_{ik} = 1$ for all i and k. Let $\{a_\tau\}$ be a sequence of positive real numbers that satisfies

$$\lim_{\tau \to \infty} a_\tau = 0 \tag{13.47}$$

and

$$\sum_{\tau=0}^{\infty} a_\tau = \infty. \tag{13.48}$$

Then the Euler method given by

$$x^{\tau+1} = P_{\mathcal{K}}(x^\tau - a_\tau F(x^\tau)), \tag{13.49}$$

where $F(x)$ is the vector defined in (13.22), converges to some imperfect market international financial equilibrium pattern.

13.6.3 A Numerical Example

In this section we present a numerical example to illustrate both the Euler method and the modified projection method applied to an imperfect market international financial equilibrium problem. The utility functions of the sectors of the countries were quadratic, as given by (13.16), with the portfolio optimization problem of a sector assumed to be given by (13.17), subject to (13.18) and (13.19). The variational inequality formulation of the governing equilibrium conditions was, hence, given by (13.20). Note that for this model, both the modified projection method and the Euler method decompose the problem into network subproblems as depicted in Figure 13.4.

The Euler method, described in Section 13.6.2, was coded in FORTRAN, as was the modified projection method, described in Section 13.6.1, and both algorithms were implemented on an IBM SP2. The CPU time for each example is reported exclusive of input/output times. The asset and liability subproblems were solved using exact asset and liability equilibration, as described in Section 9.3, and the prices were solved in closed form.

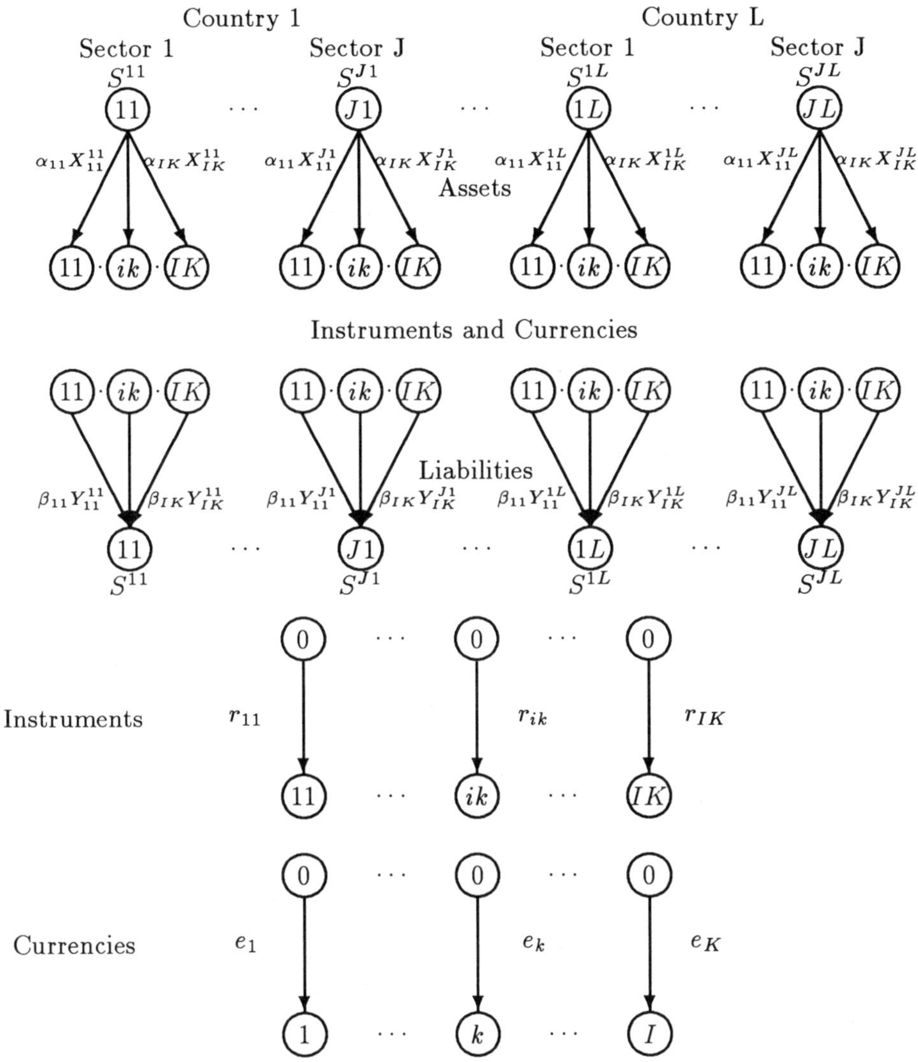

Fig. 13.4. Network structure of decomposed subproblems in the case of budget constraints with transaction costs

In the numerical example we initialized the algorithms as follows: $r_{ik} = 1$ and $e_k = 1$ for all i and k. The capital volumes of the sectors was set as: $S^{11} = S^{12} = S^{21} = S^{22} = 1$; $S^{31} = S^{32} = 2$. In order to maintain feasibility, we set $X_{11}^{jl} = \frac{S^{jl}}{\alpha_{11}}$, $Y_{11}^{jl} = \frac{S^{jl}}{\beta_{11}}$, for all j and l; the remaining X_{ik}^{jl} and Y_{ik}^{jl} were set to 0.

The convergence criterion was: $|x_b^{\tau+1} - x_b^{\tau}| \leq .001$, for all $b = 1, \ldots, n$, for both algorithms. We set $\{a_\tau\}$=.2$\{1, \frac{1}{2}, \frac{1}{2}, \frac{1}{3}, \frac{1}{3}, \ldots, \}$ for the Euler method and $\gamma = .2$ for the modified projection method.

Example 13.1: 3 Countries, 2 Sectors, 2 Currencies, 2 Instruments

The example consisted of three countries, with two sectors in each country, two currencies, and two instruments. The variance/covariance matrices for all sectors in all countries were as in Example 11.3.

We set the taxes $\mathcal{T}_{ik}^{jl}$ as follows: $\mathcal{T}_{11}^{11} = .15$, $\mathcal{T}_{12}^{11} = .02$, $\mathcal{T}_{21}^{11} = .10$, $\mathcal{T}_{22}^{11} = .20$, $\mathcal{T}_{11}^{12} = .20$, $\mathcal{T}_{12}^{12} = .01$, $\mathcal{T}_{21}^{12} = .25$, $\mathcal{T}_{22}^{12} = .10$, $\mathcal{T}_{11}^{21} = .30$, $\mathcal{T}_{12}^{21} = .05$, $\mathcal{T}_{21}^{21} = .10$, $\mathcal{T}_{22}^{21} = .10$, $\mathcal{T}_{11}^{22} = .15$, $\mathcal{T}_{12}^{22} = .05$, $\mathcal{T}_{21}^{22} = .10$, $\mathcal{T}_{22}^{22} = .20$, $\mathcal{T}_{11}^{31} = .30$, $\mathcal{T}_{12}^{31} = .15$, $\mathcal{T}_{21}^{31} = .10$, $\mathcal{T}_{22}^{31} = .20$, $\mathcal{T}_{11}^{32} = .10$, $\mathcal{T}_{12}^{32} = .05$, $\mathcal{T}_{21}^{32} = .10$, $\mathcal{T}_{22}^{32} = .25$.

The price floors and ceilings were set at: $r_{11}^F = .1$, $r_{11}^C = .5$, $r_{12}^F = .1$, $r_{12}^C = .5$, $r_{21}^F = .0$, $r_{21}^C = 1.0$, $r_{22}^F = .05$, $r_{22}^C = .5$. $e_1^F = .05$, $e_1^C = 1$, $e_2^F = .05$, $e_2^C = 1$.

The transaction costs were: $\alpha_{11} = 1.1$, $\alpha_{12} = 1.2$, $\alpha_{21} = 1.1$, $\alpha_{22} = 1.3$, $\beta_{11} = .6$, $\beta_{12} = .7$, $\beta_{21} = .8$, $\beta_{22} = .9$.

The Euler method converged in 183 iterations and .10 seconds of CPU time yielding the following solution:

Instrument Prices:

$$r_{11}^* = .225, \quad r_{12}^* = .275, \quad r_{21}^* = .100, \quad r_{22}^* = .267,$$

Exchange Rate Prices:

$$e_1^* = .499, \quad e_2^* = .804,$$

Asset and Liability Pattern:

$$X_{11}^{11*} = .099, \quad X_{12}^{11*} = .276, \quad X_{21}^{11*} = .226, \quad X_{22}^{11*} = .243,$$

$$X_{11}^{21*} = .192, \quad X_{12}^{21*} = .000, \quad X_{21}^{21*} = .212, \quad X_{22}^{21*} = .411,$$

$$X_{11}^{12*} = .000, \quad X_{12}^{12*} = .330, \quad X_{21}^{12*} = .088, \quad X_{22}^{12*} = .408,$$

$$X_{11}^{22*} = .132, \quad X_{12}^{22*} = .322, \quad X_{21}^{22*} = .087, \quad X_{22}^{22*} = .305,$$

$$X_{11}^{13*} = .127, \quad X_{12}^{13*} = .359, \quad X_{21}^{13*} = .122, \quad X_{22}^{13*} = .246,$$

$$X_{11}^{23*} = .500, \quad X_{12}^{23*} = .142, \quad X_{21}^{23*} = .680, \quad X_{22}^{23*} = .367,$$

$$Y_{11}^{11*} = .196, \quad Y_{12}^{11*} = .392, \quad Y_{21}^{11*} = .281, \quad Y_{22}^{11*} = .433,$$

$$Y_{11}^{21*} = .227, \quad Y_{12}^{21}* = .289, \quad Y_{21}^{21*} = .353, \quad Y_{22}^{21*} = .422,$$

$$Y_{11}^{12*} = .591, \quad Y_{12}^{12*} = .234, \quad Y_{21}^{12*} = .194, \quad Y_{22}^{12*} = .365,$$

$$Y_{11}^{22*} = .385, \quad Y_{12}^{22*} = .355, \quad Y_{21}^{22*} = .199, \quad Y_{22}^{22*} = .391,$$

$$Y_{11}^{13*} = .218, \quad Y_{12}^{13*} = .242, \quad Y_{21}^{13*} = .395, \quad Y_{22}^{13*} = .437,$$

$$Y_{11}^{23*} = .323, \quad Y_{12}^{23*} = .410, \quad Y_{21}^{23*} = 1.014, \quad Y_{22}^{23*} = .843.$$

Note that the markets cleared for both the instruments and for the currencies since none of the prices were at the floors or at the ceilings.

The modified projection method converged in 42 iterations and required .05 CPU seconds for convergence.

13.7 An Addendum

In this section we propose another modeling extension which is also applicable in the case of the general utility function models considered in the preceding chapters in Parts III and IV.

Observe that the general utility functions considered in this chapter with objective function (13.1) expressed that the utility of a sector was a function (in addition to the prices and the fixed tax rates) only of the asset and liability holdings of the particular sector and did not depend upon the holdings of the other sectors in the economy. One can, of course, postulate utility functions of the form: $U^{jl}(X, Y, r, e; \mathcal{T})$, in which the utility of a sector in a country depends not only on the composition of his own portfolio but also on the compositions of the portfolios of the other sectors. This would be an illustration of imperfect competition. One can also postulate noncooperative behavior among the sectors leading to a Nash-Cournot equilibrium, as defined in Definition 3.2, and as illustrated in Example 3.4; for the corresponding tatonnement process, see Example 4.3.

In the case of such utility functions and such behavior of the sectors, one would obtain, under the identical assumptions (see also (3.16)) on the utility functions, as made in this chapter, again, a variational inequality formulation of the governing equilibrium conditions with the distinction being that in inequality (13.6) one would need to replace the vectors (X^{jl^*}, Y^{jl^*}) with the vectors (X^*, Y^*) in all instances. The existence and uniqueness of an equilibrium pattern would hold under the same conditions as previously. Moreover, the projected dynamical system given by (13.24) would still be valid with the utility functions and their gradients modified accordingly.

Finally, we note that the general utility functions discussed in preceding chapters could also be extended to handle this noncooperative scenario, if need be.

13.8 Sources and Notes

In this chapter we have developed both static and dynamic imperfect market international financial models. The models in this chapter are extensions of the single country imperfect market models studied in Chapters 9 and 10. In particular, we now let each sector select his own feasible set, which need only be a closed and bounded, convex polyhedron. Of course, one may still wish to include the budget constraints as well. Dong (1996) was the first to introduce projected dynamical systems for the modeling and stability analysis of an imperfect market single country financial model. Nagurney and Siokos (1997b), in turn, extended the results to the international domain and also discussed the Euler method, along with convergence results.

Section 13.1

The models presented in this section are new and generalize, for example, the model in Nagurney and Siokos (1997b) by considering more general feasible sets for the sectors in the countries.

Section 13.2

The qualitative properties of the variational inequality formulation of the governing equiibrium conditions are adapted from analogous results in earlier chapters.

Section 13.3

This section is adapted from Nagurney and Siokos (1997b).

Section 13.4

The results in this section were also reported earlier in Nagurney and Siokos (1997b).

Section 13.5

The network optimization reformulation of the equilibrium conditions in the case of special utility functions and only taxes is an extension of the single country results presented in Section 9.3.

Section 13.6

The modified projected method for the computation of the imperfect market equilibrium pattern is proposed here for the first time. The numerical example, along with the Euler method, was proposed earlier in Nagurney and Siokos (1997b).

Section 13.7

This section discusses how imperfect competition can be captured within the variational inequality/projected dynamical system framework for the study of multi-sector, multi-instrument financial equilibrium problems.

References

Constantinides, G., "Capital Market Equilibrium with Transaction Costs," *The Journal of Political Economy* **94** (1986) 842-862.

Davis, M., and Norman, A., "Portfolio Selection with Transaction Costs," *Mathematics of Operations Research* **15** (1990) 676-713.

Dong, J., "Dynamic Model and Stability Analysis of General Financial Equilibrium with Policy Interventions," presented at the Second International Conference on Computing in Economics and Finance, Geneva, Switzerland, 1996.

Eun, C., and Janakiramanan, S., "A Model of International Asset Pricing with a Constraint on the Foreign Equity Ownership," *Journal of Finance* **41** (1986) 879-914.

Grauer, F., Litzenberger, R., and R. Stehle, "Sharing Rules and Equilibrium in an International Capital Market Under Uncertainty," *Journal of Financial Economics* **3** (1976) 233-256.

Grubel, H., "Internationally Diversified Portfolios: Welfare Gains and Capital Flows," *American Economic Review* **58** (1968) 1299-1314.

Hufbauer, G., and Schott, J., **NAFTA: An Assessment**, Institute of International Economics, Washington, DC, 1993.

Leape, J., "Taxes and Transaction Costs in Asset Market Equilibrium," *Journal of Public Economics* **33** (1987) 1-20.

Lessard, D., "World Country Industry Relationships in Equity Returns: Implications for Risk Reduction through International Diversification," *Financial Analysts Journal* **32** (1973) 2-8.

Miller, M., "Debt and Taxes," *Journal of Finance* **32** (1977) 261-275.

Nagurney, A., and Siokos, S., "Variational Inequalities for International General Financial Equilibrium Modeling and Computation," *Mathematical and Computer Modelling* **25** (1997a) 31-49.

Nagurney, A., and Siokos, S., "Projected Dynamical Systems for International Financial Modeling and Computation," in **Computational Approaches to Economic Problems**, pp. 175-192, H. M. Amman, B. Rustem, and A. Whinston, editors, Kluwer Academic Publishers, Boston, Massachusetts, 1997b.

Rosenthal, G., and Cafruny, A., **The State of the European Community. The Maastricht Debates and Beyond**, Liener Longman, Boulder, Colorado, 1993.

Silva, M., and Sjörgen, B., **Europe 1992 and the New World Power Game**, John Wiley & Son Publishers, New York, New York, 1990.

Solnik, B., "Equilibrium Model of the International Market," *Journal of Economic Theory* **8** (1974) 500-524.

Stulz, R., "On the Effects of Barriers to International Investments," *Journal of Finance* **36** (1981) 923-934.

Thore, S., **Programming the Network of Financial Intermediation**, Universitetsforlaget, Oslo, Norway, 1980.

Part V Flow of Funds and Estimation

14 Flow of Funds Models

As we have been emphasizing throughout this volume, the structure of financial markets and policy intervention is changing, perhaps more rapidly than in any other time in history. Moreover, new technologies are allowing the development of financial instruments and management strategies that were thought to be unrealistically complicated only a short time ago. Accompanying the increased sophistication of financial instruments and their management has come increased participation in complex financial transactions by all sectors of the economy. Hence, the development of rigorous analytic tools for the study of national and international financial activity has been the subject of increasing research interest.

As noted in Nagurney and Hughes (1992) and Hughes and Nagurney (1992), an important goal is to develop empirical general equilibrium models that highlight the role of economic behavior in the determination of financial capital flows between sectors. Such models can then be utilized for the evaluation of alternative financial policy interventions on a consistent basis. A prerequisite for developing these general equilibrium models, however, is a balanced set of financial accounts. In this chapter this is our principal topic of interest.

The origin of flow of funds accounting dates to Copeland (1952). Cohen (1987) presents an updated treatise on flow of funds in theory and in practice. The flow of funds accounts portray a system in which all net financial transactions in the economy have been captured. Thus, they potentially provide the complete set of information necessary to describe all financial behavior in an economy.

In the United States, the Federal Reserve Board maintains the financial flow of funds accounts and these were the first and remain the most well-known of the published national accounts. These accounts, beginning with 1952, have been quarterly and seasonally adjusted and are printed in the *Federal Reserve Bulletin*. Earlier versions of the accounts, dating to 1939, contained also nonfinancial data. For a history of the accounts, see Cohen (1972); see the Federal Reserve (1980) for the structure of the accounts.

In Canada, national transactions accounts, later referred to as financial flow accounts, are maintained by Statistics Canada. Other countries that regularly publish financial flow of funds accounts include: Australia, the United Kingdom, Belgium, Finland, France, Germany, Italy, and Norway (cf. Cohen (1987) and Thore (1980), and the references therein). For example, British tables are published in the *Quarterly Bulletin of the Bank of England*; see Alford (1986) for a further discussion.

In addition, the OECD publishes flow of funds data (cf. OECD (1981)) and uses the financial flow of funds statistics for analysis purposes. Indeed, as noted in Cohen (1987), and recognized by Dudler and Chouraqui (1977), the flow of funds identities provided important information for policy makers in the early 1970s in their analysis of the effects of economic shocks.

Due to the complexities of measurement, however, the published financial flow of funds accounts, oftentimes, do not satisfy a basic accounting identity. Hence, the accounts must be "balanced" before they can provide the basis for general equilibrium modeling of financial activity. A methodology for reorganizing and reconciling flow of funds data is, therefore, required. To accomplish this, we identify the underlying network structure of financial flows and relate this structure to the network models in Part III. We then generalize the Splitting Equilibration Algorithm of Chapter 5, which can be used to resolve the published accounts into categories suitable for a general equilibrium model of financial activity.

Recall from Chapter 1, that the modeling of the circular flow of funds as a network problem has its roots in the work of Quesnay (1785). More recently, as was also discussed in Chapter 1, Thore (1969), Thore (1970), and Thore and Kydland (1972) have introduced network models of financial credit activity. In this chapter our presentation follows the work of Nagurney and Hughes (1992) and Hughes and Nagurney (1992) in the presentation of network models for financial flow of funds accounts and their estimation.

This chapter is organized as follows. In Section 14.1 we present network models for financial flow of funds accounts. In Section 14.2 we then describe the Splitting Equilibration Algorithm for the estimation of financial flow of funds accounts. In Section 14.3 we provide a numerical example.

14.1 Network Models

In this section we describe a general network model of financial flow of funds accounting and then highlight special cases. The network model permits the reequilibration of the entire financial system by resolving discrepancies that may occur in the datasets. The model captures, as special cases, a variety of models which can then be applied depending upon the requirements of the particular financial dataset. In particular, it contains, as special cases, models in which the sector volumes and/or the instrument volume totals are fixed.

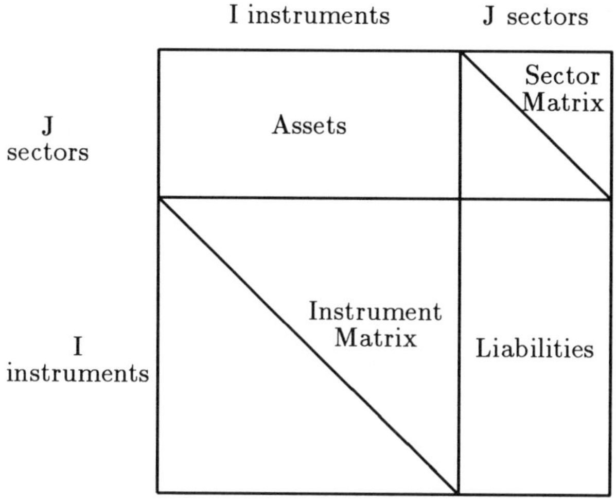

Fig. 14.1. Financial flow of funds accounts

For completeness, we first present a brief overview of the financial flow of funds balance sheet accounting system, which is presented schematically in Figure 14.1. The flow of funds data has been arranged in order to emphasize the two sets of accounting identities implicit in the framework that are critical to the network model.

As in the single country models of Chapters 6 through 10, we assume that there are J sectors in the economy into which all of the agents are grouped and I classifications of financial instruments. The flow of funds matrix is then a $(J + I) \times (I + J)$ matrix with the first J rows corresponding to the sectors and the next I rows corresponding to the instruments. The first I columns in the matrix correspond to the instruments, whereas the next J columns correspond to the sectors.

This matrix can then be subdivided into four submatrices. The first submatrix is the $J \times I$ upper left-most matrix, the entries of which represent the assets of the sectors in the economy. The second submatrix is the $J \times J$ upper right-most matrix. This matrix is a diagonal matrix, which we will, henceforth, refer to as the *sector* matrix. The third submatrix, is the $I \times J$ lower left-most matrix, and this matrix is also diagonal. This matrix will, henceforth, be referred to as the *instrument* matrix. Finally, the fourth submatrix is the $I \times I$ lower right-most matrix, the entries of which represent the liabilities of the sectors in the economy.

Two identities that must be satisfied in the flow of funds accounts matrix are the balance sheet identity and the instrument volume identity. The sector balance sheet identity states that the elements of the diagonal sector matrix representing the respective totals of the assets for a given sector must be equal to the total liabilities for the same sector. Thus, the j-th row sum of the first submatrix equals the (j, j)-th element of the second submatrix, as well as the j-th column sum of the fourth sub-matrix. The instrument volume identity, on the other hand, states that the diagonal instrument matrix, which represents the total volume outstanding of each instrument over all the sectors, must be equal to the demand for each instrument over all of the sectors. Thus, the i-th column sum of the first submatrix equals the (i, i)-th element of the third submatrix, as well as the i-th row sum of the fourth submatrix.

We will now construct the network model of financial flow of funds accounts, the solution of which will yield asset and liability levels which satisfy both the sectoral balance sheet and the instrument volume identities. As in the preceding financial modeling chapters, in this network model, the nodes of the network nomenclature become sector asset and liability portfolios and the types of instruments. Links abstract the relationships between the instruments and the sector portfolios. Flows associated with each of the links, in turn, represent the levels of the assets and liability estimates, the levels of outstanding instruments, and here, in addition, the overall size of sector portfolios. We require that the instrument volume estimates that balance the accounts lie "close" to the original data by associating penalty weights with the gap between the estimates and the original data. Similarly, we require that the sector volume estimates that balance the accounts also lie close to the original data.

We refer the reader to Figure 14.2 for a graphical depiction of this general network model of financial flow of funds accounts. We denote the uppermost nodes in the network by j; $j = 1, \ldots, J$. These nodes represent the asset portfolios of the J sectors defined in the funds matrix of Figure 14.1. The next layer of the nodes in the network are denoted by i; $i = 1, \ldots, I$. This second layer of the nodes represents the instruments recorded as assets and defined in the first I column headings of Figure 14.1. A link (j, i) is constructed from node j to node i if there exists some asset volume in location j, i of the asset submatrix. In other words, if the asset portfolio of sector j includes instrument i as an asset. Note the bipartite structure (cf. Figure 5.3) of the asset submatrix network representation, which will be exploited in the development of the algorithm in the subsequent section.

Next, we label the third layer of nodes i'; $i' = 1', \ldots, I'$; and the fourth layer of nodes j'; $j' = 1', \ldots, J'$. These layers denote instrument i' recorded as a liability, and the sector liability portfolio j', respectively. They are associated, respectively, with the I rows and the J columns of the fourth submatrix in Figure 14.1. We also construct links (i', j') corresponding to

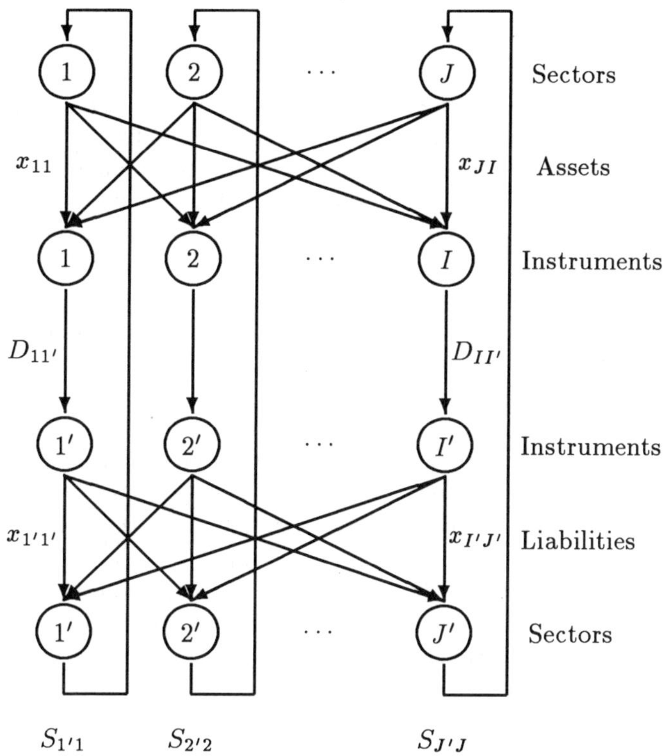

Fig. 14.2. Network model of financial flow of funds accounts (elastic sector and instrument total volumes)

possible instrument issues represented in the sector liability portfolios. This network subproblem corresponding to the liability submatrix also possesses the bipartite network structure which is crucial to the network decomposition approach (cf. Figure 5.3).

We then construct I links (i, i') relating the entry of each instrument as a liability on sector books with its entry on sector books as an asset. We let $D^0_{ii'}$ denote the i-th diagonal entry in the instrument submatrix and $D_{ii'}$ the estimated volume of instrument i on link (i, i').

Finally, we construct J "feedback" links, each such feedback link (j', j) relating sector j's total assets in his portfolio with his total liabilities. We let $S^0_{j'j}$ denote the j-th diagonal entry in the sector submatrix, and $S_{j'j}$, the estimated volume of sector j's portfolio on link (j', j). Recall that in this general model we assume that the sector volumes are not known and fixed a priori and, hence, the need for such feedback links.

We now describe the penalty procedure that requires the estimated values to lie "close" to the original data. We first let x_{ji} denote the ji-th element of the asset submatrix, and we let $x_{i'j'}$ denote the ij-th element of the liability submatrix. With each such link (k, l) we then associate the penalty equal to $w_{kl}(x_{kl} - x^0_{kl})^2$, where x^0_{kl} denotes the original kl-th element in the asset submatrix for $k = 1, \ldots, J$; $l = 1, \ldots, I$; or the corresponding element in the liability submatrix for $k = 1', \ldots, I'$; $l = 1', \ldots, J'$, with the variables x_{kl} being defined analogously. We assume that the weights w_{kl} are positive and note that then x_{kl} corresponds to the flow on link (k, l).

The penalty associated with the estimated-observed discrepancy value of the link (i, i'), in turn, is defined as: $w_{ii'}(D_{ii'} - D^0_{ii'})^2$, where the flow is $D_{ii'}$. Similarly, the penalty associated with the estimated-observed discrepancy value of the link (j', j) is defined as: $w_{j'j}(S_{j'j} - S^0_{j'j})^2$, with the corresponding flow on the feedback link (j', j) being equal to $S_{j'j}$.

Mathematically, the instrument volume conditions implicit in the instrument matrix state that:

$$D_{ii'} = \sum_{j=1}^{J} x_{ji}, \quad i = 1, \ldots, I \tag{14.1a}$$

$$D_{ii'} = \sum_{j'=1'}^{J'} x_{i'j'}, \quad i = 1, \ldots, I. \tag{14.1b}$$

The sector portfolio volume conditions implicit in the sector matrix, in turn, state that:

$$S_{j'j} = \sum_{i=1}^{I} x_{ji}, \quad j = 1, \ldots, J \tag{14.2a}$$

$$S_{j'j} = \sum_{i'=1'}^{I'} x_{i'j'}, \quad j = 1, \ldots, J. \tag{14.2b}$$

The sets of equations (14.1) and (14.2) are the conservation of flow equations of the network constructed above and pictured in Figure 14.2.

The complete model, hence, with the objective function, is given by:

$$\text{Minimize} \quad \sum_{ji} w_{ji}(x_{ji} - x^0_{ji})^2 + \sum_{i'j'} w_{i'j'}(x_{i'j'} - x^0_{i'j'})^2$$

$$+ \sum_{ii'} w_{ii'}(D_{ii'} - D^0_{ii'})^2 + \sum_{j'j} w_{j'j}(S_{j'j} - S^0_{j'j})^2 \tag{14.3}$$

subject to constraints (14.1) and (14.2), and the nonnegativity constraints:

$$x_{kl} \geq 0, \quad \text{for all links} \quad kl. \tag{14.4}$$

The above model captures several distinct network models for financial flow of funds accounts as special cases. For example, if the values of the instrument volumes and the sector volumes are known with certainty then we can set $D_{ii'} = D^0_{ii'}$, for all $i = 1, \ldots, I$, and $S_{j'j} = S^0_{j'j}$, for all $j = 1, \ldots, J$. The right-hand sides of constraints (14.1a), (14.1b), (14.2a), and (14.2b), hence, take on these known values in this case, whereas the objective function (14.3) then consists only of the first two terms. The model then collapses to two uncoupled bipartite network problems (cf. Figure 5.3), each of which has the form of a classical constrained matrix problem discussed in Section 5.2. This may be viewed as the most rigid model. Its network structure is depicted in Figure 14.3. This network optimization problem, hence, is amenable to solution via the Splitting Equilibration Algorithm discussed in Section 5.2 where each bipartite network problem depicted in Figure 14.3 is solved via this algorithm independently.

On the other hand, in the case where only the volumes $S^0_{j'j}$; $j = 1, \ldots, J$, are known with certainty, then we may make the substitution: $S_{j'j} = S^0_{j'j}$, for each $j = 1, \ldots, J$. In this case, only the first three terms in the objective function (14.3) would appear, and the constraints (14.2a) and (14.2b) would have fixed values for the sector asset and liability volume totals. This would yield the network structure in Figure 14.4. In Section 14.2 we provide a version of the Splitting Equilibration Algorithm for financial flow of funds estomation for this particular network problem.

Finally, in the special case where only the total instrument volumes $D^0_{ii'}$; $i = 1, \ldots, I$, are known with certainty, the network model becomes as depicted in Figure 14.5. In this case, we make the substitution: $D_{ii'} = D^0_{ii'}$, for each $i = 1, \ldots, I$, and objective function (14.3) then consists of the first two terms and the fourth term. Constraints (14.1a) and (14.1b), in turn, have their right-hand side values replaced by $D^0_{ii'}$.

It is worthwhile to relate the network problems depicted in Figures 14.2 through 14.5 to the network models of financial equilibrium in Part III of this book. First, note the similarity of the network depicted in Figure 14.4 and the network of the single country financial equilibrium problem depicted

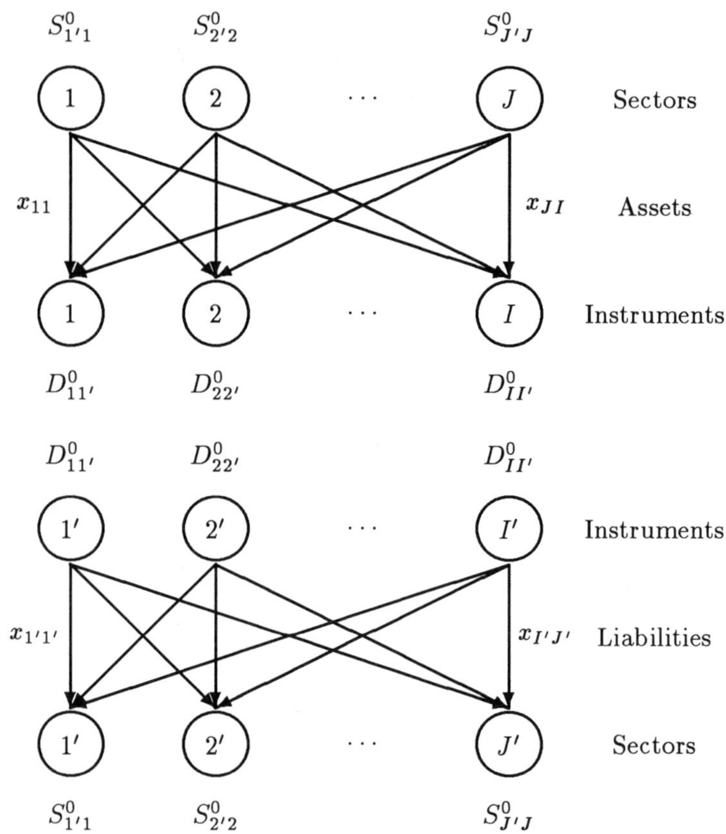

Fig. 14.3. Network model of financial flow of funds accounts (fixed sector and instrument total volumes)

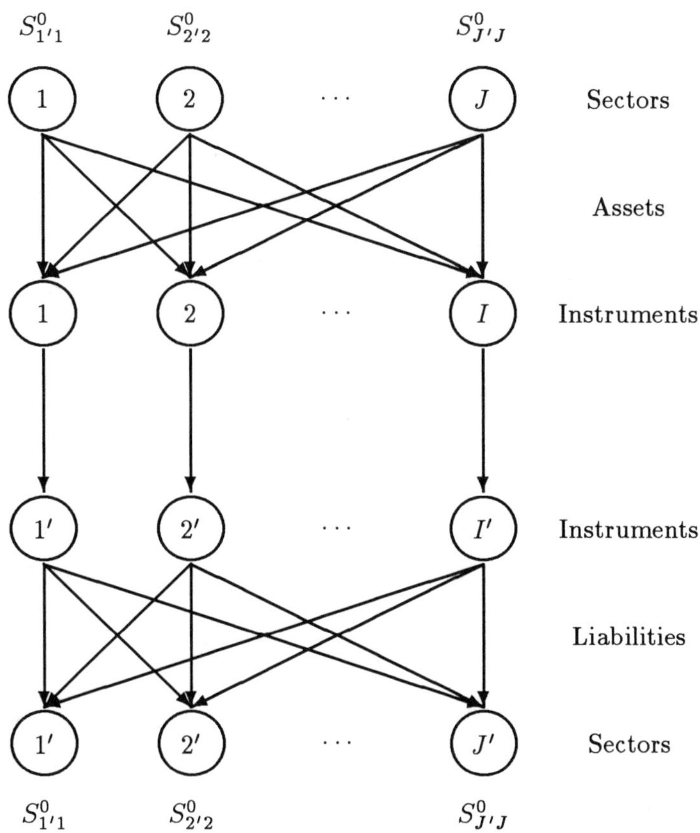

Fig. 14.4. Network model of financial flow of funds accounts (fixed sector volumes but elastic instrument total volumes)

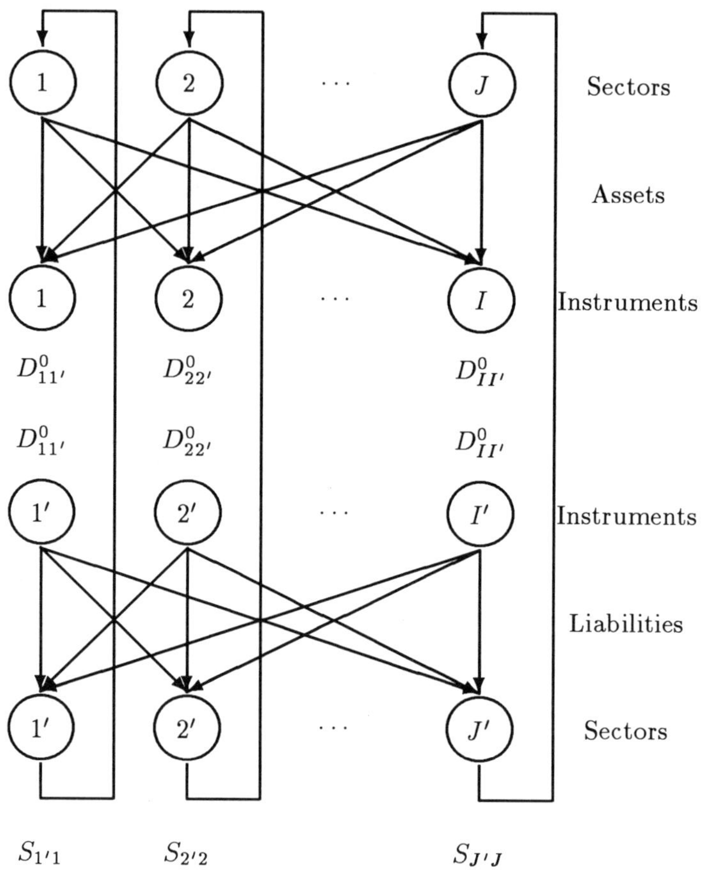

Fig. 14.5. Network model of financial flow of funds accounts (elastic sector volumes but fixed instrument total volumes)

in Figure 6.2. Note that the only distinction between these two networks is that in the network in Figure 14.4 we have another layer of instrument nodes in order to be able to estimate the (unknown) instrument total volumes. This has been done since here we are interested in the estimation problem. Nevertheless, the network in Figure 14.4 is consistent with the equilibrium network. This connection also illustrates the fact that the models in the preceding chapters have been formulated with eventual empirical application in mind. Moreover, these models provide a synthesis of both theory and practice. Indeed, although here we have utilized network optimization notation and terminology as in Chapter 5, we note that there is a clear mapping between the notation and variables here and those in the single country financial models of Part III. For example, cf. Chapter 6, the flow on an asset link (j, i) of a financial flow of funds network model can be mapped into X_i^j, which denotes the volume of instrument i held as an asset by sector j, wherea the flow on a liability link (i', j') can be mapped into Y_i^j, which denotes the volume of instrument i held as a liability by sector j. In addition, a sector volume here, denoted by $S_{j'j}$ corresponds to S^j in the models of Part III. These connections are also obvious through the structure of the financial flow of funds networks and the equilibrium networks of Part III.

On the other hand, if the models of Chapter 6, for example (see also the addendum in Chapter 13), assumed that the sector volumes were to be determined and were not fixed, then an equilibrium network model would have a structure similar to the network model depicted in Figure 14.2, but, of course, with the instrument nodes consisting of only a single layer.

Finally, note that the fundamental identities in the flow of funds accounts are: **(1).** that a sector's assets must be equal to a sector's liabilities and **(2).** in equilibrium, the supply of each instrument must be equal to the demand for the instrument. The first identity has been explicitly incorporated into all of the financial models of Chapters 6 through 12 (and implicitly in the models of Chapter 13) through the definition of the constraints underlying a sector's portfolio optimization problem. The second identity, on the other hand, has been established theoretically for all the financial models studied in Part III (and in Part IV) in the case of perfect markets and in the case of certain market imperfections, provided that the budget constraint is incorporated into the sectors' feasible sets. Hence, our modeling framework is also consistent with financial flow accounts.

14.2 SEA for Financial Flow of Funds Estimation

We now present a generalization of the Splitting Equilibration Algorithm (SEA) discussed in Section 5.2 that fully exploits the underlying network structure of the financial flow of funds estimation problem (cf. Figure 14.2) by decomposing the problem defined by (14.1) through (14.4) into two series of bipartite network subproblems: the column subproblems and the row sub-

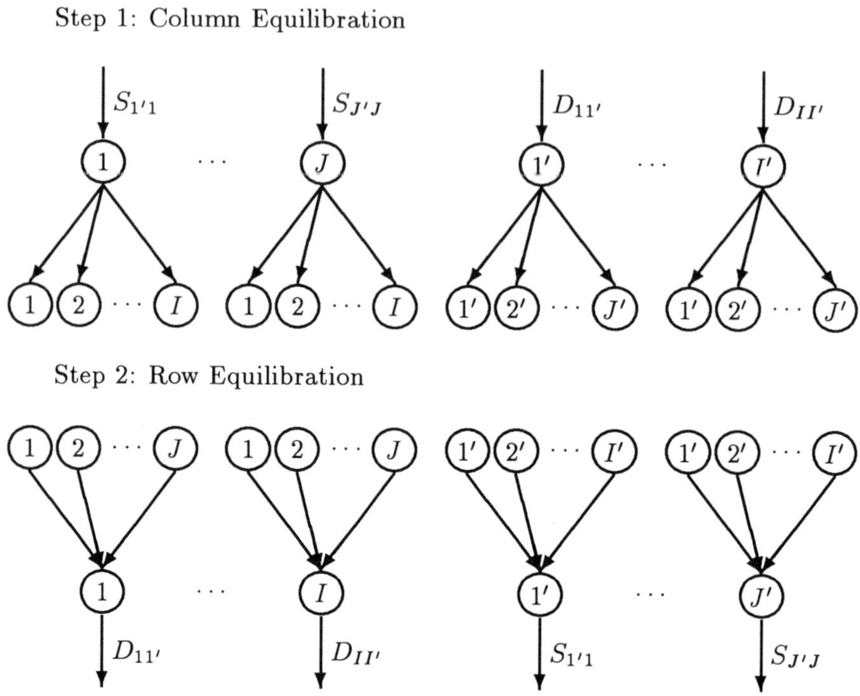

Fig. 14.6. Structure of column and row equilibration subproblems

problems, with the objective function (14.3) modified appropriately. Note that in the first financial application here, SEA (in contrast to the exposition in Section 5.2) assumes "elastic" rather than fixed supply and demand totals. Here, also, without loss of generality, we first present the column equilibration step and then the row equilibration step. We subsequently specialize SEA for the solution of the network optimization problem depicted in Figure 14.4 in which the sector volumes are assumed to be known and fixed.

The column equilibration phase consists of $I + J$ "elastic" column subproblems, in which the values $D_{ii'}; i = 1, \ldots, I$, and $S_{j'j}$; $j = 1, \ldots, J$, are to be determined along with the values for the assets, the x_{ji}'s, and the liabilities, the $x_{i'j'}$'s, subject to only the column constraints (14.1a) for the assets and the column constraints (14.2b) for the liabilities, and the nonnegativity constraints (14.4). The row equilibration phase, in turn, consists of $J + I$ elastic row subproblems in which the same values are to be determined, but now subject to only the row constraints (14.1b) for the assets and the row constraints (14.2a) for the liabilities, along with constraints (14.4).

For a graphical depiction of the two phases that emphasizes the special underlying network structure of the decomposition, see Figure 14.6. Each of the decomposed column/row subproblems can, hence, be solved exactly in closed form using an exact elastic demand/supply equilibration algorithm, which we will present in Section 14.2.1. This algorithm is an extension of the exact equilibration algorithm presented in Section 5.2.3 to the case that the supplies/demands are not fixed a priori but need to be determined as well.

This Splitting Equilibration Algorithm computes a solution to problem (14.3), that is,

$$\text{Minimize} \quad f(x, x', D, S) = \sum_{ji} w_{ji}(x_{ji} - x_{ji}^0)^2 + \sum_{j'i'} w_{i'j'}(x_{i'j'} - x_{i'j'}^0)^2$$

$$+ \sum_{ii'} w_{ii'}(D_{ii'} - D_{ii'}^0)^2 + \sum_{j'j} w_{j'j}(S_{j'j} - S_{j'j}^0)^2$$

subject to constraints (14.1), (14.2), and (14.4).

SEA for Financial Flow of Funds Estimation (Elastic Sector Volumes and Total Instrument Volumes)

Step 0: Initialization Step

Let $\lambda^1 \in R^J = 0, \bar{\lambda}^1 \in R^I = 0$. Set $\tau := 1$.

Step 1: Column Equilibration

Find $(X(\lambda^\tau, \bar{\lambda}^\tau), X'(\lambda^\tau, \bar{\lambda}^\tau), D(\lambda^\tau, \bar{\lambda}^\tau), S(\lambda^\tau, \bar{\lambda}^\tau))$ such that

$$(X(\lambda^\tau, \bar{\lambda}^\tau), X'(\lambda^\tau, \bar{\lambda}^\tau), D(\lambda^\tau, \bar{\lambda}^\tau), S(\lambda^\tau, \bar{\lambda}^\tau)) \rightarrow$$

$$\min_{x,x',D,S} f(x, x', D, S) - \sum_{j=1}^{J} \lambda_j^\tau (\sum_{i=1}^{I} x_{ji} - S_{j'j}) - \sum_{i=1}^{I} \bar{\lambda}_i^\tau (\sum_{j'=1'}^{J'} x_{i'j'} - D_{ii'}) \quad (14.5)$$

subject to:

$$D_{ii'} = \sum_{j=1}^{J} x_{ji}, \quad i = 1, \ldots, I \quad (14.6a)$$

$$S_{j'j} = \sum_{i'=1'}^{I'} x_{i'j'}, \quad j = 1, \ldots, J \quad (14.6b)$$

$$x_{ji} \geq 0, \quad x_{i'j'} \geq 0, \quad \text{for all} \quad j, i; i'j'.$$

Compute the corresponding Lagrange multiplers $\bar{\mu}_i^{\tau+1}$, $\mu_j^{\tau+1}$ for this problem where:
$\bar{\mu}_i^{\tau+1}$=$2w_{ii'}D_{ii'}^0$-$2w_{ii'}D_{ii'}(\lambda^\tau, \bar{\lambda}^\tau)$-$\bar{\lambda}_i^\tau$, for $i = 1, \ldots, I$,
and $\mu_j^{\tau+1}$=$2w_{j'j}S_{j'j}^0 - 2w_{j'j}S_{j'j}(\lambda^\tau, \bar{\lambda}^\tau) - \lambda_j^\tau$, for $j = 1, \ldots, J$.

Step 2: Row Equilibration

Find $(X(\mu^{\tau+1},\bar{\mu}^{\tau+1}),X'(\mu^{\tau+1},\bar{\mu}^{\tau+1}),D(\mu^{\tau+1},\bar{\mu}^{\tau+1}),S(\mu^{\tau+1},\bar{\mu}^{\tau+1}))$ such that

$$(X(\mu^{\tau+1},\bar{\mu}^{\tau+1}),X'(\mu^{\tau+1},\bar{\mu}^{\tau+1}),D(\mu^{\tau+1},\bar{\mu}^{\tau+1}),S(\mu^{\tau+1},\bar{\mu}^{\tau+1}))\rightarrow$$

$$\min_{x,x',D,S} f(x,x',d,s)-\sum_{j=1}^{J}\mu_j^{\tau+1}(\sum_{i'=1'}^{I'}x_{i'j'}-S_{j'j})-\sum_{i=1}^{I}\bar{\mu}_i^{\tau+1}(\sum_{j=1}^{J}x_{ji}-D_{ii'}) \tag{14.7}$$

subject to:

$$S_{j'j}=\sum_{i=1}^{I}x_{ji},\quad j=1,\ldots,J \tag{14.8a}$$

$$D_{ii'}=\sum_{j'=1'}^{J'}x_{i'j'},\quad i=1,\ldots,I \tag{14.8b}$$

$$x_{ji}\geq 0,\quad x_{i'j'}\geq 0,\quad \text{for all}\quad j,i;i',j'.$$

Compute the corresponding Lagrange multipliers $\lambda_j^{\tau+1}$, $\bar{\lambda}_i^{\tau+1}$ for this problem where:
$\lambda_j^{\tau+1}$=$2w_{j'j}S_{j'j}$- $2w_{j'j}S_{j'j}(\mu^{t+1},\bar{\mu}^{\tau+1})-\mu_j^{\tau+1}$, for $j=1,\ldots,J$,
and $\bar{\lambda}_i^{\tau+1}$=$2w_{ii'}D^0_{ii'}$-$2w_{ii'}D_{ii'}(\mu^{\tau+1},\bar{\mu}^{\tau+1})$-$\bar{\mu}_i^{\tau+1}$, for $i=1,\ldots,I$.

Step 3: Convergence Verification

If $|\sum_{j=1}^{J}x_{ji}^{\tau+1}-D_{ii'}^{\tau+1}|\leq\epsilon$ for all i, and $|\sum_{i'=1'}^{I'}x_{i'j'}^{\tau+1}-S_{j'j}^{\tau+1}|\leq\epsilon$ for all j, terminate; else, set $\tau:=\tau+1$, and go to Step 1.

For a theoretical analysis of the algorithm, see Nagurney and Hughes (1992). Note that in the case where one wishes to use non-diagonal weighting matrices, one can use the ideas of Chapter 5 to develop such a financial flow of funds estimation model and use the projection method to construct subproblems of the form above (see, e.g., Nagurney and Eydeland (1992)).

We now present a special case of the above SEA for the solution of the network optimization problem depicted in Figure 14.4. For theoretical analysis see Hughes and Nagurney (1992). Hence, this version of SEA computes a solution to:

$$\text{Minimize}\quad f(x,x',D)=\sum_{ji}w_{ji}(x_{ji}-x^0_{ji})^2+\sum_{j'i'}w_{i'j'}(x_{i'j'}-x^0_{i'j'})^2$$

$$+\sum_{ii'}w_{ii'}(D_{ii'}-D^0_{ii'})^2$$

subject to constraints (14.1) and (14.4), with (14.2) being replaced by:

$$S^0_{j'j} = \sum_{i=1}^{I} x_{ji}, \quad j = 1, \ldots, J \tag{14.9a}$$

$$S^0_{j'j} = \sum_{i'=1'}^{I'} x_{i'j'}, \quad j = 1, \ldots, J. \tag{14.9b}$$

SEA for Financial Flow of Funds Estimation (Fixed Sector Volumes and Elastic Total Instrument Volumes)

Step 0: Initialization Step

Let $\lambda^1 \in R^J = 0, \bar{\lambda}^1 \in R^I = 0$. Set $\tau := 1$.

Step 1: Column Equilibration

Find $(X(\lambda^\tau, \bar{\lambda}^\tau), X'(\lambda^\tau, \bar{\lambda}^\tau), D(\lambda^\tau, \bar{\lambda}^\tau))$ such that

$$(X(\lambda^\tau, \bar{\lambda}^\tau), X'(\lambda^\tau, \bar{\lambda}^\tau), D(\lambda^\tau, \bar{\lambda}^\tau)) \rightarrow$$

$$\min_{x,x',D} f(x, x', D) - \sum_{j=1}^{J} \lambda_j^\tau (\sum_{i=1}^{I} x_{ji} - S^0_{j'j}) - \sum_{i=1}^{I} \bar{\lambda}_i^\tau (\sum_{j'=1'}^{J'} x_{i'j'} - D_{ii'}) \tag{14.10}$$

subject to:

$$D_{ii'} = \sum_{j=1}^{J} x_{ji}, \quad i = 1, \ldots, I \tag{14.11a}$$

$$S^0_{j'j} = \sum_{i'=1'}^{I'} x_{i'j'}, \quad j = 1, \ldots, J \tag{14.11b}$$

$$x_{ji} \geq 0, \quad x_{i'j'} \geq 0, \quad \text{for all} \quad j, i; i'j'.$$

Compute the corresponding Lagrange multiplers $\bar{\mu}_i^{\tau+1}$, $\mu_j^{\tau+1}$ for this problem where:
$\bar{\mu}_i^{\tau+1}$=$2w_{ii'}D^0_{ii'}$-$2w_{ii'}D_{ii'}(\lambda^\tau, \bar{\lambda}^\tau)$-$\bar{\lambda}_i^\tau$, for $i = 1, \ldots, I$,
and $\mu_j^{\tau+1}$=$2w_{i'j'}X'_{i'j'}(\lambda^t, \bar{\lambda}^t) - 2w_{i'j'}x^0_{i'j'} - \bar{\lambda}_j^\tau$, for $j = 1, \ldots, J$.

Step 2: Row Equilibration

Find $(X(\mu^{\tau+1}, \bar{\mu}^{\tau+1}), X'(\mu^{\tau+1}, \bar{\mu}^{\tau+1}), D(\mu^{\tau+1}, \bar{\mu}^{\tau+1}))$ such that

$$(X(\mu^{\tau+1}, \bar{\mu}^{\tau+1}), X'(\mu^{\tau+1}, \bar{\mu}^{\tau+1}), D(\mu^{\tau+1}, \bar{\mu}^{\tau+1})) \rightarrow$$

$$\min_{x,x',D} f(x, x', D) - \sum_{j=1}^{J} \mu_j^{\tau+1} (\sum_{i'=1'}^{I'} x_{i'j'} - S^0_{j'j}) - \sum_{i=1}^{I} \bar{\mu}_i^{\tau+1} (\sum_{j=1}^{J} x_{ji} - D_{ii'}) \tag{14.12}$$

subject to:

$$S^0_{j'j} = \sum_{i=1}^{I} x_{ji}, \quad j = 1, \ldots, J \tag{14.13a}$$

$$D_{ii'} = \sum_{j'=1'}^{J'} x_{i'j'}, \quad i = 1, \ldots, I \tag{14.13b}$$

$$x_{ji} \geq 0, \quad x_{i'j'} \geq 0, \quad \text{for all} \quad j, i; i', j'.$$

Compute the corresponding Lagrange multipliers $\lambda_j^{\tau+1}$, $\bar{\lambda}_i^{\tau+1}$ for this problem where:
$\lambda_j^{\tau+1} = 2w_{ji}X_{ji}(\mu^{\tau+1}, \bar{\mu}^{\tau+1}) - 2w_{ji}x^0_{ji} - \bar{\mu}_i^{\tau+1}$, for $j = 1, \ldots, J$,
and $\bar{\lambda}_i^{\tau+1}$=$2w_{ii'}D^0_{ii'}$-$2w_{ii'}D_{ii'}(\mu^{\tau+1}, \bar{\mu}^{\tau+1})$-$\bar{\mu}_i^{\tau+1}$, for $i = 1, \ldots, I$.

Step 3: Convergence Verification

If $|\sum_{j=1}^{J} x_{ji}^{\tau+1} - D_{ii'}^{\tau+1}| \leq \epsilon$ for all i, and $|\sum_{i'=1'}^{I'} x_{i'j'}^{\tau+1} - S^0_{j'j}| \leq \epsilon$ for all j, terminate; else, set $\tau := \tau + 1$, and go to Step 1.

Note that in order to solve the column and row subproblems corresponding to constraints (14.11b) and (14.13a) one can use the exact equilibration algorithm, whereas to solve the subproblems corresponding to constraints (14.11a) and (14.13b) one can use to elastic exact equilibration algorithm that immediately follows. The structure of the row and column equilibration subproblems is , nevertheless, again, as depicted in Figure 14.6, with the exception that the sector volumes $S^0_{j'j}$ now replace $S_{j'j}$ for all sectors j.

14.2.1 An Elastic Exact Equilibration Algorithm

In this subsection we present an elastic exact equilibration algorithm that can be embedded in the above Splitting Equilibration Algorithm for the solution of an elastic row or column subproblem. This algorithm is an extension of the fixed demand exact equilibration algorithm of Section 5.2.3. For easy reference, we write down the problem to be solved in an analogous format to problem (5.41) subject to constraints: (5.42) and (5.43):

$$\text{Minimize} \quad \sum_{i=1}^{n} q_i x_i^2 + c_i x_i + r(\sum_{i=1}^{n} x_i)^2 - t(\sum_{i=1}^{n} x_i), \tag{14.14}$$

where all terms: q_i, c_i, r, and t are assumed to be positive for all i, subject to:

$$x_i \geq 0, \quad \forall i. \tag{14.15}$$

Note that here we have embedded the demand constraint: $\sum_{i=1}^{n} x_i$ directly into the objective function (14.14).

Mathematically, the Kuhn-Tucker optimality conditions for this problem take the form (cf. (5.44)): For each i; $i = 1, \ldots, n$:

$$2q_i x_i^* + c_i \begin{cases} = -2r\sum_{i=1}^n x_i^* + t, & \text{if} \quad x_i^* > 0 \\ \geq -2r\sum_{i=1}^n x_i^* + t, & \text{if} \quad x_i^* = 0. \end{cases} \tag{14.16}$$

The algorithm for the solution of this problem is now presented. It is a finite algorithm, in that the problem is solved in a finite number of steps and is very easy to implement.

Elastic Exact Equilibration Algorithm

Step 0: Sort

Sort the c_i's in nondescending order and relabel the c_i's accordingly. We assume, henceforth, that they are relabeled. Define $c_{n+1} \equiv \infty$. If $q \leq c_1$, then set all $x_i^* = 0$; $i = 1, \ldots, n$ and stop; else, set $v := 1$ and go to Step 1.

Step 1: Computation

Compute

$$\lambda^v = \frac{\sum_{i=1}^v \frac{c_i}{2q_i} + \frac{t}{2r}}{\sum_{i=1}^v \frac{1}{2q_i} + \frac{1}{2r}}. \tag{14.17}$$

Step 2: Evaluation

If $c_v < \lambda^v \leq c_{v+1}$, then stop, set $s' = v$, and go to Step 3. Otherwise, let $v := v + 1$, and go to Step 1.

Step 3: Update

Set

$$x_i^* = \frac{\lambda^{s'} - c_i}{2q_i}, \quad i = 1, \ldots, s' \tag{14.18}$$

$$x_i^* = 0, \quad i = s' + 1, \ldots, n.$$

Example 14.1

We now present a small example to illustrate the application of the elastic exact demand equilibration algorithm. The example is a n elastic demand version of Example 5.3.

Let $n = 3$, and let the data (cf. Example 5.3) be as follows:

$$q_1 = .5, \quad q_2 = 1, \quad q_3 = .5$$

$$c_1 = 5, \quad c_2 = 10, \quad c_3 = 2,$$

but now we no longer have a fixed demand but, rather, what may be viewed as a demand price function λ, where, for this example, we have that

$$\lambda = -.5d + 18.5 = -.5\sum_{i=1}^3 x_i + 10,$$

and, consequently, in the above notation, we have that $r = 1$ and $t = 18.5$. Then the optimization problem (14.14), subject to (14.10) for this specific example is:

$$\text{Minimize} \quad 0.5x_1^2 + 1x_2^2 + 0.5x_3^2 + 5x_1 + 10x_2 + 2x_3 + (\sum_{i=1}^{3} x_i) - 18.5(\sum_{i=1}^{3} x_i)$$

subject to:

$$x_1,\, x_2,\, x_3 \geq 0.$$

Applying the elastic exact equilibration algorithm yields the following optimal solution:

$$x_1^* = 3.5, \quad x_2^* = 0, \quad x_3^* = 6.5,$$

and, hence, $d^* = \sum_{i=1}^{3} x_i^* = 10$.

Note that the optimality conditions (14.16) are satisfied. Indeed, we have that

$$2q_1x_1^* + c_1 = 2q_3x_3^* + c_3 = 8.5 = -2r\sum_{i=1}^{3} x_i^* + t \leq 2q_2x_2^* + c_2 = 10.$$

14.3 A Numerical Example

In this section we illustrate the Splitting Equilibration Algorithm by applying it to a financial dataset for 1989 from the Federal Reserve Board (FRB). In particular, we consider the case of elastic sector volumes and instrument totals. Hence, we consider the solution of the network optimization problem depicted in Figure 14.2. For a numerical example of Figure 14.4, see Hughes and Nagurney (1992).

The goal is to estimate a dataset that stays as close as possible to the FRB data while at the same time satisfying the accounting identities used in economic general equilibrium analysis. The illustrative use of SEA provides a solution set that can be utilized in future research as base-line data for the calibration of a general equilibrium model of financial activity and for macromonetary policy analysis.

Recall that, as was illustrated in Figure 14.1, the accounting framework required for modeling a general equilibrium of financial activity has several specific properties. In particular, the accounting identities must be satisfied. First, aggregating across instruments (including tangible assets and net worth), the balance sheets of each sector must be balanced. Second, aggregating across sectors, each instrument must have a unique total outstanding volume which is the same whether calculated from the asset submatrix or from the liability submatrix.

The FRB balance sheet data was consolidated into 9 sectors and 30 instruments as listed in Table 14.1. The dataset consisted of balanced sector

Table 14.1. List of sector and instrument groupings

Sectors	**Instruments**
1. Households & Nonprofits	1. Tangible Assets, Gold & SDR's /System Net Worth
2. Private Domestic Business	2. IMF Position
3. State & Local Governments	3. Official Foreign Exchange
4. Foreign Sector	4. Treasury Currency & SDR CTFS
5. US Government	5. Private Domestic Checkable Deposits& Currency
6. Government-Sponsored Agencies& Mortgage Pools	6. Foreign Checkable Deposits
7. Monetary Authority	7. US Government Checkable Deposits&Currency
8. Commercial Banking	8. Small-Time & Savings Deposits
9. Private Non-Bank Financial Institutions	9. Money Market Fund Shares
	10. Large-Time Deposits
	11. Federal Funds & Security RP's
	12. Deposits Abroad
	13. Life Insurance Reserves
	14. Pension Fund Reserves
	15. Interbank Claims
	16. Mutual Fund Shares
	17. Corporate Equities
	18. US Treasury S's*
	19. Federal Agency S's
	20. Tax-Exempt S's
	21. Corporate & FB's**
	22. Mortgages
	23. Consumer Credit
	24. Bank Loans N. E.
	25. Open-Market Paper
	26. Other Loans
	27. Security Credit
	28. Trade Credit
	29. Taxes Payable
	30. Miscellaneous
*: Securities; **: Foreign Bonds	

balance sheets, but unbalanced instrument volumes. There are several measurement incompatibilities that lead the FRB data values to not conform to the instrument volume balances. The most common discrepancy arises from a difference in timing and recording of transactions by the agents involved, e.g., bank float. Another discrepancy arises in that two of the financial instruments subject to capital gains were left unbalanced in the original data, "Other Equities," and "Miscellaneous". The final set of discrepancies are the "Gold and SDR's" and "Tangible Assets" categories. These last two categories have no corresponding liability in terms of balance sheet entries because they are net assets in the system. A further, inadvertent, source of discrepancy that arises is the difference in timing of recalculation by the FRB of the various subsets of the accounts. Furthermore, several of the instrument types in the original data were not very close to conforming to the instrument volume balance condition.

The absolute maximum difference for any instrument volume as computed by summing the respective asset matrix column, and the respective liability row was equal to 3,330,000, with an average absolute difference over all instruments of 168,253.37. Hence, the initial data was very unbalanced. We would also like to emphasize the wide spread of the entries in the asset and liability matrices, with the data ranging from zero to the tens of millions, which is challenging from the numerical analysis point of view.

SEA was coded in FORTRAN and the system used for the numerical work was the IBM 3090-600J. The program was compiled using the FORTVS compiler at optimization level 3. Recall that SEA assumes that the flows to be estimated are nonnegative. Hence, five elements in the initial asset/liability matrices which had negative values were brought over to the other matrix, with the totals being adjusted accordingly. All of the weights were set equal to one. The initial estimate for the j-th instrument volume, $D^0_{ii'}$ was set equal to $.5 \times (\sum_{j=1}^{J} x^0_{ji} + \sum_{j'=1'}^{J'} x^0_{i'j'})$.

The stopping criterion used for the algorithm was: $|(\sum_{j=1}^{J} x_{ji} - D_{ii'})| \leq 10$ and $|\sum_{i'=1'}^{I'} x_{i'j'} - S_{j'j}| \leq 10$. The algorithm converged in 592 iterations and required only 1.34 CPU seconds for convergence (without the input/output time). The absolute maximum difference for any instrument volume as computed by summing the respective asset matrix column, and the respective liability row was equal to 4.68, with an average absolute difference over all instruments equal to 1.34. This is to be contrasted with the absolute maximum difference in the original data which was equal to 3,330,000, with an average absolute difference over all instruments of 168,253.37. The improvement, hence, was on the order of five orders of magnitude in accuracy.

14.4 Sources and Notes

This chapter focused on financial flow of funds accounts, in general, and in their estimation, in particular, in light of discrepancies that exist in such financial datasets. The financial accounts must be balanced in order to be able to develop general equilibrium models that reflect the role of economic behavior in the determination of capital flows between sectors.

In particular, we provided some background on such accounts and then developed network models of financial flow of funds. These network models were then utilized to provide balanced sets of accounts through the application of a generalization of the Splitting Equilibration Algorithm discussed in Chapter 5.

It is important to note that the financial flow of funds accounts maintained by different countries are not identical in structure. Hence, here we have focused principally on the flow of funds accounts for the United States maintained by the Federal Reserve Board since these are the best known. Cohen (1987) points out, however, that the closest to an idealized set of accounts is the integrated set of accounts proposed by the United Nations Statistical Office (cf. United Nations (1968)), sometimes referred to as the UN System of National Accounts, or SNA, for short.

Section 14.1

This section follows the paper of Nagurney and Hughes (1992) which was also used in Chapter 9 of Nagurney (1993). Here, however, we provide graphic illustrations of special cases of the network model of financial flow of funds.

Section 14.2

The Splitting Equilibration Algorithm discussed here where the sector volumes and the instrument total volumes are elastic is due to Nagurney and Hughes (1992) and this section is adapted from that paper. A version of the algorithm in the case that sectoral volumes are known is studied in Hughes and Nagurney (1992) and is also presented here, for completeness. Here we have also presented an elastic exact equilibration algorithm reported in Dafermos and Nagurney (1989) for the solution of the embedded elastic row and column equilibration subproblems.

Section 14.3

This example is due to Nagurney and Hughes (1992) and has also been reported in Chapter 9 in Nagurney (1993).

References

Alford, R. F. G., **Flow of Funds**, Aldershot, England, 1986.

Cohen, J., "Copeland's Money Flows After Twenty-Five Years: A Survey," *Journal of Economic Literature* **10** (1972) 1-25.

Cohen, J., **The Flow of Funds in Theory and Practice**, Financial and Monetary Studies, volume 15, Kluwer Academic Publishers, 1987.

Copeland, M. A., **A Study of Money flows in the United States**, National Bureau of Economic Research, New York, 1952.

Dafermos, S., and Nagurney, A., "Supply and Demand Equilibration Algorithms for a Class of Market Equilibrium Problems," *Transportation Science* **23** (1989) 118-124.

Dudler, H., and Chouraqui, J. C., **Flow of Funds Analysis in Short-Term Context**, Banque de France, Seminaire d Banques Centrales et des Institutions Internationale, Paris, France, April, 1977.

Federal Reserve Board, **Introduction to Flow of Funds**, Washington, DC, June, 1980.

Nagurney, A., **Network Economics: A Variational Inequality Approach**, Kluwer Academic Publishers, Boston, Massachusetts, 1993.

Hughes, M., and Nagurney, A., "A Network Model and Algorithm for the Analysis and Estimation of Financial Flow of Funds," *Computer Science in Economics and Management* **5** (1992) 23-39.

Nagurney, A., and Eydeland, A., "A Splitting Equilibration Algorithm for the Computation of Large-Scale Constrained Matrix Problems: Theoretical Analysis and Applications," in **Computational Economics and Econometrics**, pp. 65-105, H. M. Amman, D. A. Belsley, and L. Pau, editors, Kluwer Academic Publishers, Dordrecht, The Netherlands, 1992.

Nagurney, A., and Hughes, M., "Financial Flow of Funds Networks," *Networks* **22** (1992) 145-161.

OECD, Committee on Financial Markets, **Financial Statistics: Methodological Supplement**, 1981.

Quesnay, F., **Tableau Economicque** (1758), reproduced in facsimile with an introduction by H. Higgs by the British Economic Society, 1895.

Thore, S., "Credit Networks," *Economica* **36** (1969) 42-55.

Thore, S., "Programming a Credit Network Under Uncertainty," *Journal of Money, Banking, and Finance* **2** (1970) 219-246.

Thore, S., **Programming the Network of Financial Intermediation**, Universitetsforlaget, Oslo, Norway, 1980.

Thore, S., and Kydland, F., "Dynamic Flow of Funds Networks," in **Applications of Management Science in Banking and Finance**, S. Eilon and T. R. Fowkes, editors, Epping, England, pp. 259-276, 1972.

United Nations, **A System of National Accounts**, New York, New York, 1968.

Part VI Empirical Results

15 Empirical Analysis

In this chapter we examine different issues that may arise in the empirical analysis of the models proposed in this book and we investigate how these models can be adjusted to real data. In addition, we suggest future directions for research and conclude with a summary of the book.

As in all equilibrium models in the literature, our models are based on some fundamental assumptions and, therefore, some real world elements may be simplified or assumed away. Since the theoretical framework for the models has been established, the next step must be to examine the relationship between our models and real world phenomena.

As one would expect, the above well-justified statement suggests a new series of questions. For example, which empirical tests are meaningful for a particular theory? How can one test which variant of a model causes particular problems and how can one overcome these problems? In addition, how can the models, if need be, then be extended to capture more realistic situations?

In this chapter we attempt to provide answers to such questions acknowledging that by their nature they are broad and not always easy to answer. Our first concern is to identify the problems that arise in the empirical analysis of such types of models as ours and to examine how similar problems have been handled in the existing literature. Second, we investigate how our models can be adjusted to real data applications. Note that, in terms of financial applications, this a first attempt to connect the theoretical frameworks of variational inequalities and projected dynamical systems for finance with empirical analysis.

We recall that the models discussed in this book relaxed many of the assumptions of classical equilibrium models. For example, in comparison to the CAPM (see Chapter 2), we relaxed the assumptions of no transaction costs and no taxes, which obviously are highly unrealistic, as well as the homogeneity of expectations among investors of different background and origin. Moreover, in contrast to some existing models, we assumed that the way that investors allocate their money affects the prices of different instruments and currencies, since the corresponding supplies and demands are affected. Finally, sectors are not limited to hold assets and liabilities solely from their own country or in their home currency, but they can invest in any instrument in any currency that is more "beneficial" for them.

We must also emphasize that we do not assume that the instrument and currency prices follow some specific probability distributions. Note that, very often, prices are assumed to follow normal distributions, which cannot adequately characterize reality for two reasons. First, even though prices of instruments or currencies cannot be negative, a normal distribution admits any value both positive and negative. Second, the normal distribution cannot account for compounding, and, consequently, the assumption of a normal distribution can lead to false results.

One can easily observe that the most commonly tested model is that of the CAPM. However, since many researchers and practitioners have found some of the CAPM assumptions to be untenable, a significant part of the literature has focused on the empirical analysis of CAPM-type models. The primary goal of that ongoing research is to examine how much reality is distorted by the particular assumptions, and how realistic the outcome of such models is. In many cases the results are contradictory since they are based on different assumptions. Nevertheless, such tests of the CAPM suggest a way in which future equilibrium models can be tested and evaluated.

Obviously, it is beyond the scope of this book to discuss in detail all the tests that have been conducted on the CAPM. However, during the course of this chapter we will often address issues of empirical analysis that appear both in CAPM models and in our models. For an extensive discussion of the empirical analysis of the CAPM we refer the reader to Miller and Scholes (1972), Fama and McBeth (1973), Roll (1980, 1981), Cornell (1981), Gibbons (1982), Stambaugh (1982), and, finally, to Breeden, Gibbons, and Litzenberger (1989).

As has been mentioned several times in this book, Markowitz started a new era in financial economics by introducing the mean-variance optimization model. Interestingly, after over forty years and a series of dynamic changes in the marketplace, the principles of his model still hold. The goal of every investor or portfolio manager still focuses on the asset allocation that offers the maximum return for the minimum possible risk.

The mean-variance optimization approach is, hence, commonly used in financial economics. However, from an empirical point of view, there are several problems that one may face. For example, the estimated expected returns and variance-covariance matrix must be consistent, which means that if two instruments are perfectly correlated their rates of return must be close to each other. In addition, since many models based on the mean-variance optimization approach require inversion of the variance-covariance matrix, the matrix has to be of full rank which cannot hold true for all data. Moreover, if some elements of the variance-covariance matrix are quite large then the model may lead to *corner* solutions for the asset allocation process and, hence, to false results. Consequently, one must be very careful as to the construction of the variance-covariance matrix and must thoroughly investigate if the particular matrix fulfills the requirements that the specific model imposes on this matrix. Clearly, this will also be the case for the mean-variance models that we presented in this book.

It is important to realize that the performance evaluation of all utility-based optimization models heavily depends on the quality of the input. Most scientists believe that well-conceived input data provides good results, whereas everyone agrees that ad-hoc type or ill-conceived data can lead to misleading results.

Chapter 15 is divided into four different sections. In Section 15.1 we discuss some issues that arise in empirical analysis (e. g., the estimation of inputs to the financial process, the collection of data, etc.), whereas in Section 15.2 we examine how real world data can be adjusted for our models. Section 15.3 focuses on possible extensions of the suggested models that incorporate complex utility functions and additional constraints. Finally, in Section 15.4, we discuss the results of the aforementioned empirical analysis and we briefly summarize the material presented in this book.

15.1 Estimation of Inputs to Financial Processes

The most commonly used input for financial models is based on historical estimates. Its popularity is based on the availability, as well as, the accessibility of data, and on the fact that people can easily relate to such input.

Apart from the above advantages, historical estimates embody a strong assumption, that is, the future behavior of a financial process will follow its past historical pattern which, however, does not hold true for most financial applications. Indeed, the use of more observations improves the efficiency of the estimation, but at the expense of potential bias, if the characteristics of the distribution change over time.

Moreover, even if a model has worked well in the past, it does not mean that it will be able to capture irregularities or special abnormalities that might take place in the future. This is another reason that many practitioners object to the use of estimates based solely on historical data and are turning to more advanced and sophisticated approaches, some of which will be discussed later in this chapter.

Most of historical estimates are based on *time series* data. We recall that the term time series refers to a set of ordered observations of a quantitative variable taken at subsequent points in time. Depending on the application, the time interval between observation varies.

Since an ordered sample of data does not have the same properties as a random sample of observations drawn from a known population, we cannot apply typical analysis which assumes statistical independence. Clearly, successive observations are statistically dependent and, therefore, classical assumptions, such as the independence of observations and approaches, cannot hold.

The most significant and commonly encountered problem is that of *autocorrelation* where the value of an observation is correlated and is not independent from the value of the same variable from the previous period. As a result, calculated errors in a regression analysis may be wrongly estimated. Usually, researchers try to make observations mutually independent by removing any trends or regularly recurring fluctuations.

Until recently, in analyses of macroeconomic data, time series were typically studied as homoscedastic processes, but in the early eighties a series of significant papers (cf. Engle (1982, 1983) and Cragg (1982)) found substantial evidence that in some cases the disturbance variances are less stable than it had been assumed previously, leading to the development of special models such as the AutoRegressive Conditionally Heteroscedastic (ARCH) model (cf. Engle (1982, 1983), Engle and Rothschild (1992)) and its generalized version GARCH (see Bollerslev (1986)), which is commonly used by many theoreticians and practitioners.

Since the future always incorporates uncertainty, no statistical technique can provide a forecast with certainty. Even so, understanding how the past has worked can help us to approximate what the future may be like. In the following paragraphs we present the basic quantitative forecasting methods that are currently in use.

The most frequently used time series methods of forecasting are based on determining the weights that must be assigned to previous observations. The variety of time-series methods is based on the fact that there are many alternative ways to assign these different weights.

Moving Average

This is one of the simplest ways of reducing the randomness of individual forecasts, which tries to average all the past values by assigning equal weights to all of them. In particular, the method assigns an equal weight $1/N$ to all of the last N observations. As new data become available, they can be used in the average, making it a *moving* average. This method is commonly used when the time horizon for forecasting is fairly short.

Exponential Smoothing

This methodology is similar to the Moving Average approach, but instead of assigning constant weights to all observations, we assign an exponentially set of weights so that the recent observations receive more weight than older ones. The advantage of this method is that it utilizes less computer memory since it does not need to store all past observations. This methodology has witnessed a series of different variations in order to incorporate adjustments that handle such issues as trend and seasonal patterns.

Auto-Regressive/Moving Average (ARMA)

A more advanced methodology of determining which weights must be assigned to past observations is a series of methods classified under the nomenclature *Auto-Regressive/Moving Average*. The most well-known of this class of methodologies is the one developed by Box and Jenkins (1976), which introduced a statistical approach to determining all the different parameters in the forecasting procedure.

This type of method not only assigns different weights to different observations, but also identifies the number of observations that must be included in the forecasting procedure. In addition, ARMA models have the advantage of including weighted terms for not only the past observations of the item to be forecasted, but also for the past values of the forecast errors.

Econometrics

Econometrics is not only based on past values of the object whose value is to be forecasted, but also on the past values of other variables that have a *causal* relationship with the value of the item. This method is the most commonly used in finance, since instrument and currency prices are affected by a series of different factors.

This type of method has the advantage of including many equations that can be solved simultaneously, and, therefore, tends to provide a more accurate and realistic representation of the interrelationship among different factors. This advantage, however, is accompanied by a higher cost, so it is basically used only for highly aggregated data.

Clearly, the computational complexity of econometric methods heavily depends on the number and type of factors that one wants to incorporate in the forecasting.

During the last three decades a large part of the literature has been debating (starting with Naylor, Seaks, and Wicherin (1972), Nelson (1972), and Fromm and Klein (1973)), which forecasting approach is better for specific applications. A simple answer cannot be given since each method is more appropriate for specific types of problems. The length of the time horizon, the cost of data storage, and the number of forecasting items are all important in determining the best method.

In the single country context, a series of empirical research papers (cf. Fama and French (1988), Campbell and Shiller (1988)), has shown that the returns as well as the variances of different instruments and currencies are predictable on the basis of a group of different variables. For example, stock returns can be determined in terms of many factors such as the dividend yield and the spread between corporate and government bonds.

In an international context, however, the correlation between prices and the same factors is not always strong (see, e. g., Cutler, Poterba, and Summers (1991), Harvey (1991), and Bekaert and Hodrick (1992)) and, therefore, predictions are much harder to obtain. For example, even though the model developed by Elton and Gruber (1973) was able to forecast the dependence structure of single country share prices, it was proven to be incapable of forecasting the pairwise relationship between several international share prices (for details see Eun and Resnick (1984)).

15.1.1 Collection of Data

Due to differences in definitions, very often, compatibility of data from different sources is an issue. For the types of models that we present in this book the way that an economy is divided into different sectors, as well as the industrial classifications and geographical breakdown, may lead to problematic inconsistencies in realistic applications, although the modeling framework developed here provides great flexibility theoretically.

Many financial and economic cooperations and organizations (e. g., the Organization for Economic Cooperation and Development (OECD), Merrill Lynch, Morgan Stanley Capital International (MSCI), and Salomon Brothers) provide some standardized comprehensive statistics in a standardized format combining sectoral and geographical breakdowns for flow of capital, financial instrument prices, and asset allocation. Depending on the application, different sources of data or a different segmentation of the economy may be needed.

One must, however, be extremely careful, since very often data are presented under different definitions and time horizons, and national data are not reported according to some universal codes or standardized format. In addition, in many cases, some types of data have not been reported until very recently, and, as a consequence, further analysis may be needed in order to obtain accurate results.

Instrument Prices and Exchange Rates

In most cases, data on instrument prices and exchange rates are usually not a problem to obtain. Of course, this does not always hold true for exotic stocks and hedging instruments. In general, however, there are many different sources that someone can use in order to obtain such data. In particular, if one is interested in a very simple type of data, he can refer to relatively cheap services. If, on the other hand, detailed and statistically analyzed data are needed, one must turn to more sophisticated and, typically, more expensive sources.

Depending on the application, portfolio managers as well as researchers turn to organizations that can provide such high quality data (e. g., OECD, MSCI, etc.). Of course, even this information is not perfect, but it usually provides accurate spot as well as forward prices for many different types of instruments and currencies accompanied by a detailed analysis of different indices. The data based on the instrument, as well as on the currency prices, can then be used for the determination of the utility function of a sector. For example, in the case of the quadratic models presented in this

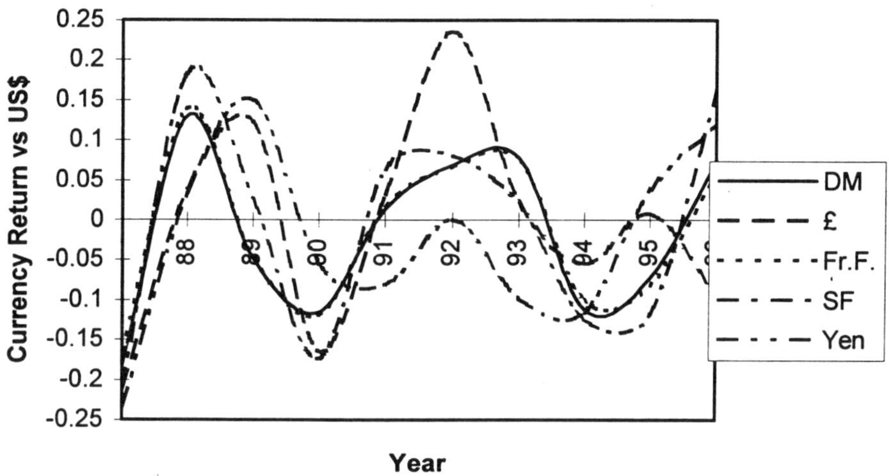

Fig. 15.1. Several currency returns in terms of the United States Dollar (1986-1996)

book, data on instrument prices and exchange rates can be used for the construction of variance-covariance (or correlation) matrices for all the different investment options (see Section 2.4). For demonstration reasons, in Figure 15.1, we depict the appreciation of some major currencies versus the United States dollar, between 1986 and 1996, whereas in Table 15.1, we present the correlation matrix between these appreciations.

Transaction Costs

One of the most difficult tasks in terms of data collection is the determination of transaction costs associated with different instruments, markets,

Table 15.1. Correlation matrix of currency returns in terms of the U.S. Dollar (1986-1996)

	DM	**£**	**FF**	**SF**	**Y**
German Mark (DM)	1.00	0.59	0.94	0.93	0.48
British Pound (£)	0.59	1.00	0.59	0.57	0.48
French Franc (FF)	0.94	0.59	1.00	0.93	0.43
Swiss Franc (SF)	0.93	0.57	0.93	1.00	0.61
Japanese Yen (Y)	0.48	0.48	0.43	0.61	1.00

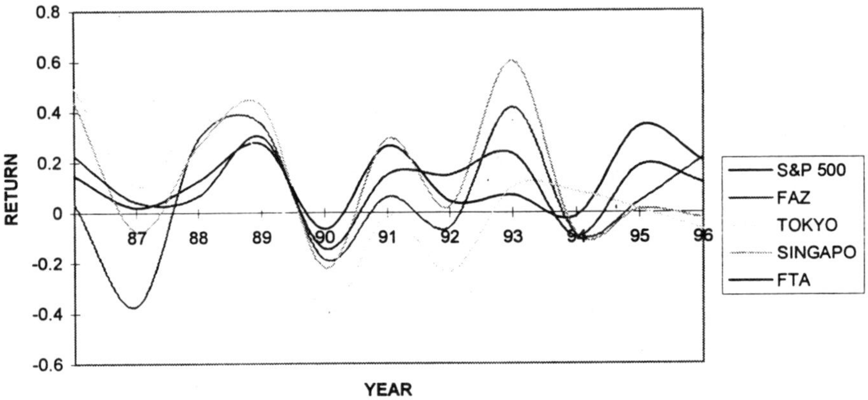

Fig. 15.2. Returns of some major stock markets (1986-1996)

and currencies. This difficulty is based on the fact that there are many ways that commissions can be charged (variable schedule, negotiable between different participants, bid-ask spread, etc.), and, hence, there are several ways of defining transaction costs. For example, commissions for bonds tend to be lower in general than commissions for stocks, and, consequently, for each type of financial instrument one must follow a different approach in order to collect the data.

According to Solnik (1996), costs of internationally diversified portfolios tend to be higher as compared to domestic portfolios. This effect is more obvious for investors that come from countries with lower transaction costs, such as the United States, and less evident for investors living in high living-cost countries, such as Switzerland, the Netherlands, and Sweden.

It is worth noting, though (for details see Oldier and Solnik (1993)), that even though international investments incorporate higher transaction costs, they still offer more return-risk benefits than investing domestically. Such effects are more pronounced (cf. Eun and Resnick (1988), Longin and Solnik (1995)), if the portfolio is diversified among markets with low correlation. For example, an investor will, on the average, have better return-risk results if he diversifies his assets between German and Japanese assets than between German and British assets, since German figures show lower correlation with the Japanese market than with the British market (see Figure 15.2 and Table 15.2).

Also, it is worth noting that the calculation of the correlation between

Table 15.2. Correlation matrix of major stock markets (1986-1996)

	NY	**Frankfurt**	**Tokyo**	**Singapore**	**London**
NY	1.0000	0.4883	0.3163	0.3881	0.7115
Frankfurt	0.4883	1.0000	0.3771	0.7464	0.6229
Tokyo	0.3163	0.3771	1.0000	0.6482	0.4677
Singapore	0.3881	0.7464	0.6482	1.0000	0.7806
London	0.7115	0.6229	0.4677	0.7806	1.0000

different markets or even assets depends on many different factors. For example, if one includes data starting from the mid-seventies instead of the mid-eighties in the data presented in Table 15.2, the correlation matrix will be different (cf. Solnik (1996)), since a series of major changes took place in the international financial market during those last years. More precisely, in the seventies, Asian markets were much smaller and less liberalized (for example, the markets of Japan, Singapore, and Hong Kong combined were 14.3% of the 1976 world stock markets, where now they account for an outstanding 32.3%). In contrast, the North American equity market was more than half of the worlds' market (61.4% in 1976), which now is limited to almost a third of the worlds' equity market (34.7% in 1996). In addition, while the European Union was more of an idea than a reality in the seventies, new members have been introduced since then (e. g., Greece, Spain, Portugal in the eighties, and Austria, Finland, and Sweden in the nineties) and it has significantly expanded its influence zone. This has been accompanied by major breakthrough treaties such as the Maastricht treaty that permanently changed the financial, as well as the political, map of Europe.

Taxes

Collecting data related to taxes is definitely a complicated task that needs a lot of expertise. Local, as well as international, laws and treaties are in constant change, and, therefore, one needs many resources in order to obtain accurate data on taxation systems. Unfortunately, even though the collection of data in a single country case is far simpler than in an international case it is still not trivial, since such data are not reported in any compact form by corporations and organizations.

Every country has a different tax system and very often investors of different origins pay different taxes. Taxes also depend on the type of instrument, as well as the type of investor. Moreover, international investments incorporate the possibility of paying taxes in various countries, which may be of an entirely different form. For example, throughout the European Union it is common for an investor to face a Value Added Tax (VAT) on commissions (e. g., 18.6% in France), whereas in Japan investors usually face a small tax rate (around 0.3%) on sales and not on purchases.

We recall that the imperfect market models presented in this book incorporate transaction costs and taxes that depend both on the origin of the investor, as well as, on the type of the instrument. This is the most general case for modeling transaction costs and taxes, and it can be appropriately adjusted for every application.

It is also worth noting that the vast majority of models in the literature (as ours) assume transaction costs and taxes to be constant. This assumption is justified and does not cause any problems with short or medium investment horizons. However, a model utilized for long-term horizons must take into consideration some adjustments of the related taxation systems, transaction costs, and, finally, different monetary interventions.

In the United States and Japan this is not much of an issue, since changes in taxes, transaction costs, and policy interventions are minimal and more predictable in comparison to the rest of the world. For country members of the European Union, the suggestions of the Commission of the European Communities are usually good predictors of future developments in transactions costs and taxes, and they can serve as excellent guidelines. Similarly, OECD financial reports for its members offer usually good predictors of future developments in transactions costs and taxes, and they can serve as excellent guidelines.

Sector-Specific Data

Another type of data that in many cases is not easy to obtain, is data related to specific sectors in different countries. Very often, a common breakdown of the economy is not available, and/or data are suppressed for confidentiality reasons. In addition, one of the major reasons for incompatibility of data is frequency as well as the form that they become available to the public. For example, in the United States (as well as in the United Kingdom, and very often in Japan) one can easily obtain data for specific sectors in the economy since all large companies publish quarterly results and are available after some weeks. In contrast, in France, firms publish their earnings six months after the end of their fiscal year, and, as a result, direct comparison of similar figures can be misleading, since these data are outdated. Clearly, these problems are application-specific and they are not always easy to overcome.

For the models presented in this book, the amount of capital that each sector has available for investments, which we denoted as S^{jl} for sector j of country l, has to be measured. One approach for the determination of the corresponding S^{jl} is to collect reports on the total assets of every sector, and to translate them into the basic currency. Then one can use these values directly, or can scale them in terms of a benchmark. The latter is more preferable since it provides a better feeling as to the effect that each sector may have on the market.

Furthermore, the risk tolerance (see Section 2.2) of each sector in each country needs also to be measured for the construction of the corresponding utility function. Many different approaches have been suggested in the literature (see, e. g., Breeden (1978), Adler and Dumas (1983)) for the measurement of the risk tolerance of each sector. In finance, a function of β that characterizes each specific sector is sometimes used as a basic approximation of sector risk preferences. One has to be careful, however, so that all the different β's are based on the same benchmark, which is obviously more complicated to ascertain in international applications. In theory, the indicator that we discussed in (2.25) is commonly used as a measure of risk aversion. Very often, the value of this indicator is assumed to be equal to 0.5 (cf. Adler and Dumas (1983)), but for real applications the corresponding risk tolerances must be estimated.

In general, sector-related data can be obtained either from the data that individual firms publish (e. g., *10-K* reports), or from reports that different organizations and institutions publish on a regular basis (e. g., several publications of OECD such as the International Direct Investment Statistics Yearbooks (started in 1993), or several publications of Morgan Stanley Capital International (MSCI)). In addition, these publications offer a series of analyzed statistical results that can be of further use and can provide valuable information for trend analysis and intersectoral comparisons even on a single instrument or currency basis. It is worth noting, however, that one has to be extremely careful, since in some cases translated data may not even meet some standard accounting constraints due to inconsistency of data sources, a fact that is not always reported.

Even in the case that there are data available on the assets of different sectors in various countries, it is still difficult to identify the amount of capital that each sector has available for investments in different markets.

Note that the international models presented in this book can also be used at a higher macroeconomic level, where one is interested in asset allocation and currency price determination on a country level rather than a sector level. The selection of country related data without the need of specific sector segmentation is obviously simpler.

Hedging Instruments

A large portion of the literature has focused on examining different types of hedging strategies that use several formats of data (e. g., Madura and Reiff (1985), Jorion (1985, 1986), and Eun and Resnick (1988)), and on demonstrating the benefits of hedging. Everyone agrees that there is no globally accepted hedging strategy because, if one existed, there would be no need for all the different types of financial hedging products.

The models presented in this book that incorporated hedging instruments did not suggest any particular hedging strategy. Our goal was to demonstrate how hedging instruments can be embodied in such type of modeling. Obviously, it would be very interesting to explore the pros and the cons of different hedging strategies through our models, but this is beyond the scope of this book. We refer the reader who is interested in the comparison of existing hedging strategies to several of the references presented in Chapters 7 and 12.

The data needed for our models that incorporate hedging instruments (e. g., exercise price, premiums) can be easily obtained from the same sources suggested previously for the instrument prices as well as the currency exchange rates. The collection of such data is more complicated in this case, since there are many different types of futures and options and there are several more variables connected with each contract. Fortunately, practitioners and theoreticians can have access today (usually for a fee) to good sources of financial data with detailed information and explicitly analyzed documentation. It is worth noting, hence, that for each type of application, and every form of modeling, there are many different ways that one can obtain data related to different hedging instruments.

15.2 Numerical Examples

In this section we will present some examples of how the models presented in the previous chapters can be adjusted for some real applications. We will consider data based on annual returns. Obviously, although for reasons of compactness we select our observation period to be a year, one can a have a different time fragmentation depending on the specific application.

Single Country Example

Initially, we will present an example based on portfolios that are diversified across different indices for groups of stocks from the Standards & Poor (500) (S & P 500) in the United States. In particular, in Figures 15.3 and 15.4, we depict the returns of nine different groups of stocks traded at the New York Stock Exchange and are incorporated into the S & P 500 composite index (S & P 500 Comp (Cmp)), that is, the indices for Aerospace Industry (Aero), Auto manufacturers (Auto), Building (Buil), Chemical companies (Che), Financial companies (Fin), Oil companies (Oil), Power industry (Pow), and, finally, computer software developers (Soft), from 1-1-86 to 12-31-96.

Table 15.3 presents the correlation matrix for the returns of these equity based indices, where, for demonstration reasons, we also present the S & P 500 Comp. This correlation matrix can serve as part of the matrix Q that we used in this book for the quadratic models. In addition, in Figure 15.5, we depict the mean and variance of each of this type of equity-based index, based on data from the same time period.

For simplicity, we only consider twelve different sectors of the United States economy. Clearly, there are several ways that one could perform the sector fragmentation, and this is just one of them. In Figure 15.6, we depict the fragmentation of the sectors based on the data that we used, whereas in the second column of Table 15.4, we present the corresponding S^j with j; $j = 1, \ldots, 12$ (note that l and k are both equal to 1, since we consider a

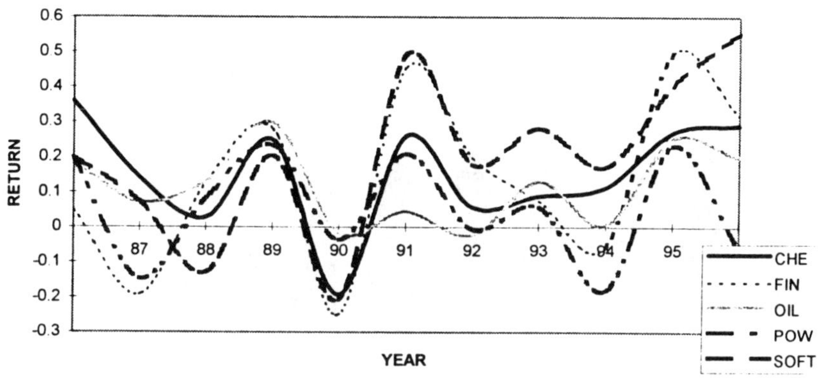

Fig. 15.3. Returns of some stock groups in the S&P 500 (1986-1996)

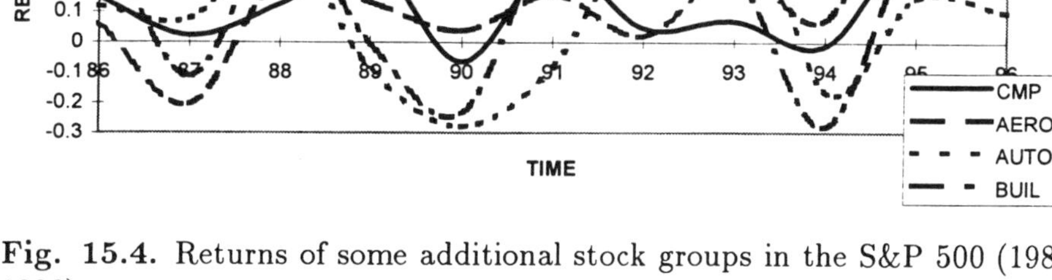

Fig. 15.4. Returns of some additional stock groups in the S&P 500 (1986-1996)

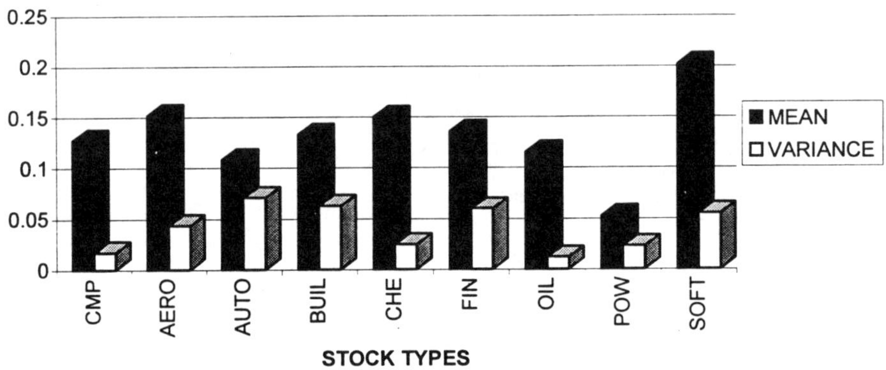

Fig. 15.5. Mean and variance on the returns of some stock groups in the S&P 500 (1986-1996)

Table 15.3. Correlation matrix on returns of some stock groups in the S&P 500 (1986-1996)

	Cmp	**Aero**	**Auto**	**Buil**	**Che**	**Fin**	**Oil**	**Pow**	**Soft**
Cmp	1.00	0.68	0.03	0.61	0.75	0.91	0.77	0.79	0.67
Aero	0.68	1.00	0.21	0.48	0.31	0.72	0.56	0.51	0.49
Auto	0.03	0.21	1.00	0.60	0.05	0.18	0.11	0.10	0.12
Buil	0.61	0.48	0.60	1.00	0.48	0.67	0.36	0.68	0.40
Che	0.75	0.31	0.05	0.48	1.00	0.63	0.65	0.47	0.77
Fin	0.91	0.72	0.18	0.67	0.63	1.00	0.51	0.67	0.76
Oil	0.77	0.56	0.11	0.36	0.65	0.51	1.00	0.62	0.38
Pow	0.79	0.51	0.10	0.68	0.47	0.67	0.62	1.00	0.29
Soft	0.67	0.49	0.12	0.40	0.77	0.76	0.38	0.29	1.00

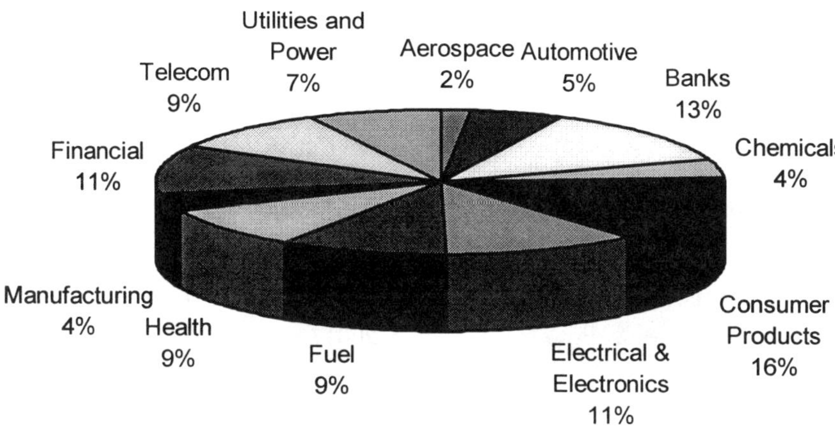

Fig. 15.6. An example of fragmentation of the U.S. economy into different sectors

single country, single currency economy) in millions of United States dollars (US \$), assuming that the values for all S^j are based on profits (net income before extraordinary items) for the economic year 1996. In the last column we present, for illustration purposes, a way of scaling these volumes of capital, in the case that we consider the assets of the Aerospace sector (the minimum) as a basis. Scaling is often recommended for computation as well as computer memory purposes, especially in large-scale applications.

Obviously, the values for all S^j have to be readjusted for an accurate analysis, since part of these sectors' assets and liabilities are "locked" and cannot be reassigned. In addition, the risk characteristics and preferences for each sector must be determined and incorporated into the utility function of each sector, along with sector-specific investment preferences. In practice, all sectors (in an individual company level), use hedging techniques in order to diversify specific types of risk, and these techniques must also be taken into account since they affect the output of all models.

An International Example

In an international application one of the first decisions that one has to make is to determine which currency will be the basic currency that every instrument and currency price will be translated on. In order to avoid some of the problems mentioned in the previous section, we suggest that, if possible, the basic currency is not one of the currencies involved in the decision process. In practice, the US dollar, the Japanese Yen, the Deutsche Mark, the British

Table 15.4. An example of S^j values for different sectors in the U.S. economy

Sector	Profits ($ millions)	Scaled
1. Aerospace	4867	1.0
2. Automotive	14445	2.96
3. Banks	35868.7	7.37
4. Chemicals	11365.2	2.33
5. Consumer Products	40609.5	8.34
6. Electronics	31152	6.40
7. Fuel	26052.4	5.35
8. Health Care	25844.5	5.31
9. Manufacturing	10808.3	2.22
10. Non-Bank Financial	30526.2	6.27
11. Telecommunication	26222.7	5.38
12. Utilities & Power	20617.8	4.23

Pound, and, recently, the *Euro* (European Union common currency) are very often used as basic currencies.

For the example discussed here we let the United States dollar be the basic currency, assuming that investors can invest in any of the five largest bond markets within the borders of European Union, that is, the markets of France, Germany, Italy, Netherlands, and United Kingdom (UK). The correlation matrix between the returns of all these markets in terms of United States dollars (US$) from 1-1-1976 to 1-1-1996 is presented in Table 15.5.

Sector fragmentation is, once again, very subjective and application-specific. For example, one may want to investigate how the banking sectors in each of the specific countries will allocate their assets in the different bond markets. For simplicity, we only consider the two largest banks in each country in terms of assets in US$. In particular, we consider Crédit Lyonnais and Crédit Agricole from France, Deutsche Bank, and Dresdner Bank from Germany, HSBC Holdings and Barclays Bank from UK, ABN-AMRO, and Rabobank from the Netherlands, and, finally, Banca di Roma and Banca San Paolo di Torino from Italy.

In the second column of Table 15.6 we present the corresponding S^l for $l = 1, \dots, 5$, in billions of US$, and in the third column we scale these assets in terms of the asset holdings of the Italian banks just for demonstration reasons, whereas in Figure 15.7 we depict the sector fragmentation for the specific bond market.

Table 15.5. Correlation matrix on the returns of major bond markets in the EU

	France	Germany	Italy	Netherlands	UK
France	1.00	0.81	0.68	0.79	0.49
Germany	0.81	1.00	0.55	0.95	0.50
Italy	0.68	0.55	1.00	0.63	0.42
Netherlands	0.79	0.95	0.63	1.00	0.22
UK	0.49	0.50	0.42	0.22	1.00

Table 15.6. An example of S^l values for banking sectors in countries of the EU

Country	Assets ($ billions)	Scaled
France	619.30	2.20
Germany	558.90	1.99
Italy	280.90	1.00
Netherlands	382.20	1.36
UK	530.40	1.89

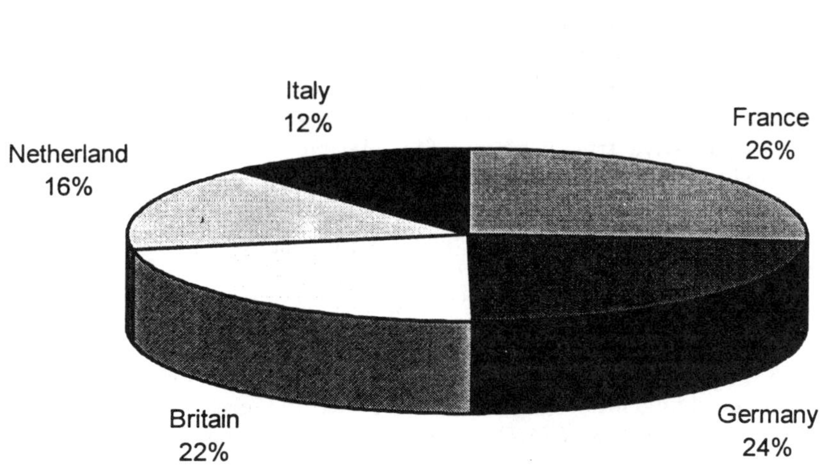

Fig. 15.7. An example of sector fragmentation of the specific bond market

15.3 Future Directions for Research

For many of the models presented in the preceding chapters, the goal of each sector was to maximize the return of his portfolio as well as to minimize the risk that this portfolio entails. Clearly, in reality, sectors may have other objectives which may depend on the nature as well as on the interests of each specific sector (for example, the solvency ratio, that is, the ratio of capital equity to all weighted assets for all banks in European Union is required to be greater than 8% following the suggestion of the Commission of the European Communities; see Commission of the European Communities (1989), and Giokas and Vassiloglou (1991)). Note that many of the basic models did include utility functions that could incorporate other behavioral issues and that in Chapter 13 we considered more general feasible sets than simply the accounting budget constraints.

In addition, in practice, many portfolio managers try to outperform a standardized market benchmark, and, consequently, our models may be extended to incorporate different benchmarks. Various reasons exist for this increased emphasis on the passive investment in existing benchmarks in contrast to a more active investment in portfolios which attempts to outperform the cited benchmark. One reason for the growing interest in passive indices (e. g., Standards & Poor 500, Salomon Brothers World Equity Index, etc.) is that, over the years, many investors have come to believe that active managers have underperformed the relative passive benchmark. While academic research has indicated that the failure of certain active portfolios to replicate passive portfolios is due to the unique risk patterns in various markets, in contrast to the risk profile of the benchmark, many investment firms have decided that direct investment in passive indices has benefits over more active manager selection. To the degree that an investor is concentrating more on benchmark performance, active managers are increasingly being forced to monitor not only the absolute risk of their portfolios but also the risk relative to the measured benchmark.

Considerable research exists on both the measurement of an investment stand-alone absolute (e. g., variance, semi-variance) as well as on alternative measures of relative tracking error (correlation, absolute error). There is disagreement, however, as to the alternative means of measuring not only absolute risk of a security or portfolio but also its relative risk within a portfolio (covariance tracking) as well as its relative risk to a proscribed benchmark.

In most cases, an appropriate benchmark depends on the country, the type of the investor, and on the assets that he is holding. For example, for stocks in the United States, the S&P 500 Composite index is one of the most commonly used benchmarks, whereas, for stocks in Germany, the Frankfurter Allgemeine Zeitung index (FAZ) is a more appropriate benchmark. Table 15.7 and Table 15.8 present a nonexhaustive list of some of the commonly used benchmarks for stocks and bonds, respectively.

Table 15.7. Major benchmarks for stocks

Country	Exchange	Index
Germany	Frankfurt	1. FAX
Germany	Frankfurt	2. DAX
France	Paris	3. CAC
France	Paris	4. SBF
Japan	Tokyo	5. Nikkei Average
Japan	Tokyo	6. Topix
Switzerland	Zurich	7. SBC
Switzerland	Zurich	8. SMI
United Kingdom	London	9. FT-SE (100)
United Kingdom	London	10. FT-All Shares
United States	New York	11. S&P 500
United States	New York	12. NYSE Composite
United States	Over the counter	13. NASDAQ
United States	New York	14. Dow Jones Industrial

Table 15.8. Major benchmarks for U.S.-based bonds

1. Lehman Brothers Corporate Index
2. Lehman Brothers Government Index
3. Merrill Lynch Corporate Master
4. Merrill Lynch Government Master
5. Merrill Lynch Domestic Master
6. Salomon Brothers Broad Investment Grade Index
7. Salomon Brothers Corporate Index

Benchmark quality became the subject of extensive discussion after benchmarks for portfolios were introduced at the beginning of the eighties. Since institutional investors are more concerned with minimizing volatility relative to a benchmark than minimizing total volatility, a large portion of the literature (see, e. g., Roll (1980, 1981), Reilly, Kao, and Wright (1992), Reilly and Akhtar (1995)) focused on evaluating different benchmarks as well as benchmark quality. Consequently, a question as to what are the correct criteria for an appropriate benchmark have received several, and, often contradictory, answers. Clearly, a good benchmark depends primarily on the investor and the financial instruments and currencies that he holds his assets and liabilities in.

The paper by Bailey (1992) presents a very good collection of the criteria that a benchmark should fulfill. A good benchmark should have similar style exposures to those of the manager's portfolio, it should be accompanied by weights in all assets that the investor can hold at all times, and it should also have a low proportion of the benchmark total market comprised of securities purchased at rebalancing (low turnover). In addition, most of the assets in the portfolio must be incorporated in the benchmark (high coverage), and its performance must get characterized by a low tracking error, which is the difference between the performance of the portfolio and that of the benchmark.

Moreover, for simplicity, and, for the sake of compactness, most of our models incorporated only a limited number of constraints, that is, balance accounting constraints, and nonnegativity constraints. More constraints can be included for different applications as long as they fulfill the theoretical limitations that our models assume (e. g., that the feasible set be convex (and a polyhedron)). Indeed, with only some simple changes, one can also explicitly add "environmental constraints," such as constraints imposed by the monetary authorities, the market, and the legal system. These types of models can then serve as extensions of the imperfect market models presented in Chapters 9 and 13.

In addition, other policy and behavioral constraints for each specific sector can also be incorporated. These constraints usually reflect restrictions imposed by financial accounting ratios or other financial measurements, such as liquidity ratios, proportions of an asset class to total asset holdings, and so forth.

As is the case in mean-variance models, the quadratic models that we presented throughout this book only diversify residual risk. If one wishes to diversify systematic risk one can impose a target *beta* (see Section 2.1) level. If, for example, we let β_{ik} be the beta factor for instrument i of currency k, and let β_b denote a benchmark value for beta, then one can diversify systematic risk on a mean-variance model with the incorporation of a constraint similar to:

$$\sum_{i=1}^{I}\sum_{k=1}^{K}\beta_{ik}X_{ik}^{jl} = \beta_b \tag{15.1}$$

Further extensions of the models presented here should also include additional time-dependent variables. For example, the introduction of time-dependent variables might also allow the sector portfolio volumes, S^{jl}, to vary. In addition, the incorporation of time-dependent risk premiums (e. g., variance-covariance matrix) would explore a new dimension of the suggested models, similar to the work presented by Engel and Rodrigues (1988) for the CAPM model.

As was pointed out earlier in Chapter 12, the models proposed here that incorporate hedging instruments can also be further explored and generalized. For example, one may wish to incorporate different types of contracts on every instrument and currency and to include contracts with different expiration dates and exercise prices. In addition, the following subjects are all topics for future research: establishing the relationship between the existing futures and options pricing models and our hedging models, comparing our models with specific models in the literature that incorporate hedging instruments (cf. Witte (1980), Dumas (1986), Poncet and Portait (1987), Huang (1987), Black (1989), Sellin and Werner (1993), Sorensen, Mezrich, and Thadani (1993)), and the evaluation of the performance of different portfolios and hedging strategies in terms of different single or customized benchmarks to be incorporated into our models.

15.4 Conclusions and Summary

In this chapter we discussed several different issues that are related to the empirical analysis of the models that were presented in this book. It became evident that for each specific application different considerations must be taken into account. Unfortunately, as one would expect, there is no optimal way to resolve all the issues simultaneously.

The goal of this chapter was to discuss some issues of empirical analysis that may be encountered in the study and application of our models. Through the numerical examples presented here we wished to demonstrate how real world applications could be captured through the models as well as to provide different sources of data and problems that might be encountered. We acknowledge that since our approach is new, additional research is needed for the empirical analysis.

Moreover, since this is the last section of this book, we believe that it would be beneficial for the reader not to only summarize the material presented in this chapter, but to also provide a brief summary of the book and its goals.

The first aim of this book was to introduce an integrated mathematical framework to the rapidly growing field of computational financial economics based on the visualization of such systems as networks consisting of nodes and links and the associated flows. Visualizing modeling and computation methodologies in such a way provides a consistent overall context for understanding the real nature of the underlying financial concepts and their evolution over time.

This volume suggested a fresh new approach to financial modeling and computation, based on the methodologies of finite-dimensional variational inequality theory for the exploration of statics and equilibrium states, and on projected dynamical systems theory for the study of dynamics and disequilibrium behavior. At the same time, visualization and formulation of financial problems as network flow problems provided one with the opportunity of applying network-based algorithms, coupled with the aforementioned methodologies, for computational purposes. The combination of these methodologies has the ability to provide an integrated conceptual backdrop for the economic, financial, and mathematical dimensions of the problems.

The scope of this text was not solely limited to the presentation of new approaches and methodologies, but it also aimed to explain the broader context of how and where these models can be successfully applied so that they can be used by both theoreticians and practitioners.

Starting with a single country, multi-sector, multi-instrument model in a perfect market environment, the problems gradually advanced to more complicated settings, relaxing most of the initial assumptions. In particular, in this book we presented models that incorporated such market imperfections as transaction costs, taxes, and price policy interventions, along with models that were based on the presence of hedging instruments, such as futures and options. In addition, models of an international dimension that incorporate multiple countries and multiple currencies were also considered and many issues involved in an international setting were addressed. The static, together with the dynamic, nature of the problems were thoroughly discussed, analyzed, and interconnected in a way so that the reader can readily understand the properties of the underlying financial processes.

The models presented in this text were accompanied by a detailed qualitative analysis, obtaining, for example, under certain assumptions, the existence and uniqueness of the equilibrium patterns, along with general sensitivity analysis and stability analysis results. The stability analysis established a clear connection between the dynamic and the static counterparts of each problem. After the qualitative properties of each model were extensively investigated, some computational methodologies were proposed. The algorithms suggested were just a sample of the algorithms that could be utilized, and their convergence was also addressed. The advantage of the proposed algorithms are based on their ability to decompose the problem into smaller and easier subproblems that can be solved (typically) explicitly and in closed form.

Hence, the methodologies presented in this book provide a rigorous framework for the modeling and computation of general financial equilibrium and can handle large-scale problems frequently encountered in practice.

Finally, in the last chapter of this book we addressed several issues that arise in empirical applications, and we suggested possible alternatives that the reader can use for different applications. For demonstration purposes, we also presented examples of how real world applications can be adjusted to some of our models.

The intended audience for this book includes students, researchers, monetary authorities, and practitioners in finance, in computational economics, and in operations research and management science, who are interested in the formulation, qualitative analysis, and computation of financial equilibrium problems in both static and dynamic settings. We hope that the material presented in this book will add fruitful new ideas and approaches to the growing field of computational financial economics.

15.5 Sources and Notes

In this chapter we briefly discussed a series of different problems commonly encountered in empirical analysis of financial equilibrium modeling, and we focused on empirical issues related to the specific models presented in this book. In addition, we demonstrated how real world data can be adjusted so that it can be utilized in the context of the financial models.

Obviously, within the limits of a book chapter it is not possible to discuss in detail all the problems that empirical analysis embodies. Our goals were to discuss the different issues that arise in empirical analysis and to provide a series of different references so that the reader can be ready for future investigation.

Section 15.1

In this section we addressed several issues that arise in the input estimation of different financial processes and we discussed some well-known approaches that have being suggested in the literature and are commonly applied by practitioners and theoreticians.

Obviously, it is impossible to present in detail all the issues as the contents of a single section. Moreover, it is beyond our scope to address in detail all the issues that arise in time-series data and in different forecasting methodologies. Hence, we refer the reader to the books by Judge, Hill, Griffiths, Lee, and Lütkepohl (1982), Taylor (1986), Lütkepohl (1991), and Greene (1993), as well as to the papers by Domowitz and Hakkio (1985), Engle and Rothschild (1992) for a more detailed analysis on time-series issues, and to Makridakis (1976), Makridakis and Wheelwright (1978, 1979), and Montgomery and Johnson (1976) for a more detailed discussion on forecasting methodologies.

Section 15.2

In this section we presented examples of how the suggested models can be adjusted for some real applications. The main source of for the data was the online service of Datastream International Limited. Supplemental data was obtained from several different publications of Morgan Stanley Capital International, the Organization of Economic Cooperation and Development, and Business Week magazine (March 3, 1997).

Section 15.3

In this section we suggested future directions for research based on the models presented in this book.

Section 15.4

In the last section of this book, we included some final thoughts.

References

Adler, M., and Dumas, B., "International Portfolio Choice and Corporation Finance: A Synthesis," *Journal of Finance* **38** (1983) 925-984.

Bailey, J. V., "Evaluating Benchmark Quality," *Financial Analysts Journal* (June 1992) 33-39.

Bekaert, G., and Hodrick, R. J., "Characterizing Predictable Components in Excess Returns on Equity and Foreign Exchange Markets," *Journal of Finance* **47** (1992) 467-508.

Black, F., "Equilibrium Exchange Rate Hedging," National Bureau of Economic Research, Working Paper 2947, April, 1989.

Bollerslev, T., "Generalized Autoregressive Conditional Heteroscedasticity," *Journal of Econometrics* **31** (1986) 307-327.

Box, G. E. P., and Jenkins, G. M., **Time Series Analysis: Forecasting and Control**, Holden-Day, Inc., San Francisco, California, 1976.

Breeden, D. T., "An Intertemporal Asset Pricing Model with Stochastic Consumption and Investment Opportunities," *Journal of Financial Economics* **7** (1978) 265-296.

Breeden, D. T., Gibbons, M., and Litzenberger, R., "Empirical Tests of the Consumption-Oriented CAPM," *Journal of Finance* **44** (1989) 231-262.

Campbell, J. Y., and Shiller, R., "The Dividend-Price Ratio and Expectations of Future Dividends and Discount Factors," *Review of Financial Studies* **1** (1988) 195-228.

Commission of the European Communities, "Proposal for Directive Concerning the Solvency Ratio for Credit Institutions," *COM(89)239* (1989).

Cornell, B., "The Consumption Based Asset Pricing Model: A Note on Potential Tests and Applications," *Journal of Financial Economics* **9** (1981) 103-108.

Cragg, J., "Estimation and Testing in Time-Series Regression Models with Heteroscedastic Disturbances," *Journal of Econometrics* **20** (1982) 135-157.

Cutler, D. M., Poterba, J.M., and Summers, L.H., "Speculative Dynamics," *Review of Economic Studies* **58** (1991) 529-546.

Domowitz, I., and Hakkio, C., "Conditional Variance and the Risk Premium in the Foreign Exchange Market," *Journal of International Economics* **19** (1985) 47-66.

Dumas, B., "Two-Person Dynamic Equilibrium: Trading in the Capital Market," National Bureau of Economic Research, Working Paper 2016, September, 1986.

Elton, E., and Gruber, M., "Estimating the Dependence Structure of Share Prices. Implications for Portfolio Selection," *Journal of Finance* **28** (1973) 1203-1232.

Engel, C., and Rodrigues, A. P., "Tests of International CAPM with Time-Varying Covariances," *Journal of Applied Econometrics* **4** (1988) 119-138.

Engle, R., "Autoregressive Conditional Heteroscedasticity with Estimates of the Variations of The United Kingdom Inflations," *Econometrica* **50** (1982) 987-1008.

Engle, R., "Estimates of the Variance of U.S. Inflation Based on the ARCH Model," *Journal of Money, Credit and Banking* **15** (1983) 286-301.

Engle, R., and Rothschild, R., "ARCH Models in Finance," *Journal of Econometrics* **52** (1992) 115-132.

Eun, C., and Resnick, B., "Exchange Rate Uncertainty, Forward Contracts, and International Portfolio Selection," *The Journal of Finance* **39** (1984) 1311-1324.

Eun, C., and Resnick, B., "Estimating the Correlation Structure of International Share Prices," *The Journal of Finance* **43** (1988) 197-215.

Fama, E., and French, K., "Dividend Yields and Expected Stock Returns," *Journal of Financial Economics* **22** (1988) 3-26.

Fama, E., and MacBeth, J., "Risk, Return and Equilibrium: Empirical Tests," *Journal of Political Economy* **71** (1973) 607- 636.

Fromm, G., and Klein, L. R., "A Comparison of Eleven Econometric Models of the United States," **Proceedings of the American Economic Association**, pp. 385-401, May, 1973.

Gibbons, M. R., "Multivariate Tests of Financial Models: A New Approach," *The Journal of Financial Economics* **1** (1982) 3-28.

Giokas, D., and Vassiloglou, M., "A Goal Programming Model for Bank Assets and Liabilities Management," *European Journal of Operational Research* **50** (1991) 48-60.

Greene, W. H., **Econometric Analysis**, Prentice-Hall, Inc., Englewood Cliffs, New Jersey, 1993.

Hansen, L. P., and Singleton, K., "Generalized Instrumental Variables Estimation of Nonlinear Rational Expectations Models," *Econometrica* **50** (1982) 1269-1285.

Harvey, C., "The World Price of Covariance Risk," *Journal of Finance* **46** (1991) 111-158.

Huang, C. F., "An Intertemporal General Equilibrium Asset Pricing Model: The Case of Diffusion Information," *Econometrica* **55** (1987) 117-142.

Jorion, P., "International Portfolio Diversification with Estimation Risk," *Journal of Business* **58** (1985) 259-278.

Jorion, P., "Bayes-Stein Estimation for Portfolio Analysis," *Journal of Financial and Quantitative Analysis* **21** (1986) 279-292.

Judge, G. G., Hill, C., Griffiths, W., Lee, T., and Lütkepohl, H., **An Introduction to the Theory and Practice of Econometrics**, John Wiley & Sons, Inc., New York, New York, 1982.

Longin, F., and Solnik, B., "Is the Correlation of Equity Returns Constant: 1960-1990?" *Journal of International Money and Finance* (February 1995) 3-26.

Lütkepohl, H., **Introduction to Multiple Time Series Analysis**, Springer-Verlag, Inc., Berlin, Germany, 1991.

Madura, J., and Reiff, W., "A Hedge Strategy for International Portfolios," *Journal of Portfolio Management* **11** (1985) 70-74.

Makridakis, S., "A Survey of Time Series," *International Statistical Review* **44** (1976) 29-70.

Makridakis, S., and Wheelright, S. C., **Forecasting: Methods and Applications**, Wiley-Hamilton, Inc., Santa Barbara, California, 1978.

Makridakis, S., and Wheelright, S. C., editors, **Forecasting**, North-Holland, Inc., Amsterdam, Netherlands, 1979.

Miller, M. H., and Scholes, M., "Rates of Return in Relation to Risk: A Re-Examination of Some Recent Findings," in **Studies in the Theory of Capital Markets**, M. Jensen, editor, Praeger, New York, New York, 1972.

Montgomery, S., and Johnson, L. A., **Forecasting and Time Series Analysis**, McGraw-Hill, Inc., New York, New York, 1976.

Naylor, C. R., Seaks, T. G., and Wicherin, D. W., "Box-Jenkins Methods: An Alternative to Econometric Forecasting," *International Statistical Review* **40** (1972) 123-137.

Nelson, C. R., "The Prediction Performance of the FRB-MIT-PENN Model of the U.S. Economy," *The American Economic Review* **62** (1972) 901-917.

Oldier, P., and Solnik, B., "Lesson for International Asset Allocation," *Financial Analysts Journal* (March/April 1993) 63-78.

Poncet, P., and Portait, R., "Futures Markets: Clarification on the Theories of Hedging and Equilibrium," *Finance* **8** (1987) 55-76.

Reilly, F. K., and Akhtar, R. A., "The Benchmark Error Problem with Global Capital Markets," *Journal of Portfolio Management* **11** (1995) 33-52.

Reilly, F. K., Kao, G. W., and Wright, D. J., "Alternative Bond Market Indexes," *Financial Analysts Journal* (June 1992) 44-58.

Roll, R., "Performance Evaluation and Benchmark Error I," *Journal of Portfolio Management* **6** (1980) 5-12.

Roll, R., "Performance Evaluation and Benchmark Error II," *Journal of Portfolio Management* **7** (1981) 17-22.

Sellin, P., and Werner, I., "International Investment Barriers in General Equilibrium," *Journal of International Economics* **34** (1993) 137-151.

Solnik, B., **International Investments**, third edition, Addison-Wesley Publishing Company, Inc., New York, New York, 1996.

Sorensen, E. H., Mezrich, J. J., and Thadani, D. N., "Currency Hedging through Portfolio Optimization," *Journal of Portfolio Management* **19** (1993) 78-85.

Stambaugh, R. F., "On the Exclusion of Assets from Tests of the Two-Parameter Model: A Sensitivity Analysis," *Journal of Financial Economics* **3** (1982) 237-268.

Taylor, S., **Modelling Financial Time Series**, Wiley, Chichester, United Kingdom, 1986.

Wilmott, P., Dewynne, J., Howison, S., **Option Pricing Mathematical Models and Computation**, Oxford Financial Press, Oxford, United Kingdom, 1995.

Witte, W. E., "Trade Hedging and the Dynamic Stability of the Foreign Exchange Market," *Quarterly Journal of Economics* **94** (1980) 15-30.

Appendix A Linear Algebra and Analysis

This appendix reviews fundamental notions, definitions, and ideas related to vectors, matrices, real analysis, convexity theory, and mathematical optimization, which are relevant to the material presented in this book. Its goal is to provide the minimal mathematical background needed for an adequate understanding of the models discussed in this book.

The appendix is divided into three different sections. Section A.1 covers the fundamentals from the area of linear algebra. Section A.2 presents ideas, definitions, and theorems from the area of real analysis. Section A.3 discusses the foundations of optimization theory. For a more detailed presentation of the aforementioned areas, we refer the reader to the books by Kolmogorov and Fomin (1970), Bradley, Hax, and Magnanti (1977), Bazaraa, Jarvis, and Sherali (1990), and Bazaraa, Sherali, and Shetty (1993).

A.1 Linear Algebra

In this section we present some of the fundamentals of linear algebra.

A.1.1 Vectors

A *vector* is an ordered set of numbers assigned in a row or column format. It can also be defined as an array of n scalars: $x_1, x_2, \ldots, x_n$, where the element x_i is said to be the i-th *element* of the vector. The collection of all n-dimensional vectors where all the elements are real numbers forms the n-dimensional space of real numbers, which is denoted as R^n.

Vector Addition and Multiplication by a Scalar

Let x and y be two row (column) vectors in R^n. Then the sum of these vectors is another row (column) vector of the same dimension, denoted as $x + y$, whose i-th element is equal to $x_i + y_i$. If we consider ϕ to be a scalar, then the product of this scalar with vector x is another n-dimensional vector denoted as ϕx, whose i-th element is equal to ϕx_i.

Inner Product

Consider two vectors x and y defined in R^n and assume that x and y are both column vectors, then the *inner product* of vectors x and y is denoted as $\langle x^T, y\rangle$ and is defined as:

$$\langle x^T, y\rangle = \sum_{i=1}^{n} x_i y_i, \tag{A.1}$$

where x^T is the *transpose* of the vector x and is a row vector. Sometimes, the inner product of the vectors x and y is denoted by: $x^T \cdot y$.

Norm of a Vector

Let x be a vector in R^n. Then the (Euclidean) *norm* of this vector is denoted by $||x||$ and is equal to:

$$||x|| = \left(\sum_{i=1}^{n} x_i^2\right)^{1/2}. \tag{A.2}$$

Note that for any two vectors x and y of the same dimension:

$$||x+y||^2 = ||x||^2 + ||y||^2 + 2\langle x^T, y\rangle$$

and

$$|\langle x^T, y\rangle| \leq ||x|| ||y||,$$

where the above inequality is known as the *Schwartz Inequality*.

Linear Dependence and Independence of Vectors

A set of k n-dimensional vectors: $x^1, x^2, \ldots, x^k$ is *linearly dependent* if there exist real numbers: $a_1, a_2, \ldots, a_k$ not all zero, such that:

$$a_1 x^1 + a_2 x^2 + \ldots + a_k x^k = 0.$$

If the only set of a_i's for which the previous equation holds are: $a_1 = a_2 = \ldots = a_k = 0$, then the k vectors are said to be *linearly independent*.

An n-dimensional vector Θ is said to be dependent in the vectors: x^1, x^2, ..., x^k if Θ can be written as a linear combination of these vectors, that is:

$$\Theta = \mu_1 x^1 + \mu_2 x^2 + \ldots + \mu_k x^k, \tag{A.3}$$

for some real numbers: $\mu_1, \mu_2, \ldots, \mu_k$.

A.1.2 Matrices

A *matrix* of dimension $m \times n$ is a rectangular array of numbers denoted as:

$$A = [a_{ij}] = \begin{pmatrix} a_{11} & a_{12} & \dots & a_{1n} \\ a_{21} & a_{22} & \dots & a_{2n} \\ \vdots & \ddots & \ddots & \vdots \\ a_{m1} & a_{m2} & \dots & a_{mn} \end{pmatrix}, \qquad (A.4)$$

where all the elements of the matrix are denoted as $a_{row\,column}$.

Special Matrices

Let A be an $m \times n$ matrix. The *transpose* of matrix A, denoted as A^T, is the $n \times m$ matrix whose (ij)-th element is equal to a_{ji}. If, moreover, $m = n$, then A is called a *square* matrix. In the special case, that $m = n$ and $A = A^T$, then A is said to be *symmetric*. There are several types of symmetric matrices that are commonly used in financial economics and mathematical programming. One of them is the *diagonal* matrix, which has all of its nonzero elements on the main diagonal, that is, the diagonal that runs from the upper left to the lower right of the matrix. The special case in which a diagonal matrix has all of its elements equal to a specific number is called a *scalar* matrix. In the particular case that a scalar matrix has all of its elements equal to one, we obtain the *identity* matrix, denoted as I_n, where n is the size of the matrix, also known as the *order*.

Addition of Matrices

Let A and B be two matrices of the same dimension. Then their sum, denoted as $A + B$, is a matrix of the same dimension whose (i,j)-th element is the summation of the (i,j)-th elements of matrices A and B.

Example A.1

Let A and B be two 3×3 matrices such that:

$$A = \begin{pmatrix} 4 & 8 & 0 \\ 5 & -5 & 35 \\ 6 & -2 & -11 \end{pmatrix}, \quad B = \begin{pmatrix} 6 & 17 & -12 \\ 8 & 0 & -35 \\ 6 & -2 & -10 \end{pmatrix}.$$

Then their sum is another 3×3 matrix, denoted as $A + B$, which is equal to:

$$A + B = \begin{pmatrix} 10 & 25 & -12 \\ 13 & -5 & 0 \\ 12 & -4 & -21 \end{pmatrix}.$$

Multiplication of Matrices

Let A be an $m \times n$ dimensional matrix and let B be an $n \times p$ dimensional matrix. Then the product of these two matrices is denoted as AB and yields an $m \times p$ dimensional matrix C whose (i,j)-th element, c_{ij}, is given by:

$$c_{ij} = \sum_{k=1}^{n} a_{ik} b_{kj}, \text{ for } i = 1, \ldots, m; \quad j = 1, \ldots, p. \tag{A.5}$$

Example A.2

Let A and B be two 3×3 matrices such that:

$$A = \begin{pmatrix} 2 & 1 & 0 \\ 4 & 1 & 3 \\ 3 & 2 & 2 \end{pmatrix}, \quad B = \begin{pmatrix} 2 & 7 & 1 \\ 5 & 0 & 1 \\ 6 & 5 & 4 \end{pmatrix}.$$

Then the product of these matrices is another 3×3 matrix denoted by AB given by:

$$AB = \begin{pmatrix} 2(2)+1(5)+0(6) & 2(7)+1(0)+0(5) & 2(1)+1(1)+0(4) \\ 4(2)+1(5)+3(6) & 4(7)+1(0)+3(5) & 4(1)+1(1)+3(4) \\ 3(2)+2(5)+2(6) & 3(7)+2(0)+2(5) & 3(1)+2(1)+2(4) \end{pmatrix}$$

$$= \begin{pmatrix} 9 & 14 & 3 \\ 31 & 43 & 17 \\ 28 & 31 & 13 \end{pmatrix}.$$

The Rank of a Matrix

Let A be an $m \times n$ matrix. The *rank* of A is the maximum number of linearly independent rows (or columns) of matrix A. Furthermore, matrix A is said to be of *full rank,* if its rank is equal to the minimum of (m, n).

Determinant of a Matrix

Let A be an $n \times n$ (square) matrix. The *determinant* of A, which is commonly denoted as $\det(A)$ or $|A|$, is defined as:

$$|A| = \sum_{i=1}^{n} a_{ij}(-1)^{i+j}|A_{ij}|, \tag{A.6}$$

where A_{ij} is the matrix obtained from A by deleting row i and column j. The determinant of A_{ij} is called the *minor* of A and when the correct sign $(-1)^{i+j}$ is added it is termed the *cofactor*. In the case that A is a two-dimensional matrix, say,

$$A = \begin{pmatrix} a_{11} & a_{12} \\ a_{21} & a_{22} \end{pmatrix},$$

the determinant is defined as:

$$|A| = a_{11}a_{22} - a_{21}a_{12}. \tag{A.7}$$

The calculation of the determinant of a 3×3 matrix by using equation $(A.6)$ is demonstrated through the following example.

Example A.3

Consider the 3×3 matrix A such that:

$$A = \begin{pmatrix} 3 & 6 & 11 \\ 2 & -5 & 6 \\ 8 & 2 & -6 \end{pmatrix}.$$

The determinant of A is then, according to equation $(A.6)$, equal to:

$$|A| = 3(-1)^2 \begin{pmatrix} -5 & 6 \\ 2 & -6 \end{pmatrix} + 6(-1)^3 \begin{pmatrix} 2 & 6 \\ 8 & -6 \end{pmatrix} + 11(-1)^4 \begin{pmatrix} 2 & -5 \\ 8 & 2 \end{pmatrix}$$
$$= 898.$$

A square matrix A is said to be *singular (nonsingular)* if $|A| = 0$ ($|A| \neq 0$).

Inverse of a Matrix

A square matrix A^{-1} is called the *inverse* of matrix A, if

$$AA^{-1} = A^{-1}A = I. \tag{A8}$$

Only square nonsingular matrices have an inverse, and, if it exists, it is unique.

Partition of a Matrix

Very often in financial economics a matrix is partitioned into submatrices. For example, an $m \times n$ matrix Q can be *partitioned* as follows:

$$Q = \begin{pmatrix} Q_{11} & Q_{12} \\ Q_{21} & Q_{22} \end{pmatrix}, \tag{A9}$$

where Q_{11} is $m_1 \times n_1$, Q_{12} is $m_1 \times n_2$, Q_{21} is $m_2 \times n_1$, and Q_{22} is $m_2 \times n_2$, so that, $m_1 + m_2 = m$ and $n_1 + n_2 = n$.

Definite and Semi-Definite Matrices

Let A be an $n \times n$ symmetric matrix. Let x denote any n-dimensional column nonzero vector. Then A is:

- *Positive Definite* if $x^T Ax > 0$, for all such x.
- *Positive Semi-Definite* if $x^T Ax \geq 0$, for all such x.
- *Negative Definite* if $x^T Ax < 0$, for all such x.
- *Negative Semi-Definite* if $x^T Ax \leq 0$, for all such x.
- *Indefinite* if none of the above conditions hold.

In practice, if we let Δ_i denote the i-th minor of A for $i = 1, \ldots, n$, then A is:

- *Positive Definite* if and only if $\Delta_i > 0$ for $i = 1, 2, \ldots, n$.
- *Positive Semi-Definite* if some of the Δ_i are zero, but none is negative for $i = 1, 2, \ldots, n$.
- *Negative Definite* if and only if $(-1)^i \Delta_i > 0$ for $i = 1, 2, \ldots, n$, and the principal minors alternate in sign with $\Delta_1 < 0$.
- *Negative Semi-Definite* if the minors are zero, or $(-1)^i$, with the minors alternating in sign, for $i = 1, 2, \ldots, n$.
- *Indefinite* if it does not fulfill any of the above conditions.

Example A.4

Consider the 3×3 matrix A, such that:

$$A = \begin{pmatrix} 4 & 6 & 0 \\ 6 & 12 & 1 \\ 0 & 1 & 1 \end{pmatrix}$$

with $\Delta_3 = 44 - 36 = 8 > 0$, $\Delta_2 = 48 - 36 = 12 > 0$, $\Delta_1 = 4 > 0$. Hence, A is a positive definite matrix. The notion of a definite matrix is extremely useful in determining the convexity of constraints and objective functions as it will be shown in subsequent sections of this appendix.

A.2 Real Analysis

A.2.1 Sets

A *set* is defined as a collection of objects or elements that share some common properties. If we let Ω be a set and let ω be one of its elements then we can mathematically denote this relationship as $\omega \in \Omega$. Moreover, if $\mathcal{K}$ is a subset of Ω then this can be denoted as $\mathcal{K} \subset \Omega$. Finally, a set with no elements is called the *empty* set, and is denoted as $\emptyset$.

Operations on Sets

Let $\mathcal{X}$ and Ψ be two given sets. Then the set:

- $\mathcal{K} = \mathcal{X} \cup \Psi = \{y : \ y \in \mathcal{X}, \text{ or } y \in \Psi\}$ is called the *union* of $\mathcal{X}$ and Ψ.
- $\mathcal{K} = \mathcal{X} \cap \Psi = \{y : \ y \in \mathcal{X}, \text{ and } y \in \Psi\}$ is called the *intersection* of $\mathcal{X}$ and Ψ.

Furthermore, we say that a set Ω is a *pairwise disjoint family* of sets $\mathcal{X}$ and Ψ, if $X \cap \Psi = \emptyset$ when $\mathcal{X} \in \Omega$, $\Psi \in \Omega$, and $\mathcal{X} \neq \Psi$.

Hyperplanes, Halfspaces and Polyhedral Sets

A set $H \in R^n$ is said to be a *hyperplane* in R^n if it is of the form $(x : \alpha x = \theta)$ where α is a nonzero vector in R^n and θ is a scalar. Vector α is usually called the *normal* or the *gradient* to the hyperplane.

A hyperplane divides the n-dimensional space of real numbers into two regions, called *halfspaces*. Therefore, a halfspace is a set of the form $\{x : \alpha x \geq \theta\}$ or $\{x : \alpha x \leq \theta\}$ where α is a nonzero vector in R^n and θ is a scalar. The union of the two halfspaces $\{x : \alpha x \geq \theta\}$ and $\{x : \alpha x \leq \theta\}$ is R^n.

The intersection of a finite number of halfspaces is called a *polyhedral set* or a *polyhedron*, whereas a bounded polyhedral set is called *polytope*.

Supremum and Infimum of a Set

Let Ω be a set of real numbers. Then the scalar α for which $\alpha \geq x$ for every $x \in \Omega$ is said to be the *supremum* of set Ω, denoted by $sup\{x : x \in \Omega\}$. Similarly, the scalar β for which $\beta \leq x$ for every $x \in \Omega$ is said to be the *infimum* of set Ω, denoted by $inf\{x : x \in \Omega\}$.

Products of Sets

Consider two sets $\mathcal{X}$ and Ψ. Then the *Cartesian Product* of these two sets is a another set denoted as $\mathcal{X} \times \Psi$ such that:

$$\mathcal{X} \times \Psi = \{(x, \psi) : x \in \mathcal{X} \text{ and } \psi \in \Psi\}.$$

Neighborhood of a Point

Let $x \in R^n$, and also let $\delta > 0$. Then the set $B(x, \delta)$, which is a ball with radius δ and center x, is given by:

$$B(x, \delta) = \{Z : ||Z - x|| \leq \delta\} \tag{A.10}$$

is called a *δ-neighborhood* of x.

Interior and Boundary Points of a Set

Consider Ω to be a subset of R^n and let $x \in \Omega$. Then x is called:

- *An interior point* of Ω if there is a ball $B(x, \delta)$ that is contained in Ω. More precisely, x is an interior point if there is a $\delta > 0$ such that if $||Y - x|| \leq \delta$ then $Y \in \Omega$. The collection of all the interior points of Ω is called the *interior* of Ω and is denoted as Ω^0.

- *A boundary point* of Ω if for every $\delta > 0$, the ball $B(x, \delta)$ contains a point in Ω and a point outside of Ω. The collection of all the boundary points of Ω is called the *boundary* of Ω and is denoted as $\partial\Omega$.

Open, Closed, Bounded, and Compact Sets

A set $\Omega \subset R^n$ is defined as:

- *Open* if all of its points are interior points.

- *Closed* if $\Omega = \overline{\Omega}$ where $\overline{\Omega}$ is defined as the *closure* of Ω and represents all the points that are arbitrarily close to set Ω. More precisely, $x \in \overline{\Omega}$ if for each $\delta > 0$, $\Omega \cap B(x, \delta) \neq \emptyset$.

- *Bounded* if it can be contained within a neighborhood $B(x, \delta)$ of finite radius.

- *Compact* if it is both closed and bounded.

Convex Sets

A set $\Omega \subset R^n$ is called a *convex* set if for given any two points x_1 and x_2 in Ω, then $\lambda x_1 + (1-\lambda)x_2 \in \Omega$, for every $\lambda \in [0,1]$. In other words, a set is called convex if the line that interconnects any two points in that set lies also in the interior of that set.

Convergence and Limits

A sequence of points: $\{x^i\} = x^1, x^2, \ldots, x^i, \ldots$ in R^n is said to *converge* to a point $x \in R^n$ if every neighborhood $B(x, \delta)$ of x contains all points x^i starting from a specific index. This is mathematically denoted as $x^i \to x$ as $i \to \infty$. The point x is called the *limit* of the sequence $\{x^i\}$.

A.2.2 Functions

A *function* f valued on a set Φ and defined on a set Ω is an association of every point $\omega \in \Omega$ with a point $\phi \in \Phi$. This association is mathematically denoted as $f : \Omega \mapsto \Phi$. In particular, if $\Phi = R$, where R is the set of real numbers, then function f is said to be a *real-valued* function.

Continuous Functions

A function $f : \Omega \mapsto R$ is said to be *continuous* at $x \in \Omega$ if for any given $\epsilon > 0$ there is a $\delta > 0$ such that $\psi \in \Omega$ and $||\psi - x|| < \delta$ imply that $|f(\psi) - f(x)| < \epsilon$.

Absolutely Continuous Functions

Let $a < b$ and be in R. Then a function $f : [a, b] \mapsto R$ is said to be *absolutely continuous* on $[a, b]$ if for any given $\epsilon > 0$ there exists a $\delta > 0$ such that if n is the total finite number of pairwise disjoint subintervals of $[a, b]$ satisfying $\sum_{j=1}^{n}(b_j - a_j) < \delta$ then

$$\sum_{j=1}^{n} |f(b_j) - f(a_j)| < \epsilon. \tag{A.11}$$

Differentiable Functions

Consider a nonempty set Ω such that $\Omega \subset R^n$, a column vector x lying in the interior of Ω, and let f be a function such that $f : \Omega \mapsto R$. Then f is said to be *differentiable*, if there exists a column vector $\nabla f(x) \in R^n$, called the *gradient* of f at x, defined as:

$$\nabla f(x)^T = \left(\frac{\partial f(x)}{\partial x_1}, \frac{\partial f(x)}{\partial x_2}, \ldots, \frac{\partial f(x)}{\partial x_n} \right), \tag{A.12}$$

and a function $\beta(x;y) \rightarrow 0$ as $y \rightarrow x$ such that:

$$f(y) = f(x) + \nabla f(x)^T (y - x) + ||y - x|| \beta(x;y), \quad \forall y \in \Omega. \tag{A.13}$$

Moreover, f is said to be *twice differentiable* at x if, in addition to the gradient vector, there exists an $n \times n$ matrix $H(x)$, called the *Hessian matrix* of function f at x, defined as:

$$H = \begin{pmatrix} \frac{\partial f^2}{\partial x_1 \partial x_1} & \frac{\partial^2 f}{\partial x_1 x_2} & \cdots & \frac{\partial^2 f}{\partial x_1 x_n} \\ \frac{\partial^2 f}{\partial x_1 x_2} & \frac{\partial^2 f}{\partial x_2 \partial x_2} & \cdots & \frac{\partial^2 f}{\partial x_2 x_n} \\ \vdots & \ddots & \ddots & \vdots \\ \frac{\partial^2 f}{\partial x_1 x_n} & \cdots & \cdots & \frac{\partial^2 f}{\partial x_n \partial x_n} \end{pmatrix} \tag{A.14}$$

and a function $\beta(x;y) \rightarrow 0$ as $y \rightarrow x$ such that:

$$f(y) = f(x) + \nabla f(x)^T (y - x)$$

$$+ \frac{1}{2} (y - x)^T H(x) (y - x) + ||y - x||^2 \beta(x;y), \quad \forall y \in \Omega. \tag{A.15}$$

Convex and Concave Functions

Let Ω be a nonempty convex set and consider a function $f : \Omega \mapsto R$. Then the function $f(x)$ is said to be *convex function* on Ω if for any two distinct points $x_1, x_2 \in \Omega$ and for all $\lambda \in [0, 1]$, the following holds:

$$f[\lambda x_2 + (1 - \lambda) x_1] \leq \lambda f(x_2) + (1 - \lambda) f(x_1). \tag{A.16}$$

The function f is said to be *strictly convex* on Ω if the above inequality holds as a strict inequality. A function $f(x)$ is said to be *concave* (*strictly concave*) if $-f(x)$ is convex (strictly convex).

Simply stated, a function $f(x)$ is convex (concave) if a line segment joining any two points: $[x_1, f(x_1)]$, $[x_2, f(x_2)]$, on the surface of $f(x)$ lies on or above (below) that surface.

The previous definition can be used directly to establish whether a function is convex or not. If we assume that function $f(x)$ is continuous and that it has second order partial derivatives over Ω, then an alternative way is to evaluate whether the Hessian of the function is positive definite. In particular, if the Hessian matrix H of second order partial derivatives is positive definite, then $f(x)$ is convex, and if H is negative definite, then $f(x)$ is concave.

Example A.5

Consider the following function:

$$f(x_1, x_2, x_3) = x_1^2 + 3x_2^2 + 0.5x_3^2 + x_1x_2 + 2x_2x_3 - 8x_1 + 4x_2 - 3x_3 + 15.$$

Then its first and second order partial derivatives are given by:

$$\frac{\partial f}{\partial x_1} = 2x_1 + x_2 - 8, \quad \frac{\partial f}{\partial x_2} = 6x_2 + 2x_3 + x_1 + 4, \quad \frac{\partial f}{\partial x_3} = x_3 + 2x_2 - 3,$$

$$\frac{\partial^2 f}{\partial x_1 \partial x_1} = 2, \quad \frac{\partial^2 f}{\partial x_2 \partial x_2} = 6, \quad \frac{\partial^2 f}{\partial x_3 \partial x_3} = 1,$$

$$\frac{\partial^2 f}{\partial x_1 x_2} = 1, \quad \frac{\partial^2 f}{\partial x_1 x_3} = 0, \quad \frac{\partial^2 f}{\partial x_2 x_3} = 2,$$

and, hence, the Hessian H is equal to:

$$H = \begin{pmatrix} 2 & 1 & 0 \\ 1 & 6 & 2 \\ 0 & 2 & 1 \end{pmatrix},$$

with the corresponding minors given by:

$$\Delta_1 = 2 > 0, \ \Delta_2 = \begin{pmatrix} 2 & 1 \\ 1 & 6 \end{pmatrix} = 11 > 0, \ \Delta_3 = \begin{pmatrix} 2 & 1 & 0 \\ 1 & 6 & 2 \\ 0 & 2 & 1 \end{pmatrix} = 3 > 0.$$

Therefore, $f(x)$ is convex over R^3.

Quasiconvex and Quasiconcave Functions

Let Ω be a nonempty convex set and consider a function $f : \Omega \mapsto R$. The function $f(x)$ is said to be a *quasiconvex function* on Ω, if for any two distinct points $x_1, x_2 \in \Omega$ and $\forall \lambda \in [0, 1]$, we have:

$$f\left[\lambda x_2 + (1 - \lambda)\, x_1\right] \leq \text{maximum } \left(f(x_1), f(x_2)\right).$$

The function $f(x)$ is said to be *quasiconcave* on Ω if $-f(x)$ is quasiconvex.

Pseudoconvex and Pseudoconcave Functions

Let Ω be a nonempty convex set and consider a function $f : \Omega \mapsto R$ which is differentiable on Ω. Then the function $f(x)$ is said to be a *pseudoconvex function* on Ω, if for any two distinct points $x_1, x_2 \in \Omega$ with $\nabla f(x_1)^T (x_2 - x_1) \geq 0$ we have $f(x_2) \geq f(x_1)$.

The function $f(x)$ is said to be *pseudoconcave* on Ω if $-f(x)$ is pseudoconvex.

Monotonicity of Functions

The function $f : \Omega \mapsto R^n$ is said to be:

- *Monotone* on Ω if for every x and y in Ω,

$$[f(x) - f(y)]^T \cdot (x - y) \geq 0, \tag{A.17}$$

- *Strictly Monotone* on Ω if for any distinct x and y in Ω,

$$[f(x) - f(y)]^T \cdot (x - y) > 0, \tag{A.18}$$

- *Strongly Monotone* on Ω if for any x and y in Ω, and for some scalar $\alpha > 0$,

$$[f(x) - f(y)]^T \cdot (x - y) > \alpha ||x - y||^2. \tag{A.19}$$

Lipschitz Continuous Functions

The function $f : \Omega \mapsto R^n$ is said to be *Lipschitz continuous* on Ω if there exists an $L > 0$ such that:

$$||f(x) - f(y)|| \leq L||x - y||, \quad \forall x, y \in \Omega. \tag{A.20}$$

Lebesgue Outer Measure

Lebesgue measure is a function that assigns to each subset of R a number in $[0, \infty]$ in such a way that each interval is assigned its length. In particular, consider an interval $I = [a, b] \in R^n$ and let the length of I be denoted by: $|I| = b - a$. Then for $\Omega \subset R$, the *Lebesgue measure* of Ω is the number:

$$\lambda(\Omega) = inf \, \{\sum_{I \in Z} |I|\}, \tag{A.21}$$

such that Z is a countable family of open intervals with $\Omega \subset \cup Z$.

It must be noted that if I is an interval of R then $\lambda(I) = |I|$, and that $\lambda(\emptyset) = 0$. Finally, if $\Omega \subset K \subset R$ then $\lambda(\Omega) \leq \lambda(K)$.

A.3 Optimization

One of the principal goals of financial economic theory is the determination of an optimal solution for a series of different problems. In this section we present the fundamentals of optimization theory along with some of the notions and ideas that are utilized throughout this book.

An optimization problem in R^n is a problem in which we seek to optimize a function f, which is said to be the *objective function*, subject to some constraints. A point $x^0 \in R^n$ is called a *feasible solution* to the optimization problem if it satisfies all the constraints of the problem. Moreover, a point $x^* \in R^n$ is called an *optimal solution* to the optimization problem, if it is a feasible solution and it provides the best possible value for the objective function.

A.3.1 Karush-Kuhn-Tucker Optimization Conditions

In this subsection we discuss important conditions for optimality.

Global Maximum and Minimum

The function $f : \Omega \mapsto R^n$ is said to take its *global maximum* at point x^* if:

$$f(x) \leq f(x^*), \quad \forall x \in \Omega. \tag{A.22a}$$

Similarly, the function $f : \Omega \mapsto R^n$ is said to take its *global minimum* at point ψ^* if:

$$f(\psi) \geq f(\psi^*), \quad \forall \psi \in \Omega. \tag{A.22b}$$

Local Maximum and Minimum

The function $f : \Omega \mapsto R^n$ is said to take its *local maximum* at point x^* if there exists a $\delta > 0$ such that for every $x \neq x^*$ that belongs to Ω and is in a δ-neighborhood of x^*, the following holds:

$$f(x) \leq f(x^*) \quad \forall x \in (\Omega \cap B(x^*, \delta))\,. \tag{A.23a}$$

Similarly, the function $f : \Omega \rightarrow R^n$ is said to take its *local maximum* at point ψ^* if there exists a $\delta > 0$ such that for every $\psi \neq \psi^*$ that belongs to Ω and is in a δ-neighborhood of ψ^*, the following holds:

$$f(\psi) \geq f(\psi^*) \quad \forall \psi \in (\Omega \cap B(\psi^*, \delta))\,. \tag{A.23b}$$

Karush-Kuhn-Tucker (KKT) Conditions

Karush (1939) and Kuhn and Tucker (1951) independently developed a set of necessary and sufficient conditions for an optimal solution of a general mathematical problem. Their work provided the mathematical framework upon which all the computational methods in optimization have been based. In this subsection, we aim to present a compact presentation of these conditions.

Karush-Kuhn-Tucker Necessary Conditions

Let K be a nonempty open set such that $K \subset R^n$, and let $\{f : R^n \mapsto R\}$, $\{g_i : R^n \mapsto R\}$ for $i = 1, 2, \ldots, m$ and $\{h_j : R^n \mapsto R\}$ for $j = 1, 2, \ldots, t$. Moreover, consider the general optimization problem of the following form:

$$\text{Minimize} \quad f(x)$$

subject to:

$$g_i(x) \leq 0, \quad \text{for } i = 1, 2, \ldots, m$$
$$h_j(x) = 0, \quad \text{for } j = 1, 2, \ldots, t$$
$$x \in K.$$

Let x^* be a feasible solution and let $\Theta = \{i : g_i(x^*) = 0\}$. Furthermore, assume that f and g_i are differentiable at x^* for $i \in \Theta$, and that the g_i are continuous at x^* for $(i,l) \in \Theta$. Finally, assume that the h_j are continuously differentiable at x^* for all $j = 1, 2, \ldots, t$. Moreover, suppose that $\nabla g_i(x^*)$ for $i \in \Theta$ and $\nabla h_j(x^*)$ for $j = 1, 2, \ldots, t$, are linearly independent. If x^* locally solves the minimization problem then there exist unique scalars u_i for $i \in \Theta$, and w_j for $j = 1, 2, \ldots, t$, such that:

$$\nabla f(x^*) + \sum_{i \in \Theta} u_i \nabla g_i(x^*) + \sum_{j=1}^{t} w_j \nabla h_j(x^*) = 0 \tag{A.24}$$

$$u_i g_i(x^*) = 0, \text{ for } i \in \Theta \tag{A.25}$$

$$u_i \geq 0, \text{ for } i \in \Theta. \tag{A.26}$$

The scalars u_i and w_j are called *Lagrange* multipliers. There is one Lagrange multiplier associated with each constraint and they represent the marginal rate of change in the objective function f with respect to each per unit change in the right-hand side of the corresponding constraint.

The condition that x^* has to be feasible is called *primal feasibility (PF)* condition, whereas the set of equations (A.24) and (A.26) are called *dual feasibility (DF)* conditions. Equations (A.25) are called the *complementary slackness (CS)* conditions. Any point that satisfies the KKT conditions is called a *KKT point*.

Sometimes the optimization problem includes nonnegativity constraints for the variables involved, that is, $x \geq 0$. Obviously, the KKT conditions that we just presented will still hold. Many times, however, for reasons of convenience and simplification the Lagrange multipliers associated with those constraints are eliminated, and the conditions are reduced to:

$$\nabla f(x^*) + \sum_{i \in \Theta} u_i \nabla g_i(x^*) + \sum_{j=1}^{t} w_j \nabla h_j(x^*) \geq 0 \tag{A.27}$$

$$\left[\nabla f(x^*) + \sum_{i \in \Theta} u_i \nabla g_i(x^*) + \sum_{j=1}^{t} w_j \nabla h_j(x^*) \right]^T x = 0 \tag{A.28}$$

$$u_i g_i(x^*) = 0, \text{ for } i \in \Theta \tag{A.29}$$

$$u_i \geq 0, \text{ for } i \in \Theta. \tag{A.30}$$

A geometric interpretation of the KKT conditions is that a vector x^* is a KKT point if and only if $-\nabla f(x^*)$ lies in the cone spanned by the gradients of the binding constraints.

Karush-Kuhn-Tucker Sufficient Conditions

Let, again, K be a nonempty open set such that $K \subset R^n$, and let $\{f : R^n \mapsto R\}$, $\{g_i : R^n \mapsto R\}$ for $i = 1, 2, \ldots, m$ and $\{h_j : R^n \mapsto R\}$ for

$j = 1, 2, \ldots, t$. Moreover, consider, once again, the general optimization problem of the following form:

$$\text{Minimize} \quad f(x)$$

subjcct to:

$$g_i(x) \leq 0, \quad \text{for } i = 1, 2, \ldots, m$$

$$h_j(x) = 0, \quad \text{for } j = 1, 2, \ldots, t$$

$$x \in K.$$

Let x^* be a feasible solution, and let $\Theta = \{i : g_i(x^*) = 0\}$. Assume that the KKT conditions hold at x^*. In other words, assume that there exist scalars $\overline{u}_i \geq 0$ with $i \in \Theta$ and $\overline{w}_j$ with $j = 1, 2, \ldots, t$, such that:

$$\nabla f(x^*) + \sum_{i \in \Theta} \overline{u}_i \nabla g_i(x^*) + \sum_{j=1}^{t} \overline{w}_j \nabla h_j(x^*) = 0. \tag{A.31}$$

Let $J = \{j : \bar{w}_j > 0\}$ and $L = \{j : \bar{w}_j < 0\}$. Further, suppose that f is pseudoconvex at x^*, the constraints g_i are quasiconvex at x^* for $i \in \Theta$, h_j is quasiconvex for the $j \in J$ and quasiconcave for the $j \in L$. Then x^* is a global optimal solution to the general minimization problem.

For a maximization problem, the KKT conditions are similar, where now the function f has to be pseudoconcave.

Lagrangian Function

Consider, once again, the general minimization problem used in the previous section. Then the function such that:

$$\phi(x, u, w) = f(x) + \sum_{i=1}^{m} u_i g_i(x) + \sum_{j=1}^{t} w_j h_j(x) \tag{A.32}$$

is said to be the *Lagrangian function* of the general optimization problem.

Moreover, if we let x^* be a KKT point to the general optimization problem with u^*, w^* being the Lagrange multipliers that correspond to the constraints of the problem, then the function:

$$L(x) \equiv \phi(x, u^*, w^*) = f(x) + \sum_{i \in \Theta} u_i^* g_i(x) + \sum_{j=1}^{t} w_j^* h_j(x) \tag{A.33}$$

is said to be the *restricted Lagrangian function*.

Let $\nabla^2 L$ denote the Hessian of (A.33). Then if $\nabla^2 L$ is:

- Positive semi-definite for all x in the feasible set, x^* is a global minimum.

- Positive semi-definite for all x in the feasible set and in a δ-neighborhood $B(x^*, \delta)$, for a $\delta > 0$, x^* is a local minimum.

- Positive definite, x^* is a strict local minimum.

References

Bazaraa, M. S., Jarvis, J.J., and Sherali, H. D., **Linear Programming and Network Flows**, John Wiley & Sons, Inc., second edition, New York, New York, 1990.

Bazaraa, M. S., Sherali H. D., and Shetty, C. M., **Nonlinear Programming: Theory and Algorithms**, John Wiley & Sons, Inc., second edition, New York, New York, 1993.

Bradley, S. P., Hax, A., and Magnanti, T. L., **Applied Mathematical Programming**, Addison-Wesley Publishing Company, Inc., Reading, Massachusetts, 1977.

Karush, W., "Minima of Functions of Several Variables with Inequalities as Side Conditions," M.S. Thesis, Department of Mathematics, University of Chicago, Chicago, Illinois, 1939

Kolmogorov, A. N., and Fomin, S.V., **Introductory Real Analysis**, translated and edited by R. A. Silverman, Dover Publications, Inc., Mineola, New York 1970.

Kuhn, H. W., and Tucker A. W., "Nonlinear Programming," in **Proceedings of Second Berkeley Symposium on Mathematical Statistics and Probability,** pp. 481-492, J. Neyman, editors, University of California Press, Berkeley, California, 1951.

Appendix B Probability

In this Appendix we present an introduction to issues from basic probability theory. In particular, in Section B.1, we review notions, definitions, and ideas from the area of probability theory. For an extensive background on probability theory, we refer the reader to Papoulis (1984) and Devore (1995).

B.1 Probability Theory

Sample Space

The set that is formed by all distinctly different possible outcomes of an experiment is called the *sample space* of that experiment and is denoted as S.

Events

Any group of outcomes contained in the sample space of an experiment is said to be an *event*. For every event A there is a number $0 \leq P(A) \leq 1$ associated with it, which is defined as *the probability of event* A, and which provides an exact measure of the possibility of event A happening. Obviously, the summation of the probabilities of all events occurring in a sample space is equal to one.

Conditional Probability

Let A and B be any two events, where $P(B) > 0$. Then the probability of A happening, given that B has already taken place, is said to be the *conditional probability* of A, given B, is denoted as $P(A \mid B)$, and given by:

$$P(A \mid B) = \frac{P(A \cap B)}{P(B)}. \qquad (B.1)$$

Law of Total Probability

Consider k mutually exclusive events, that is, a set of events in which no two of them have a common outcome, and denote them as: $B_1, \ldots, B_k$, whose union is S. According to the *law of total probability*, for any other event A, which is a subset of S, the following holds:

$$P(A) = \sum_{i=1}^{k} P(B_i)P(A \mid B_i). \tag{B.2}$$

Bayes' Theorem

Consider $B_1, B_2, \ldots, B_k$ to be mutually exclusive events whose union is the S. Then according to Bayes' Theorem, for any event B_j, the following holds:

$$P(B_j \mid A) = \frac{P(B_j)P(A \mid B_j)}{\sum_{i=1}^{k} P(B_i)P(A \mid B_i)}. \tag{B.3}$$

Independent Events

Two events A_1 and A_2 are independent if $P(A_1 \mid A_2) = P(A_1)$, and dependent, otherwise; equivalently, two events A_1 and A_2 are independent if and only if

$$P(A_1 \cap A_2) = P(A_1)P(A_2). \tag{B.4}$$

B.1.1 Random Variables and Probability Distributions

In this subsection we discuss random variables and probability distributions.

Random Variables

For a given sample space S, a *random variable* is any mapping that associates a specific number with every possible outcome in S. Moreover, if the set of all possible values is discrete (continuous) then the random variable is said to be *discrete (continuous)*.

Probability Distributions

The *probability distribution* or *probability mass function (pmf)* of a discrete random variable is defined for every possible number x as:

$$p(x) = P(X = x) = P(all\ \omega \in S:\ X(\omega) = x). \tag{B.5}$$

Furthermore, the following should hold:

$$0 \leq p(x) \leq 1 \tag{B.6}$$

and

$$\sum_{all\ possible\ x} p(x) = 1. \tag{B.7}$$

The *probability distribution* or *probability density function (pdf)* of a continuous random variable X is a function $f(x)$ such that:

$$P(a_1 \leq X \leq a_2) = \int_{a_1}^{a_2} f(x)dx \tag{B.8}$$

with $a_1, a_2 \in R$ and $a_1 \leq a_2$. Note that, the probability of a continuous function on an interval $[a_1, a_2]$ is equal to the area under the graph of $f(x)$ between points a_1 and a_2. Moreover, the following should always hold:

$$f(x) \geq 0 \tag{B.9}$$

and

$$\int_{-\infty}^{\infty} f(x) = 1. \tag{B.10}$$

Example B.1 (Uniform Distribution)

For illustration purposes, we present a simple example of a continuous random variable X, which follows a uniform distribution on the interval $[a_1, a_2]$. For a uniformly distributed random variable, the pdf of X is given by:

$$f(x) = \begin{cases} \frac{1}{a_2 - a_1}, & a_1 \leq x \leq a_2, \\ 0, & \text{otherwise.} \end{cases} \tag{B.11}$$

Cumulative Distribution Function

For a random variable X, the probability that the value of X will be less than or equal to a value x is denoted as $F(x)$, and is said to be the *cumulative distribution (cdf)* of X.

For a discrete random variable the cdf is:

$$F(x) = \sum_{X \leq x} p(x). \tag{B.12}$$

Similarly, the cdf for a continuous random variable is:

$$F(x) = \int_{-\infty}^{x} f(z)dz \tag{B.13}$$

and

$$f(x) = \frac{dF(x)}{dx}. \tag{B.14}$$

For both discrete and random variables the following should always hold:

- $0 \leq F(x) \leq 1$
- If $x > y$ then $F(x) \geq F(y)$
- $F(+\infty) = 1$ and $F(-\infty) = 0$
- $Prob(\alpha < x \leq \beta) = F(\beta) - F(\alpha)$.

Example B.2

Consider the uniform distribution presented in Example B.1. Then one can easily prove through the definition (B.13) that the cdf of the uniform distribution is equal to:

$$F(x) = \begin{cases} 0, & x < a_1 \\ \frac{x-a_1}{a_2-a_1}, & a_1 \leq x \leq a_2 \\ 1, & x > a_2. \end{cases} \qquad (B.15)$$

B.1.2 Expectations of a Random Variable

We now discuss the expected value of a random variable and related notions.

Expected Value

The *mean* or *expected value* of a random variable X is denoted by $E(X)$ and is given by:

$$E(X) = \mu_x = \begin{cases} \sum_i x_i p(x_i), & \text{if X is discrete} \\ \int_{-\infty}^{\infty} x f(x) dx, & \text{if X is continuous,} \end{cases} \qquad (B.16)$$

provided that the integral in the second case exists. The expected value does not have to be taken from the random variable. For example, the expected number of getting a head from tossing a coin is 0.5, while the random variable does not take this value.

Expected Value of a Function

The *expected value* of a function $g(X)$ of a random variable X is denoted by $E(g(X))$ and is given by:

$$E(g(X)) = \mu_{g(X)} = \begin{cases} \sum_i g(x_i) p(x_i), & \text{if X is discrete} \\ \int_{-\infty}^{\infty} g(x) f(x) dx, & \text{if X is continuous,} \end{cases} \qquad (B.17)$$

provided that the integral in the second case exists.

Variance

The *variance* of the random variable X is a positive number that measures the dispersion of the distribution that variable X follows. It is defined to be the expected value of $(X - \mu_X)^2$ and is denoted by: $\sigma_X^2 = Var(X)$. It is given by

$$\sigma_X^2 = \begin{cases} \sum_i (x_i - \mu)^2 p(x_i), & \text{if X is discrete} \\ \int_{-\infty}^{\infty} (x - \mu)^2 f(x) dx, & \text{if X is continuous.} \end{cases} \qquad (B.18)$$

The *standard deviation* of the random variable X is equal to:

$$\sigma_X = \sqrt{\sigma_X^2}. \qquad (B.19)$$

Furthermore, the following holds for the variance of a random variable X:

$$\sigma_X^2 = E(X^2) - (E(X))^2 . \qquad (B.20)$$

Example B.3

Consider, once again, the random variable with the uniform distribution that was presented in Example B.1. The expected value of the distribution is given by:

$$\mu_X = \int_{a_1}^{a_2} xf(x)dx = \frac{1}{a_2 - a_1}\int_{a_1}^{a_2} xdx = \frac{a_1 + a_2}{2}.$$

Similarly, the variance of the uniform distribution is:

$$\sigma_X^2 = \int_{a_1}^{a_2} (x-\mu_X)^2 f(x)dx = \frac{1}{a_2 - a_1}\int_{a_1}^{a_2} (x-\mu_X)^2 dx = \frac{(a_2 - a_1)^2}{12}.$$

Skewness and Kurtosis

Skewness measures the asymmetry of a distribution and is given by

$$\text{Skewness} = E\left[(X-\mu)^3\right] . \qquad (B.21)$$

On the other hand, *kurtosis* measures the thickness of the tails of the distribution and is equal to

$$\text{Kurtosis} = E\left[(X-\mu)^4\right] . \qquad (B.22)$$

B.1.2.1 Normal Distribution

A continuous random variable X is said to be normally distributed with parameters $\mu \in R$ and $\sigma \in R_+$, if the pdf of X is given by:

$$f(x) = \frac{1}{\sqrt{2\pi}\sigma} e^{-\frac{(x-\mu)^2}{2\sigma^2}}, \quad \forall x \in R. \qquad (B.23)$$

In the case that $\mu = 0$ and $\sigma = 1$, the variable X is said to be *standardly normally distributed* and is denoted by Z, where the pdf is the one given by $(B.23)$ for $\mu = 0$ and $\sigma = 1$.

B.1.2.2 Joint Distributions

Joint Probability Functions

Let X and Y be two discrete random variables. Then we denote the *joint probability mass function* of variables X and Y, by $p(x,y)$, which specifies how much probability mass is allocated for each pattern of values (x,y).

Similarly, if we let X and Y be two continuous random variables, then we define as $f(x,y)$ the *joint probability density function* of variables X and Y.

Marginal Probability Functions

The *marginal probability mass functions* of discrete random variables X and Y are denoted by $p_X(x)$ and $p_Y(y)$ and are given by:

$$p_X(x) = \sum_y p(x,y) \text{ and } p_Y(y) = \sum_x p(x,y). \qquad (B.24)$$

Similarly, the *marginal probability density functions* of continuous random variables X and Y are denoted by $f_X(x)$ and $f_Y(y)$ and are given by:

$$f_X(x) = \int_{-\infty}^{\infty} f(x,y)dy \text{ and } f_Y(y) = \int_{-\infty}^{\infty} f(x,y)dx. \qquad (B.25)$$

Covariance

Consider two random variables X and Y. We denote the covariance between these two variables as $Cov(X,Y)$, where

$$Cov(X,Y) = E\left[(X-\mu_X)(Y-\mu_Y)\right]$$

$$= \begin{cases} \sum_x \sum_y (x-\mu_X)(y-\mu_Y)p(x,y), & \text{if X is discrete} \\ \int_{-\infty}^{\infty}\int_{-\infty}^{\infty}(x-\mu_X)(y-\mu_Y)f(x,y)dxdy, & \text{if X is continuous.} \end{cases} \qquad (B.26)$$

Correlation

The *correlation coefficient* of variables X and Y is a measure of the degree of the linear relationship between these two variables, and is denoted as ρ_{XY}, where:

$$\rho_{XY} = \frac{Cov(X,Y)}{\sigma_X \sigma_Y}. \qquad (B.27)$$

The strongest positive possible linear relationship between variables X and Y is indicated by $\rho_{XY} = 1$, whereas, the strongest negative linear relationship between variables X and Y is indicated by $\rho_{XY} = -1$.

References

Devore, J. L., **Probability and Statistics for Engineering and the Sciences**, Duxbury Press, fourth edition, Belmont, California, 1995.

Papoulis, A., **Probability, Random Variables and Stochastic Processes**, McGraw Hill, Inc., New York, New York, 1984.

Appendix C Black and Scholes Model

In this appendix we outline the Black and Scholes (1973) option pricing model, which is considered to be the basis of option pricing. For a detailed discussion of this model, as well as a detailed analysis of other existing option pricing models, we refer the reader to the original paper by Black and Scholes (1973), and to the books by Kolb (1991), McMillan (1992), Hull (1993), and Wilmott, Dewynne, and Howison (1993).

The Black and Scholes Option Pricing Model

The price of an option depends on a series of different financial factors (see Table C.1), which are directly related to the underlying security, its time to expiration, and the present financial environment. Black and Scholes suggested a relatively simple formula that takes into consideration these different factors and manages to derive a relatively accurate price for every option contract.

In particular, the Black and Scholes option pricing model is based on the following assumptions about these factors:

- There exists a constant risk-free interest rate.
- Prices are distributed lognormaly with constant volatility.
- There are no taxes and transaction costs.
- Security trading is continuous.
- There are no dividends during the life of the underlying security.
- Market participants can sell short.
- Options are exercisable only at expiration (European).

Table C.1. Effect on price of a call/put option of an increase in factors

Factor (increase)	Call Option	Put Option
Spot Price	*up*	*down*
Exercise Price	*down*	*up*
Time to Expiration	*up*	*up*
Volatility	*up*	*up*
Interest Rates	*up*	*down*
Dividends	*down*	*up*

It can readily verified that almost all the assumptions of the Black and Scholes model are violated in practice. Nevertheless, the model can be adjusted to accommodate situations that violate some of its assumptions (see Hull (1993), Wilmott, Dewynne, and Howison (1993)).

For example, even though security trading is assumed to be continuous, discrete filters are acceptable on a portfolio basis. In addition, adjustments can be made to handle transaction costs, taxes, and derivatives, as well as the case of American options. Clearly, there are many situations in which the model will not behave well, since no adjustments can overcome all the limitations imposed by the model. For example, the theory will not behave well in markets in which participants cannot sell short (e. g., Japanese equity warrants), or in cases that the price distributions of the underlying assets are not lognormally distributed.

The following expression gives the Black and Scholes option pricing model for a call option:

$$C = [sN(\beta_1)] - \left[EN(\beta_2)e^{-rt}\right] \qquad (C.1)$$

with

$$\beta_1 = \frac{\left[ln\left(\frac{s}{E}\right) + \left(r + 0.5\sigma^2\right)t\right]}{\sqrt{\sigma^2 t}} \qquad (C.2)$$

and

$$\beta_2 = \beta_1 - \sqrt{\sigma^2 t}, \qquad (C.3)$$

where $N(\cdot)$ denotes the cumulative normal distribution of a normally distributed variable, with a mean value equal to zero, and a standard deviation equal to one. In addition, s denotes the spot price of the underlying stock, E denotes the exercise price of the option contract, r and t denote, respectively, the risk-free interest rate of the market, and the time to expiration of the specific option contract. Finally, σ^2 corresponds to the variance of the underlying stock.

References

Black, F., and Scholes, M., "The Pricing of Options and Corporate Liabilities." *Journal of Political Economy* **81** (1973) 637-659.

Hull, J., **Options, Futures, and Other Derivatives,** Prentice Hall Inc., Englewood Cliffs, New Jersey, 1993.

Kolb, R. W., **Options: An Introduction**, Kolb Publishing Company, Miami, Florida, 1991.

McMillan, L. G., **Options as a Strategic Investment,** New York Institute of Finance, New York, New York, 1992.

Wilmott, P., Dewynne, J., and Howison, S., **Option Pricing: Mathematical Models and Computation,** Oxford Financial Press, Oxford, United Kingdom, 1993.

List of Figures

List of Tables

Index

Advances in

Spatial and Network Economics

B. M. Roehner

Theory of Markets

Trade and Space-time Patterns of Price Fluctuations. A Study in Analytical Economics

1995. XVIII, 405 pp. 149 figs., Hardcover DM 190,- ISBN 3-540-58815-9

M. J. Beckmann, T. Puu

Spatial Structures

1990. IX, 139 pp. 40 figs. Hardcover DM 84,- ISBN 3-540-51957-2

Please **order** by Fax: +49 30/827 87-301
e-mail: orders@springer.de
or through your bookseller

Visit the **Springer-Website** to find out more about our books and journals.

Springer-Verlag Berlin Heidelberg
http://www.springer.de

Springer-Verlag New York
http://www.springer-ny.com

T.C. Miller, F.L. Friesz, R.L. Tobin

Equilibrium Facility Location on Networks

1995. X, 242 pp. 14 figs., 47 tabs.
Hardcover DM 128,- ISBN 3-540-60563-0

This book emphasizes the interdependence of the location, production and distribution decisions made by a firm operating over a network. It examines why and how a firm must evaluate the link between these interdependent decisions and the equilibrium conditions on the network where it locates. In doing so, this book offers several intriguing new paradigms for facility location on networks.

A. Sen, T.E. Smith

Gravity Models of Spatial Interaction Behavior

1995. XVI, 572 pp. 13 figs., 28 tabs.
Hardcover DM 178,- ISBN 3-540-60026-4

This book presents an up-to-date, consistent and unified approach to the theory, methods and applications of the gravity model – which spans from the axiomatic foundations of such models all the way to practical hints for their use. "I have found no better general method for use in applied research dealing with spatial interaction... It is against this background that the present book by Sen and Smith is most welcomed."

Walter Isard

Springer

Tm.BA97.03.03

New in Transportation

B. Ran, D. Boyce

Modeling Dynamic Transportation Networks

An Intelligent Transportation System Oriented Approach

2nd rev. ed. 1996. XX, 356 pages.
51 figures, 29 tables.
Hardcover DM 128,–
ISBN 3-540-61139-8

Intelligent transportation systems have provided a welcome stimulus to research on dynamic urban transportation network models. This book presents a new generation of models for solving dynamic travel choice problems including traveller's destination choice, departure/arrival time choice and route choice. Additionally, a summary of the neccessary mathematical background is given.

Please order from
Springer-Verlag Berlin
Fax: + 49 / 30 / 8 27 87- 301
e-mail: orders@springer.de
or through your bookseller

Prices subject to change without notice.
In EU countries the local VAT is effective.

L. Bianco, P. Toth (Eds.)

Advanced Methods in Transportation Analysis

1996. XVI, 619 pages. 146 figures,
49 tables (Transportation Analysis).
Hardcover DM 198,–
ISBN 3-540-61118-5

A survey of the most important current research efforts in mathematical modelling for transportation analysis. Particular emphasis laid is on transportation planning, transportation management and vehicle management. Readers will find models, solution algorithms and computational results which allow them to deal with the most complex problems in the above-mentioned fields.

Springer

Springer-Verlag, P. O. Box 31 13 40, D-10643 Berlin, Germany. IMCA.3501/MNT/E/1

Printing: Druckhaus Beltz, Hemsbach
Binding: Buchbinderei Schäffer, Grünstadt